D0780141

The
Garland Library
of
War and Peace

The
Garland Library
of
War and Peace

Under the General Editorship of

Blanche Wiesen Cook, *John Jay College, C.U.N.Y.*

Sandi E. Cooper, *Richmond College, C.U.N.Y.*

Charles Chatfield, *Wittenberg University*

The Eagle and The Dove

The American Peace Movement
and
United States Foreign Policy,
1900-1922

edited by

John Whiteclay Chambers II

Garland Publishing, Inc., New York & London

WITHDRAWN

1976

39579

Copyright © 1976

Garland Publishing, Inc.

All Rights Reserved

Library of Congress Cataloging in Publication Data
Main entry under title:

The Eagle and the dove.

(The Garland library of war and peace)
Bibliography: p.
1. Peace--History--Addresses, essays, lectures.
2. United States--Foreign relations--20th century--
Addresses, essays, lectures. 3. Pacifism--History--
Addresses, essays, lectures. I. Chambers, John
Whiteclay. II. Series.
JX1961.U6E24   327'.172'0973   79-147763
ISBN 0-8240-0503-1

For my Mother
Le-Arie P. Chambers

Administrative Assistant
to the National Executive Secretary
of The Women's International
League for Peace and Freedom,
1944-1952

Contents

CONTENTS

CONTENTS

CONTENTS

CONTENTS

CONTENTS

Preface

The War in Vietnam taught an entire generation of Americans about opposition to war. In fact, the most unpopular conflict in the nation's history produced millions of peace enthusiasts in only a handful of years. During the late 1960s and early 1970s, the debilitating experience in Southeast Asia contributed to a massive and direct challenge to the U.S. government's war policies and to a reassessment of many of the attitudes and programs of the Cold War era.

Resistance to war continued even after U.S. troops left South Vietnam. In the reluctance of Americans to support new military ventures, the post-Vietnam period reflected many of the same attitudes as the two decades after World War I. However effective this hesitancy to apply military solutions might be in forcing the government to use diplomatic, political, or economic methods instead, it posed a problem of its own. Without a constructive program for peace, the popular response to the Vietnamese War might generate a renewed political isolationism and an apathy to international conditions. Such inattention to world affairs could contribute to future conflicts which in turn could threaten American security. A lack of understanding of peace could lead to war once again.

For there must be more to a truly effective peace movement than merely opposition to war. Building the basis for conflict resolution through both structural and procedural change represents an essential element in the elimination of major world conflagrations. There is a need for a new foreign policy in the aftermath of the war in Vietnam. The peace movement can play an important role in such a reassessment and redirection. It can bring new idealism, new priorities, new methods and new resources to policymaking and to the relationship between the United States and the rest of the world in the last quarter of the 20th century. It had done so before. One such earlier experience is the focus of this book.

This volume examines the emergence of the modern American peace movement in the first two decades of this century. In an introductory essay and the accompanying documents, it provides exemplary material and an analysis for understanding the movement and its impact upon American foreign policy between 1900 and 1922. It is the only anthology to examine the effects as well as the development of the peace movement in the United States. It demonstrates the transformation of the old-line pacifist organizations into a more broadly based social movement for restructuring international relations. It sets forth the specific proposals of the peace groups: disarmament, arbitration, conciliation, mediation, the establishment of international law and a world court, a confederation of nations, and world government. It presents some of the criticism directed at such proposals. And it seeks to show the response of the United States government.

Documents included in this anthology were selected from a variety of sources to illustrate the attitudes and actions of the peace advocates, their critics, and the government. All of these are primary sources, written during the period by participants in the debate over foreign policy. They include excerpts from correspondence, pamphlets, leaflets, handbills, cartoons, periodicals, newspapers, conference proceedings, congressional hearings, debates, and resolutions, presidential proclamations, speeches, and letters and informal diplomatic exchanges and formal notes, memoranda, and treaties. The nearly one-hundred documents reprinted here have been arranged in chronological order in sections relating to the major developments of the period.

The compilation and interpretation of these documents would not have been possible without the work of a number of other historians who have sought to reconstruct and assess the peace movement in the early 20th century. The pioneering work of Merle Curti of the University of Wisconsin deserves special credit. So do more specialized studies of the peace movement between the 1890s and the 1920s. Among those whose works I have drawn upon are Charles Chatfield of Wittenberg University; Blanche Wiesen Cook of John Jay College of the City University of New York; Charles DeBenedetti of the University of Toledo; Arthur Ekirch, Jr. of the State University of New York at Albany; Sondra Herman of DeAnza College in California; Warren Kuehl of the University of

PREFACE

Akron; Michael Lutzker of Richmond College of the City University of New York; C. Roland Marchand of the University of California at Davis; and David Patterson of Rice University. My own investigation of the debate over U.S. military and foreign policy in the World War I period contributed to my knowledge of the peace movement, its critics, and U.S. policymakers. I also learned much about the foreign policy of the period from the works of Arthur Link of Princeton University, Richard Leopold of Northwestern University, and Ernest May of Harvard University.

In the preparation of this volume, I am especially indebted to a number of persons. Bernice Nichols and Nina Walls assisted me in using the manuscripts of the Swarthmore College Peace Collection, the single most important depository for the study of pacifism in America. My research assistant, Jay Weiser, helped to locate and photocopy materials at a number of libraries in New York City. Carol Irelan guided the manuscript through the publishing process with both patience and expertise. As always, I am indebted to the editors of this series, particularly to Blanche Wiesen Cook, for numerous acts of kindness and aid.

Like pacifism itself, this work has been in many ways an effort of cooperation and friendship. Perhaps in some manner it may contribute to the understanding which is necessary for the achievement of just and lasting peace in the world.

John Whiteclay Chambers II
Department of History
Barnard College
Columbia University

June 1975

Introductory Essay

Probably never in its erratic history has the American peace movement experienced a more volatile course than during the first two decades of the 20th century. Within a single generation, it soared to heights of influence and expectation, then plunged like a roller coaster to the depths of impotence and despair during American belligerency in World War I, only to climb back to importance in the years following the armistice. It was an amazing performance by the conglomeration of individuals and groups known collectively as the peace movement.

Among the most dramatic aspects of the peace movement were not only its resiliency, but also its diversity. While this social movement sought to reduce or eliminate warfare in international relations, it was plagued by disagreement over both means and ends. The majority of adherents could be most appropriately called peace advocates. They wanted to move the world away from warfare, but while they sought other means of settling disputes such as international law and a world court, they were willing in extraordinary conditions to employ some kind of force if necessary.

A more extreme minority was composed of pacifists—absolute non-resistants—who refused to sanction the use of collective violence in any case. Despite their differences, both peace advocates and pacifists considered themselves members of the peace movement and endeavored to redirect American foreign policy and international relations during this period.

As one aspect of the broad movement to reform American institutions in the Progressive Era the peace movement met with both successes and failures in its campaign. Supported by some of the nation's most prestigious people, including the President of the United States, it established arbitration and conciliation as accepted methods for this country to settle secondary disputes. It won American participation in both Hague peace conferences and in the working of the Hague Tribunal. Yet it was unable to achieve binding arbitration for all disputes, and it failed to establish the United States as chief mediator in a league of neutral nations during the European War that broke out in 1914. American participation in the World War splintered, drained, and radicalized the peace movement. Rebounding in the postwar period, the movement helped to defeat peacetime conscription and to achieve the first step towards comprehensive naval disarmament. However, it failed completely in its long-range goal of establishing the basis for lasting international peace.

The twisting history of the peace movement in these years can only be understood in relation to changing developments in the United States and the world. Industrialism, nationalism, and imperialism had brought immense changes by the turn of the century. Technological revolutions in transportation, communication, industry, and warfare had greatly increased the power and ambition of major nations. Provided with weapons by the new technology, the armies and navies of Britain, France, Germany, Italy, Russia and Japan carried their nations' banners into Asia and Africa in a new surge of imperial expansion. Politically and economically, the face of the world changed within a few years. The aspirations and the forces of the expanding nations often clashed with those of indigenous peoples and those of other imperialist nations. Finally in 1914, Europe itself marched to war initiating a conflict which, within three years, led to American military intervention across the Atlantic.

As the United States entered the 20th century a burgeoning, urban-industrial giant in a rapidly changing world, Americans had already begun to re-examine and redefine many of the institutions which had been formed in years when the country had been more agrarian and isolated. Nowhere was that reappraisal more evident than in the field of international relations. The Venezuela controversy with Britain, the Spanish-American War, the acquisition of an island empire sweeping from Puerto Rico to the Philippines, and the extension of American interests to the Far East demonstrated that the United States was redefining its relations with other nations and exercising its increasing power.

INTRODUCTION

The search for a proper foreign policy for the new industrial America in a world of arming and ambitious nations elicited a variety of proposed solutions. One was a reaffirmation of the traditional policies designed to avoid involvement in European dynastic conflicts and turmoil. Specific doctrines included political isolationism—the avoidance of permanent alliances which would restrict American freedom of action—and the policy of neutrality towards wars between other nations.

The traditional isolationist program received much support. It was particularly popular in the rural South and Midwest. However, these agrarian regions were not in favor of complete withdrawal from world affairs. They endorsed expanded trade, defense of the nation's shores, and prevention of any additional European colonies in the Western Hemisphere, the essence of the Monroe Doctrine. To the isolationists, Americans could continue to rely upon their traditional defense—the breadth of the Atlantic and Pacific Oceans, the weakness of their Canadian and Mexican neighbors, the balance of power among major nations abroad, and the defense ability of the navy and the small regular army, supported by millions of Americans who would volunteer when needed.

Other Americans, however, sought to break with a tradition they considered inadequate for the new domestic and international circumstances. Militant expansionists like Theodore Roosevelt, Admiral Alfred Thayer Mahan, and General Leonard Wood sought to commit the United States to an active use of diplomatic, economic, military, and naval power in pursuit of broadened goals. Viewing continued expansion as inevitable and desirable, they concluded that this country should secure its strategic position in the Western Hemisphere, and both vigorously pursue investment and trade throughout the world and ensure the shipping routes necessary to maintain that commerce. To support this foreign policy, they urged the building of a large modern navy and merchant marine, the establishment of far-flung coaling stations, naval bases, and entrepôts, and the creation of an efficient and expandable army and massive numbers of pretrained reservists. Additionally, they advocated a much more active diplomacy. The cornerstones of their policy were, first, active cooperation with Great Britain in maintaining the balance of power and freedom of the seas and, second, the prevention of threats to American interests in East Asia and the Western Hemisphere from powerful expanding nations like Germany and Japan. A different suggestion for adjusting America's relationship with the world was made by those internationalists who also wanted the United States to play a more active world role economically and diplomatically, but who hoped to curtail or even eliminate the use of military and naval force. Unlike the militant expansionists, these people put their hope in arbitration, mediation, adjudication and international cooperation rather than naked power to safeguard U.S. interests and security and world peace. This reform of the international order and American foreign policy was advocated most strongly in the first two decades of the 20th century by members of the peace movement.

To a certain extent, these broad categories of foreign policy attitudes are analytical devices imposed upon the past to help understand the processes of historical development. They are accurate only as general descriptions of broad tendencies. There was, in fact, considerable overlapping, especially as time progressed. Most members of the peace movement were reform internationalists, but when some specific issue such as military or naval expansion or U.S. entry into World War I arose, some of them appealed to traditional isolationism. Conversely, some isolationists belonged to peace organizations because they saw the movement as a means of safeguarding U.S. interests without active intervention abroad. Some militant expansionists, like Theodore Roosevelt, were willing to support reform internationalism in minor matters while continuing to believe that expansion would ultimately generate conflicts that could only be resolved by force. Thus with considerable subtlety and complexity, these three broad strategies for foreign policy—isolationism, militant expansionism, and reform internationalism (organizationally expressed in the peace movement)—helped to shape American foreign policy during the first two decades of the 20th century.

INTRODUCTION
I
(1900-1914)

The American peace movement grew dramatically during the first decade and a half of the new century after years of relative lethargy. Since its inception during the reform outburst of the 1830s, the movement had been composed primarily of Quakers and other religious pacifists and a handful of New England reformers. Its foremost leaders, William Ladd, Elihu Burritt, Alfred Love and Benjamin Trueblood, had advocated an international court, periodic congresses of nations, the use of arbitration, and the neutralization of zones of conflict. Yet they generated little enthusiasm. In 1900, even the largest and oldest group, the American Peace Society, remained a small, Boston-centered organization with an annual budget of less than six thousand dollars. Change, however, came quickly.

Beginning around 1905 the traditional peace movement began to be transformed under the pressure of events and changing attitudes. Central to this were the imperialist rivalries among the major European powers, the growing naval arms race between Britain and Germany, the emergence of peace sentiments and organizations in many western nations, the first Hague Peace Conference of 1899, and the increasing American attention to international events. More specifically, the pressure for a more effective peace movement came as a result of the Spanish-American War of 1898, the bloody American suppression of the Philippine insurrection between 1899 and 1902, the Russo-Japanese War of 1904-1905, and the call for a Second Hague Peace Conference.

Under pressure from a number of peace advocates, including several congressmen, President Theodore Roosevelt, during the 1904 election, called for another international conference to be held at The Hague in 1907. Alarmed by the enormous casualties of the Russo-Japanese conflict—the first war between major powers in thirty-five years and the first to be fought with rapid-firing artillery and machine guns—many Americans ardently supported Roosevelt's summons. The historian Warren Kuehl has suggested that the anticipation of the Second Hague Conference and the preparations for it contributed directly to the unprecedented activity and growth of the peace movement which began in 1905.

In the following decade, the ranks of the established peace groups swelled and a number of new organizations were created. The American Peace Society grew from seven branch chapters in 1909 to thirty-one in 1914, an increase of 340 per cent. By 1914, the Society counted seven thousand dues-paying members, an increase of 600 per cent in seven years. Furthermore, the expansion of the traditional peace groups was matched by the enlistment of new groups in the effort to eliminate war. C.R. Marchand and M.A. Lutzker have demonstrated that the assumptions of the peace movement about the need to restrain popular emotions which led to war and the necessity of achieving social and international harmony found favor with many American business and civic leaders. Many of these men were already concerned about threats to American domestic peace and stability from new immigrants and from increasingly class-conscious groups like the Socialists. Thus concern about both external and internal disorder helped contribute to the growth of the peace movement and its programs in this period.

A number of alternative strategies were offered as the peace movement grew in strength and diversity in the early years of the 20th century. While not all adherents supported each with equal intensity, the methods were generally endorsed by the groups within the movement.

Many of the prestigious new peace advocates—lawyers, educators, and businessmen—sought to establish an international common law through a world court and its decisions. The number of international attorneys had been increasing with the growth of world trade and investment in the late 19th Century. In 1905, a number of them, led by Dean George Kirchwey of Columbia Law School, founded the American Society of International Law. Five years later, James Brown Scott, the State Department solicitor, led another group in organizing the American Society for the Judicial Settlement of International Disputes. Viewing international arguments narrowly as specific grievances rather than broader clashes of

INTRODUCTION

economic and political interests, these legalistic peace advocates sought to substitute world law and an international
judiciary for European-style power politics. It was in essence,
a modest program, involving only slight constriction of national sovereignty and little change in the traditional reluctance of Americans to intervene politically or militarily in
European affairs. The plan called for the United States to
agree to submit justiciable disputes—which would not involve
vital matters of self-defense—to a world court that would
solve international disagreements through judicial action.

The growth of world trade and communications seemed to
some Americans to be making war a wasteful anachronism. A
number of peace-minded businessmen and publicists believed
that economic growth and prosperity depended upon stable
international conditions and uninterrupted trade. To them, the
uncertainty produced by conflict and war scares disrupted
economic conditions and jeopardized profits for most businessmen except unscrupulous speculators. Scholars like William
Graham Sumner asserted that in the evolution of society,
commerce and industry produced a more rationalized and less
warlike world than the warrior-dominated societies of feudal
times. The English writer Norman Angell contended in his
influential book *The Great Illusion* that modern war was becoming so costly in life and property that it was unprofitable
to wage it.

Peace advocates sought to educate the American public to
the need for thinking in terms of international order and peaceful settlement of disputes. Among the most prominent businessmen joining this campaign were Edward Ginn and Andrew
Carnegie. A wealthy Boston publisher, Ginn established the
World Peace Foundation in 1910 with a gift of one million
dollars, one-third of his fortune. It financed a massive promotional effort among young people on behalf of peace. Within a
year, Carnegie, a retired steel magnate, dwarfed Ginn's gesture
by creating the Carnegie Endowment for International Peace
through a grant of ten million dollars. Headed by lawyers like
Elihu Root and James Scott and educators such as Nicholas
Murray Butler, the president of Columbia University, the
Endowment promoted scholarly research into the causes of

war and the peaceful settlement of international problems. It also subsidized most of the peace societies and soon became influential in determining their leadership and policies.

A multilateral approach to peace was attempted at the Second Hague Conference which met in 1907. Many peace advocates hoped the delegates from various nations would agree to limit armaments, codify international law, and create a permanent and effective international court. However, not all agreed. Elihu Root, then Secretary of State, instructed the American delegates to avoid entangling alliances and to oppose disarmament since the U.S. Navy had not yet completed its new superbattleships. While the Americans did work for extension of arbitration and a more precise statement of the rights and duties of neutrals in wartime, the conference was a disappointment to many. The Germans defeated a U.S. proposal for a permanent treaty of arbitration, and the British blocked American attempts to insure greater protection of neutral rights in war. In the end, the Conference merely urged represented governments to consider the problem of armaments. The delegates' chief accomplishment, an improved formula for a permanent court of arbitral justice, failed to be ratified.

Other suggestions for achieving world peace were put forward by bolder members of the peace movement. Proposals for disarmament ranged from suggestions for multilateral arms reductions to cries from non-resistants for unilateral abolition of armaments and the elimination of standing armies. Others called for some kind of federation of nations. One alternative was Andrew Carnegie's plan for a league of peace in which the major powers would use economic sanctions and an international police force against aggressors. Another was the plan of Hamilton Holt, editor of *The Independent* magazine, for a world government which would include both a legislature to develop laws and procedures for peace and an executive to apply decisions to specific cases.

An even more extreme alternative solution was advocated by a few pacifistic social reformers. Jane Addams, the founder of Hull House in Chicago, proposed the creation of an international welfare community as a substitute for war. As early as 1904, she suggested that the labor movement, with its ideal of human solidarity, and the social reform effect, with its trust in the masses, could serve as moral substitutes for international conflict. She offered these as alternative outlets for individual desires for patriotism, adventure, self-sacrifice and glory. The idea greatly appealed to William James, the Harvard philosopher. Six years later, he called publicly for a different equivalent for war. Concluding that martial tendencies were innate, James sought to redirect them into socially-useful purposes. As a consequence, he urged that young people be recruited into non-military teams to help improve the conditions of life in the new industrial metropolises. Such direct alternatives to martial ventures were adopted by the Boy Scouts and a few other youth groups, but they did not become governmental programs until the Civilian Conservation Corps of the 1930s and the Peace Corps of the 1960s.

The peace movement, however, did have an influence on American foreign policy in the years before World War I. In part this was due to the fear of the new technological warfare demonstrated in the Russo-Japanese War. To some extent it was caused by the widespread belief that war had outlasted its usefulness and was wasteful and archaic. Partly, this influence was a result of the belief in this reform period that patterns of behavior—even international relations—could be improved through the application of human intelligence. And to a certain degree, it was a product both of the activity of the peace movement and of the location of a number of peace advocates in important positions in the government.

This influence was especially felt in the State Department. There, Secretaries of State Elihu Root (1905-1909), William Jennings Bryan (1913-1915), and Robert Lansing (1915-1920) had been, at other points in their careers, officers of peace groups. Furthermore, between 1906 and 1915, the department's chief legal officers—James Brown Scott, Chandler P. Anderson, John Bassett Moore, and Robert Lansing—had been members of the original executive committee of the American Society of International Law. Additionally, Presidents William Howard Taft and Woodrow Wilson were both partisans of the movement for international peace.

INTRODUCTION

A number of Americans received Nobel Peace Prizes during this period. Theodore Roosevelt won the prize in 1906 for his mediation of the Russo-Japanese War and his support of international conferences to reduce world tensions. He accepted the prize in 1910 after leaving office. Elihu Root was awarded the prize in 1912 for his work on behalf of international law and arbitration; he did not deliver his acceptance speech until 1914. Woodrow Wilson was the recipient of the Nobel Prize for 1919 for his proposals for international peace in the postwar period, but because of his illness was unable to journey to Norway to deliver an acceptance speech. A decade later, in 1931, two of the leading peace advocates of this period—Jane Addams and Nicholas Murray Butler—jointly received the Nobel Prize for their work for peace.

There was no doubt that peace was popular with many citizens and political leaders during the first two decades of the 20th century, but the various attempts to ensure peace produced mixed results.

The movement to establish a world court, which would construct an international common law, met with both success and failure. The First Hague Conference in 1899 had established a Permanent Court of Arbitration. Not a permanent sitting court, despite its name, this body consisted of a panel of more than one hundred potential arbitrators. Critics said these jurists and diplomats often compromised and split differences regardless of law or equity and that this deterred nations with strong cases from using the Hague Tribunal.

Theodore Roosevelt and his secretary of state sought to invigorate this international agency. In an attempt to rescue it from inactivity, the President referred a minor American controversy with Mexico to it in 1902 and the following year persuaded Britain, Germany and Italy to end their blockade of Venezuela and submit their grievances over unpaid debts to the Tribunal. From the State Department, Elihu Root tried to create a permanent court of sitting jurists which could substitute decisions based upon law for diplomatic compromises. In 1907, he played a key role in the creation of a Central American Court of Justice and he instructed the American delegates

INTRODUCTION

to the Second Hague Conference to work to convert the Hague Tribunal into a similar court.

A permanent international court with broad powers failed to come into existence until after World War I, however. The Second Hague Conference could not agree on the manner of choosing a small number of jurists since that would eliminate some nations from representation. It was not until 1921, that a World Court was created by the League of Nations with jurists chosen by a vote of the member nations. Despite the efforts of the peace movement and of President Wilson and Secretary Lansing, the Senate refused to allow the United States to join the court. Nevertheless, several American jurists were elected to it. Before it was succeeded by the International Court of Justice of the United Nations in 1945, the World Court rendered nearly three dozen judgments and over two dozen advisory opinions. The most important of these was the disallowance in 1933 of Norway's claim to the north coast of Greenland and the affirmation of Danish sovereignty in that area.

Numerous attempts to establish arbitration as the basis for settling various types of difficulties between the United States and other nations were made under the impetus of peace advocates and in the wake of international events. In the 19th century, the U.S. had used the technique several times in regard to boundary disputes and property claims. The most famous of these was the 1872 award by an international arbitration board of fifteen million dollars in gold to the United States as a result of the damages caused by the British-built Confederate raider *Alabama* during the Civil War. Twenty-five years later, following a war scare between Britain and the United States over a Venezuelan boundary dispute, the administration of Grover Cleveland provided in the Olney–Pauncefote Treaty of 1897 for arbitration of several kinds of property and territorial disputes between the two nations if they should occur. However, Anglophobia and the Senate's own sense of prerogative combined to prevent the two-thirds majority needed in the upper chamber to approve the treaty.

The popularity of the idea of arbitration grew slowly in succeeding years. It received the endorsement of the First

Hague Conference as the most effective and equitable means of settling legal questions. Further evidence of support came during the 1904 election year when President Roosevelt sponsored a series of bilateral pacts requiring the U.S. to arbitrate certain classes of disputes. Once again, the Senate, cautious of its prerogative and American security, bridled at such suggestions. When it amended Secretary of State John Hay's treaties to such an extent that they became almost meaningless, except as general statements, the President refused to submit the modified treaties to the other signatory governments.

A compromise was worked out in the second Roosevelt administration. In the winter of 1908–1909, Secretary of State Root signed twenty-four bilateral arbitration treaties with other nations. In deference to the Senate, these treaties exempted disputes involving America's vital interests, independence, and national honor and, equally as important, upheld the Senate's authority to define the scope of arbitration in every case. Thus restricted, the five–year treaties were overwhelmingly approved. While Roosevelt and Root viewed arbitration as an occasionally useful, semijudicial device to settle minor international disputes or to allow a nation to retreat from an untenable or embarrassing position without loss of prestige, the succeeding Taft administration took a much bolder position.

William Howard Taft and his Secretary of State, Philander Knox, wanted to make arbitration a vital tool in reshaping international relations into peaceful channels. They already encouraged private American investment in underdeveloped nations—the so-called "dollar diplomacy"—as a means of expanding American trade and avoiding instability and military intervention. In a bid to increase his sagging popularity, the Chief Executive in 1910 proposed to submit almost all international disputes relating to the United States—even those involving national honor—to judicial arbitration. The program divided Americans and split the peace movement. Roosevelt and Root, for example, argued that the United States should not accept an arbitration decision against its vital interests. Despite an intensive educational and lobbying campaign by the White House and most of the peace groups, the Senate refused to accept Taft's treaties with Britain and France but rewrote them into general statements in favor of arbitration without compelling the United States to any specific action. Angrily, Taft rejected the Senate's amended treaties. After three such clashes between the Executive and the Legislature in fifteen years, the limits of U.S. acceptance of the arbitral process had been clearly defined. Arbitration could be used only in regard to disputes of relatively minor importance. The Senate refused to jeopardize its power in foreign affairs, to endanger the Monroe Doctrine or U.S. security, to alienate Southerners who feared the claims of foreign holders of Confederate bonds, to aggravate Westerners concerned about Oriental immigration restriction, or to anger Americans, especially those of German or Irish ancestry, who feared that the treaties created a virtual Anglo-American alliance. The upper chamber determined that the U.S. government would not make sweeping promises in peaceful times which it would not fulfill in periods of crisis. Apparently the Wilson administration agreed, for it did not adopt Taft's position, but was content to renew Root's treaties in 1913 and 1914 when they approached expiration.

In the early years of the 20th century, the United States did employ arbitration in at least three disputes with its neighbors. In 1903, it agreed to submit a Canadian-Alaskan boundary controversy which had flared after the discovery of gold in that area. With the support of the British and American delegates, a tri-national panel decided in favor of the U.S. claims. Seven years later, the Hague Tribunal settled a dispute over American fishing rights off the Newfoundland Canadian fisheries through a compromise which gave some recognition to the position of both sides. Also in 1910, the United States and Mexico agreed to submit the contested Chamizal tract issue to a panel. Despite these cases, the U.S. Government refused to arbitrate such important matters as Colombia's grievances regarding American support of the Panamanian revolution in 1903, the interpretation of the Hay-Pauncefote Treaty in the quarrel over the U.S. exception from Panama Canal tolls in 1912, or the many differences between the policies of President

INTRODUCTION

Wilson and President Victoriano Huerta during the early stages of the Mexican Revolution in 1913 and 1914.

While the Wilson administration proved reluctant to arbitrate these issues, Secretary of State Bryan did seek to provide conciliation machinery to avert wars. Bryan had opposed American military conquest of the Philippines and had become a Christian pacifist after a visit with Count Leo Tolstoy in Russia in 1902. The leader of the agrarian wing of the Democratic Party, Bryan found enthusiastic response in the rural South and Midwest to his religious rhetoric on behalf of peace. It was primarily the opinion makers in the metropolitan areas of the country who publicly belittled his aptitude for being Secretary of State. During 1913 and 1914, Bryan negotiated thirty bilateral treaties which provided that every dispute, even those involving national honor, should be submitted to an international commission for investigation. Uniquely, the signatory nations—including most major powers except Germany and Japan—agreed to a one-year "cooling-off" period while the commission investigated such disputes. Even though he realized that the disputant nations could then reject the conciliating agency's recommendation, Bryan hoped that overheated tempers would cool in the waiting period and world opinion for peace would be mobilized. While the conciliation treaties were never used, they did help to influence peace-keeping policies in the period after World War I.

Although peace advocates attempted to establish machinery which would eliminate war, they differed in their opinion over whether some degree of force might be necessary to ensure international order and whether the United States should, therefore, arm or disarm. Many of those like Ginn, Holt, and the Quakers Lucia Ames Mead and William Hull, who favored a world federation wanted an international peace-keeping force with limited powers. They advocated national disarmament. On the other hand, international lawyers like Root, Moore, and Scott held national military power necessary for defense of vital interests. A number of peace society trustees were also affiliated with organizations which supported the expansion of American military and naval power, such as the Navy League and the National Security League. In Roosevelt's cabinet, Root had been secretary of war before he became secretary of state. While these people sought peace through arbitration, they were prepared to rely upon force if other means failed.

Many peace advocates urged disarmament, or at least arms reduction, rather than expansion. The idea was an old one; Americans had inherited a suspicion of large standing armies from their colonial period. During the 19th Century, the United States, Britain, and Canada had averted a threatened arms race on the Great Lakes and along the Canadian border by demilitarizing the area during a forty-year period between the Rush-Bagot Agreement of 1817 and the Treaty of Washington in 1871. Soon, however, the issue of the necessity of armaments arose from another area.

In the late 19th and early 20th centuries, a naval arms race began among leading powers. Germany began to challenge British naval supremacy and triggered a naval building spree. Furthermore, the Japanese Navy showed its prowess by demolishing the Russian ships in Far Eastern waters. In his first administration, President Roosevelt launched a major warship building program. Naval appropriations leaped nearly 40 per cent from $85 million to $118 million a year and the U.S. Navy became the second largest fleet in the world. Roosevelt's "Big Navy" program generated considerable opposition, and a coalition to stop it formed among many peace advocates, anti-imperialists, rural isolationists, and labor unionists. In Congress, a small, but vocal bipartisan bloc criticized the shipbuilding program as a jingoistic and unnecessary waste of tax revenues fostered by the President, navalists, and the steel and munitions manufacturers. Led by Republican Senator Eugene Hale of Maine, the chairman of the Naval Affairs Committee, and Republican Congressman Theodore Burton of Ohio, the "Little Navy" group was able by 1906 —in the middle of Roosevelt's second term—to trim the President's requests for new battleships. Taft continued the policy of naval expansion, but faced an increasingly hostile Congress. Between 1910 and 1913, the legislators balked several times in voting funds for more warships. Twice they adopted resolutions urging the Chief Executive to seek to limit the naval arms race through an international agreement. Despite this expression of opinion from Capitol Hill, however, the escalation of weaponry continued, except for a brief pause in the early years of the Wilson administration when the Democratic President curtailed the requests of the admirals.

In the first decade and a half of the 20th century, the United States appeared a paradox as it emerged as an active world power. These years witnessed both an unprecedented peacetime naval building program and also the dramatic revitalization of the peace movement as an important force in American foreign policy. The United States seemed to be represented by both the eagle and the dove.

Swollen in numbers, wealth, and prestige, the peace organizations in this period suggested alternative means of assuring national security and fulfilling what many saw as America's mission of redeeming the world through its liberal, democratic, capitalistic institutions. The peace strategists rejected involvement in European-style power politics and balance of power formulas. They also refused to continue traditional American political isolationism. Between 1900 and 1914, several proposals of the peace movement—arbitration, conciliation, disarmament, and the establishment of international peace conferences, international law, and a world court—reached the stage of national debate in the pages of the mass media and in the halls of the national government. Most of these proposals—except disarmament—were adopted to a limited degree as national goals, although U.S. foreign policy continued to be based in the short-run primarily on the defense of expanding American interests through economic, diplomatic, and military measures.

The extent to which the United States relied upon nonforceful means of diplomacy represented both the strength of the peace movement and of the belief in the sanctity of treaties and the pledged word of governments. Moreover, this was also a period in which neither American vital interests nor the world balance of power, which helped to protect these, was confronted by a major military challenge. The beliefs and circumstances of this period were abruptly confronted by dramatic new forces when the general European war broke out in August 1914.

II
(1914-1917)

War is a transforming event. The war which broke out in the summer of 1914 and raged for four bloody years had a profound impact upon the peace movement and U.S. foreign policy even before the nation joined the fray as a belligerent in 1917. Gradually, between 1914 and 1917, the world's most powerful neutral edged into the maelstrom across the Atlantic. As a result, the peace movement splintered into conservative and radical wings, each pursuing different strategies. While many of the established peace societies became moribund or dormant under the changed circumstances, several new peace-oriented organizations emerged and pursued much more activist roles. In the meantime, the Wilson administration moved from attempts at mediation to the decision for American military intervention. The period of American neutrality during the first three years of the European War thus proved to be a time of re-examination of the attitudes and policies of the peace movement and of testing its influence upon American foreign policy.

Members of the peace movement had been shocked and dismayed by the bloodshed that began in 1914, but they divided in their response to the European war. Many of those in the prewar peace organizations came to support the Allied cause, especially after a German submarine sank the Cunard passenger liner *Lusitania* on its way from New York to Southampton. The brutality and recklessness of the U-boat campaign and the German challenge to British supremacy of the seas led some to condemn the Kaiser's actions as a threat to both American security and prosperity and to international law and order.

A number of the more conservative prewar organizations suspended their major efforts for world peace until after the

INTRODUCTION

conclusion of the war. They advocated the defeat of Germany as essential to progress towards the establishment of international relations based upon cooperation and judicial principles, and many of them, therefore, supported increased military and naval spending by the United States. Led by its secretary James Brown Scott, the Carnegie Endowment for International Peace proved instrumental in persuading many peace groups not to try to stop the current war by mediation but to encourage an Allied victory or at least to concentrate on postwar plans. Subsidized organizations like the American Peace Society and the International Peace Bureau soon accepted that general position. So did many members of the American Society of International Law, the American Society for Judicial Settlement of International Disputes, the New York Peace Society, and the World Peace Foundation.

However, many of the more conservative peace advocates joined in creating a new organization designed to work for a postwar league of nations which would use force if necessary to maintain peace and order. Under the impetus of President A. Lawrence Lowell of Harvard University, who had been a member of several peace organizations, these men founded the Association for a League to Enforce Peace. The idea of a league of nations was not entirely new. It had been advocated in various forms since the 17th century by people as disparate as the Duc de Sully, William Penn, and Immanuel Kant. The Holy Alliance and the First Hague Conference had been steps towards it in the 19th century. In the early 20th century, it was endorsed by Andrew Carnegie in 1904 and by Theodore Roosevelt in his Nobel Peace Prize Address in 1910. Yet these proposals had been largely ignored even by the peace movement. Not until the World War undermined the competing notion that nations could be restrained from going to war by public opinion or moral force, did the concept of a league with sanctions begin to gain widespread support.

The 1915 proposal for a league to enforce peace combined the idea of deliberation and delay in times of crisis with the processes of arbitration and adjudication and the ultimate sanction of force. According to the Association's proposal issued in January of that year, member nations would have to agree to submit justiciable questions to a world court and abide by the result. All other questions—the most important ones—would be submitted to a council of conciliation, made up of the major powers, for recommendation. Economic and military force could be used against nations which refused to abide by these recommendations or which were judged guilty of aggression.

With deliberation and adroitness, the Association for a League to Enforce Peace put forward its program in an attempt to influence both the public and key governmental decision-makers. Its prestigious leadership was headed by William Howard Taft, former president of the United States. Its program was widely publicized by a number of other prewar peace advocates including Hamilton Holt, Theodore Marburg and John Bates Clark. Seeking broad-based mainstream support, the association emphasized the postwar nature of its program and shunned discussion of proposals to end the present war through compromise. And it avoided contact with the various new pacifist groups which emerged and did advocate such a program after the outbreak of the European war.

Unlike the conservative peace advocates and the Association for a League to Enforce Peace, the new peace organizations which appeared after 1914 worked to conclude the bloody conflict as quickly and as fairly as possible. In fact, the new activist organizations which sprang up between 1914 and 1916 came into being to a great extent because the old-time and conservative peace societies refused to discuss proposals for ending the current war peacefully and in a number of cases even supported measures for increased military preparedness.

The new spectrum of groups virtually reconstituted the peace movement, at least one wing of it. Included were short-lived associations like the League to Limit Armaments and the Emergency Peace Federation and more enduring organizations like the Women's Peace Party and the American Union against Militarism. This shifting coalition, as historians Charles Chatfield and Blanche Wiesen Cook have noted, was made up of action-oriented peace advocates who were also feminists, social workers, journalists, labor lawyers, and social-gospel clergymen. While hostile to the Kaiser's actions, they were also critical of many Allied policies as well.

Drawing upon liberal thought in both Europe and America, these pacifist progressives urged the United States to play an active but peaceful role in ending the war and preventing future conflagrations. They called upon the Wilson administration to summon a conference of neutral nations which would offer to mediate between the belligerents. They also advocated terms which they believed would ensure a just and lasting peace. The liberal peace proposals provided for no annexations or indemnities, an end to secret treaties and entangling alliances, elimination of trade barriers and colonial empires, and the reduction of large armies and navies. In their place, the liberal pacifists urged disarmament, neutralization of the sea lanes, self-determination of peoples, democratic governments, open diplomacy, and international machinery for the judicial settlement of disputes between nations.

The most lasting of the new liberal pacifist organizations was the Women's Peace Party which soon became known as The Women's International League for Peace and Freedom (W.I.L.P.F.) and has continued to work for peace ever since. Founded in January 1915 by a score of women's groups, the organization represented forty thousand affiliated members. It was led by American feminists such as Jane Addams, Carrie Chapman Catt, Anna Garlin Spencer, and Charlotte Perkins Gilman, and European feminists like Rosika Schwimmer of Hungary and Emmeline Pethick-Lawrence of Britain. They claimed that women had a special revulsion against war and a particular responsibility for the future of the human race. Endorsing mediation and the liberal peace proposals, they also recommended that the President appoint a commission to work to prevent war.

In April 1915, forty-five delegates from the Women's Peace Party attended an International Congress of Women at The Hague. In conjunction with women from belligerent and other neutral nations, they formed the W.I.L.P.F. and elected Addams as its first chairperson. In a dramatic effort, the women called for a continuous conference of neutral nations to offer mediation to the belligerents. A delegation took the proposal directly to statesmen in the fighting countries, but since none of the men was willing to initiate proposals for peace, the conference was never organized.

A subsequent attempt to force the neutral governments to offer mediation to the belligerents ended in one of the most dramatic diplomatic episodes of 1915. It centered on the private initiative for peace launched by Henry Ford, the automobile manufacturer. A pacifist who believed war wasteful in both lives and property, Ford became convinced that the main stumbling block to ending the war had become the ineffectiveness of the diplomats. Psychologically and financially prepared to make a bold bid for peace, Ford was persuaded by Madame Schwimmer to send a mission of distinguished persons across the Atlantic to join leading Europeans in compelling the neutral nations either to extend their good offices for mediation or, failing that, to offer suggestions for peace themselves.

Maladroitly promising to "get the boys out of their trenches and back to their homes by Christmas Day," Ford chartered the steamship *Oscar II* early in December 1915 to carry a peace mission to Europe later that month. Derided by the press, his effort was crippled before it began. Many public figures subsequently declined Ford's invitation to sail, and the auto magnate himself deserted the expedition as soon as the vessel landed in Scandinavia. Nevertheless, the "peace ship" mission did organize a Neutral Conference for Continuous Mediation at Stockholm. As historian Merle Curti has explained, the Conference remained until 1917 a nongovernmental clearinghouse for suggestions for peaceful means to end the war.

While some of the new peace groups emphasized the need for the United States to help mediate to end the war, the American Union against Militarism (A.U.A.M.) was formed in New York City in November, 1915 primarily to dissuade the U.S. government from expanding the Army and Navy. Originally, the new organization was established in response to the so-called preparedness campaign led by Theodore Roosevelt, General Leonard Wood, and groups like the National Security League, the Navy League, and the Military Training

INTRODUCTION

Camps Association. By the fall of 1915, these bodies and the international situation had convinced President Wilson to recommend an expansion of the armed services. In opposition, the A.U.A.M. was created by a number of progressives, including social workers like Addams and Lillian Wald, journalists like Oswald Garrison Villard of *The Nation* and the New York *Evening Post* and Max Eastman af *The Masses,* labor lawyers such as his sister Crystal Eastman, Amos Pinchot, and Hollingsworth Wood, and social-gospel clergymen like John Haynes Holmes, and Rabbi Stephen Wise.

By the end of 1916, the American Union against Militarism had become the largest antimilitarist organization in the country. With branches in twenty-two cities, it counted over six thousand members and had another fifty thousand sympathizers on its mailing list. Through its adherents and its propaganda campaign, it sought to build a coalition of aroused farmers, workers, pacifists, immigrants and radicals against expansion of the military and the introduction of universal military training which most of the preparedness also advocated. On a budget of $35,000 a year, the A.U.A.M. sent out more than six-hundred thousand pieces of literature and accurately claimed to provide the only active nation-wide press service against militarism. It employed a full-time lobbyist on Capitol Hill and its leaders met directly with President Wilson on several occasions.

While not completely successful, the A.U.A.M. campaign against expansion of the armed forces was to some degree effective. Although it did not prevent the Congress from voting substantial increases in the military and naval services, it did aid in preventing the preparedness organizations from obtaining their full program, including conscription, and it even helped to modify the President's defense program. Furthermore, the antimilitarists obtained a Congressional declaration that the United States approved in principle of the reduction rather than expansion of armaments. Attached to the Naval Expansion Act of August, 1916 was a rider introduced by Representative Walter L. Hensley of Missouri which not only made such a statement of congressional opinion but also requested the President to invite an international conference

INTRODUCTION

on general disarmament and the creation of a true world court. If a disarmament agreement were reached, the Chief Executive was authorized to suspend the naval building program which Congress had just enacted.

The American Union against Militarism directed its efforts at international peace as well as the prevention of the expansion of armaments. In a statement of principles entitled "Towards a Peace that Shall Last," the organization endorsed the liberal peace program. The leaders of the A.U.A.M. opposed war because it endangered the concepts of liberty and of the preciousness of human life. They also believed that war threatened to terminate the progressive movement's attempt to achieve social reform and to uplift humanity.

In the area of international peacekeeping, the A.U.A.M.'s most significant historical accomplishment was in helping to prevent a war between Mexico and the United States in 1916. Relations between the two nations, tense since the outbreak of the Mexican Revolution in 1910, had been further strained when irregulars led by Francisco "Pancho" Villa crossed the border and killed a number of Americans in 1916. As a result, a punitive expedition under General John J. Pershing pursued Villa and his men several hundred miles into Mexico. Although the Americans failed to catch the irregulars, they came into conflict with Mexican federal soldiers.

On June 21, two troops of Pershing's cavalry encountered a detachment of 250 government troops near the town of Carrizal. A skirmish resulted in the deaths of twelve Americans and twenty-nine Mexicans. The next day, *The New York Times* and many other newspapers charged, under screaming headlines, that the American cavalrymen had been treacherously ambushed. War fever reached the government as well and President Wilson prepared to ask for a full-scale invasion of northern Mexico.

Seeking to counter the pressure for war, the A.U.A.M. moved swiftly. It obtained a first-hand account of the Carrizal incident from an American officer which showed that the U.S. cavalry, not the Mexican troops, had initiated the fighting. In a number of advertisements, it reprinted the officer's testimony, asserted that the incident was not a valid cause for war, and urged people to write to the government. Shaken by this new information and by a flood of anti-war telegrams, Wilson reversed his initial judgment and worked to avoid a major conflict, as did Venustiano Carranza, the Mexican chief of state. Consequently, the A.U.A.M. helped to launch negotiations by convening a commission of conciliation, made up of several leading private citizens from both sides, which served as a transitional body while an official Joint High Commission was created. Through its quick initiative, the A.U.A.M. had helped to avert war, although relations between the two countries remained extremely tense until the worsening European situation caused President Wilson to remove Pershing's forces from Mexico and formally recognize Carranza's government in March, 1917.

At the left wing of the peace movement in the years 1914 to 1917 stood the American Socialists. Although they sought to keep the United States out of the European War, the Socialists seldom worked with the peace societies. Nor did they share many of the assumptions or long-range goals of the liberal peace advocates. Indeed, the Socialists considered the peace groups thoroughly capitalistic and middle-class in orientation and generally held them in contempt. Unlike the liberals who believed the war had been caused by a combination of militarism, imperialism, nationalism, and the alliance system, the Socialists asserted the primacy of the economic motive. It was a businessmen's war, they argued, encouraged by the lust of merchants, manufacturers, and financiers for markets, trade, and colonies to exploit. Marxist-Leninist theory held that conflict between expanding capitalistic economies was an inevitable consequence of the profit-seeking of wealthy elites.

Socialists on both sides of the Atlantic proved ineffective in ending the war or in preventing the entry of the United States as a belligerent, although they offered a number of strategies to do both. With a few exceptions, most European Socialist leaders endorsed their nation's war efforts, compromising their Marxist principles to retain the support of the trade unions which generally were strongly nationalistic. American Socialists, with less strength in the labor movement, remained closer to Marx's principles of opposition to capitalist

INTRODUCTION

wars. To ensure U.S. neutrality, American Socialists like Eugene V. Debs, Allan Benson, Morris Hillquit, and Kate Richards O'Hare denounced preparedness, recommended an embargo against all belligerents, and urged that a national referendum be held before a declaration of war. William "Big Bill" Haywood, leader of the Industrial Workers of the World, the radical wing of the Socialists, suggested that the workers should stage a general strike rather than fight in a capitalist war, but the proposal was not endorsed by the majority of Socialists. Neither the American Socialists nor the "Wobblies" seem to have had much impact on the conduct of American foreign policy.

Woodrow Wilson had been influenced for some time by the growth of the peace movement and the ideas of international organization and world law. While aware of the movement, he had largely ignored it until its transformation around the time of the Second Hague Conference. In 1908 as president of Princeton, he had joined other leading educators in becoming an active member and speaker in the American Peace Society. Three years later, as governor of New Jersey, he had endorsed President Taft's arbitration treaties.

In the White House, Wilson continued to be attentive to the peace movement and its proposals. He endorsed Secretary of State Bryan's conciliation treaties. And in early 1914, he agreed to mediation by Argentina, Brazil and Chile to avoid war between the United States and Mexico over U.S. non-recognition of President Huerta and temporary American occupation of the ports of Tampico and Vera Cruz. Bryan remained in the cabinet until his resignation in the spring of 1915 over what he considered the harshness and partiality of the President's warning to Germany after the sinking of the *Lusitania*. Nevertheless, Wilson continued to learn of the views of representatives of various peace groups—the Association of the League to Enforce Peace, the Women's Peace Party, the American Union against Militarism, the American Neutral Conference Committee (founded in June 1916), and others--through notes and proposals they submitted to him directly or through his confidant, Colonel Edward M. House. While some urged increasing aid to the Allies to defeat Germany, others advocated mediation for a compromise peace. The divisions within the peace movement over both means and goals, reduced the effectiveness of the peace advocates. Such differences in the peace movement, together with deep divisions within American society over preparedness, munitions trade with the Allies, and Germany's submarine warfare, allowed President Wilson greater freedom of action in pursuing his own foreign policy.

Wilson eagerly sought to maintain this freedom of action in his role as head of the most powerful neutral nation. His initial desire was for an early end to the fighting in Europe in a compromise peace settlement that would maintain the balance of power and thus protect U.S. security. While playing the peacemaker, the President pursued his own policies, not those of the pacifists. Within four months after the outbreak of the war, he sent Colonel House as an unofficial emissary on a secret mission to the foreign offices of both sides. In a series of visits in 1915 and 1916, House proposed a compromise solution in which Germany would be granted wider scope in colonial areas and overseas markets if it would end its challenge to British naval superiority.

In 1916, Colonel House signed an agreement with British Foreign Secretary Edward Grey (the House-Grey Memorandum) which stated that when and if the moment proved opportune for Britain and France, President Wilson would call for a peace conference. If the Kaiser's government refused to participate, the United States in the words of the agreement "would probably enter the war against Germany." Because both sides believed they could still break the military deadlock and win the war, they did not respond to the Wilson administration's secret proposals for a negotiated peace. The House–Grey strategy was abandoned.

Wilson's cautious approach to America's policy was at odds with the dramatic proposals of the mediationists for U.S. leadership in ending the war. The keystone of their appeal was for the United States to take the lead in calling a convention of neutral nations to tempt the belligerents into peace negotiations. In view of German military dominance on the continent and the emerging submarine issue which threatened to draw the United States into the war, the President refused to agree to such a proposal. Neutral mediation seemed a remote issue to most Americans who were more concerned with Germany's submarine warfare, the President's policy of insisting on the right of Americans to travel on belligerent's ships (challenged by the unsuccessful Gore-McLemore Resolution in 1915), the growing munitions trade with the Allies, and the controversy over military preparedness. Wilson, in several meetings with the mediationists, indicated a reluctance to participate in any joint mediation schemes. His most important objections to American leadership in 1915 and 1916 in a neutral conference were, first, the unsettled difficulties with the German government over the submarine issue; second, the military situation on the Continent which was so unfavorable to the Allies that they would brand any American peace overtures as unneutral; and third, his belief that he should reserve judgment on the problem until the changing military situation made it fairly clear that both sides would accept American mediation. Wilson feared that if he committed himself prematurely to a specific mediation proposal, he might be rejected by the belligerents as a peace maker and therefore lose whatever influence he might have for ending the war at an opportune moment.

Despite his vacillation for two years without publicly offering mediation, Woodrow Wilson did not alienate the majority of peace workers. He met with their delegations on more than a dozen occasions between 1914 and 1917, listened to their pleas, and answered their letters. He sincerely admired people like Jane Addams, Lillian Wald, Hamilton Holt and Paul Kellogg and sympathized with their hopes for restoring peace in the world. He also hoped to bring an end to the war before the submarine controversy led to American belligerency. As a result, in the 1916 election, most of the mediationists supported him against the Republican nominee, Charles Evans Hughes, whose party had taken a more bellicose and nationalistic position on America's role in the war. Thus Wilson had skillfully pursued a foreign policy which did not alienate either the mediation advocates or those neutralist-isolationists who wanted to keep the United States aloof from Europe's problems. He won re-election in 1916 campaigning on the slogans of peace and prosperity. Many liberal pacifists campaigned and voted for him.

After his re-election, President Wilson began an intensive and public effort to mediate an end to the war based on the principles of the "new diplomacy" — open covenants and international cooperation. His note of Dec. 18, 1916, asked both sides to state their war aims publicly. When the Germans refused and the Allies offered terms clearly unfavorable to the Central Powers—withdrawal from all conquered territories, payment of indemnities, and the break-up of the Austro-Hungarian Empire—Wilson announced his own program for a desirable peace. He had come increasingly to believe that mediation had to be tied to the goals of the liberal peace program in order to ensure not only the proper conclusion of the world war, but the prevention of its recurrence. In the spring of 1916, he had endorsed the idea of a postwar league of nations and asserted, in the Democratic Party platform, that the United States had a duty to join any reasonable association of nations after the conflict. In a major address before the Senate on January 22, 1917, he called for a "peace without victory" and endorsed the liberal peace aims, including an international organization to guarantee world peace. While he dismayed those like Theodore Roosevelt who demanded unconditional surrender of Germany, the President's call for mediation and a compromise peace to establish a new framework of international relations won the applause of reform internationalists and peace advocates in both Europe and the United States.

The influence of the peace movement upon the President's decision to attempt publicly to mediate the war was relatively slight according to historian David Patterson. Occasionally indecisive and often politically expedient, Woodrow Wilson nevertheless had strong personal opinions. It was his own assessment of the changing international circumstances in 1916, rather than the suggestions of his advisors or of the mediation workers, which led to Wilson's peace moves. He believed that

INTRODUCTION

jettisoning the House-Grey Memorandum and adopting a more favorable position towards Germany might persuade the belligerents to allow him to negotiate. At the same time, the Allies increasing economic dependence upon the United States might enable him to force them to the conference table.

While the peace workers had little effect on the timing of Wilson's mediation attempt and failed to convince him of the usefulness of a conference of neutral nations, they did have significant influence on the President. Patterson has concluded that their persistent efforts between 1914 and 1916 helped nourish Wilson's interest in mediation even during the darkest hours as they gave him emotional support and relayed reports of anti-war sentiment from the European nations. Thus they helped to convince him that his independent peace move would receive support from moderates in both the United States and Europe. Additionally, the peace workers also helped to stimulate Wilson's interest in the liberal program for the reform of international relations. The President consciously drew upon the resolutions of the Women's Congress at The Hague and the pronouncements of British and American liberals in formulating his own maturing approach in 1916 to the postwar settlement.

Ironically, it was partly to achieve the principles of international reform that President Wilson took the United States into the World War in April 1917. His mediation proposals had failed to bring peace in the winter of 1916-17. Instead, the German government, under the influence of the military, decided upon all-out submarine warfare beginning February 1st against neutral as well as belligerent shipping in an attempt to starve the British into suing for peace. Events followed each other in rapid and almost compelling order: the announcement of unrestricted submarine wafare, the American severance of diplomatic relations with Germany, the publication of the Zimmermann telegram proposing a German alliance with Mexico against the United States, and the torpedoing and sinking of several American merchantships. On April 2, the President asked Congress to declare that a state of war already existed between the United States and Germany. He asserted that America would go to war to make the world safe for the spread of democratic principles.

The period between February and April 1917 witnessed the most extreme crisis to confront the peace movement in the early decades of the 20th century. The drift towards American belligerency in those nine weeks increased the fragmentation within the movement, while driving some activist groups towards even more intensive actions. Conservative organizations like the Carnegie Endowment and the American Peace Society, which had already decided against immediate peace efforts, concluded that U.S. intervention had become inevitable and even desirable to obtain world peace. Although divided, the more activist peace organizations refused to acquiesce. The Women's Peace Party, the American Union against Militarism, and a newly formed coalition, the Emergency Peace Federation, tried to arouse the country. They staged anti-war demonstrations, prepared petitions, and lobbied in Washington. A delegation from the A.U.A.M. visited the President in February to encourage him to prevent the jingoes from pushing the United States into the war.

Alternatives were offered to full belligerency. William Jennings Bryan spoke to mass audiences and urged that the submarine dispute be submitted to a joint high commission for investigation and recommendation for settlement following the war, just as the contested aspects of the British blockade had been relegated to postwar claims. In the meantime, he suggested that Americans be prohibited from sailing on ships carrying contraband and that perhaps all American ships should be ordered not to enter the war zone, a position taken unsuccessfully the previous year by a number of Congressmen in the Gore-McLemore Resolution. If a declaration of war became inevitable, it should be submitted to the people in a referendum Bryan argued, before the nation actually took up arms. A less extreme alternative to this acquiescence in the submarine blockade was offered by Carlton J.H. Hayes, an historian at Columbia University, who recommended armed neutrality. With its ships protecting themselves, the United States could uphold its rights while waging only defensive combat. Some argued that the United States should lead in forming a league of armed neutrals which would also include the Netherlands and the Scandinavian, Iberian, and Latin American countries. Such a coalition could provide the naval vessels needed to keep the sea lanes open to neutral trade.

While President Wilson knew of these proposals, he did not choose to use them. He decided instead for full belligerency. His reasons, according to his biographer Arthur Link of Princeton University, included his complete mistrust of Germany, his desire to maintain as much domestic unity as possible, his underestimation of the military effort that would be required and, most importantly, his conviction that American intervention, guaranteeing a place at the peace conference, would be the most effective means of establishing an early peace and reform of international relations.

In Congress, the President faced the opposition of a rural Southern and Midwestern coalition of anti-interventionists led by Senators Robert LaFollette of Wisconsin and George Norris of Nebraska and House majority leader Claude Kitchin of North Carolina. Ignoring their warnings that the United States was going to war to protect the investment of bankers and munitions makers in the Allied war effort, Congress passed the war resolution by a vote of 82 to 6 in the Senate and 373 to 50 in the House. On April 6, 1917, the United States officially entered the World War.

III
(1917-1918)

When the war came to the United States, it altered both the structure of the peace movement and its relationship to the government. Rapidly following the declaration of war in April, came a dramatic change in the social and political environment. The range of acceptable debate narrowed as the nature of loyalty and the legitimacy of dissent were re-evaluated in a wartime context. Much of what had been permissable before became unwise or illegal in the wake of proscriptive new laws, such as the espionage and sedition acts, and the increased power of governmental authorities.

INTRODUCTION

With victory over the Kaiser's regime the proclaimed national goal, efforts for an immediate or compromise peace could be viewed as disloyal. Government officials, editorial writers, and irate mobs assailed the more activist dissenters, including many of those peace advocates who continued to work for an end to the European War even after it became an American war as well. The years 1917 and 1918 represented both the peak of dedication by a relative handful of pacifists and the nadir of the scope and impact of the peace movement as it withered under the forces of alienation and repression.

Confronted with the choice of supporting the war effort or challenging the government's policy, most of the leaders of the peace movement rallied behind the President's decision for belligerency. In his message to Congress, Wilson argued that Germany had thrust the war upon the United States and that this country, in entering the conflict, sought only to defend itself and to help ensure a just and lasting international peace. A few groups such as the Women's Peace Party took a neutral position and refused either to condemn or endorse American entry into the war. However, the government's decision was upheld by most peace groups including the American Peace Society, the Association of the League to Enforce Peace, the Church Peace Union, the American School Peace League, the World Peace Foundation, and the Carnegie Endowment for International Peace. These bodies pledged their loyalty and urged Americans to unite behind the war effort. To help demonstrate their patriotism, the directors of the Carnegie Endowment turned over the organization's offices to the government's main propaganda agency, the Committee on Public Information.

Most of these peace organizations spent the period of American belligerency working for a postwar settlement which they hoped would ensure permanent peace. However, their members differed over immediate aims and methods. Some like John Spencer Bassett and journalist Norman Hapgood advocated a federated world government. Others like Nicholas Murray Butler and Elihu Root favored conservative evolutionary legalism and supported organic growth through international law and a world court. William Howard Taft, president of the

INTRODUCTION

Association of the League to Enforce Peace, and a number of other people occupied a middle ground and sought a kind of limited internationalism. They urged collective security and order enforced by an association of nations with only partial abrogation of national sovereignty.

There were important differences over the use of force by an international organization. James Brown Scott of the Carnegie Foundation opposed the League of Nations because he doubted whether the United States would allow a combination of foreign countries to use military force against it. A majority of American peace leaders who met in May 1917 at the National Conference on Foreign Relations also opposed a commitment which bound members to use force against offenders or to concede that such coercion might be used against themselves. While a few peace advocates like Root approved of the League as a coalition of the Allies, most wanted a universal association created after the war, one which would include Germany and not be another "Holy Alliance" of victors designed to maintain the settlement they had won. The Women's Peace Party and others also continued to advocate the liberal peace program including disarmament and popular control of foreign policy, including the election of some delegates to conferences to supplement the appointed governmental representatives.

As the war continued, the peace advocates sought to win Woodrow Wilson's endorsement of their particular program. A combination of both foreign and domestic pressures, as well as his own sense of leadership resulted in the President's endorsement of the liberal peace program. The Allies faced a growing demand in 1917 for a statement of war aims and for a negotiated peace. In the wake of the Russian Revolution, the Kerensky Social Democratic government assumed office in May pledged to promote a peace based upon self-determination of peoples and without any annexations or indemnities. In August, Pope Benedict XV urged the belligerents to negotiate on a similar basis. He also urged the consideration of freedom of the seas, the substitution of arbitration for war, and the examination of territorial claims in a "spirit of equity and justice." The Wilson administration and the other Allied

49

governments refused to deal with the Kaiser, however, and the offer produced no results.

When in September, 1917, President Wilson asked Colonel House to begin an investigation into the problems of a postwar peace conference and the appropriate policies for the United States, his unofficial adviser sought out the internationalist peace-advocates for advice. Among those consulted were Taft, Lowell, and Hamilton Holt of the Association of the League to Enforce Peace, Mrs. Fannie Fern Andrews of the American School Peace League and the Central Organization for a Durable Peace, and Nicholas Murray Butler and Elihu Root of the Carnegie Endowment for International Peace. Over a period of time, House conveyed their suggestions to Wilson. The President drew upon some of their recommendations and ignored others as he formulated his own ideas about the peace settlement.

The winter of 1917–18 witnessed increased pressure for a statement of war aims. Following the November Revolution in Russia, the Bolsheviks published the secret Allied treaties (which called for punishing Germany and parceling her colonies among the victors) as evidence of the imperialistic nature of the war. Like a number of other groups on both sides of the Atlantic, the Women's Peace Party urged the meeting of an Inter-Allied Conference, composed of both selected and elected delegates, to formulate and announce new liberal peace aims including a postwar league of nations. When govermental representatives at an Inter-Allied Conference in Paris met and failed to agree upon such a program, President Wilson assumed the leadership of the movement for a liberal peace settlement in a dramatic speech to Congress on January 8, 1918.

Wilson's "Fourteen Points" speech encapsulated the liberal alternative to the imperialism of the secret treaties and to the revolutionary restructuring proposed by V.I. Lenin and the Bolsheviks. According to the President, the "only possible program" for peace as far as the United States was concerned would include open diplomacy, freedom of the seas, equality of trade, disarmament, impartial adjustment of colonial claims giving equal weight to the claims of the colonial power and the native population, withdrawal from territory conquered by the Central Powers, self-determination of autonomous peoples in Eastern Europe and the Turkish Empire, and finally a general association of nations to guarantee political independence and territorial integrity of all the member nations. Significantly, Wilson did not elaborate about the league at the time for he had not decided upon its nature. In fact, he believed public discussion of it premature until the conclusion of the war.

Although the peace organizations which had supported American belligerency may have helped President Wilson to arrive at this position, the antiwar groups in the peace movement after April 1917 became further alienated from the administration. They were also subjected to internal division, and suppressed by local, state, and national authorities.

The American Union Against Militarism, for example, had split over the proper course to follow after the declaration of war. Paul Kellogg, Lillian Wald, and Stephen Wise led a minority of the founders out of the organization when the majority decided to establish a National Civil Liberties Bureau (later the A.C.L.U.) to protect the civil rights of conscientious objectors and others who dissented from the government's war policies. Those who remained within the A.U.A.M. joined with remnants of the Emergency Peace Federation and antiwar Socialists to form the People's Council of America for Peace and Democracy.

Led by Roger Baldwin, a pacifist social worker, Louis Lochner, a journalist and internationalist, Emily Balch, Crystal Eastman, and Morris Hillquit, the People's Council campaigned for civil liberties during wartime, repeal of conscription, and the establishment of a quick peace which would include no annexations and no indemnities. The pacifist-socialist leadership tried to build a coalition of farm and labor groups behind their program of opposition to the war and support for dramatic economic and social change. Although large meetings were held in several cities, a grand Constituent Assembly planned for September was blocked by officials in several Midwestern states.

The Socialist Party took the most outspoken stand of any organization against the American war effort. Delegates to an

51

emergency party conference in Saint Louis, the day after the declaration of war, adopted a report written by Morris Hillquit and Charles Ruthenberg which indicted both the war and U.S. belligerency. Declaring their "unalterable opposition" to the conflict, the antiwar majority urged the "workers of all countries to refuse to support their governments because wars of the contending national groups of capitalists are not the concern of the workers." Although a minority of important Socialists bolted the party and supported the administration, the majority recommended active opposition to the war through mass petitions, demonstrations, and "all other means within our power." The Socialist Party also counseled resistance to many of the administration's war measures such as conscription, war taxes, war bonds, and the curtailment of civil liberties. By a vote of approximately twenty-one thousand to eight thousand, Socialist Party members supported the resolution in national balloting. The majority of Socialists joined with the Industrial Workers of the World and with Emma Goldman and Alexander Berkman of the anarchists to endorse active wartime dissent.

Socialist opposition to the war was demonstrated in a number of ways. Although no general strike took place, Socialists did encourage draft evasion and resistance. The only major incident of violence against the war came in the fields of Oklahoma where many debt-ridden tenant farmers belonged to the I.W.W. or the Socialist Party. When drafting began in August, 1917, a number of these sharecroppers shot a deputy sheriff and made plans to destroy a railroad bridge and cut telegraph wires to block the operation of conscription. The rebels planned a protest march to Washington, gathering support as they went and provisioning themselves enroute with barbecued steers and unripened corn. This so-called "Green Corn Rebellion" never matured, however, because a sheriff's posse galloped into a meeting of the protesters and scattered them before the march had begun. Within a week some 450 men had been arrested.

Less violent but perhaps more significant were the impressive Socialist gains at the polls in the municipal elections in the fall of 1917. Capitalizing on antiwar sentiment, inflation, and other sources of discontent, Socialist candidates polled 22 per cent of the total municipal vote in fifteen cities in the Northeast. In New York City, the Socialists elected ten state assemblymen, seven aldermen, and a municipal judge. Their candidate, Morris Hillquit, placed third–ahead of the regular Republican candidate—in a four-party race for the mayoralty.

The Socialists also sought to encourage international co-operation to end the war, but they were stopped by the U.S. Government. In May, 1917, delegates from the Socialist Party of America sought to join other members of the Second International in Stockholm to discuss means of initiating peace negotiations and ending the war. However, Hillquit and the other representatives were prevented from attending by the State Department. Agents seized their passports under the Logan Act of 1799 which prohibited private citizens from conducting diplomatic negotiations.

During the war, the federal government launched a major campaign to suppress the Socialists and other radicals who dissented against the military or economic policies of the administration. In his Flag Day speech in June 1917, President Wilson condemned the antiwar movement as treasonous and labeled its members as conscious agents or unwitting tools of the German militarists. New wartime legislation, including the espionage and sedition acts, gave the government extensive powers and made it a crime to obstruct the draft or enlistment, or to criticize the government or its war policies.

Acting under these provisions, the federal government moved against radical dissenters. It was joined by local authorities as well. By denying full mailing privileges, Postmaster General Albert Burleson suppressed a number of left-wing newspapers and magazines, including the New York *Call,* the Milwaukee *Leader, The Masses,* and *The American Socialist.* Local district attorneys and the Justice Department· obtained indictments and convictions of leading Socialists such as Kate Richards O'Hare, Rose Pastor Stokes (Victor Berger and Max Eastman were indicted but acquitted) and Eugene V. Debs, titular head of the party. Federal agents, under orders from Attorney General Thomas Gregory, raided the offices of the I.W.W. More than one hundred "Wobbly" leaders including

Haywood were convicted of antiwar activity in a mass trial in Chicago. Anarchist leaders like Goldman and Berkman who had organized a No-Conscription League and held rallies against the draft were convicted, imprisoned, and subsequently deported to Russia. Wartime suppression destroyed the Wobblies and anarchists as organized movements and left the Socialist Party greatly weakened, its press impotent, and many of its leaders imprisoned.

The liberal pacifists who continued to criticize the war effort did not suffer the same degree of persecution as the radicals but they were no more effective in influencing the foreign policy of the Wilson administration. They failed completely to block enactment of the espionage and sedition laws or to prevent or repeal conscription. Only in regard to conscientious objectors did they eventually have some success.

Sympathetic recognition of sincere objectors to military service was advocated by sects like the Quakers and Mennonites and by new organizations like the National Civil Liberties Bureau headed by Roger Baldwin and the Fellowship of Reconciliation, a group of religious pacifists led by Norman Thomas, a Presbyterian minister. From the beginning, they urged that any draft law provide for recognition of not only religious but political objectors who included a number of Socialists, individualists, and German and Austrian-Americans. Despite their lobbying in Congress and personal appeals to President Wilson and Secretary of War Newton Baker, the pacifists were disappointed in the provisions of the draft act. The new law provided only for recognition of conscientious objectors who belonged to traditional pacifist sects, and declared that these would be assigned to noncombatant work within the armed forces.

During the war, the liberal pacifists appealed to the administration to modify this initial decision, but Wilson and Baker were cautious until they determined that the number of objectors was limited. Draft boards recognized 57,000 men as C.O.s and 21,000 of these had been inducted into the 3.5 million-man Army by 1918. Segregated in camp under Baker's orders, nearly 80 per cent of the C.O.s changed their minds. Out of a sense of isolation and rejection, they decided to rejoin their outfits. When only 4,000 men continued to refuse to train for combat, the administration advised camp commanders to treat them with tact and consideration. Nevertheless, many objectors were beaten with sticks, drenched with cold water, jabbed with bayonets, and starved on bread and water in solitary confinement. At least two objectors died as a result. Vigorously protesting this treatment, the civilian pacifist groups obtained from the Wilson administration orders in 1918 which directed most of these objectors into noncombatant service or furloughed them to work on farms or in factories. Nevertheless, 500 conscientious objectors were court-martialed and imprisoned with sentences that averaged over ten years each.

President Wilson had the greatest single influence in ending the fighting of World War I. Once again, Wilson's own sense of leadership and his desire to achieve a settlement which would not only protect American interests but which would ensure lasting world peace within a liberal, capitalistic, reform framework proved more important than the influence of particular groups. When the deteriorating military position in the fall of 1918 forced the German Government to seek an armistice, it asked for peace negotiations based on Wilson's Fourteen Points rather than the Allies war aims. The President made the decision to agree to an early and negotiated settlement. In so doing, he rejected the pleas of those like Theodore Roosevelt and Gen. John J. Pershing, the commander of the American Expeditionary Force, who wanted to drive the Germans back across the Rhine and to obtain an unconditional surrender. In order to force the British and French governments to accept less than total victory, Wilson had to threaten to take the United States out of the war and make a separate peace with the Germans.

Wilson's pressure proved effective in obtaining an armistice. The British and French agreed to the cease-fire and negotiations based upon the Fourteen Points rather than their own secret treaties, with two exceptions. The British refused to endorse freedom of the seas, lest England be deprived of using a blockade in future wars. And the French demanded that Germany restore the territory it had conquered and pay reparation for war damages. Under these conditions, and with the abdication of the Kaiser, with whom Wilson had refused to negotiate, a new German Republican government signed the armistice which ended the World War on November 11, 1918.

Because of Wilson's rejection of total military victory as the goal, the war ended a year earlier than most of the Allied officials and military leaders expected. As a result of his action, Germany was not forced to surrender unconditionally and the Allied imperialistic war aims were not automatically achieved. Wilson had used the power of his office and of the United States to work for the general goals of the liberal internationalist peace movement. However, the end of the fighting did not mean that he had accomplished those goals. In fact, the struggle had just begun.

IV
(1919-1922)

With the armistice and the end of the wartime strictures, the peace movement resumed its full range of activity. The immediate focal points of its work were the peace settlement for World War I, the creation of international machinery to reduce or eliminate the possibilities of such conflicts in the future, the demobilization of armies, and reduction of wartime armaments. In the years between 1919 and 1922, the United States determined its postwar international position. This did not mean affiliation with the League of Nations, but it did include attempts to maintain both peace and national interest through the limitation of armaments and the establishment of multilateral regional agreements to protect the *status quo* in the Far East.

In regard to the shaping of the postwar settlement in the winter and early spring of 1919, the peace movement in general found itself awaiting the outcome of the decision of the representatives of the big powers at Paris. President Wilson

INTRODUCTION

had seized the initiative by deciding to attend the peace conference himself, the first American chief executive to visit Europe while in office. As the leader of the hand-picked delegation, he exercised absolute personal control over the American position at the sessions. Wilson failed to sound out public or congressional opinion before leaving, but in the negotiations, he claimed to speak for the American people. The peace treaty hammered out in France was shaped by his conception of the needs of America and the world, and the demands of the other major statesmen on behalf of Britain, France, Italy and Japan. The peace movement had little direct influence in the formulation of its terms.

The Treaty of Versailles which Wilson presented to the United States Senate in July 1919 departed significantly from the hopes of peace advocates. It was not a peace without victory, but was a vindictive settlement. It forced Germany to accept sole guilt for the war, to disarm unilaterally, and to pay reparations ultimately fixed at $56 billion. It stripped the Germans of their colonies and concessions in Africa and Asia and turned these over to the victorious Allies. It demilitarized the right bank of the Rhine, put the left bank under Paris' control for fifteen years, authorized the French to occupy the Saar for a similar period, and returned Alsace-Lorraine to France. In eastern Germany and in Russia, it re-established Poland as an independent state with a corridor to the Baltic.

The peace treaty departed signficantly from many of the Fourteen Points. It said nothing about freedom of the seas or reduction of tariffs. Under pressure from the European leaders, Wilson had sacrificed these to prevent an even more severe treaty such as the French proposed, one which would have permanently dismembered the Rhineland.

In accepting deviations from the liberal peace program such as these, Wilson hoped that the settlement would be ameliorated through the work of a League of Nations. He insisted that the League be made a part of the peace treaty. The covenant of the new international organization provided for a small but powerful executive council dominated by the major Allied powers (the United States, Britain, France, Italy, and Japan), a large assembly in which each nation would have one vote, and a permanent secretariat in the neutral capital of Geneva. In the controversial Article X, member nations accepted the principle of collective security. They pledged themselves to preserve each other's independence and territorial integrity against external attacks. They also agreed to submit all disputes which could lead to war to the League. They also consented to employ military and economic sanctions against nations resorting to war, to reduce armaments, to cooperate in setting up a Permanent Court of International Justice, and to place the former colonies of the Central Powers under a mandate status in which the new colonial authorities would have to report to the League on steps being taken to prepare the native populations for self-government.

The drafters of the covenant used some of the ideas of the peace movement, but they neglected many others. The preamble, expressing the aim of world co-operation, peace and security and avoidance of war, echoed pacifist hopes. The covenant urged arbitration, advanced the principle of a continuous world conference, and achieved a congress of nations. However, its provisions for force seemed far removed from the mainstream of the peace movement and internationalist thought. Most peace advocates had rejected the possibilities of such open-ended use of force. The League of Nations also differed from the legalistic and procedural approach of internationalists like Root and Taft. Wilson's organization failed to have a Court created as a co-equal body and lacked the machinery to create or determine international law. Furthermore, the association was clearly dominated by the great powers and tied to a vindictive peace settlement. It lacked a major focus on advancing democracy or justice, as pacifists like Addams and Villard had urged.

By 1919, the legalist wing of the American peace movement had achieved general agreement on a number of principles. Among those were the belief that a league should be established, but that it should be limited in its powers. International disputes should be settled peacefully through procedural action, but a new system for world order should evolve gradually. The legalists also believed that the use of force should be limited under strict safeguards.

INTRODUCTION

As created, the League of Nations reflected this desire for a conference of nations, but it went far beyond these peace advocates' proposals. The Allies established the League upon a political rather than a legal foundation. While the covenant recognized arbitration, it provided only peripherally for a judicial body. Wilson apparently did not envision the World Court as an integral part of the international machinery as had the legalistic peace advocates. The more conservative internationalists were also shocked by Wilson's bold attempt to create a system of world government virtually overnight. They wanted to build upon previous experiences and achievements in a slower and more reassuring manner.

The majority of peace advocates were appalled by Articles X and XVI which obligated the signatories to use force if the association so determined. The idea that a league of states would defend the territory and independence of its members had appeared before 1919 in only a few plans for an association of nations. Even then its adherents, such as Hamilton Holt and Theodore Roosevelt, qualified the concept by insisting that force be applied only in accordance with procedures involving law and justice. They envisioned an international judicial system which would prevent any autocratic action on the part of the organization. The position taken by President Wilson, who gave the League a political base and authority to compel military action, represented a minority view within the peace movement.

Many pacifists and liberals were disillusioned by the degree to which the covenant departed from democratic ideals, especially in its emphasis upon the council where big powers dominated, and the lack of legislative power in the assembly which meant that no body of international law could be constructed by the organization. Thus, the covenant failed to reflect the prevailing patterns of thought in the peace movement. The legalists wished to create a judicial system which would evolve into a world organization. Wilson created a world organization which he hoped would establish an international system under which peace and prosperity could be maintained.

When the details of the League of Nations were learned, the peace movement supported the general idea, but urged various

INTRODUCTION

modifications. Advanced peace advocates like Holt, Marburg, and Nasmyth wanted to strengthen and improve the League by creating a stronger world legislature, electing delegates by popular vote, and establishing an international police force to uphold disarmament agreements. More moderate internationalists like Taft and Lowell and even some active pacifists like Jordan and Bryan, sought to protect traditional American policies by exempting immigration laws and the Monroe Doctrine from League consideration. A third group, led by Elihu Root, supported the League only reluctantly, fearing it endangered U.S. sovereignty and that it lacked detailed provisions for arbitration and a world court.

The Congress held in Zurich in the spring of 1919 by the Women's International League for Peace and Freedom was the first public body to protest against the terms of peace. It attacked the treaty as vindictive and, while gratified by the League, criticized many of its aspects. Led by Jane Addams, Lillian Wald, and Emily Greene Balch, the Women's Congress urged immediate disarmament, free trade and travel, guarantees for the rights of minorities, full equality for women, abolition of child labor, abrogation of regional understandings such as the Monroe Doctrine when they were inconsistent with the Covenant of the League, free access to raw materials for all nations on equal terms, abolition of the protection of capital investments in foreign countries, and the abandonment of military action as a means of enforcing League decisions.

Many peace organizations found their membership divided over the proposed League of Nations. The Women's Peace Party split, some members supporting the League whole-heartedly, others only with reservations, and still others refusing to endorse the organization which they said approved of force to maintain a vindictive peace settlement. Within the Association for a League to Enforce Peace, most members wanted some modifications. A few, like Albert Shaw and John Bates Clark, were completely opposed to the proposal because of its failure to emphasize the judiciary. The organization could not agree on what changes to recommend. As a liberal alternative to the interventionist-oriented League to Enforce Peace, the League of Free Nations Association (later the Foreign Policy

INTRODUCTION

Association) was founded in 1918 by Columbia Professor James T. Shotwell, who was to become one of the leading advocates of international cooperation, and a number of people from the old American Union against Militarism, especially Lillian Wald and Paul Kellogg. The American Peace Society noted the lack of judicial processes in Wilson's League, called it authoritarian and coercive in emphasis, and refused to endorse it. The Society suggested a Third Hague Conference instead. Both the World Peace Foundation and the Carnegie Endowment also declined to take official stands on the League.

Even though Wilson obtained a number of modifications when he returned to Paris in the spring of 1919 for a second round of negotiations, the revised covenant still did not reflect those legal and procedural ideas which were held by most peace advocates. They wanted a court as an integral part of the League and its major agency, not as a derivative organ to be established sometime in the future. They desired separate but clearly-defined bodies to hear different types of disputes. And they wished a league with the power to formulate and codify international law.

On the other hand, those who supported Wilson's League used several arguments to counter this criticism. They praised the League as an outstanding advance towards world peace in the tradition of the Hague Conferences and the arbitration treaties. Claiming that the majority of Americans supported U.S. membership in the League, they introduced resolutions passed by thirty-two state legislatures by the middle of 1919 as partial evidence. In their most emotional appeal, many advocates, including Wilson himself, argued that the League would be a bulwark not only against the return of German-style militarism but also against the spread of Bolshevik-sponsored revolution.

The Versailles Treaty was debated in the Senate as well as in the forum of public opinion in the United States in 1919 and 1920. The senators responded to the provisions of the covenant, the territorial, economic, and political aspects of the peace settlement, to Wilson's leadership, and to sectional and partisan advantage. A sizable Republican opposition existed, including a few who were irreconcilably opposed to U.S. membership in any league and a larger number who supported the demand of Henry Cabot Lodge, chairman of the Senate Foreign Relations Committee, for substantial modifications. A militant expansionist and nationalist who wanted to maintain American freedom of action in foreign policy, Lodge had earlier insisted on safeguarding clauses in the Roosevelt and Taft arbitration treaties. In 1919 he feared that Wilson's League was an armed alliance which could control the forces of the United States and interfere in American domestic affairs.

The Association of the League to Enforce Peace and President Wilson sought to counter objections through a massive publicity campaign in favor of U.S. membership in the League of Nations. The President spoke out vigorously for the Treaty. He refused to allow the Lodge reservations which he argued, probably incorrectly, would destroy the League. During a nine thousand-mile speaking tour, the health of the Chief Executive broke. He suffered a stroke which incapacitated him for several months and increased his determination not to compromise. In November, 1919, the Senate voted twice on the Treaty. A combination of Democrats and moderate Republicans rejected the Lodge reservations. Then the irreconcilables and Lodge's supporters rejected Wilson's League without the reservations.

The peace movement does not appear to have played a major role in the Senate decision against the League. The verdict at that stage was in the hands of the President and the Senators. The impotence of the peace movement at that critical moment seems to have been due primarily to its failure to coalesce behind a single position. The peace advocates found themselves badly divided and as a result, their influence was muted.

The most effective action taken by the peace societies in regard to the League was a campaign arousing the American people to force the Senate to reconsider the Treaty. For the first time in the Treaty fight, the internationalists acted together. In January and February of 1920, representatives of twenty-six groups which favored U.S. entry into the League and which claimed to represent fifty million people sent delegates to Washington to press for reconsideration. The Senate did take up the Treaty a third time, but Wilson, Lodge, and the irreconcilables had not changed their positions. They were not willing to compromise and the stalemate continued. Once again the treaty with the Lodge reservations failed to obtain the necessary two-thirds majority. Enough Democrats followed Wilson's orders and joined the irreconcilables to prevent passage.

Ironically, President Wilson had contributed to the defeat of his own creation. With a stubbornness intensified by his illness and his own personal involvement in the definition of America's wartime and postwar aims, Wilson refused to compromise and accept the modifications Lodge demanded. Both Wilson's clash with Lodge and his lack of cooperation with the internationalists helped to prevent U.S. membership in the League.

Wilson had taken an advanced position on world organization, one far removed from prevailing thought. By March 1920, nearly all of the peace advocates favored reservations to the covenant. The struggle was not fought over whether the United States should join the League, but what kind of a league the United States should join. Wilson's individualistic course, his failure to heed the internationalists who had spent years exploring the idea of a league of nations, and his inadequate knowledge of the prevailing American ideas on the subject, all contributed to the defeat of his own league. Furthermore, Wilson himself helped to prevent the creation of Lodge's league. Historian Warren Kuehl has concluded that Wilson's real error lay not in his refusal to compromise on Article X, the commitment to force, but in including it at all. Neither the peace movement nor the majority of American people in those years was willing to bind the country to what was in essence a defensive alliance with the major countries of Europe and Asia.

In the wake of the Senate rejection, even the slightest American relations with the League of Nations came only gradually. In the summer of 1920, the Congress terminated the state of war with Germany and Austria-Hungary through a simple joint resolution. Afrer initially refusing any connection with the association in Geneva, the Republican administrations of the 1920s slowly increased American cooperation, at first in economic and social matters and later in diplomatic affairs. Without officially joining the League, the United States participated in its reparations commissions, the international opium conference of 1924, the conference on communication and transportation in 1926, and on trade and taxation in 1927 and 1928. By 1931, the United States had been represented at forty League meetings and had five officials at Geneva to represent American interests.

The World Court was created by the League in 1921 with judicial rather than the purely arbitral and diplomatic functions of the old Hague Tribunal. It had a permanent body of eleven sitting jurists. Numerous attempts were made by peace organizations to persuade the United States Government to join the World Court. The Harding Administration endorsed adherence to its protocol. Consequently, in 1925, Congress passed favorable resolutions but the Senate included such reservations that the Court rejected the American terms for membership. President Hoover submitted a formula for U.S. participation worked out by both Elihu Root and the members of the Court. However, the irreconcilables in the Senate postponed consideration until 1935 when the formula was defeated by isolationists despite the support of President Franklin D. Roosevelt. Not until after World War II did the United States join an international association of nations—the United Nations—and a new World Court.

In the immediate postwar years, the peace movement was much more successful in its attempts to prevent expansion of the American military and naval establishments than it had been in its efforts to join the League and the World Court. Indeed, it helped to achieve a limited degree of disarmament among the Army and Navy. Some elements of the peace movement also worked in an additional campaign, one to obtain amnesty for imprisoned war resisters. Their efforts which began after the armistice in 1918 eventually succeeded, but only after a long and sustained effort.

INTRODUCTION

The Wilson administration resisted the postwar drive for amnesty for those pacifists, Socialists, and members of the Industrial Workers of the World, and others convicted of resistance to the draft or violation of the Espionage or Sedition Acts because they had spoken out against the war. Efforts to free several hundred such prisoners began almost immediately after the armistice. By early 1919, a number of organizations were carrying on an amnesty campaign in the metropolitan press, in liberal periodicals, in petitions, and in personal meetings with President Wilson and Secretary of War Baker. The American Civil Liberties Union, created by the American Union against Militarism, was especially active in the campaign, as were the League for Amnesty of Political Prisoners, the Washington D.C. Citizens' Amnesty Committee, some labor unions, and liberal periodicals like the *Dial*, the *New Republic,* and the *Nation*. The movement gained increasing support as a result of newspaper and congressional investigations in 1919 into the equity of military justice.

While the administration refused to grant a general amnesty, it did release some opponents of war on an individual basis. In 1919, one hundred conscientious objectors were released from Fort Leavenworth after a War Department Board of Inquiry found them to be sincere in their objection, and judged that their sentences had been too harsh. But the President supported his attorneys general, Thomas Gregory and later A. Mitchell Palmer, in resisting pressure for the release of violators of the Espionage and Sedition Acts, including the most prominent political prisoner, Eugene V. Debs, the Socialist presidential nominee then being held in the Atlanta penitentiary.

Authorities even moved to curb the amnesty agitation itself. In the postwar fear of Bolshevism, the Department of Justice indicted and obtained convictions, under wartime statutes, of three Syracuse men who were working for the release of political prisoners. The Espionage Act remained in effect until the war was officially declared at an end in November, 1921. Police and patriotic groups broke up several amnesty meetings in 1919 and disrupted a Fifth Avenue parade in New York City on behalf of the prisoners on Christmas Day.

INTRODUCTION

Although the fear of radicalism in 1919 and early 1920 militated against a general policy of amnesty, the Wilson administration released a number of political prisoners on an individual basis under growing pressure from the amnesty organizations, the American Federation of Labor, the press, and several Congressmen, led by Senator William E. Borah, the progressive isolationist from Idaho. On November 23, 1920—two years after the Armistice—Secretary Baker ordered the last thirty-three conscientious objectors released. However, Debs and the more than one hundred other dissenters remained in prison.

With the arrival of President Harding and the Republican administration in Washington in March, 1921, the amnesty committees obtained a more sympathetic hearing. The new Chief Executive listened to the pleas of Samuel Gompers of the American Federation of Labor and others. Following the approval of the formal peace proclamation on November 14, 1921, Harding freed Debs and twenty-three other political prisoners on Christmas Day. Despite the fact that additional individual inmates were pardoned or had their sentences commuted, 113 dissenters remained in federal penitentiaries in 1922 and hundreds more were still incarcerated in state prisons. At congressional hearings into the matter, Albert De Silver, the head of the A.C.L.U., testified in favor of amnesty because wartime hysteria had prevented fair trials and because the laws under which these people had been convicted were no longer in effect. However, many Congressmen and others continued to link the amnesty movement to socialism, Bolshevism, and anarchism.

By 1923, the amnesty campaign had expanded dramatically and had produced significant results. Many prominent church leaders, governors, educators, journalists, and a number of national organizations joined the movement. In June, Harding offered conditional freedom to twenty-four I.W.W.'s, but they rejected his gesture because they said acceptance would amount to a confession of disloyalty. The last thirty-one federal political prisoners from World War I were released by Harding's successor, President Calvin Coolidge, on December 15, 1923. When Franklin D. Roosevelt became

President in 1933, he issued a formal pardon to those who had been political prisoners in World War I, thus restoring their legal and political rights to full citizenship.

The peace movement achieved more immediate success in its postwar efforts to limit the military and naval establishments. Specifically, it helped to trim the Army back to its prewar size and to prevent compulsory military training in peacetime, and to cut down the fleet and the naval building program. In these cases, it ran into opposition from the Wilson administration, the officer corps, and civilian support groups such as the American Legion, the American Defense Society, the Military Training Camps Association, and the Navy League.

In his attempt to win American support for U.S. entry into the League of Nations, President Wilson warned that the alternative to collective security would be a costly isolation for the United States. "If we must stand apart and be the hostile rivals of the rest of the world. . . ," he wrote to the Senate Foreign Relations Committee in 1919, "we must be physically ready for anything that comes. . . . We must see to it that every man in America is trained in arms." He proposed a dramatic increase in the Army and Navy in case the United States failed to join the League. In 1919, Wilson and Secretary Baker endorsed the General Staff's recommendations for a permanent Regular Army of 500,000 men (five times the prewar Army) and civilian reserves prepared through compulsory universal military training of three months for each able-bodied young male citizen.

With the war over, however, the country was in no mood for such a departure in American military traditions. Old-line antimilitary groups such as the American Federation of Labor, the National Farmers Union and the National Grange quickly came out against the proposal. So did many clergymen, educators, and liberal journalists. Coordinating the opposition to the administration's program for the Army and conscription was a revitalized American Union against Militarism headed by publisher Oswald Garrison Villard. Effectively, it united the opposition, especially in the South and West, against the scheme which it said would Prussianize America. In the Congress, even most of the House Democrats revolted against the proposal of their President and party leader.

The National Defense Act of June 1920, which prescribed the postwar military, represented the will of Congress, not of the Executive. It limited the Regular Army to 280,000 men (in fact Congress made appropriations for only 175,000 in 1920 and for 137,000 in 1922), rejected conscription in peacetime, and continued the traditional reliance upon the state militia—the National Guard—to provide trained reservists. The virtual return to the prewar model in this respect resulted from the resumption of peace and a demand for an end to wartime taxes and conscription. The adroit lobbying of the American Union against Militarism played a key part in the decision.

However, the problems of disarmament and of militarism after World War I involved the Navy much more than the Army. Although the three-year naval building program, adopted in 1916 to make the U.S. Navy equal to Britain's, had not yet been completed, President Wilson and Secretary of the Navy Josephus Daniels recommended in December 1919 an additional three-year construction program. In the immediate post-armistice period, the United States built more warships than the rest of the world combined. Considering Japan the next potential enemy, the United States also transferred half of its fleet to the Pacific and constructed naval bases there. Wilson seems to have been motivated not only by concern with increasing Japanese power and ambitions in the Far East, but also by his desire to use the expansion program as a bargaining tool to coerce the British and the American public into supporting his concept of the League in exchange for a reduction of American warship-building.

Once again, the American Union against Militarism was in the forefront of opposition to the administration's proposals to expand the defense establishment. It coordinated the efforts of groups traditionally opposed to naval expansion. These included farmers, workers, clergymen, educators, and pacifists, and a number of important businessmen and financiers who had become convinced by wartime spending and postwar inflation of the necessity of cutting government spending and taxes. Faced with British acceptance of the League and with strong opposition from Congress and the American public to navalism, the administration withdrew its proposal in May 1919. In the Republican administration of President Harding two years later, the powerful new Secretary of the Treasury, Andrew Mellon, led in urging arms reductions. The resulting Appropriations Act of 1921 eliminated the proposed additional naval expansion and confined warship-building to completion of the 1916 authorization, an action which reflected the growing sentiment against navalism and for disarmament.

Elements in the peace movement continued to press for international disarmament in the postwar period and they scored probably their most dramatic success when the naval arms limitation treaty was signed in Washington in 1922. The international conference in that city resulted from both the Republicans' attempt to provide an alternative to the League and the increasing public pressure for disarmament even without U.S. membership in an association of nations. Despite the American rejection of membership, the League of Nations in the fall of 1920 invited the United States to take part in consultations regarding limitation of armaments. Public opinion supported disarmament and even a number of leading military figures like Generals John J. Pershing and Tasker H. Bliss called for the United States to take the lead in arms reduction.

Within the Republican Party, arms limitation found advocates among those who wanted to ensure America's security with less expense and without the departure from traditional unilateral action demanded by Wilson's proposal for collective security. Even before the Harding administration took office in March 1921, some Congressional Republicans had seized the initiative. Replying to Geneva's invitation, Senator Borah, an irreconcilable opponent of the League, introduced a resolution on Dec. 14, 1920 which revived the Hensley Amendment to the Naval Act of 1916. It undercut the League's action by authorizing the President to call an American-sponsored naval disarmament conference. The Borah Resolution served as the focus for the further mobilization of public opinion by advocates of disarmament and tax reduction.

INTRODUCTION

The movement for arms limitation at the Washington Conference grew rapidly in 1921 on the basis of sensational disclosures and a powerful new coalition of interests.

Sentiment for disarmament was fueled by a number of important events. Already disillusioned by the war, many Americans were shocked by the apparent resumption of a naval race, this time by the United States, Britain, and Japan. Furthermore, in the summer of 1921, the bombers of General William "Billy" Michell sank several unmanned German battleships in target practice off the Atlantic Coast, a demonstration of how vulnerable even the largest naval vessels were to aerial bombardment. Antiwar sentiment was further exacerbated the same year by the publication of a startling book by the popular correspondent Will Irwin. Grimly entitled *The Next War—a Common Sense View,* it detailed War Department plans to use poison gas on a large scale in the next major conflict. A sermon by a rising young New York preacher named Harry Emerson Fosdick on the immorality of these military plans and others to employ germ warfare was also circulated nationally and helped to build the cry for disarmament and the abolition of war.

The movement received widespread support as the public came to believe that disarmament could be achieved in one conference which would result in not only an end to warfare but a dramatic reduction in taxes. Disarmament committees sprang up in major cities. Catholic, Jewish, and Protestant leaders endorsed it. So did the various peace groups. Two new organizations took the leadership in bringing public opinion to bear on Congress. One was the Women's Committee for World Disarmament, headed by the former suffragist leader Carrie Chapman Catt. The other was the National Council for the Limitation of Armaments, soon called the National Council for the Prevention of War. It was initiated by Philadelphia Quakers and led by Frederick J. Libby, a Maine-born educator and minister. Together these two committees marshalled women's organizations, church and peace groups, farm, labor, and educational associations behind the demand for disarmament. Most of the press vigorously endorsed the movement and exerted additional pressure upon the government to achieve results.

INTRODUCTION

The campaign for arms limitation put the Harding administration in a difficult position. The President had been reluctant to call such a conference because of the warnings of Big Navy advocates like Senator Lodge who cautioned against the growing power of Japan. Additionally, the administration had its own plan for U.S. membership in an "association of nations" which would be less controlling than Wilson's League. This association would then work for disarmament, codification of international law, and the establishment of a world court. Opposition to immediate arms limitation had also come from the Army and Navy and some advocates of U.S. membership in the League of Nations who considered the renunciation of military force without alternative collective security to be unrealistic. However, under public and congressional pressure for disarmament and tax cuts, and pressed by British and Japanese naval-building, the administration endorsed Senator Borah's resolution. When the proposal was passed by Congress in July 1921, President Harding summoned an international conference to meet in Washington that winter.

Secretary of State Charles E. Hughes startled the delegates on the opening day of the conference in November 1921 by proposing immediate disarmament and the scrapping of specific vessels. As delegates, including admirals from the major powers, sat bolt upright, Hughes proposed a ten-year moratorium on the construction of new major warships. He announced that the United States was willing to destroy thirty battlewagons and he suggested that Britain and Japan sink thirty-six of theirs, so the three nations would maintain the current ratio of capital ships at 5-5-3. Within thirty minutes, Hughes had demolished sixty-six battleships, totalling nearly two million tons, more than all the admirals of the world had sunk over the centuries.

After much deliberation, the delegates on February 6, 1922 signed the Five-Power Treaty between the United States, Britain, Japan, France, and Italy. It represented the first voluntary acceptance by large nations of restrictions on their liberty to possess weapons of war. It was based on the principles of limiting the ratio to the *status quo* and of eliminating construction or continued existence of ships that would alter that balance. Shrewdly, Hughes had sought a defensive maintenance of the existing balance of power in the Far East. Combined with the other treaties signed at the Washington Conference, the disarmament pact temporarily interrupted the naval race between the United States and Japan and replaced the Anglo-Japanese Alliance of 1902 with a regional nonaggression agreement which included all the major powers involved in East Asia.

The disarmament wing of the peace movement played an important role in the success of the deliberations at Washington. It helped to force the administration to summon the meeting, lobbied continually during the three-month conference, and conducted a drive for the ratification of the treaties. Despite the opposition of navalists and others who considered it unrealistic, the treaty won approval in the Senate on March 29, 1922 by an overwhelming vote of 74 to 1, clear indication of its popularity.

Nevertheless, the Washington Treaty was only a preliminary step. In succeeding years, the disarmament forces in the peace movement worked to extend its principles. The 1922 treaty applied only to capital ships, limiting battleships, battlecruisers, and aircraft carriers. Significantly cruisers, destroyers, and submarines were not included under the Washington restrictions. A separate agreement, also signed on February 6, 1922, tried to govern the operation of submarines, but it was not ratified by France and failed to go into effect.

Encouraged by the National Council for the Prevention of War, public opinion supported further attempts at naval arms limitation, but these efforts did not succeed. Between 1923 and 1925, Congress on three occasions asked the President to call a new conference to consider limiting cruisers. Even a three-nation meeting sponsored by the United States in 1927 failed to reach agreement, and in 1929, Congress authorized the country to enter the cruiser-building race already begun by Britain and Japan.

A final attempt to curb the growing naval arms race was made at the London Naval Arms Conference in 1930. The resulting treaty pledged the United States, Britain and Japan to limit cruiser and submarine construction, but under a new ratio of 10:10:7 which proved more favorable to the Japanese than the 1922 agreements. The United States thus ensured its ability to achieve its goal of keeping naval parity with England while maintaining a 30 per cent superiority over Japan, without having to pay for a huge building program. But the price of the agreement was a weak treaty which contained a number of escape clauses and which many contemporary observers saw would last no more than six years. Indeed, by the mid-1930s, the naval arms race had begun once again. Nevertheless, conditions and the disarmament treaties beginning in 1922 had kept such a development restricted for more than a dozen years.

V
Conclusion

Analysis of these developments in the first two decades of the 20th century indicates that the modern American peace movement first took shape in this period. Like many other collective efforts to reassess institutions effected by industrialization during the late 19th and early 20th centuries, the attempt to re-orient U.S. foreign policy and international relations became a powerful social movement. As with the women's movement and the labor movement, the peace movement represented collective action taken on behalf of social change. It remained, however, primarily an elite rather than a mass movement, concerned as it was with an issue which generally did not directly affect most Americans. Yet it did have some significant successes in the course of its growth.

The peace movement found unity in its discontent with the anarchy and warfare which characterized international relations at the turn of the century when the United States emerged as a world power. The European arms race, the bloody Russo-Japanese War, and, in a different way, the First Hague Conference served as inducements to the internationalists. So did the peace advocates' belief in their ability to improve domestic and foreign institutions. Additionally, Theodore Roosevelt's mediation at Portsmouth and the call for a second Hague

INTRODUCTION

Conference served as the precipitating events which catalyzed scattered American discontent into action. A series of new organizations and leaders soon revitalized the remnants of the 19th-century peace movement. Aided by new and generous financing from prominent businessmen, the internationalists sought to apply what they considered America's unique institutions to its historic mission of offering an enlightened example to humanity. These peace advocates tried to achieve both international peace and order which would aid both the United States and the world.

Yet within this larger aim, a variety of lesser goals were attempted by various new American peace workers. The new leaders ranged from Elihu Root, a corporation lawyer and former secretary of war, to Jane Addams, a settlement house worker, social reformer, and suffragist. They included radicals and conservatives, businessmen, clergymen, journalists, feminists, educators, and politicians. A plethora of organizations, new and old, clustered in specific, issue-oriented movements which differed over the means for achieving world peace. The means included international law, world government, disarmament, and U.S. neutrality and mediation.

In general, the political strategy of these different groups was remarkably similar. Confident of their position and of the operation of the American political system, they placed primary reliance upon persuasion for achieving their goals. They sought to convince the decision-makers and the public of the desirability of peace and their means for achieving it. With the exception of some radicals, most of the peace advocates did this within the existing framework of nationalism (accepting the sense of America's uniqueness and mission) and within the structure of decision-making in the United States. It was on the whole a movement moderate in its means. Most peace organizations, led by men and women of high prestige, supported in many cases by substantial funding and organizational and promotional skills, exuded confidence in the ultimate success of their educational campaign. They endeavored to awaken public opinion to the need to pursue their programs. Generally, they also tried to counter the influence of other groups which pressed for a more aggressive foreign policy backed up by expanded military and naval forces. Pacifists in particular portrayed these opponents as autarchical militarists, representing a danger to peace and to American institutions.

During the first twenty years of this century, the peace movement underwent a number of changes. Its development was strikingly cyclical, characterized by an intermittent pattern of growth, decline, and resumption. After a period of dramatic expansion, the peace movement, on the whole, went into hibernation in World War I, only to emerge once again in rejuvenated form after the armistice.

The peace movement had been transformed after 1905 by the influx of members, money, and new organizations dedicated to finding world order. The older peace societies had been overwhelmed and literally engulfed by the new enthusiasts. The movement gained the legitimation provided by affiliation with leading businessmen, educators, and political figures, including the President of the United States. With such leadership and financial support, the abolition of war had seemed to some to be within reach.

The outbreak of the European War in 1914 had proven a painful antidote to such optimism. Confronted with such a massive and bloody conflict, peace advocates redefined the aims and methods of their movement. The more conservative members decided to suspend activities or to work for the long-range achievement of peace rather than to try to stop the current war or to prevent American involvement in it. This decision split the movement. The more radical opponents of international conflict determined to confront the problems of the current war. They formed new, more activist, issue-oriented organizations, like the League to Limit Armaments and the American Union against Militarism. They tried to prevent the expansion of the military establishment and American entry into the war. The activists worked to persuade the Wilson administration to play a major role in mediating among the belligerents. Unlike the more conservative peace organizations, these new groups endeavored not only to reduce the possibilities of future wars, but to end the current conflict.

American entry into full belligerency further fragmented the peace movement in 1917 and 1918. Only the most militant and dedicated pacifists proved willing to risk the charge of treason or subversion and to actively continue in opposition after the congressional declaration of war. While moderates grew silent, radicals formed new organizations like the People's Council and the National Civil Liberties Bureau and, despite popular and governmental repression, worked to end the war and to curtail the erosion of civil liberties under the intensive wartime chauvinism. Non-pacifist, antiwar organizations, like the Industrial Workers of the World and the Socialist Party, which had long incurred the hostility of more powerful groups, suffered such active persecution that they were virtually eliminated during the war.

In the postwar period, while the peace movement resumed its activities, its internal divisions remained. Conservative, legalistic organizations, like the Carnegie Endowment, continued to eschew mass action campaigns. They preferred to concentrate on cooperation with governmental decision-makers and on scholarly research into the causes of war. Their goals included codification of international law, American participation in the World Court, and the convocation of a Third Hague Conference. However, the newer, more activist organizations which had developed since the outbreak of war in 1914 continued to function in a different manner and after the armistice, they were joined by a number of new organizations.

Much of the postwar peace movement differed from its predecessors in being more activist, more issue-oriented, and more successful in obtaining legislation in the 1920s and 1930s. It seemed to fit into the new interest-group bargaining arrangement which emerged in the nation's capital in the first third of the 20th century as power shifted to Washington and additional groups organized on a national basis. Thus, the League of Nations Non-Partisan Association and the Foreign Policy Association lobbied for American entry into the new international organization. They did not hesitate to seek to mobilize popular support and congressional and executive opinion behind specific programs aimed at rationalizing international relations. Similarly, the work of the Women's International League for Peace and Freedom and the National Council for the Prevention of War showed that public opinion

INTRODUCTION

could be aroused, activists coordinated, coalitions formed with labor, farm, business, education, and religious groups, and influence brought to bear on federal foreign and military policy. No longer merely educational devices, the organizations in the postwar peace movement worked as effective lobbies at the nation's capital. They remained so for the next two decades, until Pearl Harbor and U.S. entry into World War II.

The success of the peace movement in achieving its goals by influencing American governmental policy varied during the first two decades of the 20th century. Its achievements were affected by changes in international and domestic circumstances, by the strength of counter-pressures exerted by opposing organizations, by divisions within the peace movement itself, by public opinion, and by the receptivity of the President of the United States as well as the heads of other governments. The degree of success also depended upon the specific immediate goal and strategy of particular elements of the peace movement.

Attempts by peace advocates to stop actual combat between the armed forces of the United States and other nations between 1900 and 1922 proved much less influential than military circumstances themselves. In addition to numerous uses of contingents of Marines in Caribbean countries, the United States during this period was involved in substantial military operations in the Philippines, China (during the Boxer Rebellion), Mexico, France and Russia during World War I. U.S. military successes or failures rather than the efforts of peace workers generally led to the termination of these hostilities. The antiwar movement seems to have been relatively ineffectual in concluding American conflicts during this period.

Somewhat more effective were those peace advocates who encouraged the mediation of international disputes that broke out during the first two decades of the century. President Roosevelt showed that the United States could play the role of mediator and peacemaker when he helped negotiate the settlement of the Russo-Japanese War at Portsmouth, New Hampshire in 1905 and in acting as conciliator among the

INTRODUCTION

European nations at the Algeciras Conference in Spain in 1905 and 1906.

During World War I, peace activists urged President Wilson to play the role of mediator and employ a conference of neutral nations to initiate negotiations. While the mediation movement failed to influence Wilson's efforts, it did bolster his hopes and stimulate his interest in leading the world to abandon the old diplomacy of secret treaties and military alliances. Ironically, the President eventually concluded, in the face of the German submarine offensive, that only by going to war could he help achieve the new diplomacy of international cooperation to maintain a liberal, capitalist world order. Mediationists proved more successful in averting war between the United States and Mexico in 1916. Their talks among private citizens of the two countries helped lead to formal negotiations between the two governments and the easing of tensions.

Those members of the peace movement who sought to establish a world government proved somewhat less successful. They too fell short of obtaining their goal. They did, however, contribute to President Wilson's acceptance of the idea of an association of nations. Nevertheless, the League of Nations failed to embody the kind of unified world organization, with legislative, judicial, and executive powers, that these peace advocates desired. Despite their hope that it would lead to true world government, they were unable to obtain Senate approval for American membership in the League.

While opposing such a sweeping goal as world government, many legalistic internationalists supported arbitration, adjudication, and the construction of an international common law through a world court. These friends of peace were particularly successful in obtaining the adoption of their program for arbitration by the Roosevelt and Taft administrations. However, the Senate, jealous of its prerogatives and wary of compromising national interests, refused to allow the executive to commit the United States to arbitration of vital matters. In the Wilson administration, Secretary of State Bryan, one of the spokesmen of the peace movement, obtained less restrictive treaties of conciliation with a number of countries, but these were never used and eventually expired.

The idea of a world court received much support by American Presidents. The Roosevelt administration used the Hague Tribunal to settle several minor differences involving the United States and other countries, and the Wilson administration tried to establish an inter-American court of international justice. While Wilson also endorsed a world court, many peace activists were disappointed that it was not established simultaneously with the League, but only later as a creature of the association of nations. Despite repeated efforts by internationalists, the United States never joined the World Court. Thus while highly successful in affecting the chief U.S. policymakers, the advocates of international arbitration and adjudication and a world court found themselves restricted by nationalism, isolationism, and political concern reflected within the United States Senate.

It was when the two branches of government supported them that the peace advocates found themselves most effective. Such was the case in the naval arms limitation treaty of 1922. Even then, however, the reduction applied only to the largest ships of the leading powers. Furthermore, the disarmament movement had not always been even that successful. It had exercised little constraint on the naval expansion encouraged by Theodore Roosevelt. Nor did it prevent the massive construction program of 1916–1918 authorized during the Wilson administration. In the postwar period, however, arms limitation coincided with the attitudes of the majority in the country and Congress. Then, disarmament advocates were able to block the efforts of the administration and the admirals and generals who sought to maintain a large naval and military establishment. Thus in 1919 and 1922, the peace movement proved perhaps most effective in obtaining its immediate goal of disarmament.

The study of the influence of the peace movement upon U.S. foreign policy between 1900 and 1922 also provides insights into the operation of the American political system and into the development of the United States as a world power. Our examination of one aspect of those phenomena suggests hypotheses about both the effectiveness of the peace movement and the nature of influence upon foreign policy within the American polity in the early years of the 20th century.

From the preceding evidence, it appears that the peace movement was most effective when its goals coincided with public sentiment which was being shaped by other forces as well. The antipathy to war and armaments which followed World War I represented a dramatic example. Americans saw little justification for large defense expenditures in a period of little external danger and high domestic taxes. Within such a setting, peace advocates could provide both the arguments and the apparatus for catalyzing public opinion and channeling it into political action. The peace movement could become an especially effective lobby when it aimed at achieving limited and negative goals, such as reducing tax appropriations for armaments. In periods of little plausible danger to the national interest, peace workers could act as an effective counter to the recommendations of those who wished to maintain or expand large military and naval establishments.

Conversely, the peace movement seems to have been least effective during wartime, especially in the course of a relatively popular, short, and successful war, when public opinion and those who help to shape it were, on the whole, either apathetic or hostile to the pleas of peace activists. Pacifists appeal to people's hopes; the military appeals to their fears. At the outbreak of war, the military's arguments almost automatically gain legitimacy.

A declaration of war also provides increased power for the agencies of social control—the government, the judiciary, the clergy, and the mass media—to restrict those who continue to dissent from national policy. Persuasion by the authorities is enhanced by appeals to loyalty, patriotism, the symbols of national unity and history, and the ability to repudiate the more radical dissenters as people who willingly or unconsciously are aiding the enemy. Increased governmental control over the channels of information increases its power and, conversely, limits the means of these dissenters to extend their message. The government's ability to use sanctions also increases in wartime through both new enabling legislation and

INTRODUCTION

through the acquiescence of the normally countervailing power centers, public or private. Authorities can, and in World War I did, prevent communications by some dissenters, by breaking up meetings, denying mailing privileges, and confiscating printed publications. They can fine, imprison, or exile activist dissenters. They can encourage divisions within dissenting groups, and they can act to prevent American citizens from operating outside official channels in attempts to open private negotiations with other governments. As long as a particular war is supported by the overwhelming majority of people, such constraints can curtail effective action by the peace movement. Such was the case during American belligerency in World War I.

Such moments of suppression as in 1917–1918, or of achievement as in 1922, do not, however, appear typical of the peace movement during the first two decades of the 20th century.

The main function of the peace movement during that period seems to have been to present alternatives to American foreign policymakers and then to lobby for their acceptance and implementation. Not all of these options were accepted by the Presidents, but a number were. Arbitration, the use of an international tribunal, and mediation of international disputes all became official U.S. policy. The Chief Executive, however, frequently failed to follow the specific advice of the peace organizations. Instead, the Presidents tended to use the alternatives and support of the peace advocates when these coincided with their own thought or needs and to disregard them at other times.

Sometimes, the peace movement scored a dramatic tactical success, as in the prevention of war between the United States and Mexico over the Carrizal incident of 1916 or in the achievements of the Washington Naval Conference of 1922. At other times it was able to help modify U.S. policy, as in the arbitration agreements of the Roosevelt administration, the conciliation treaties and the Treaty of Versailles of the Wilson administration.

It should be remembered, however, that the peace movement was not unified and that it was itself only one of the interest-groups which sought to influence foreign policy in Washington.

INTRODUCTION

Business, agricultural, religious, military, and ethnic organizations were also active. Each of these jockeyed for influence upon Congress, the State Department, and the White House. Furthermore, the peace movement was so broad that its constituent groups seldom worked together as they pursued their specific immediate goals. This heterogeneity of membership and diversity of immediate goals frequently hampered the effectiveness of the peace workers.

Like the other interest-groups, the peace organizations operated on the whole between the decision-makers and the media and members of an attentive public, in this case, those concerned with foreign policy. The peace activists tried to use the one to influence the other. As such, their political role was primarily communicative and educational. Their prestige and their arguments proved to be their major tools of persuasion, but they had their most significant effect when they could demonstrate great popular support as well.

In retrospect, the most important trend of the period in the relationship of the United States to the rest of the world was the increased willingness of Americans to have the United States play the international role to which its economic strength and military potential entitled it. The first three Presidents of the century, Roosevelt, Taft, and Wilson, led the country into new political, military, economic, and diplomatic involvement in international affairs.

The peace movement helped the Presidents in their attempts to convince Americans to accept this increased international activity. While they did not support the expanded military role, and some questioned the increased economic involvement, the majority of peace activists, through their educational campaigns, encouraged a more cosmopolitan world view among many Americans. Thus they helped to erode the traditional isolationism—more accurately, political unilateralism—that had characterized the American attitude towards the nations outside the Western Hemisphere. In some cases, such as the attempt to prevent American entry into World War I or the effort to achieve military and naval disarmament, elements of the peace movement reversed themselves and appealed to traditional isolationism, but overall, peace advocates urged an expanded American role and mission in the world. In their view, this would not be a military role, but a political and perhaps economic one which would be in keeping with what they saw as America's unique destiny of bringing enlightened, humane, and just relations among peoples.

To peace advocates as to many other Americans, the United States remained the world's last, best hope. They maintained their faith in that vision even through the agony of World War I. They coupled it with an intensive, new effort to bring lasting peace to the global community. Their faith in America and in the pragmatic application of intelligence to human problems sustained them.

Part I

*Awakening of the Modern
American Peace Movement,
1900-1914*

Document No. 1 The First Hague Conference (1899)
Source: William M. Malloy, compiler, *Treaties, Conventions, International Acts, Protocols and Agreements between the United States of America and other Powers, 1776-1909* (2 vols.; Washington, D.C.: U.S. Government Printing Office, 1910), II, pp. 2016-2032.

CONVENTIONS CONCLUDED AT THE FIRST INTERNATIONAL PEACE CONFERENCE, HELD AT THE HAGUE, 1899.

1899.[a]

CONVENTION FOR THE PACIFIC SETTLEMENT OF INTERNATIONAL DISPUTES.

Concluded July 29, 1899; ratification advised by Senate February 5, 1900; ratified by President April 7, 1900; ratifications deposited with the Netherlands Government September 4, 1900; proclaimed November 1, 1901.

ARTICLES.

Title I. Maintenance of general peace.

I. Pacific settlement of international differences.

Title II. Mediation.

II. Good offices.
III. Offer of mediation.
IV. Mediator.
V. Termination of mediator's duties.

VI. Effect of mediation.
VII. Acceptance of mediation.
VIII. Special mediation; choosing mediators, etc.

Title III. International commissions of inquiry.

IX. Investigations by commission.
X. Special agreement; jurisdiction.
XI. Formation.

XII. Facilities supplied commission.
XIII. Report.
XIV. Effect of report.

Title IV. International arbitration.

Chapter I. System of arbitration.

XV. Object.
XVI. Recognition.
XVII. Questions considered.

XVIII. Submission to award.
XIX. Extension of arbitration.

[a]Adhered to by the Argentine Republic, Bolivia, Brazil, Chile, Colombia, Cuba, Dominican Republic, Ecuador, Guatemala, Haiti, Nicaragua, Panama, Paraguay, Peru, Salvador, Uruguay, and Venezuela.
The convention for the pacific settlement of international disputes, concluded at The Hague, October 18, 1907 (second international conference) Article XCI provides, "The present convention, duly ratified, shall replace, as between the contracting powers, the convention for the pacific settlement of international disputes of the 29th July, 1899."

Chapter II. Permanent court of arbitration.

Chapter III. Arbitral procedure.

[Translation.]

His Majesty the Emperor of Germany, King of Prussia; His Majesty the Emperor of Austria, King of Bohemia etc. and Apostolic King of Hungary; His Majesty the King of the Belgians; His Majesty the Emperor of China; His Majesty the King of Denmark; His Majesty the King of Spain and in His Name Her Majesty the Queen Regent of the Kingdom; the President of the United States of America; the President of the United Mexican States; the President of the French Republic; Her Majesty the Queen of the United Kingdom of Great Britain and Ireland, Empress of India; His Majesty the King of the Hellenes; His Majesty the King of Italy; His Majesty the Emperor of Japan; His Royal Highness the Grand Duke of Luxemburg, Duke of Nassau; His Highness the Prince of Montenegro; Her Majesty the Queen of the Netherlands; His Imperial Majesty the Shah of Persia; His Majesty the King of Portugal and of the Algarves etc.; His Majesty the King of Roumania; His Majesty the Emperor of all the Russias; His Majesty the King of Servia; His Majesty the King of Siam; His Majesty the King of Sweden and Norway; the Swiss Federal Council; His Majesty the Emperor of the Ottomans and His Royal Highness the Prince of Bulgaria

Animated by a strong desire to concert for the maintenance of the general peace;

Resolved to second by their best efforts the friendly settlement of international disputes;

Recognizing the solidarity which unites the members of the society of civilized nations;

Desirous of extending the empire of law, and of strengthening the appreciation of international justice;

Convinced that the permanent institution of a Court of Arbitration, accessible to all, in the midst of the independent Powers, will contribute effectively to this result;

Having regard to the advantages attending the general and regular organization of arbitral procedure;

Sharing the opinion of the august Initiator of the International Peace Conference that it is expedient to record in an international Agreement the principles of equity and right on which are based the security of States and the welfare of peoples;

Being desirous of concluding a Convention to this effect, have appointed as their Plenipotentiaries,

• • • •

TITLE I.—ON THE MAINTENANCE OF THE GENERAL PEACE.

ARTICLE I.

With a view to obviating, as far as possible, recourse to force in the relations between States, the Signatory Powers agree to use their best efforts to insure the pacific settlement of international differences.

TITLE IV.—ON INTERNATIONAL ARBITRATION.

CHAPTER I.—*On the System of Arbitration.*

ARTICLE XV.

International arbitration has for its object the settlement of differences between States by judges of their own choice, and on the basis of respect for law.

ARTICLE XVI.

In questions of a legal nature, and especially in the interpretation or application of International Conventions, arbitration is recognized by the Signatory Powers as the most effective, and at the same time the most equitable, means of settling disputes which diplomacy has failed to settle.

ARTICLE XVII.

The Arbitration Convention is concluded for questions already existing or for questions which may arise eventually.

It may embrace any dispute or only disputes of a certain category.

ARTICLE XVIII.

The Arbitration Convention implies the engagement to submit loyally to the Award.

89

Article XIX.

Independently of general or private Treaties expressly stipulating recourse to arbitration as obligatory on the Signatory Powers, these Powers reserve to themselves the right of concluding, either before the ratification of the present Act or later, new Agreements, general or private, with a view to extending obligatory arbitration to all cases which they may consider it possible to submit to it.

Chapter II.—*On the Permanent Court of Arbitration.*

Article XX.

With the object of facilitating an immediate recourse to arbitration for international differences, which it has not been possible to settle by diplomacy, the Signatory Powers undertake to organize a permanent Court of Arbitration, accessible at all times and operating, unless otherwise stipulated by the parties, in accordance with the Rules of Procedure inserted in the present Convention.

Article XXI.

The Permanent Court shall be competent for all arbitration cases, unless the parties agree to institute a special Tribunal.

Article XXII.

An International Bureau, established at The Hague, serves as record office for the Court.

This Bureau is the channel for communications relative to the meetings of the Court.

It has the custody of the archives and conducts all the administrative business.

The Signatory Powers undertake to communicate to the International Bureau at The Hague a duly certified copy of any conditions of arbitration arrived at between them, and of any award concerning them delivered by special Tribunals.

They undertake also to communicate to the Bureau the Laws, Regulations, and documents eventually showing the execution of the awards given by the Court.

Article XXIII.

Within the three months following its ratification of the present Act, each Signatory Power shall select four persons at the most, of known competency in questions of international law, of the highest moral reputation, and disposed to accept the duties of Arbitrators.

The persons thus selected shall be inscribed as members of the Court, in a list which shall be notified by the Bureau to all the Signatory Powers.

Any alteration in the list of Arbitrators is brought by the Bureau to the knowledge of the Signatory Powers.

Two or more Powers may agree on the selection in common of one or more Members.

The same person can be selected by different Powers.

The Members of the Court are appointed for a term of six years. Their appointments can be renewed.

In case of the death or retirement of a member of the Court, his place shall be filled in accordance with the method of his appointment.

ARTICLE XXIV.

When the Signatory Powers desire to have recourse to the Permanent Court for the settlement of a difference that has arisen between them, the Arbitrators called upon to form the competent Tribunal to decide this difference, must be chosen from the general list of members of the Court.

Failing the direct agreement of the parties on the composition of the Arbitration Tribunal, the following course shall be pursued:—

Each party appoints two Arbitrators, and these together choose an Umpire.

If the votes are equal, the choice of the Umpire is intrusted to a third Power, selected by the parties by common accord.

If an agreement is not arrived at on this subject, each party selects a different Power, and the choice of the Umpire is made in concert by the Powers thus selected.

The Tribunal being thus composed, the parties notify to the Bureau their determination to have recourse to the Court and the names of the Arbitrators.

The Tribunal of Arbitration assembles on the date fixed by the parties.

The Members of the Court, in the discharge of their duties and out of their own country, enjoy diplomatic privileges and immunities.

ARTICLE XXV.

The Tribunal of Arbitration has its ordinary seat at The Hague.

Except in cases of necessity, the place of session can only be altered by the Tribunal with the assent of the parties.

ARTICLE XXVI.

The International Bureau at The Hague is authorized to place its premises and its staff at the disposal of the Signatory Powers for the operations of any special Board of Arbitration.

The jurisdiction of the Permanent Court, may, within the conditions laid down in the Regulations, be extended to disputes between non-Signatory Powers, or between Signatory Powers and non-Signatory Powers, if the parties are agreed on recourse to this Tribunal.

Article XXVII.

The Signatory Powers consider it their duty, if a serious dispute threatens to break out between two or more of them, to remind these latter that the Permanent Court is open to them.

Consequently, they declare that the fact of remindingn the conflicting parties of the provisions of the present Convention, and the advice given to them, in the highest interests of peace, to have recourse to the Permanent Court, can only be regarded as friendly actions.

Article XXVIII.

A Permanent Administrative Council, composed of the Diplomatic Representatives of the Signatory Powers accredited to The Hague and of the Netherland Minister for Foreign Affairs, who will act as President, shall be instituted in this town as soon as possible after the ratification of the present Act by at least nine Powers.

This Council will be charged with the establishment and organization of the International Bureau, which will be under its direction and control.

It will notify to the Powers the constitution of the Court and will provide for its installation.

It will settle its Rules of Procedure and all other necessary Regulations.

It will decide all questions of administration which may arise with regard to the operations of the Court.

It will have entire control over the appointment, suspension or dismissal of the officials and employés of the Bureau.

It will fix the payments and salaries, and control the general expenditure.

At meetings duly summoned the presence of five members is sufficient to render valid the discussions of the Council. The decisions are taken by a majority of votes.

The Council communicates to the Signatory Powers without delay the Regulations adopted by it. It furnishes them with an annual Report on the labours of the Court, the working of the administration, and the expenses.

Article XXIX.

The expenses of the Bureau shall be borne by the Signatory Power in the proportion fixed for the International Bureau of the Universal Postal Union.

Chapter III.—*On Arbitral Procedure.*

The said Convention was signed by the Plenipotentiaries of the United States of America under reservation of the following declaration:

"Nothing contained in this convention shall be so construed as require the United States of America to depart from its traditional policy of not intruding upon, interfering with, or entangling itself in the political questions of policy or internal administration of any foreign state; nor shall anything contained in the said convention be construed to imply a relinquishment by the United States of America of its traditional attitude toward purely American questions;"

In pursuance of the stipulations of Article LVIII of the said Convention the ratifications of the said Convention were deposited at The Hague on the 4th. day of September, 1900, by the Plenipotentiaries of the Governments of the United States of America, Germany, Austria-Hungary, Belgium, Denmark, Spain, France, Great Britain, Italy, the Netherlands, Persia, Portugal, Roumania, Russia, Siam, Sweden and Norway and Bulgaria; on the 6th. day of October, 1900, by the Plenipotentiary of the Government of Japan; on the 16th. day of October, 1900, by the Plenipotentiary of the Government of Montenegro; on the 29th. day of December, 1900, by the Plenipotentiary of the Government of Switzerland; on the 4th. day of April, 1901, by the Plenipotentiary of the Government of Greece; on the 17th. day of April, 1901, by the Plenipotentiary of the Government of Mexico; on the 11th day of May, 1901, by the Plenipotentiary of the Government of Servia; and on the 12th. day of July, 1901, by the Plenipotentiary of the Government of Luxembourg.

Document No. 2   John W. Foster, "The Year's Progress in Peace" (1903)
Source: *The Independent,* LV (July 2, 1903), pp. 1551-1553.

The Year's Progress in Peace

By John W. Foster

Ex-Secretary of State

HAVING been requested by THE INDEPENDENT to contribute to its Fourth of July number, I have thought it appropriate to furnish a review of the events of the past year respecting arbitration. In no aspect of our international relations has our country been more distinguished than in its attitude on this subject. In our exultation on the return of our national anniversary we should not forget that some of our most glorious victories have been those of peace. Ours is not a military Government, and let us so shape its policy with other nations that it may never become such.

It is a matter of congratulation for us that the United States was the first to set an example to the world of a resort to The Hague Tribunal. It was announced a year ago that this country and Mexico were just concluding an agreement to submit to that international court a question much discussed and of long standing. That case has already been submitted to the Tribunal, and with a promptness and celerity almost unknown in international judicatures a decision has been rendered. Altho the amount of the award is large, the debtor nation has cheerfully accepted the result.

Even for her the result was so much more satisfactory than the constant irritation growing out of the continued agitation of the question that it was better to pay the award, even tho regarded as inequitable, and be at peace with her neighbor.

Probably the most edifying and auspicious event has occurred in a quarter of the world to which Anglo-Saxons have not been inclined to look for helpful examples in good government and salutary public law. In the lower extreme of the South American continent there have arisen during the last century two prosperous and aspiring republics. As a rule they have sustained good administration, maintained excellent foreign credit, and have greatly advanced in wealth and resources. For a time they arrayed themselves in a rivalry for supremacy on that continent, and following the example of the greater nations they largely increased their armies and navies. A controversy over a boundary line threatened to light the torch of war and thrust these two peaceful, prosperous and industrious peoples into a sanguinary and exhausting conflict. But better counsels prevailed, and Chile and Argentina agreed to submit the bound-

94

ary question to the arbitration of the King of England. His award has been rendered and accepted by both nations.

But that is only the beginning of the narrative. The two nations have entered into a treaty whereby they agree to submit all questions which cannot be settled by diplomacy to arbitration, the only exception being those involving principles of their constitutions. They further agreed to stop the construction of more naval vessels and to sell those which were ordered at the time the war fever was raging, and as a result there are now in the naval dockyards of Europe several war vessels of the two nations seeking customers. They also agreed to reduce their armies to a peace footing and to so maintain them, and to partially disarm their naval vessels at home.

As a result of this disarmament we are informed by recent press news from Buenos Aires that the Minister of Marine has tendered to the Minister of Agriculture two of his unoccupied men-of-war to transport grain and meat products to South Africa, where the Government is seeking to open up a new market for their superabundant harvests. With a slight change in the Biblical metaphor, may we regard this as the beginning of that millennium era, foretold by the ancient prophet, when the people " shall beat their swords into plowshares and their spears into pruning-hooks; nation shall not lift up a sword against nation, neither shall they learn war any more "?

From these far away countries, where we have been so prone to expect war and disorder, comes this inspiring and hopeful example. They are a people, too, of a different religion and race from the most of us—Catholics, not Protestants—Spanish Americans of the Latin race, not the boastful Anglo-Saxon. May we not learn from this to be a little more charitable in our criticism of the countries to the South of us in their struggles to free themselves from the customs which enchained them during so many centuries of misrule?

Some notice must be taken of the Venezuela complication. Three of the most powerful nations of the world combined in a hostile demonstration against one of the feeblest of the smaller nations.

The alleged cause of this combined armed expedition was one for which neither of them, nor all three combined, would have had the temerity to make war against any nation with even moderate military resources. When in 1861 the United States was solicited by three of the great nations of Europe to unite with them in an armed demonstration against Mexico for a similar reason, Secretary Seward replied that our Government was not disposed to enter upon warlike measures to enforce claims against a friendly Power. Such a reason for hostilities has certainly not gained in strength with the lapse of half a century of enlightenment. The point which I wish to emphasize is that the public sentiment of the world, and especially of the British people, brought those three powerful nations to a halt. It is encouraging to know that in this era it is not so easy to inaugurate or prosecute an unjust war as it was a century or more ago.

On the other hand, the event shows some of the evil effects of transforming the populous nations into great military Powers. While the vast naval armaments and standing armies of Great Britain, France, Germany, Russia and other nations make them very cautious about provoking each other to a conflict, they offer a temptation to occupy these forces in expeditions and adventures against weaker nations. There was little risk to Germany, Great Britain and Italy in seizing or sinking the infantile flotilla of Venezuela and in bombarding its antiquated forts. Hence, in the interest of the weaker nations and of the world's peace, it is of the utmost importance that a public sentiment be created among the enlightened nations which will restrain the great military Powers from entering upon schemes of adventure or oppression and which will support the smaller independent nations in their appeal to the arbitration of their differences with the more powerful.

In this connection it is gratifying to us as Americans to note the attitude of our Government in the existing controversy of the European nations with China. After they, by their territorial aggressions upon that empire, had provoked its people to rise in blind resentment against foreigners, and then punished them by the levy of an enormous indemnity, they insisted with this helpless nation upon the exaction of the last "pound of flesh" by a technical construction of the protocol, which made it annually more and more difficult for the empire to comply with its terms. It was a generous and magnanimous act on the part of Secretary Hay to construe the protocol most favorably for China, and heartily to support that Government in its appeal for submission of the question in dispute to The Hague Tribunal. How it would exalt the Christian nations in the eyes of those whom we style the heathen if this appeal should be granted!

The Venezuela embroglio has also served to bring into prominence the value of arbitration and the utility of The Hague Tribunal. It was a high compliment to President Roosevelt to be solicited to act as arbitrator of that dispute. But it enhanced his reputation still more to decline the offer and to refer the contending parties to the Tribunal which his own Government has done so much to create.

In no country did this act of President Roosevelt receive greater commendation than in France, some of whose representatives at The Hague Conference were the most ardent supporters of the scheme adopted by that body. Only a few days ago the press announced that the Parliamentary arbitration organization of Senators had received some notable accessions from the ranks of its public men, and that the cause of international arbitration had been given a new impetus in that enlightened country.

Not the least of the events of the past year tending to peace is the treaty between the Governments of the United States and Great Britain to refer the controverted question of the Alaskan boundary to a mixed tribunal of American and British jurists. It is not an arbitration, and, from the state of the question and of public sentiment in the United States, it could not well be such. It is an illustration of the fact that even so excellent a principle as arbitration has its limitations in practice. It was not possible to have secured a treaty to entrust the settlement of the Alaskan boundary to the award of a neutral foreign arbitrator. It may sound strange to be told that some of the most earnest advocates of The Hague Tribunal were strongly opposed to the Alaskan boundary treaty. But I regard it as a wise measure and one which redounds to the credit of President Roosevelt and Secretary Hay. It provides a safe method of adjusting a long pending and vexed question, which threatened to disturb the relations of neighbors who ought to be the closest friends; and I entertain the confident expectation that the six distinguished jurists to whom the matter is referred will find a solution honorable to both parties.

Should it have this greatly to be desired outcome, it cannot fail to increase the prospects of a permanent arbitration treaty between the United States and Great Britain. It will be remembered that six years ago Secretary Olney and Lord Pauncefote signed a general arbitration convention to continue for five years only, but it failed to receive the approval of the Senate largely because of this boundary dispute. The Alaskan boundary treaty, approved by the Senate last February, is the method of settlement provided in the Olney-Pauncefote convention. If it shall prove effective we may have renewed hope of seeing at no distant day a general arbitration treaty between these two kindred peoples, who have a common heritage and a common mission in the world. It must not be that the twin Latin Republics of South America shall put us to very shame when we are claiming to hold aloft as a model for all peoples our much vaunted Anglo-Saxon Christian civilization. We should concentrate our efforts in favor of a general arbitration treaty between the American and British Governments on the lines of the unratified convention of 1897. To this end public sentiment should be brought to bear upon the Senate of the United States. That distinguished body is a fair representation of the American people, and when the latter shall express themselves as favorable to such a treaty the Senate will ratify their verdict. Let all lovers of peace and of their country concentrate their efforts to bring about that greatly desired result.

WASHINGTON, D. C.

Document No. 3 Lucia Ames Mead, "International Police" (1903)
Source: *The Outlook,* LXXIV (July 18, 1903), pp. 705-706.

International Police
By Lucia Ames Mead

" I BELIEVE in arbitration, of course, and in a stated International Congress—I have worked to promote that," said a Senator in the Massachusetts Legislature to me ; "but when you peace people talk about ending war, I can't follow you. I think you will have to wait until the millennium ; for so long as there is sin in the world there must needs be force." Doubtless there are some "peace men" who, like Tolstoi, decry all use of force ; but the ordinary sensible man who is working to abolish national armaments, when the shrieks from Kishenev and the Congo ring in his ears, calls for a strong hand, and no milk-and-water policy. As he remembers the two thousand gangs of American anarchists who have torn open jail doors and hanged and burned untried men, and themselves gone unpunished, he believes there is still use in this world for the soldier.

But if he is a peace man who wants to make himself effective, he will not waste time in discussing the horrors of war and the beauties of peace. He will try to let in a light on a subject about which much sophistry has befogged the public's mind. His first proposition will be that the organized, authoritative force of this world is of two essentially different kinds. The one that we know most about is of comparatively recent origin ; it is the police force. Time was, and not more than two or three centuries ago, when every man carried his own weapon and avenged his own wrong. To-day, in thoroughly civilized communities, he who avenges his own wrong becomes a criminal. The State has established a disinterested method of settling disputes according to evidence and justice. Force is employed, but not to settle the dispute. The policeman brings the contestants to a court. That is his function—to bring to court—and he uses only that modicum of force which is necessary to bring contestants to court. Often they come of their own accord, or, when brought, they usually venture little or no resistance. Then twelve men hear evidence for and against. No man may be a juror who is interested personally in the dispute. Witnesses are brought, lawyers employed, law books studied. When the verdict is given, an impartial judge decrees sentence according to statutes made by another disinterested set of men called legislators. The whole transaction means that the result depends upon law and justice, not accident or the bulk of the contestants. The child has as good a chance of justice as the man. The function of the police is to bring to court and to take to prison according as the court orders. The policeman himself inflicts no punishment, and uses only such force as may be necessary to bring a stubborn man to trial. Let this be emphasized, for this use of force is almost universally confounded with that totally different use of force employed by armies and navies. National armies and navies have no analogy with the police, though nine college graduates out of ten argue as if they were analogous. The function of the police is to bring to court. The function of national armies and navies and the powers behind them is to execute without trial. Were the nations not living in anarchic relations with each other, armies and navies would be simply gigantic, organized lynches. They listen to no arguments, weigh no testimony, are not disinterested, and do not force their antagonist to come to any court. Their settlement is made, not according to justice, but by brute force. Almost every attribute of the police force is lacking in army and navy. And yet we are incessantly told by some of the best and ablest of men that the navy polices our coast, that the army is our national police. The most fundamental and palpable divergence of functions is ignored, and the solution of the world's greatest problem is relegated to the millennium because of this curious kink in the reasoning faculties of many leaders of thought.

At the recent Mohonk Arbitration Conference I listened anxiously for one word on this confusing subject. Only one speaker, Mr. Edwin Ginn, the publisher, casually used the word that, if said with emphasis and heeded, would have thrown a flood of light on what to most men seems hopelessly obscured. He said "the International Police." What would an international police do? It would bring stubborn nations to the World's Court with the same efficiency as the city police separate two men glaring at each other with murderous knives unsheathed, and drag them to the Police Court. Of what would the International Police be composed? Of a small body of armed men and battle-ships paid and organized by practically all the nations of the world and controlling them through a World Legislature which would make laws to be carried out by the Hague Court. We have the Hague Court. Next winter Congress will be asked to propose to the nations to establish an International Congress to meet at regular intervals to discuss international problems. This will not be a World Legislature, as its delegates will have, as at the Hague Conference, no power to do more than to refer questions to their nations for ratification. It must be a little time before the Congress can be formed. It may be decades before it develops into a genuine Legislature with power. But a World Legislature is as definitely bound to come as the Isthmian canal or the Cape to Cairo railroad. Not until it is established, and perhaps several decades after that, can we talk practically about forming an International Police; we must first, of course, all pledge ourselves to carry international differences to court. But though the period of complete national disarmament may be relegated to another century, it is of immense importance for the world to know that it is approximately near, that we need not wait until sin and quarrels have been banished from the earth before we find a rational way of treating them.

The police force will remain to bring men to court. The militia will remain to compel riotous mobs and lynchers to leave their quarrels and their vengeance to the courts. The international police will supplant the national, paid bodies of executioners who, under our present anarchic system of international relations, execute in absence of law, according to national whim or passion or prejudice. The reign of law has come in families, in cities, in the States, in the nations. It is coming between the nations. There is no new principle to be invented, simply the extension of an old and tried principle.

We shall not arbitrate with savages, but the civilized nations will arbitrate about the lands and rights of savages. No one nation will be permitted by the other nations to steal their land and exploit them. The mutual self-interest of great nations, if nothing more, will demand justice for the weaker ones. Human nature will, no doubt, still have the tiger latent in it; but the tiger will be left dormant as there is less and less occasion to arouse it. Sin and cruelty and avarice will persist, but we shall treat them calmly, disinterestedly, not with the senseless passion of war. Civil war may remain an abstract possibility. The International Police is not an academic question, but a live, practical question. There is nothing that need prevent its being realized within a hundred years, if the leaders of thought in Europe and America see clearly and do what they are perfectly capable of doing. The action of the allied armies in China in the suppression of the "Boxers" gives a hint of what International Police may do.

For years Dr. Hale and others in America went up and down the land crying, "We must have an International Court;" when it came we welcomed it as a familiar thought. While we are busy making this court more and more efficient by enlarging the scope of cases brought to it, we must familiarize men with the next step to goals ahead of us—the World Legislature and the World Police. We must arouse the hopeless and give new courage to pessimists who assume that Christendom must continue to sink three billion [1] dollars annually simply to keep the peace. We must show a way out of the quagmires in which their hopes are sunk. City, State, and nation have been organized and put under the reign of law. The world will likewise be organized and put under the reign of law, and when that is done we shall not have abolished force, or wickedness, or punishment for wickedness, or civil war, but we shall have abolished wars between nations and national armies and navies.

---

[1] This includes interest on debt for past wars and part of the wages lost by millions of unproductive soldiers.

Document No. 4 Andrew Carnegie, *A League of Peace: A Rectoral Address Delivered to the Students in the University of St. Andrew,* Oct. 17, 1905 (N.Y.: The New York Peace Society, 1911), pp. 32-37.

• • • •

It may surprise you to learn that from the date of the Jay Treaty, one hundred and eleven years ago, no less than five hundred and seventy-one international disputes have been settled by arbitration. Not in any case has an award been questioned or disregarded, except I believe in one case, where the arbiters misunderstood their powers. . If in every ten of these differences so quietly adjusted without a wound, there lurked one war, it follows that peaceful settlement has prevented fifty-seven wars—one every two years. More than this, had the fifty-seven wars, assumed as prevented by arbitration, developed, they would have sown the seeds of many future wars, for there is no such prolific mother of wars as war itself. Hate breeds hate, quarrel breeds quarrels, war breeds war—a hateful progeny. It is the poorest of all remedies. It poisons as it cures. No truer line was ever penned than this of Milton's, "For what can war but endless war still breed?"

No less than twenty-three International Treaties of Arbitration have been made within the past two years. The United States made ten with the principal Powers, which only failed to be formally executed because the Senate, which shares with our Executive the treaty-making power to the extent that its approval is necessary, thought it advisable to change one word only—"treaty" for "agreement"—which proved unsatisfactory to the Executive. The vote of the Senate was almost unanimous, showing an over-whelming sentiment for arbitration. The internal difference will no doubt be adjusted.

You will judge from these facts how rapidly arbitration is spreading. Once tried, there is no backward step. It produces peace and leaves no bitterness. The parties to it become better friends than before; war makes them enemies.

Much has been written upon the fearful cost of war in our day, the ever-increasing blood tax of nations, which threatens soon to approach the point of exhaustion in several European lands. To-day France leads with an expenditure of £3 14s and a debt of £31 3s 8d per head. Britain follows with an annual expenditure of £3 8s 8d and a debt of £18 10s 5d per head. Germany's expenditure is in great contrast—only £1 15s 4d, not much more than one-third; her debt £2 12s 2d, not one-sixth that of Britain. Russia's expenditure is £1 14s 6d, about the same as the German; her debt £5 9s 9d per head.

The military and naval expenditure of Britain is fully half of her total expenditure; that of the other great Powers, though less, is rapidly increasing.

All the great national debts, with trifling exceptions—Britain's Eight Hundred Millions, France's Twelve Hundred Millions Sterling—are the legacies of war.

This drain, with the economic loss of life added, is forcing itself upon the nations concerned as never before. It threatens soon to become dangerous unless the rapid increase of recent years be stopped; but it is to be feared that not till after the financial catastrophe occurs will nations devote themselves seriously to apply the cure.

The futility of war as a means of producing peace between nations has often been dwelt upon. It is really the most futile of all remedies, because it embitters contestants and sows the seeds of future struggles. Generations are sometimes required to eradicate the hostility engendered by one conflict. War sows dragons' teeth, and seldom gives to either party what it fought for. When it does, the spoil generally proves Dead Sea fruit. The recent terrible war just concluded is another case in point. Neither contestant obtained what he fought for, the reputed victor being most of all disappointed at last with the terms of peace. Had Japan, a very poor country, known that the result would be a debt of two hundred millions Sterling loading her down, or had Russia known the result, differences would have been peacefully arbitrated. Such considerations find no place, however, in the fiery furnace of popular clamor; as little do those of cost or loss of life. Only if the moral wrong, the sin in itself, of man-slaying is brought home to the conscience of the masses may we hope speedily to banish war. There will, we fear, always be demagogs in our day to inflame their brutal passions and urge men to fight, as a point of honor and patriotism, scouting arbitration as a cowardly refuge. All thoughts of cost or loss of human life vanish when the brute in man, thus aroused, gains sway.

It is the crime of destroying human life by war and the duty to offer or accept peaceful arbitration as a substitute which needs to be established, and which, as we think, those of the Church, the Universities, and of the Professions are called upon to strongly emphasize.

If the principal European nations were not free thru conscription from the problem which now disturbs the military authorities of Britain, the lack of sufficient numbers willing to enter the man-slaying profession, we should soon hear the demand formulated for a League of Peace among the nations. The subject of war can never be studied without recalling this simplest of all modes for its abolition. Five nations co-operated in quelling the recent Chinese disorders and rescuing their representatives in Pekin. It is perfectly clear that these five nations could banish war. Suppose even three of them formed a League of Peace—inviting all other nations to join—and agreed that since war in any part of the civilized world affects all nations, and often seriously, no nation shall go to war, but shall refer international disputes to the Hague Conference or other arbitral body for peaceful settlement, the League agreeing to declare non-intercourse with any nation refusing compliance. Imagine a nation cut off today from the world. The League also might reserve to itself the right, where non-intercourse is likely to fail or has failed to prevent war, to use the necessary force to maintain peace, each member of the League agreeing to provide the needed forces, or money in lieu thereof, in proportion to her population or wealth. Being experimental and upon trial, it might be deemed advisable, if necessary, at first to agree that any member could withdraw after giving five years' notice, and that the League should dissolve five years after a majority vote of all the members. Further provisions, and perhaps some adaptations, would be found requisite, but the main idea is here.

The Emperor of Russia called the Hague Conference, which gave us an International Tribunal. Were King Edward or the Emperor of Germany or the President of France, acting for their Governments, to invite the nations to send representatives to consider the wisdom of forming such a League, the invitation would no doubt be responded to and probably prove successful.

The number that would gladly join such a League would be great, for the smaller nations would welcome the opportunity.

The relations between Britain, France, and the United States to-day are so close, their aims so similar, their territories and fields of operation so clearly defined and so different, that these Powers might properly unite in inviting other nations to consider the question of such a League as has been sketched. It is a subject well worthy the attention of their rulers, for of all the modes of hastening the end of war this appears the easiest and the best. We have no reason to doubt that arbitration in its present optional form will continue its rapid progress, and that it in itself contains the elements required finally to lead us to peace, for it conquers wherever it is tried; but it is none the less gratifying to know that there is in reserve a drastic mode of enforcement, if needed, which would promptly banish war.

Notwithstanding all the cheering signs of the growth of arbitration, we should delude ourselves if we assumed that war is immediately to cease, for it is scarcely to be hoped that the future has not to witness more than one great holocaust of men to be offered up before the reign of peace blesses the earth. The scoria from the smoldering mass of the fiery past, the seeds that great wars have sown, may be expected to burst out at intervals more and more remote, until the poison of the past is exhausted. That there is to be perfect unbroken peace in our progress to this end we are not so unduly sanguine as to imagine. We are prepared for more than one outbreak of madness and folly in the future as in the past; but that peace is to come at last, and that sooner, much sooner than the majority of my hearers can probably credit, I for one entertain not one particle of doubt.

• • • •

Document No. 5 President Theodore Roosevelt to Andrew Carnegie, August 6, 1906
Source: *The Letters of Theodore Roosevelt,* edited by Elting E. Morison and John Blum (8 vols.; Cambridge, Mass.: Harvard University Press, 1951-1954), V, pp. 345-346.

;993 · TO ANDREW CARNEGIE   *Roosevelt Mss.*

Personal and private   Oyster Bay, August 6, 1906

My dear Mr. Carnegie: Your letter is most interesting. Do you know, I sometimes wish that we did not have the ironclad custom which forbids a President ever to go abroad. If I could meet the Kaiser and the responsible authorities of France and England, I think I could be of help in this Hague Conference business; which is now utterly impossible, and as facts are unadvisable. In any such matter the violent extremists who favor the matter are to be dreaded almost or quite as much as the Bourbon reactionaries who are against it. This is as true of the cause of international peace as it is of the cause of economic equity as between labor and capital at home. I do not know whether in the French Revolution I have most contempt and abhorrence for the Marat, Hébert, Robespierre and Danton type of revolutionists, or for the aristocratic, bureaucratic and despotic rulers of the old regime; for the former did no good in the revolution, but at the best simply nullified the good that others did and produced a reaction whi i re-enthroned despotism; while they made the name of liberty a word of shuddering horror for the time being.

I hope to see real progress made at the next Hague Conference. If it is possible in some way to bring about a stop, complete or partial, to the race in adding to armaments, I shall be glad; but I do not yet see my way clear as regards the details of such a plan. We must always remember that it would be a fatal thing for the great free peoples to reduce themselves to impotence and leave the despotisms and barbarisms armed. It would be safe to do so if there was some system of international police; but there is now no such system; if there were, Turkey for instance would be abolished forthwith unless it showed itself capable of working real reform. As things are now it is for the advantage of peace and order that Russia should be in Turkestan, that France should have Algiers, and that England should have Egypt and the Sudan. It would be an advantage to justice if we were able in some way effectively to interfere in the Congo Free State to secure a more righteous government; if we were able effectively to interfere for the Armenians in Turkey, and for the Jews in Russia. But at present I do not see how we can interfere in any of these three matters, and the one thing I won't do is to bluff when I cannot make good; to bluster and threaten and then fail to take the action if my words need to be backed up.

I have always felt that our special peace champions in the United States were guilty of criminal folly in their failure to give me effective support in my contest with the Senate over the arbitration treaties. In this contest I had the support of certain Senators, headed by the very best man in the Senate — O. H. Platt of Connecticut. But the Senate, which has undoubtedly shown itself at certain points not merely an inefficient but often a dangerous body as regards its dealings with foreign affairs, so amended the treaties as to make them absolutely worthless. Yet there were some people — including, for instance, a man named Love[1] or Dove, who is the head of the peace conference that meets at Lake Mohonk — who in their anxiety to get anything, no matter how great a sham, and in their ignorance of the fact that foreign powers would undoubtedly have refused to ratify the amended treaties, declined entirely to give me any support and thereby committed a very serious wrong against the cause of arbitration.

You have doubtless seen how well the Pan-American Conference has gone off. Root's going there was a great stroke. Gradually we are coming to a condition which will insure permanent peace in the Western Hemisphere. If only the Senate will ratify the Santo Domingo treaty, we shall have taken another stride in this direction. At The Hague I hope we can work hand in hand with France and England; but all three nations must be extremely careful not to get led off into vagaries, and not to acquiesce in some propositions such as those I am sorry to say Russia has more than once made in the past — propositions in the name of peace which were really designed to favor military despotisms at the expense of their free neighbors. I believe in peace but I believe that as things are at present, the cause not only of peace but of what is greater than peace, justice, is favored by having those nations which really stand at the head of civilization show, not merely by words but by action, that they ask peace in the name of justice and not from any weakness.

With warm regards to Mrs. Carnegie, believe me, *Faithfully yours*

[1] Alfred Henry Love, Philadelphia merchant, Quaker, uncompromising, often naïve pacifist, vocal opponent of the Civil and Spanish-American wars, long-time president of the Universal Peace Society.

Document No. 6   Secretary of State Elihu Root, Instructions to the American Delegates to the Hague Conference of 1907
Source: James B. Scott, ed., *Instructions to the American Delegates to the Hague Peace Conferences and Their Official Reports* (N.Y.: Oxford University Press, 1916), pp. 69-85.

INSTRUCTIONS TO THE AMERICAN DELEGATES TO THE HAGUE CONFERENCE OF 1907

DEPARTMENT OF STATE,
WASHINGTON, May 31, 1907.

To Messrs. Joseph H. Choate, Horace Porter, Uriah M. Rose, David Jayne Hill, George B. Davis, Charles S. Sperry, and William I. Buchanan.

GENTLEMEN: You have been appointed delegates plenipotentiary to represent the United States at a Second Peace Conference which is to meet at The Hague on the 15th of June, 1907.

The need of such a Conference was suggested to the Powers signatory to the acts of The Hague Conference of 1899 by President Roosevelt in a circular note by my predecessor, Mr. Hay, dated October 21, 1904, and the project met with a general expression of assent and sympathy from the Powers; but its realization was postponed because of the then existing war between Japan and Russia. The conclusion of the peace which ended that war presenting a favorable moment for further developing and systematizing the work of the First Conference, the initiative was appropriately transferred to His Imperial Majesty the Emperor of Russia as initiator of the First Conference.   The Russian Government proposed that the program of the contemplated meeting should include the following topics:

1. Improvements to be made in the provisions of the Convention relative to the peaceful settlement of international disputes as regards the court of arbitration and the international commissions of inquiry.
2. Additions to be made to the provisions of the Convention of 1899 relative to the laws and customs of war on land—among others, those concerning the opening of hostilities, the rights of neutrals on land, etc.   Declarations of 1899.   One of these having expired, question of its being revived.

[1] *Foreign Relations of the United States,* 1907, pt. 2, p. 1128; Scott, *The Hague Peace Conferences of 1899 and 1907,* vol. ii, p. 181.

3. Framing of a convention relative to the laws and customs of maritime warfare, concerning—

The special operations of maritime warfare, such as the bombardment of ports, cities, and villages by a naval force; the laying of torpedoes, etc.

The transformation of merchant vessels into war-ships.

The private property of belligerents at sea.

The length of time to be granted to merchant ships for their departure from ports of neutrals or of the enemy after the opening of hostilities.

The rights and duties of neutrals at sea; among others, the questions of contraband, the rules applicable to belligerent vessels in neutral ports; destruction, in cases of *vis major*, of neutral merchant vessels captured as prizes.

In the said convention to be drafted, there would be introduced the provisions relative to war on land that would also be applicable to maritime warfare.

4. Additions to be made to the Convention of 1899 for the adaptation to maritime warfare of the principles of the Geneva Convention of 1864.

We are advised by the Ambassador of Russia, in a note dated March 22/April 4, 1907, that all of the Powers have declared their adhesion to this tentative program. The following remarks, however, have been made in respect thereof:

The Government of the United States has reserved to itself the liberty of submitting to the Conference two additional questions, viz., the reduction or limitation of armaments and the attainment of an agreement to observe some limitations upon the use of force for the collection or ordinary public debts arising out of contracts.

The Spanish Government has expressed a desire to discuss the limitation of armaments.

The British Government has given notice that it attaches great importance to having the question of expenditures for armament discussed at the Conference, and has reserved to itself the right of raising it.

The Governments of Bolivia, Denmark, Greece, and the Netherlands have reserved to themselves, in a general way, the right to submit to the consideration of the Conference subjects not specially enumerated in the program.

Several Governments have reserved the right to take no part in any discussion which may appear unlikely to produce any useful result.

The Russian note proposing the program declared that the deliberations of the contemplated meetings should not deal with the political relations of the different States, or the condition of things established by treaties; and that neither the solution of the questions brought up for discussion, nor the order of their discussion, nor the form to be given to the decisions reached, should be determined in advance of the Conference. We understand this view to have been accepted.

In regard to the two questions which were not included in the proposed program, but which the United States has reserved the right to present to the Conference, we understand that notice of the reservation has been communicated to all the Powers by note similar to that from the Russian Ambassador dated March 22/April 4, 1907; so that each Power has had full opportunity to instruct its delegates in respect thereof. The United States understands that as to the topics included in the program the acceptance of the program involves a determination that such topics shall be considered by the Conference, subject to the reserved rights of particular Powers to refrain from discussion of any topic as to which it deems that discussion will not be useful; but that as to the two topics which we have reserved the right to present, there has been no determination one way or the other, the question whether they shall be considered by the Conference remaining for the determination of the Conference itself in case they shall be presented.

It is not expedient that you should be limited by too rigid instructions upon the various questions which are to be discussed, for such a course, if pursued generally with all the delegates, would make the discussion useless and the Conference a mere formality. You will, however, keep in mind the following observations regarding the general policy of the United States upon these questions:

1. In the discussions upon every question it is important to remember that the object of the Conference is agreement, and not compulsion. If such Conferences are to be made occasions for trying to force nations into positions which they consider against their interests, the Powers can not be expected to send representatives to them. It is important also that the agreements reached shall be genuine and not reluctant. Otherwise they will inevitably fail to receive approval when submitted for the ratification of the Powers represented. Comparison of views and frank and considerate explanation and discussion may frequently resolve doubts, obviate difficulties, and lead to

real agreement upon matters which at the outset have appeared insurmountable. It is not wise, however, to carry this process to the point of irritation. After reasonable discussion, if no agreement is reached, it is better to lay the subject aside, or refer it to some future Conference in the hope that intermediate consideration may dispose of the objections. Upon some questions where an agreement by only a part of the Powers represented would in itself be useful, such an agreement may be made, but it should always be with the most unreserved recognition that the other Powers withhold their concurrence with equal propriety and right.

The immediate results of such a Conference must always be limited to a small part of the field which the more sanguine have hoped to see covered; but each successive Conference will make the positions reached in the preceding Conference its point of departure, and will bring to the consideration of further advances toward international agreements opinions affected by the acceptance and application of the previous agreements. Each Conference will inevitably make further progress and, by successive steps, results may be accomplished which have formerly appeared impossible.

You should keep always in mind the promotion of this continuous process through which the progressive development of international justice and peace may be carried on; and you should regard the work of the Second Conference, not merely with reference to the definite results to be reached in that Conference, but also with reference to the foundations which may be laid for further results in future Conferences. It may well be that among the most valuable services rendered to civilization by this Second Conference will be found the progress made in matters upon which the delegates reach no definite agreement.

With this view you will favor the adoption of a resolution by the Conference providing for the holding of further Conferences within fixed periods and arranging the machinery by which such Conferences may be called and the terms of the program may be arranged, without awaiting any new and specific initiative on the part of the Powers or any one of them.

Encouragement for such a course is to be found in the successful working of a similar arrangement for international conferences of the American republics. The second American Conference, held in Mexico in 1901–2, adopted a resolution providing that a third conference should meet within five years and committed the time and place and the program and necessary details to the Department of State and representatives of the American States in Washington. Under this authority the Third Conference was called and held in Rio de Janeiro in the summer of 1906 and accomplished results of substantial value. That Conference adopted the following resolution:

The governing board of the International Bureau of American Republics (composed of the same official representatives in Washington) is authorized to designate the place at which the Fourth International Conference shall meet, which meeting shall be within the next five years; to provide for the drafting of the program and regulations and to take into consideration all other necessary details; and to set another date in case the meeting of the said Conference can not take place within the prescribed limit of time.

There is no apparent reason to doubt that a similar arrangement for successive general international conferences of all the civilized Powers would prove as practicable and as useful as in the case of the twenty-one American States.

2. The policy of the United States to avoid entangling alliances and to refrain from any interference or participation in the political affairs of Europe must be kept in mind, and may impose upon you some degree of reserve in respect of some of the questions which are discussed by the Conference.

In the First Conference the American delegates accompanied their vote upon the report of the committee regarding the limitation of armaments by the following declaration:

That the United States, in so doing, does not express any opinion as to the course to be taken by the States of Europe. This declaration is not meant to indicate mere indifference to a difficult problem, because it does not affect the United States immediately, but expresses a determination to refrain from enunciating opinions upon matters into which, as concerning Europe alone, the United States has no claim to enter. The words drawn up by M. Bourgeois, and adopted by the first commission, received also the cordial interest and sympathy with which the United States, while carefully abstaining from anything that might resemble interference, regards all movements that are thought to tend to the welfare of Europe.

Before signing the arbitration convention of the First Conference the delegates of the United States put upon record the following declaration:

> Nothing contained in this Convention shall be so construed as to require the United States of America to depart from its traditional policy of not intruding upon, interfering with, or entangling itself in the political questions or policy or internal administration of any foreign State; nor shall anything contained in the said Convention be construed to imply a delinquishment by the United States of America of its traditional attitude toward purely American questions.

These declarations have received the approval of this Government, and they should be regarded by you as illustrating the caution which you are to exercise in preventing our participation in matters of general and world-wide concern from drawing us into the political affairs of Europe.

3. The attitude of the United States as to consideration of the subject of limiting armaments was stated in a letter from the Secretary of State to the Russian ambassador dated June 7, 1906. That letter, after expressing assent to the enumeration of topics in the Russian programme, proceeded to say:

> The Government of the United States is, however, so deeply in sympathy with the noble and humanitarian views which moved His Imperial Majesty to the calling of the First Peace Conference that it would greatly regret to see those views excluded from the consideration of the Second Conference. [Quoting from the call for the First Conference.]
>
> The truth and value of the sentiments thus expressed are surely independent of the special conditions and obstacles to their realization by which they may be confronted at any particular time. It is true that the First Conference at The Hague did not find it practicable to give them effect, but long-continued and patient effort has always been found necessary to bring mankind into conformity with great ideals. It would be a misfortune if that effort, so happily and magnanimously inaugurated by His Imperial Majesty, were to be abandoned.
>
> This Government is not unmindful of the fact that the people of the United States dwell in comparative security, partly by reason of their isolation and partly because they have never become involved in the numerous questions to which many centuries of close neighborhood have given rise in Europe. They are, there-

fore, free from the apprehensions of attack which are to so great an extent the cause of great armaments, and it would ill become them to be insistent or forward in a matter so much more vital to the nations of Europe than to them. Nevertheless, it sometimes happens that the very absence of a special interest in a subject enables a nation to make suggestions and urge considerations which a more deeply interested nation might hesitate to present. The Government of the United States, therefore, feels it to be its duty to reserve for itself the liberty to propose to the Second Peace Conference, as one of the subjects of consideration, the reduction or limitation of armaments, in the hope that, if nothing further can be accomplished, some slight advance may be made toward the realization of the lofty conception which actuated the Emperor of Russia in calling the First Conference.

The First Conference adopted the following resolutions:

> The Conference is of opinion that the restriction of military charges, which are at present a heavy burden on the world, is extremely desirable for the increase of the material and moral welfare of mankind.
> The Conference expresses the wish that the Governments, taking into consideration the proposals made at the Conference, may examine the possibility of an agreement as to the limitation of armed forces by land and sea and of war budgets.

Under these circumstances this Government has been and still is of the opinion that this subject should be regarded as unfinished business, and that the Second Conference should ascertain and give full consideration to the results of such examination as the Governments may have given to the possibility of an agreement pursuant to the wish expressed by the First Conference. We think that there should be a sincere effort to learn whether, by conference and discussion, some practicable formula may not be worked out which would have the effect of limiting or retarding the increase of armaments.

There is, however, reason to believe not only that there has been the examination by the respective Governments for which the First Conference expressed a wish, but that the discussion of its results has been forestalled by a process of direct communication between a majority of the Governments having the greatest immediate interest in the subject. These communications have been going on actively among the different Governments for nearly a year, and as a result at least four of the European Powers have announced their unwillingness to continue the discussion in the Conference. We regret that the discussion should have taken place in this way rather than at the Conference, for we are satisfied that a discussion at the Conference would have afforded a greater probability of progress toward the desired result. The fact, however, can not be ignored.

If any European Power proposes consideration of the subject, you will vote in favor of consideration and do everything you properly can to promote it. If, on the other hand, no European Power proposes consideration of the subject, and no new and affirmative evidence is presented to satisfy you that a useful purpose would be subserved by your making such a proposal, you may assume that the limitations above stated by way of guidance to your action preclude you from asking the Conference to consider the subject.

4. The other subject which the United States specifically reserved the right to propose for consideration is the attainment of an agreement to observe some limitation upon the use of force for the collection of ordinary public debts arising out of contract.

It has long been the established policy of the United States not to use its army and navy for the collection of ordinary contract debts due to its citizens by other Governments. This Government has not considered the use of force for such a purpose consistent with that respect for the independent sovereignty of other members of the family of nations which is the most important principle of international law and the chief protection of weak nations against the oppression of the strong. It seems to us that the practice is injurious in its general effect upon the relation of nations and upon the welfare of weak and disordered States, whose development ought to be encouraged in the interests of civilization; that it offers frequent temptation to bullying and oppression and to unnecessary and unjustifiable warfare. It is doubtless true that the non-payment of such debts may be accompanied by such circumstances of fraud and wrongdoing or violation of treaties as to justify the use of force; but we should be glad to see an international consideration of this subject which would discriminate between such cases and the simple nonperformance of a contract with a private person, and a resolution in favor of reliance upon peaceful means in cases of the latter class.

The Third International Conference of the American States, held at Rio de Janeiro in August, 1906, resolved:

To recommend to the Governments therein that they consider the point of inviting the Second Peace Conference at The Hague to examine the question of the compulsory collection of public debts, and, in general, means tending to diminish between nations conflicts having a peculiarly pecuniary origin.

You will ask for the consideration of this subject by the Conference. It is not probable that in the first instance all the nations represented at the Conference will be willing to go as far in the establishment of limitations upon the use of force in the collection of this class of debts as the United States would like to have them go, and there may be serious objection to the consideration of the subject as a separate and independent topic. If you find such objections insurmountable, you will urge the adoption of provisions under the head of arbitration looking to the establishment of such limitations. The adoption of some such provisions as the following may be suggested, and, if no better solution seems practicable, should be urged:

The use of force for the collection of a contract debt alleged to be due by the Government of any country to a citizen of any other country is not permissible until after—

1. The justice and amount of the debt shall have been determined by arbitration, if demanded by the alleged debtor.

2. The time and manner of payment, and the security, if any, to be given pending payment, shall have been fixed by arbitration, if demanded by the alleged debtor.

5. In the general field of arbitration two lines of advance are clearly indicated. The first is to provide for obligatory arbitration as broad in scope as now appears to be practicable, and the second is to increase the effectiveness of the system so that nations may more readily have recourse to it voluntarily.

You are familiar with the numerous expressions in favor of the settlement of international disputes by arbitration on the part both of the Congress and of the Executive of the United States.

So many separate treaties of arbitration have been made between individual countries that there is little cause to doubt that the time is now ripe for a decided advance in this direction. This condition, which brings the subject of a general treaty for obligatory arbitration into the field of practical discussion, is undoubtedly largely due to the fact that the Powers generally in the First Hague Conference committed themselves to the principle of the pacific settlement of international questions in the admirable convention for voluntary arbitration then adopted.

The Rio Conference of last summer provided for the arbitration of all pecuniary claims among the American States. This convention has been ratified by the President, with the advice and consent of the Senate.

In December, 1904, and January, 1905, my predecessor, Mr. Hay, concluded separate arbitration treaties between the United States and Great Britain, France, Germany, Spain, Portugal, Italy, Switzerland, Austria-Hungary, Sweden and Norway, and Mexico. On the 11th of February, 1905, the Senate advised and consented to the ratification of these treaties, with an amendment which has had the effect of preventing the exchange of ratifications. The amendment, however, did not relate to the scope or character of the arbitration to which the President had agreed and the Senate consented. You will be justified, therefore, in assuming that a general treaty of arbitration in the terms, or substantially in the terms, of the series of treaties which I have mentioned will meet the approval of the Government of the United States. The first article of each of these treaties was as follows:

> Differences which may arise of a legal nature, or relating to the interpretation of treaties existing between the two contracting parties, and which it may not have been possible to settle by diplomacy, shall be referred to the permanent court of arbitration established at The Hague by the Convention of the 29th July, 1899, provided, nevertheless, that they do not affect the vital interests, the independence, or the honor of the two contracting States, and do not concern the interests of third parties.

To this extent you may go in agreeing to a general treaty of arbitration, and to secure such a treaty you should use your best and most earnest efforts.

Such a general treaty of arbitration necessarily leaves to be determined in each particular case what the questions at issue between the two Governments are, and whether those questions come within the scope of the treaty or within the exceptions, and what shall be the scope of the Powers of the arbitrators. The Senate amendment which prevented the ratification of each of these treaties applied only to another article of the treaty which provided for special agreements in regard to these matters and involved only the question who should act for the United States in making such special agreements. To avoid having the same question arise regarding any general treaty of arbitration which you may sign at The Hague, your signature should be accompanied by an explanation substantially as follows:

> In signing the general arbitration treaty the delegates of the United States desire to have it understood that the special agreements provided for in article — of said treaty will be subject to submission to the Senate of the United States.

The method in which arbitration can be made more effective, so that nations may be more ready to have recourse to it voluntarily and to enter into treaties by which they bind themselves to submit to it, is indicated by observation of the weakness of the system now apparent. There can be no doubt that the principal objection to arbitration rests not upon the unwillingness of nations to submit their controversies to impartial arbitration, but upon an apprehension that the arbitrations to which they submit may not be impartial. It has been a very general practice for arbitrators to act, not as judges deciding questions of fact and law upon the record before them under a sense of judicial responsibility, but as negotiators effecting settlements of the questions brought before them in accordance with the traditions and usages and subject to all the considerations and influences which affect diplomatic agents. The two methods are radically different, proceed upon different standards of honorable obligation, and frequently lead to widely differing results. It very frequently happens that a nation which would be very willing to submit its differences to an impartial judicial determination is unwilling to subject them to this kind of diplomatic process. If there could be a tribunal which would pass upon questions between nations with the same impartial and impersonal judgment that the Supreme Court of the United States gives to questions arising between citizens of the different States, or between foreign citizens and the citizens of the United States, there can be no doubt that nations would be much more ready to submit their controversies to its decision than they are now to take the chances of arbitration. It should be your effort to bring about in the Second Conference a development of the Hague tribunal into a permanent tribunal composed of judges who are judicial officers and nothing else, who are paid adequate salaries, who have no other occupation, and who will devote their entire time to the trial and decision of international causes by judicial methods and under a sense of judicial responsibility. These judges should be so selected from the different countries that the different systems of law and procedure and the principal languages shall be fairly represented. The court should be made of such dignity, consideration, and rank that the best and ablest jurists will accept appointment to it, and that the whole world will have absolute confidence in its judgments.

The arbitration convention signed at the First Hague Conference contained no authority for the adherence of non-signatory Powers, but provided:

> The conditions on which the Powers who were not represented at the International Peace Conference can adhere to the present Convention shall form the subject of a separate agreement among the contracting Powers.

This left all the Central and South American States outside of the treaty. The United States has from time to time endeavored to secure an opportunity for them to adhere, and it has now been arranged that this shall be accomplished as a necessary preliminary to their taking part in the Second Conference. The method arranged is that on the day before the opening of the Conference a protocol shall be signed by the representatives of all the Powers signatory to the treaty substantially as follows:

> The representatives at the Second Peace Conference of the States signatories of the convention of 1899 relative to the peaceful settlement of international disputes, duly authorized to that effect, have agreed that in case the States that were not represented at the First Peace Conference, but have been convoked to the present Conference, should notify the Government of the Netherlands of their adhesion to the above-mentioned convention they shall be forthwith considered as having acceded thereto.

It is understood that substantially all the Central and South American States have notified the Government of the Netherlands of their adherence to the Convention, and upon the signing of this protocol their notices will immediately take effect and they will become parties competent to take part in the discussions of the Second Conference looking toward the amendment and extension of the arbitration convention. You will sign the protocol in behalf of the United States pursuant to the full powers already given you.

6. You will maintain the traditional policy of the United States regarding the immunity of private property of belligerents at sea.

On the 28th of April, 1904, the Congress of the United States adopted the following resolution:

> *Resolved by the Senate and House of Representatives of the United States of America in Congress assembled,* That it is the sense of the Congress of the United States that it is desirable, in the interests of uniformity of action by the maritime States of the world in time of war, that the President endeavor to bring about an understanding among the principal maritime Powers with a view of incorporating into the permanent law of civilized nations, the principle of the exemption of all private property at sea, not contraband of war, from capture or destruction by belligerents. Approved April 28, 1904.

This resolution is an expression of the view taken by the United States during its entire history. Such a provision was incorporated in the treaty of 1775 with Prussia, signed by Benjamin Franklin, Thomas Jefferson, and John Adams, and it was proposed by the United States as an amendment to be added to the privateering clause of the Declaration of Paris in 1856. The refusal of the other Powers to accompany prohibition of privateering by such a provision caused the Government of the United States to refuse its adherence to the declaration.

The Congressional resolution was in response to the recommendation of President Roosevelt's message to Congress in December, 1903, quoting and enforcing a previous message by President McKinley in December, 1898, which said:

> The United States Government has for many years advocated this humane and beneficent principle, and is now in a position to recommend it to other Powers without the imputation of selfish motives.

Whatever may be the apparent specific interest of this or any other country at the moment, the principle thus declared is of such permanent and universal importance that no balancing of the chances of probable loss or gain in the immediate future on the part of any nation should be permitted to outweigh the considerations of common benefit to civilization which call for the adoption of such an agreement.

In the First Peace Conference the subject of the immunity of private property at sea was not included in the program. Consideration of it was urged by the delegates of the United States and was supported by an able presentation on the part of Mr. Andrew D. White. The representatives of several of the great Powers declared, however, that in the absence of instructions from their Governments they could not vote upon the subject; and, under the circumstances, we must consider that gratifying progress was made when there was included in the Final Act of the Conference a resolution expressing—

> The wish that the proposal which contemplates the declaration of the inviolability of private property in naval warfare may be referred to a subsequent Conference for consideration.

The subject has accordingly been included in the present program and the way is open for its consideration.

It will be appropriate for you to advocate the proposition formulated and presented by the American delegates to the First Conference, as follows:

> The private property of all citizens or subjects of the signatory Powers, with the exception of contraband of war, shall be exempt from capture or seizure on the high seas, or elsewhere by the armed vessels or by the military forces of any of the said signatory Powers. But nothing herein contained shall extend exemption from seizure to vessels and their cargoes which may attempt to enter a port blockaded by the naval forces of any of the said Powers.

7. Since the code of rules for the government of military operations on land was adopted by the First Peace Conference there have been occasions for its application under very severe conditions, notably in the South African war and the war between Japan and Russia. Doubtless the Powers involved in those conflicts have had occasion to observe many particulars in which useful additions or improvements might be made. You will consider their suggestions with a view to reducing, so far as is practicable, the evils of war and protecting the rights of neutrals.

As to the framing of a convention relative to the customs of mari time warfare, you are referred to the naval war code promulgated in General Orders 551 of the Navy Department of June 27, 1900, which has met with general commendation by naval authorities throughout the civilized world, and which, in general, expresses the views of the United States, subject to a few specific amendments suggested in the volume of international law discussions of the Naval War College of the year 1903, pages 91 to 97. The order putting this code into force was revoked by the Navy Department in 1904, not because of any change of views as to the rules which it contained, but because many of those rules, being imposed upon the forces of the United States by the order, would have put our naval forces at a disadvantage as against the forces of other Powers, upon whom the rules were not binding. The whole discussion of these rules contained in the volume to which I have referred is commended to your careful study.

You will urge upon the Peace Conference the formulation of international rules for war at sea and will offer the Naval War Code of 1900, with the suggested changes and such further changes as may be made necessary by other agreements reached at the Conference, as a tentative formulation of the rules which should be considered.

8. The clause of the program relating to the rights and duties of neutrals is of very great importance and in itself would furnish matter for useful discussion sufficient to occupy the time and justify the labors of the Conference.

The various subjects which the Conference may be called upon to consider are likely to bring out proposals which should be considered in their relation to each other, as standing in the following order of substantial importance:

(1) Provisions tending to prevent disagreements between nations.

(2) Provisions tending to dispose of disagreements without war.

(3) Provisions tending to preserve the rights and interests of neutrals.

(4) Provisions tending to mitigate the evils of war to belligerents.

The relative importance of these classes of provisions should always be kept in mind. No rules should be adopted for the purpose of mitigating the evils of war to belligerents which will tend strongly to destroy the right of neutrals, and no rules should be adopted regarding the rights of neutrals which will tend strongly to bring about war. It is of the highest importance that not only the rights but the duties of neutrals shall be most clearly and distinctly defined and understood, not only because the evils which belligerent nations bring upon themselves ought not to be allowed to spread to their peaceful neighbors and inflict unnecessary injury upon the rest of mankind, but because misunderstandings regarding the rights and duties of neutrals constantly tend to involve them in controversy with one or the other belligerent.

For both of these reasons, special consideration should be given to an agreement upon what shall be deemed to constitute contraband of war. There has been a recent tendency to extend widely the list of articles to be treated as contraband; and it is probable that if the belligerents themselves are to determine at the beginning of a war what shall be contraband, this tendency will continue until the list of contraband is made to include a large proportion of all the articles which are the subject of commerce, upon the ground that they will be useful to the enemy. When this result is reached, especially if the doctrine of continuous voyages is applied at the same time, the doctrine that free ships make free goods and the doctrine that blockades in order to be binding must be effective, as well as any rule giving immunity to the property of belligerents at sea, will be deprived of a large part of their effect, and we shall find ourselves going backward instead of forward in the effort to prevent every war from becoming universally disastrous. The exception of contraband of war in the Declaration of Paris will be so expanded as to very largely destroy the effect of the declaration. On the other hand, resistance to this tendency toward the expansion of the list of contraband ought not to be left to the neutrals affected by it at the very moment when war exists, because that is the process by which neutrals become themselves involved in war. You should do all in your power to bring about an agreement upon what is to constitute contraband; and it is very desirable that the list should be limited as narrowly as possible.

With these instructions there will be furnished to you copies of the diplomatic correspondence relating to the conference, the instructions to the delegates to the First Conference which are in all respects reaffirmed and their report, the international law discussions of the Naval War College of 1903, the report of the American delegates to the Conference of the American Republics at Rio de Janeiro in 1906, and the report of the American delegates to the Geneva Conference of 1906 for the revision of the Red Cross Convention of 1864.

Following the precedent established by the commission to the First

Conference, all your reports and communications to this Government will be made to the Department of State for proper consideration and eventual preservation in the archives. The record of your commission will be kept by your secretary, Mr. Chandler Hale. Should you be in doubt at any time regarding the meaning or effect of these instructions, or should you consider at any time that there is occasion for special instructions, you will communicate freely with the Department of State by telegraph. It is the President's earnest wish that you may contribute materially to the effective work of the Conference and that its deliberations may result in making international justice more certain and international peace more secure.

I am, gentlemen, your obedient servant,

ELIHU ROOT.

Document No. 7   The Second Hague Conference (1907)
Source: William M. Malloy, compiler, *Treaties, Conventions, International Acts, Protocols and Agreements between the United States of America and other Powers, 1776-1909* (2 vols.; Washington, D.C.: U.S. Government Printing Office, 1910), II, pp. 2220-2248.

CONVENTIONS CONCLUDED AT THE SECOND INTERNATIONAL PEACE CONFERENCE, HELD AT THE HAGUE, 1907.

I.

1907.[a]

CONVENTION FOR THE PACIFIC SETTLEMENT OF INTERNATIONAL DISPUTES.

Concluded October 18, 1907; ratification advised by the Senate April 2, 1908; ratified by the President February 23, 1909; ratifications deposited with the Netherlands Government November 27, 1909; proclaimed February 28, 1910.

ARTICLES.

PART I.—*Maintenance of general peace.*

I. Pacific settlements of international differences.

PART II.—*Good offices immediation.*

PART III.—*International commissions of inquiry.*

[a] The ratifications of this convention were deposited at the Hague November 27, 1909, by Germany, the United States of America, Austria Hungary, China, Denmark, Mexico, The Netherlands, Russia, Sweden, Bolivia, and Salvador.

[Translation.]

His Majesty the German Emperor, King of Prussia; the President of the United States of America; the President of the Argentine Republic; His Majesty the Emperor of Austria, King of Bohemia, &c., and Apostolic King of Hungary; His Majesty the King of the Belgians; the President of the Republic of Bolivia; the President of the Republic of the United States of Brazil; His Royal Highness the Prince of Bulgaria; the President of the Republic of Chile; His Majesty the Emperor of China; the President of the Republic of

Colombia; the Provisional Governor of the Republic of Cuba; His Majesty the King of Denmark; the President of the Dominican Republic; the President of the Republic of Ecuador; His Majesty the King of Spain; the President of the French Republic; His Majesty the King of the United Kingdom of Great Britain and Ireland and of the British Dominions beyond the Seas, Emperor of India; His Majesty the King of the Hellenes; the President of the Republic of Guatemala; the President of the Republic of Haïti; His Majesty the King of Italy; His Majesty the Emperor of Japan; His Royal Highness the Grand Duke of Luxemburg, Duke of Nassau; the President of the United States of Mexico; His Royal Highness the Prince of Montenegro; His Majesty the King of Norway; the President of the Republic of Panamá; the President of the Republic of Paraguay; Her Majesty the Queen of the Netherlands; the President of the Republic of Peru; His Imperial Majesty the Shah of Persia; His Majesty the King of Portugal and of the Algarves, &c.; His Majesty the King of Roumania; His Majesty the Emperor of All the Russias; the President of the Republic of Salvador; His Majesty the King of Servia; His Majesty the King of Siam; His Majesty the King of Sweden; the Swiss Federal Council; His Majesty the Emperor of the Ottomans; the President of the Oriental Republic of Uruguay; the President of the United States of Venezuela:

Animated by the sincere desire to work for the maintenance of general peace;

Resolved to promote by all the efforts in their power the friendly settlement of international disputes;

Recognizing the solidarity uniting the members of the society of civilized nations;

Desirous of extending the empire of law and of strengthening the appreciation of international justice;

Convinced that the permanent institution of a Tribunal of Arbitration accessible to all, in the midst of independent Powers, will contribute effectively to this result;

Having regard to the advantages attending the general and regular organization of the procedure of arbitration;

Sharing the opinion of the august initiator of the International Peace Conference that it is expedient to record in an International Agreement the principles of equity and right on which are based the security of States and the welfare of peoples;

Being desirous, with this object, of insuring the better working in practice of Commissions of Inquiry and Tribunals of Arbitration, and of facilitating recourse to arbitration in cases which allow of a summary procedure;

Have deemed it necessary to revise in certain particulars and to complete the work of the First Peace Conference for the pacific settlement of international disputes;

The High Contracting Parties have resolved to conclude a new Convention for this purpose, and have appointed the following as their Plenipotentiaries:[a] • • • •

---

[a] The names of Plenipotentiaries in President's proclamation appear in French only.

PART I.—*The Maintenance of General Peace.*

ARTICLE I.

With a view to obviating as far as possible recourse to force in the relations between States, the Contracting Powers agree to use their best efforts to ensure the pacific settlement of international differences.

PART II.—*Good Offices and Mediation.*

ARTICLE II.

In case of serious disagreement or dispute, before an appeal to arms, the Contracting Powers, agree to have recourse, as far as circumstances allow, to the good offices or mediation of one or more friendly Powers.

ARTICLE III.

Independently of this recourse, the Contracting Powers deem it expedient and desirable that one or more Powers, strangers to the dispute, should, on their own initiative and as far as circumstances may allow, offer their good offices or mediation to the States at variance.

Powers strangers to the dispute have the right to offer good offices or mediation even during the course of hostilities.

The exercise of this right can never be regarded by either of the parties in dispute as an unfriendly act.

ARTICLE IV.

The part of the mediator consists in reconciling the opposing claims and appeasing the feelings of resentment which may have arisen between the States at variance.

ARTICLE V.

The functions of the mediator are at an end when once it is declared, either by one of the parties to the dispute or by the mediator himself, that the means of reconciliation proposed by him are not accepted.

ARTICLE VI.

Good offices and mediation undertaken either at the request of the parties in dispute or on the initiative of Powers strangers to the dispute have exclusively the character of advice, and never have binding force.

ARTICLE VII.

The acceptance of mediation cannot, unless there be an agreement to the contrary, have the effect of interrupting, delaying, or hindering mobilization or other measures of preparation for war.

If it takes place after the commencement of hostilities, the military operations in progress are not interrupted in the absence of an agreement to the contrary.

ARTICLE VIII.

The Contracting Powers are agreed in recommending the application, when circumstances allow, of special mediation in the following form:—

In case of a serious difference endangering peace, the States at variance choose respectively a Power, to which they intrust the mission of entering into direct communication with the Power chosen on the other side, with the object of preventing the rupture of pacific relations.

For the period of this mandate, the term of which, unless otherwise stipulated, cannot exceed thirty days, the States in dispute cease from all direct communication on the subject of the dispute, which is regarded as referred exclusively to the mediating Powers, which must use their best efforts to settle it.

In case of a definite rupture of pacific relations, these Powers are charged with the joint task of taking advantage of any opportunity to restore peace.

PART III.—*International Commissions of Inquiry.*

ARTICLE IX.

In disputes of an international nature involving neither honour nor vital interests, and arising from a difference of opinion on points of fact, the Contracting Powers deem it expedient and desirable that the parties who have not been able to come to an agreement by means of diplomacy, should, as far as circumstances allow, institute an International Commission of Inquiry, to facilitate a solution of these disputes by elucidating the facts by means of an impartial and conscientious investigation.

ARTICLE X.

International Commissions of Inquiry are constituted by special agreement between the parties in dispute.

The Inquiry Convention defines the facts to be examined; it determines the mode and time in which the Commission is to be formed and the extent of the powers of the Commissioners.

It also determines, if there is need, where the Commission is to sit, and whether it may remove to another place, the language the Commission shall use and the languages the use of which shall be authorized before it, as well as the date on which each party must deposit its statement of facts, and, generally speaking, all the conditions upon which the parties have agreed.

If the parties consider it necessary to appoint Assessors, the Convention of Inquiry shall determine the mode of their selection and the extent of their powers.

ARTICLE XI.

If the Inquiry Convention has not determined where the Commission is to sit, it will sit at The Hague.

The place of meeting, once fixed, cannot be altered by the Commission except with the assent of the parties.

If the Inquiry Convention has not determined what languages are to be employed, the question shall be decided by the Commission.

ARTICLE XII.

Unless an undertaking is made to the contrary, Commissions of Inquiry shall be formed in the manner determined by Articles XLV and LVII of the present Convention.

ARTICLE XIII.

Should one of the Commissioners or one of the Assessors, should there be any, either die, or resign, or be unable for any reason whatever to discharge his functions, the same procedure is followed for filling the vacancy as was followed for appointing him.

ARTICLE XIV.

The parties are entitled to appoint special agents to attend the Commission of Inquiry, whose duty it is to represent them and to act as intermediaries between them and the Commission.

They are further authorized to engage counsel or advocates, appointed by themselves, to state their case and uphold their interests before the Commission.

ARTICLE XV.

The International Bureau of the Permanent Court of Arbitration acts as registry for the Commissions which sit at The Hague, and shall place its offices and staff at the disposal of the Contracting Powers for the use of the Commission of Inquiry.

ARTICLE XVI.

If the Commission meets elsewhere than at The Hague, it appoints a Secretary-General, whose office serves as registry.

It is the function of the registry, under the control of the President, to make the necessary arrangements for the sittings of the Commission, the preparation of the Minutes, and, while the inquiry lasts, for the charge of the archives, which shall subsequently be transferred to the International Bureau at The Hague.

ARTICLE XVII.

In order to facilitate the constitution and working of Commissions of Inquiry, the Contracting Powers recommend the following rules, which shall be applicable to the inquiry procedure in so far as the parties do not adopt other rules.

ARTICLE XVIII.

The Commission shall settle the details of the procedure not covered by the special Inquiry Convention or the present Convention, and shall arrange all the formalities required for dealing with the evidence.

ARTICLE XIX.

On the inquiry both sides must be heard.

At the dates fixed, each party communicates to the Commission and to the other party the statements of facts, if any, and, in all cases, the instruments, papers, and documents which it considers useful for ascertaining the truth, as well as the list of witnesses and experts whose evidence it wishes to be heard.

ARTICLE XX.

The Commission is entitled, with the assent of the Powers, to move temporarily to any place where it considers it may be useful to have recourse to this means of inquiry or to send one or more of its members. Permission must be obtained from the State on whose territory it is proposed to hold the inquiry.

ARTICLE XXI.

Every investigation, and every examination of a locality, must be made in the presence of the agents and counsel of the parties or after they have been duly summoned.

ARTICLE XXII.

The Commission is entitled to ask from either party for such explanations and information as it considers necessary.

ARTICLE XXIII.

The parties undertake to supply the Commission of Inquiry, a fully as they may think possible, with all means and facilities neces sary to enable it to become completely acquainted with, and to accu rately understand, the facts in question.

They undertake to make use of the means at their disposal, under their municipal law, to insure the appearance of the witnesses or experts who are in their territory and have been summoned before the Commission.

If the witnesses or experts are unable to appear before the Commission, the parties will arrange for their evidence to be taken before the qualified officials of their own country.

ARTICLE XXIV.

For all notices to be served by the Commission in the territory of a third Contracting Power, the Commission shall apply direct to the Government of the said power. The same rule applies in the case of steps being taken on the spot to procure evidence.

The requests for this purpose are to be executed so far as the means at the disposal of the Power applied to under its municipal law allow. They cannot be rejected unless the Power in question considers they are calculated to impair its sovereign rights or its safety.

The Commission will equally be always entitled to act through the Power on whose territory it sits.

ARTICLE XXV.

The witnesses and experts are summoned on the request of the parties or by the Commission of its own motion, and, in every case, through the Government of the State in whose territory they are.

The witnesses are heard in succession and separately, in the presence of the agents and counsel, and in the order fixed by the Commission.

ARTICLE XXVI.

The examination of witnesses is conducted by the President.

The members of the Commission may however put to each witness questions which they consider likely to throw light on and complete his evidence, or get information on any point concerning the witness within the limits of what is necessary in order to get at the truth.

The agents and counsel of the parties may not interrupt the witness when he is making his statement, nor put any direct question to him, but they may ask the President to put such additional questions to the witness as they think expedient.

ARTICLE XXVII.

The witness must give his evidence without being allowed to read any written draft. He may, however, be permitted by the President to consult notes or documents if the nature of the facts referred to necessitates their employment.

Article XXVIII.

A Minute of the evidence of the witness is drawn up forthwith and read to the witness. The latter may make such alterations and additions as he thinks necessary, which will be recorded at the end of his statement.

When the whole of his statement has been read to the witness, he is asked to sign it.

Article XXIX.

The agents are authorized, in the course of or at the close of the inquiry, to present in writing to the Commission and to the other party such statements, requisitions, or summaries of the facts as they consider useful for ascertaining the truth.

Article XXX.

The Commission considers its decisions in private and the proceedings are secret.

All questions are decided by a majority of the members of the Commission.

If a member declines to vote, the fact must be recorded in the Minutes.

Article XXXI.

The sittings of the Commission are not public, nor the Minutes and documents connected with the inquiry published except in virtue of a decision of the Commission taken with the consent of the parties

Article XXXII.

After the parties have presented all the explanations and evidence and the witnesses have all been heard, the President declares the inquiry terminated, and the Commission adjourns to deliberate and to draw up its Report.

Article XXXIII.

The Report is signed by all the members of the Commission.

If one of the members refuses to sign, the fact is mentioned; but the validity of the Report is not affected.

Article XXXIV.

The Report of the Commission is read at a public sitting, the agents and counsel of the parties being present or duly summoned.

A copy of the Report is given to each party.

Article XXXV.

The Report of the Commission is limited to a statement of fac and has in no way the character of an Award. It leaves to the parties entire freedom as to the effect to be given to the statement.

ARTICLE XXXVI.

Each party pays its own expenses and an equal share of the expenses incurred by the Commission.

PART IV.—*International Arbitration.*

CHAPTER I.—*The System of Arbitration.*

ARTICLE XXXVII.

International arbitration has for its object the settlement of disputes between States by Judges of their own choice and on the basis of respect for law.

Recourse to arbitration implies an engagement to submit in good faith to the Award.

ARTICLE XXXVIII.

In questions of a legal nature, and especially in the interpretation or application of International Conventions, arbitration is recognized by the Contracting Powers as the most effective, and, at the same time, the most equitable means of settling disputes which diplomacy has failed to settle.

Consequently, it would be desirable that, in disputes about the above-mentioned questions, the Contracting Powers should, if the case arose, have recourse to arbitration, in so far as circumstances permit.

ARTICLE XXXIX.

The Arbitration Convention is concluded for questions already existing or for questions which may arise eventually.

It may embrace any dispute or only disputes of a certain category.

ARTICLE XL.

Independently of general or private Treaties expressly stipulating recourse to arbitration as obligatory on the Contracting Powers, the said Powers reserve to themselves the right of concluding new Agreements, general or particular, with a view to extending compulsory arbitration to all cases which they may consider it possible to submit to it.

CHAPTER II.—*The Permanent Court of Arbitration.*

ARTICLE XLI.

With the object of facilitating an immediate recourse to arbitration for international differences, which it has not been possible to settle by diplomacy, the Contracting Powers undertake to maintain the Permanent Court of Arbitration, as established by the First Peace Conference, accessible at all times, and operating, unless otherwise stipulated by the parties, in accordance with the rules of procedure inserted in the present Convention.

ARTICLE XLII.

The Permanent Court is competent for all arbitration cases, unless the parties agree to institute a special Tribunal.

ARTICLE XLIII.

The Permanent Court sits at The Hague.

An International Bureau serves as registry for the Court. It is the channel for communications relative to the meetings of the Court; it has charge of the archives and conducts all the administrative business.

The Contracting Powers undertake to communicate to the Bureau, as soon as possible, a certified copy of any conditions of arbitration arrived at between them and of any Award concerning them delivered by a special Tribunal.

They likewise undertake to communicate to the Bureau the laws, regulations, and documents eventually showing the execution of the Awards given by the Court.

ARTICLE XLIV.

Each Contracting Power selects four persons at the most, of known competency in questions of international law, of the highest moral reputation, and disposed to accept the duties of Arbitrator.

The persons thus selected are inscribed, as members of the Court, in a list which shall be notified to all the Contracting Powers by the Bureau.

Any alteration in the list of Arbitrators is brought by the Bureau to the knowledge of the Contracting Powers.

Two or more Powers may agree on the selection in common of one or more members.

The same person can be selected by different Powers. The members of the Court are appointed for a term of six years. These appointments are renewable.

Should a member of the Court die or resign, the same procedure i followed for filling the vacancy as was followed for appointing him In this case the appointment is made for a fresh period of six years

ARTICLE XLV.

When the Contracting Powers wish to have recourse to the Per manent Court for the settlement of a difference which has arise: between them, the Arbitrators called upon to form the Tribun with jurisdiction to decide this difference must be chosen from th general list of members of the Court.

Failing the direct agreement of the parties on the composition of the Arbitration Tribunal, the following course shall be pursued:—

Each party appoints two Arbitrators, of whom one only can be its national or chosen from among the persons selected by it as members of the Permanent Court. These Arbitrators together choose an Umpire.

If the votes are equally divided, the choice of the Umpire is intrusted to a third Power, selected by the parties by common accord.

If an agreement is not arrived at on this subject each party selects a different Power, and the choice of the Umpire is made in concert by the Powers thus selected.

If, within two months' time, these two Powers cannot come to an agreement, each of them presents two candidates taken from the list of members of the Permanent Court, exclusive of the members selected by the parties and not being nationals of either of them. Drawing lots determines which of the candidates thus presented shall be Umpire.

Article XLVI.

The Tribunal being thus composed, the parties notify to the Bureau their determination to have recourse to the Court, the text of their " Compromis," [a] and the names of the Arbitrators.

The Bureau communicates without delay to each Arbitrator the " Compromis," and the names of the other members of the Tribunal.

The Tribunal assembles at the date fixed by the parties. The Bureau makes the necessary arrangements for the meeting.

The members of the Tribunal, in the exercise of their duties and out of their own country, enjoy diplomatic privileges and immunities.

Article XLVII.

The Bureau is authorized to place its offices and staff at the disposal of the Contracting Powers for the use of any special Board of Arbitration.

The jurisdiction of the Permanent Court may, within the conditions laid down in the regulations, be extended to disputes between non-Contracting Powers or between Contracting Powers and non-Contracting Powers, if the parties are agreed on recourse to this Tribunal.

Article XLVIII.

The Contracting Powers consider it their duty, if a serious dispute threatens to break out between two or more of them, to remind these latter that the Permanent Court is open to them.

Consequently, they declare that the fact of reminding the parties at variance of the provisions of the present Convention, and the advice given to them, in the highest interests of peace, to have

---

[a] The preliminary Agreement in an international arbitration defining the point at issue and arranging the procedure to be followed.

recourse to the Permanent Court, can only be regarded as friendly actions.

In case of dispute between two Powers, one of them can always address to the International Bureau a note containing a declaration that it would be ready to submit the dispute to arbitration.

The Bureau must at once inform the other Power of the declaration.

Article XLIX.

The Permanent Administrative Council, composed of the Diplomatic Representatives of the Contracting Powers accredited to The Hague and of the Netherland Minister for Foreign Affairs, who will act as President, is charged with the direction and control of the International Bureau.

The Council settles its rules of procedure and all other necessary regulations.

It decides all questions of administration which may arise with regard to the operations of the Court.

It has entire control over the appointment, suspension, or dismissal of the officials and employés of the Bureau.

It fixes the payments and salaries, and controls the general expenditure.

At meetings duly summoned the presence of nine members is sufficient to render valid the discussions of the Council. The decisions are taken by a majority of votes.

The Council communicates to the Contracting Powers without delay the regulations adopted by it. It furnishes them with an annual Report on the labours of the Court, the working of the administration, and the expenditure. The Report likewise contains a résumé of what is important in the documents communicated to the Bureau by the Powers in virtue of Article XLIII, paragraphs 3 and 4.

Article L.

The expenses of the Bureau shall be borne by the Contracting Powers in the proportion fixed for the International Bureau of the Universal Postal Union.

The expenses to be charged to the adhering Powers shall be reckoned from the date on which their adhesion comes into force.

CHAPTER III.—*Arbitration Procedure.*

Article LI.

With a view to encouraging the development of arbitration, the Contracting Powers have agreed on the following rules, which are applicable to arbitration procedure, unless other rules have been agreed on by the parties.

Article LII.

The Powers which have recourse to arbitration sign a " Compromis," in which the subject of the dispute is clearly defined, the time allowed for appointing Arbitrators, the form, order, and time in which the communication referred to in Article LXIII must be made, and the amount of the sum which each party must deposit in advance to defray the expenses.

The " Compromis " likewise defines, if there is occasion, the manner of appointing Arbitrators, any special powers which may eventually belong to the Tribunal, where it shall meet, the language it shall use, and the languages the employment of which shall be authorized before it, and, generally speaking, all the conditions on which the parties are agreed.

ARTICLE LIII.

The Permanent Court is competent to settle the " Compromis," if the parties are agreed to have recourse to it for the purpose.

It is similarly competent, even if the request is only made by one of the parties, when all attempts to reach an understanding through the diplomatic channel have failed, in the case of :—

1. A dispute covered by a general Treaty of Arbitration concluded or renewed after the present Convention has come into force, and providing for a " Compromis " in all disputes and not either explicitly or implicitly excluding the settlement of the " Compromis " from the competence of the Court. Recourse cannot, however, be had to the Court if the other party declares that in its opinion the dispute does not belong to the category of disputes which can be submitted to compulsory arbitration, unless the Treaty of Arbitration confers upon the Arbitration Tribunal the power of deciding this preliminary question.

2. A dispute arising from contract debts claimed from one Power by another Power as due to its nationals, and for the settlement of which the offer of arbitration has been accepted. This arrangement is not applicable if acceptance is subject to the condition that the " Compromis " should be settled in some other way.

ARTICLE LIV.

In the cases contemplated in the preceding Article, the " Compromis " shall be settled by a Commission consisting of five members selected in the manner arranged for in Article XLV, paragraphs 3 to 6.

The fifth member is President of the Commission ex officio.

ARTICLE LV.

The duties of Arbitrator may be conferred on one Arbitrator alone or on several Arbitrators selected by the parties as they please, or chosen by them from the members of the Permanent Court of Arbitration established by the present Convention.

Failing the constitution of the Tribunal by direct agreement between the parties, the course referred to in Article XLV, paragraphs 3 to 6, is followed.

Article LVI.

When a Sovereign or the Chief of a State is chosen as Arbitrator, the arbitration procedure is settled by him.

Article LVII.

The Umpire is President of the Tribunal *ex officio*.
When the Tribunal does not include an Umpire, it appoints its own President.

Article LVIII.

When the " Compromis " is settled by a Commission, as contemplated in Article LIV, and in the absence of an agreement to the contrary, the Commission itself shall form the Arbitration Tribunal.

Article LIX.

Should one of the Arbitrators either die, retire, or be unable for any reason whatever to discharge his functions, the same procedure is followed for filling the vacancy as was followed for appointing him.

Article LX.

The Tribunal sits at The Hague, unless some other place is selected by the parties.
The Tribunal can only sit in the territory of a third Power with the latter's consent.
The place of meeting once fixed cannot be altered by the Tribunal, except with the consent of the parties.

Article LXI.

If the question as to what languages are to be used has not been settled by the " Compromis," it shall be decided by the Tribunal.

Article LXII.

The parties are entitled to appoint special agents to attend the Tribunal to act as intermediaries between themselves and the Tribunal.
They are further authorized to retain for the defence of their rights and interests before the Tribunal counsel or advocates appointed by themselves for this purpose.
The members of the Permanent Court may not act as agents, counsel, or advocates except on behalf of the Power which appointed them members of the Court.

Article LXIII.

As a general rule, arbitration procedure comprises two distinct phases: pleadings and oral discussions.

The pleadings consist in the communication by the respective agents to the members of the Tribunal and the opposite party of cases, counter-cases, and; if necessary, of replies; the parties annex thereto all papers and documents called for in the case. This communication shall be made either directly or through the intermediary of the International Bureau, in the order and within the time fixed by the "Compromis."

The time fixed by the "Compromis" may be extended by mutual agreement by the parties, or by the Tribunal when the latter considers it necessary for the purpose of reaching a just decision.

The discussions consist in the oral development before the Tribunal of the arguments of the parties.

Article LXIV.

A certified copy of every document produced by one party must be communicated to the other party.

Article LXV.

Unless special circumstances arise, the Tribunal does not meet until the pleadings are closed.

Article LXVI.

The discussions are under the control of the President.

They are only public if it be so decided by the Tribunal, with the assent of the parties.

They are recorded in minutes drawn up by the Secretaries appointed by the President. These minutes are signed by the President and by one of the Secretaries and alone have an authentic character.

Article LXVII.

After the close of the pleadings, the Tribunal is entitled to refuse discussion of all new papers or documents which one of the parties may wish to submit to it without the consent of the other party.

Article LXVIII.

The Tribunal is free to take into consideration new papers or documents to which its attention may be drawn by the agents or counsel of the parties.

In this case, the Tribunal has the right to require the production of these papers or documents, but is obliged to make them known to the opposite party.

Article LXIX.

The Tribunal can, besides, require from the agents of the parties the production of all papers, and can demand all necessary explanations. In case of refusal the Tribunal takes note of it.

Article LXX.

The agents and the counsel of the parties are authorized to present orally to the Tribunal all the arguments they may consider expedient in defence of their case.

Article LXXI.

They are entitled to raise objections and points. The decisions of the Tribunal on these points are final and cannot form the subject of any subsequent discussion.

Article LXXII. ′

The members of the Tribunal are entitled to put questions to the agents and counsel of the parties, and to ask them for explanations on doubtful points.

Neither the questions put, nor the remarks made by members of the Tribunal in the course of the discussions, can be regarded as an expression of opinion by the Tribunal in general or by its members in particular.

Article LXXIII.

The Tribunal is authorized to declare its competence in interpreting the "Compromis," as well as the other Treaties which may be invoked, and in applying the principles of law.

Article LXXIV.

The Tribunal is entitled to issue rules of procedure for the conduct of the case, to decide the forms, order, and time in which each party must conclude its arguments, and to arrange all the formalities required for dealing with the evidence.

Article LXXV.

The parties undertake to supply the Tribunal, as fully as they consider possible, with all the information required for deciding the case.

Article LXXVI.

For all notices which the Tribunal has to serve in the territory of a third Contracting Power, the Tribunal shall apply direct to the Government of that Power. The same rule applies in the case of steps being taken to procure evidence on the spot.

The requests for this purpose are to be executed as far as the means at the disposal of the Power applied to under its municipal law allow. They cannot be rejected unless the Power in question considers them calculated to impair its own sovereign rights or its safety.

The Court will equally be always entitled to act through the Power on whose territory it sits.

Article LXXVII.

When the agents and counsel of the parties have submitted all the explanations and evidence in support of their case the President shall declare the discussion closed.

Article LXXVIII.

The Tribunal considers its decisions in private and the proceedings remain secret.

All questions are decided by a majority of the members of the Tribunal.

Article LXXIX.

The Award must give the reasons on which it is based. It contains the names of the Arbitrators; it is signed by the President and Registrar or by the Secretary acting as Registrar.

Article LXXX.

The Award is read out in public sitting, the agents and counsel of the parties being present or duly summoned to attend.

Article LXXXI.

The Award, duly pronounced and notified to the agents of the parties, settles the dispute definitively and without appeal.

Article LXXXII.

Any dispute arising between the parties as to the interpretation and execution of the Award shall, in the absence of an Agreement to the contrary, be submitted to the Tribunal which pronounced it.

Article LXXXIII.

The parties can reserve in the "Compromis" the right to demand the revision of the Award.

In this case and unless there be an Agreement to the contrary, the demand must be addressed to the Tribunal which pronounced the Award. It can only be made on the ground of the discovery of some new fact calculated to exercise a decisive influence upon the Award and which was unknown to the Tribunal and to the party which demanded the revision at the time the discussion was closed.

Proceedings for revision can only be instituted by a decision of the Tribunal expressly recording the existence of the new fact, recognizing in it the character described in the preceding paragraph, and declaring the demand admissible on this ground.

The "Compromis" fixes the period within which the demand for revision must be made.

Article LXXXIV.

The Award is not binding except on the parties in dispute.

When it concerns the interpretation of a Convention to which Powers other than those in dispute are parties, they shall inform all the Signatory Powers in good time. Each of these Powers is entitled to intervene in the case. If one or more avail themselves of this right, the interpretation contained in the Award is equally binding on them.

Article LXXXV.

Each party pays its own expenses and an equal share of the expenses of the Tribunal.

Chapter IV.—*Arbitration by Summary Procedure.*

Article LXXXVI.

With a view to facilitating the working of the system of arbitration in disputes admitting of a summary procedure, the Contracting Powers adopt the following rules, which shall be observed in the absence of other arrangements and subject to the reservation that the provisions of Chapter III apply so far as may be.

Article LXXXVII.

Each of the parties in dispute appoints an Arbitrator. The two Arbitrators thus selected choose an Umpire. If they do not agree on this point, each of them proposes two condidates taken from the general list of the members of the Permanent Court exclusive of the members appointed by either of the parties and not being nationals of either of them; which of the candidates thus proposed shall be the Umpire is determined by lot.

The Umpire presides over the Tribunal, which gives its decisions by a majority of votes.

Article LXXXVIII.

In the absence of any previous agreement the Tribunal, as soon as it is formed, settles the time within which the two parties must submit their respective cases to it.

Article LXXXIX.

Each party is represented before the Tribunal by an agent, who serves as intermediary between the Tribunal and the Government who appointed him.

Article XC.

The proceedings are conducted exclusively in writing. Each party, however, is entitled to ask that witnesses and experts should be called.

The Tribunal has, for its part, the right to demand oral explanations from the agents of the two parties, as well as from the experts and witnesses whose appearance in Court it may consider useful.

Part V.—*Final Provisions.*

Article XCI.

The present Convention, duly ratified, shall replace, as between the Contracting Powers, the Convention for the Pacific Settlement of International Disputes of the 29th July, 1899.

Article XCII.

The present Convention shall be ratified as soon as possible.
The ratifications shall be deposited at The Hague.

The first deposit of ratifications shall be recorded in a *procès-verbal* signed by the Representatives of the Powers which take part therein and by the Netherland Minister for Foreign Affairs.

The subsequent deposits of ratifications shall be made by means of a written notification, addressed to the Netherland Government and accompanied by the instrument of ratification.

A duly certified copy of the *procès-verbal* relative to the first deposit of ratifications, of the notifications mentioned in the preceding paragraph, and of the instruments of ratification, shall be immediately sent by the Netherland Government, through the diplomatic channel, to the Powers invited to the Second Peace Conference, as well as to those Powers which have adhered to the Convention. In the cases contemplated in the preceding paragraph, the said Government shall at the same time inform the Powers of the date on which it received the notification.

Article XCIII.

Non-Signatory Powers which have been invited to the Second Peace Conference may adhere to the present Convention.

The Power which desires to adhere notifies its intention in writing to the Netherland Government, forwarding to it the act of adhesion, which shall be deposited in the archives of the said Government.

This Government shall immediately forward to all the other Powers invited to the Second Peace Conference a duly certified copy of the notification as well as of the act of adhesion, mentioning the date on which it received the notification.

Article XCIV.

The conditions on which the Powers which have not been invited to the Second Peace Conference may adhere to the Present Convention shall form the subject of a subsequent Agreement between the Contracting Powers.

Article XCV.

The present Convention shall take effect, in the case of the Powers which were not a party to the first deposit of ratifications, sixty days after the date of the *procès-verbal* of this deposit, and, in the case of the Powers which ratify subsequently or which adhere, sixty days after the notification of their ratification or of their adhesion has been received by the Netherland Government.

Article XCVI.

In the event of one of the Contracting Parties wishing to denounce the present Convention, the denunciation shall be notified in writing to the Netherland Government, which shall immediately communicate a duly certified copy of the notification to all the other Powers informing them of the date on which it was received.

The denunciation shall only have effect in regard to the notifying Power, and one year after the notification has reached the Netherland Government.

Article XCVII.

A register kept by the Netherland Minister for Foreign Affairs shall give the date of the deposit of ratifications effected in virtue of Article XCII, paragraphs 3 and 4, as well as the date on which the notifications of adhesion (Article XCIII, paragraph 2) or of denunciation (Article XCVI, paragraph 1) have been received.

Each Contracting Power is entitled to have access to this register and to be supplied with duly certified extracts from it.

In faith whereof the Plenipotentiaries have appended their signatures to the present Convention.

Done at The Hague, the 18th October, 1907, in a single copy, which shall remain deposited in the archives of the Netherland Government, and duly certified copies of which shall be sent, through the diplomatic channel, to the Contracting Powers.

1. Pour l'Allemagne:	Marschall.
	Kriege.
2. Pour les Etats Unis d'Amérique: Sous réserve de la Déclaration faite dans la séance plénière de la Conférence du 16 octobre 1907.	Joseph H. Choate.
	Horace Porter.
	U. M. Rose.
	David Jayne Hill.
	C. S. Sperry.
	William I. Buchanan.
3. Pour l'Argentine:	Roque Saenz Peña.
	Luis M. Drago.
	C. Rúez Larreta.
4. Pour l'Autriche-Hongrie:	Mérey.
	Bon Macchio.
5. Pour la Belgique:	A. Beernaert.
	J. Van den Heuvel.
	Guillaume.

6. Pour la Bolivie: CLAUDIO PINILLA.
7. Pour le Brésil: Avec réserve RUY BARBOSA.
sur l'article 53, alinéas 2, 3
et 4.
8. Pour la Bulgarie: GÉNÉRAL-MAJOR VINAROFF.
IV. KARANDJOULOFF.
9. Pour le Chili: Sous la ré- DOMINGO GANA.
serve de la déclaration for- AUGUSTO MATTE.
mulée à propos de l'article CARLOS CONCHA.
39 dans la septième séance
du 7 octobre de la première
Commission.
10. Pour la Chine: LOU TSENG-TSIANG.
TSIEN-SUN.
11. Pour la Colombie: JORGE HOLGUIŃ.
S. PEREZ TRIANA.
M. VARGAS.
12. Pour la République de Cuba: ANTONIO S. DE BUSTAMANTE.
GONZALO DE QUESADA.
MANUEL SANGUILY.
13. Pour le Danemark: C. BRUN.
14. Pour la République Domini- DR. HENRIQUEZ Y CARVAJAL.
caine: APOLINAR TEJERA.
15. Pour l'Equateur: VICTOR M. RENDON.
E. DORN Y DE ALSÚA.
16. Pour l'Espagne: W. R. DE VILLA URRUTIA.
JOSÉ DE LA RICA Y CALVO.
GABRIEL MAURA.
17. Pour la France: LÉON BOURGEOIS.
D'ESTOURNEILES DE CONSTANT.
L. RENAULT.
MARCELLIN PELLET.
18. Pour la Grande-Bretagne: EDW. FRY.
ERNEST SATOW.
REAY.
HENRY HOWARD.
19. Pour la Grèce. Avec la ré- CLÉON RIZO RANGABÉ.
serve de l'alinéa 2 de l'ar- GEORGES STREIT.
ticle 53.
20. Pour le Guatémala: JOSÉ TIBLE MACHADO.
21. Pour le Haïti: DALBÉMAR JN JOSEPH.
J. N. LÉGER.
PIERRE HUDICOURT.
22. Pour l'Italie: POMPILJ.
G. FUSINATO.
23. Pour le Japon. Avec ré- AIMARO SATO.
serve des alinéas 3 et 4 de
l'article 48, de l'alinéa 2 de
l'article 53 et de l'article
54.

24. Pour le Luxembourg:	EYSCHEN.
	CTE. DE VILLERS.
25. Pour la Mexique:	G. A. ESTEVA.
	S. B. DE MIER.
	F. L. DE LA BARRA.
26. Pour le Monténégro:	NELIDOW.
	MARTENS.
	N. TCHARYKOW.
27. Pour le Nicaragua.	
28. Pour la Norvège:	F. HAGERUP.
29. Pour le Panama:	B. PORRAS.
30. Pour le Paraguay:	J. DU MONCEAU.
31. Pour les Pays-Bas:	W. H. DE BEAUFORT.
	T. M. C. ASSER.
	DEN BEER POORTUGAEL.
	J. A. ROELL.
	J. A. LOEFF.
32. Pour le Pérou:	C. G. CONDAMO.
33. Pour la Perse:	MOMTAZOS-SALTANEH M. SAMAD KHAN.
	SADIGH UL MULK M. AHMED KHAN.
34. Pour le Portugal:	Marquis DE SOVERAL.
	Conde DE SÉLIR.
	ALBERTO D'OLIVEIRA.
35. Pour la Roumanie. Avec les mêmes réserves formulées par les Plénipotentiaires Roumains à la signature de la Convention pour le Règlement pacifique des conflits internationaux du 29 juillet 1899.	EDG. MAVROCORDATO.
36. Pour la Russie:	NELIDOW.
	MARTENS.
	N. TCHARYKOW.
37. Pour le Salvador:	P. J. MATHEU.
	S. PEREZ TRIANA.
38. Pour la Serbie:	S. GROUÏTCH.
	M. G. MILOVANOVITCH.
	M. G. MILITCHEVITCH.
39. Pour le Siam:	MOM CHATIDEJ UDOM.
	C. CORRAGIONI D'ORELLI.
	LUANG BHÜVANARTH NARÜBAL.
40. Pour la Suède:	JOH. HELLNER.
41. Pour le Suisse. Sous réserve de l'article 53, chiffre 2°.	CARLIN.
42. Pour la Turquie. Sous réserve des déclarations portées au procès verbal de la 9° séance plénière de la Conférence du 16 octobre 1907.	TURKHAN.

43. Pour l'Uruguay: JOSÉ BATLLE Y ORDOÑEZ.
44. Pour le Venézuéla: J. GIL FORTOUL.

RESOLUTION OF RATIFICATION BY THE SENATE OF THE CONVENTION FOR
THE SETTLEMENT OF INTERNATIONAL DISPUTES, SIGNED AT THE HAGUE,
1907.

APRIL 2, 1908.

Resolved (*two-thirds of the Senators present concurring therein*),
That the Senate advise and consent to the ratification of a convention
signed by the delegates of the United States to the Second International Peace Conference, held at The Hague from June sixteenth to
October eighteenth, nineteen hundred and seven, for the pacific settlement of international disputes, subject to the declaration made by the
delegates of the United States before signing said convention, namely:
"Nothing contained in this convention shall be so construed as to
require the United States of America to depart from its traditional
policy of not intruding upon, interfering with, or entangling itself in
the political questions of policy or internal administration of any foreign state; nor shall anything contained in the said convention be
construed to imply a relinquishment by the United States of its traditional attitude toward purely American questions."

Resolved further, as a part of this act of ratification, That the United
States approves this convention with the understanding that recourse
to the permanent court for the settlement of differences can be had
only by agreement thereto through general or special treaties of arbitration heretofore or hereafter concluded between the parties in dispute; and the United States now exercises the option contained in
article fifty-three of said convention, to exclude the formulation of
the " compromis " by the permanent court, and hereby excludes from
the competence of the permanent court the power to frame the " compromis " required by general or special treaties of arbitration concluded or hereafter to be concluded by the United States, and further
expressly declares that the " compromis " required by any treaty
of arbitration to which the United States may be a party shall
be settled only by agreement between the contracting parties, unless
such treaty shall expressly provide otherwise.

Document No. 8 W.T. Stead, "Internationalism as an Ideal for the Youth of America" (1909)
Source: *The Chautauquan,* LIV (May, 1909), pp. 333-337.

Internationalism as an Ideal for the Youth of America*

By W. T. Stead

Editor of *The Review of Reviews,* London.

WHAT are the political ideals which glow resplendent before the eyes of the youth of America?

Perhaps it would be better to ask first are there any political ideals which have a pull upon the hearts of American youth?

To many it is to be feared the conjunction of the word ideal with the word politics will seem grotesque. Politics as they are often understood are the negation of the ideal. To speak of idealism in politics is like speaking of virtue in sin. To most men now-a-days politics is little better than the regulating of the rush of the swine to the feeding trough so that the rival herd shall not get all the swill.

But the soul of youth is nourished on ideals, and the zest of life lies in the hope of realizing them.

---

*The first article of this series, "The European Equilibrium and the Peace of the World," by Victor S. Yarros, appeared in the September CHAUTAUQUAN; the second article, by the same author, "Danger Points About the Globe," in the October number. In November, "The Story of the Peace Movement," by Benjamin F. Trueblood; December, "Armies the Real Promoters of Peace," by Col. W. C. Church; January, "The Human Harvest," by David Starr Jordan; and "International Aspects of Socialism," by A. N. Simons; February, "What is International Law?" by Henry Wade Rogers; and "The Sanction of International Law," by Elihu Root; March, "Modern Economic Forces Against War," Charles A. Conant; April, "The Family of Nations in Conference at the Hague," William I. Hull.

This faith in some ideal Good
Under whatever mortal name it masks
Freedom, Law, Country, * * *
Shall be a wisdom that we set above
All other skills and gifts to culture dear.

The best service the University, School, the Teacher, can confer upon the student is to kindle in his soul a passion to realize some lofty ideal. What ideal is there at the present day capable of forcing the imagination or the youth of America?

Their forefathers lived and labored and many of them were glad to die in the service of the ideal of national independence. The following generation was not less keen to spend and be spent in the service of the ideal of national union. What is the ideal which the Twentieth Century offers to those who will be the Masters of the Republic for the next half century?

No internal foe threatens the liberty, independence or integrity of the United States. No internal foe threatens to destroy the union which links in a peaceful federation all the sovereign states between the Atlantic and the Pacific.

Ideals are usually born of an acute realization of the dangers or disadvantages of the Actual. There are two such ideals confronting the youth of the world common to every land although appealing with varying degrees of force to different nations. One is the thirst for a more complete realization of fraternity and equality in the possession of this world's goods, which is crudely described as Socialism. The other is a not less divine aspiration after a more complete realization of justice and brotherhood in the external relations of States which is usually labelled Internationalism. Of these two Socialism appeals with greater force to the students of Russia (where nearly every College boy or girl is a Socialist) than it does to American students. It is quite otherwise with Internationalism. This is an ideal which should appeal more forcibly to the youth of America than to the youth of any other nation.

The world progresses with ever increasing velocity towards the ideal of internationalism. Steam and Electricity have made all the nations of the world next door neighbors. What the locomotive and the steamship have left undone the aeroplane will finish. Frontiers will be wiped out and almost before we know where we are mankind will find itself a political unit. Unfortunately progress in mechanical contrivances for the application of the discoveries of science has far outstripped the progress that has been made by the nations in the improvement of their international political relations. To speed up political progress towards international justice and friendship is the most urgent duty lying before the human race.

There are some who imagine the ideal of International Peace will stimulate our youth to energetic action. It will do no such thing. No one will ever die for Peace, and an ideal for which men do not care to shed their blood has no magic lure for the human heart. Peace is negative, the mere absence of war. Peace is as admirable as happiness, but if either is made the objective of life we neither generate enthusiasm not attain our aim. Peace is a by-product of international justice. For Justice men will die. The ideal of national unity filled the youth of Italy with a divine thirst for martyrdom. If this was possible when the ideal was only that of the unity of a peninsula, how much greater the appeal to the heart and the imagination that is made by the Unity of the Planet?

I wish I could rouse the youth of America to a realizing sense of the splendor of the opportunity which is theirs today, and still more to a sense of the immense responsibility that lies upon their shoulders. Towards the International World State other nations are groping blindly, wandering hither and thither without compass, without guide. The Americans walk confidently along a familiar path to a clearly defined goal. It is for the youth of America to send the American idea sweeping in triumph round the globe.

What is the American political idea? It is simplicity itself. It is the equal sovereignty of every independent State, and the federation of all these Sovereign States in a great federal pact, the provisions of which are interpreted by a central Supreme Court and enforced in case of need by the combined forces of all the federated States. It ought to be regarded as the proudest privilege of young America to secure for the disunited States of the world the political advantages which are enjoyed by the United States of America. To them much has been given, from them much will be expected.

When the American idea fired the imagination of the French they were not content with making their own Revolution. They were seized with a sacred zeal to make liberty, fraternity, and equality the common possession of all the nations of Europe. I do not wish to suggest that young America should aspire to make the Stars and Stripes make the tour of the world as the Tricolor made the tour of Europe. But I do wish that Americans would realize their pride of place and apply themselves seriously to expedite the federation of the world.

For the federation of the world is inevitably the Americanization of the World, the recasting of the Old World systems in the new mould of the American idea. Here is a world ideal worthy the ambition of the proudest patriot. I would venture to suggest as I have more than once suggested before that every American College and University should recognize the duty of contributing its share to the Americanization of the World. An American Collegiate Mission appealing in the first place to the Collegiate youth of the other countries to coöperate in federating the world would not merely have a great effect abroad. It would react powerfully upon America. It would give the youth of America something to dream of, to pray for, to labor at and if need be to die for. For the International World State, like all smaller federations, will not come into being without those pangs of labor which we call war. But we shall but fight to end our fighting, for we shall replace the armed anarchy of the nations by the established order of a World State based on liberty and defended by law administered by a Supreme Court of Justice and Arbitration.

That is the ideal to which I wish the youth of America to turn their eyes. It is infinitely more glorious than that of Imperial conquest or of political domination. And it is preëminently the work that lies to the hand of the Americans for they alone have practised on a Continental scale the doctrines which had heretofore been confined to the closets of philosophers or the laboratory of the Swiss Republic.

Document No. 9   Theodore Roosevelt, Nobel Peace Prize Speech (1910)
Source: *The Works of Theodore Roosevelt,* Herman Hagedorn, editor,
Memorial Edition (20 vols.; N.Y.: Charles Scribner's Sons, 1925), XVIII, pp.
410-415.

INTERNATIONAL PEACE *

It is with peculiar pleasure that I stand here to-day
to express the deep appreciation I feel of the high honor
conferred upon me by the presentation of the Nobel
Peace Prize. The gold medal which formed part of the
prize I shall always keep, and I shall hand it on to my
children as a precious heirloom. The sum of money
provided as part of the prize by the wise generosity of
the illustrious founder of this world-famous prize system I did not, under the peculiar circumstances of the
case, feel at liberty to keep. I think it eminently just
and proper that in most cases the recipient of the prize
should keep for his own use the prize in its entirety.
But in this case, while I did not act officially as President of the United States, it was nevertheless only because I was President that I was enabled to act at all;
and I felt that the money must be considered as having
been given me in trust for the United States. I therefore used it as a nucleus for a foundation to forward the
cause of industrial peace, as being well within the general purpose of your committee; for in our complex industrial civilization of to-day the peace of righteousness and justice, the only kind of peace worth having,
is at least as necessary in the industrial world as it is
among nations. There is at least as much need to curb
the cruel greed and arrogance of part of the world of

* Address before the Nobel Prize Committee, delivered at Christiania, Norway,
May 5, 1910.

capital, to curb the cruel greed and violence of part of the world of labor, as to check a cruel and unhealthy militarism in international relationships.

We must ever bear in mind that the great end in view is righteousness, justice as between man and man, nation and nation, the chance to lead our lives on a somewhat higher level, with a broader spirit of brotherly good-will one for another. Peace is generally good in itself, but it is never the highest good unless it comes as the handmaid of righteousness; and it becomes a very evil thing if it serves merely as a mask for cowardice and sloth, or as an instrument to further the ends of despotism or anarchy. We despise and abhor the bully, the brawler, the oppressor, whether in private or public life; but we despise no less the coward and the voluptuary. No man is worth calling a man who will not fight rather than submit to infamy or see those that are dear to him suffer wrong. No nation deserves to exist if it permits itself to lose the stern and virile virtues; and this without regard to whether the loss is due to the growth of a heartless and all-absorbing commercialism, to prolonged indulgence in luxury and soft effortless ease, or to the deification of a warped and twisted sentimentality.

Moreover, and above all, let us remember that words count only when they give expression to deeds or are to be translated into them. The leaders of the Red Terror prattled of peace while they steeped their hands in the blood of the innocent; and many a tyrant has called it peace when he has scourged honest protest into silence. Our words must be judged by our deeds; and in striving for a lofty ideal we must use practical methods; and if we cannot attain all at one leap, we must advance toward it step by step, reasonably content so long as we do actually make some progress in the right direction.

Now, having freely admitted the limitations to our work, and the qualifications to be borne in mind, I feel that I have the right to have my words taken seriously when I point out where, in my judgment, great advance can be made in the cause of international peace. I speak as a practical man, and whatever I now advocate I actually tried to do when I was for the time being the head of a great nation, and keenly jealous of its honor and interest. I ask other nations to do only what I should be glad to see my own nation do.

The advance can be made along several lines. First of all, there can be treaties of arbitration. There are, of course, states so backward that a civilized community ought not to enter into an arbitration treaty with them, at least until we have gone much farther than at present in securing some kind of international police action. But all really civilized communities should have effective arbitration treaties among themselves. I believe that these treaties can cover almost all questions liable to arise between such nations, if they are drawn with the explicit agreement that each contracting party will respect the other's territory and its absolute sovereignty within that territory, and the equally explicit agreement that (aside from the very rare cases where the nation's honor is vitally concerned) all other possible subjects of controversy will be submitted to arbitration. Such a treaty would insure peace unless one party deliberately violated it. Of course, as yet there is no adequate safeguard against such deliberate violation, but the establishment of a sufficient number of these treaties would go a long way toward creating a world opinion which would finally find expression in the provision of methods to forbid or punish any such violation.

Secondly, there is the farther development of the Hague Tribunal, of the work of the conferences and courts at The Hague. It has been well said that the first Hague Conference framed a Magna Charta for the nations; it set before us an ideal which has already to some extent been realized, and toward the full realization of which we can all steadily strive. The second Conference made further progress; the third should do yet more. Meanwhile the American Government has more than once tentatively suggested methods for completing the Court of Arbitral Justice, constituted at the second Hague Conference, and for rendering it effective. It is earnestly to be hoped that the various governments of Europe, working with those of America and of Asia, shall set themselves seriously to the task of devising some method which shall accomplish this result. If I may venture the suggestion, it would be well for the statesmen of the world in planning for the erection of this world court, to study what has been done in the United States by the Supreme Court. I cannot help thinking that the Constitution of the United States, notably in the establishment of the Supreme Court and in the methods adopted for securing peace and good relations among and between the different States, offers certain valuable analogies to what should be striven for in order to secure, through The Hague courts and conferences, a species of world federation for international peace and justice. There are, of course, fundamental differences between what the United States Constitution does and what we should even attempt at this time to secure at The Hague; but the methods adopted in the American Constitution to prevent hostilities between the States, and to secure the supremacy of the Federal Court in certain classes of cases, are well worth the study of those who seek at The Hague to obtain the same results on a world scale.

In the third place, something should be done as soon as possible to check the growth of armaments, especially vital armaments, by international agreement. No one power could or should act by itself; for. it is eminently undesirable, from the standpoint of the peace of righteousness, that a power which really does believe in peace should place itself at the mercy of some rival which may at bottom have no such belief and no intention of acting on it. But, granted sincerity of purpose, the great powers of the world should find no insurmountable difficulty in reaching an agreement which would put an end to the present costly and growing extravagance of expenditure on naval armaments. An agreement merely to limit the size of ships would have been very useful a few years ago, and would still be of use; but the agreement should go much further.

Finally, it would be a master stroke if those great powers honestly bent on peace would form a League of Peace, not only to keep the peace among themselves, but to prevent, by force if necessary, its being broken by others. The supreme difficulty in connection with developing the peace work of The Hague arises from the lack of any executive power, of any police power, to enforce the decrees of the court. In any community of any size the authority of the courts rests upon actual or potential force; on the existence of a police, or on the knowledge that the able-bodied men of the country are both ready and willing to see that the decrees of judicial and legislative bodies are put into effect. In new and wild communities where there is violence, an honest man must protect himself; and until other means of securing his safety are devised, it is both foolish and wicked to persuade him to surrender his arms while the men who are dangerous to the community retain theirs. He should not renounce the right to protect himself by his own efforts until the community is so organized that it can effectively relieve the individual of the duty of putting down violence. So it is with nations. Each nation must keep well prepared to defend itself until the establishment of some form of international police power, competent and willing to prevent violence as between nations. As things are now, such power to command peace throughout the world could best be assured by some combination between those great nations which sincerely desire peace and have no thought themselves of committing aggressions. The combination might at first be only to secure peace within certain definite limits and certain definite conditions; but the ruler or statesman who should bring about such a combination would have earned his place in history for all time and his title to the gratitude of all mankind.

Document No. 10   American Peace Society, "The Commission for World
Peace" (1910)
Source: The Advocate of Peace, LXXII (July and August, 1910), p. 153.

Advocate of Peace.

VOL. LXXII.   BOSTON, JULY AND AUGUST, 1910.   No. 7

THE AMERICAN PEACE SOCIETY,
PUBLISHERS,
31 BEACON STREET, BOSTON, MASS.
Cable Address, "Peace, Boston."

MONTHLY, ONE DOLLAR PER YEAR.   TEN CENTS PER COPY
Entered at the Boston Post Office as Second Class Matter.
Make all checks payable to the American Peace Society. To personal
checks on Western and Southern banks add ten cents for collecting.

The Commission for World Peace.

The following joint resolution was adopted by the
United States House of Representatives on June 20
and by the Senate on June 24 :

" Resolved, by the Senate and House of Representatives
of the United States of America in Congress assembled,
that a commission of five members be appointed by the
President of the United States to consider the expediency
of utilizing existing international agencies for the purpose
of limiting the armaments of the nations of the world by
international agreement, and of constituting the combined
navies of the world an international force for the preservation of universal peace, and to consider and report upon
any other means to diminish the expenditures of government for military purposes and to lessen the probabilities
of war."

This resolution is the outcome of efforts made with
Congress by the New York Peace Society, the World
Federation League (a department of the New York
Peace Society), the Peace Committee of the National
German Alliance, and other organizations, in behalf
of world federation, limitation of armaments, etc.

Resolutions were introduced into Congress at the
request of these societies by Mr. Bartholdt of Missouri
and Mr. Bennet of New York, asking for the appointment of a commission by our government to study
and report on these pressing international questions.

The hearing on these resolutions given by the
House Committee on Foreign Affairs developed much
interest and clearly indicated that Congress was
ready to take any practicable step possible in the
direction of further international coöperation to assure
the peace of the world and relief from the present
heavy and growing burdens of armaments.

This resolution, though it is in part vague and indefinite, puts into the foreground the urgent question
of limitation of armaments, the matter of an international naval police being only incidental. It is
well, however, that it leaves to the commission the
largest latitude, for it will be found that the problem
of arrest of armaments is inextricably bound up with
the various phases of the problem of world organization — an international parliament, a court of arbitral
justice, etc.

The appointment of this commission by our government, if it is made up of the right type of statesmen,
as it certainly will be, may easily prove to be one of
the greatest steps that has ever been taken in the
working out of the practical problem of world peace.
It has been evident for a long time that no real progress toward the solution of the problem of limitation of armaments can be made until the subject has
been first thoroughly and exhaustively studied by an
international Commission. That was the difficulty
at the Hague Conferences ; no preliminary study of
the problem of armaments had been made. A good
deal of advancement has been made through the
Hague Conferences toward the establishment of a
regular parliament of the world, a complete system
of arbitration and a high court of nations. But so
far nothing practical has been done toward the removal of the immense obstacle which the current
rivalry of armaments offers to the further progress of
international unity and peace. This Commission has
not been provided for a moment too soon. We shall
await with interest the announcement of the names of
the statesmen who shall compose it and the inauguration of their work. It will take at least two years,
and probably twice that time, for them to be joined by
similar commissions of other powers and to examine
thoroughly and comprehensively the details of the
immensely important problem that is intrusted to them

Document No. 11 Hamilton Holt, "A League of Peace" (1911)
Source: *The Independent,* LXX (May 11, 1911), pp. 995-999.

A League of Peace

BY HAMILTON HOLT

[The article which follows is the substance of the address made by Mr. Holt as president of the Third National Peace Congress held last week in Baltimore. For a discussion of the work of the Congress the reader is referred to our editorial pages.—EDITOR.]

THE first National Peace Congress of the United States was held in New York City from April 14 to 17, 1907—just two months before the convening of the Second Hague Conference. In the personnel of its officers, speakers and delegates, it was the most distinguished unofficial gathering ever held in the United States.

As was to be expected, the main attention of the Congress was focused on the coming Hague Conference. Nearly all the speakers discussed it, and the two most important resolutions passed were those favoring the negotiation of a general treaty of arbitration and the turning of the Hague Conference into a permanent international body.

The Hague Conference, thanks in large measure to the leadership of the United States delegation, took a long step toward making these two propositions realities. The principle of obligatory arbitration was unanimously adopted by all the nations, and had not Germany and Austria and a few of the smaller European states objected strenuously a general treaty in accordance with that principle would have been drafted and approved.

The nations also took the first step toward turning the Hague Conference into an automatic and periodic world congress, by taking the third conference out of the hands of Russia and putting it in charge of an international preliminary committee which was to meet about 1913 and determine its method of organization and program.

When the Second National Peace Congress of the United States was convened in Chicago exactly two years ago this very day and hour, the Second Hague Conference had already passed into history and the world was just beginning to realize what a great work it had accomplished for international justice and peace. As Elihu Root has so truly said, that conference "presents the greatest advance ever made at a single time toward the reasonable and peaceful regulation of international conduct, unless it be the advance made at the Hague Conference of 1899."

The Chicago Congress was not content, however, with passing congratulatory resolutions on things already accomplished. Like the New York Congress it set its face toward the future and spoke out brave and strong. Not only did it declare that war was "out of date" in this age of Hague conferences, courts and arbitration treaties, but it demanded as the most pressing "next steps" in the peace movement the creation of a peace commission by our Government to study the whole peace question, a general treaty of obligatory arbitration, and the establishment of a League of Peace, to make the recurrence of war impossible. Two years have now elapsed since these three recommendations were uttered. Has any progress been made toward their realization?

Last June the Congress of the United States passed unanimously the following joint resolution:

"Resolved, etc., 'That a commission of five members be appointed by the President of the United States to consider the expediency of utilizing existing international agencies for the purpose of limiting the armaments of the nations of the world by international agreement and of constituting the combined navies of the world an international force for the preservation of universal peace, and to consider and report upon any other means to diminish the expenditures of government for military purposes and to lessen the probabilities of war.'"

In his annual message to Congress, dated December 16, 1910, President Taft stated:

"I have not as yet made appointments to the commission because I have invited and am awaiting the expressions of foreign governments as to their willingness to co-operate with us in the appointment of a similar commission or representatives who would meet with our commissions and by joint action seek to make their work effective."

It is impossible to overestimate this epoch-making document and the action of the President upon it. When the President appoints the commission, for the first time in the annals of history a great nation in time of peace will prepare for peace.

It is in the realm of arbitration, however, that the greatest cause for rejoicing exists. The world, to be sure, has not yet obtained the desired general treaty of obligatory arbitration. It has got, however, what is of vastly more importance. President Taft's statement that he is willing to settle all disputes, even those supposed to involve national honor, by arbitration, the most momentous declaration ever made in favor of peace by a man in his position. The proposed arbitration treaty of unlimited scope with Great Britain is the practical application of this declaration. Already it has transfigured the whole peace movement. Eventually it will render the code of war obnoxious if not obsolete. And this is the situation that confronts the world as we assemble here today at the opening of the Third National Peace Congress of the United States. It is our duty to look ahead thru the vista opened up by President Taft's high statesmanship and to take as resolute and progressive a stand here as the New York and Chicago congresses did four and two years ago.

There are many pressing problems before us waiting to be solved. The judicial arbitration court created by the Second Hague Conference, all but the detail of the method of the selection of the judges, is yet to be constituted. No attention has yet been paid to the requests of both the First and the Second Hague Conferences that the governments give themselves over to the serious study of the limitation of armaments. It is not yet provided that the future Hague conferences become automatc, periodic and self-governing bodies, as our delegation suggested at the Conference of 1907. The Peace Commission is not yet appointed. We should consider all these and many other questions where our voice may be of help to governments, and peace societies both here and abroad. But the one all important issue before us is the pending arbitration treaty with Great Britain; for this treaty is destined to make war hereafter impossible between the English-speaking peoples of the earth.

The peace movement, we have now come to realize, is nothing but the process of substituting law for war. The world has already learned to substitute law for war in hamlets, towns, cities, states, and even within the forty-six sovereign civilized nations. But in that international realm over and above each nation in which each nation is equally sovereign, the only way at the present moment for a nation to secure its rights is by the use of force. Force, therefore, or war as it is called when exerted by a nation against another nation—is at present the only legal and final method of settling international differences. The world is now using a Christian code of ethics for individuals, and a pagan code for nations, tho there is no double standard of ethics in the moral world. In other words, the nations are in that state of civilization where without a qualm they claim the right to settle their disputes in a manner which they would actually put their own subjects to death for imitating. Thus the peace problem is nothing but the ways and means of doing *between* the nations what has already been done *within* the nations. International law follows private law. The "United Nations" follow the United States.

At present international law has reached the same state of development that private or municipal law had attained in the tenth century. Furthermore, a careful study of the formation o. the thirteen American colonies from separate States into our present compac Union discloses the fact that the nation today are in the same stage of development that the American colonies were a about the time of their first confederation As the United States came into existenc by the establishment of the Articles o Confederation and the Continental Con gress, so the "United Nations" at thi very moment exists by the fact of th Hague Court and the recurring Hagu Conferences: the Hague Court bein the promise of the Supreme Cour of the World and the Hagu Conferences being the prophecy o the Parliament of Man. We ma look with confidence therefore to a fu ture in which the world will have an established court with jurisdiction over all questions, self-governing conferences with power to legislate on all affairs of common concern, and an executive power of some form to carry out the decrees of both. To deny this is to ignore all the analogies of private law and the whole trend of the world's political history since the Declaration of Independence. As Secretary Knox has said in his great address delivered last June at the commencement of the University of Pennsylvania:

"We have reached a point when it is evident that the future holds in store a time when war shall cease: when the nations of the world shall realize a federation as real and vital as that now subsisting between the component parts of a single state."

I recall no more far-visioned statement than this ever emanating from the chancellery of a great state. It means nothing less than that the age-long dreams of the poets, the prophets and the philosophers have at last entered the realms of practical statesmanship and that the world is on the threshold of the dawn of universal peace.

The political organization of the world, therefore, is the task of the twentieth century. But the formation of a world government must be a very slow process. Such a federal government when complete would be, as the historian Freeman has said, "the most finished and the most artificial production of political ingenuity." To accomplish it is surely not the work of a day or a year.

How then can this movement be hastened? There are only two ways. First, by the education of the public opinion of the world so as to induce the governments to move at successive Hague conferences or at special international conferences, and, second, by a few of the more enlightened nations organizing themselves together for peace in advance of the others. This latter method is already being adopted extensively. The Judicial Arbitration Court will be constituted by only a few of the nations at first. England and the United States will not wait for a general treaty of obligatory arbitration before establishing a model one between themselves. Chile and Argentina did not delay for concurrent action on the part of the whole world be-

fore they commenced to disarm, as the statue of the Christ on the summit of the Andes so eloquently attests. Why, then, should not a few nations here and now form among themselves a League of Peace to hasten the ultimate world federation?

The idea of a League of Peace is not novel. All federal governments and confederations of governments, both ancient and modern, are essentially leagues of peace, even tho they may have functions to perform which often lead directly to war.

The ancient Achaian League of Greece, the Confederation of Swiss Cantons, the United Provinces of the Netherlands, and the United States of America are the most perfect systems of federated government known to history. Less perfect, but none the less interesting to students of government, are the Latin League of thirty cities, the Hanseatic League, and in modern times the German Confederation. Even the Dual and Triple Alliances and the Concert of Europe might be called more or less inchoate leagues of peace.

Any league of peace, however, likely to be established in the immediate future must differ from all previous and present leagues, alliances and confederations in total abstinence from the use of force. The ancient leagues as well as the modern confederations have generally been unions of offense and defense. They stood ready, if they did not actually propose, to use their common forces to compel outside states to obey their will. Thus they were as frequently leagues of oppression as leagues of peace.

The problem of the League of Peace is therefore the problem of the use of force. Shall the members of the League "not only keep the peace themselves but prevent by force, if necessary, its being broken by others," outside of the League, as ex-President Roosevelt has suggested? Or shall its force be exercised only within its membership and thus be on the side of law and order and never on the side of arbitrary will or tyranny? Or, rather, shall it never use force at all? Whichever of these three possibilities is ultimately adopted, I think that at first it would be unwise for a League of Peace to attempt to use force for any purpose whatsoever. Besides, the use of force will probably be found unnecessary. When nations arrive at that state of civilization in which they are ready to settle their differences by arbitration rather than by war, they are ready peaceably to abide by the decision of arbitral tribunals. The history of arbitration clearly demonstrates this. With but one or two insignificant exceptions, the nations have lived up to all arbitral awards, both in the letter and the spirit of the judgment; and there have been hundreds of such awards. We need a policeman to use force on criminals. But happily there is no such thing nowadays as a criminal nation.

Moreover, to project a League of Peace at the present moment with a specially constituted international force at its disposal would instantly beget suspicion, if not alarm, on the part of all nations not invited to join. They would consider it an alliance against themselves, and would very likely proceed forthwith to start a counter alliance to preserve the balance of power.

With the idea in view, then, that the League of Peace shall not have any specially constituted common army and navy at its disposal, I offer herewith, for whatever they may be worth, the following suggestions for a League of Peace in the hope that they may possibly serve as a basis for further study:

1. The nations in the League shall refer all disputes of whatsoever a nature to arbitration.

2. The Hague Court or other duly constituted Courts shall decide all disputes that cannot be settled by diplomacy.

3. The League shall provide a periodical convention or assembly to make all rules for the League, such rules to become law unless vetoed by a nation within a stated period.

4. Each member of the League shall have the right to arm itself according to its own judgment.

5. Any member of the League shall have the right to withdraw on due notice.

The advantages that a nation would gain in becoming a member of such a league are manifest. The risk of war would be eliminated between the members of the league, and a method would be devised whereby they could develop their common intercourse and interests as far and as fast as they could unanimously agree on ways and means. It is conceivable that such a league might in time reduce tariffs and postal rates and in a thousand other ways promote commerce and comity among its members. Indeed, the possibilities of such a league are almost infinite, even tho it attempts to employ no force whatsoever to compel obedience to its will.

Assuming, then, the desirability of such a League of Peace, how is it to be brought about?

Surely the first step is to conclude the arbitration treaty now being negotiated with Great Britain. Once this treaty is upon the international statute books, and as surely as daylight follows dawn it will be followed by similar treaties with other nations. Japan and France are said to be ready—even anxious—to negotiate similar treaties with us. Indeed, it is by no means impossible that there will be a race between England and Japan on the one hand and France and the United States on the other to see which can conclude the second model arbitration treaty of the world.

Thus the time is likely soon to come when several of the nations, having bound themselves each to each by eternal chains of peace, will be ready to take the next logical step and negotiate a general treaty of arbitration among themselves. This, to all intents and purposes, would constitute a League of Peace. And it would inevitably grow in power and prestige until all the nations of the world entered its concordant and prosperous circle.

Indeed, it might be a stroke of statesmanship if an article were added to the proposed arbitration treaty between Great Britain and the United States inviting other nations to adhere to it. This would save much time and effort and obviate the necessity for each of the forty-six nations to negotiate a special treaty with every other. Thus only one treaty would have to be negotiated instead of 1,034. But whether Great Britain and the United States ask other nations to adhere to their model treaty or not, the principle of unlimited arbitration will grow—first by a few nations adopting it, then by more, until finally the whole world will agree to enthrone reason rather than might as the arbiter of their destinies, and war shall reign no more.

First, an unlimited arbitration treaty between Great Britain and the United States. Second, a League of Peace. Third, the Federation of the World.

Is all this a dream? I have already quoted the weighty words of Secretary Knox prophesying the eventual coming of a world state. Let me close with the equally prophetic utterance of an equally responsible and distinguished statesman. On March 17 last, at the dinner of the International Arbitration League, the Right Honorable Sir Edward Grey, the British Secretary of State for Foreign Affairs, said:

"If an arbitration treaty is made between the two great countries on the lines sketched out by the President of the United States, . . . don't let them set narrow bounds to their hopes of the beneficent results which may develop from it in the course of time—results which I think must extend far beyond the two countries originally concerned. The effect on the world at large of the example would be bound to have beneficent consequences. To set a good example is to hope that others of the great powers will follow it, and if they did follow there would eventually be something like a League of Peace."

NEW YORK CITY.

Document No. 12   President William Howard Taft, "World-Peace and the General Arbitration Treaties" (1911)
Source: *World's Work*, XXIII (December, 1911), pp. 143-149.

WORLD-PEACE AND THE GENERAL ARBITRATION TREATIES

SWIFTLY-GATHERING SENTIMENT ENCOURAGES HOPE FOR AN AREOPAGITIC COURT OF THE NATIONS — THE TREATIES AWAITING RATIFICATION A, LONG, ADVANCE IN CIVILIZATION — ARE WE IN FAVOR OF ARBITRATION OR WAR?

BY

WILLIAM HOWARD TAFT

(REPORTED BY WILLIAM BAYARD HALE)

IT *was an autumn day at Beverly-by-the-Sea. The cold wind that swept up the hill made the log that crackled in the study fire-place a pleasure to the eye and a comfort to the back. The last detail of a long journey through twenty-four states of the Union, to be entered upon on the morrow, was completed. A last official act — the exchanging of adieux with the late ambassador of Japan, just called home to become his Emperor's Minister of Foreign Affairs — was over. A loyal delegation of New England's business men had come, offered their stirrup-cup of cheer, and departed, and the President had an hour all his own. He sat back in his chair, and talked — talked of a thing that lies perhaps nearer his heart than anything else in the world — talked of peace on earth among the nations of the earth, and the prospect of it. The sun was going down in a particularly fine exhibition of its best colors.*

When a President relaxes before his study fire late on a fine autumn afternoon, he is pretty certain to say something interesting. Mr. Taft said a great many things interesting. Some of them discretion scarcely suggests the advisability of printing. But some other things which the President said so manifestly ought to be printed — ought to be heard not by a solitary listener but by the nation and the world, both on account of their intrinsic interest and of their significance coming from the occupant of so exalted an office — that I asked permission to write them out. And obtained it, with the qualification that I should make it clear I was recording an unpremeditated, informal conversation.

Thus, then, the President, to the best of his interlocutor's recollection:

Do you know that one of the most notable phenomena of the day is the swiftness with which belief in permanent international peace is growing?

Yes, this sentiment, comparatively new in the world, has made enormous strides within the past few years. Wherever I go I find the most eager interest in anything I say on the subject of war and peace. Crowds grow silent as I approach that theme; men put a hand behind the ear and stand on tiptoe leaning forward so as not to miss a word. There is astir a profound revolution in the popular thought on the subject of war, a moral awakening to the hideous wickedness of armed combat between man and man, and an economic perception of the wastefulness and folly not only of war but of the great armaments which the present jealousy of the Powers makes it necessary to maintain.

Workingmen have brought it home to me as I have seen and talked with them in all parts of the country that they are against war. They have to pay the bills, and what do they gain? What interest have they in the common run of disputes between governments — matters of boundary, matters of dynasty, matters of so-called "honor"? And if they feel any interest in the dispute, they want to know why it can't be settled in some way less archaic, less barbarous, less wasteful, than the marching out of armies of men bent on killing one another.

It is indeed a barbarous thing, a thing worthy of the Stone Age, that men with common interests, a common destiny, with all the great common causes, common battles to fight against nature, common marches to make up the ascent of civilization — a barbarous thing that men should cease from their common war to engage in mutual slaughter and destruction, should batter and disfigure and maim and slay one another.

With this feeling in the mind of the workingman, war to-day does not afford the glittering prospects it once did. It is, for instance, no longer advisable to resort to conflict with another country as a means of reuniting a country distracted by internal problems. On the contrary, war is distinctly dangerous to a country torn by internal dissensions. The increased burden of taxation, the tightness of money, the inconvenience of living, the unpopularity of war, the absence of troops, abnormal conditions generally, and especially the vivid realization that the interests of the rulers are not the interests of the people — these things are likely to provoke and encourage domestic disaffection.

The birth and growth of this peace sentiment (and I tell you it is acquiring amazing strength) is not to be wondered at; it would have been a cause of wonder if it had not been born. We have advanced in everything else; we have lagged far behind in this serious and terrible matter of international disputes, allowing them to settle themselves according to the rude and savage methods of days long past. Now we have at last taken up that matter, I am inclined to think that we shall advance with it much more swiftly than some will believe.

The evening papers on the table had cables from Peking telling of the gravity of the insurrection in a Chinese province; cables from Paris, Berlin, and Rome agreeing in pessimistic views of the outcome of the European crisis. But the President talked on — of permanent peace among the nations.

I say boldly that what I look forward to is nothing less than a court of the nations — an Areopagitic court, to whose conscientious and impartial judgment peoples shall submit their disputes, to be decided according to the eternal principles of law and equity.

Civilization demands that, and it is coming. The treaties with Great Britain and France lately negotiated, will, if ratified by the Senate, mark a long step into the path along which the world must now advance.

Everyone recognizes that our existing treaties with England and France — which agree to arbitrate all questions except those which affect the vital interests or the national honor of the Powers concerned — make an advance in international relations. Yet, of course, when any question comes up, either nation might convince itself that its vital interests or its national honor were involved, and refuse to arbitrate. There are very few questions which might not be so construed in the opinion of one or the other nation. I mean to say that the exception in the present treaties is so phrased that it really leaves very little to be arbitrated; it leaves us definitely committed to very little indeed. In effect, we merely declare that we are in favor of arbitration, and that, when a question arises which we are willing to arbitrate, we will arbitrate it — if the other nation also is willing.

Now, that is all very well — but it doesn't go very far toward permanent peace — toward providing a means for the settling of those serious questions which lead to wars.

The new treaties do provide that means; the new treaties do really commit us, and the nations which sign with us, to seek a settlement of all disputes, even the most serious, without armed conflict. The new treaties do not leave it to the excited, momentary opinion of the countries involved to decide whether or not the question which has arisen is one that may honorably be arbitrated. The new treaties provide a judicial means of settling that initial question. They es-

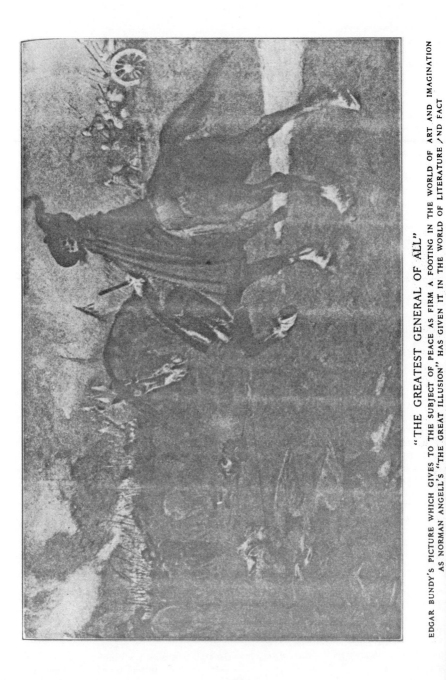

"THE GREATEST GENERAL OF ALL"

EDGAR BUNDY'S PICTURE WHICH GIVES TO THE SUBJECT OF PEACE AS FIRM A FOOTING IN THE WORLD OF ART AND IMAGINATION AS NORMAN ANGELL'S "THE GREAT ILLUSION" HAS GIVEN IT IN THE WORLD OF LITERATURE AND FACT

tablish a Joint High Commission to pass on that question.

This device of the Joint High Commission is the centre and the point of the whole plan. I repeat there is nothing gained for the cause of peace by agreeing to arbitrate what and when we feel inclined. There is everything gained for it by agreeing to arbitrate whatever an impartial tribunal says is arbitrable. These treaties establish such a tribunal; under the plan it will always be constituted of an equal number of citizens of the United States and of the other country involved — three of each. It is a mistake to say that the Joint High Commission might be made up of foreigners. That could not possibly be; there must always be in it three American citizens and three citizens or subjects of the other nation; and unless five of the six agree that the issue is an international one which may be settled by the just application of the principles of law and equity in which the whole civilized world agree — arbitration may not be had. If five of the six members agree that it is capable of just settlement by the impartial principles of law and equity, then the Executive and the Senate are bound to take the steps necessary to submit the question to a board of arbitration.

We should not be forced to arbitrate anything, and, of course, on the other hand, we should not be able to secure arbitration for anything, unless two of our own three members agree on it.

The treaties themselves naturally do not state how the members of the Joint High Commission are to be selected. Each nation will name them as it sees fit. The Senate can, if it like, reserve to itself the right to confirm nominations made by the President. I see no objection to that.

IN BALTIMORE ON MAY 3, 1911
PRESIDENT TAFT, THE OFFICIAL HEAD OF THE ARMY AND NAVY, AND SECRETARY OF WAR DICKINSON ARRIVING AT THE PEACE CONFERENCE

There is another feature which has not been appreciated as much as it deserves. In the first place, under these treaties,-before we come to actual arbitration or even to reference to the Joint High Commission for a decision as to whether arbitration is or is not to be had, it is provided that either party to a dispute may postpone action for one year, in order to afford an opportunity for diplomatic discussion and adjustment.

Now, that year's delay would prevent almost any possible war. Wars almost invariably spring from the swift passions of a moment. Almost invariably governments are hurried into some belligerent act by the sudden passion of a people aroused by an accident, a misunderstanding, or an error, which a few days' delay would cure, and a few months' time would erase from the memory. The necessity for a very little delay, the making it impossible for two Powers to rush into hostilities, would remove far more than half the peril of war.

Objection has been made, you know, that the ratification of these treaties would obligate us to submit to outsiders questions so vital as, for instance, the restriction of immigration, the Monroe Doctrine, and the payment of Confederate bonds. Senator Root has proposed to put into the resolution ratifying the treaties a qualification to the effect that they do not authorize the submission to arbitration of "any questions which depend upon or involve the maintenance of the traditional attitude of the United States concerning American questions or other purely Governmental policy."

Senator Root's resolution does no harm, but the subjects which it excepts from those which may be arbitrated were never among them. The treaties as they now stand do not contemplate the arbitration of any questions connected with immigration or the Monroe Doctrine. These are all domestic matters, matters of internal policy, which no other power could bring into question.

What is the good of such a qualification? It is already implicit in the treaties as they stand. All of us in our daily lives are fully subject to the courts of the land. We are responsible for our every act, and we may be haled before the court viding that we shall be free to restrict immigration and to enforce the Monroe Doctrine. Those are national matters — not international. They would never be arbitrated, Root resolution or no Root resolution. As to immigration, there can't be an instant's doubt that it is a purely domestic matter. As to the Monroe Doctrine, I believe that the study of that subject will demonstrate that it, too, is by all the world recognized and accepted as a settled national policy of the United

THE PRESIDENT ON HIS FAVORITE SUBJECT

"CROWDS GROW SILENT AS I APPROACH THAT THEME ; MEN PUT A HAND BEHIND THE EAR AND STAND ON TIP-TOE LEANING FORWARD SO AS NOT TO MISS A WORD"

and our acts questioned, and the decision of the court pronounced. Yet people do not worry lest they have to submit to the judge the internal conduct of their own households.' They don't deem it necessary to draft a bill of rights guaranteeing that a man shall be secure in his inalienable privilege of marrying either a blonde or a brunette as his taste and the opinions of the girls decide. That would be no more absurd than is the amendment pro-

States. A policy which has been continually adhered to for a century, publicly and in the eyes and ears of the whole world, without challenge by any Power, has ceased to be open to question. Prof. John Bassett Moore, than whom there is no higher authority, takes the position that it is a strictly national policy. Sir Edward Grey, Great Britain's Minister of Foreign Affairs, has in words so described it — which makes it probable that

both the French and British governments would acquiesce in that view.

While I am expressing my own views, I may as well say that personally I would go further than these treaties go in the matter of deciding what questions are justiceable. I should be willing to leave the question of whether or not an issue arising between two nations is arbitrable to the decision — not of a Joint High Commission whose finding is practically controlled by a majority of our own representatives upon it — but of the Board of Arbitration itself, which is ultimately

Now, those who object to these treaties in their hearts object to any arbitration; that is all there is about it. They do not realize it themselves, but that is the truth. They will agree to arbitrate everything — which they may themselves fit to arbitrate. That will not go very far.

Either we are in favor of arbitration of issues which are likely to lead to war or we are not.

If we are in favor of war as the only means of settling questions of importance between countries, then let us recognize

A PROUD MOMENT FOR THE PRESIDENT
THE SIGNING OF THE ARBITRATION TREATY, AUGUST 3, 1911, BETWEEN ENGLAND AND THE UNITED STATES BY AMBASSADOR BRYCE. SECRETARY KNOX, AT THE OTHER END OF THE TABLE IS PUTTING HIS NAME TO THE TREATY BETWEEN FRANCE AND THE UNITED STATES. THESE TREATIES ARE NOW AWAITING CONFIRMATION BY THE SENATE

to decide the issue, if it be arbitrable. I should be willing to have that board pass not only upon the merits of the question, but also upon the jurisdiction. In time I have no doubt we shall come to that, but these treaties do not go that far. They do take away from the Executive and the Senate the absolute power to withhold a question from arbitration just because they do not choose to arbitrate it, and yet they do leave the question of arbitration in the hands of a Commission practically controlled by our own members.

it as a principle and decline all arbitration. But if we are really in favor of arbitration as a means of avoiding war, then why should we not be willing to submit to impartial men the decision upon a question rather than leave it to the result of a bloody battle, in which, with the fair cause, we may be beaten, or with an unjust cause, we may conquer? If we are going to substitute reason for force, law for clashing individual wills, the court for the duel, the reign of right for the rule of might — well, we shall-just have to substitute them. It won't do to say we believe in arbitration, and then refuse to arbitrate anything but minor questions about which we care nothing, which we are certain of winning, or which we are willing to lose. You can't have a court on such terms. You can't enforce international law and equity over the affairs of nations by playing fast and loose like that. It is no good talking about the grand principle of international arbitration — and then excepting from the application of that principle all that makes it of any significance.

Of course, a man who in his heart of hearts believes in war and likes it, who is convinced that it is a noble game, strengthening the body and elevating the soul — of course, that man can not be expected to support real arbitration treaties. There are those who were born with this spirit in their breast and who probably do sincerely regard as invertebrate milksops us who are opposed to war.

Some of us really believe in arbitration — believe not only in talking about it, but also in practising it. Some of us so hate war, while we so love the peace of righteousness, that we are willing to submit all our disputes to disinterested judges. We believe that the method of judicial determination is as much juster, wiser, more righteous, more advantageous than war, as the day is clearer, more revealing, more beautiful than the night

President Taft is a man profoundly, religiously impressed with the wickedness of war. He is, furthermore, through all his veins, a believer in the processes of legal judgment. He does not believe that it is necessary to be a man of Berseker soul in order to understand the glory of conflict. He holds that in the battle against disease and ignorance, the battle to win the truths of science and to subjugate nature, man, the man of the future, will find, in a nobler fashion of fighting, a "moral equivalent for war." He does not believe that the gallant soldierly virtues will die out because fields are no longer strewn with dead and widows left weeping in smoldering cities. He believes that finer courage, nobler heroism, will have its opportunity when the leaders of the nations have found wisdom to "guide our feet into the way of peace."

Document No. 13   Arbitration Treaty between the United States and Great Britain (1911)
Source: *International Conciliation* (N.Y., 1912), Pamphlet No. 48, pp. 3-8.

THE TEXT

The United States of America and His Majesty the King of the United Kingdom of Great Britain and Ireland and of the British Dominions beyond the Seas, Emperor of India, being equally desirous of perpetuating the peace, which has happily existed between the two nations, as established in 1814 by the Treaty of Ghent, and has never since been interrupted by an appeal to arms, and which has been confirmed and strengthened in recent years by a number of treaties whereby pending controversies have been adjusted by agreement or settled by arbitration or otherwise provided for; so that now for the first time there are no important questions of difference outstanding between them, and being resolved that no future differences shall be a cause of hostilities between them or interrupt their good relations and friendship;

The High Contracting Parties have, therefore, determined, in furtherance of these ends, to conclude a treaty extending the scope and obligations of the policy of arbitration adopted in their present arbitration treaty of April 4, 1908, so as to exclude certain exceptions contained in that treaty and to provide means for the peaceful solution of all questions of difference which it shall be found impossible in future to settle by diplomacy, and for that purpose they have appointed as their respective Plenipotentiaries:

The President of the United States of America, the Honorable Philander C. Knox, Secretary of State of the United States; and

His Britannic Majesty, the Right Honorable James Bryce, O.M., his Ambassador Extraordinary and Plenipotentiary at Washington;

Who, having communicated to one another their full

powers, found in good and due form, have agreed upon the following articles:

ARTICLE I

All differences hereafter arising between the High Contracting Parties, which it has not been possible to adjust by diplomacy, relating to international matters in which the High Contracting Parties are concerned by virtue of a claim of right made by one against the other under treaty or otherwise, and which are justiciable in their nature by reason of being susceptible of decision by the application of the principles of law or equity, shall be submitted to the Permanent Court of Arbitration established at The Hague by the Convention of October 18, 1907, or to some other arbitral tribunal, as *shall* [may] be decided in each case by special agreement, which special agreement shall provide for the organization of such tribunal if necessary, to define the scope of the powers of the arbitrators, the question or questions at issue, and settle the terms of reference and the procedure thereunder.

The provisions of Articles 37 to 90 inclusive, of the Convention for the Pacific Settlement of International Disputes concluded at the Second Peace Conference at The Hague on the 18th October, 1907, so far as applicable, and unless they are inconsistent with or modified by the provisions of the special agreement to be concluded in each case, and excepting Articles 53 and 54 of such Convention, shall govern the arbitration proceedings to be taken under this Treaty.

The special agreement in each case shall be made on the part of the United States by the President of the United States, by and with the advice and consent of the Senate thereof, His Majesty's Government reserving the right before concluding a special agreement in any matter affecting the interests of a self-governing dominion of the British Empire to obtain the concurrence therein of the government of that dominion.

Such agreements shall be binding when confirmed by the two Governments by an exchange of notes.

Article II

The High Contracting Parties further agree to institute as occasion arises, and as hereinafter provided, a Joint High Commission of Inquiry to which, upon the request of either Party, shall be referred for impartial and conscientious investigation any controversy between the Parties within the scope of Article I, before such controversy has been submitted to arbitration, and also any other controversy hereafter arising between them even if they are not agreed that it falls within the scope of Article I; provided, however, that such reference may be postponed until the expiration of one year after the date of the formal request therefor, in order to afford an opportunity for diplomatic discussion and adjustment of the questions in controversy, if either Party desires such postponement.

Whenever a question or matter of difference is referred to the Joint High Commission of Inquiry, as herein provided, each of the High Contracting Parties shall designate three of its nationals to act as members of the Commission of Inquiry for the purposes of such reference; or the Commission may be otherwise constituted in any particular case by the terms of reference, the membership of the Commission and the terms of reference to be determined in each case by an exchange of notes.

The provisions of Articles 9 to 36, inclusive, of the Convention for the Pacific Settlement of International Disputes concluded at The Hague on the 18th October, 1907, so far as applicable and unless they are inconsistent with the provisions of this Treaty, or are modified by the terms of reference agreed upon in any particular case, shall govern the organization and procedure of the Commission.

Article III

The Joint High Commission of Inquiry, instituted in each case as provided for in Article II, is authorized to examine into and report upon the particular questions or matters referred to it, for the purpose of facilitating the solution of disputes by elucidating the facts, and to define the issues presented by such questions, and also to include in its report such recommendations and conclusions as may be appropriate.

The reports of the Commission shall not be regarded as decisions of the questions or matters so submitted either on the facts or on the law and shall in no way have the character of an arbitral award.

It is further agreed, however, that in cases in which the Parties disagree as to whether or not a difference is subject to arbitration under Article I of this Treaty, that questions shall be submitted to the Joint High Commission of Inquiry; and if all or all but one of the members of the Commission agree and report that such difference is within the scope of Article I, it shall be referred to arbitration in accordance with the provisions of this Treaty.

ARTICLE IV

The Commission shall have power to administer oaths to witnesses and take evidence on oath whenever deemed necessary in any proceeding, or inquiry, or matter within its jurisdiction under this Treaty; and the High Contracting Parties agree to adopt such legislation as may be appropriate and necessary to give the Commission the powers above mentioned, and to provide for the issue of subpœnas and for compelling the attendance of witnesses in the proceedings before the Commission.

On the inquiry both sides must be heard, and each Party is entitled to appoint an Agent, whose duty it shall be to represent his Government before the Commission and to present to the Commission, either personally or through counsel retained for that purpose, such evidence and arguments as he may deem necessary and appropriate for the information of the Commission.

ARTICLE V

The Commission shall meet whenever called upon to make an examination and report under the terms of this Treaty, and the Commission may fix such times and places for its meetings as may be necessary, subject at all times to special call or direction of the two Governments. Each Commissioner, upon the first joint meeting of the Commission after his appointment, shall, before proceeding with the work of the Commission, make and subscribe a solemn declaration in writing that he will faithfully and impartially perform the duties imposed upon him under this Treaty, and such declaration shall be entered on the records of the proceedings of the Commission.

The United States and British sections of the Commission may each appoint a secretary, and these shall act as joint secretaries of the Commission at its joint sessions, and the Commission may employ experts and clerical assistants from time to time as it may deem advisable. The salaries and personal expenses of the Commission and of the agents and counsel and of the secretaries shall be paid by their respective Governments and all reasonable and necessary joint expenses of the Commission incurred by it shall be paid in equal moieties by the High Contracting Parties.

ARTICLE VI

This Treaty shall supersede the Arbitration Treaty concluded between the High Contracting Parties on April 4, 1908, but all agreements, awards, and proceedings under that Treaty shall continue in force and effect and this Treaty shall not affect in any way the provisions of the Treaty of January 11, 1909, relating to questions arising between the United States and the Dominion of Canada.

ARTICLE VII

The present treaty shall be ratified by the President of the United States of America, by and with the advice and consent of the Senate thereof, and by His Britannic Majesty. The ratifications shall be exchanged at Washington as soon as possible and the treaty shall take effect on the date of the exchange of its ratifications. It shall thereafter remain in force continuously unless and until terminated by twenty-four months' written notice given by either High Contracting Party to the other.

In faith whereof the respective Plenipotentiaries have signed this Treaty in duplicate and have hereunto affixed their seals.

Done at Washington the third day of August, in the year of our Lord one thousand nine hundred and eleven.

[SEAL]   PHILANDER C. KNOX
[SEAL]   JAMES BRYCE

I certify that the foregoing is a true copy of the original treaty this day signed.

PHILANDER C. KNOX
Secretary of State

AUGUST 3, 1911

NOTE:—The Treaty with France is identical with that of Great Britain, with the exception of the appropriate verbal changes.

Document No. 14 Lake Mohonk Conference, "The Business Man and International Law" (1911)
Source: *Report of the Seventeenth Annual Lake Mohonk Conference on International Arbitration,* May 24-26, 1911 (Lake Mohonk Conference, 1911), pp. 188-189.

BUSINESS MEN'S BULLETIN NO. 10

THE BUSINESS MAN AND INTERNATIONAL LAW

There is at least one thing upon which business men agree. *Commercial endeavor is best served when law is certain.* This principle is universally recognized and of easy and usual application in domestic trade law. Its force is many times overlooked, however, in the broader fields of business activity even though there is infinitely greater reason for its recognition.

Whether or not one's business is large or small, domestic or foreign, it is affected by the uncertainty of international law. It works out this way. We manufacture and raise more goods and produce in eight months than we consume at home in twelve. The four months' surplus must be either exported or the home capacity for consumption greatly increased. Merchants who have secured foreign markets not only open the avenues to their own output, but by lessening the competition at home, materially assist the man whose business is local. Merchants who supply the home market are interested in an uninterrupted continuance of foreign exports, because any disturbance of foreign trade throws back upon this country goods which must be sold in direct competition with theirs. Therefore, whatever disturbs or embarrasses free commerce, such as war, internal revolution, fear of war or an uncertain international law is a detriment to all commercial activity. The wise business man has taken the cue; he is considering the to-morrows of trade as well as the to-days.

This tendency is best illustrated by comparing the texts of the two Hague Conferences. Read them, The First (1899) was dominated by the monarch and the moralist. Humane conventions predominated. But throughout the Second (1907) may be traced the influence of the business man. In defining and enlarging the rights of neutral nations and nationals, their commerce and shipping, it achieved a work second to none in the field of national endeavor. There is not a business man on the corners who does not profit by some one of its provisions.

No matter how steady the hand, how cool the nerve, how well known the flag, commercial predominance that depends upon battleships, coaling stations and state secrets is at best a thing temporary, containing within itself the germs of its own possible destruction. Gunboat government tends to lawless law. Is it any wonder that our private international law which feebly attempts to harmonize the rules of nations upon such topics as contracts and their interpretation, agency, judgments, bankruptcy, patents, etc., is languishing?

Now that business men realize that the people of other lands are prospective if not actual customers, now that they are thinking in terms of hemispheres, now that they see that successful domestic business leans upon a constant export trade, it is for them to place international relations upon a safe foundation—one that will make possible a certain, universal law. This means that they must discredit the war game no matter who stands ready and willing to play it. War and commercial certainty, like disgruntled litigants, are not on speaking terms.

There are plenty of existing agencies about which to rally in support of international arbitration, treaties of arbitration, international courts, conferences and other forces making for a better and more certain law of nations. The main thing is active co-operation for the desired end.

_____

The foregoing bulletin is taken, by permission, from an article by Harry E. Hunt, Esq., of Detroit, to whom acknowledgment is made.

JAMES WOOD, Mt. Kisco, N. Y., *Chairman*
HARLOW N. HIGINBOTHAM, Chicago
WILLIAM McCARROLL, New York
MARCUS M. MARKS, New York
GEORGE FOSTER PEABODY, New York
ELWYN G. PRESTON, Boston
CHARLES RICHARDSON, Philadelphia
CLINTON ROGERS WOODRUFF, Philadelphia
Committee on Business Organizations

MOHONK LAKE, N. Y., *May 1, 1911.*

Document No. 15 President William Howard Taft, Dollar Diplomacy (1912)
Source: *Supplement to the Message and Papers of the Presidents Covering the Administration of Taft,* pp. 8152-8153.

DOLLAR DIPLOMACY
Extract from Fourth Annual Message of President Taft
December 3, 1912

CHINA

In China the policy of encouraging financial investment to enable that country to help itself has had the result of giving new life and practical application to the open-door policy. The consistent purpose of the present administration has been to encourage the use of American capital in the development of China by the promotion of those essential reforms to which China is pledged by treaties with the United States and other powers. The hypothecation to foreign bankers in connection with certain industrial enterprises, such as the Hukuang railways, of the national revenues upon which these reforms depended, led the Department of State early in the administration to demand for American citizens participation in such enterprises, in order that the United States might have equal rights and an equal voice in all questions pertaining to the disposition of the public revenues concerned. The same policy of promoting international accord among the powers having similar treaty rights as ourselves in the matters of reform, which could not be put into practical effect without the common consent of all, was likewise adopted in the case of the loan desired by China for the reform of its currency. The principle of international cooperation in matters of common interest upon which our policy had already been based in all of the above instances has admittedly been a great factor in that concert of the powers which has been so happily conspicuous during the perilous period of transition through which the great Chinese nation has been passing.

CENTRAL AMERICA NEEDS OUR HELP IN DEBT ADJUSTMENT

In Central America the aim has been to help such countries as Nicaragua and Honduras to help themselves. They are the immediate beneficiaries. The national benefit to the United States is twofold. First, it is obvious that the Monroe doctrine is more vital in the neighborhood of the Panama Canal and the zone of the Caribbean than anywhere else. There, too, the maintenance of that doctrine falls most heavily upon the United States. It is therefore essential that the countries within that sphere shall be removed from the jeopardy involved by heavy foreign debt and chaotic national finances and from the ever-present danger of international complications due to disorder at home. Hence the United States has been glad to encourage and support American bankers who were willing to lend a helping hand to the financial rehabilitation of such countries because this financial rehabilitation and the protection of their customhouses from being the prey of would-be dictators would remove at one stroke the menace of foreign creditors and the menace of revolutionary disorder.

The second advantage of the United States is one affecting chiefly all the southern and Gulf ports and the business and industry of the South. The Republics of Central America and the Caribbean possess great natural wealth. They need only a measure of stability and the means of financial regeneration to enter upon an era of peace and prosperity, bringing profit and happiness to themselves and at the same time creating conditions sure to lead to a flourishing interchange of trade with this country.

I wish to call your especial attention to the recent occurrences in Nicaragua, for I believe the terrible events recorded there during the revolution of the past summer—the useless loss of life, the devastation of property, the bombardment of defenseless cities, the killing and wounding of women and children, the torturing of noncombatants to exact contributions, and the suffering of thousands of human beings—might have been averted had the Department of State, through approval of the loan convention by the Senate, been permitted to carry out its now well-developed policy of encouraging the extending of financial aid to weak Central American States with the primary objects of avoiding just such revolutions by assisting those Republics to rehabilitate their finances, to establish their currency on a stable basis, to remove the customhouses from the danger of revolutions by arranging for their secure administration, and to establish reliable banks.

Document No. 16 David Starr Jordon, "The Impossible War," (1913)
Source: *The Independent*, LXXIV (Feb. 27, 1913), pp. 467-468.

The Impossible War

By David Starr Jordan, M.D., Ph.D., LL.D.

[The remarkable fact that the Great Powers of Europe have refrained from hostilities during the Balkan war, the dilatory negotiations at London and the renewal of the war are the best of evidence that the "power behind the thrones"—*The Unseen Empire*, as President Jordan calls it in his recent book by that title—has decided that it will not pay to provoke a conflict altho it does obviously pay to make people believe that a war is imminent. If such a delicate and involved question as the disposition of European Turkey—the fruitful cause of wars in the past—can be settled by those immediately concerned without involving other nations, it is hard to believe that any difficulty is likely to arise in the future which may not be settled by peaceful methods. President Jordan has in recent years devoted much of his time to the peace movement, which as a biologist he considers primarily from the standpoint of eugenics. His latest contributions to THE INDEPENDENT on the subject are: November 14, 1912, "A Dream of Invasion"; July 6, 1911, "Concerning Sea Power," and December 21, 1905, "War and Peace Decadence."—EDITOR.]

What shall we say of the Great War of Europe, ever threatening, ever impending and which never comes? We shall say that it will never come. Humanly speaking, it is impossible.

Not in the physical sense, of course, for with weak, reckless and godless men nothing evil is impossible. It may be, of course, that some half-crazed archduke or some harassed minister of state will, half unknowing, give the signal for Europe's conflagration. In fact, the agreed signal has been given more than once within the last few months. The tinder is well dried and laid in such a way as to make the worst of this catastrophe. All Europe cherishes is ready for the burning. Yet Europe recoils and will recoil, even in the dread stress of spoil-division of the Balkan War.

Behind the sturdy forms of the Bulgarian farmers lurks the sinister figure of Russian intrigue. Russia and Austria, careless of their neighbors, careless of obligations, find in this their opportunity. And the nations of Europe in their degree are bound to one or the other of these malcontents. Neither Russia nor Austria can be trusted to keep the peace even in her own interest, for both,

thru debt abroad and discontent at home, are in a condition of perpetual crisis.

But accident aside, the Triple Entente lined up against the Triple Alliance, we shall expect no war. Some glimpses of the reasons why appear daily in the press. We read that German and that Austrian banks try in vain to secure short loans in New York, even at 8 per cent. We learn that great bankers refuse absolutely to loan on any terms for war. We learn that on the day of Montenegro's declaration of war the nominal value of stocks and bonds in Europe fell to the extent of nearly 7,000,000,-000. The loss of France alone, the creditor of Europe, is given at $800,-000,000.

At the same time the house of Krupp, greatest builders of war tools, reports a surplus for the year of $12,500,000. A 12 per cent dividend was declared, besides the setting apart of $4,000,000 for welfare work and capital reserves.

The gains of war and war-talk go to the vultures. The cost falls on the people. Whatever else happens the common man stands to lose in war. In such a war as this they all lose mightily.

The number of men who might be

engaged in a general war are thus tabulated by Prof. Charles Richet, of the University of Paris:

	Men.
Austria	2,600,000
England	1,500,000
France	3,400,000
Germany	3,600,000
Italy	2,800,000
Rumania	300,000
Russia	7,000,000
	21,200,000

If these nations, supposed to be diplomatically concerned in the question of whether the obscure Albanian port of Durazzo should fall to Servia or to Austria, neither of the two having the slightest claim to it, should rush into the fight, the expense would run at $55,000,000 per day, a sum to be greatly increased with the sure rise of prices.

The table of Richet (here changed from francs to dollars) deserves most careful attention.

Daily cost of a great European war:

Feed of men	$12,600,000
Feed of horses	1,000,000
Pay (European rates)	4,250,000
Pay of workmen in arsenals and ports	1,000,000
Transportation (60 miles 10 days)	2,100,000
Transportation of provisions.	4,200,000
Munitions: Infantry, 10 cartridges a day	4,200,000
Artillery, 10 shots per day.	1,200,000
Marine, 2 shots per day....	400,000
Equipment	4,200,000
Ambulances, 500,000 wounded or ill ($1 per day)	500,000
Cuirassés	500,000
Reduction of imports	5,000,000
Help to the poor (20c. per day to 1 in 10)	6,800,000
Destruction of towns	2,000,000
Total per day	$54,900,000

To all this we may add the horrors of the air, the cost of aeroplanes and of burning cities which this monstrous abomination of murder may render inhumanly possible. The nation which uses instruments like these against a sister nation can boast no advance over the Red Indian and his scalping knife.

In this connection we must remember that Europe still owes $27,000,-000,000 for old war debts; that her present nominal capital of floating bonds is estimated at $150,000,000,-000; that she has in circulation at present ten to twelve billion dollars of bank notes and that in all her banks and vaults there exists but seven or eight billion dollars of actual coin or bullion, a third of this locked up or tied up in vaults from which it cannot escape. The total of coin money and bullion in circulation in the whole world is not far from $10,000,000,000.

The growth of credit in the last forty years has been without conceivable precedent. The movable credit of Europe in 1871 did not exceed $40,000,000,000.

The masters of credit are staggered at the hazards of present-day war. Wars of a certain class may be tolerated, others may be connived at in the interest of local exploitation, but the great wars—ending perhaps, whoever is victorious, in the total destruction of credit—present appalling risks unknown to any earlier generation.

The bankers will not find the money for such a fight, the industries of Europe will not maintain it, the statesmen cannot. So whatever the bluster or apparent provocation, it comes to the same thing at the end. There will be no general war until the masters direct the fighters to fight. The masters have much to gain, but vastly more to lose and their signal will not be given.

It is not alone the paralysis of debt which checks the rush of armies. The common man is having a word to say. While the waning aristocracy is everywhere for war, and while the man with nothing to lose repeats the echo, the good citizen sees the world in a new light. He is not so ready for a fool's errand to Durazzo as he was a couple of generations ago to enter Sebastopol. The cause of peace has moved forward in these years, and in the only way in which real progress in civilization can be made, the enlightenment of the people.

Stanford University.

Document No. 17   Secretary of State Bryan; A Pacifist in Charge of Our
Foreign Relations (1913)
Source: *The Literary Digest,* XLVI (May 31, 1913), p. 1207-1209.

THE LITERARY DIGEST

PUBLIC OPINION (New York) combined with THE LITERARY DIGEST

Published by Funk & Wagnalls Company (Adam W. Wagnalls, Pres.; Benj. F. Funk, Vice-Pres.; Robert J. Cuddihy, Treas.; W. J. Funk, Sec'y), 44–60 E. 23d St.,New York

Vol. XLVI., No. 22   NEW YORK, MAY 31, 1913   WHOLE NUMBER 1206

TOPICS OF THE DAY

A PACIFIST IN CHARGE
OF OUR FOREIGN RELATIONS

IN THE BRIEF TIME that he has held the portfolio of
State, William Jennings Bryan has shown, in the felicitous
words of a fellow speaker at a recent banquet, "that so far
as he can, he is not going to permit humanity to be crucified on a
cross of war, but instead, that he will work to have it crowned
with the golden crown of peace." Not that the universal
recognition of the Secretary's stand means anything like a
unanimous commendation of what he has said and done. His
course "is winning him new and unaccustomed esteem," in the
opinion of the New York *Evening Post,* which adds graciously
that this is "not the least pleasing aspect of his peace policy."
But other editors grumble at the sight of the Secretary of State
"gadding about" to talk "generalities," and cannot find anything of practical merit in the plans he has announced. According to *The Army and Navy Journal's* way of thinking there is even
danger that the Secretary of State may be hurting the nation's
interest, at the present time, "by his attendance at peace meetings and his declarations that every question should be settled
in a peaceful manner." Mr. Bryan evidently has no such mis-
givings. He has had to carry on difficult negotiations dealing
with protests from a Power sometimes thought of as our great
future rival, yet the faith within him remains unshaken, and he
remarks serenely:

"I made up my mind before I accepted the office of Secretary
of State that I would not take the office if I thought there was to
be a war during my tenure. When I say this I am confident
that I shall have no cause to change my view, for we know no
cause to-day that can not be settled better by reason than by war.

"I believe that there will be no war while I am Secretary of State, and I believe that there will be no war so long as I live, and I hope that we have seen the last great war."

Mr. Bryan's fanciful "two-battleship program," a vision of the day when our Navy shall be made up of the dreadnoughts *Friendship* and *Fellowship*, whose "shells carry good-will" and "are projected by the smokeless powder of love," is of course received by the press either derisively or with kindly good humor. But the Secretary has offered a concrete plan for the promotion of peace which has compelled the newspapers to take it on its merits and to give it serious criticism or commendation. This proposition has been laid before the Senate Foreign Relations Committee, and has been presented to the entire diplomatic corps, assembled expressly for that purpose. The Brooklyn *Eagle* sees in the Bryan plan simply an adaptation to diplomatic purposes of the homely advice: "When angry, count fifty; when very angry, count a hundred." "The prescription for the Bryan 'cooling off' and 'getting sober' medicine," as the New York *Commercial* calls it, is simply the suggestion that all nations adopt, in addition to any arbitration treaties they may be bound by, an agreement something like this:

"The parties hereto agree that all questions of whatever character and nature in dispute between them shall, when diplomatic efforts fail, be submitted for investigation and report to an international commission (the composition to be agreed upon); and the contracting parties agree not to declare war or begin hostilities until such investigation is made and report submitted.

"The investigation shall be conducted as a matter of course upon the initiation of the commission without the formality of a request from either party; the report shall be submitted within (time to be agreed upon) from the date of the submission of the dispute; that the parties hereto reserve the right to act independently of the subject-matter in dispute after the report is considered."

While this is evidently as much an Administration measure as the Taft arbitration treaties, and while Secretary Bryan insists that to President Wilson belongs all credit for "the latest and longest step toward peace," the New York *Herald* (Ind.) contends that W. J. Bryan is really "its proud daddy." And it quotes as authority this passage from Mr. Bryan's own *Commoner:*

"The peace plan which the President authorized the Secretary of State to present to the representatives of foreign nations was presented by Mr. Bryan to a peace congress in London in 1906 and unanimously indorsed by it."

At one of the many dinners that have been given to the delegates who are arranging for the celebration of one hundred years of peace between this country and England, the Secretary of State said of this Wilson-Bryan plan:

"I believe, my friends, that this proposition is as long a step in the direction of peace as has ever been proposed. It does not mean to take the place of arbitration treaties; make all you can; submit to arbitration every question which you can agree to submit; but when you are through you will find, at least we have found thus far, that there are certain questions that are excepted.

"And they are so important that they themselves become the cause of war. And it is the purpose of this plan to close the gap and to leave no question to become a cause of war. It is the belief of the President, it is his earnest hope, that when these treaties have been made, or agreements if you prefer to call them such, agreements between this nation and all the other nations severally, by which there will be investigation before hostilities begin, it is his belief, it is his hope, that war will become practically impossible."

This proposition "places the United States in the leadership of the peace movement," declares the Pittsburg *Dispatch* (Rep.),

THE NEW MARINE PAINTER.
—Berryman in the Washington *Star*.

and the Indianapolis *News* (Ind.), New York *Evening Post* (Ind.), Boston *Advertiser* (Rep.), and Chicago *Tribune* (Prog.) are equally confident of its value. The New York *Times* (Ind.) speaks of it as "one of those rare ventures in the field of world affairs of which it may be said that it can do no possible harm, and may do much good." True,

"It would by no means necessarily prevent all wars, for war is sometimes the only final arbitrament. But it would tend to prevent all but the truly inevitable contests. It would, moreover, be in the direct line of the traditional policy of the United States with reference to the peaceful adjudication of international disputes, and it would very powerfully reinforce that policy. It would, indeed, in most cases, make resort to arbitration unnecessary, for if we engaged to study all causes of difference, in cooperation with the other Government, for a year or half a year, the chances are many that we should come to an agreement without outside aid. . . . It will be a national and an international gain if it be adopted."

Yet the Brooklyn *Eagle* (Dem.), which believes that nations would often find the "cooling-off" process of distinct value, notes this "serious objection" to the Bryan plan:

"It does not and can not prevent a nation secretly resolved on war from carrying on preparations for war during the whole period of investigation by the proposed international commission. It is quite conceivable that the opportunity given for the 'cooling-off' process might be abused by one of the contracting parties so far as to obtain a distinct advantage over the other when the time came to throw diplomacy and arbitration overboard."

Other dailies, like the Philadelphia *Inquirer* (Rep.), Detroit *Free Press* (Ind.), and Chicago *Inter Ocean* (Rep.), think the Administration's plan "harmless, but futile." *The Inter Ocean* argues that modern wars are not entered upon in sudden anger. It takes two typical instances:

"The blowing up of the *Maine* but struck into flame the smoldering conviction of two or three generations of Americans that some day we would have to kick Spain out of Cuba. The Balkan declaration of war was unexpected to those who assumed the inevitable military superiority of the Turk, but the Bulgarians had been preparing to fight ever since the Treaty of Berlin."

In a recent Sunday peace sermon in Washington, Secretary Bryan paid his respects to the business interests and the newspapers which he says are behind the "war-scare" talk. To quote from his remarks given in the press accounts:

"The world is learning that back of much of the furor for war, back of much of the stirring of the passions of the people, is the interest in armor-plate and in battle-ships on the part of corporations whose business it is to build those battle-ships and to make this armor-plate. It has even been found that men in one country will spend the money to stir up in another country a feeling against their own country. If you can think of a baser use of money than that you will have an inventive genius of which you may be proud.

"Not only that, but I believe that with a larger intelligence the people will begin to discriminate between patriotic newspapers and newspapers which are more interested in big headlines and sensational news than in the spread of truth."

The new and "refreshing thing" in all this, according to the New York *Evening Post*, "is to have a Secretary of State, especially concerned as he is in maintaining friendly relations with other countries, take the public into his confidence and courageously point out the selfish and insidious enemies of peace."

But *The Army and Navy Journal* (New York) takes a far different view of Mr. Bryan's utterances. Such a remark as "I know no cause that can not be settled better by reason than by arms" may easily, it declares, "be misconstrued by foreign jingoes as an evidence of national weakness." Further:

"It may not only create in Japan a misinterpretation of the temper of the American people, but it is likely to show the people of California that the negotiations with Japan are being conducted by the State Department through the intermediary of a doctrinaire who is actuated more by devotion to his abstract theories of right than by a just estimate of the actual conditions confronting the Californians."

We have already seen, says *The Journal*, melancholy examples

BUSY DAYS FOR THE HANDY MAN.
—Sykes in the Philadelphia *Public Ledger*.

185

"of a wrong reading of the fighting pulse of a nation." One was the erroneous opinion in the South before the Civil War that the North lacked fighting spirit. "Again, before the Spanish-American War, the people of Spain had been deluded into the belief that their navy was superior to that of the United States." These examples inspire *The Journal* to ask whether, in this case,

"Mr. Bryan is not treading dangerously near the border-line not only of good taste, but also of diplomatic propriety, in raising his voice now in favor of settling all questions without war."

Document No. 18 President Woodrow Wilson, "A New Latin-American Policy" (1913)
Source: *The Public Papers of Woodrow Wilson,* edited by Ray S. Baker and William E . Dodd, (4 vols.; N.Y.: Harper and Brothers, 1926), Vol. III, *The New Democracy,* pp. 64-69.

A NEW LATIN-AMERICAN POLICY

ADDRESS DELIVERED BEFORE THE SOUTHERN COM-
MERCIAL CONGRESS AT MOBILE, ALA., OCTOBER 27,
1913. FROM OFFICIAL PUBLICATION IN MR. WIL-
SON'S FILES.

IT is with unaffected pleasure that I find myself here to-day. I once before had the pleasure, in another southern city, of addressing the Southern Commercial Congress. I then spoke of what the future seemed to hold in store for this region, which so many of us love and toward the future of which we all look forward with so much confidence and hope. But another theme directed me here this time. I do not need to speak of the South. She has, perhaps, acquired the gift of speaking for herself. I come because I want to speak of our present and prospective relations with our neighbors to the south. I deemed it a public duty, as well as a personal pleasure, to be here to express for myself and for the Government I represent the welcome we all feel to those who represent the Latin American States.

The future, ladies and gentlemen, is going to be very different for this hemisphere from the past. These States lying to the south of us, which have always been our neighbors, will now be drawn closer to us by innumerable ties, and, I hope, chief of all, by the tie of a common understanding of each other. Interest does not tie nations together; it sometimes separates them. But sympathy and understanding does unite them, and I believe that by the new route that is just about to be opened, while we physically cut two continents asunder, we spiritually unite them. It is a spiritual union which we seek.

I wonder if you realize, I wonder if your imaginations have been filled with the significance of the tides of commerce. Your governor alluded in very fit and striking terms to the voyage of Columbus, but Columbus took his voyage under compulsion of circumstances. Constantinople had been captured by the Turks and all the routes of trade with the East had been suddenly closed. If there was not a way across the Atlantic to open those routes again, they were closed forever, and Columbus set out not to discover America, for he did not know that it existed, but to discover the eastern shores of Asia. He set sail for Cathay and stumbled upon America. With that change in the outlook of the world, what happened? England, that had been at the back of Europe with an unknown sea behind her, found that all things had turned as if upon a pivot and she was at the front of Europe; and since then all the tides of energy and enterprise that have issued out of Europe have seemed to be turned westward across the Atlantic. But you will notice that they have turned westward chiefly north of the Equator and that it is the northern half of the globe that has seemed to be filled with the media of intercourse and of sympathy and of common understanding.

Do you not see now what is about to happen? These great tides which have been running along parallels of latitude will now swing southward athwart parallels of latitude, and that opening gate at the Isthmus of Panama will open the world to a commerce that she has not known before, a commerce of intelligence, of thought and sympathy between North and South. The Latin American States, which, to their disadvantage, have been off the main lines, will now be on the main lines. I feel that these gentlemen honoring us with their presence to-day will presently find that some part, at any rate, of the center of gravity of the world has shifted. Do you realize that New York, for example, will be nearer the western coast of South America than she is now to the eastern coast of South America? Do you realize that a line drawn northward parallel with the greater part of the western coast of South America will run only about 150 miles west of New York? The great bulk of South America, if you will look at your globes (not at your Mercator's projection), lies eastward of the continent of North America. You will realize that when you realize that the canal will run southeast, not southwest, and that when you get into the Pacific you will be farther east than you were when you left the Gulf of Mexico. These things are significant, therefore, of this, that we are closing one chapter in the history of the world and are opening another, of great, unimaginable significance.

There is one peculiarity about the history of the Latin American States which I am sure they are keenly aware of. You hear of "concessions" to foreign capitalists in Latin America. You do not hear of concessions to foreign capitalists in the United States. They are not granted concessions. They are invited to make investments. The work is ours, though they are welcome to invest in it. We do not ask them to supply the capital and do the work. It is an invitation, not a privilege; and States that are obliged, because their territory does not lie within the main field of modern enterprise and action, to grant concessions are in this condition, that foreign interests are apt to dominate their domestic affairs, a condition of affairs always dangerous and apt to become intolerable. What these States are going to see, therefore, is an emancipation from the subordination, which has been inevitable, to foreign enterprise and an assertion of the splendid character which, in spite of these difficulties, they have again and again been able to demonstrate. The dignity, the courage, the self-possession, the self-respect of the Latin American States, their achievements in the face of all these adverse circumstances, deserve nothing but the admiration and applause of the world. They have had harder bargains driven with them in the matter of loans than any other peoples in the world. Interest has been exacted of them that was not exacted of anybody else, because the risk was said to be greater; and then securities were taken that destroyed the risk—an admirable arrangement for those who were forcing the terms! I rejoice in nothing so much as in the prospect that they will now be emancipated from these conditions, and we ought to be the first to take part in assisting in that emancipation. I think some of these gentlemen have already had occasion to bear witness that the Department of State in recent months has tried to serve them in that wise. In the future they will draw closer and closer to us because of circumstances of which I wish to speak with moderation and, I hope, without indiscretion.

We must prove ourselves their friends, and champions upon terms of equality and honor. You cannot be friends upon any other terms than upon the terms of equality. You cannot be friends at all except upon the terms of honor. We must show ourselves friends by comprehending their interest whether it squares with our own interest or not. It is a very perilous thing to determine the foreign policy of a nation in the terms of material interest. It not only is unfair to those with whom you are dealing, but it is degrading as regards your own actions.

Comprehension must be the soil in which shall grow all the fruits of friendship, and there is a reason and a compulsion lying behind all this which is dearer than anything else to the thoughtful men of America. I mean the development of constitutional liberty in the world. Human rights, national integrity, and opportunity as against material interests—that, ladies and gentlemen, is the issue which we now have to face. I want to take this occasion to say that the United States will never again seek one additional foot of territory by conquest. She will devote herself to showing that she knows how to make honorable and fruitful use of the territory she has, and she must regard it as one of the duties of friendship to see that from no quarter are material interests made superior to human liberty and national opportunity. I say this, not with a single thought that anyone will gainsay it, but merely to fix in our consciousness what our real relationship with the rest of America is. It is the relationship of a family of mankind devoted to the development of true constitutional liberty. We know that that is the soil out of which the best enterprise springs. We know that this is a cause which we are making in common with our neighbors, because we have had to make it for ourselves.

Reference has been made here to-day to some of the national problems which confront us as a Nation. What is at the heart of all our national problems? It is that we have seen the hand of material interest sometimes about to close upon our dearest rights and possessions. We have seen material interests threaten constitutional freedom in the United States. Therefore we will now know how to sympathize with those in the rest of America who have to contend with such powers, not only within their borders but from outside their borders also.

I know what the response of the thought and heart of America will be to the program I have outlined, because America was created to realize a program like that. This is not America because it is rich. This is not America because it has set up for a great population great opportunities of material prosperity. America is a name which sounds in the ears of men everywhere as a synonym with individual opportunity because a synonym of individual liberty. I would rather belong to a poor nation that was free than to a rich nation that had ceased to be in love with liberty. But we shall not be poor if we love liberty, because the nation that loves liberty truly sets every man free to do his best and be his best, and that means the release of all the splendid energies of a great people who think for themselves. A nation of employees cannot be free any more than a nation of employers can be.

In emphasizing the points which must unite us in sympathy and in spiritual interest with the Latin American peoples we are only emphasizing the points of our own life, and we should prove ourselves untrue to our own traditions if we proved ourselves untrue friends to them.

Do not think, therefore, gentlemen, that the questions of the day are mere questions of policy and diplomacy. They are shot through with the principles of life. We dare not turn from the principle that morality and not expediency is the thing that must guide us and that we will never condone iniquity because it is most convenient to do so. It seems to me that this is a day of infinite hope, of confidence in a future greater than the past has been, for I am fain to believe that in spite of all the things that we wish to correct the nineteenth century that now lies behind us has brought us a long stage toward the time when, slowly ascending the tedious climb that leads to the final uplands, we shall get our ultimate view of the duties of mankind. We have breasted a considerable part of that climb and shall presently—it may be in a generation or two—come out upon those great heights where there shines unobstructed the light of the justice of God.

Document No. 19   Frederick Lynch, "Peace and War in 1913" (1914)
Source: The Yale Review, III, new series (January, 1914), pp. 272-284.

PEACE AND WAR IN 1913

By Frederick Lynch

THE peace advocates during 1913 have daily been subjected to the irritating experience of the Psalmist, who
was taunted with the question: "Where is now thy God?"
"Where now is your peace movement?" has been the query
on many lips.   It has been asked, too, not only by the
scoffers but by the well-wishers—those who had hoped, until
1913, that the dawn of law, good-will, international fraternity, was in sight.   It is not strange that even some of those
who have hoped and worked for the cause should have
become discouraged, and surely the scoffer seems to have
had some grounds for his cynicism.   For months two great
groups of people, the allied Balkan States on one side, and
Turkey on the other, throwing away all semblance of civiliza-
on, ignoring all rules of modern warfare, determined only
o exterminate each other, were grappling in the maddest and
most cruel fighting Europe has witnessed for generations.
The warfare did not stop with the soldiers; but women and
children were slain with equal ferocity and inhumanities
practised which all men thought had disappeared forever.
Another discouraging element was the absolute ignoring of
the Hague Tribunal, and any suggestion that the issues at
stake be settled by arbitration.   The questions were all of
a judicial nature, could have been amicably adjusted before
an impartial tribunal, or at least the attempt could have been
made and the nature of the dispute have been clearly defined
before the world.   But the Balkan States would have none
of this.   The time had come when, combined, they could get
revenge on Turkey—drive her out, get her European hold-
ings.   And without the semblance of seeking justice a war
began, a war which, from the beginning, has been marked

by no spirit higher than revenge, acquisition of territory, and lust of fighting.

At the conclusion of this war, and after enormous losses on both sides, the Turks were driven back into Constantinople. Then the allied states, already depleted and exhausted beyond recovery, turned upon one another with a ferocity surpassing that shown towards the Turks. Europe advised and offered mediation. The friends of the Balkan States said that they were committing suicide and pleaded. But it was all of no avail. The lust of killing had been aroused and could not be quenched. Old hatreds welled up again. Mutual jealousies and fears over the division of the spoils taken from the Turks dissipated all hope of future unity; and as a result, these wars, whose atrocities the newspapers could not print, broke loose. The pages of these wars are among the blackest Europe has known and can only be matched in the days of the Huns and Vandals. Indeed, men who visited the fields of battle, believe that no wars of the savagest races of any time ever stained Europe with such foul deeds. It is quite easy, from all one can gather from history, to believe that the ancient tribes of Gaul and Germany did not cut little babies to pieces before their mothers' eyes, although they probably did enjoy cutting of the ears and noses of their victims as much as the Allies did. The whole conflict was a signal illustration of a truth which those who have studied wars learned long ago: that war breed not peace, but more wars.

While these wars were in progress, Germany—perhaps frightened by the uneasiness in the European situation caused by the Balkan strife—suddenly announced her intention of increasing the war budget by $250,000,000. This meant that in a time of peace, the army and navy should practically be put upon a war basis. The burden of this extra $250,000,000 can only be imagined when one remembers what Germany was already spending upon preparation for war. At first there was much protest. But finally the proposal was accepted by the people in a great wave of patriotism, undulled by the revelation of the share that the armament makers had in securing this new appropriation; and even the Social Democrats, the avowed enemies of armament and war, were drawn into the maelstrom of patriotism, Bebel himself having written, shortly before he died, a letter defending the increased military preparations of the Emperor.

In the nature of things, this act of Germany compelled every other nation in Europe to hasten to increase its military strength in the same proportion that Germany had increased hers. France immediately took a great and costly step and added one year to the period of military service. This meant, as Anatole France pointed out, the diversion not only of millions of dollars from industry, science, education, and art, but the quenching of the best genius of the land—the genius just awakening in youth. It will now go to waste in barracks. Austria, Italy, Russia, and of course England, prepared for great increases, and even little neutral countries, such as Belgium, caught the military fever and began to arm. It has now reached such a stage that the next thing is, as Mr. Alfred Noyes has said, "the bottomless pit."

The year 1913 has also witnessed an unusually active war propaganda, not only on the part of the militarists and those who believe in war as a necessity of national defense and existence, or who distrust the efficacy of arbitration and World Courts, but also on the part of those who believe that war in itself is a good thing. General von Bernhardi of Germany has published a widely read book openly praising war, and hinting that the best thing that could possibly happen would be for Germany to make war upon France at once, to expand her territory by force before it is too late, and to have nothing to do with arbitration and Hague Courts. The adoption of arbitration spells ruin. War is even a Christian institution. In England, Lord Roberts has been stumping the country in favor of compulsory military service, and painting dire conditions of England's fate. In Australia, conscription has become a law, and the boys who do not run away (as many are doing) are taken out of school and trades in order to be trained how to kill somebody instead of how to make something. In our own country, the militarists and the Navy League have been more active than ever. Foiled in one direction, they turned in others. All this advocacy, during 1913, of paid militia, training boys in school to shoot, introducing military instruction into colleges, building up vast navies, betrays an unusual activity of militarists and manufacturers who profit from war. Their success has not been conspicuous; but their activity has been very great, and that is our present point.

It is no wonder, then, that some people ask: "What has become of the peace movement? Are not the peace workers discouraged before this outburst of savagery, before this revival of militarism? Has the peace cause made any gains in the face of these things? Can it show any cause for our allegiance and our energies?" The answer is that, in spite of all these seeming setbacks, the peace movement, proceeding quietly along beside the din of war, has made during 1913 some of the most notable gains of recent years; and one or two steps have been taken that hold more promise of the ultimate substitution of judicial methods for war in the settlement of international disputes than anything that has happened since the calling of the First Hague Conference. It is well to emphasize these gains constantly in this year of wars and frenzied militarism.

First of all, let us remember that it was in this year that Mr. Bryan made his proposals to the nations to sign treatie with the United States, whereby the contracting partie should agree not to go to war over any kind of dispute, o even make preparations for war, until an international com mittee of five members had thoroughly examined the poin at issue to see whether it could not be amicably adjusted b judicial methods. A year is allowed for the investigations, deliberations, and report of this committee. Each nation is free to abide by the recommendations of this committee or not, as it chooses. But if Mr. Bryan can get the nations to sign these treaties—and he says the outlook is decidedly favorable,—and if our reactionary Senate can be coerced into ratifying them, the greatest step forward that the peace movement has known, will have been taken. They practically amount to absolute treaties. For it is almost inconceivable to think that any two civilized nations would ever go to war over any question whatsoever, after a year had elapsed in which passions could cool, and after a commission, chosen by both parties to the dispute, had recommended, as the result of careful study, that the question was justiciable. At this writing, one nation has already signed one of these treaties with the United States. America has the opportunity, in the ratification of these treaties by her Senate, to become preëminently the leader of the nations into the realm of justice and good will. In after years they will be remembered as the finest fruit of 1913, when Turkish-Balkan wars are forgotten.

Another thing which astute students of international politics are rightly construing as among the most marked signs of a new spirit in Europe, surely due to the agitation of the peace movement and the Hague Conferences, is this: that the five great powers of Europe—Great Britain, Russia, Germany, France, and Austria—have worked together through this whole Balkan crisis in a concert hitherto unknown. Professor John B. Clark, of Columbia University, has referred to this as a most remarkable sign of the impression the peace movement has made upon Europe; and Sir Edward Grey has publicly called the attention of Europe to the fact with great satisfaction. Mr. Norman Angell, author of "The Great Illusion," and an astute observer of international politics, considers this the most advanced step in the peace movement; in a letter written for the War Number of "Life"—entitled "How Long Before Universal Peace?"—he singled out this fact for special emphasis. His words are so significant that we quote them here. Mr. Angell calls attention to the fact that the cessation of military conflict between such powers as France and Germany, Germany and England, and Germany and Russia, has come already; that the nation which we have all been taught to regard as the most military in the world—Germany—has not gone to real war for forty years; that it is becoming more and more evident that nothing will induce these nations to use their preposterous military instruments if they can possibly avoid it. He then says: "All the military wiseacres prophesied the Armageddon apropos of the break-up of Turkey. We were told that the conflicts which would arise would inevitably throw the great powers at one another. Yet every imaginable situation of high politics has been created, and every imaginable interest touched during the course of the Balkan trouble, and the more dangerous the situation got, the less was shown by either nations or governments the disposition to go to war." This same truth has recently been emphasized by President David Starr Jordan. "Great international wars," he says, "are already practically at an end. This the 'Concert of Europe' has shown. Powerless for anything else, it keeps the peace." And it surely is significant that when Mr. Carnegie was passing by the German Emperor at the grand reception during the recent Jubilee, the Emperor, the moment he saw Mr. Carnegie, shouted in a loud voice: "Twenty-five years of peace, Mr. Carnegie, and I hope there will be twenty-five more."

The year 1913 has witnessed another event full of happy augury for the future triumph of law over war, justice over might, namely: the dedication of the Peace Palace at The Hague on the twenty-ninth of August. It is not possible to overestimate its significance. Soon after the First Hague Conference in 1889, the Hon. Andrew D. White had a conference with **Mr.** Carnegie at Skibo Castle, Scotland, in which he suggested how desirable it would be for the Hague Tribunal, and the Hague Court, after it should be organized, to have a home. This would also serve as a meeting place for future Hague Conferences and international gatherings. He was reinforced by Baron d'Estournelles de Constant, who laid before Mr. Carnegie the fact that the world would hold the Hague Tribunal in infinitely higher respect if it had a home. As a result of these conversations with Dr. White and Baron d'Estournelles, Mr. Carnegie conceived the idea of the Palace of Peace, a great structure, which was to include what had been suggested and much more; it was to be indeed a temple of justice, law, good will, and human brotherhood. The Palace was completed last August and dedicated with imposing ceremonies in the presence of delegates from every nation. All the nations of the world have contributed to its furnishings. Here the periodic Hague Conferences will meet; here the Tribunal will be assembled to sit on cases, awaiting the organization of the Permanent Court. But the mere fact of a building and a room being ready for this court will enable the coming Third Hague Conference to hasten the formation of this permanent court of nations, corresponding to the Supreme Court of the United States.

It should also be a great source of encouragement to all who seek peace that, while war has been rampant and the militarists insistent, the peace cause has attracted more attention than ever, its strength has greatly increased, and the peace workers have been more active. Thus, there have been in 1913 eight or ten of the most successful and widely reported peace congresses that have yet been held. The national congresses in England, Germany, France, and the United States, have far surpassed those of previous years, both in the character of those attending them and in the general interest shown. The American congress, held in St. Louis in May, is a good instance. Not only was it large in numbers but the most representative men were in attendance—statesmen, jurists, ministers, educators, editors, and business men of national reputation. Indeed, so far as our own country is concerned, the leading men in all ranks of life are becoming more and more actively interested in the movement to substitute judicial methods for war, and courts for battles—for that is the peace movement, or, to put it in other words, it is to persuade nations to have recourse to those methods of settling disputes that all civilized individuals everywhere pursue. Mr. Hamilton Holt, in a speech at the dinner given at New York, on September eighteenth, to the visiting *Corda Fratres,* the students' Cosmopolitan Clubs of Europe, remarked that he knew only two college presidents in America who were not in heartiest sympathy with the peace movement. Over sixty chambers of commerce have passed resolutions. The leading pastors of the churches are enrolled in the great Church Peace League of America, of which Bishop David H. Greer, of New York, is President. The Lake Mohonk Conference of 1913 brought together over four hundred of the most distinguished men of America. The meeting of the International Peace Congress at The Hague last August was more largely attended than any previous congress, and by more representative men. It was followed by the meeting of the Interparliamentary Union, which devoted much of its time to impressing the importance of Mr. Bryan's peace proposals upon the world. And while the war was raging in the Balkans, a large delegation of representative Englishmen was spending a week in America with representative Americans, planning not only how to celebrate the one hundred years of unbroken peace between the British Empire and the United States but how to perpetuate it another hundred years. In New York, a large group of eminent men has met three times to urge upon the nations immediate steps for calling the Third Hague Conference.

We should also bear in mind that there has been in 1913

a remarkable increase in peace literature. Every month has seen a production of such books as Mrs. Spencer Trask's "In the Vanguard," President David Starr Jordan's "Unseen Empire," Mrs. Lucia Ames Mead's "Swords and Ploughshares," and Wilhelm Lamszu's "The Human Slaughterhouse" (which has reached a sale of 100,000 copies in Germany). The periodicals have printed ten times more peace articles than ever, while several prizes for peace essays have been offered to the college students of America and England. In 1913, too, have been founded the two great Church Peace Leagues of Canada and the United States, lining up in their membership thousands of the clergy and church workers of both countries.

A most significant fact of 1913 has been the increase of friendly feeling between Germany and England, after several years of tension which has often been near the breaking point. When one considers that everywhere Germany turns in her new era of expansion, she finds England occupying the earth; that the Englishman is sometimes arrogant in his lordly appropriation of creation; that the German is also feeling his new position of power in the world; that a mad race of armaments has been going on for years; that in both nations there are groups of so-called statesmen, editors, generals, and manufacturers, who have been spending all their energies in the endeavor to plunge England and Germany into war—when one remembers all this, he realizes the hold that the peace movement has upon these two nations, inasmuch as it has been able not only to restrain them from war, but slowly to establish a more friendly relationship between them. Last summer a French statesman told the writer of this paper—we had just come from a session of the Interparliamentary Union in Geneva, where British and German relationships were being discussed—that "if there had not been in Europe two Hague Conferences, at which the nations had morally, if not by treaty, committed themselves to the arbitrational ideal, and where they had all had their minds turned towards the possibility of the peaceable methods of settling disputes, Germany and France would certainly have gone to war over the Moroccan incident, and Germany and England would probably not have been able to keep the peace, considering the irritation that existed." I am inclined to think that there is much truth in my friend's remark, and I have heard it corroborated by many other eminent men in Europe. The year 1913 has at last found Germany and England talking the possibilities of peace, and all the European nations have come to recognize the sentiment for peace as something to be considered. The sudden activity of the militarists, already referred to, is largely due to the rapidly growing extent of this movement to substitute judicial processes for war. It has come to be a movement that must be reckoned with. General Bernhardi's book betrays this fear on every page; and the English book, "The Struggle for Bread," by "A Rifleman," is a direct answer to Norman Angell's "Great Illusion."

While Germany and England have come more closely together, a meeting of German and French parliamentarians at the Berne Peace Bureau last summer should not be overlooked, for they separated with the promise to use all their powers to counteract those fire-eaters who would plunge the two great nations into war. Indeed, this event is one of the most significant happenings of the year. Dr. Albert Gobat, Director of the Berne Bureau, persuaded several members of the Swiss National Council to unite with him in inviting a selected list of members of the French and German parliaments to meet in Berne with the view of discussing what could be done to increase friendly understanding between Germany and France. The invitations were accepted by over two hundred French Deputies and Members of the Reichstag. At this meeting, the following resolutions were unanimously passed; and Baron d'Estournelles de Constant, who presided, did well to ask if these resolutions did not mark a new departure in European politics:

The first conference of members of the French and German parliaments, assembled at Berne on May 11, 1913, energetically repudiates any share in the detestable campaigns of chauvinistic incitations of all kinds, and the guilty speculations which threaten to mislead the good sense and patriotism of the people on both sides of the frontier.

It knows, and publicly affirms, that the immense majority in both countries are firmly attached to peace as the only condition of progress.

It undertakes constant action in order to dissipate misunderstandings and to prevent conflicts, and it heartily thanks the representatives of Alsace-Lorraine for having, by their noble declarations, adopted unanimously, facilitated an understanding between the two countries for the common work of civilization.

It invites its members to make every effort to persuade the governments of the great powers to reduce their naval and military expenditure.

The conference warmly supports the proposal of Mr. Bryan, Secretary of State of the United States of America, with reference to treaties of arbitration. It urges that any disputes which may arise between the two countries, and which cannot be settled by diplomacy, may be referred to the arbitration of The Hague Court, and it relies on its members to carry on an energetic and sustained action in this direction.

It considers that an understanding between France and Germany would facilitate the *entente* between the two great European groups, and thereby prepare the establishment of a lasting peace.

The work of the two great Peace Foundations has gone steadily on during the year. There has been considerable feeling abroad that somehow or other the Carnegie Endowment, with the large sums at its disposal, is not exercising the influence that it should in the movement. A careful perusal of its Year Book should be made, however, before judgment is passed. Evidently the Endowment intends to devote itself to the more academic side of the movement, with the feeling that in the long run it will aid the peace cause best by laying deep foundations for future civilizations, which shall be based on justice rather than on force. Yet, many think that it missed the greatest opportunity it will have in years to advance the sentiment against war.

Just when Europe and America were so outraged over the unspeakable horrors of the Balkan War, perhaps it should have taken every cent of its income—a million dollars would not have been too much—and flooded the nation with pamphlets giving the fullest details of the atrocities, and containing articles by the best writers of the two continents showing what war really is, and how it breeds only more war.   There are times when one great stroke at the psychological moment counts for more than years of academic investigation.   The Endowment did send a commission to the Balkans after the wars were over to gather what information it could. Professor Samuel T. Dutton, of Teachers College, Columbia University, was the American representative, and his report contains many facts and suggestions of great value.   But the Endowment might have rendered unparalleled service to the peace movement had it had a group of men in the Balkans during the whole war, and let the entire world know just what was going on.   An Englishman recently remarked: "Pierre Loti's letter from the Balkans in the 'Daily Telegraph' for August twenty-fourth has done more for the peace cause than anything that has happened in twenty years."   And yet the work the Endowment is doing is valuable,—if it will only remember that no one cares how much *money* wars cost.

In closing this review of forces making for peace, too much emphasis cannot be placed on the fact that the wars themselves have been great factors in promoting peace sentiment.   The Balkan War has made innumerable converts to the peace cause.   It has revolted the twentieth-century conscience.   It has made thousands ask the question that "Life" asked under its famous picture: "Must It Always Be?"   More men than ever have said, "Surely there must be some better way!"   Many are saying, "Is what one gets worth the price paid for it?"   This change of heart has been noticeable in the daily press.   There has been a distinct progress towards the advocacy of judicial methods during the year. This has not all been due to the exhibition of savage hatred in the Balkans, nor to the inhuman atrocities perpetrated by all concerned, but it has partly come about from the revelation of the futility of it all. Hundreds and thousands of lives have been lost, thousands of homes are fatherless and poverty stricken, the nations are bankrupt and without resources for the future; for the next hundred years taxes will be of abnormal proportions; worst of all, there are no young men left to breed a future race. The Allies have gained nothing after all this fearful cost. They have come more than ever under the dominance of the great powers, for every war loan increases this dominance. In the partition of territory by the powers, some of the states are worse off than ever, and hatreds and jealousies have been engendered which simply mean future wars unless the powers intervene. It has all caused many to ask if wars accomplish anything in the long run that could not much better be gained by judicial and peaceable methods. I have a lurking suspicion, from what I heard in Italy last year, that many Italians feel the same way after the war in Tripoli. However this may be, the wars of 1913 have produced a very noticeable reaction, and the friends of peace would do well to make the most of it. Moreover, the scandals in Germany, where a very strong suspicion has been aroused that manufacturers of war materials have been deliberately fermenting war scares to frighten nations into buying more armaments, have thoroughly disgusted great crowds of people with the whole military system. Everywhere, in England and America, as well as in Germany, many have been asking: "Who starts war scares? Who advocates increase of armaments and big navies?" Yes, "Who originates wars themselves?" After twenty years of most intimate contact with the peace movement, I feel very strongly that in 1913 the sentiment is more widely held than ever before that the time has come to base civilization on law instead of war, justice instead of brute force, gospel instead of guns.

Document No. 20 Conciliation or "Cooling-off" Treaty between the United States and Great Britain (1914)

Source: U.S. Congress, Senate Document No. 348, *Treaties, Conventions, International Acts, Protocols, and Agreements between the United States and Other Powers, 1910-1923,* 67th Congress, 4th Session, (Washington, D.C.: U.S. Government Printing Office, 1923), III, pp. 2642-2644.

1914.

Treaty for the Advancement of Peace.

Signed at Washington September 15, 1914; ratification advised by the Senate September 25, 1914; ratified by the President November 4, 1914; ratified by Great Britain October 8, 1914; ratifications exchanged at Washington November 10, 1914; proclaimed November 11, 1914.

(Treaty Series, No. 602; 38 Statutes at Large, 1853.)

ARTICLES.

I. All disputes not settled by diplomacy or under existing agreements to be referred to commission before resort to hostilities.

II. Composition and appointment of commission.

III. Reference of disputes; procedure if British self-governing dominions are concerned; time and effect of report.

IV. Does not affect provisions of Canadian boundary waters treaty of 1909.

V. Ratification; duration.

The President of the United States of America and His Majesty the King of the United Kingdom of Great Britain and Ireland and of the British Dominions beyond the Seas, Emperor of India, being desirous to strengthen the bonds of amity that bind them together and also to advance the cause of general peace, have resolved to enter into a treaty for that purpose, and to that end have appointed as their plenipotentiaries:

The President of the United States, the Honorable William Jennings Bryan, Secretary of State of the United States; and

His Britannic Majesty, the Right Honorable Sir Cecil Arthur Spring-Rice, G. C. V. O., K. C. M. G., etc., His Ambassador Extraordinary and Plenipotentiary at Washington;

Who, after having communicated to each other their respective full powers, found to be in proper form, have agreed upon and concluded the following articles:

ARTICLE I.

The High Contracting Parties agree that all disputes between them, of every nature whatsoever, other than disputes the settlement of which is provided for and in fact achieved under existing agreements between the High Contracting Parties, shall, when diplomatic methods of adjustment have failed, be referred for investigation and report to a permanent International Commission, to be constituted in the manner prescribed in the next succeeding article; and they agree not to declare war or begin hostilities during such investigation and before the report is submitted.

ARTICLE II.

The International Commission shall be composed of five members, to be appointed as follows: One member shall be chosen from each country, by the Government thereof; one member shall be chosen by each Government from some third country; the fifth member shall be chosen by common agreement between the two Governments, it being understood that he shall not be a citizen of either country. The expenses of the Commission shall be paid by the two Governments in equal proportions.

The International Commission shall be appointed within six months after the exchange of the ratifications of this treaty; and vacancies shall be filled according to the manner of the original appointment.

ARTICLE III.

In case the High Contracting Parties shall have failed to adjust a dispute by diplomatic methods, they shall at once refer it to the International Commission for investigation and report. The international Commission may, however, spontaneously by unanimous agreement offer its services to that effect, and in such case it shall notify both Governments and request their cooperation in the investigation.

In the event of its appearing to His Majesty's Government that the British interests affected by the dispute to be investigated are not mainly those of the United Kingdom but are mainly those of some one or more of the self governing dominions, namely, the Dominion of Canada, the Commonwealth of Australia, the Dominion of New Zealand, the Union of South Africa, and Newfoundland, His Majesty's Government shall be at liberty to substitute as the member chosen by them to serve on the International Commission for such investigation and report another person selected from a list of persons to be named one for each of the self governing dominions but only one shall act, namely, that one who represents the dominion immediately interested.

The High Contracting Parties agree to furnish the Permanent International Commission with all the means and facilities required for its investigation and report.

The report of the International Commission shall be completed within one year after the date on which it shall declare its investigation to have begun, unless the High Contracting Parties shall limit or extend the time by mutual agreement. The report shall be prepared in triplicate; one copy shall be presented to each Government, and the third retained by the Commission for its files.

The High Contracting Parties reserve the right to act independently on the subject matter of the dispute after the report of the Commission shall have been submitted.

ARTICLE IV.

This treaty shall not affect in any way the provisions of the Treaty of the 11th January, 1909,[1] relating to questions arising between the United States and the Dominion of Canada.

Article V.

The present treaty shall be ratified by the President of the United States of America, by and with the advice and consent of the Senate thereof, and by His Britannic Majesty; and the ratifications shall be exchanged at Washington as soon as possible. It shall take effect immediately after the exchange of ratifications, and shall continue in force for a period of five years; and it shall thereafter remain in force until twelve months after one of the High Contracting Parties have given notice to the other of an intention to terminate it.

In witness whereof the respective plenipotentiaries have signed the present treaty and have affixed thereunto their seals.

Done in duplicate at Washington on the 15th day of September, in the year of our Lord nineteen hundred and fourteen.

[SEAL.]   WILLIAM JENNINGS BRYAN
[SEAL.]   CECIL SPRING RICE

---

[1] For text see above, p. 2607.

Document No. 21 Elihu Root, Nobel Peace Prize Speech (1914)
Source: Robert Scott and James Brown, eds., *Addresses on International
Subjects by Elihu Root* (Cambridge: Harvard University Press, 1916), pp.
153-174.

NOBEL PEACE PRIZE ADDRESS

REQUIRED BY THE STATUTES OF THE NOBEL FOUNDATION
UPON THE AWARD OF THE PEACE PRIZE
FOR THE YEAR 1912

The Swedish scientist, Alfred Nobel, inventor of dynamite, died December 10,
1896, and established by his will a fund of approximately nine million dollars, the
interest of which should every year be distributed to those who had contributed
most to " the good of humanity." The interest thus provided for was to be divided
into five equal shares and distributed " one to the person who in the domain of
physics has made the most important discovery or invention, one to the person who
has made the most important chemical discovery or invention, one to the person
who has made the most important discovery in the domain of medicine or physi-
ology, one to the person who in literature has provided the most excellent work of
an idealistic tendency, and *one to the person who has worked most or best for the
fraternization of nations, and the abolition or reduction of standing armies, and the
calling and propagating of peace congresses.*"

The fund became available in the year 1901, and the individual prize, amounting to
about $40,000, is awarded annually on the anniversary of Mr. Nobel's death.

The Nobel Peace Prize for 1912, reserved, in conformity with article 5 of the
statutes, for the year 1913, was conferred upon Elihu Root. The committee made
its decisions known to the public on December 10, 1913, the anniversary of Mr.
Nobel's death, in the hall of the Nobel Institute at Christiania. Mr. Lövland,
president of the committee, presided at the ceremony. The secretary of the committee, Mr. Moe, delivered an address on Mr. Root's political career, from which
the following is an extract:

In August, 1899, he [Mr. Root] was appointed Secretary of War by President McKinley and remained in office during Mr. Roosevelt's administration
until February, 1904. Upon the death of Secretary of State John Hay, in July,
1905, Mr. Root succeeded to that office and directed the foreign affairs of the
United States up to the expiration of Mr. Roosevelt's term, in March, 1909.
It was his task, as Secretary of War, to lay the bases of the plan for the reorganization of Cuba and the Philippines in their relation to the United States
after the Spanish-American war.

As Secretary of State, he made a notable journey to South America, during
which he visited the Third Pan-American Congress at Rio de Janeiro. In 1907,
he visited Mexico. The object of these visits was to remove the long-standing
distrust of their Anglo-Saxon sister on the part of the Latin Republics, and to
further the efforts made in the interest of Pan-Americanism. In 1908 there
was founded at Washington the Pan-American Bureau, under the direction
of the Secretary of State of the United States, in coöperation with the
Ministers of the American Republics accredited to Washington. Mr. Root
took the initiative in calling a Central American Peace Congress at Washington

in 1907. The following year a permanent court for the Central American states was created at Cartago, Costa Rica.

The most difficult task that fell to Mr. Root as Secretary of State was the settlement of the dispute between the United States and Japan on the question of Japanese immigrants in California, in 1906–07. It is impossible to give here the history of this great question, which assumed a threatening aspect in the winter of 1907. It will suffice to say that the peaceful settlement of the dispute, clinched by the action of the Congress at Washington in passing the immigration act of March 19, 1907, followed by the identic note of November, 1908, was due to the efforts of Mr. Root.

Long alone among American statesmen in his stand on the question, he vigorously attacked the act of August, 1912, providing for the free passage of American coastwise vessels through the Panama Canal. His eloquent speech in the Senate on January 21, 1913, was distributed among the friends of peace throughout the entire world. Since his retirement Mr. Root has been recognized as the leader of the peace movement in the United States. He is President of the American Society of International Law and of the great Carnegie Endowment for International Peace.[1]

In accordance with the statutes of the Nobel Foundation, the laureate of the Peace Prize is required to deliver an address in person at Christiania, Norway. The date for the delivery of Mr. Root's address was set for September 8, 1914, but delivery was prevented by the outbreak of the European war.

The address prepared by Mr. Root for that occasion is here printed exactly as it was prepared for delivery before the outbreak of the war, without the change of a word or syllable.

THE humanitarian purpose of Alfred Nobel in establishing the peace prize which bears his name was doubtless not merely to reward those who should promote peace among nations, but to stimulate thought upon the means and methods best adapted, under the changing conditions of future years, to approach and ultimately attain the end he so much desired.

The apparent simplicity of the subject is misleading. Recognition of the horrors of war and the blessings of peace, acceptance of the dogma " War is wrong and to keep the peace a duty," are so universal that upon the surface it seems only necessary to state a few incontrovertible truths and to press them upon the attention of mankind, in order to have war end and peace reign perpetually.

Yet the continual recurrence of war and the universally increasing preparations for war based upon expectation of it among nations all of whom declare themselves in favor of

[1] Translated from *Les Prix Nobel en 1913*, Stockholm (1914), pp. 64–65.

peace, indicate that intellectual acceptance of peace doctrine is not sufficient to control conduct, and that a general feeling in favor of peace, however sincere, does not furnish a strong enough motive to withstand the passions which lead to war when a cause of quarrel has arisen. The methods of peace propaganda which aim at establishing peace doctrine by argument and by creating a feeling favorable to peace in general, seem to fall short of reaching the springs of human action and of dealing with the causes of the conduct which they seek to modify. It is much like treating the symptoms of disease instead of ascertaining and dealing with the cause of the symptoms. The mere assemblage of peace-loving people to interchange convincing reasons for their common faith; mere exhortation and argument to the public in favor of peace in general fall short of the mark.

They are useful, they serve to strengthen the faith of the participants, they tend very gradually to create a new standard of conduct, just as exhortations to be good and demonstrations that honesty is the best policy have a certain utility by way of suggestion. But they do not, as a rule, reach or extirpate or modify the causes of war.

Occasionally some man with exceptional power of statement or of feeling, and possessed by the true missionary spirit, will deliver a message to the world, putting old truths in such a way as to bite into the consciousness of civilized peoples and move mankind forward a little, with a gain never to be altogether lost. But the mere repetition of the obvious by good people of average intelligence, while not without utility and not by any means to be despised as an agency for peace, nevertheless is subject to the drawback that the unregenerate world grows weary of iteration and reacts in the wrong direction. The limitation upon this mode of promoting peace lies in the fact that it consists in an appeal to the civilized side of man, while war is the product of forces proceeding from man's original savage nature. To deal with the true causes of war one must begin by recognizing as of prime relevancy to the solution of the problem the familiar fact that civilization is a partial, incomplete, and, to a great extent, superficial modification of barbarism. The point of departure of the process to which we wish to contribute is the fact that war is the natural reaction of human nature in the savage state, while peace is the result of acquired characteristics. War was forced upon mankind in his original civil and social condition. The law of the survival of the fittest led inevitably to the survival and predominance of the men who were effective in war and who loved it because they were effective. War was the avenue to all that mankind desired. Food, wives, a place in the sun, freedom from restraint and oppression, wealth of comfort, wealth of luxury, respect, honor, power, control over others, were sought and attained by fighting. Nobody knows through how many thousand of years fighting men have made a place for themselves while the weak and peaceable have gone to the wall. Love of fighting was bred in the blood of the race, because those who did not love fighting were not suited to their environment and perished. Grotius himself sets war first in the title of his great work, *De Jure Belli ac Pacis*, as if, in his mind, war was the general and usual condition with which he was to deal, and peace the occasional and incidental field of international relation. And indeed the work itself deals chiefly with war, and only incidentally with peaceful relations.

In attempting to bring mankind to a condition of permanent peace in which war will be regarded as criminal conduct, just as civilized communities have been brought to a condition of permanent order, broken only by criminals who war against society, we have to deal with innate ideas, impulses and habits, which became a part of the cave man's nature by necessity from the conditions under which he lived; and these ideas and impulses still survive more or less dormant under the veneer of civilization, ready to be excited to action by events often of the most trifling character. As Lord Bacon says " Nature is often hidden, sometimes overcome, seldom extinguished." To eradicate or modify or curb the tendencies which thus survive among civilized men is not a matter of intellectual conviction or training. It is a matter primarily of development of character and the shifting of standards of conduct — a long, slow process in which advance is to be measured, not by days and years but by generations and centuries in the life of nations.

The attractive idea that we can now have a parliament of man with authority to control the conduct of nations by legislation or an international police force with power to enforce national conformity to rules of right conduct is a counsel of perfection. The world is not ready for any such thing, and it cannot be made ready except by the practical surrender of the independence of nations, which lies at the basis of the present social organization of the civilized world. Such a system would mean that each nation was liable to be lawfully controlled and coerced by a majority of alien powers. That majority alone could determine when and for what causes and to what ends the control and coercion should be exercised. Human nature must have come much nearer perfection than it is now, or will be in many generations, to exclude from such a control prejudice, selfishness, ambition and injustice. An attempt to prevent war in this way would breed war, for it would destroy local self-government and drive nations to war for liberty. There is no nation in the world which would seriously consider a proposal so shocking to the national pride and patriotism of its people.

To help in the most practical and efficient way towards making peace permanent, it is needful to inquire with some analysis what are the specific motives and impulses, the proximate causes which, under the present conditions of the civilized world, urge nations to the point where the war passion seizes upon them. And then we should inquire what are the influences which naturally tend or may be made to tend towards checking the impulse, destroying the motive, preventing the proximate cause, before passion has become supreme and it is too late.

It is to be observed that every case of war averted is a gain in general, for it helps to form a habit of peace, and community habits long continued become standards of conduct. The life of the community conforms to an expectation of their continuance, and there comes to be an instinctive opposition to any departure from them.

The first and most obvious cause for international controversy which suggests itself is in the field of international rights and obligations. Claims of right and insistence upon obligations may depend upon treaty stipulations or upon the rules of international law or upon the sense of natural justice applied to the circumstances of a particular case, or upon disputed facts. Upon all these there are continually arising controversies as to what are the true facts; what is the rule of international law applicable to the case; what is the true interpretation of the treaty; what is just and fair under the circumstances. This category does not by any means cover the entire field out of which causes of war arise, but no one should underestimate its importance. Small differences often grow into great quarrels, and honest differences of opinion frequently produce controversies in which national *amour propre* is involved and national honor, dignity and prestige are supposed to be at stake. Rival claimants to an almost worthless strip of land along a disputed boundary, a few poor fishermen contesting each others' rights to set nets in disputed waters, may break into violence which will set whole nations aflame with partisanship upon either side. Reparation demanded for injury to a citizen or an insult to a flag in foreign territory may symbolize in the feeling of a great people their national right to independence, to respect, and to an equal place in the community of nations. The people of a country, wholly mistaken as to their national rights, honestly ignorant of their international obligations, may become possessed of a real sense of injustice, of deep resentment, and of a sincere belief that the supreme sacrifice of war is demanded by love of country, its liberty and independence, when in fact their belief has no just foundation whatever.

In this field the greatest advance is being made towards reducing and preventing in a practical and effective way the causes of war, and this advance is proceeding along several different lines. First, by providing for the peaceable settlement of such controversies by submission to an impartial tribunal. Up to this time that provision has taken the form of arbitration, with which we are all familiar. There have been occasional international arbitrations from very early times, but arbitration as a system, a recognized and customary method of diplomatic procedure rather than an exceptional expedient, had its origin in The Hague Conference of 1899. It is interesting to recall the rather contemptous reception accorded to the Convention for the Pacific Settlement of International Disputes concluded at that conference, and to the Permanent Court at The Hague which it created. The convention was not obligatory. No power was bound to comply with it. The cynicism with which the practical diplomatist naturally regards the idealist pronounced it a dead letter. But the convention expressed, and, by expressing, established, a new standard of international conduct which practical idealism had long been gradually approaching, for which thoughtful men and women in all civilized lands had been vaguely groping, which the more advanced nations welcomed and the more backward nations were ashamed to reject. Let me quote the recitals with which the delegates prefaced their work:

Animated by a strong desire to concert for the maintenance of the general peace;

Resolved to second by their best efforts the friendly settlement of international disputes;

Recognizing the solidarity which unites the members of the society of civilized nations;

Desirous of extending the empire of law, and of strengthening the appreciation of international justice;

Convinced that the permanent institution of a Court of Arbitration, accessible to all, in the midst of the independent Powers, will contribute effectively to this result;

Having regard to the advantages attending the general and regular organization of arbitral procedure;

Sharing the opinion of the august initiator of the International Peace Conference that it is expedient to record in an international agreement the principles of equity and right, on which are based the security of states and the welfare of peoples, etc.

These declarations, although enforced by no binding stipulation, nevertheless have become principles of action in international affairs, because, through the progress of civilization and the influence of many generations of devoted spirits in the cause of humanity, the world had become ready for the setting up of the standard. The convention would have been a dead letter if the world had not been made ready for it, and, because the world was ready, conformity to the standard year by year has become more universal and complete. Since this convention, which was binding upon no state, one hundred and thirteen obligatory general treaties of arbitration have been made between powers who have taken part in The Hague Conferences, and sixteen international controversies have been heard and decided, or are pending before that tribunal according to the last report of the Administrative Council of the Court.

Quite apart from the statistics of cases actually heard or pending, it is impossible to estimate the effect produced by the existence of this court, for the fact that there is a court to which appeal may be made always leads to the settlement of far more controversies than are brought to judgment. Nor can we estimate the value of having this system a part of the common stock of knowledge of civilized men, so that, when an international controversy arises, the first reaction is, not to consider war but to consider peaceful litigation.

Plainly, the next advance to be urged along this line is to pass on from an arbitral tribunal, the members of which are specifically selected from the general list of the court for each case, and whose service is but an incident in the career of a diplomatist or a publicist, to a permanent court composed of judges who devote their entire time to the performance of judicial duties and proceed in accordance with a sense of judicial obligation, not to adjust or compromise differences, but to decide upon rights in accordance with the facts and the law. Long steps in this direction were made in the Second Hague Conference by the convention for the establishment of a permanent international prize court and by the formulation and adoption of a draft convention relative to the creation of a general judicial arbitration court. This draft convention lacked nothing of completion except an agreement upon the method by which the judges were to be selected. Towards the creation of such a court the best efforts of those who wish to promote peace should be directed.

The second line of advance in this same field of international controversy is in pressing forward the development of international law and the agreement of nations upon its rules. Lord Mansfield described the law of nations as "founded upon justice, equity, convenience, the reason of the thing, and confirmed by long usage." There are multitudes of events liable to occur frequently in the intercourse of nations, regarding which there has never been any agreement as to what is just, equitable, or convenient, and, as to many of the classes of controversy, different views are held by different nations, so that in a large part of the field with which an arbitral tribunal or international court should deal there is really no law to be applied. Where there is no law, a submission to arbitration or to judicial decision is an appeal, not to the rule of law but to the unknown opinions or predilections of the men who happen to be selected to decide. The development of the peaceable settlement of international disputes by the decision of impartial tribunals waits therefore upon the further development of international law by a more complete establishment of known and accepted rules for the government of international conduct.

In this direction also great progress has been made within

recent years. The ordinary process of reaching rules of international law through the universal assent of nations, expressed as particular cases arise from time to time in the ordinary course of international affairs, is so slow that, instead of making progress towards a comprehensive law of nations by such a method, the progress of the law has been outstripped by the changes of condition in international affairs, so that the law has been growing less and less adequate to settle the questions continually arising. The Declaration of Paris, in 1856, by a few simple rules dealing, not with particular cases, but looking to the future through an agreement of the powers signing the convention, was a new departure in the method of forming international law. That method has developed into the action of the two Hague Conferences of 1899 and 1907, which were really law-making bodies, establishing, by the unanimous vote of the powers, rules of conduct for the future, covering extensive portions of the field of international conduct. The action of The Hague Conferences would have been impossible if it had not been for the long continued and devoted labors of the *Institut de Droit International*, which, in its annual meetings for forty years, has brought together the leaders of thought in the science of the law of nations in all the countries of the civilized world to discuss unofficially, with a free and full expression of personal opinion, the unsettled problems as to what the law is and ought to be. The conclusions of that body furnished to the successive Hague Conferences the matured results of years of well directed labor and bore the same relation to the deliberations of the conferences as the report of a committee of a legislative body in furnishing the basis for deliberation and action. Their work should be encouraged and their example should be followed.

Further Hague Conferences should be insisted upon. They should be made to recur at regular periods without requiring the special initiative of any country. The process of formulating and securing agreement upon rules of international law should be pressed forward in every direction.

There is a third line of progress, little, if any, less important than the two already mentioned, and that is, the instruction of students and of the great bodies of the people of civilized countries in the knowledge of international law. Under the modern development of constitutional governments, with varying degrees of extension of suffrage, more and more the people who cast the ballots determine the issues of peace and war. No government now embarks in war without the assurance of popular support. It is not uncommon in modern times to see governments straining every nerve to keep the peace, and the people whom they represent, with patriotic enthusiasm and resentment over real or fancied wrongs urging them forward to war. Nothing is more important in the preservation of peace than to secure among the great mass of the people living under constitutional government a just conception of the rights which their nation has against others and of the duties their nation owes to others. The popular tendency is to listen approvingly to the most extreme statements and claims of politicians and orators who seek popularity by declaring their own country right in everything and other countries wrong in everything. Honest people, mistakenly believing in the justice of their cause, are led to support injustice. To meet this tendency there should be not merely definite standards of law to be applied to international relations, but there should be general public understanding of what those standards are. Of course it is not possible that all the people of any country can become familiar with international law, but there may be such knowledge and leadership of opinion in every country on the part of the most intelligent and best educated men that in every community mistaken conceptions can be corrected and a true view of rights and obligations inculcated. To attain this end much has been done and much is in contemplation. Societies of international law have been formed in many countries for the discussion of international questions and the publication and distribution of the results. Many journals of international law have been established and are rapidly increasing their circulation and influence. More and more colleges and universities are establishing chairs and giving instruction in international law to their students. A further step is about to be taken at The Hague by the establishment there of an international school of international law to which scholars from all over the civilized world will come and in which the great masters of the science have undertaken to give instruction. There can be no better augury for the success of the new institution than the fact that it found its origin in the general enthusiasm of Ludwig von Bar of Göttingen, of Otfried Nippold of Frankfort, of Demetrius Sturdza of Roumania, and of T.M.C. Asser of Holland; and that it has for its president Louis Renault of France. The distinctive feature of this new departure is that it will bring together teachers and students from many countries; so that their intercourse and instruction will tend towards the unification of rules and the establishment of a general standard of law instead of perpetuating the differing and often antagonistic conceptions which obtain within the limits of different nations.

Along all these lines of practical effort for peace in the development of arbitration and judicial decision in the development of a definite system of law determining the rights and obligations of nations, and in the enlightenment of the civilized nations as to what their rights and obligations are, the present generation has rendered a service in the cause of peace surpassing that of many centuries gone before, and in further development along these same lines the present generation has before it a golden opportunity for further service.

There is, however, another class of substantive causes of war which the agencies I have described do not reach directly. This comprises acts done or demanded in pursuance of national policy, and ordinarily either for the enlargement or protection of territory or for trade or industrial advantage.

The conduct of a nation under such a policy is often regarded by other nations as unwarranted aggression or as threatening their safety or their rights. Illustrations of this kind of question are to be found in the protean forms of the Eastern question and of the balance of power in Europe, in the assertion of the Monroe Doctrine by the United States; in the position of Germany regarding the settlement of Morocco, before the Conference of Algeciras; in the attitude of Great Britain regarding Agadir, after that conference. It is plain that, under the present organization of civilization in independent nationalities, questions of public policy supposed to be vital cannot be submitted to arbitration, because that would be an abdication of independence and the placing of government *pro tanto* in the hands of others. The independence of a state involves that state's right to determine its own domestic policy and to decide what is essential to its own safety.

It does not follow, however, that we are without opportunity to promote and strengthen specific influences tending to diminish or prevent causes of war of this description. In the first place, when there is a policy of intentional aggression, inspired by a desire to get possession of the territory or the trade of another country, right or wrong, a pretext is always sought. No nation now sets forth to despoil another upon the avowed ground that it desires the spoils. Some ground of justification is always alleged. The wolf always charges the lamb with muddying the stream. The frank and simple days of the Roman proconsul and of the robber baron have passed, and three things have happened: First, there has come to be a public opinion of the world; second, that opinion has set up a new standard of national conduct which condemns unjustified aggression; and third, the public opinion of the world punishes the violation of its standard. It has not been very long since the people of each country were concerned almost exclusively with their own affairs, and, with but few individual exceptions, neither knew nor cared what was going on outside their own boundaries. All that has changed. The spread of popular education; the enormous increase in the production and circulation of newspapers and periodicals and cheap books; the competition of the press, which ranges the world for news; the telegraph, which carries instantly knowledge of all important events everywhere to all parts of the world; the new mobility of mankind, which availing itself of the new means of travel by steamship and railroad, with its new freedom under the recently recognized right of expatriation and the recently established right of free travel, moves to and fro by the million across the boundaries of the nations; the vast extension of international commerce; the recognition of interdependence of the peoples of different nations engendered by this commerce and this intercourse; their dependence upon each other for the supply of their needs and for the profitable disposal of their products, for the preservation of health, for the promotion of morals and for the increase of knowledge and the advance of thought; — all these are creating an international community of knowledge and interest, of thought and feeling. In the hundreds of international associations reported by Senator LaFontaine's *L'Office Central* at Brussels, men of all nations are learning to think internationally about science and morals and hygiene and religion and society and business. Gradually, everything that happens in the world is coming to be of interest everywhere in the world, and, gradually, thoughtful men and women everywhere are sitting in judgment upon the conduct of all nations. Some very crass and indefensible things have been done by nations within the past few years, but no one can read the discussions about those national acts without seeing that the general judgment of mankind has sunk deep into the hearts of the people of the countries responsible; that a great new force is at work in international affairs; that the desire for approval and the fear of condemnation by the contemporary opinion of the civilized world is becoming a powerful influence to control national conduct. True, we are but at the beginning, but it is the beginning of a great new era in which the public opinion of mankind renders judgment, not upon peace and war, for a vast majority of mankind is in favor of war when that is necessary for the preservation of liberty and justice, but upon the just and unjust conduct of nations, as the public opinion of each community passes upon the just and unjust conduct of its individual members. The chief force which makes for peace and order in the community of individuals is not the police officer, with his club, but it is the praise and blame, the honor and shame, which follow observance or violation of the community's standards of right conduct. In the new era that is dawning of the world's public opinion we need not wait for the international policeman, with his artillery, for, when any people feels that its government has done a shameful thing and has brought them into disgrace in the opinion of the world, theirs will be the vengeance and they will inflict the punishment.

Two conclusions from all these considerations are quite obvious: First, that the development and understanding of international law and the habit of submitting international controversies to judicial decision will continually tend to hinder wanton aggression, because it will tend to make it more difficult to find pretexts, excuses, or justification. Second, that quite apart from argument and exhortation concerning war and peace, there is a specific line of effort along which those who seek to promote peace may most usefully proceed; by insisting upon a willingness to do justice among nations, and this, not justice according to the possibly excited and warped opinion of the particular nation, but according to the general public judgment of the civilized world; by condemning injustice on the part of nations as we condemn injustice on the part of individuals; by pressing upon the peoples of the earth a consciousness that if they are arrogant and grasping and overbearing and use their power

223

to oppress and despoil the weak, they will be disgraced in the estimation of mankind. Such an effort is not a denial of the innate impulses of the race, but is an appeal to them. It accords with the line of historic development. The taboo of savage tribes is nothing else. The social penalties of civilized communities are the same thing. The theoretical postulate of all diplomatic discussion between nations is the assumed willingness of every nation to do justice. The line of least resistance in the progress of civilization is to make that theoretical postulate real by the continually increasing force of the world's public opinion.

Yet there are other influences tending in the same direction which may be usefully promoted. The self-interest which so often prompts nations to unjust aggression can no longer safely assume that its apparent profit is real; for a nation which has been built up by the industry and enterprise of its people, which depends upon its products and the marketing of them, upon its commerce and the peaceful intercourse of commerce for its prosperity, the prize of aggression must be rich indeed to counterbalance the injury sustained by the interference of war with both production and commerce. At the same time, freedom of trade regardless of political control is diminishing the comparative value of extension of territory. The old system of exploitation of colonies and the monopolization of their trade for the benefit of the mother country has practically disappeared. The best informed men are coming to understand that, under modern conditions, the prosperity of each nation is enhanced by the prosperity of all other nations; and that the government which acquires political control over new territory may gratify pride and minister to ambition, but can have only a slight effect to advance the welfare of its people.

The support of these statements rests upon the facts of economic science. If they are true, as I am sure we all believe them to be, they should be forced upon the attention of the peoples, not by mere assertion, which avails but little, but by proof drawn from the rich stores of evidence to be found in the history of mankind. For the accomplishment of this purpose a meeting of eminent economists and publicists was held three years ago at Berne. They came from Denmark, Holland, Belgium, Great Britain, France, Germany, Switzerland, Italy, Austria-Hungary, the United States and Japan. For some weeks they devoted themselves to the preparation of a program for systematic, scientific investigation into the historical and economic causes and effects of war. For the three years which have ensued they have been engaged, with ample and competent assistance, in pursuing their investigations. The first installments of their work are ready for publication, and they reconvened last month to review what has been done and to lay down the lines of further work. The results of their labors, when made available, should be eagerly sought by every lover of peace who is competent by tongue or pen to be a teacher of his fellow-men, for we may be confident they will show that while the sacrifice of war may be demanded for justice, for liberty, for national life, yet war is always a sacrifice, and never is a rational mode of promoting material prosperity.

There yet remain certain disposing causes, which, quite apart from real substantive questions in controversy, operate upon national feeling and give injurious effect to trifling or fancied occasions for offense. There is no international controversy so serious that it cannot be settled if both parties really wish to settle it. There are few controversies so trifling that they cannot be made the occasion for war if the parties really wish to fight. Among these disposing causes which create an atmosphere of belligerency are:

Race and local prejudice, breeding dislike and hatred between the peoples of different countries.

Exaggerated national *amour propre*, which causes excessive sensitiveness and excessive resentment of foreign criticism or opposition.

With these go the popular assumption, often arrogant,

often ignorant, that the extreme claims of one's country are always right and are to be rigidly insisted upon as a point of national honor. With them go intolerance of temperate discussion, of kindly consideration, and of reasonable concession.

Under these feelings insulting words and conduct towards foreign governments and people become popular, and braggart defiance is deemed patriotic. Under them the ambitious aspirants of domestic politics seek preferment through avenues of military success.

And under them deep and real suspicions of the sinister purpose of other nations readily take possession of a people, who become ready to believe that an attack by their own country is the only recourse to guard effectually against an attack upon their country by others, and that patriotism requires them to outstrip other countries in armament and preparation for war.

Prejudice and passion and suspicion are more dangerous than the incitement of self-interest or the most stubborn adherence to real differences of opinion regarding rights. In private life more quarrels arise, more implacable resentment is caused, more lives are sacrificed, because of insult than because of substantial injury. And it is so with nations.

The remedy is the same. When friends quarrel we try to dissipate their misunderstandings, to soften their mutual feelings, and to bring them together in such a way that their friendship may be renewed. Misunderstanding and prejudice and dislike are, as a rule, the fruits of isolation. There is so much of good in human nature that men grow to like each other upon better acquaintance, and this points to another way in which we may strive to promote the peace of the world. That is, by international conciliation through intercourse, not the formal intercourse of the traveller or the merchant, but the intercourse of real acquaintance, of personal knowledge, of little courtesies and kindly consideration; by the exchange of professors between universities, by the exchange of students between countries; by the visits to other countries on the part of leaders of opinion, to be received in private hospitality and in public conference; by the spreading of correct information through the press; by circulating and attracting attention to expressions of praise and honor rather than the reverse; by giving public credit where credit is due and taking pains to expose and publish our good opinions of other peoples; by coöperation in the multitude of causes which are world-wide in their interest; by urging upon our countrymen the duty of international civility and kindly consideration; and by constant pressure in the right direction in a multitude of ways — a slow process, but one which counts little by little if persisted in.

Each separate act will seem of no effect but all together they will establish and maintain a tendency towards the goal of international knowledge and broad human sympathy. There is a homely English saying, "Leg over leg the dog went to Dover." That states the method of our true progress. We cannot arrive at our goal *per saltum*. Not by invoking an immediate millenium, but by the accumulated effects of a multitude of efforts, each insignificant in itself, but steadily and persistently continued, we must win our way along the road to better knowledge and kindliness among the peoples of the earth which the will of Alfred Nobel describes as " the fraternity of nations."

There are many reasons to believe that progress toward the permanent prevalence of peace may be more rapid in the future than in the past.

Standards of conduct are changing in many ways unfavorable to war.

Civilized man is becoming less cruel. Cruelty to men and to the lower animals as well, which would have passed unnoticed a century ago, now shocks the sensibilities and is regarded as wicked and degrading. The severity of punishments for minor offenses which formerly prevailed now seems to us revolting. The torture of witnesses or of criminals has become unthinkable. Human life is held in much higher esteem and the taking of it, whether in private quarrel or by judicial procedure, is looked upon much more seriously than it was formerly. The social reaction from the theories of the individualistic economists of the last century has brought with it a very wide-spread sense that men have some sort of responsibility to cause affairs to be so ordered in civilized communities that their fellow-men have a chance to live. The Hague Conventions to regulate the conduct of war and the Geneva Conventions to ameliorate its horrors have a significance which goes beyond their professions. They mark the changing attitude of the world towards the subject to which they relate; and they introduce into the business of warfare obligatory considerations of humanity and respect for human rights which tend to destroy the spirit upon which alone the business itself can continue. No one can read those conventions closely without being struck by the similarity of the process of regulation and limitation which they exhibit with the historic process by which private war was ultimately regulated out of existence in the greater part of the civilized world. The growth of modern constitutional government compels for its successful practice the exercise of reason and considerate judgment by the individual citizens who constitute the electorate. The qualities thus evoked in the training schools of domestic affairs are the qualities which make for national self-restraint and peace in international affairs. History is being rewritten, and the progress of popular education is making men familiar with it; and as the world, which worships strength and has most applauded military glory, grows in knowledge, the great commanding figures rising far above the common mass of mere fighters, the men who win the most imperishable fame have come to be the strong, patient, great-hearted ones like Washington, and Lincoln, and William the Silent, and Cavour, whose genius inspired by love of country and their kind urges them to build up and not to destroy. The sweetest incense offered to the memory of the soldier is not to the brutal qualities of war but to the serene courage ennobled by sympathy and courtesy of a Bayard or a Sidney. The hero-worshipper is gradually changing from the savage to the civilized conception of his divinities. Taken all in all the clear and persistent tendencies of a slowly developing civilization justify cheerful hope.

We may well turn from Tripoli and Mexico and the Balkans with the apocryphal exclamation of Galileo, " And still the world moves."

Part II

*Responding to War in Europe
and
Revolution in Mexico,
1914-1917*

Document No. 22 Wilson's Appeal for Neutrality; Message to Senate, August 19, 1914
Source: U.S. 63 Congress, 2nd Sess. *Senate Doc. 566.*

WILSON'S APPEAL FOR NEUTRALITY
Message to Senate, August 19, 1914

My fellow countrymen: I suppose that every thoughtful man in America has asked himself, during these last troubled weeks, what influence the European war may exert upon the United States, and I take the liberty of addressing a few words to you in order to point out that it is entirely within our own choice what its effects upon us will be and to urge very earnestly upon you the sort of speech and conduct which will best safeguard the Nation against distress and disaster.

The effect of the war upon the United States will depend upon what American citizens say and do. Every man who really loves America will act and speak in the true spirit of neutrality, which is the spirit of impartiality and fairness and friendliness to all concerned. The spirit of the Nation in this critical matter will be determined largely by what individuals and society and those gathered in public meetings do and say, upon what newspapers and magazines contain, upon what ministers utter in their pulpits, and men proclaim as their opinions on the street.

The people of the United States are drawn from many nations, and chiefly from the nations now at war. It is natural and inevitable that there should be the utmost variety of sympathy and desire among them with regard to the issues and circumstances of the conflict. Some will wish one nation, others another, to succeed in the momentous struggle. It will be easy to excite passion and difficult to allay it. Those responsible for exciting it will assume a heavy responsibility, responsibility for no less a thing than that the people of the United States, whose love of their country and whose loyalty to its Government should unite them as Americans all, bound in honor and affection to think first of her and her interests, may be divided in camps of hostile opinion, hot against each other, involved in the war itself in impulse and opinion if not in action.

Such divisions amongst us would be fatal to our peace of mind and might seriously stand in the way of the proper performance of our duty as the one great nation at peace, the one people holding itself ready to play a part of impartial mediation and speak the counsels of peace and accommodation, not as a partisan, but as a friend.

I venture, therefore, my fellow countrymen, to speak a solemn word of warning to you against that deepest, most subtle, most essential breach of neutrality which may spring out of partisanship, out of passionately taking sides. The United States must be neutral in fact as well as in name during these days that are to try men's souls. We must be impartial in thought as well as in action, must put a curb upon our sentiments as well as upon every transaction that might be construed as a preference of one party to the struggle before another.

My thought is of America. I am speaking, I feel sure, the earnest wish and purpose of every thoughtful American that this great country of ours, which is, of course, the first in our thoughts and in our hearts, should show herself in this time of peculiar trial a Nation fit beyond others to exhibit the fine poise of undisturbed judgment, the dignity of self-control, the efficiency of dispassionate action; a Nation that neither sits in judgment upon others nor is disturbed in her own counsels and which keeps herself fit and free to do what is honest and disinterested and truly serviceable for the peace of the world.

Shall we not resolve to put upon ourselves the restraints which will bring to our people the happiness and the great and lasting influence for peace we covet for them?

Document No. 23 John H. Holmes, "War and the Social Movement" (1914)
Source: *The Survey*, XXXII (Sept. 26, 1914), pp. 629-630.

WAR AND THE SOCIAL MOVEMENT—BY JOHN HAYNES HOLMES, CHURCH OF THE MESSIAH, NEW YORK CITY

IN THE STORM and stress of the stupendous conflict now raging in Europe, it is inevitable that our attention should be absorbed by the more obvious horrors of the situation. Captured cities, burning harvest fields, desolate homes, bleeding men, weeping women and children—these are the things which are holding our interest to the exclusion of everything else. Yet there must be quiet moments, now and then, when we see more clearly and think more deeply than is possible in the hours of reading newspapers and watching bulletin boards.

Then it is that we begin to understand that there is a calamity in this warfare which is more permanently terrible than any of the surface incidents of the struggle. I refer to the awful fact that suddenly, as in the wink of an eye, three hundred years of progress is cast into the melting-pot. Civilization is all at once gone, and barbarism come. And the one gone and the other come not for today merely, nor yet for the actual period of the armed conflict, but for years and perhaps generations thereafter.

As Harold Begbie put it recently, "Already now civilization stops—stops dead. . . . Religion, philosophy, literature. painting, and chief of all perhaps, science, with its torch at the head of our human hosts, are suddenly flung backward; they become of no moment. Who wants to know about Immanence? Who cares to hear what Bergson and Eucken think? Who bothers about books and pictures? Who is ready to endow a laboratory or listen to the chemist and the biologist?" And who, we may add here, cares a fig about the social movement?

It was only a few months ago that I heard Walter Rauschenbusch, in the course of a speech at a public dinner, give urgent warning on this very point. He was trying to impress upon his hearers the obligation of unremitting endeavor in the prosecution of the great movements for political and industrial reform—the peril of undue patience in "biding our time"—the need of haste, as he put it. "At any moment," he said, among other things, "a great war may break upon us, and the social movement. as we know it today, will be dead for a generation, if not a century." And lo! with a suddenness and upon a scale which Professor Rauschenbusch could not have conceived even in darkest moments of foreboding, the war is here, and the social movement, along with art, literature, philosophy and religion, is indeed dead!

For who is talking in England today about national insurance, woman suffrage, or the breaking of the land monopoly? Who is interested in the enactment of the plural voting bill? What chance has Lloyd-George of living to complete his program of social legislation? Where is the campaign for franchise reform in Germany? Who cares about co-operation in Belgium, or syndicalism in France, or socialism anywhere? Is there an international labor movement any longer; and if there can be said to be such a movement, what does it amount to?

Nor is it only in the countries immediately concerned in this awful struggle that the social movement has vanished. We are three thousand miles away from the smoke and flame of combat, and have not a single regiment or battleship involved. And yet—who in these United States is thinking at this moment of recreation centers, improved housing, or the minimum wage? Who is going to fight the battle for widows' pensions, push the campaign against child labor, or study exhaustively the problem of unemployment? Where is the strike in Colorado and the Industrial Relations Commission? What hope have the tuberculosis workers of selling their red seals this coming Christmas? What are the suffragists going to do to stir a ripple of interest in their cause? THE SURVEY itself, to me the most fascinating magazine now being published, is at this moment about as thrilling as last year's almanac; and I venture to prophesy that its columns will have only a little better chance of attracting public attention during the next twelvemonth than my pulpit.

Nor can we hope for any revival of the social movement with the conclusion of the war. If, as now seems probable, the nations fight to the point of exhaustion, the question facing the world at the conclusion of peace will not be that of social progress at all, but simply and solely that of social survival! For days and weeks after the flood went through Dayton, the question before the community was exclusively that of feeding the hungry, clothing the naked, nursing the wounded, and cleaning the streets of mud, debris and wreckage. Only with the rebuilding of offices and homes, and the restoration of normal conditions of life, did the people give even a passing thought to issues of municipal reform and social betterment. So with the civilized world, when "the grievousness of war" has at last swept by! With commerce disorganized, industry demoralized, wealth destroyed, fields wasted and cities razed, thousands of men slain and greater thousands wounded and crippled, multitudes everywhere perishing of starvation and wretchedness—the urgent problem for the moment will be that of keeping the world going; and for years to come that of rebuilding the shattered mechanism of civilization, creating new stores of wealth, breeding a new race of men—in a word, of recovering "by painful steps and slow" the ground gained by centuries of struggle and sacrifice, and lost, alas! in one black night of madness. Not for generations will the world's life again be normal, and men be free to think not merely of living, but of *better* living!

The situation is terrible! And yet, may it not be that this calamity, like every calamity, will work at last to final and universal good? Can we not say today what Lincoln said in 1865, "The Almighty has his own purposes"? Too long have we left unsilenced and unrebuked the apologists for blood and iron. Too long have we regarded war as a passing incident and mayhap a partial good. But, now, if we do not hate this "sum of all villanies" with a perfect hatred, and highly resolve that the dead now rotting on the plains of Europe "shall not have died in vain," we are not even human!

From this moment on, every lover of civilization and servant of human kind —the social worker first among them all —must be a *peace fanatic*. He must seek for nothing before this, care for nothing above this, strive for everything through this. He must fight war as Cato fought Carthage, as Voltaire fought *L'enfame*, as Garrison fought slavery.

Nor must he be content to urge this fight in the dilettante, academic, pinktea, high-brow way too much practiced hitherto by the organized peace movement. He must join forces, without apology or reserve with Labor, and strike straight and sure not so much at war, as at the things which make war— first, militarism; second, political autocracy; and third, commercialism. The axe must be laid at the roots of the tree —which are armaments, dynasties, and exploitation.

And when, years hence, the works of civilization are restored and the voice of the social worker is again heard in the land, may it not be that he will see a changed world, wherein his task is easy? May it not be that he will look in vain for battleships and thrones and selfish business? And when he consults the history books, to discover when and how these things were wrought, may it not be that he will find himself reading of the War of the Nations in 1914?

Document No. 24 Hamilton Holt, "The Way to Disarm: A Practical Proposal" (1914)
Source: The Independent, LXXIX (Sept. 28, 1914), pp. 427-429.

VOLUME 79   MONDAY, SEPTEMBER 28, 1914   NUMBER 3433

THE WAY TO DISARM: A PRACTICAL PROPOSAL

BY HAMILTON HOLT

N his famous essay, *Perpetual Peace,* published in 1795, Emmanuel Kant, perhaps the greatest intellect the world has ever produced, declared that we never can have universal peace until the world is politically organized and it will never be possible to organize the world politically until the people, not the kings, rule.

If this be the true philosophy of peace, then when the Great War is over, and the stricken sobered peoples set about to rear a new civilization on the ashes of the old, they cannot hope to banish war from the earth unless they are prepared to extend democracy everywhere, and to organize the international realm on a basis of law rather than force.

The question of the extension of democracy is a domestic one. It can hardly be settled by joint action of the nations. World organization and disarmament, however, can be provided for in the terms of peace or by international agreement thereafter. As the United States seems destined to play an important part in the grea reconstruction at the end of the war, this is perhaps the most important question now before American statesmanship.

LAW OR WAR

THE only two powers that ever have governed or ever can govern human beings are reason and force—law and war. If we do not have the one we must have the other.

The peace movement is the process of substituting law for war. Peace follows justice, justice follows law, law follows political organization. The world has already achieved peace, thru justice, law and political organization in hamlets, towns, cities, states and even in the forty-six sovereign civilized nations of the world. But in that international realm over and above each nation, in which each nation is equally sovereign, the only way for a nation to secure its rights is by the use of force. Force, therefore—or war as it is called when exerted by a nation against another nation—is at present the only legal and final method of settling international differences. In other words, the nations are in that state of civilization today where, without a qualm, they claim the right to settle their disputes in a manner which they would actually put their own subjects to death for imitating. The peace problem, then, is nothing but the problem of finding ways and means of doing *between* the nations what has already been done *within* the nations. International law follows private law. The "United Nations" follow the United States.

At present international law has reached the same state of development that private law reached in the tenth century. Professor T. J. Lawrence (in his essay *The Evolution of Peace*) distinguishes four stages in the evolution of private law:

1. Kinship is the sole bond; revenge and retaliation are unchecked, there being no authority whatever.
2. Organization is found an advantage and tribes under a chief subdue undisciplined hordes. The right of private vengeance within the tribe is regulated but not forbidden.
3. Courts of justice exist side by side with a limited right of vengeance.
4. Private war is abolished, all disputes being settled by the courts.

It is evident that in international relations we are entering into the third stage, because the nations have already created an international tribunal which exists side by side with the right of self-redress or war.

LIKE THE AMERICAN CONFEDERATION

FURTHERMORE, a careful study of the formation of the thirteen American colonies from separate states into our present compact Union discloses the fact that the nations today are in the same stage of development that the **American** colonies were about the time of their first confederation. As the United States came into existence by the establishment of the Articles of Confederation and the Continental Congress, so the "United Nations" will come into existence thru the development of **The Hague Court** and the recurring Hague Conferences; The Hague Court being the promise of the Supreme Court of the world and The Hague Conferences being the prophecy of the parliament of man. We may look with confidence, therefore, to a future in which the world will have an established court with jurisdiction over all questions, self-governing conferences with power to legislate on all affairs of common concern, and an executive power of some form to carry out the decrees of both. To deny this is to ignore all the analogies of private law and the whole trend of the world's political history since the Declaration of Independence. As Secretary of State Knox said not long ago:

> We have reached a point when it is evident that the future holds in store a time when war shall cease, when the nations of the world shall realize a federation as real and vital as that now subsisting between the component parts of a single state.

It would be difficult to recall a more far-visioned statement than this emanating from the chancellery of a great state. It means nothing less than that the age-long dreams of the poets, the prophets and the philosophers have at last entered the realms of practical statesmanship.

But now the Great War has come upon us. "When the storm is spent and the desolation is complete; when the flower of the manhood of Europe has past into eternal night; when famine and pestilence have taken their tithe of childhood and age," will then the exhausted and beggared that live on be able to undertake the task of establishing that World Government which the historian Freeman has called "the most finished and the most artificial production of political ingenuity"?

THE HAGUE OR THE LEAGUE OF PEACE

IF it can be done at all it can only be done in one of two ways.

First. By building on the foundations already laid at The Hague the Federation of the World.

Second. By establishing a Great Confederation or

League of Peace, composed of those few nations who thru political evolution or the suffering of war have at last seen the light and are ready here and now to disarm.

It is obvious that the time is scarcely ripe for voluntary and universal disarmament by joint agreement. There are too many medieval-minded nations still in existence. The Federation of the World must still be a dream for many years to come. It must be developed slowly, step by step.

The immediate establishment of a League of Peace, however, would in fact constitute a first step toward world federation and does not offer insuperable difficulties. The idea of a League of Peace is not novel. All federal governments and confederations of governments, both ancient and modern, are essentially leagues of peace, even tho they may have functions to perform which often lead directly to war.

The ancient Achaian League of Greece, the Confederation of Swiss Cantons, the United Provinces of The Netherlands, the United States of America, and the Commonwealth of Australia are the most nearly perfect systems of federated governments known to history. Less significant, but none the less interesting to students of government, are the Latin League of thirty cities, the Hanseatic League, the Holy Alliance, and in modern times, the German Confederation. Even the recent Concert of Europe was a more or less inchoate League of Peace. The ancient leagues as well as the modern confederations have generally been unions of offense and defense. They stood ready, if they did not actually propose, to use their common forces to compel outside states to obey their will. Thus they were as frequently leagues of oppression as leagues of peace.

THE PROBLEM OF FORCE

THE problem of the League of Peace is therefore the problem of the use of force. Force internationally exprest is measured in armaments. The chief discussion which has been waged for the past decade between the pacifists and militarists has been over the question of armaments. The militarists claim that armaments insure national safety. The pacifists declare they inevitably lead to war. Both disputants insist that the present war furnishes irrefutable proof of their contentions.

As is usual in cases of this kind the shield has two sides. The confusion has arisen from a failure to recognize the threefold function of force:

1. Force used for the maintenance of order—police force.
2. Force used for attack—aggression.
3. Force used to neutralize aggression—defense.

Police force is almost wholly good.

Offense is almost wholly bad.

Defense is a necessary evil, and exists simply to neutralize force employed for aggression.

The problem of the peace movement is how to abolish the use of force for aggression, and yet to maintain it for police purposes. Force for defense will of course automatically cease when force for aggression is abolished.

The chief problem then of a League of Peace is this: Shall the members of the League "not only keep the peace themselves, but prevent by force if necessary its being broken by others," as ex-President Roosevelt suggested in his Nobel Peace Address delivered at Christiania, May 5, 1910? Or shall its force be exercized only within its membership and thus be on the side of law and order and never on the side of arbitrary will or tyranny? Or shall it never be used at all? Whichever one of these conceptions finally prevails the Great War has conclusively demonstrated that as long as War Lords exist defensive force must be maintained. Hence the League must be prepared to use force against any nations which will not forswear force. Nevertheless a formula must be devised for disarmament. For unless it is a law of nature that war is to consume all the fruits of progress disarmament some how and some way must take place. How then can the maintenance of a force for defense and police power be reconciled with the theory of disarmament?

THE CONSTITUTION OF THE LEAGUE

IN this way: Let the League of Peace be formed on the following five principles:

First. The nations of the League shall mutually agree to respect the territory and sovereignty of each other.

Second. All questions that cannot be settled by diplomacy shall be arbitrated.

Third. The nations of the League shall provide a periodical assembly to make all rules to become law unless vetoed by a nation within a stated period.

Fourth. The nations shall disarm to the point where the combined forces of the League shall be a certain per cent higher than those of the most heavily armed nation or alliance outside the League. Detailed rules for this pro rata disarmament shall be formulated by the Assembly.

Fifth. Any member of the League shall have the right to

withdraw on due notice, or may be expelled by the unanimous vote of the others.

The advantages that a nation would gain in becoming a member of such a league are manifest. The risk of war would be eliminated within the League. Obviously the only things that are vital to a nation are its land and its independence. Since each nation in the League will have pledged itself to respect the territory and the sovereignty of every other, a refusal to do so will logically lead to expulsion from the League. Thus every vital question will be automatically reserved from both war and arbitration. All other questions are of secondary importance and can readily be arbitrated.

By the establishment of a periodical assembly a method would be devised whereby the members of the League could develop their common intercourse and interests as far and as fast as they could unanimously agree upon ways and means. As any law could be vetoed by a single nation, no nation could have any fear that it would be coerced against its will by a majority vote of the other nations. By such an assembly the League might in time agree to reduce tariffs and postal rates and in a thousand other ways promote commerce and comity among its members.

As a final safeguard against coercion by the other members of the League, each member will have the right of secession on due notice. This would prevent civil war within the League. The right of expulsion by the majority will prevent one nation by its veto power indefinitely blocking all progress of the League.

THE SCRAP OF PAPER

BUT it will be said that all these agreements will have no binding effect in a crisis. A covenant is a mere "scrap of paper" whose provisions will be violated by the first nation which fancies it is its interest to do so. In order to show that their faith is backed up by deeds, however, the nations on entering the League agree to disarm to a little above the danger point, and put all their defensive power under a federal authority. This is the real proof of their conversion to the peace idea.

Thus the nations which join the League will enjoy all the economic and political advantages which come from mutual coöperation and the extension of international friendship and at the same time will be protected by an adequate force against the aggressive force of the greatest nation or alliance outside the League. The League therefore reconciles the demand of the pacifists for the limitation of armaments and eventual disarmament and the demand of the militarists for the protection that armament affords. Above all the establishment of such a league will give the liberal parties in the nations outside the League an issue on which they can attack their governments so as sooner or later to force them to apply to the League for membership. As each one enters there will be another pro rata reduction of the military forces of the League down to the armament of the next most powerful nation or alliance outside it; until finally the whole world is federated in a brotherhood of universal peace and armies and navies are reduced to an international police force.

This is the plan for a League of Peace. Is the hour about to strike when it can be realized? If only the United States, France, and England would lead in its formation, Belgium, Holland, Switzerland, Denmark, Norway, Sweden, Argentina, Brazil, Chile and others might perhaps join. Even if Russia and Germany and Japan and Italy stayed out, the League would still be powerful and large enough to begin with every auspicious hope of success.

THE DESTINY OF THE UNITED STATES

IT would seem to be the manifest destiny of the United States to lead in the establishment of such a league. The United States is the world in miniature. The United States is the greatest league of peace known to history. The United States is a demonstration to the world that all the races and peoples of the earth can live in peace under one form of government, and its chief value to civilization is a demonstration of what this form of government is.

Prior to the formation "of a more perfect union" our original thirteen states were united in a confederacy strikingly similar to that now proposed on an international scale. They were obliged by the articles of this confederacy to respect each other's territory and sovereignty, to arbitrate all questions among themselves, to assist each other against any foreign foe, not to engage in war unless called upon by the confederation to do so or actually invaded by a foreign foe, and not to maintain armed forces in excess of the strength fixed for each state by all the states in congress assembled.

It is notable that security against aggression from states inside or outside the American Union accompanied the agreement to limit armaments. Thus danger of war and size of armaments were decreased contemporaneously.

It is also notable that from the birth of the Republic to this hour every President of the United States has advocated peace thru justice. From the first great Virginian to the last, all have abhorred what Thomas Jefferson called "the greatest scourge of mankind."

When the Great War is over and the United States is called upon to lead the nations in reconstructing a new order of civilization, why might not Woodrow Wilson do on a world scale something similar to what George Washington did on a continental scale?

Stranger things than this have happened in history. Let us add to the Declaration of Independence a Declaration of Interdependence.

TO THE PEACE
PALACE AT THE HAGUE

BY ROBERT UNDERWOOD JOHNSON

Builded of Love and Joy and Faith and Hope,
Thou standest firm beyond the tides of war
That dash in gloom and fear and tempest-roar,
Beacon of Europe!—tho wise pilots grope
Where trusted lights are lost; tho the dread scope
Of storm is wider, deadlier than before;
Ay, tho the very floods that strew the shore
Seem to obey some power turned misanthrope.

For thou art witness to a world's desire,
And when—oh, happiest of days!—shall cease
The throes by which our Age doth bring to birth
The fairest of her daughters, heavenly Peace,
When Man's red folly has been purged in fire,
Thou shalt be Capitol of all the Earth.

Document No. 25   Hamilton Holt, "The Enforcement of Peace" (1914)
Source: *The Independent,* LXXX (Oct. 12, 1914), pp. 43-44.

| VOLUME 80 | MONDAY, OCTOBER 12, 1914 | NUMBER 3435 |

THE ENFORCEMENT OF PEACE

OUR readers will be glad to know that the article by the Editor of The Independent entitled "The Way to Disarm," published two weeks ago, has already attracted wide comment. We are receiving by every mail newspaper clippings and letters commending or criticizing it. A few of these we are reserving for future publication.

In the meantime it seems profitable to continue the discussion of the function of force under a reign of law, for that is the core of the whole peace problem.

In an article published in The Independent July 5, 1906, the Hon. John Basset Moore, long recognized as the leading living international lawyer in the United States, wrote:

> The great problem confronting those who wish to do away with war is how to employ the force necessary to the restraint or repression of evil without producing the legal condition known as a state of war. The most striking imperfection in the international system today is the lack of a common agency for the enforcement of law. If, at the present time, a contest by force breaks out between two nations, the conflict is recognized as a war, and other nations assume the attitude of neutrals, even tho the cause of the conflict be the flagrant disregard by one of the contending parties of a well-settled principle of international law. Such a condition of things involves an obvious incongruity, the remedy for which would be the organization of a common agency for the enforcement of law; the addition, in other words, to judicial and legislative power of what we call executive power.

IN our proposal for the constitution of a League of Peace we made no attempt to define how the force of the League shall be exerted. That was left for the decision of the Assembly of the League. We simply suggested that "the nations shall disarm to the point where the combined forces of the League shall be a certain per cent higher than those of the most heavily armed nation or alliance outside the League." This implies that the forces of the League shall be used for the neutralization of the aggressive force of nations outside the League— that is, for defense. As the Great War has absolutely demonstrated that defense is a necessity as long as war lords exist, there can no longer be any doubt of the importance of defense for those nations who prize their sovereignty and independence. But shall not the force of the League be also used as police power, that is, to maintain aggressively international law and order? A League with power to exert its will without any constitutional limitations might easily become a League of Oppression. It would have the right to be judge and sheriff in its own cause, a violation of the first principles of justice.

It would not, in our judgment, be over-sanguine to expec⁺ that the Assembly of the League would vote that the armaments of the League should be brought into regular and concerted action for compelling obedience to the judicial decisions of the Court of the League both among members of the League and those outside who have agreed to this method of settling their disputes. It may even be anticipated that the force of the League will be used to assist one of the members of the League in a controversy with a nation outside the League that has not previously agreed to resort to arbitration and that refuses so to agree upon request. Such an agreement would tend to enthrone law and suppress arbitrary action. Entering a League with such a policy would not subject the United States to the necessity of waging war thru the erroneous action of its allies in an "entangling alliance," but only to extend the reign of law. This is the fundamental purpose of our Government and perhaps the United States is now ready to go thus far.

BUT the question of the proper use of force for preserving peace is practical only after the nations have *federated* themselves for that purpose.

Given a World Confederation or League of Peace, the problem of the establishment and exercize of an international police force to maintain international law and order and to neutralize the aggressive force of any nation outside the League will present no greater difficulties than the similar problem which confronted the framers of the United States Constitution or even of the

Articles of Confederation. It must ever be borne in mind, however, that the constitution of a League of Peace will differ in this important respect from the Constitution of the United States. Our Constitution is both an instrument for federating the states and for guaranteeing each citizen within the Union certain rights; the proposed constitution of the League of Peace has no relation whatsoever to any so-called "world-citizen."

Thus the whole problem of the League of Peace resolves itself into this: The League follows the example of the United States in the relationship its members hold to one another and the example of England in the relationship it holds to outside nations. Within the League danger of war and size of armaments will decrease contemporaneously as happened with the formation of the United States. Between the League and outside nations an excess of armaments will be maintained over the heaviest armed outside nation or alliance, as England maintains a navy equal to any two likely to be brought against her.

In urging the United States to take the lead at the end of the war in organizing the world for peace, we are not unmindful that such a proposal contemplating the use of the armed forces of the United States under the federal authority of the League may require a constitutional amendment for its adoption. The power to declare war under our Constitution is vested in Congress alone, and even in time of war Congress is forbidden to make military appropriations for more than two years ahead. Nevertheless, the organization of an international government is essential to further progress of the peace movement. All obstacles will have to give way, even constitutional ones. The monster of war must be dethroned. The majesty of law co-extensive with human intercourse can alone achieve this beneficent and inevitable result.

Document No. 26   Nicholas M. Butler, "The Work of Reconstruction"
(1914)
Source: *Advocate of Peace*, LXXVI (November, 1914), pp. 234-235.

TheWork of Reconstruction.*

By Nicholas Murray Butler.

. . . We are a neutral nation, and the President
has rightly enjoined us all to observe neutrality in
speech and in deed. But neutrality is not indifference;
it is not the neutrality of the casual passer-by who views
with amused carelessness a fight between two street
rowdies; it is the neutrality of the just judge who aims,
without passion and without prejudice, to render judgment on the proved facts. We cannot if we would refrain from passing judgment upon the conduct of men,
whether singly or in nations, and we should not attempt
to do so.

In the first place, the moral judgment of the American people, as to this war and as to the several steps in
the declaration and conduct of it, is clear, calm, and
practically unanimous. There is no beating of drums
and blowing of bugles, but rather a sad pain and grief
that our kin across the sea, owing whatever allegiance
and speaking whatever tongue, are engaged in public
murder and destruction on the most stupendous scale
recorded in history. This of itself proves that the education of public opinion has proceeded far, and, whatever the war-traders and militarists may say, that the
heart of the American people is sound and its head well-
informed. . . .

Next, it must not be forgotten that this war was
made by kings and by cabinets; it was not decreed by
peoples. I can testify that the statement that kings and
cabinets were forced into the war by public sentiment is
absolutely untrue, so far at least as several of the belligerent nations are concerned. Certainly in not more
than two cases were the chosen representatives of the
people consulted at all. A tiny minority in each of several countries may have desired war, but the militarist
spirit was singularly lacking among the masses of the
population. People generally have simply accepted with
grim resignation and reluctant enthusiasm the conflict
which in each case they are taught to believe has been
forced on them by another's aggression. . . .

*From the address of President Butler at the opening ex-
ercises of the academic year of Columbia University, September 23, 1914.

Again, a final end has now been put to the contention, always stupid and often insincere, that huge armaments are an insurance against war and an aid in maintaining peace. This argument was invented by the war-traders who had munitions of war to sell, and was nothing more than an advertisement for their business. Sundry politicians, many newspapers, and not a few good people who are proud to have their thinking done for them accepted this advertisement as a profound political truth. Its falsity is now plain to every one. Guns and bullets and armor are not made to take the place of postage stamps and books and laboratories and other instruments of civilization and of peace; they are made to kill people. Since war is an affair of governments and of armies, one result of the present war should be to make the manufacture and sale of munitions of war a government monopoly hereafter. This is a case where invasion of the field of liberty by government would do good, not harm. Then, too, the export of munitions of war from one country to another should be absolutely forbidden. When that happens, the taxpayer will be able to see just how his money is spent and to check the expenditure, and the powerful war-trader, with his lines of influence in every parliament house and in every chancellery, will be eliminated.

It seems pretty clear that when the present huge supplies of guns and ammunition are used up in the contest now going on no civilized people will ever again permit its government to enter into a competitive armament race. The time may not be so very far distant when to be the first moral power in the world will be a considerably greater distinction than to be the first military power or even the second naval power, which latter goal is so constantly and so subtly urged on the people of the United States. How any one, not fit subject for a madhouse, can find in the awful events now happening in Europe a reason for increasing the military and naval establishments and expenditures of the United States is to me wholly inconceivable.

Another great gain is to be found in the fact that no one is willing to be responsible for this war. Every combatant alleges that he is on the defensive, and summons his fellow-countrymen who are scientists and philosophers to find some way to prove it. The old claim that war was a part of the moral order, a God-given instrument for the spreading of enlightenment and the only real training school for the manly virtues, is just now in a state of eclipse. Each one of the several belligerent nations insists that it and its government are devoted friends of peace, and that it is at war only be-

cause war was forced upon it by the acts of some one
else. As to who that some one else is it has not yet
been possible to get a unanimous agreement. What we
do know is that no one steps forward to claim credit for
the war or to ask a vote of thanks or a decoration for
having forced it upon Europe and upon the world.
Everybody concerned is ashamed of it and apologetic
for it.

. . . In the Europe of tomorrow there will be no
place for secret treaties and understandings, for huge
systems of armed camps and limitless navies, for sleepless international enmity and treachery, for carefully
stimulated race and religious hatred, or for wars made
on the sole responsibility of monarchs and of ministers.
Moral, social, and political progress will refuse longer
to pay the crushing tolls which a conventional diplomacy and an unenlightened statesmanship have demanded of them. It is not the Slav or the Teuton, the
Latin or the Briton, the Oriental or the American who
is the enemy of civilization and of culture. Militarism;
there is the enemy!

The first notable victim of the Great War was the
eloquent and accomplished French parliamentarian, M.
Jaurès. He was murdered by a war-crazed fanatic. In
the course of a long and intimate conversation with
M. Jaurès shortly before his tragic death he dwelt much
on the part that America could play in binding the nations of Europe together. He spoke of the success of
the policies that had been worked out here to make the
United States and Germany and the United States and
France better known to each other, and he thought that
through the agency of the United States it might eventually be practicable to draw Germany and France together in real trust and friendship. As we parted his
last words to me were: "Do not leave off trying. No
matter what the difficulties are, do not leave off trying."
Today the words of this great socialist leader of men
seem like a voice from beyond the grave. They are true.
We must not leave off trying. When exhaustion, physical and economic, brings this war to an end, as I believe
it will at no distant day, the task of America and Americans will be heavy and responsible. It will be for us to
bind up the war's wounds, to soften the war's animosities, and to lead the way in the colossal work of reconstruction that must follow. Then if our heads are clear,
our hearts strong, and our aims unselfish—and if our
nation continues to show that it means always to keep
its own plighted word—we may gain new honor and imperishable fame for our country. We may yet live to
see our great policies of peace, of freedom from entan-

gling alliances, of a world concert instead of a continental balance of power, of an international judiciary and an international police, of international co-operation instead of international suspicion, generally assented to, and as a result the world's resources set free to improve the lot of peoples, to advance science and scholarship, and to raise humanity to a level yet unheard of. Here lies the path of national glory for us, and here is the call to action in the near future.

Document No. 27 Jane Addams and William J. Bryan, "Is the Peace Movement a Failure?" (1914)
Source: *The Ladies' Home Journal,* XXXI (November, 1914).

THE LADIES' HOME JOURNAL
VOLUME XXXI NUMBER 11 · PHILADELPHIA NOVEMBER 1914

Is the Peace Movement a Failure?

PERSONAL STATEMENTS BY

Jane Addams
of Hull-House, Chicago

and

William Jennings Bryan
Secretary of State

IT WAS only a few weeks ago that people were led to believe that never in the history of the world was universal peace among the nations of the earth so nearly attained, when suddenly Europe was hurled into the most gigantic war in the history of the world. Naturally many have tried to square the theory and the fact and have asked themselves: "How about universal peace now?" This question was submitted to the two most prominent advocates of universal peace, Miss Addams and Mr. Bryan, and their statements follow. THE EDITORS OF THE LADIES' HOME JOURNAL.

THE many advocates of peace will give widely different explanations of the European war, but certainly they will agree that no one ever ventured to claim that arbitration had as yet become firmly established as an International usage.

Although the Tribunal at The Hague gave a concrete and living expression to International law and precedent war did not become impossible simply because International disputes might be adjudicated with honor and just dealing.

The question of International arbitration seems, at moments, to resolve itself into one of time. Its most ardent promoters could never do more than ask themselves if the resort to arbitration without compulsion was psychologically possible for a sufficient length of time so that the custom could be built up between nations, as the resort to law between individuals has already been established in all civilized States.

The occurrence of this great war cannot stamp International arbitration as a failure. The mistake of judging such a situation too hastily may be illustrated from our own National experience: When the thirteen original States united, and each agreed to make no attempt to defend its own borders, but to submit all differences to a supreme court of the federated States, the founders of our republic had every right to look forward to centuries of unbroken peace, although in less than seventy-five years these States were engaged in a prolonged civil war. Yet no one would call our Federal Government a failure nor the establishment of the Supreme Court a mistake.

Over and over again the Conferences at The Hague attempted without success to limit, through mutual agreement, the huge standing armies of Europe, whose very existence means that the maneuvers of war become the daily business of thousands of men during the very best years of their lives.

If, as the war adherents claim, it is impossible for the world to get along without war in man's present state of developm⟨;⟩t, may it not be because these impressive preparations have themselves made for war?

ADVOCATES of peace have published elaborate calculations demonstrating that the armed peace of Europe was only less costly than war itself. Millions of idle men supported at public expense, interest on war debts and all the rest, during the current year, cost the various nations of the earth two billions of dollars, according to an estimate of David Starr Jordan, who also insists that the high cost of living all over the world is due to this senseless waste.

Many years ago I heard Professor James, at a great meeting of the International Peace Society, urge the necessity for "moral substitutes" for war. It is doubtless true that "every man should some time in his life make a definite renunciation of ease and comfort for his country's good"; that he should have the stimulation of "fear nobly resisted"; that he should submit to an impersonal discipline and lose himself in "the heart of a people beating with one desire"; but certainly it is possible to achieve all of these without warfare, if we have courage to insist that much of what the past forced us to accept is not good enough for the present. Certainly the increased moral sensitiveness to the outrage and wrong of warfare has been widely expressed in American newspapers and is evinced in cartoons published every day since the war began.

The rulers of the nations involved in the war have each carefully explained that there was no alternative for him, that some one else was responsible for this war. When, even in the excitement of the first weeks, the neutral nations condemned and the warring nations apologized, may we not say that public sentiment has at last turned against war and that the unconscious reservists of the army of peace are reënforcing the vanguard?

Hull-House, Chicago   *Jane Addams*

NO, THE peace movement is not a failure. The European war may better be interpreted as the final object lesson needed to convince mankind of the folly of war. This war will teach a truth that will not soon be forgotten, namely, that "preparedness" directly encourages the very carnage which it is supposed to prevent. We have been told that peace rests upon fear. This is in harmony with the views of a school of philosophers whose members contend that nations can be held together in the bonds of amity only when each nation is fully equipped for battle.

If preparedness were a preventive surely Europe had a guarantee of permanent peace, for they were all ready to take up arms at a moment's notice. Hereafter preparation for wars—preparation for wars that should never come—must be defended upon some other ground than that it preserves peace. The peace argument, based upon preparedness, overlooks the fact that such preparedness cannot be continuous without a cultivation of the war spirit, and the war spirit is impossible unless there is some real or imaginary foe against whom the nation's antagonism can be directed. Passions must be fanned in the name of patriotism, and man-killing devices must be planned in the alleged interest of brotherhood! This war may be worth its awful cost if it buries forever this fallacious theory.

WAR, in so far as it is not a matter of desire, is a state of mind, and it is possible to effect a change in both the desire and the thought of a nation. It is just as easy to stimulate a public favorable to peaceful methods as to cultivate the idea that war is a legitimate means of securing an International advantage. With moral growth it should become more and more easy to substitute the doctrine that Right makes Might for the doctrine that Might makes Right.

See what mediation has done. The possibility of war in the Western Hemisphere has been made more remote by the offer of mediation by Brazil, Argentina and Chile, and its acceptance by the United States and Mexico. Henceforth it will be easier in the Americas to preserve peace and more difficult to excite discord.

A good omen is to be found in the recent ratification of eighteen treaties, binding this country to Central America, to the leading countries of South America and to six of the nations of Europe, by conventions providing that there shall be no war until the matter in dispute is investigated. This Government offered to link itself to any and every other nation, without regard to the size or strength of the nation, in an agreement that there shall be time for deliberation before the beginning of hostilities, and twenty-two treaties of this kind have already been signed.

Here, then, are the two systems: one puts its trust in force, the other in reason. Only those of little faith can doubt the triumph of the latter.

DIPLOMACY is the art of keeping cool. We go far toward insuring peace when we agree that there shall be a period during which the real issues may be set forth and questions of honor be separated from questions of fact. Man excited is quite different from man when calm. When we are angry we talk of what we *can* do; when our anger has passed away we consider what we *should* do.

Truth is vindicated in two ways—first by its success when tried, and second by the failure of error when error is put to the test. The truth embodied in the peace movement is receiving a double vindication at this time. The ultimatum will yet give place to the motto: Nothing is final between friends.

Department of State,
  Washington

William Jennings Bryan

Document No. 28   Mrs. F.W. Pethick Lawrence, "Motherhood and War" (1914)
Source: *Harper's Weekly,* LIX (Dec. 5, 1914), p. 542.

Motherhood and War
By MRS. F. W. PETHICK LAWRENCE

FROM time to time the current of the world's life is quickened by some new stream that is poured into it. The emergence of the middle class into political life wrought a commercial revolution in Great Britain. The emancipation of the working classes changed the national outlook upon many industrial and social questions. Today the new force that is entering into the woman's life is that of an awakened and still rapidly awakening womanhood.

At the very moment that this new force has been generated, the whole world is standing aghast at the contemplation of its own disruption. We are witnessing in the present European War something that resembles a "twilight of the gods" the passing away in blood and fire of an epoch. It is from the ruins that a new civilization will have to be built up.

Even at a moment like this, the thoughts of all men and women who live at all in the wider life of humanity must be occupied in preparing for the work of reconstruction. The foundations of such reconstruction must inevitably be the peace that sooner or later will supervene upon the present war.

For, whether there is decisive victory for one side or the other, or whether there is not, peace must come within a measurable distance of time for the simple reason that war cannot feed itself. War is absolutely destructive. It subsists on the resources which can only be accumulated in time of peace. When the substance of the people is almost eaten up, when our life blood is almost sucked away, then exhaustion and bankruptcy will be allowed to withdraw humanity from the clutches of the glutted vampire of war.

But what kind of peace will it be when it comes? That is the question. Who is going to determine it? Who will arrange its conditions? Everything depends upon that. If the same people who by secret diplomacies brought war upon Europe, without the consent, without even the knowledge of their respective democracies, settle in this same way the conditions of peace, then the new peace will only be once again the prelude of a new war, which will ensue some generations hence and will be vaster and more destructive even than the present colossal conflict.

It has been claimed that the aim of the present war is to end war. But war cannot end war, neither can militarism destroy militarism. The only thing that can end war is the birth of a new spirit embodied in a constructive peace hitherto new to the world. It is possible that even now, amongst the non-combatant of the world, a new spirit may find embodiment in some great organization that may bring influence to bear upon this question when the opportune moment comes.

There are only two forces that can withstand the force of the war's spirit when it seizes upon the world. The one is the force of an independently thinking free, and articulate democracy. The other is the force of an instructed and enlightened public opinion.

But the democracies, one and all, are utterly impotent in present conditions to inspire, or to criticise, or to direct the foreign policy of their respective nationalities. This condition of things must be brought to an end and some constitutional machinery must be found for the future exercise of democratic control of foreign policy. International treaties and alliances should not be ratified without the consent of the peoples whose destinies they control. In this, and in many other respects, the new epoch must see the rise of a reinforced democracy.

The new force of the woman's movement should be seized upon to further this end. It is vital to the deepest interests of the human race that the mother half of humanity should now be admitted into the ranks of the articulate democracies of the world, in order to strengthen them and to enable them to combine the more effectively in their own defense against the deadly machinery of organized distruction that threatens in the future to crush the white races and to overwhelm civilization.

The bed-rock of humanity is motherhood. The solidarity of the world's motherhood, potential or otherwise, underlies all cleavages of nationality. Men have conflicting interests and ambitions. Women all the world over, speaking broadly, have one passion and one vocation, and that is the creation and preservation of human life. Deep in the hearts of the women of the peasant and industrial classes of every nation, there lies beneath their readiness to endure their full share of their nations' toll of sacrifice and suffering, a denial of the necessity of war. There is a rooted revolt against the destruction of the blossoming manhood of the race. This revolt is now for the first time finding expression, as the race soul of the womanhood of the world comes in this twentieth century to consciousness. The woman's movement has awakened women to their great responsibilities as the natural custodians of the human race. It is vital to the interests of the human race itself that the mother half of humanity should now be admitted to articulate citizenship. The emancipation of women must be included in the program of those who would lay a broad foundation of constructive peace for the rebuilding of the modern world.

IT would be a great thing if the woman's movement all over the world should enter now upon a great organized campaign of preparation for peace, allying itself with all the other forces now at work in the same direction and setting itself the task, first, in the great neutral nation of America, and then, in all other countries, of awakening and educating public opinion with regard to the supreme value of human life and of racial evolution. Peace movements in the past have been negative. That is where they have failed.

Since public opinion cannot be educated solely by words, such a campaign, if started, should be linked with certain definte propositions to be decided upon in conference between the men and women who should initiate it. These propositions should be urged as some of the conditions of constructive peace. I tabulate by way of illustration the following suggestions that civilized peoples should unite in demanding from their respective countries:

FIRST, the broadening and strengthening of the democracies by the admission of the mother-half of the human race into the body politic.

Second, the creation, where none already exists, of some adequate machinery for insuring democratic control of foreign policy.

Third, the assurance that no treaty arrangement or undertaking be entered upon, in the name of the country, without the sanction of the people concerned expressed through their representatives.

Fourth, that the manufacture of armaments and ammunition be taken over by the nation itself, and that the export of armaments to other countries be prohibited.

Fifth, that at the termination of the war, the influence of the nation be used to discourage the transfer of any of the European provinces from one government to another without the consent by plebiscite of the population of such province, and that the plebiscite should include the women who have borne the burden of suffering equally with the men.

Sixth, that there should be some representation of women at the Hague conference.

IN addition to such concrete proposals as these, public opinion has to be enlightened and organized towards the ideal of international agreement. "We must labor", as says ex-President Roosevelt, "for an international agreement among the great civilized nations which shall put the full force of all of them, back of anyone of them, and of any well-behaved weak nation which is wronged by any other power."

By the initiation throughout the States of a popular campaign carried out upon lines indicated by these suggestions, led by influential men and women, aided by the President, reinforced by great public meetings, America would give a much needed lead to the democracies of Europe.

The better, happier world that we hope for in the future must be built up by the people themselves, upon the foundations of a constructive, lasting peace. This task cannot be left to the detached and secret agencies of Governments. It should be begun now. There is not a moment to lose.

Document No. 29 Addresses at the Woman's Peace Party Conference
(1915)
Source: Pamphlet located at the Swarthmore College Peace Collection,
Swarthmore, Pa.

ADDRESSES

GIVEN AT THE

ORGANIZATION CONFERENCE

OF THE

WOMAN'S PEACE PARTY

WASHINGTON, D. C.
JANUARY 10, 1915

WOMAN'S PEACE PARTY
National Headquarters
116 So. Michigan Ave.
CHICAGO, ILL.

Price 5 cents

257

ROLL OF CHARTER MEMBERS OF THE WOMAN'S PEACE PARTY

ORGANIZED JANUARY 9-11, 1915
REVISED TO FEBRUARY 6, 1915

LIST OF THOSE PRESENT AND REPORTING:

AMERICAN PEACE SOCIETY
Mrs. Anna Garlin Spencer, Meadville, Pa.
Miss Lyra D. Trueblood, 309 Falkstone Courts, Washington.
Mrs. Arthur D. Call, 1820 Newton., N. W., Washington.
Miss Marion Tilden Burritt, 507 Fifth Ave., New York.
Miss Jane Addams, Hull House, Chicago.
Mrs. Jas. L. Slayden, San Antonio, Tex. (The Concord, Washington).
Miss Susan R. Cutts, 613 Colorado Bldg., Washington.
Mrs. Rose Morgan French. San Francisco, Cal. (Temporarily Hotel McAlpin, Greeley Square, New York.)

NATIONAL AMERICAN WOMEN'S SUFFRAGE ASS'N.
Rev. Anna Howard Shaw, Pres., 1706, 505 Fifth Ave., New York.
Mrs. Susan Walker Fitzgerald, 7 Greenough Ave., Jamaica Plain, Mass.
Mrs. Henry Villard, 540 Park Ave., New York.
Miss Caroline Ruutz-Rees, Greenwich, Conn.
Mrs. Antoinette Funk, Munsey Bldg., Washington.

NATIONAL COUNCIL OF WOMEN
Mrs. Kate Waller Barrett, Pres., 408 Duke St., Alexandria, Va.
Mrs. Lucia Ames Mead, Chairman Peace Dept., 39 Newbury St., Boston.
Mrs. Cassius E. Wright, 200 A St., S. E., Washington.
Mrs. Mary W. Story, 628 A St., S. E., Washington.
Mrs. Frank P. Woodbury, 601 Howard Place. Washington.
Mrs. Emma J. Price, 2332 First St., N. W., Washington.

NATIONAL WOMAN'S CHRISTIAN TEMPERANCE UNION
Mrs. Emma S. Shelton, Cypress St., Chevy Chase, Md.
Mrs. Margaret D. Ellis, The Driscoll, Washington.
Mrs. Ella Hoover Thacher, 1627 Mass. Ave., Washington.

FRIENDS EQUAL RIGHTS ASSOCIATION
Mrs. Guion Miller, Easton, Talbot Co., Md.

NATIONAL SOCIETY, DAUGHTERS OF THE AMERICAN REVOLUTION
Mrs. George M. Sternberg, (representing Mrs. Wm. C. Story, Pres., 2005 Mass Ave., Washington).
Mrs. George T. Smallwood, 3520 16th St., Washington.
Mrs. S. Ella Wood Dean, 5000 Drexel Blvd., Chicago.

ASSOCIATION OF COLLEGIATE ALUMNAE
Miss Elsie M. Hill, Central High School, Washington.

INTERNATIONAL KINDERGARTEN UNION
Miss Catherine R. Watkins, 1720 Oregon Ave., Washington.
Miss A. M. Winchester, U. S. Bureau of Education, Washington.
Miss Helen Gordon, 1527 Park Road, Washington.

NATIONAL LEAGUE OF TEACHERS' ASSOCIATIONS
Miss Mollie R. Hobbs, 823 N. Fremont Ave., Baltimore, Md.

NATIONAL FEDERATION OF SETTLEMENTS
Miss Mary E. McDowell, Pres., U. of Chicago Settlement, 4630 Gross Av Chicago.
Mrs. Vladimir G. Simkhovitch. Greenwich House, 26 Jones St., New York.

NATIONAL WOMEN'S TRADE UNION LEAGUE
Mrs. Lydia M. Schmidt, Chicago.
Miss Marie Schmidt, Chicago.

WOMAN'S NATIONAL COMMITTEE, SOCIALIST PARTY
Mrs. Charles Edward Russell, 1025, 15th St., Washington.

AMERICAN SCHOOL PEACE LEAGUE
Mrs. Fannie Fern Andrews, 405 Marlborough St., Boston, Mass.

WORLD PEACE FOUNDATION
Mrs. Anna S. Duryea, 40 Mt. Vernon St., Boston, Mass.

AMERICAN ASSOCIATION FOR INTERNATIONAL CONCILIATION
Mrs. George F. Whicher, 709 West Nevada St., Urbana, Ill.

VITAL CONSERVATION ASSOCIATION
Mrs. James Pryor Tarvin, 1758 Q St., Washington.

FEDERAL SUFFRAGE ASSOCIATION
Mrs. Clara Bewick Colby, 522 Sixth St., Washington.

SPANISH-AMERICAN WAR NURSES
Mrs. Anita Newcomb McGee, M. D., 1620 P St., Washington.

AMERICAN PEACE AND ARBITRATION LEAGUE
Mrs. Mary Cruttenden Percy, 254 West 76th St., New York.

INDIVIDUALS
Mrs. Carrie Chapman Catt, 2 West 86th St., New York.
Mrs. John Jay White, 2306 Mass Ave., Washington.
Mrs. Glendower Evans, 12 Otis Place, Boston, Mass.
Mrs. Joseph Fels, 3640 Chestnut St., Philadelphia, Pa.
Mrs. Caroline M. Hill, c/o N. Y. Peace Society, 507 Fifth Ave., New York.
Mrs. Charlotte Perkins Gilman, 627 West 136th St., New York.
Mrs. Juliet Barrett Rublee, 1105, 16th St., Washington.
Mrs. William Kent, 1925 F St., Washington.
Miss Julia Lathrop, The Ontario, Washington.
Mrs. Louis F. Post, 2513, 12th St., Washington.
Mrs. Robert M. LaFollette, 3320 16th St., Washington.
Miss Mary R. Cabot, 501 Beacon St., Boston, Mass.
Mrs. Frank F. Williams, 54 Irving Place, Buffalo, N. Y.
Mrs. Frances Greeno Barr, Junction City, Kans. (Temporary address 1753 18th St., Washington).
Mrs. C. E. Ellicott, Equal Suf. Lea. of Balt., Brown Arcade 107, Baltimore, Md.

REPRESENTING LOCAL BRANCHES OF WOMAN'S PEACE PARTY

CHICAGO BRANCH
Miss Florence Holbrook, 562 Oakwood Blvd., Chicago.
Mrs. Bertram W. Sippy, 5615 Woodlawn Ave., Chicago.
Mrs. Frank R. Lillie, 5801 Kenwood Ave., Chicago.
Mrs. H. M. Wilmarth, Congress Hotel, Chicago.
Mrs. Wm. Bross Lloyd, Winnetka, Ill.
Mrs. Edgar Martin, 1719 East 55th St., Chicago.

WASHINGTON BRANCH
Mrs. Christian D. Hemmick, 1626 Rhode Island Ave., Washington.
Miss Aline E. Solomons, 1205 K St., Washington.
Mrs. J. I. Chamberlain, The Highlands, Washington.
Mrs. George Odell, The Rochambeau, Washington.
Dr. C. S. Ludlow, The Ethelhurst, Washington.
Miss Janet E. Richards, The Wyoming, Washington.
Mrs. Huntington W. Jackson, 1304 Conn. Ave., Washington.
Mrs. Olive Powell Ransdell, 1726 M St., Washington.
Mrs. Winston Churchill, 1109 16th St., Washington.
Mrs. Nina E. Allender, The Harford, 1315 Clifton St., Washington.
Mrs. J. N. Speel, 1516 K St., Washington.
Mrs. Frances L. Adams, 5605 14th St., Washington.
Mrs. Nevil Monroe Hopkins, 2128 Bancroft Pl., Washington.
Mrs. Gilson Gardner, The Rochambeau, Washington.

MASSACHUSETTS PEACE SOCIETY
Mrs. J. Malcolm Forbes, 280 Adams St., Milton, Mass.

CONNECTICUT PEACE SOCIETY
Mrs. Josepha Whitney, 188 Bishop St., New Haven, Conn.

MARYLAND DAUGHTERS OF THE AMERICAN REVOLUTION
Mrs. Robert G. Hogan, Catonsville, Md.

COLORADO WOMAN'S CHRISTIAN TEMPERANCE UNION
Mrs. Ruth H. Spray, 245 W. 8th St., Salida, Colo. (Temporary address 800 Reservoir St., Baltimore, Md.)

DISTRICT OF COLUMBIA WOMAN'S CHRISTIAN TEMPERANCE UNION
Miss Lucy S. Patrick, Peace Supt., The Sherman, Washington.

WASHINGTON, D. C. PEACE SOCIETY
Mrs. Mabel Harte Ramsay, Euclid and 14th Sts., Washington.

PHILADELPHIA PEACE ASSOCIATION OF FRIENDS
Mrs. Jonathan Mowry Steere, Haverford, Pa.

HONORARY MEMBERS OF WOMAN'S PEACE PARTY
Mrs. Pethick-Lawrence, London, England.
Mme. Roŝika Schwimmer, Budapest, Hungary. (Temporarily, Hotel McAlpin, Greenley Sq., New York).

Addresses Given at the Organization Conference of the Woman's Peace Party

On the 10th and 11th of January, 1915, a conference was held in Washington, at which representatives from all the leading women's organizations and movements assembled to consider measures for promoting and formulating peace sentiment in this country and, perhaps throughout the world.

The meetings of the first day and a half, presided over by Miss Janet Richards, were spent in drafting a platform and explanatory statement, with a plan of work. On the afternoon of the second day a great public meeting was held, at which the platform was unanimously adopted. The Woman's Peace Party was formally launched.

Mrs. Carrie Chapman Catt, of New York, presided over this meeting, which she opened with the following statement:

"This meeting has been called as a part of a conference of women held in Washington to review the general situation concerning the great problem of peace, and looking to a national, and probably international, organization among women. The women of this country were lulled into inattention to the great military question of the war by reading the many books put forth by great pacifists who had studied the question deeply and who announced that there never could be another world war. But when the great war came and the women of this country waited for the pacifists to move, and they heard nothing from them, they decided all too late to get together themselves and to try to do something at this eleventh hour."

Mrs. Anna Garlin Spencer then presented the preamble with the platform.

Preamble

WE, WOMEN OF THE UNITED STATES, assembled in behalf of World Peace, grateful for the security of our own country, but sorrowing for the misery of all involved in the present struggle among warring nations, do hereby band ourselves together to demand that war be abolished.

Equally with men pacifists, we understand that planned-for, legalized, wholesale, human slaughter is today the sum of all villainies.

As women, we feel a peculiar moral passion of revolt against both the cruelty and the waste of war.

As women, we are especially the custodians of the life of the ages. We will not longer consent to its reckless destruction.

As women, we are particularly charged with the future of childhood and with the care of the helpless and the unfortunate. We will not longer endure without protest that added burden of maimed and invalid men and poverty stricken widows and orphans which war places upon us.

As women, we have builded by the patient drudgery of the past the basic foundation of the home and of peaceful industry. We will not longer endure without a protest that must be heard and heeded by men, that hoary evil which in an hour destroys the social structure that centuries of toil have reared.

260

As women, we are called upon to start each generation onward toward a better humanity. We will not longer tolerate without determined opposition that denial of the sovereignty of reason and justice by which war and all that makes for war today render impotent the idealism of the race.

Therefore, as human beings and the mother half of humanity, we demand that our right to be consulted in the settlement of questions concerning not alone the life of individuals but of nations be recognized and respected.

We demand that women be given a share in deciding between war and peace in all the courts of high debate—within the home, the school, the church, the industrial order, and the state.

So protesting, and so demanding, we hereby form ourselves into a national organization to be called the Woman's Peace Party.

We hereby adopt the following as our platform of principles, some of the items of which have been accepted by a majority vote, and more of which have been the unanimous choice of those attending the conference that initiated the formation of this organization. We have sunk all differences of opinion on minor matters and given freedom of expression to a wide divergence of opinion in the details of our platform and in our statement of explanation and information, in a common desire to make our woman's protest against war and all that makes for war, vocal, commanding and effective. We welcome to our membership all who are in substantial sympathy with that fundamental purpose of our organization, whether or not they can accept in full our detailed statement of principles.

Platform

THE PURPOSE of this Organization is to enlist all American women in arousing the nations to respect the sacredness of human life and to abolish war. The following is adopted as our platform:

1. The immediate calling of a convention of neutral nations in the interest of early peace.
2. Limitation of armaments and the nationalization of their manufacture.
3. Organized opposition to militarism in our own country.
4. Education of youth in the ideals of peace.
5. Democratic control of foreign policies.
6. The further humanizing of governments by the extension of the franchise to women.
7. "Concert of Nations" to supersede "Balance of Power."
8. Action toward the gradual organization of the world to substitute Law for War.
9. The substitution of an international police for rival armies and navies.
10. Removal of the economic causes of war.
11. The appointment by our Government of a commission of men and women, with an adequate appropriation, to promote international peace.

The following speakers were introduced by Mrs Catt:

Mrs. Charlotte Perkins Gilman, of New York:

I think we are all of one mind as to the general purpose or purposes of this convention, but it is of even more importance that we settle upon some single immediate definite possible action, and that we then set in motion large, carefully planned, efficient measures to promote that one action. In every program which I have seen advanced there is an agreement on that one point so warmly welcomed here, of the calling of an international conference and calling it quickly. We feel that there is a greater necessity for immediate action than was ever before the world up to this date; that nothing could make a more tremendous appeal for immediate action than that continuous horror which is going on in Europe today. We are all agreed that that is the thing to do, and that it remains for us to decide on the method of doing it. We want it done nationally, officially, governmentally. If at present it is not so done, it remains in the hands of the American people by millions and millions to express their definite will in the matter. To that end, the thing that I want to leave before this house is a suggestion as to active propaganda in the interests of our already established purpose. It is an interesting thing in this country to watch the nation-wide, swift, confident, efficient action of a political party when it wishes to influence public opinion, whether it is on free silver or a gold standard, or any other subject. There is an organized body whose business it is to distribute information, and not only information, but emotional appeal. That sort of work is what has to be done now; to get together and start the definite machinery for distribution through the press, the platform, the pulpit, the college, the school, through every medium of reaching the public that is open to us of as much of this program as they will take, and most especially to have before them all one simple, definite and concrete proposition that no one can object to. Surely that proposition is the one that stands first with us all—the calling of the international conference to discuss measures for the ending of this war and the prevention of further wars. I cannot imagine any body of people in this country, any large organization, that could withhold its backing to such a proposition as that. Peace is a thing between nations, as war is a thing between nations. One cannot make peace all alone, any more than one can make war all alone. In order to procure and maintain peace, we have got to get together the nations of the world. That call most properly comes from the nation that represents the idea of federal union as fully as does ours. Now, if this simple proposition can be brought before the American public all up and down the land, laid before the women's clubs and the men's associations, and all the great bodies of people, and backed up by the alliance of body after body, having for its signatories not merely individuals, but representative groups; if we can roll up millions upon millions of organized public opinion in America, then surely a representative government will express the will of the people and call as soon as it is humanely possible that conference of representative delegates which alone can take the further measures to promote the end for which we are all gathered here.

Mrs. Pethick-Lawrence, of London:

Madam Chairman, Ladies and Gentlemen: As I understand it, th woman's movement in America for constructive peace has naturally been great moral idea, and this idea was expressed yesterday by one of the mo: revered pioneers of the peace movement in the following words, so far as can remember them. She said to us: "We must remember that it is ours t demonstrate the principle that human life is sacred and inviolable." It is th supreme duty of women, who give birth to human life, to stand for this trut against the whole world, and to band themselves together to insist upon i recognition as a fundamental moral law. Human life is sacred and inviolabl It follows, therefore, that the human body, without respect to nation, to se: or to color, is the temple of the holy spirit, and that the human soul is mor precious than any accumulation of wealth. My friends, this is not a ne idea. It is a very old idea; it is the fundamental idea of all the great religion all down the ages, and yet at the present day it is this principle which being blasphemed by the world in which we live. Hold that in your mind, and then turn your eyes, the eyes of your imagination, for one moment to those hundreds of miles of trenches in that old country which has been looked upon as the birthplace of modern civilization, the stronghold of the Christian religion. Think of those miles and miles of trenches where organized deliberate murder is being done even now as we speak, and continuously by day and by night; think of those battlefields sodden with the blood of our human fellow beings; not only piled with dead, as the newspapers describe it, but piled with shrieking, writhing, agonized manhood; think of those shelterless and fugitive women, bearing in their violated bodies the unborn children of the next generation; think of those mothers stifling the wailing of their children in their arms, hiding in the woods and ditches of those desolated villages; think of those trains bearing back to their homes the dead to be burned upon the refuse heaps; think of those things, and then say whether this iniquity is to be tolerated any longer. In answer to that question, I say no! It is not to be tolerated! I say no on behalf of the women and men assembled in this room; no on behalf of the womanhood of the whole world. If men can tolerate it, women can not! We who, speaking collectively, have purchased every living human frame in this world with our blood and with our life. What does this no mean? If you have said it with me, it means that there is not a woman here, nor a man, that can go out of this meeting without making a protest every single day that the war goes on, a protest that is in action, a protest not only by words, but by deeds. We must make it very clear, we must grasp the idea very, very clearly that there is no conceivable end of any value to the human race to be gained by any conceivable eventualit of the present war—nobody knows better than some of our soldiers who are fighting at the front.

There is only one power that stands up against this madness of war, and that is the power of public opinion, and public opinion in this, the greatest democracy of all the world. It has but to be fixed, educated, organized, and it can then be brought to bear upon the governments of all the world through your own government and through your representative, President Wilson, who will be called into the council of nations, and who has proved himself to be a man both of peace and of good will. He can act only with the power that you give him. Remember, it is not statesmen who can organize public opinion, for public opinion has to organize the statesman; and the business of the democracy of America is so to organize public opinion that it may put the voice of the whole people behind President Wilson and strengthen his hand when it acts. One thing let us be determined upon—that when peace comes to be made, it shall be made on behalf of the democracies who did not make the war—that it shall not be made by these international political gamblers, or these degenerate rulers who have not the interest of the people at stake, but only their own dynastic, financial or political purpose.

There is not a moment to lose—not a moment. Every day that war goes on we must be preparing for an advantageous peace which alone can end wars in the future.

My friends, the crisis is urgent. The hour is great. Every man and woman in this audience must determine here and now to become the active soldiers in the great cause of peace, which is the cause of liberty, which is the cause of democracy, which is the cause of the progress of the human race.

Mrs. Kate Waller Barrett, President, National Council of Women:

As you know, the National Council of Women of the United States was represented at the international conference at Rome last summer, at which were represented thirty-six national councils, representing all the nations that are now at war, and many of the neutral nations; and it has been my privilege in the last few weeks to receive letters from every one of those organized groups of women, and it has been a sad, but at the same time a pleasant, privilege to read these letters, and while every group of women is trying to be faithful to the country in which they have been born and bred, there is a deepseated desire on the part of every organized group of women for just the thing that we American women are here today to demand of the world. The only reason that the women of Europe are not demanding what we are demanding is that we are privileged to be American women, and I stand before you today privileged as an American woman to say what I please; there is no power in the United States that can stop me. I bring to you the desire expressed by the National Council of Women of the Netherlands that the women of the United States join with them in trying to bring about a federation of Europe similar to the federation of the United States of America. I bring to you an expression of opinion from the women of Switzerland that we do everything possible to bring about the least possible suffering among the women and children and non-combatants and foreigners in the countries that are now at war with each other. I bring to you a plea from the women of Austria, from the women of Hungary, that we unite with them in an effort to stop this war, to end the needless suffering of women and children and non-combatants in the war zone. So you see that these foreign women look to us for help—with broken hearts and bleeding bodies are looking to us American women, who are at the same time powerful and free, to help them

Madame Rosika Schwimmer, of Budapest, Hungary:

I think when the time comes that we European people will try to express our gratitude to you, the people of the United States, we will try all kinds of things, and maybe some of us will think of trying to become finally a citizen of your nation, and by this showing that we would call it the greatest honor to be a citizen of this nation. But I am afraid that this kind of gratitude would be more of a burden than you should care for, yet I wonder whether you realize how great this gratitude is which we feel for the American women who have taught us European women; whether you realize that by the thing that you have done today you have added so much to that for which we are already so grateful. By adopting this platform of peace, then by adopting this program for action—for active, not theoretical peace—you have laid down the foundations for a new Europe, for a Europe which seemed to many of us European people as hopelessly broken down. The adoption of the resolution of these women here today, representing the organized women of your nation, not to wait until the unspeakable sufferings of Europe go so far that it is not worth while to save it, your resolution to try to save what can be saved, is the greatest historic act that we can put on record of what women have done for the world. You have shown us European women that you are what we expect you to be, not only teachers of the European women as you have been in the past, but teachers of the men of the world. You have begun today to teach them their lesson that there is a courage, a new kind of courage, which is more valuable than the courage for which men have stood until today. You have shown that moral courage to express your will and your wish in spite of all old-fashioned ideas and diplomatic difficulties. And this sign of your moral courage is the first lesson of these lessons which you are going to bring the world if you carry out the program for a new, for an active peace, which you have laid down here at this meeting.

Our old-fashioned idea was that a man must have the courage to face death, not only for something that is worth dying for, but even for a whim. It is a wonderful thing that you women of the United States are teaching us of the old world, teaching the men of the world that there is a greater courage than the physical one—the courage to stand for a principle, the high human courage.

When the wires bring the message over to poor, unhappy Europe, to the women who in agony and anxiety, as none of you can imagine, are living days that are dark as night, living sleepless nights; when your message comes to these unhappy people there in Europe, it will be the first glance of hope that has come to them since this terrible massacre began. You cannot know how you will be blessed by every one who hears your message that is going out today from this place. But every great and good thing that you have done has not been done only for us European people; you have not only lightened the terrible burden on us; you have not only brought consolation to the women who weep and cry for the millions of men who have already been killed in these five months of the war; you have not only brought consolation to those tortured women who are the sole protectors of their children; you have done something for yourselves, you women of the United States, today. Many of you are still in the terrible position in which we European women are. Many of you in so many of your states are not yet able to say, "I am going to do my share in making the world a safe place for my sons and daughters." Most of you who are not citizens, only daughters or wives of citizens, must be afraid and trembling and full of anxiety that an incident may bring your children what has happened to our children. Only those women who can say, "We have the power in our hands to avert it, we are going to safeguard the great home, called the state, for our children"; only those who can do something for the safety of their children are free. For the others who are not yet free, who have not yet the means to protect their children, for them, I think, you have done today the greatest thing you could do.

I thank you in the name of the European women, in the name of the European men whose lives your action will save. I thank you for your resolution to continue the work for peace which one man of your nation has begun. A man of your nation has given the world a palace of peace, and you have laid down today the foundation for an empire of peace. I thank you in the name of the European women, and let me tell you that we promise you that what with hands and hearts and brains we can contribute on our part to make this empire beautiful and safe for future generations, we will not only for our sake, but out of gratitude to you who here tonight taught us to build the new empire.

Miss Jane Addams, of Chicago:

After the eloquent speeches you have heard from women who have come from the field of battle, as it were, a speech from one representing American women, thousands of miles away from the devastation and carnage, must seem tame and scarcely deserving a hearing. But there are certain things now being destroyed by war in which from the beginning of time women, as women, have held a vested interest, and I beg to draw your attention to three or four of them.

One thing war is now destroying, and which is being "thrown back" in the scientific sense, is the conception of patriotism gradually built up during thousands of years. Europe has had one revolution after another in which women as well as men have taken part, that a patriotism might be established which should contain liberty as well as loyalty.

At the present moment, however, thousands of men marching to their death are under compulsion, not of this higher type of patriotism, but of a tribal conception which ought to have left the world long since.

A state founded upon such a tribal ideal of patriotism has no place for women within its councils, and women have a right to protest against the destruction of that larger ideal of the state in which they had won a place, and to deprecate a world put back upon a basis of brute force—a world in which they can play no part.

Women also have a vested right in the developed conscience of the world. At this moment, because of war, the finest consciences in Europe are engaged in the old business of self-justification, utilizing outgrown myths to explain the course of action which their governments have taken.

And last, shall we not say that that sensitiveness to human life so highly developed in women has been seriously injured by this war. Thousands of people in the United States and Europe had become so convinced that the sanctity of life was an accepted tenet of civilization that they deemed war had become forever impossible. That belief has been rudely overturned and we are now at the foot of the ladder, beginning again to establish the belief that human life is secured above all else that the planet contains.

I do not assert that women are better than men — even in the heat of suffrage debates I have never maintained that— but we would all admit that there are things concerning which women are more sensitive than men, and that one of these is the treasuring of life. I would ask you to consider with me five aspects concerning this sensitiveness, which war is rapidly destroying.

The first is the protection of human life. The advanced nations know very accurately, and we had begun to know in America, how many children are needlessly lost in the first years of infancy. Measures inaugurated for the prevention of infant mortality were slowly spreading from one country to another. All that effort has been scattered to the winds by the war. No one is now pretending to count the babies who are dying throughout the villages and countrysides of the warring nations.

The second aspect is the nurture of human life. From the time a soldier is born to the moment he marches in his uniform to be wantonly destroyed, it is largely the women of his household who have cared for him. War overthrows not only the work of the mother, the nurse and the teacher, but at the same time ruthlessly destroys the very conception of the careful nurture of life.

The third aspect is the fulfillment of human life. Every woman who cares for a little child, fondly throws her imagination forward to the time when he shall have become a great and heroic man. Every baby is thus made human and is developed by the hope and expectation which surrounds him. But no one in Europe in the face of war's destruction can consider any other fulfillment of life than a soldier's death.

The fourth aspect is the conservation of human life; that which expresses itself in the state care of dependent children, in old age pensions, the sentiment which holds that every scrap of human life is so valuable that the human family cannot neglect the feeblest child without risking its own destruction. At this moment, none of the warring countries of Europe can cherish the aged and infirm. The State cannot give care to its dependents when thousands of splendid men are dying each day. Little children and aged people are dying, too; in some countries in the proportion of five to one soldier killed on the field; but the nation must remain indifferent to their suffering.

And last of all is that which we call the ascent of human life; that which leads a man to cherish the hope that the next generation shall advance beyond the generation in which he lives; that generous glow we all experience when we see that those coming after us are equipped better than we have been. We know that Europe at the end of this war will not begin to build where it left off; we know that it will begin generations behind the point it had reached when the war began.

If we admit that this sensitiveness for human life is stronger in women than in men because women have been responsible for the care of the young and the aged and those who need special nurture, it is certainly true that this senitiveness, developed in women, carries with it an obligation.

Once before in the history of the world, in response to this sensitiveness, women called a halt to the sacrifice of human life, although it then implied the abolition of a religious observance long believed to be right and necessary. In the history of one nation after another, it was the mothers who first protested that their children should no longer be slain as living sacrifices upon the altars of the tribal gods, although the national leaders contended that human sacrifice was bound up with the traditions of free religion and patriotism and could not be abolished.

The women led a revolt against the hideous practice which had dogged the human race for centuries, not because they were founding a new religion, but because they were responding to their sensitiveness to life. When at last a brave leader here and there gave heed to the mother of the child, he gradually found that courage and religion were with the abolition of human sacrifice, and that the protesting women had anticipated the conscience of the future.

Many of us believe that throughout this round world of ours there are thousands of men and women who have become convinced that the sacrifice of life in warfare is unnecessary and wasteful. It is possible that if women in Europe—in the very countries which are now at war—receive a message from the women of America solemnly protesting against this sacrifice, that they may take courage to formulate their own.

We are today trying to do a difficult thing and are doubtless doing it bunglingly; it is never easy to formulate the advanced statement. Our protest reflects our emotions as well as our convictions, but still more it is the result of the deepest human experiences. We believe that we are endeavoring to express that which is grounded in the souls of women all over the world— that when this war is over—as in time it must be, if only through the exhaustion of the contending powers—there will be many men to say, "Why didn't women call a halt before thousands, and even millions, of men had needlessly lost their lives?" Certainly, if women's consciences are stirred in regard to warfare, this is the moment to formulate a statement of their convictions.

Document No. 30 George W. Nasmyth, "Constructive Mediation: An Interpretation of the Ten Foremost Proposals" (1915)
Source: *The Survey*, XXXIII (March 6, 1915), pp. 616-620.

Constructive Mediation

An Interpretation
of the Ten Foremost Proposals
By George W. Nasmyth

DIRECTOR WORLD PEACE FOUNDATION

"**O**UR FRIENDSHIP can be accepted and is accepted without reservation, because it is offered in a spirit and for a purpose which no one need ever question or suspect. Therein lies our greatness. We are champions of peace and of concord . . . it is our dearest present hope that this character and reputation may presently, in God's providence, bring us an opportunity such as has seldom been vouchsafed any nation, the opportunity to counsel and obtain peace in the world and reconciliation and a healing settlement of many a matter that has cooled and interrupted the friendship of nations."—*President Wilson's message to Congress.*

THE year 1915 presents many suggestive points of similarity with the year 1815, which marked the close of Napoleonic wars. Then, as now, the futility of military force when used for aggression had been demonstrated. A century ago, at the end of the campaigns which had devastated the continent of Europe and destroyed millions of the population, the world was sick of war and humanity was longing passionately for a stable and permanent peace. Wise men saw that the only way to put an end to war was to replace the system of international anarchy by a system of international organization, based upon the principle of a common European responsibility.

A number of treaties of alliance had been made in the preceding years, and in June, 1815, the Tsar Alexander I of Russia, proposed the formation of a confederation of Europe. The proposal was accepted by the Emperor Francis I of Austria, and by King Frederick William II of Prussia, and the confederation was formed on September 26, 1815. The three sovereigns who formed the nucleus of the confederation called upon all the Powers to become members, and the invitation was accepted by Louis XVIII of France and the English Prince Regent.

The loose confederation was developed into a stronger political alliance under the guidance of Prince Metternich. The rulers held their Congresses, going from city to city, meeting at Aachen in 1818, at Troppau in 1820, at Laybach in 1821, and at Verona in 1822, nd developing the details of the confederation.

The Holy Alliance corresponded to a real need in the development of the world, and it did secure peace for a generation and opened the way for an extraordinary development of civilization, but it was founded upon a wrong principle and could not last.

If we were to choose a committee to draw up a constitution for the federation of the world today, we should hardly elect the Tsar of Russia, the Emperor of Austria, and the King of Prussia, and expect to get a stable democratic constitution as the result. The Holy Alliance had the splendid ideal of applying Christianity to politics and it aimed at "the liberal promotion of all economic, intellectual, and social life"; but "political liberalism was to be suppressed or held in check in order to reserve the administration of public affairs to the government as especially ordained thereto." It became finally an evil thing, standing in the way of democracy and progress, and it had to go.

THE time has come to make the attempt once more to form a confederation of the world, this time upon the basis of democracy instead of autocracy, with the initiative coming from America, which has already worked out the problem of voluntary federation of forty-eight states on the principle of "government of the people, by the people, for the people," instead of from Russia, which proceeds upon the principle of compulsory federation resting upon military power. The people in all the European countries are saying "as far as is humanly possible, this must be the last war," and they are looking to President Wilson to extend, when the right moment arrives, not merely a formal offer of mediation, but a constructive plan, based upon a thorough knowledge of the situation and of the real needs of all the people involved, which will prevent another such breakdown of civilization in the future. For professional and technical reasons, the passionate longings of the people in the countries at war cannot find expression through the usual diplomatic channels; and if the making of the treaty of peace which shall end this war, is to be left to the diplomats and rulers who declared it, we shall have a blood-stained and brutalized Europe rising from this nightmare to prepare for forty-four years more of the same armament competition leading to another and still greater Armageddon.

A bold initiative coming from America, however, cannot be kept out of the censored press of Europe and would meet with wide-spread democratic support on the part of influential political groups in all the countries involved, who would put pressure upon their governments and force them to consider favorably the proposals for a constructive peace. The longer such international mediation is delayed, the stronger will be the forces which are pressing in the direction of peace. On the other hand, if the war is allowed to drag on too far towards exhaustion and bankruptcy, the danger of anarchy increases in Austria and other countries on the one hand, and of a war between the victorious Allies, such as England and Russia, analogous to the second Balkan War, on the other. A constructive offer of mediation, put forward as a basis for discussion would enable the diplomats on both sides to "save their faces," and would be effective long before one side would be so far reduced in strength as to sue for peace.

AS an indication of the nature of the constructive mediation which would meet with widespread popular support on the part of the mass of the people in all countries, programs of constructive peace, put forward by the important political groups, representing in some cases scores of millions of the population in the European and American countries, are most significant. An analytical table of ten of the most important of these constructive peace programs is printed on another page. The ten programs which have been selected as the most representative are, those of the Union of Democratic Control in Great Britain, which includes among its leaders, Norman Angell, J. Ramsey MacDonald, M.P., Charles Trevelyan, M.P., E. D. Morel, Arthur Ponsonby, M.P.; of the South German Social Democrats; of the National Executive Committee of the American Socialist party; of the International Peace Bureau, composed of the leading pacifists of all countries with Senator H. La Fontaine of Belgium as president; of the Emergency Federation of Peace Forces (Chicago Branch), which includes more than twenty political organizations in

Chicago; of the Women's Peace Party which is being organized throughout the United States, with Jane Addams as president; of the Anti-War Council of Holland, composed of many of the leading statesmen, journalists, business men, and professors of Holland, with the Jongheer van Beek en Donk, of the Department of Justice, as secretary; of the World Peace Foundation of Boston; the New York Peace Society, and the plan for a League of Peace, put forward by Hamilton Holt in *The Independent.*

In addition to the movements whose programs are given, the wide-spread aspiration for and belief in a better condition of things held by the immense mass of the public in all countries is witnessed by the movement for a Ligue des Pays Neutres of Switzerland and the proposal for a League of Peace, backed by an international police force, as outlined by ex-president Roosevelt in *The Independent;* by the manifests of the Committee for The European Federation, in Holland, and by the projects for a "United States of Europe," emanating from such widely separated sources as President Butler, of the Division of Intercourse and Education of the Carnegie Endowment for International Peace, and from Mr. Hyndman, leader of the British Socialist Party; by the program of the Woman's Movement for Constructive Peace, proposed by Mrs. Pethick-Lawrence of London.

These programs, arising from so many different centers, are indications that the people of all countries would be willing to give a fair trial to boldly constructive proposals which at the present moment their official representatives would probably declare to be pure Utopianism. It is important to note that these great aspirations of the masses of the people are practically unrepresented in the orthodox diplomatic circles at the present time and that the only way in which they can find expression is through the courageous initiative of the American democracy.

The analysis of ten constructive peace programs shows a remarkable unanimity of the public opinion of all the countries represented, on the most essential points. The necessity for a concert of the powers to replace the old shipwrecked theory of the "balance of power" as a means of keeping the peace, is found in some form in all the programs.

IN this connection it is significant to note that even Sir Edward Grey recognized the urgent need of some kind of a concert of the powers to protect Germany against the fear of aggression on the part of Russia, France and England. This proposal was put forward on July 30, 1914, at the eleventh hour of the crisis, when the air was so full of suspicion and fear that no constructive action was possible. When all other means had failed, Sir Edward Grey telegraphed to Berlin[1] as follows:

"If the peace of Europe can be preserved, and the present crisis safely passed, my own endeavor will be to promote some arrangement to which Germany could be a party, by which she could be assured that no aggressive or hostile policy would be procured against her or her allies by France, Russia, and ourselves, jointly or separately. I have desired this and worked for it, so far as I could, through the last Balkan crisis, and, Germany having a corresponding object, our relations constantly improved. The idea has hitherto been too Utopian to form the subject of definite proposals, but if this present crisis, so much more acute than any that Europe has gone through for a generation, be safely passed, I am hopeful that the relief and reaction which will follow may make possible some more definite rapprochement between the Powers than has been possible hitherto."

It is evident that such a concert of the powers, towards which some of the great states, England and Germany, have been working for years represents the only stable guaranty for a permanent peace in the future.

Even the militarists, usually most

[1]British White Papers on the European Crisis, Dispatch No. 101.

short-sighted in international relations, have come to realize that a policy of isolation is no longer possible and that a country must depend for its safety, not upon its own armaments alone, but upon treaties and alliances with other countries. It is but a short step from this position to the idea of a general league of peace for the protection of all against any aggression. The Wilson-Bryan treaties for the advancement of peace, which have been signed between the United States and nearly all the nations of the world, providing for a commission of inquiry to investigate the disputes between nations with a period of delay up to one year before any hostile action can be taken, constitute an important step towards such a league of peace. The experience of 1914 shows that mobilization partial or complete must be defined as hostile action.

THE programs are unanimous in proposing international disarmament as a condition for permanent peace. It is probable that the financial condition of the nations after the war will be such as to render the continuance of the "organized insanity" of armament competition impossible, and the necessity for putting an end to this great waste will be one of the most pressing reasons for forming the Concert of the Powers. It is significant that most of the programs urge the nationalization of the manufacture of armaments as a step towards international disarmament. Recent exposures of the activities of armament rings in promoting war-scares and wars in England, Germany, France, and Japan, have demonstrated to the world that the possibility of making private profit out of the flesh and blood of human beings is too dangerous a condition to be longer tolerated.

The majority of the programs favor an international police force and the proposals under this head include neutralization of the seas and of such maritime trade routes as the Bosporus, the Dardanelles, the Suez, Panama and Kiel canals, and the Straits of Gibraltar. The abolition of the right of capture of private property at sea is also discussed in one of the programs on account of its effect in diminishing the necessity for the protection of commerce.

Nearly all the programs agree that the principle of nationality should govern any changes of territory, i. e., that no province should be transferred from one country to another without the consent of the population obtained by a plebiscite, in order that the treaty of peace which ends this war should not plant the seed of future wars.

This principle would mean of course the restoration of Belgium and Luxemburg; and if applied to the territories in dispute, should mean the removal from the map of Europe of some at least of the centers of political inflammation, such as Alsace and Lorraine, the Danish part of Schleswig, Poland, Finland, the Italian population under Austrian rule in Trentino and Trieste, the Servian population in Bosnia and Herzegovina, the Rumanian population in Transylvania and Bessarabia, the Bulgarian population in the part of Macedonia occupied by Servia and Greece, etc. In Alsace-Lorraine, the alternative of autonomy should also be presented to the people and in all cases the plebiscite should be taken by an international commission from the neutral nations. A general adjustment of geographical boundaries to fit the national aspirations of the people would go far towards relieving tension and laying foundations for a secure peace in Europe.

The abolition of secret diplomacy and the democratic control of foreign policy finds almost unanimous support, and in four of the programs guaranties of democratic government within the countries are suggested as additional securities for peace. The social and economical changes suggested include national and international action towards removing the economic causes of war; making incitements to international hatred in the press, in speech or by other means, punishable by penal laws; organized opposition to militarism; education of the youth in ideas of peace; free trade;

equal treatment of all nations in the colonies, and prohibition of loans to belligerents by neutral nations. Wherever the question of indemnities is touched upon in the programs for constructive peace, there is a general agreement that no indemnity should be extorted by the victor. This principle would probably be understood to include a return of all indemnities and military levies assessed during the war.

Among the immediate steps recommended in the programs are,—the calling of a conference of the neutral powers to offer mediation; the federation of all possible peace forces in support of a minimum peace program; and agitation for the immediate adoption of this program as official in every nation, to constitute a standing offer of federation.

In one program, a meeting of the Third Hague Conference immediately after the conclusion of peace is urged. In this connection the action of the Pan-American Union, composed of the twenty-one republic of North, Central, and South America, is significant. At a meeting of the governing board of the Pan-American Union, at which the Secretary of State, as chairman, and all the members of the board were present, a resolution was passed calling for the definition of the rights of neutrals in the direction of establishing the principle of the liberty of commerce, and appointing a special neutrality committee to study the problems presented by the present European war and to submit to the governing board suggestions that may be of common interest.

This official action, together with the American protest to England and the formal proposal of Venezuela for a conference of the neutral powers on the rights of neutrals, marks the beginning of a new attitude towards international law and war. The interests of neutral nations are beginning to take shape corresponding to the interests of the general public in an industrial war, an interest which has come to be considered as paramount in settling the issues involved. Heretofore, the legislation of the Hague Conferences, which have included a large proportion of military experts, has been made from the point of view of nations which expect to commit war in the future and which do not desire to have their liberty of action as belligerents restricted. Hence the phrase, "as far as military necessities permit," and similar expressions, and the indefinite wording of much of the international law of the past. It is this intentional looseness of wording, rather than the lack of an international police force, which has prevented effective protest being made at some of the actions of the belligerents which have shocked the moral sense and the public opinion of the civilized world. In future Hague Conferences, marking successive steps toward the federation of the world, the whole attitude towards war and the rights of neutrals as against those of belligerents, is likely to undergo a revolutionary change, and we may look forward in the next few years to the development of a real code of international law, based upon the principle of reciprocity: Nations should do unto nations as they would be done by.

THE importance of the preservation of a strict moral neutrality by America becomes apparent as soon as we realize how intimate is the connection between our keeping the friendship and confidence of all the warring nations, on the one hand, and our ability to aid them in bringing about a just and permanent peace, on the other. All pressure put upon the administration to intervene on behalf of one side or the other, or to make futile protests against alleged violations of international law should be firmly resisted. The good that might be accomplished in this way sinks into insignificance when compared with the service which America can render to the world if its full power is reserved for such constructive mediation as is clearly indicated by the peace programs, which represent the passionate longings and democratic aspirations of the mass of people in all countries,—that this may be the last war.

Document No. 31 The Socialist Party of America, Statements on the War (1915)
Source: Alexander Trachtenberg, ed., *The American Socialists and the War* (N.Y.: Rand School of Social Science, 1917), pp. 14-19.

The American Socialists and the War

edited by

Alexander Trachtenberg

THE LUSITANIA CRISIS

When the sinking of the Lusitania gave the militarists and jingoes of this country the opportunity to demand an immediate declaration of war upon Germany, the National Committee of the Socialist Party assembled at its annual meeting, May, 1915, addressed a manifesto to the American people warning them against the influence of the interests which were laboring hard to stampede the United States into war. It called upon the workers to oppose war agitation and to refuse to support the ambitions of those who profit by war.

TO THE PEOPLE OF THE UNITED STATES
Fellow Citizens:

The insidious propaganda of American militarism has received a powerful impetus through the destruction of American lives as a result of the war-operations in Europe. The jingo press of the country is busily engaged in reckless efforts to turn the cries of natural indignation of the people into 'a savage howl of revenge. Short-sighted "patriots" and professional militarists are inflaming the minds and blinding the reason of their fellow citizens by appeals to national vanity. The sinister influences of the armament ring work through thousands of hidden channels to stimulate a war sentiment, which to it means business and profits.

In this grave hour of national crisis, the Socialist Party of the United States raises its voice in solemn and emphatic protest against this dangerous and criminal agitation, and proclaims its undying opposition to militarism and war. No disaster, however appalling, no crime, however revolting, justifies the slaughter of nations and the devastation of countries.

The destruction of the Lusitania and the killing of hundreds of non-combatants, men, women and children on board the steamer, brings more closely home to us the fiendish savagery of warfare and should inspire us with stronger determination than ever to maintain peace and civilization at any cost.

Strong armaments and military preparations inevitably and

irresistibly lead to war as the tragic example of the nations of Europe has conclusively demonstrated.

We call upon the people of the United States to profit by the lesson of our unfortunate brothers on the other side of the Atlantic Ocean and to throttle all efforts to draw this country into the dangerous paths of international quarrels, imperialism, militarism and war.

We call particularly upon the workers of America to oppose war and all agitation for war by the exercise of all the power in their command, for it is their class who pays the awful cost of warfare, without receiving any of its rewards. It is the workers who primarily furnish the soldiers on the battlefield and give their limbs and lives in the senseless quarrels of their masters.

Let us proclaim in tones of unmistakable determination: "Not a worker's arm shall be lifted for the slaying of a fellow-worker of another country, nor turned for the production of mankilling implements or war supplies! Down with war! Forward to international peace and the world-wide solidarity of all workers!"

NO INDEMNITIES. NO ANNEXATIONS. FREE DEVELOPMENT OF NATIONS

The battle cry of the Russian Council of Workmen's and Soldiers' Deputies in their efforts to secure a just and durable peace to war-torn Europe was proclaimed by the American Socialist Party two years ago. The National Committee adopted at the meeting on May, 1915 a peace platform, a draft of which was widely discussed in the party press prior to the meeting of the Committee.

The manifesto contained a searching analysis of the causes which make for war and pointed out the reasons for the Socialist opposition to war and militarism. The manifesto was followed by a peace program, which, in the opinion of the National Committee, the Socialists should work for in order to remove the possibility of friction in the future, as well as to aid in establishing a universal and lasting peace.

The proposed terms of peace, calculated to insure the advance of internationalism, demanded among other things, the adoption of the principles: no indemnities, no forcible annexations and the free development of nations. The program also advocated the international federation of the world, universal disarmament, extension of democracy, and the removal of the economic causes making for war.

The supreme crisis in human history is upon us.

European civilization is engulfed. The world's peace is shattered. The future of the human race is imperilled.

The immediate causes of the war are obvious. Previous wars and terms of settlement which created lasting hatreds and bred thoughts of revenge; imperialism and commercial rivalries; the Triple Alliance and the Triple Entente dividing all Europe into

276

two hostile camps; secret intrigue of diplomats and lack of democracy; vast systems of military and naval equipment; fear and suspicion bred and spread by a vicious jingo press in all nations; powerful armament interests that reap rich harvests out of havoc and death, all these have played their sinister parts. But back of these factors lie the deeper and more fundamental causes, causes rooted in the very system of capitalist production.

Every capitalist nation on earth exploits its people. The wages received by the workers are insufficient to enable them to purchase all they need for the proper sustenance of their lives. A surplus of commodities accumulates. The capitalists cannot consume all. It must be exported to foreign countries.

In every capitalist nation it becomes increasingly difficult for the capitalists to re-invest their accumulated profits to advantage in their own country, with their people destitute and their resources fully developed and exploited. The capitalists are constantly forced to look for new and foreign fields of investment.

In many countries of Europe, limited territorially and densely populated, the supply of natural resources is insufficient to support the large volume of industrial requirements. The capitalists must look for new sources of raw materials and supplies to less developed foreign countries.

Hence arise the commercial struggles between the nations, the rivalries for the acquisition of foreign colonies, the efforts to defend and extend the oversea "possessions"; the policies of imperialism, the conflicts for commercial supremacy, ever growing more intense and fierce as the nations expand and the world's field of conquest narrows. Hence arise the policies of armaments every year more immense and monstrous. Hence arise the strategy, the intrigues of secret diplomacy, till all the world is involved in a deadly struggle for the capture and control of the world market.

Thus capitalism, inevitably leading to commercial rivalry and imperialism and functioning through the modern state with its vast armaments, secret diplomacies and undemocratic governments, logically leads to war.

Reactionary ruling classes sometimes also deliberately plunge countries into war for the purpose of crushing progressive movements by creating false patriotic excitement and thus sidetracking the real class issues. Every war, furthermore, is used by the capitalists in order to destroy the organized forces of the labor movement.

For more than half a century the Socialist movement has warned the world of this impending tragedy. With every power at their command the Socialists of all nations have worked to prevent it. But the warning has gone unheeded and the Socialist propaganda against imperialism, militarism and war has been ignored by the ruling powers and the majority of the people of all nations.

To-day our prediction has been only too swiftly and too tragically fulfilled. War, with all its horrors is upon us.

And it has come as the logical and inevitable outcome of the forces of capitalist system. It has come in spite of the warnings and protests of the Socialist and labor movements and indeed in spite of the personal desires of many of the capitalists themselves. The capitalist system is a modern Frankenstein which is destroying its own creators.

If this unspeakable tragedy shall serve to demonstrate to the world, and particularly to the workers of all nations, the real and fundamental causes of war, so that by removing these causes man henceforth may live at peace, the war may be worth the cost.

If, on the other hand, the people shall remain blind to the terrible lessons of this war, and leave the destinies of the world in the hands of unscrupulous, war-inciting capitalist rulers, then indeed is this world-war an unmitigated curse. For, if the causes that brought on this war are left to operate, then this war will not be the last. It will be only the first of a series of wars more terrible and more tragic, until one mighty and monstrous imperialism has drenched the world in blood and subdued the peoples in abject slavery. Socialism alone will ultimately save mankind from the standing menace of self-destruction.

The supreme duty of the hour is for us, the Socialists of all the world, therefore, to summon all labor forces of the world, for an aggressive, an uncompromising opposition to the whole capitalist system, and, to every form of its most deadly fruits—militarism and war—to strengthen the bonds of working-class solidarity; to deepen the currents of conscious internationalism, and to proclaim to' the world a constructive program leading towards permanent peace.

The Socialists of America extend the hand of comradeship to their unfortunate brothers in all countries now ravaged by the war, the sufferers and victims of the vicious system which has engulfed them in fratricidal carnage. We convey to them our unfaltering faith in the world-wide class-struggle, in international Socialism and in the brotherhood of man. We proclaim our determination to join our comrades in the task of rebuilding the Socialist International upon such a basis that henceforth it cannot be shaken by the most violent storms of capitalist conflicts.

To the Socialist and labor forces in all the world and to all who cherish the ideals of justice, we make our appeal, believing that out of the ashes of this mighty conflagration will yet arise the deeper internationalism and the great democracy and peace.

As measures calculated to bring about these results we urge:

I. TERMS OF PEACE AT THE CLOSE OF THE PRESENT WAR must be based on the following provisions:

 1. No indemnities.
 2. No transfer of territory except upon the consent and by vote of the people within the territory.
 3. All countries under foreign rule be given political independence if demanded by the inhabitants of such countries.

II. INTERNATIONAL FEDERATION—THE UNITED STATES OF THE WORLD:

 1. An international congress with legislative and administrative powers over international affairs and with permanent committees in place of present secret diplomacy.
 2. Special Commissions to consider international disputes as they may arise. The decisions of such commissions to be enforced without resort to arms. Each commission to go out of existence when the special problem that called it into being is solved.
 3. International ownership and control of strategic waterways such as the Dardanelles, the Straits of Gibraltar and the Suez, Panama and Kiel Canals.
 4. Neutralization of the seas.

278

III. DISARMAMENT.
1. Universal disarmament as speedily as possible.
2. Abolition of manufacture of arms and munitions of war for private profit, and prohibition of exportation of arms, war equipments and supplies from one country to another.
3. No increase in existing armaments under any circumstances.
4. No appropriations for military or naval purposes.

IV. EXTENSION OF DEMOCRACY.
1. Political democracy.
   (a) Abolition of secret diplomacy and democratic control of foreign policies.
   (b) Universal suffrage, including woman suffrage.
2. Industrial democracy.

RADICAL SOCIAL CHANGES IN ALL COUNTRIES TO ELIMINATE ECONOMIC CAUSES FOR WAR, such as will be calculated to gradually take the industrial and commercial processes of the nations out of the hands of the irresponsible capitalist class and place them in the hands of the people, to operate them collectively for the satisfaction of human wants and not for private profits in co-operation and harmony and not through competition and war.

V. IMMEDIATE ACTION.
Immediate and energetic efforts shall be made through the organizations of the Socialist parties of all nations to secure universal co-operation of all Socialist and labor organizations and all true friends of peace to obtain the endorsement of this program.

279

Document No. 32   A.H. Jacobs to Jane Addams, A Visit with President
Wilson (1915)
Source: The Jane Addams Papers, Swarthmore College Peace Collection,
Swarthmore, Pa.

Sept. 15, 1915

Dear Miss Addams,

I saw the President at noon. I told him what
I had to say and asked him the several questions.
He was very kind and manlike as well as gentleman-
like. His answers were very diplomatical. In short
it was:"The U.S. were now in such great difficulties
with the belligerents that a definite answer in one
way or another was impossible. The Pres. was very
thankful for the information I brought, but about
his attitude towards peace he could not say a word.
Every-day that attitude could be changed, according
to the circumstances and even a quite unofficial
statement in one way or another could bind him in a
certain degree. He wants to remain free to act in
the best way as he sees the things himself."

I then left Washington by the first train I
could catch and went up to Moylan, to spend a day
with Miss Shaw. Arriving there I found her house
closed and heard from the neighbours that she is
in New Jersey for a series of suffrage-meetings.
I then went to the hotel "Idlewild" where I shall
stay overnight and come tomorrow to New-York.

I hope to hear soon from you and if there is
an opportunity to meet you before I return to
Europe. Please give my kind greetings to Miss
Smith, Miss Wald will be in N.Y. now, where I hope
to meet her soon.

With my best wishes for your health,

Cordially yours,

Aletta H. Jacobs

Document No. 33 Emily Greene Balch, "The Time to Make Peace" (1915)
Source: *The Survey,* XXXV (Oct. 2, 1915), pp. 24-25.

The Time to Make Peace

By Emily Greene Balch

ASSOCIATE PROFESSOR OF POLITICAL ECONOMY, WELLESLEY COLLEGE

THERE is a widespread feeling that this is not the moment to talk of a European peace. On the contrary there is reason to believe that the psychological moment may be very close upon us. If, in the wisdom that comes after the event, we see that the United States was dilatory when it might have helped to open a way to end bloodshed and make a fair and lasting settlement, we shall have cause for deep self-reproach.

The question of peace is a question of terms. Every country desires peace at the earliest possible moment at which it can be had on terms satisfactory to itself. Peace is possible the moment that each side would accept what the other would grant, but from the international or human point of view a satisfactory peace is possible only when these claims and concessions are such as to forward and not to hinder human progress. If Germany's terms are the annexation of Belgium and part of France and a military hegemony over the rest of Europe, or if on the other hand the terms of France or of England include "wiping Germany off the map of Europe" there is no possibility of peace at the present time nor at any time that can be foreseen, nor does the world desire peace on these terms.

In one sense the present war is a conflict between the two great sets of belligerent powers, but in a different and very real sense it is a conflict between two conceptions of national policy. The catch words "democracy" and "imperialism" may be used briefly to indicate the opposing ideas. In every country both are represented, though in varying proportions, and in every country there is strife between them.

In each belligerent nation there are those that want to continue the fight till military supremacy is achieved, in each there are powerful forces that seek a settlement of a wiser type which, instead of containing such threats to stability as are involved in annexation, humiliation of the enemy, and in competition in armaments, shall secure rational independence all round, protect the rights of minorities and foster international co-operation.

One of the too little realized effects of the war is the overriding of the regular civil government by the military authorities in all the warring countries. The forms of constitutionalism may be undisturbed but as *inter arma leges silent* so in time of war military power —no less really because unobtrusively— tends to control the representatives of the people. Von Tirpitz, Kitchener, Joffre, have in greater or less degree over-shadowed their nominal masters.

Another effect of war is that as between the two contending voices, the one is given a megaphone, the other is muffled if not gagged. Papers and platforms are open to "patriotic" utterances as patriotism is understood by the jingo; the moderate is silenced not alone by the censor, not alone by social pressure, but also by his own sense of the effect abroad of all that gives an impression of internal division and of a readiness to quit the fight. In our own country during the height of tension with Germany, loyal Americans who believed that the case of the United States was not a strong one (and a hundred million people cannot all think alike on such an issue), those who loathe the thought of war over such a quarrel, could not and would not give any commensurate expression to their views for fear that they might make it harder for our government to induce Germany to render her warfare less inhuman.

Everywhere war puts out of sight the moderates and the forces that make for peace and gives an exaggerated influence to militaristic and jingo forces creating a false impression of the pressure for extreme terms.

Of course each country desires as favorable terms as it can get and therefore would prefer to make peace at a moment when the great struggle—which in a rough general sense is a stale-mate—is marked by some incident advantageous to itself. Germany would like to make peace from the crest of the wave of her invasion of Russia; Russia and England would like to make terms from a conquered Constantinople. If the disinterested neutrals, who alone are free to act for peace, wait for a moment when neither side has any advantage they will wait long indeed.

But the minor ups and downs of the war, shifting and unpredictable, are relatively much less important than they appear. The grim unchanging fact which affects both sides and which is to the changing fortunes of battle as the miles of immovable oceans depths are to the waves on the surface—this all outweighing fact is the intolerable burden of continued war. This it is which makes momentary advantage comparatively unimportant. All the belligerents want peace, though probably with different intensity; none of them wants it enough to cry "I surrender."

The making of peace involves not only questions of the character of the terms, of demands more or less extreme; it also involves the question of the principle according to which settle-ments are to be made. There are again two conflicting conceptions.

On the one hand is the assumption that military advantage must be represented *quid pro quo* on the terms—so much victory, so much corresponding advantage in the settlement. There is even the commercial conception of war as an investment and the idea that the fighter has a right to indemnity for what he has spent.

On the other hand it is assumed that the war having thrown certain international adjustments into the melting pot, the problem is to create a new adjustment such as shall on the whole be as generally satisfactory and contain as much promise of stability as practicable.

Even in a settlement based on such considerations the balance of physical force could not be merely ignored. Gains won by force create no claim that anyone is bound to respect yet while the expenditure of blood and treasure gives no right to reimbursement (and it is to the general interest that such expenditure, undertaken more or less on speculation, should never prove a good investment), nevertheless the arbitrament of war, being an arbitrament of violence, relative power is bound to tell in the resulting adjustment.

IT is important, therefore, to consider that, with a given balance of relative strength as between the contending sides an equilibrium may be expressed in more than one way, as there are equations which admit of more than one solution. The equilibrium of opposing claims might be secured by balancing unjust acquisition against unjust acquisition or by balancing magnanimous concession against magnanimous concession. A neutral mediator or mediating group acting in the interest of civilization in general and of the future might, without throwing any weight into the scale of one or the other side help them to find the equilibrium on the higher rather than on the lower level.

On the basis of military advantage on the basis of military costs the neutrals have no claim to be heard in the

282

settlement. The soldier is genuinely aggrieved and outraged that they should mix in the matter at all. Yet even on the plane of fighting power the unexhausted neutral may fling a sword into the scale and on the plea of costs suffered the neutral may demand a voice. It is, however, supremely as representatives of humanity and civilization and the true interests of all sides alike that those who are not in the thick of the conflict can and should be of use in the settlement and help to find it on the higher plane.

The settlement of a war by outsiders —not their mere friendly co-operation— is something that has often occurred, exhibiting that curious mixture of the crassest brute force with the most ambitious idealism which often characterizes the conduct of international dealings. The fruits of victory were refused to Russia by the Congress of Berlin in 1878, Europe forbade Japan the spoils of her war with China in 1895, the results of the Balkan wars were largely determined by those who had done none of the fighting. While mere might played a large part in such interferences from the outside there is something beside hypocrisy in the claim of the statesmen of countries which had not taken part in the war to speak on behalf of freedom, progress and peace.

A peace involving annexation of unwilling peoples could never be a lasting one. The widespread sense of irritation at all talk of peace at present seems to be due to a feeling that a settlement now would be a settlement which would leave Belgium if not part of France in German hands. Such a settlement would be as disastrous to Germany as to any other nation. It might put an end to military operations but it certainly would not bring peace if we give any moral content to that much abused word. Europe was not at peace before August, 1914, nor Ireland for long before, nor Poland, nor Alsace, nor Finland. Any community which, if it could, would fight to change its political status, may be quiet under coercion but it is not at peace. Neither would Europe be at peace with Germany in Belgium.

The question then is what sort of peace may we at least hope for now —on what terms, on what principles?

WE may be sure that each side is ready to concede more and to demand less than appears on the surface or than it is ready to advertise. The summer campaign, in which marked advantages are most likely, is nearly over and a winter in the trenches will cost on all sides money and suffering out of all proportion to the advances that can be hoped for. It must be remembered too, that the advantages hitherto gained are not all on one side but that each has something to concede. The British annexations of Egypt and Cyprus may be formal rather than substantial changes but the conquest of the German colonies large and small—South West Africa, Togo Land, Samoa, Neu Pommern, Kaiser Wilhelmsland, the Solomon, Caroline and Marshall Islands, to say nothing of Kiao-Chao—and probably Russian gains at the expense of Turkey in the East—give bargaining power to the Allies. So also, even without success in the Dardanelles, does their ability to thwart or forward the Germans in Asia Minor and Mesopotamia.

Friends of Finland and of Poland must see to it that the debatable lands of the eastern as well as of the western frontier are kept in mind. From the point of view of Poland the main thing to be desired is the union of the three dismembered parts—Russian, German and Austrian Poland—and their fusion in some sort of a buffer state, independent or at least essentially autonomous. Something like this appears to be the purpose of both Germany and Russia with the difference that this Polish state would be in the one case under Teutonic, in the other under Russian, auspices. No one knows which would be the choice as between the two of the majority of the Poles concerned. Concessions to Germany in Finland and Poland are at least conceivable and would make the concession of complete withdrawal in the West easier for her to make. Still more important are the concessions in regard to naval control of the seas which Great Britain ought to be willing to make if the safety of her commerce and intercolonial communications can be adequately secured otherwise, and this would seem to be the natural counterpart of substantial steps toward disarmament on land.

But all this is speculation. The fact, obvious to those who look below the surface, is that every belligerent power is carrying on a war deadly to itself, that bankruptcy looms ahead, that industrial revolt threatens, not at the moment but in a none too distant future, that racial stocks are being irreparably depleted. The prestige of Europe, of the Christian church, of the white race is lowered inch by inch with the progress of the struggle which is continually closer to the débâcle of a civilization.

Each power would best like peace on its own terms. Our common civilization would suffer by the imposition of extreme terms by any power. Each people would be thankful indeed to secure an early peace without humiliation a long way short of its extreme demands.

There is thus every reason to believe that a vigorous initiative by representatives of the neutral powers of the world could at this moment begin a move toward negotiations and lead the way to a settlement which, please God, shall be a step toward a nobler and more intelligent civilization than we have yet enjoyed.

Document No. 34   The Pan-American Pact (1915)
Source: Charles Seymour, ed., *The Intimate Papers of Colonel House* (4 vols.; Boston: Houghton Mifflin, 1926), I, pp. 233-234.

APPENDIX

PAN-AMERICAN PACT — REVISED DRAFT

ARTICLE I

That the high contracting parties to this solemn covenant and agreement hereby join one another in a common and mutual guaranty of territorial integrity and of political independence under republican forms of government.

ARTICLE II

To give definitive application to the guaranty set forth in Article I, the high contracting parties severally covenant to endeavor forthwith to reach a settlement of all disputes as to boundaries or territory now pending between them by amicable agreement or by means of international arbitration.

ARTICLE III

That the high contracting parties further agree, First, that all questions, of whatever character, arising between any two or more of them which cannot be settled by the ordinary means of diplomatic correspondence shall, before any declaration of war or beginning of hostilities, be first submitted to a permanent international commission for investigation, one year being allowed for such investigation; and, Second, that if the dispute is not settled by investigation, to submit the same to arbitration, provided the question in dispute does not affect the honor, independence, or vital interests of the nations concerned or the interests of third parties.

ARTICLE IV

To the end that domestic tranquillity may prevail within their territories, the high contracting parties further severally covenant and agree that they will not permit the departure from their respective jurisdictions of any military or naval expedition hostile to the established government of any of the high contracting parties, and that they will prevent the exportation from their respective jurisdictions of arms, ammunition, or other munitions of war destined to or for the use of any person or persons notified to be in insurrection or revolt against the established government of any of the high contracting parties.

November, 1915

Document No. 35 Oswald Garrison Villard, "Shall We Arm for Peace?"
(1915)
Source: *The Survey,* XXXV (Dec. 11, 1915), pp. 296-299.

Shall We Arm for Peace?

By Oswald Garrison Villard

PRESIDENT NEW YORK EVENING POST

WHO would have thought a year ago that in addition to the profound injury caused by the European war's dislocation of our financial, commercial and economic conditions, it would in a few short months bring us face to face with a political and social crisis in our national life, and one involving a grave break with a historic policy of our past, of which the nation has always been particularly proud?

Such is now the fact, however, for the President's sudden, but let us hope temporary, yielding to the militarists' arguments—after stating in his message to Congress a year ago that the country had no reason to be alarmed or excited, and that this country must not be turned into an armed camp—presents a clearcut issue of far-reaching import to all Americans, and particularly to those striving for social, economic and political betterment in this country. It means, as Mr. Bryan has said, the turning over of a new page in our history, a breaking with the past; it means an enormous drain upon the treasury of the United States, so that taxation and the cost of living must rise further, bringing burdens that no man is so rich or so poor as to be able to escape.

Now, there are two great questions before us. The first is, Shall we arm at all? Shall we deliberately say to ourselves, and let the whole world know, that we believe that force has now become the dominating factor of the world and that moral issues and our own national ideals of an armed democracy have all gone by the board; that we have returned to that stage of civilization in which every nation must be armed to the extent of its ability; that we can consider no nation a friend, but every nation a potential enemy; that we who have been warned by the father of his country against entangling alliances are now to ally ourselves with and to become a part of the worst alliance in the world—an alliance with militarism with its international ramifications, its armament factories that pollute political life, under a system by which English capital is used to make torpedoes and guns for Turks to destroy Englishmen and German capital makes arms and guns for Servians to take German lives?

We have until recently always prided ourselves on the fact that no action of our American Congress helped to fasten the dread burdens of militarism upon the poor people of any other nation, but now at the very moment when it is more than ever necessary that the United States keep itself aloof from any action which would seem to be a threat toward the rest of the world, in order that it may plead at the coming peace conference for the peace that shall last, and the freeing of mankind from this horrible slavery of arms, we are notified that we, too, must enter the ignoble competition of arms.

That is the first question, far-reac

ing and heart-searching, which the President's new position forces upon us. The second has to do with the means of defence. We are asked to give a billion for the up-keep of the army alone within the next five years, and another billion for the navy. So far as the army is concerned, we are given no assurances whatever that the sums thus expended will produce results, and that we shall have an army when this great treasure of the people has been poured out.

IF we are to judge by the past, we know that we shall not have an efficient army, for we know today that we have numerous unnecessary army posts which alone cause an annual waste of $5,500,000, upon which waste Mr. Wilson and Secretary Garrison have deliberately turned their backs. We know that our army costs from two to five times as much per man as the European armies— this on the word of a former secretary of war, Mr. Stimson.

But these details will become important only if we decide that we are to embrace this plan of preparedness. Then it will behoove militarist and pacifist alike to see that if we pay out additional billions, we get one hundred cents for every dollar invested, and that we have something worth while to show for it. But even before that is done, we ought to decide on a definite policy as to whether ours is to be an offensive or a defensive policy, and how we shall define the word "defensive." The Germans say they are now on the defensive in Servia, Turkey and Russia, and that they will soon be on the defensive in Egypt and Asia Minor if their victories continue.

Shall our navy continue to be of the offensive cross-seas-voyaging type, or shall it be a purely defensive harbor-and-coast-protecting force? This is a question that the President and Congress and the people should settle first of all. But pending discussion of this and other issues, I wish to submit at this time some of the questions involved in the President's departure, and some reasons why the opinions of military and naval experts should not be accepted on matters of national policy.

Must we arm? Is there for us nothing left but to follow in the footsteps of what we have been pleased to call the effete monarchies of Europe? Our American ideals have been of service to humanity and to liberty; to create, not to destroy; to be a refuge to the oppressed of all nations has been our chiefest aim. Millions have flocked to us from abroad to escape the evils and burdens of this very militarism we would now voluntarily embrace. Their happiness upon our soil, the eagerness with which they seek our citizenship, the passionate loyalty that a Carl Schurz, a Jacob Riis, or a Mary Antin brought to our unarmed country justify us in asserting that, more nearly than any other, our institutions, however imperfect, satisfy the human longing for equality of opportunity, for the right to rise in the social scale in accordance with ability and merit, for equality in government and in the courts of justice.

Must we now change overnight to a nation in arms, either as a citizenry or as professional soldiers? Must we devote a still larger portion of our wealth to the ignoble business of teaching men to kill by wholesale? Must we hold up to our sons the ideal of the military camp and of the battleship deck? Must we, too, denounce Bernhardi-ism but surrender to his teachings, abhor his gospel but accept of its sacrament as something better, finer, nobler, more worth while than the ideal of peace and good will America has cherished heretofore?

Let no true American believe it! And let nobody believe for a moment that this is time for a change; that there is a single thing in the terrors abroad to make us follow in their footsteps of disaster and abjure the wisest teachings of our fathers, our forefathers, and the founders of our great republic.

But there is much in the hour to make us take note of the forces about us which would make preparation for war the chief business of our lives. Let no one

287

think that all this sudden agitation for great armaments has come only as a result of fears born of the conflict abroad. For years there has been a military and naval propaganda at work in this country, of which only a few have been aware. There is no more dangerous and insidious force at work in Washington than the army and navy lobby.

The large number of retired officers of both services living in the capital, by themselves provide a military atmosphere in which discussions of war and plans for it largely figure. In addition, there are hundreds of active officers on duty in the War and Navy Departments, or stationed in the District, for one reason or another, who are steadily working with congressmen for the increase of our military and naval forces. Every year a sheaf of bills increasing the two services finds its way into the legislative hopper, and not a single year has passed since 1898 that the army or navy has not been increased, or both. One year it is the corps of army engineers which is enlarged threefold; the next it is the signal corps or the field artillery.

Our battleship strength steadily waxes, and so does the clamor for still more among the army and navy lobby, and the ship, gun, and armor manufacturers who live in part or wholly on government business.

UNDER the shadow of the War Department—yes, in the War Department itself—the propaganda goes on, for there is a National Board for the Promotion of Rifle Practice, which devotes itself to the development of rifle practice in the United States in a way to delight the hearts of all our powder makers. A few years ago this board was warmly urging the government to purchase four or five million rounds of rifle ammunition from the cartridge companies to be tested with one million rounds of government-made ammunition. At the same time, the chairman of this board was editor of a magazine which was largely supported by powder and gun makers.

The United States Infantry Association, a body comprising the bulk of the infantry officers, has maintained not only a magazine which has *demanded*—not *asked*—a much larger regular army, by which every one of its members would profit in rank and pay, but a paid press agent, as well. His activities in behalf of army legislation flourished unrebuked until he went so far as to father a story advocating a skeleton army of 200,000 men and immediate intervention in Mexico.

Then Secretary Garrison called a halt, and since then the *Infantry Journal* has piped in subdued tones. What should we think of a group of pension clerks, or of postoffice clerks, or of employes of the Agricultural Department, if under the similar plea that they were working for the welfare of the country, they were to conspire together, to lobby and to pad the press with prepared documents, in order to induce Congress to increase their rank and pay? We know what the public would think, because it has supported the government in its rigid refusal to permit such organizations in the Post Office Department or elsewhere, particularly under the administration of Theodore Roosevelt.

Yet our military and naval lobby is undisturbed, because it claims the right to speak for the nation's safety. It is, of course, more dangerous than any of the much-denounced lobbies of big business, of the sugar trust, or of any group of protected manufacturers, because it is an official lobby, or, at least, a lobby of federal officials. While other lobbyists go home to rest, this army and navy lobby is always on the job, whether Congress is in session or not, and it is a rare secretary or assistant secretary of the army or navy who does not soon become imbued with the big-navy, big-army idea.

A good deal of the criticism of Secretary Daniels has undoubtedly been due to the fact that he is not being blindly led by the big-navy crowd, and has dared, rightly or wrongly, to go counter to them in the matter of the abolition of wine, and the introduction of instruction for the enlisted man, besides having forced down the prices of the armament ring in at least one particular.

Lest anyone think that I exaggerate in this matter of the lobbying of army and navy officers, let me record that Major-. General W. W. Wotherspoon, on his retirement as chief of staff on November 16, 1914, found no more earnest message to give to the officers who tendered him a farewell banquet than to beseech them to keep away from the halls of Congress and let legislation alone.

Our army and navy officers ought no more to regulate the size of our fleets and armies than our protected manufacturers should be allowed to write our tariffs, and, therefore, say how much money shall flow into their own pockets. As well might we ask our trust magnates to write our anti-trust laws. Yet they would be as quick to assert their unselfish devotion to the public weal, their true American patriotism, as are our army and navy officers.

What class of our citizens ever waved the American flag more vigorously than the Pennsylvania and New England manufacturers who in the days of McKinley and Dingley and Quay exacted their toll and made their millions out of the American people? They, too, boasted that our American prosperity and progress were safeguarded from the foreign invader only by their coast defences of a high tariff, which they so laboriously erected and so valiantly defended until the buncoed American people drove them out of some of their intrenchments of privilege. The most fiery of them have abandoned all their nonsense about national defence against foreign cheap labor, and are at last compelled to admit that the tariff schedules might better be fixed by a tariff commission of experts, representing public and consumer, than by themselves.

Let us not reverse this policy with the militarists. Selfish interests must not be allowed to write our military laws. If we must have armies and navies, let the board to control them and fix their size

be constituted of real, unfettered representatives of the people, those upon whom the burdens chiefly fall.

As the able Ohio *State Journal* recently put it:

"Military men have no business with the question whether this nation can do without war or not. When it is decided that we cannot, then is when the military men should be consulted. Whether we should be prepared or not is a different question from whether we are prepared or not. A sewing-machine agent might as well be employed to sell the government sewing-machines as to trust it to a military man whether we should be prepared or not. He will say yes. It has never failed. We have the highest respect for a military man, but his question is not before the house."

Yet the military official is not only apt to arrogate to himself all wisdom in matters military, even though he donned his gay coat but yesterday, and was a doctor or a lawyer or a commission merchant the day before, but he thinks himself especially competent in all things relating to our foreign affairs. He is never at a loss to say just what our relations with a given nation should be, and it takes a navy officer beyond everybody else to tell you just what Japan or Germany is plotting, and how the presence of this or that ship at a given point alone saved the republic's honor and its safety.

Truly, their question is today not before the house, and their authority in such matters is wholly to be questioned, for their training and mode of thought are directly contrary to that which fits men to deal soberly and with complete detachment with questions of state and of foreign policy.

They are the more ready to demand unlimited sums, because there rests upon them no responsibility for raising the money. In this country few of them are taxpayers, none of them have ever had to concern themselves with the means of supplying the men and materials they desire, and so certain are they that disaster awaits that they deem no expenditure too great. If you tell them that the government is being starved because of the military and naval demands, the answer is usually a call for an unlimited bond issue. Would you save a few paltry millions and see the New York sub-treasury raided by England, or Japan, or Germany? Would you place dollars above national honor? But if you were to grant them all they ask today, it would satisfy them only a little while.

GERMANY has for thirty years faced the same military problems which it is today endeavoring to solve on the field of battle, but its experts have never had enough troops to satisfy them. Year after year they appeared before the Reichstag asking for just a few more regiments, until in 1913 they demanded 140,000 men and so much additional artillery and war material as to make impossible the raising of this sum by ordinary taxation. As a result, for the first time the German tax-gatherer knocked at the citizen's door not to take another tithe of his income, but a share of his capital and this had not been wholly paid before the cyclone of war burst upon them in all its horror.

There is nothing whatever in Continental army precedents to make anybody believe that if war had not come this would have been the last demand upon the property of the German people by their war-lords, whose power is so great that the German general staff can obtain large appropriations—as it did for the deadly 42-centimetre guns—without disclosing to the Reichstag the purpose for which it is asked.

AGAIN, the military experts are never of one mind as to their prescriptions, even when their diagnosis is the same. Some of ours see in the Philippines and Hawaii a great military weakness; others insist that they are points of great strategic value; still others are glad to throw heavy garrisons into them if only because they can then go to Congress and demand more troops since the alleged "necessity" of maintaining troops in Hawaii, Alaska, the Philip-

pines and the Panama Canal zone has so greatly reduced the force available for service in continental America.

Some of our experts insist that 150,-000 regulars are essential, others ask for 300,000, and still others put their figures at 500,000. The demands as to a proper reserve vary correspondingly some of them would have every man trained to bear arms either upon the Swiss or the German plan, and they would naturally take this whole question out of the hands of Congress, or of any other civilians and place it in the hands of a national defence committee to which two or three civilian officials might graciously be admitted.

But how have the prophecies of the professional soldier been made ridiculous by the events of Europe! The Germans themselves have proved through the daring and courage of their volunteers that the Prussian worship of regular troops was ill-founded. Von Hindenburg's new armies, so he and the Kaiser boast, have fought just as well and as successfully in Poland against the Russians as have the flower of the Imperial Guard. In trench warfare the recruit appears the equal of the long trained soldier.

The editors of our own *Infantry Journal* have been trying to make Congress believe that it takes two years to create infantry soldiers. Lord Kitchener through his Canadian troops has already made nonsense of this talk; he was quite willing to pit against the Germans on May 1 raw levies who never saw a regiment until enlisted seven months before. For years military experts the world over have been telling that in modern battles there could be no bayonet charges; that hand-to-hand conflicts were impossible and that the armies would be firing at one another at such ranges as to be practically invisible. The hundreds of thousands men now bent on killing one another trenches so close that hand bombs and grenades may be thrown from one to the other are a terrible blow to the finality of this judgment.

So has the submarine falsified the prophecies of the naval experts, and so has the battleship yet to prove in this war that it is worth the staggering price paid for it. And surely we ought never to hear again such balderdash and stuff as Theodore Roosevelt has written oft, that the profession of arms is necessary to preserve the pristine virtues; that long periods of peace make the craven and weakling, that military drill is necessary in order to keep alive the manly virtues.

From college, factory and shop, from palace and from hovel, have come men by the million ready to die for their cause and physically able to withstand any draughts upon their strength. The old fallacy that there was any difference in the courage of any given set of men or people has now received its quietus, for Frenchmen, Russians, natives of India, Germans, Servians, Belgians and Englishmen have all shown an equal heroism under fire, a similar readiness to face sudden death from machine gun or submarine, together with a fatalistic composure which forbids any attempt at classifying or differentiating.

But our military and naval men none the less openly advocate upsetting one of the fundamental principles of this republic—that of the complete subordination of the military to civilian authority as the truest if not the only safeguard against militarism. The founders of this republic knew what they were about, because they had had a peculiarly trying experience with British militarism; they knew what it was to be overned from afar by what were practically military governors, backed by a military force which was none the less hateful, as the Boston massacre attests, because the soldiery spoke the same language and were of the same stock. They represented not merely an alien government but military, as opposed to civilian, authority—as distasteful to the colonists as our military forces in the Philippines are to the Filipinos.

And so it is neither the duty nor the right today of any American general to instruct the people or the government as to our military policy; they belong solely to the civilian officials, the cabinet, the President and Congress. Any departure from this wise doctrine of the fathers would be fraught with gravest consequences, for it is in just such insidious ways that militarism fastens a death-grasp upon a people while they still insist that they are absolutely peaceful or anti-militaristic.

But there is still another and quite as weighty a reason why we should receive no counsel of defence or offence from naval or military men, save with far-reaching doubt. To use a legal phrase, they cannot come to the court of public opinion with clean hands; that is, they are biased consciously or unconsciously, by a *direct personal stake* in the issue. They, or their sons in the army, or their caste or their kind will profit in rank, pay and power, if we increase our forces.

No sooner are such increases of the army now being urged by the secretary of war contemplated than officers begin to figure out the promotion that will accrue to them. It is human nature and inevitable, and is the more natural because in peace times officers cannot advance themselves (except to the highest grades in the army) by their own merits.

But to hear some of our new-born Bernhardis rage, one might think that Congress had been absolutely blind and deaf to all the militaristic appeals. The contrary is the fact: in the last twenty years we have spent enormous sums upon army and navy together; from 1881 to 1915 our annual naval bill has increased from $13,000,000 to $147,538,-981.88.

WE are thus spending about seven times the endowment of Yale or Harvard Universities in a single year upon the navy alone, with nothing whatever to show for it after fifteen years at most, when the new battleships of today will be reduced to junk or shot to pieces as targets.

If we are not defenceless as alleged, the question is whether all this money has been wasted and whether we have or have not anything to show for it. That millions of it has been wasted through congressional politics in the location and upkeep of needless forts and navy-yards is as I have pointed out the testimony of more than one secretary of war or navy; that millions more have been lost by the extravagance and waste which are usually characteristic of government as compared with private enterprises is also a matter of common knowledge.

Surely, in view of the wide differences of opinion as to just what kind of a navy and army we have, it would seem the part of common-sense to begin any new policy of preparedness with a study of what we have and an official statement of its military value. Thus, Congressman Kitchin, the majority leader in the house, bases his opposition to the President's policy squarely on the assertion that our navy is a third better than Germany's, and twice as effective as that of Japan, and stakes his reputation on the accuracy of his facts. He cites three of the most prominent admirals in the navy, Badger, Winterhalter and Fletcher, the present commander of the Atlantic Fleet, as testifying before a house committee last winter that our navy was superior to that of Germany.

How astoundingly farreaching Mr. Wilson's new program is—it is the largest ever advocated in any nation at any time—Mr. Kitchin sets forth thus:

"Increases our already immensely large naval appropriation more than our total increase for the last fourteen years; more than the increase by Germany in the whole fifteen years preceding the European war, and more than the combined increase of *all the nations in the world in any one year in their history* (in times of peace)! This five-year program increases our naval appropriation over forty times more than the increase by Germany in five years preceding the European war; and by $200,000,000 more than the combined increase of all the nations in the world for the five years preceding the European war; and over $50,000,000 more than the combined increase of all the nations in the world for the whole period of ten years immediately preceding the European war. Add to this the fact that prior to the beginning of the European war we were expending annually on our navy from $20,000,000 to $30,000,000 more than Germany or any other nation (except Great Britain) was expending on its navy."

Mr. Kitchin also shows that if this program is adopted the United States at the expiration of the next five years will be spending annually "more than any nation in the world ever expended in times of peace on its army and navy more than England with her navalism more than Russia or Germany with their huge militarism." If this program goes into effect we shall be putting 70 per cent of our national outlay into militarism and navalism five years hence.

DURING the first two years of the Wilson administration, we have expended for armaments more than during the entire four years of Roosevelt rule or of Taft's government. Is it any wonder that President Wilson, a year ago—a year before he surrendered to the politicians—said to Congress: "Let there be no misconception. The country has been misinformed. We have not been negligent of national defence"?

But there are also other official testimonies as to the value of the existing defences. Testifying before the sub-committee of the House Committee on Appropriations in charge of the Fortifications Appropriation bill of 1915-1916, during February of this year, Secretary of War Garrison, in reply to a question whether in a broad sense our coast defences were adequate, replied as follows:

"Yes, sir; they certainly are adequate for the purpose for which they were placed there, qualifying only to the extent that I do not mean to say that some guns may not be on naval ships that can shoot more effectively at extreme ranges, but when you come down that you see how small a part that play those ships could not come in near the shore; they would have to lie out there and occasionally shoot, perhaps shooting on the hit-or-miss plan and doing so damage or doing no damage."

There were military experts also in attendance upon this committee. One of them was Brigadier-General Erasmus M. Weaver, chief of coast artillery whose duty it is, he said, to be "advised as to the character and sufficiency of our seacoast armament." In reply to a question, General Weaver said: "My opinion is that our system of fortifications is reasonably adequate for all defensive purposes which they are likely to be called upon to meet." A little later he again said: "I have been a close student of the whole subject for a number of years, and I know of no fortifications in the world, as far as my reading, observation and knowledge go, that compare favorably in efficiency with ours." As to our coast artillery force, General Weaver said: "I think it is at least equal to that of any coast-defence personnel in the world."

The greatest expert in this country on fortifications and guns, General William Crozier, chief of ordnance, was also called by this committee. Being asked what, in his judgment, would be the condition in our fortifications after certain alterations were made in the mounting and elevation of the existing guns in our forts, General Crozier replied: "I am of the opinion, Mr. Chairman, that they [our fortifications] will be of such power and will be recognized of such power *that naval officers would not put their ships up against them in a fight.*"

Surely, in view of all this, there is no possible excuse for haste in legislation, particularly as the President's military and naval program proves in itself that we are in no immediate danger. For it is inconceivable that if we were seriously menaced the President would be urging a military plan it will take three years to carry out and a navy-building program that cannot be completed for ten years.

But the reader may ask whether mine has not been a negative attitude; to cling fast to our national ideals, to refuse to follow military experts in matters of policy as opposed to matters of fact, to have faith in our present forces and whether I have no concrete recommendations to make?

To this, I answer that I have such a program:

First, to insist that this nation resume its rôle of chief exemplar of peace and disarmament in the world—a nation devoted primarily and whole-heartedly to the arts of peace;

Second, to spend at least the price of two battleships a year, say $25,000,000, in winning the good opinion of countries with whom we might be in danger of friction, and in acquainting ourselves and our own people with them and their aims;

Third, to demand of our cabinets and Presidents that they shall recognize that war is always a failure of statesmanship and that behind war lies too often a fear of somebody else which it must be the chief duty of responsible officials not to increase by large armaments, but to allay;

Fourth, to gain for ourselves, the plain people, such control of our foreign affairs as will make Congress alone, not a handful of men the arbiters as to whether we shall or shall not go to war.

I believe that in the years to come it will stand out as one of the blackest crimes in history that a dozen patricians, in the English cabinet could plunge that nation into the hell of war, because of a secret agreement, without a vote of Parliament, much less a vote of the people. No groups of tradesmen, none of laboring men, none of the great masses for whom the mere declaration of war spells unemployment, suffering and misery, and not a single woman were asked to say whether England should go to war or not.

I believe the time is near at hand when the masses will rise in rebellion as they ought against this whole theory of war, demanding freedom of trade and harbors throughout the world, a union of nations where there are unions of states within a nation today, and internationalism as against nationalism.

THE thing for all sane men to hope, who believe in democracy, in the brotherhood of man, is that the masses will refuse to be food for cannon at the behest of any masters, kings or queens, or whatever their titles may be; that they will see in the slavery of war the worst slavery of our times; that they will behold in it the greatest conceivable waste of the world's treasure; that they will recognize that the terrible rise in the cost of living and of government is in large part due to the staggering war tax-burdens, the waste of war and the unproductive character of all military expenditure.

This is the kind of revolution the world needs above all else at this hour—a new brand of French Revolution—a sweeping, overwhelming uniting against those who rob nations of 75 per cent of their income for war purposes, and take it away from the building of cities beautiful without slums, the reclaiming of waste lands, of our deserts and our swamps, the developing of our waterways, our water powers and our highways, the true education of our masses, the levelling of every barrier of caste and prejudice.

In short, militarism withholds vast sums from the amelioration of the lot of the poor, the ill, the suffering, the wronged, the oppressed, and I am for bitter and harsh words about it now and always; I am for turning upon those who counsel that we shall plot to murder other nations and peoples either for offense or defense as true traitors to the spirit of the nation.

Document No. 36   The House-Grey Memorandum (1916)
Source: Charles Seymour, ed., *The Intimate Papers of Colonel House* (4 vols.; Boston: Houghton Mifflin, 1926), II, pp. 201-202.

Memorandum of Sir Edward Grey

(Confidential)

Colonel House told me that President Wilson was ready, on hearing from France and England that the moment was opportune, to propose that a Conference should be summoned to put an end to the war. Should the Allies accept this proposal, and should Germany refuse it, the United States would probably enter the war against Germany.

Colonel House expressed the opinion that, if such a Conference met, it would secure peace on terms not unfavourable to the Allies; and, if it failed to secure peace, the United States would [probably] [1] leave the Conference as a belligerent on the side of the Allies, if Germany was unreasonable. Colonel House expressed an opinion decidedly favourable to the restoration of Belgium, the transfer of Alsace and Lorraine to France, and the acquisition by Russia of an outlet to the sea, though he thought that the loss of territory incurred by Germany in one place would have to be compensated to her by concessions to her in other places outside Europe. If the Allies delayed accepting the offer of President Wilson, and if, later on, the course of the war was so unfavourable to them that the intervention of the United

[1] Inserted by President Wilson, to correspond with the 'probably' three lines above and eight lines below. The value of the offer was in no way lessened by the use of the word 'probably,' which was a conventional covering expression common in diplomatic documents. Since the power to declare war resides in Congress and since the President shares with the Senate the control of foreign policy, it would have been impossible for Wilson to give a categorical guaranty of the future action of the United States. As a matter of practice, however, the President can determine the question of peace and war, and the expression of his intention appears here in the strongest permissible form.

States would not be effective, the United States would probably disinterest themselves in Europe and look to their own protection in their own way.

I said that I felt the statement, coming from the President of the United States, to be a matter of such importance that I must inform the Prime Minister and my colleagues; but that I could say nothing until it had received their consideration. The British Government could, under no circumstances, accept or make any proposal except in consultation and agreement with the Allies. I thought that the Cabinet would probably feel that the present situation would not justify them in approaching their Allies on this subject at the present moment; but, as Colonel House had had an intimate conversation with M. Briand and M. Jules Cambon in Paris, I should think it right to tell M. Briand privately, through the French Ambassador in London, what Colonel House had said to us; and I should, of course, whenever there was an opportunity, be ready to talk the matter over with M. Briand, if he desired it.

(Intd.)   E. G.

FOREIGN OFFICE
22 *February* 1916

Colonel House to Sir Edward Grey
[Telegram]

NEW YORK, *March* 8, 1916

I reported to the President the general conclusions of our conference of the 14th of February, and in the light of those conclusions he authorizes me to say that, so far as he can speak for the future action of the United States, he agrees to the memorandum with which you furnished me, with only this correction: that the word 'probably' be added after the word 'would' and before the word 'leave' in line number nine.

Please acknowledge receipt of this cable.

E. M. HOUSE

Document No. 37   The Gore-McLemore Resolution and Wilson's Reply
(February, March, 1916)
Source: Current History, April, 1916, p. 15 ff.

THE GORE-McLEMORE RESOLUTION AND WILSON'S REPLY
February, March, 1916

1. THE GORE-McLEMORE RESOLUTION

Resolved . . . That it is the sense of the Congress, vested as it is with the sole power to declare war, that all persons owing allegiance to the United States should in behalf of their own safety and the vital interest of the United States, forbear to exercise the right to travel as passengers on any armed vessel of any belligerent power, whether such vessel be armed for offensive or defensive purposes, and it is the further sense of Congress that no passport should be issued or renewed by the Secretary of State, or anyone acting under him, to be used by any person owing allegiance to the United States for the purpose of travel upon any such armed vessel of a belligerent power.

2. PRESIDENT WILSON'S LETTER TO SENATOR STONE

The White House,
Washington, February 24, 1916.

My Dear Senator: I very warmly appreciate your kind and frank letter of to-day, and feel that it calls for an equally frank reply.

You are right in assuming that I shall do everything in my power to keep the United States out of war. I think the country will feel no uneasiness about my course in that respect. Through many anxious months I have striven for that object, amidst difficulties more manifold than can have been apparent upon the surface, and so far I have succeeded. I do not doubt that I shall continue to succeed. The course which the Central European powers have announced their intention of following in the future with regard to undersea war-fare seems for the moment to threaten insuperable obstacles, but its apparent meaning is so manifestly inconsistent with explicit assurances recently given us by those powers with regard to their treatment of merchant vessels on the high seas, that I must believe that explanations will presently ensue which will put a different aspect upon it. We have had no reason to question their good faith or their fidelity to their promises in the past, and I for one feel confident that we shall have none in the future.

But in any event our duty is clear. No nation, no group of nations, has the right while war is in progress to alter or disregard the principles which all nations have agreed upon in mitigation of the horrors and sufferings of war; and if the clear rights of American citizens should ever unhappily be abridged or denied by any such action, we should, it seems to me, have in honor no choice as to what our own course should be.

For my own part, I cannot consent to any abridgment of the rights of American citizens in any respect. The honor and self-respect of the nation is involved. We covet peace, and shall preserve it at any cost but the loss of honor. To forbid our people to exercise their rights for fear we might be called upon to vindicate them would be a deep humiliation indeed. It would be an implicit, all but an explicit, acquiescence in the violation of the rights of mankind everywhere, and of whatever nation or allegiance. It would be a deliberate abdication of our hitherto proud position as spokesmen, even amidst the turmoils of war, for the law and the right. It would make everything this Government has attempted, and everything that it has achieved during this terrible struggle of nations meaningless and futile.

It is important to reflect that if in this instance we allowed expediency to take the place of principle, the door would inevitably be opened to still further concessions. Once accept a single abatement of right, and many other humiliations would certainly follow, and the whole fine fabric of international law might crumble under our hands piece by piece. What we are contending for in this matter is of the very essence of the things that have made America a sovereign nation. She cannot yield them without conceding her own impotency as a nation, and making virtual surrender of her independent position among the nations of the world.

I am speaking, my dear Senator, in deep solemnity, without heat, with a clear consciousness of the high responsibilities of my office, and as your sincere and devoted friend. If we should unhappily differ, we shall differ as friends; but where issues so momentous as these are involved we must, just because we are friends, speak our minds without reservation.

Faithfully yours,
Woodrow Wilson

Document No. 38   President Wilson's Peace Plan (1916)
Source: *Literary Digest,* LII (June 10, 1916), pp. 1683-1685.

THE LITERARY DIGEST

PUBLIC OPINION (New York) combined with THE LITERARY DIGEST

Published by Funk & Wagnalls Company (Adam W. Wagnalls, Pres.; Wilfred J. Funk, Vice-Pres.; Robert J. Cuddihy, Treas.; William Neisel, Sec'y), 354-360 Fourth Ave., New York

Vol. LII, No. 24   New York, June 10, 1916   Whole Number 1364

TOPICS - OF - THE - DAY

PRESIDENT WILSON'S PEACE-PLAN

NO HOPE of mediation in the present conflict is exprest in the President's "peace-speech" in Washington, in which he outlines an international plan to prevent other wars when this one is fought out. Nor do the European press greet his words with any such fervor as would indicate an intention to stop fighting to adopt his platform. Yet his voice "is the voice of America," declares a paper quoted below, and on this side of the Atlantic, at least, his views find hearty indorsement. Moved by the conviction that "the world is even now upon the eve of a great consummation," and that this war "has set forward the thinking of the statesmen of the world by a whole age," President Wilson on May 27 outlined before the League to Enforce Peace the fundamental principles upon which he believes the future peace of the world must rest, and declared that the United States "is willing to become a partner in any feasible association of nations formed in order to realize these objects and make them secure against violation." The following beliefs, he averred, form part of the "passionate conviction of America": "First, that every people has a right to choose the sovereignty under which they shall live; secondly, that the small States of the world have a right to enjoy the same respect for their sovereignty and for their territorial integrity that great and powerful nations expect and insist on; and, thirdly, that the world has a right to be free from every disturbance of its peace that has its origin in aggression and disregard of the rights of peoples and nations." Therefore, he went on to say, "if it should ever be our privilege to suggest or initiate a movement for peace among the nations now at war, I am sure that the people of the United States would wish their Government to move along these lines:

"*First*—Such a settlement with regard to their own immediate interests as the belligerents may agree upon. We have nothing material of any kind to ask for ourselves, and are quite aware that we are in no sense or degree parties to the present quarrel Our interest is only in peace and its future guaranties.

"*Secondly*—A universal association of the nations to maintain the inviolate security of the highway of the seas for the common· and unhindered use of all the nations of the world, and to prevent any war, begun either contrary to treaty covenants or without warning, and full submission of the causes to the opinion of the world—a virtual guaranty of territorial integrity and political independence."

Despite his disclaimer, many Washington correspondents think they see here a first step, perhaps indirect, toward American mediation in the war, and they take his words as a statement of the terms on which the President would undertake such mediation. One of them says: "As Sir Edward Grey and Chancellor von Bethmann-Hollweg have recently defined the British and German attitudes toward peace, so President Wilson took up and defined the position of America as the greatest of the neutrals." It is noticeable that the press of the Entente Allies are, with one or two exceptions, distinctly chilly toward the President's proposals, while the only clause the German editors find thoroughly to their taste is the declaration in favor of the freedom of the seas. A few of our own editorial commentators express the fear that any public discussion of peace by President Wilson at this time is in effect playing into Germany's hands, or, as one of them put it, "helping her to get away with her loot." But domestic criticism of the speech is chiefly concerned with the possibility that it may open the way for "entangling alliances," with a consequent weakening of our stand on the Monroe Doctrine. Many of our editors also hesitate to subscribe to the "freedom of the seas" doctrine, while still others regard as Utopian the theory that "every people has a right to choose the sovereignty under which they shall live." The Republican New York *Tribune*, whose pen is always poised for a thrust at the present Administration, regards the speech as a whole as "only another flagrant illustration of Mr. Wilson's instability as a statesman, his fluid sentimentalism, his servitude to winged phrases which carry him far beyond the boundary-lines of his matured thought." The Brooklyn *Times* remarks ironically that while the President can not do the slightest thing to end this war, "he can lay down a formula to prevent all future wars!" The Brooklyn *Eagle* recognizes the "nobility" of the President's dream, but sees little prospect of its speedy realization—a view in which the Washington *Post* concurs. Says the Brooklyn paper:

"The disposition of the United States to act as a mediator in the European conflict will be more graciously recognized in Berlin and Vienna than in the capitals of the Allies, because the Central Empires, having achieved substantial advantages on land, are eager for peace before the Allies can recover lost ground and before the pressure of sea-power accomplishes the slow but inevitable process of strangulation. So far as this country is concerned the sharpest imaginable division of opinion must arise on the President's proposition that the United States shall league itself with foreign nations to preserve the peace of the world on issues to which it may have no direct relation. . . . . . .

"It is not inconceivable that a peace congress to settle the unhappy differences of the Old World may yet be held in this country. A precedent for that was established in 1905, when Russia and Japan met at Portsmouth. But if that should be the case, the relation of the United States to any such conference would in all probability be limited to the assertion of those rights at sea which both groups of belligerents have flouted, one in callous disregard of human life, the other in violation of neutral

THE SEAT OF TROUBLE.
—Bradley in the Chicago *Daily News.*

interests in property and in mail service. The causes of the war were purely European. The consequences of the war must press most heavily upon Europe. The treaty of peace that shall end the war must be European-made, wherever the locality of the conference or congress in which the treaty shall be formulated and signed. The gulf at present separating the contending parties is so abysmal, the differences of purpose are so fundamental, the sacrifices entailed are so tremendous, that a compromise leaving conditions much as they were before the war began is to-day wholly unacceptable in London, Paris, Petrograd, and Rome. It will take a great deal more than the occupation of Poland, Belgium, Servia, and northeastern France to convince the Allies that they can not secure a peace other than that to which Germany is now willing to accede."

On the other hand, the Springfield *Republican* points out that "the world is alive as never before to the need of concerted

measures to reduce the risk of such catastrophic disturbances,"
and the Baltimore *Sun* is convinced that the President's words
"can not fail to make a serious impression on the minds of all the
warring Powers." In this matter "the voice of the President
is the voice of America," declares the St. Louis *Republic*, and
similar expressions of approval and indorsement confront us
from the editorial pages of hundreds of papers, among them
such representative dailies as the Chicago *Herald*, New York
Times, *World*, and *Evening Post*, Philadelphia *Public Ledger*,
Milwaukee *Evening Wisconsin*, Buffalo *Times*, Indianapolis *News*,
Columbus *Ohio State Journal*, Cleveland *Leader*, Wilmington *Star*,
Charleston *News and Courier*, and the Charlotte *Observer*. "His
is the greatest of all peace-propagandas," declares the Charlotte
paper, "because its aim is peace for all nations for all time."
With the acceptance of the doctrine of the freedom of the seas
and of the territorial rights of nations, says *The Ohio State
Journal*, "the immense navies and armies could be discarded,
and everybody put to producing something for the common
good." Most significant, thinks the Cleveland *Leader*, is the
President's "guarded but none the less unmistakable espousal
of the doctrines of those who urge that peace must be maintained by force, if necessary, before modern civilization can
fulfil its mission and vindicate its claims." In this connection
it is interesting to recall that the plan of the League to Enforce
Peace, as concisely stated by the Pittsburg *Dispatch*, is as follows:

"It would band the nations in a common agreement to submit
justiciable questions to a world-court, and all other issues to a
council of conciliation. It would enforce respect for this agreement by the joint use of their economic and, if necessary, their
military powers against any nation that violated it."

The President's position, as several papers remark, is apparently in complete harmony with this plan. His program,
declares the New York *Times*, is one that can be "accepted,
lauded, and embraced" by "pacifists and militarists, big-army
and little-army men, peace-leaguers, and security-leaguers."

Turning to the foreign press, we find cordial indorsement of the
President's speech in the *Osservatore Romano* and the *Corriere
d'Italia*, the official and the semiofficial organs of the Vatican.
Says the latter:

"This speech is the most eloquent manifestation of President
Wilson's work for peace and of his desire to be a mediator. He
was most tactful in alluding to the rights of small States, which
include the questions of the future of Belgium, Servia, Poland,
and Armenia.

"From across the ocean President Wilson answers the Pope,
who was the first to raise a voice defending principles which
the war may have momentarily obscured, but which remain
immortal.

"The President and the Pope invoke a return to justice and fraternity among the peoples. Their union is a consoling spectacle among the painful sights of this period of blood and hatred. Even if President Wilson's initiative fails the world must rejoice at his intention."

Another Italian paper, the Rome *Tribuna*, remarks that Italy is in accord with President Wilson, "but his idea resembles extraordinarily the advice given to children to put salt on a bird's tail." And in still another Entente paper, the London *Daily News*, we read:

"It would be a profound misfortune if the critics took too limited a view of President Wilson's speech. On its positive, constructive side it deserves serious treatment, especially by this country. Nothing is clearer than that on fundamental issues President Wilson and Sir Edward Grey are absolutely one. The identity of purpose between Great Britain and America in their aim for the maintenance of the world's peace is full of hope."

But, in the main, English and French comment seems to be anything but enthusiastic. "President Wilson's electioneering

THE FIRST STEP TOO HIGH.
—Tuthill in the St. Louis *Star*.

speeches are bringing him on dangerous ground," remarks the London *Times*, which adds that the Allies "will listen to proposals of peace only when they come from the beaten foe." "There can

303

be no satisfactory end until Germany has suffered a decisive military defeat," agrees the London *Express*, and the London *Daily Chronicle* is convinced that "Germany is working up a peace move in her own interests, and is plainly counting on American opinion to help her." To quote *The Chronicle* further:

"The most important objects for which the Allies have been fighting would be lost if any peace were made at this stage, for no matter what its terms it would be the peace of a victorious

EUROPE—"HARK! DID SOME ONE KNOCK?"
—Darling in the Des Moines *Register and Leader.*

Germany and would cover with fatal prestige the aggressions and crimes of which Germany has been guilty.

"The whole policy of which this war is the monstrous outcome has been made possible by the fact that in 1864, 1866, and 1870 Prussia's deliberately planned aggressions had unqualified success, and guilt was overshadowed by the military triumph of the guilty party.

"It would be an incalculable disaster to civilization were this experience repeated, as it would be if peace were concluded with an undefeated Germany. America must recognize, and we believe that an ever-growing majority of them do, that anything the United States did to help in such a result would in no distant future recoil with fatal effect on their own heads."

In Paris, correspondents tell us, the President's peace-proposals "are not taken very seriously." The *Journal* finds in his speech visions of "a new world where wolves are changed to sheep," and in Clemenceau's *L'Homme Enchaîné*, we read:

"Wilson is trying the old game of pleasing both the Allies and Germany. The first part of his speech is directed against Germany, which violated the sovereignty of Belgium, and the second part against England, because Germany has not free use of the seas."

Such comments as these move the New York *Press* to remark that "the most significant thing about President Wilson's peace-propaganda is that the Allies reject it out of hand."

"Only one Wilson idea will be received without contradiction in the whole non-English world, and that is the freedom of the seas," declares one Berlin paper. But it adds: "This is no article for a peace-treaty. It is rather a realization of a universal, valid, and vital right of all nations, great and small." Further light is thrown on Germany's attitude by the following paragraphs in the Berlin *Vossisrhe Zeitung:*

"We must recognize the fact that for the moment no really serious inclination exists in England to enter upon negotiations on any basis that could in any way be acceptable to us. England must first convince herself that the idea of Germany being starved out before the next harvest is a fantom. The French, even more than the English, are living on this fantom."

"There is no chance of peace until the Entente changes its views," declares Count Tisza, Hungarian Prime Minister. Professor Hans Delbrück, of the University of Berlin, writes that "there is something repellent to Germany in the idea of accepting President Wilson as mediator," because "his sympathies are obviously with the Entente Powers." Conservatives in the Reichstag are also quoted as saying he would be unacceptable.

Returning to our own press, we find many papers sharing the fear of the New York *Sun* that in expressing his willingness to join a league of nations in behalf of peace the President proposes to depart from our historic policy of avoiding entangling alliances. The President himself answered this criticism in his Memorial-day speech, when he said:

"Some of the public prints have reminded me, as if I needed to be reminded, of what General Washington warned us against. He warned us against entangling alliances.

"I shall never myself consent to an entangling alliance; but I would gladly assent to a disentangling alliance—an alliance which would disentangle the peoples of the world from those

305

combinations in which they seek their own separate and private interests and unite the peoples of the world to preserve the peace of the world upon a basis of common right and justice. There is liberty there, but there is not limitation. There is freedom, not entanglement."

Another point over which there is some editorial uneasiness in the American press is the President's declaration in favor of the freedom of the seas. "Does he mean that the United States should take the foremost part in establishing a league against Great Britain?" asks the New York *Evening Sun*, and the Rochester *Democrat and Chronicle* avers that freedom

GROWING BOLDER.
—Sykes in the Milwaukee *Leader*.

of the seas, according to the German understanding, "means destroying the strength of Great Britain by destroying the effectiveness of its Navy." To the Boston *Transcript* it "looks very much like putting America in line to pull Germany's chestnuts out of the fire."

Document No. 39   The Carrizal Incident: Shall We Have War with Mexico? (1916)

Source: Leaflet in the American Union against Militarism Papers, Box 4, Swarthmore College Peace Collection, Swarthmore, Pa.

Shall We Have War With Mexico?

To the President and the American People: June 26, 1916.

We are on the point of war. If war comes the American people and the other nations of the world will sit in judgment and render a verdict as to the right and justice of the cause. Every American who is patriotic in the highest sense feels that to go to war without a just cause which will bear the critical judgment of future generations would be an irreparable injury to the nation.

IS THERE A JUST CAUSE FOR WAR?

It is conceded by the State Department that up to the Carrizal engagement between American and Mexican troops nothing has happened that amounts to a substantial cause for war. As we understand it, there is little conflict of opinion in regard to this. If we go to war now it will be understood at home and abroad that it is because of the shooting of Captain Boyd's troopers by Mexican soldiers under General Gomez, outside of the town of Carrizal at about 4.30 A. M., on June 20th.

Captain Morey, wounded and under the belief that he would not reach the border alive, has given a clear, cool and detailed account of this engagement. His statement follows:

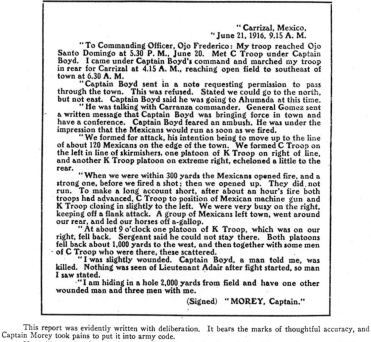

> " Carrizal, Mexico,
> "June 21, 1916, 9.15 A. M.
>
> "To Commanding Officer, Ojo Frederico: My troop reached Ojo Santo Domingo at 5.30 P. M., June 20. Met C Troop under Captain Boyd. I came under Captain Boyd's command and marched my troop in rear for Carrizal at 4.15 A. M., reaching open field to southeast of town at 6.30 A. M.
>
> "Captain Boyd sent in a note requesting permission to pass through the town. This was refused. Stated we could go to the north, but not east. Captain Boyd said he was going to Ahumada at this time.
>
> "He was talking with Carranza commander. General Gomez sent a written message that Captain Boyd was bringing force in town and have a conference. Captain Boyd feared an ambush. He was under the impression that the Mexicans would run as soon as we fired.
>
> "We formed for attack, his intention being to move up to the line of about 120 Mexicans on the edge of the town. We formed C Troop on the left in line of skirmishers, one platoon of K Troop on right of line, and another K Troop platoon on extreme right, echeloned a little to the rear.
>
> "When we were within 300 yards the Mexicans opened fire, and a strong one, before we fired a shot; then we opened up. They did not run. To make a long account short, after about an hour's fire both troops had advanced, C Troop to position of Mexican machine gun and K Troop closing in slightly to the left. We were very busy on the right, keeping off a flank attack. A group of Mexicans left town, went around our rear, and led our horses off a-gallop.
>
> "At about 9 o'clock one platoon of K Troop, which was on our right, fell back. Sergeant said he could not stay there. Both platoons fell back about 1,000 yards to the west, and then together with some men of C Troop who were there, these scattered.
>
> "I was slightly wounded. Captain Boyd, a man told me, was killed. Nothing was seen of Lieutenant Adair after fight started, so man I saw stated.
>
> "I am hiding in a hole 2,000 yards from field and have one other wounded man and three men with me.
>
> (Signed)   "MOREY, Captain."

This report was evidently written with deliberation. It bears the marks of thoughtful accuracy, and Captain Morey took pains to put it into army code.

You will note that Captain Morey says that Captain Boyd was under the impression that the Mexicans would run if fired on, and that the Americans then "formed for attack" and advanced upon the Mexicans, and that thereupon the Mexican troops opened fire. If this is true—and it seems impossible to doubt it—we submit that THE CARRIZAL EPISODE DOES NOT CONSTITUTE A JUST CAUSE OF WAR.

It has been announced by the Associated Press that the Government will not give weight to Captain Morey's statement as printed above, but will await an "official account" from him as a basis of judgment. The American people will surely not be deceived by any attempt to alter the facts presented in Captain Morey's original report.

It has been stated that the Carrizal engagement was a mere incident; and that Carranza's refusal to allow American troops to proceed further into Mexico was in itself a cause of war. HISTORY WILL NOT JUSTIFY THIS NATION in going to war because a neighboring republic, having allowed our troops to enter its territory in pursuit of a band of outlaws, demanded that these troops should not march further into its territory after the band of outlaws had been scattered and many of them killed.

The fact that Mexico is a small nation, torn by recent revolutions and now undergoing a period of reconstruction, make it a matter of national honor that we should scrupulously respect its rights. We believe that if this nation should choose to go to war rather than accept the offer of mediation made by the Latin-American Republics and accepted by Mexico, it will be a blot upon American history.

AMERICAN UNION AGAINST MILITARISM,
70 Fifth Avenue, New York City.

Write or Wire Your Congressman TO-DAY

Document No. 40   The Hensley Rider to the Naval Appropriations Act of
August 29, 1916
Source: U.S., *Statutes at Large,* December 1915 to March 1917, XXXIX,
Part I, p. 618 (Washington, D.C.: Government Printing Office, 1917).

Policy for peaceful settlement of international disputes declared.

It is hereby declared to be the policy of the United States to adjust and settle its international disputes through mediation or arbitration, to the end that war may be honorably avoided. It looks with apprehension and disfavor upon a general increase of armament throughout the world, but it realizes that no single nation can disarm, and that without a common agreement upon the subject every considerable power must maintain a relative standing in military strength.

International disarmament, etc.

Conference invited to plan tribunal for peaceful settlement of disputes.

In view of the premises, the President is authorized and requested to invite, at an appropriate time, not later than the close of the war in Europe, all the great Governments of the world to send representatives to a conference which shall be charged with the duty of formulating a plan for a court of arbitration or other tribunal, to which disputed questions between nations shall be referred for adjudication and peaceful settlement, and to consider the question of disarmament and submit their recommendation to their respective Governments for approval. The President is hereby authorized to appoint nine citizens of the United States, who, in his judgment, shall be qualified for the mission by eminence in the law and by devotion to the cause of peace, to be representatives of the United States in such a conference. The President shall fix the compensation of said representatives, and such secretaries and other employees as may be needed. Two hundred thousand dollars, or so much thereof as may be necessary, is hereby appropriated and set aside and placed at the disposal of the President to carry into effect the provisions of this paragraph.

United States representatives authorized.

Appropriation.

Suspension of new construction if tribunal established, etc.

If at any time before the construction authorized by this Act shall have been contracted for there shall have been established, with the cooperation of the United States of America, an international tribunal or tribunals competent to secure peaceful determinations of all international disputes, and which shall render unnecessary the maintenance of competitive armaments, then and in that case such naval expenditures as may be inconsistent with the engagements made in the establishment of such tribunal or tribunals may be suspended, when so ordered by the President of the United States.

Document No. 41 President Woodrow Wilson's Statement to the American Neutral Conference Committee, August 30, 1916
Source: Transcript in the Charles L. Swem Collection of Wilsonia, Princeton University Library, Princeton, N.J.

In order to say what you are entitled to hear, my real thoughts,of course, it is necessary that I should ask you to regard them as confidential, because this is a matter too important to touch just on the surface. I wish my brains were more alert than they are from having to use them to avert another war. But something that Dr. Jordan said just now is a key to part of the situation. The U.S. has nothing to gain and nothing to lose in one sense in respect of this war. She has a great deal to gain, of course, if permanent peace can be brought out of it in some way, but directly she has very little to gain or to lose and she certainly has nothing to fear. In that respect she differs from all the other nations that could be called into this conference. Even the South American nations, it has been foreseen, would in the case of certain results of the war be open to the entrance of new influences or old influences of a new shape which might operate to their very great disadvantage, so that even on this side of the water we are the only nation that has this position of independence of judgment and of interest. That means that any possible conference of neutrals that might be called would consist of one nations with disengaged interests and all the others of deeply engaged interests, interests that go to the very foundation of the life of some of them, and that have divided others in a degree that has made the conduct of their government for the time being very difficult indeed. So that we would have one vote out of say, 20, which would be cast in the interest of mankind and they would have 19 votes, let us assume, to be cast in the interests of settlements which would safeguard certain national considerations which they had in their mind.

Of course, I am assuming that we have the heart to discuss the desirability of brining war to an end; we all want that, we will all discuss one of the means and at first blush the most promising means to bring this about; but when I have thought of the U.S. voting one vote out of a large number in the settlement of an essential question and being on an entirely different footing of interest from all the other voters in the conference, I haven't been able to see a satisfactory result brought out of that. Because I have had this distressing experience. I have had it at home, but I have had it more also abroad. In most of the European chancellories disinterested motives are incredible. I have been certain of the motives of propositions that I have made to them, but I have found out that I had also to be certain that they discounted the motives that I alleged and did not

credit them. In other words, outside of America
disinterestedness in public matters isn't believed to
exist. There are a good many skeptics in America but the
most hopeless skepticism is in the European govts. Of
course, the European arrangements are arrangements that
it is hard for us even to conceive. We cannot conveive
a government like the Greeks have, a government which is
not only not of their own choice, but given them from
outside sources and resisting the whole impulse of their
own people in the determination of their own affairs.
We cannot imagine anything like that, but there are the
influences all knitted together of the various courts of
Europe, and they are all interlaced with the things
that do work and the things that don't work. The things
that do work are the official influences and the things
that don't work are the popular influences.

   If I could hold a conference of neutrals consisting
only of representatives who represented the people of
the neutral nations, I would hold it in a minute, but
inasmuch as I can't hold a conference that represents
more than one people, so far as I can see, I am afraid
to hold it. A conference consisting of representatives
of all the neutral govts. except the U.S. and the
people of the U.S. would be a conference in which the
people of the world were in a hopeless minority. Now,
that is the fundamental difficulty in my mind. Mind you,
I have received intimations from various neutral govts.
that they would--not many, two or three--that they would
like to know what our attitude was with regard to a
conference of this sort, and that they would very much
like to take the initiative, but I know the reasons and
I couldn't for one consent to it, because those reasons
were unwise. That is the difficulty frankly stated.
You see why I couldn't state that in a voice that would
reach beyond this room. It isn't because I distrust the
European statesmen. I do not. I honor those that I have
had a chance to know and to test, but their point of view
is utterly different from ours and their object is utterly
different from ours. I can illustrate it in this way.
I made an address which has been referred to before
the League to Enforce Peace, and I said in it that
with the causes and questions involved in the present
war we had no concern. I thought it was obvious that
what I meant was that we hadn't had any part in starting
the case, that is all that I meant, and that not having
any part in starting it and not having any direct
interest in what was being settled, if anybody knew
what it was that was being settled, we had nothing to
say in the way of judgment as to how it started or
anything about it, but that we would have a great deal
to say in the ways it affected the rest of the world
and in the way wars hereafter would affect the rest of
the world and were entitled to a voice in the peace

hereafter, not the settlement between the parties but the arrangements which would ensue in the world at large; but that was the one phrase in that address which was quoted everywhere in Europe and which was universally resented, because the whole attitude of those people is, either you sympathize with them or you are cold-hearted. The German feels if you don't sympathize with him you really don't know what modern culture is, and the attitude of the French is you don't know what human liberty is if you don't sympathize with them. I don't really blame them. If I were in their place I would feel exactly the same way, because they are engaged in a terrible struggle, vital to everything that they hold dear and valuable, but that is the way that an innocent effort to say that we were disengaged in our interests affects all the nations, and it was commented unfavorably in the neutral nations as it was in others. They said that the U.S. is so cold-blooded that it doesn't care about what is going on in Europe.

Now, in one sense,we don't care, for what the quarrel is, because we don't know, partly because nobody knows what the quarrel is. It is just a fight, as Professor Fisher says, to see who is strong enough to prevent the other from fighting better. I don't see anything else that is involved, so that when I imagine a conference of neutrals I imagine Sweden and Denmark and Holland—think of how those countries are shot through with the passions and the dangers of this thing—and Spain, that has been shut out in recent years from influence in European affairs, and I dare say would like to see those influences magnified; and little Switzerland inside of a circle of fire.

The whole problem on this side of the water is this Dr. Jordan said that he didn't think there would be any objection to the including of the three great govts. of South America, but one of the difficulties in South America is that the other countries don't admit that tho are the great countries of South America and are very jealous of the ABC group, and you can't do much with them if you magnify the ABC group. If we want to have any influence with them we can't invite the ABC group and exclude the rest. We have either got to invite all of them or none of them. Do you think that the European nations would wish to be outvoted by Central and South American neutral countries. Not a minute. They wouldn't consent to be outseated by Central and South America; so that we have either got to break up Pan-America, which has a hopeful future, now, in view of the coordination of the two continents of this hemisphere, or we have got to include all the American states, and if we included all the Americans states in the call, the European states probably won't respond to the call. It is a circle of difficulties and perplexities that

you open up in this. That doesn't mean that I despair
at all of the influences that are making for peace.
I believe they are growing every day, and I believe
that some of the instrumentalities are represented by
groups like this that are influential enough to get what
they said heard, who have friends enough to get what they
say spread, who have channels by which sentiment can be
released in the countries which are most interested.
The volume is growing, steadily growing, and the voice that
is calling for peace will presently be heard. It will be
heard by the govts. themselves sooner than it will be
heard by us. Those govts. hear the voices which they
suppress, or else they wouldn't suppress them. They hear
them in the very hypothesis(?). You don't suppress what
you don't know exists, and they know that this tide is
rising, and they are trying to keep it down. They know it,
as I say, very much better and very much sooner than we
do, and that tide is getting too powerful for them.

I can't observe and be confident that I am finding
the facts as fast as the result, but I am keeping in touch
with these things as well as I can, and I believe that a
psychological moment will come, I am praying that it will
come very soon, when some suggestion made out loud by
somebody that they have to listen to will be irresistible,
that they will have to begin to parley and if they once
stop fighting and begin to parley they will never begin
fighting again. My hope is that we can get them to talk to
each other, and the minute that happens the war is over.
They will never go back to it. They will never revive the
forces that will sustain them it in.

WHY WILSON?

A Statement by Social Workers

AS social workers we believe that Woodrow Wilson should be re-elected president of the United States. The rapid changes which are taking place in economic and social conditions in this country and the many new and unforeseen developments which the war is causing in our industrial and political life, as well as in our international relations, make it imperative that during the next four years there shall be in the White House a man of broad social vision, a man who stands ready, in whatever situations may arise, to initiate and direct policies with regard for the rights, the interests, and the social welfare of the whole people rather than those of any group.

We believe that Woodrow Wilson is such a man. He has shown himself to be truly democratic in his handling of the perplexing problems, both international and domestic, that have arisen during his administration.

In Mexico, his stand against aggrandizement by the United States has made possible the growth of popular government and is bringing about an era of sympathetic understanding between the American Republics.

In foreign affairs, he has stood for a diplomacy of reason and negotiation, with good will toward all peoples, rather than one of bluster and the parade of force.

In domestic affairs, the present administration comes before the country with a social program that carries assurance because of a record of pledges fulfilled and a series of legislative achievements not equaled by any other administration. Prominent among its contributions to social and industrial justice are these :

> *It has been established as a matter of law that labor is not to be considered a mere commodity or article of commerce.*
>
> *The seamen have been made free men and have been given the right, previously denied, to leave their employment when conditions become intolerable.*
>
> *The products of child labor have been excluded from interstate commerce.*
>
> *The most liberal workmen's compensation law in the world has been enacted, affecting 400,000 federal employes.*
>
> *The principle of the 8-hour day has been recognized.*
>
> *The Rural Credits Bill and the Federal Reserve Act are contributions to the welfare of the entire country.*

In his appointments President Wilson has struck a new high level by the naming of such socially-minded persons as Louis D. Brandeis to the Supreme Court, Newton D. Baker to a cabinet position, Frederic C. Howe as immigration commissioner at New York, and by his retention of Julia C. Lathrop at the head of the Children's Bureau.

Given these facts, we favor the re-election of Woodrow Wilson.

Seymour K. Barnard
Ludwig B. Bernstein
David M. Bressler
Cornelia Bradford
Howard A. Bradstreet
Margaret F. Byington
Vernon M. Cady
Kate H. Claghorn
Montrose Craiger
Robert A. Crosby
F. Elizabeth Crowell
John L. Eliot
John A. Fitch
Monroe W. Goldstein
S. S. Goldwater
Fred S. Hall
George A. Hall
Theodore W. Hannigan
Shelby M. Harrison
James P. Heaton
Edward Hochhauser
Harry L. Hopkins
Philip P. Jacobs
Frederick W. Jenkins
James Jenkins, Jr.
Arthur P. Kellogg
Paul U. Kellogg
Winthrop D. Lane
John Lathrop
Florence L. Lattimore
/ Porter R. Lee

Solomon H. Lowenstein
Frank H. Mann
Bleecker Marquette
Benjamin C. Marsh
William C. McKee
Francis H. McLean
W. Frank Persons
Louis H. Pink
Samuel Rabinovich
A. H. Richardson
Mary E. Richmond
Jane Robbins
E. G. Routzahn
Mary Swain Routzahn
Edward F. Sanderson
Karl de Schweinitz
Lester F. Scott
Benjamin Selekman
John R. Shilladay
Mabel F. Spinney
4. Franklin Thomas
Henry W. Thurston
Lilliam D. Wald
Morris D. Waldman
Joseph J. Weber
Franklin Wells
Gaylord S. White
Elizabeth Williams
C. C. Williamson
Alexander M. Wilson

In the brief time between the writing and printing of this letter, the following signatures from outside Greater New York were received, mostly by telegram :

Chicago
Jane Addams
Mary McDowell
James H. Tufts
Eugene T. Lies
James Mullenback
Charles P. Schwartz

Buffalo
Frederic Almy
William E. McClennan
John P. Sanderson

St. Louis
J. Lionberger Davis
Oscar Leonard
Roger N. Baldwin

Philadelphia
R. M. Little
Carol Aronovici
Bernard J. Newman
Martha J. Megee
Arthur Evans Wood

Cleveland
George S. Addams
Howell Wright
John H. Lotz
Starr Cadwallader
T. L. Lewis
E. J. Henry
A. R. Hatton
Allen T. Burns

Boston
Edward T. Hartman
Michael M. Davis, Jr.
J. Prentice Murphy
John F. Moors

Pittsburgh
J. Byron Deacon
Francis D. Tyson

Newark
A. W. MacDougall
D. P. Falconer

Cincinnati
William J. Norton

Document No. 43 President Wilson's Peace Proposal of Dec. 18, 1916
Source: U.S. Department of State, *Foreign Relations of the United States,*
1916 Supplement (Washington, D.C.: Government Printing Office, 1929),
pp. 97-99.

THE PRESIDENT'S SUGGESTION OF DECEMBER 18, 1916, THAT THE
BELLIGERENT GOVERNMENTS COMMUNICATE THEIR TERMS OF
PEACE—LLOYD GEORGE'S SPEECH OF DECEMBER 19, 1916

File No. 763.72119/230a

The Secretary of State to the Ambassadors and Ministers in Belligerent Countries [1]

[Circular telegram]

WASHINGTON, *December 18, 1916, 9.30 p. m.*

The President directs me to send you the following communication
to be presented immediately to the Minister of Foreign Affairs of
the government to which you are accredited, and he requests that
you present it with the utmost earnestness of support. He wishes the
impression clearly conveyed that it would be very hard for the
Government of the United States to understand a negative reply.
After yourself reading it to the Minister of Foreign Affairs and
making the oral representations suggested, please leave a copy of
this paper with him:

The President of the United States has instructed me to suggest to (substitute name of government to which you are accredited) a course of action
with regard to the present war which he hopes that the (substitute name of
government to which you are accredited) will take under consideration as suggested in the most friendly spirit and as coming not only from a friend but also
as coming from the representative of a neutral nation whose interests have
been most seriously affected by the war and whose concern for its early conclusion arises out of a manifest necessity to determine how best to safeguard
those interests if the war is to continue.

The suggestion which I am instructed to make the President has long had
it in mind to offer. He is somewhat embarrassed to offer it at this particular
time because it may now seem to have been prompted by the recent overtures
of the Central powers. It is in fact in no way associated with them in its
origin, and the President would have delayed offering it until those overtures
had been answered but for the fact that it also concerns the question of peace

---

[1] The entire telegram as follows to diplomatic officers in Great Britain, France
(for transmission also to the Belgian Government through the Consul at Havre),
Russia, Italy, Portugal, Japan, Roumania, and Greece (for transmission to the
Serbian and Montenegrin Governments). The same, with the alteration described in the following footnote, to officers in Germany, Austria-Hungary, Turkey, and Bulgaria (File No. 763.72119/230b). The "communication" and
alternative sentences to officers in neutral countries for their information (File
No. 763.72119/230c). On December 20, 1916, officers in neutral countries were
instructed to deliver copies to the governments (File No. 763.72119/230f), and
copies were sent to all representatives of foreign governments in the United
States (File No. 763.72119/256a).

315

and may best be considered in connection with other proposals which have the same end in view.[1] The President can only beg that his suggestion be considered entirely on its own merits and as if it had been made in other circumstances.

The President suggests that an early occasion be sought to call out from all the nations now at war such an avowal of their respective views as to the terms upon which the war might be concluded and the arrangements which would be deemed satisfactory as a guaranty against its renewal or the kindling of any similar conflict in the future as would make it possible frankly to compare them. He is indifferent as to the means taken to accomplish this. He would be happy himself to serve or even to take the initiative in its accomplishment in any way that might prove acceptable, but he has no desire to determine the method or the instrumentality. One way will be as acceptable to him as another if only the great object he has in mind be attained.

He takes the liberty of calling attention to the fact that the objects which the statesmen of the belligerents on both sides have in mind in this war are virtually the same, as stated in general terms to their own people and to the world. Each side desires to make the rights and privileges of weak peoples and small states as secure against aggression or denial in the future as the rights and privileges of the great and powerful states now at war. Each wishes itself to be made secure in the future, along with all other nations and peoples, against the recurrence of wars like this and against aggression or selfish interference of any kind. Each would be jealous of the formation of any more rival leagues to preserve an uncertain balance of power amidst multiplying suspicions; but each is ready to consider the formation of a league of nations to insure peace and justice throughout the world. Before that final step can be taken, however, each deems it necessary first to settle the issues of the present war upon terms which will certainly safeguard the independence, the territorial integrity, and the political and commercial freedom of the nations involved.

In the measures to be taken to secure the future peace of the world the people and Government of the United States are as vitally and as directly interested as the Governments now at war. Their interest, moreover, in the means to be adopted to relieve the smaller and weaker peoples of the world of the peril of wrong and violence is as quick and ardent as that of any other people or government. They stand ready, and even eager, to coöperate in the accomplishment of these ends, when the war is over, with every influence and resource at their command. But the war must first be concluded. The terms upon which it is to be concluded they are not at liberty to suggest; but the President does feel that it is his right and his duty to point out their intimate interest in its conclusion, lest it should presently be too late to accomplish the greater things which lie beyond its conclusion, lest the situation of neutral nations, now exceedingly hard to endure, be rendered altogether intolerable, and lest, more than all, an injury be done civilization itself which can never be atoned for or repaired.

The President, therefore, feels altogether justified in suggesting an immediate opportunity for a comparison of views as to the terms which must precede those ultimate arrangements for the peace of the world, which all desire and in which the neutral nations, as well as those at war, are ready to play their full responsible part. If the contest must continue to proceed towards undefined ends by slow attrition until the one group of belligerents or the other is exhausted, if million after million of human lives must continue to be offered

---

[1] The foregoing two sentences, in the communication for the Central powers, are changed to read as follows: "He is somewhat embarrassed to offer it at this particular time because it may now seem to have been prompted by a desire to play a part in connection with the recent overtures of the Central powers. It has in fact been in no way suggested by them in its origin and the President would have delayed offering it until those overtures had been independently answered but for the fact that it also concerns the question of peace and may best be considered in connection with other proposals which have the same end in view."

up until on the one side or the other there are no more to offer, if resentments must be kindled that can never cool and despairs engendered from which there can be no recovery, hopes of peace and of the willing concert of free peoples will be rendered vain and idle.

The life of the entire world has been profoundly affected. Every part of the great family of mankind has felt the burden and terror of this unprecedented contest of arms. No nation in the civilized world can be said in truth to stand outside its influence or to be safe against its disturbing effects. And yet the concrete objects for which it is being waged have never been definitively stated.

The leaders of the several belligerents have, as has been said, stated those objects in general terms. But, stated in general terms, they seem the same on both sides. Never yet have the authoritative spokesmen of either side avowed the precise objects which would, if attained, satisfy them and their people that the war had been fought out. The world has been left to conjecture what definitive results, what actual exchange of guaranties, what political or territorial changes or readjustments, what stage of military success even would bring the war to an end.

It may be that peace is nearer than we know; that the terms which the belligerents on the one side and on the other would deem it necessary to insist upon are not so irreconcilable as some have feared; that an interchange of views would clear the way at least for conference and make the permanent concord of the nations a hope of the immediate future, a concert of nations immediately practicable.

The President is not proposing peace; he is not even offering mediation. He is merely proposing that soundings be taken in order that we may learn, the neutral nations with the belligerent, how near the haven of peace may be for which all mankind longs with an intense and increasing longing. He believes that the spirit in which he speaks and the objects which he seeks will be understood by all concerned, and he confidently hopes for a response which will bring a new light into the affairs of the world.

LANSING

File No. 763.72119/219

Document No. 44 Debate on Peace Between William H. Taft of the League to Enforce Peace and pacifist William J. Bryan (January, 1917)
Source: *World Peace: A Written Debate Between William Howard Taft and William Jennings Bryan* (N.Y.: Doran, 1917), pp. 129-143.

WORLD PEACE

A WRITTEN DEBATE BETWEEN

WILLIAM HOWARD TAFT

AND

WILLIAM JENNINGS BRYAN

NEW YORK

GEORGE H. DORAN COMPANY

Mr. Taft's Concluding Argument

WE have now reached the end of the discussion. This tenth article offers an opportunity for a summary of the positions taken in the previous papers. The program of the League looks to a treaty binding all nations to adopt, in the settlement of controversies likely to lead to war between them, a peaceable procedure for the hearing and decision of issues capable of being settled on principles of law and of issues that may not be so settled. It does not attempt to enforce the decisions. The aim of the League is, by elucidation of the facts and arguments on both sides of the issue and by a decision of it by an impartial tribunal, to practice nations in the art of settling irritating questions by judicial investigation and conclusion. The example of our relations with Canada and the constant use of arbitration to settle our difficulties—which has been created a habit—offer a precedent from which we believe that, when such a procedure is enforced, it will train all nations to adopt it rather than to resort to war. The force of the world is to be used to compel nations to adopt this procedure before resorting to hostilities. This is the same principle, though not carried so far, which prevails in domestic communities, cities, states and nations. It is the plan of organising the force of all to suppress the lawless force of an individual or a group of individuals. Any one who opposes the use of force in such a World League must be logically led to deny the propriety of the use of force in a domestic community to maintain order and to preserve the law. Governmental force cannot be excluded from human affairs as long as force is used to violate the law and right. Such vicious force can only be restrained by greater force. For this, the state organizes a police and an army. So the family of nations may and should organize a police force to suppress the unlawful force of a nation. A pacifist who will admit a policeman to be a proper official in the community yields the whole case against the creation of an international police force in our League.

Mr. Bryan attempts to meet this argument in the sixth paper which I have not had an opportunity under the rules to answer until now. He says now that the analogy is misleading and uses these words:

"The nations cannot, in fairness, be likened to criminals, although we often describe their public acts as criminal, especially in time of war. The criminal is one who intentionally violates a law duly enacted by those having authority to make laws. He disregards an obligation confessedly binding upon him; and the policeman, acting for the outraged community, arrests the guilty party and brings him before the bar of justice. There is no international law-making power; and, if such a law-making power existed, there are certain questions upon which it would not assume to act—certain questions upon which each nation, whether large or small, is conceded the right to decide for

320

itself without regard to the views or interests of other nations. Our arbitration treaties, the most advanced in the world, contain exceptions, questions of honour, questions of independence, vital interests and the interests of third parties. These questions are not to be submitted to arbitration; and yet these are the very questions out of which wars grow."

Of all men in the world, Mr. Bryan, by reason of his general views, is the one least entitled to put forth these reasons in order to escape the analogy of state police. No one has spoken more eloquently against war as a crime than Mr. Bryan. No one has upheld more fully international law as a binding force upon the nations. International law is the law of nations agreed to between the nations and deriving its sanction from their general acquiescence. A nation which violates international law is a criminal before the bar. The exceptions from our existing treaties of arbitration of questions of vital interest and national honour, to which Mr. Bryan refers, were exceptions which were not recognized in the unratified general arbitration treaties made with France and Great Britain which Mr. Bryan approved and to which he gave effective support. More than that, the Senate itself did not seek, in its proposed amendments, to except questions of honour and vital interest from arbitration. Mr. Bryan's distinction is a forced one and has no foundation, certainly as applied to the plan of the League to Enforce Peace. The treaty forming the League is an agreement by all nations to comply with its stipulations and not only to comply with its stipulations, but, in case of non-compliance by any member to contribute their quotas to an international police to restrain and punish that member for non-compliance. In other words, it furnishes an international constitution. It creates an international law and denounces as a crime violation of the legal obligations into which the nations voluntarily enter. The very object of the League is to organize the world politically; and that means to enact law and to provide for its enforcement. I submit that the analogy of the state police is not only a fair one but a clinching and convincing one in showing the fundamental fallacy and error of those who have the international pacifist views of Mr. Bryan and still are in favour of a state and city police.

That the League is practical may be inferred from the approval which its general principles have received from the leading statesmen of the Great Powers in answer to direct questions upon the subject, and also in official expression in the correspondence between President Wilson and the belligerent powers engaged in the present war. It is practical because there is precedent for every detail in the League, and because it embodies the elemental principle of government as it should be in city, state, and nation and in the world: to wit, the organization of the force of all to suppress lawless force of the few. The lines upon which the League has been framed are very general; the plan is only a working hypothesis. That it may be changed in international conference in detail goes without saying. But that it furnishes broad and correct foundation for the political organization of the world, as Kant foresaw it, I submit is clear.

The United States should enter the League; first, because of all nations in the world, it wishes to avoid war and to make it as remote as possible; second, because its interests have now become so world-wide, and it has become so close a neighbour of all the great powers of Europe and of Asia that a general war must involve the United States. It is therefore of the highest importance to the United States in a selfish view to secure the joint effort of the world to prevent such a war or to confine it to a local struggle. The present difficulty with Germany is a most speaking demonstration of the danger in which the United States will be involved in every general war in the future, struggle as it may to escape being drawn in.

The objection, that by such a League as this the United States will have to abandon the Monroe Doctrine, is entirely unfounded. On the contrary, the League will assist the United States in maintaining that Doctrine by invoking the action of the world to hold off its violation by a European nation's making war against an American country until after a hearing and decision on the merits of the controversy. Nor will it commit the United States to any judgment in respect to the Doctrine, because, under the League, it is not the subject matter of a judgment, but only of a recommendation of a compromise which the United States is at liberty to accept or reject. The League offers no authority or opportunity to European nations to subvert American governments or colonize American territory, any more than it offers to the United States corresponding authority or opportunity for similar action in Europe.

Nor does the League involve the delegation to an international council, in which the United States has but one vote, the power to hurry this country into war. The President and the Senate sign the treaty of the League and bind the United States to its obligations. Congress is the authority which will decide whether the fact exists, calling for action by the United States, and then will take such action as the obligation requires. Should the purpose of the International Police under the League be perverted to anything other than enforcing the peaceable procedure in the settlement of international controversies, Congress will have full power to withdraw the United States forces and decline further to take part in the proceedings.

It is the duty of the United States, as potentially the leading power of the world, to bring about an international arrangement to make war less probable. The war and the weakening of the European countries have increased the primacy and influence of the United States if properly exercised. It is doubtful whether such a League can be formed unless the United States, with its power and its position of indifference to the jealousies and local interest of Europe and of Asia, does not become active in its advocacy and formation. The United States should take its full part of the responsibility for the peace of the world even though it involves some risk in doing so. The burden of preparation which it would have to assume in this regard, however, would not exceed that which it owes to itself in military and naval preparation for reasonable defence and the maintenance of its international rights, even if no League were formed. With the blessings which God has showered on this country, it should not hesitate to help the world and the family of nations to protect itself against the recurrence of such an awful disaster and retrograde movement in Christian civilization as the present war.

Mr. Bryan's Concluding Argument

THIS, the last argument of the series, is intended for recapitulation. The objections to the plan of the League to Enforce Peace are:

First, That it would necessitate a departure from the advice of the fathers and a change in our national policy—a change which would not only deprive us of the security which we have enjoyed, but would inevitably entangle us in the numerous and varied disputes of the old world.

Second, It would virtually compel a surrender of the Monroe Doctrine because we could not expect to take part in the settlement of European quarrels and at the same time exclude European nations from participation in the settlement of international disputes in the Western hemisphere.

Third, It would virtually be a surrender by Congress of the right to declare war and a delegation of that authority to a council controlled by European nations. In his ninth argument, Mr. Taft attempts to avoid this conclusion by arguing that Congress would have to act affirmatively in each case before our aid would be given. The action of Congress would, however, be a mere formality. If we enter into an agreement to join other nations in compelling a submission of every question to investigation, it will be difficult, if not impossible, to excuse ourselves from responding to a call when made. Mr. Taft would doubtless admit that he would regard it as a breach of faith for the United States to fail to respond after having pledged itself to furnish its quota.

Fourth, The League's plan substitutes physical force for moral influence; and this is a step down from the position which we have heretofore occupied. While this may seem sentimental, I venture to present it as a substantial objection. With a nation, as with the individual, the idea is vital and controls destiny. If an individual depends upon the exercise of physical force for his influence in a community, he must content himself with the inferior position awarded to men of his class. He may excite fear; but he cannot win respect.

If, however, he relies upon character and service, he will command not only confidence but increasing consideration and influence. So with the nation; if it chooses to rely upon the weapons of physical warfare, it must be content to be feared. It can not hope to be loved. And such a nation can hardly be expected to estimate its greatness in terms of world service.

Our nation has for a century been inspired by an honourable ambition to conquer with its ideals rather than with its arms; and it has rejoiced to see its political principles making progress throughout the world. Within a decade China, the sleeping giant of the Orient, has aroused itself. Breaking off its monarchial fetters, it has declared itself a republic; and, passing over imperial designations, it has honoured our nation by giving to its chief executive, the title President. We could never have won such a triumph by the employment of force.

Within the last few days Russia, the largest European nation when measured by population or territory, has overthrown its arbitrary government and commenced to build a national authority upon popular consent. Surely the American people, believing as they do in free institutions, must find great satisfaction in the increasing influence exerted by our example. Shall we exchange our moral prestige for the tinsel glory of military power?

And is not our religion involved? However

belligerent one may become in hours of excitement, he cannot, in his calmer moments, fail to understand the difference between the teachings of Christ and the threatenings of a League whose "vital principle is force." When appeals are made for the application of Christian principles to government, the usual answer is that we cannot afford to adjust our governmental methods to the teachings of the New Testament until other nations are ready to do so; but this rejoinder entirely overlooks the basic principle of Christianity, namely, that its truths are to be propagated by example.

Our religion would have never made progress if each individual had waited for other individuals to join him before putting Christ's philosophy into practice. And so the application of Christianity to government must be postponed indefinitely if each nation waits for other nations to join it. Nations have not hesitated to make war alone. Why should they hesitate to act alone in putting God's truth to the test? Why not try the international value of a philosophy that has established peace between individuals wherever applied?

As a substitute for the League's plan, I have proposed; First, the plan of separate treaties between the nations, such as we now have with thirty nations, providing for investigations of *all disputes;* Second, the establishing of an international court, which will give expression to the universal sense of justice, leaving the decision to be accepted upon its merits, or to be enforced by the nations immediately concerned; Third, provision for a referendum on war, except in case of actual invasion; Fourth, the reduction of armaments. In my ninth argument, I suggested a fifth plan which I do not deem necessary, but which is much to be preferred to the League's plan; namely, the announcement of an *intention* to take part in future wars *when the excuse for the war is such as to commend itself to our nation,* the sufficiency of the excuse to be determined by our Congress when the time for action arrives and the issue is clearly defined.

I venture to express the hope that the proposed League, being a child, so to speak, of the European war and being nourished by the spirit of preparedness which has been so assiduously cultivated in this country, will find its final repose in the calm that will follow the restoration of peace. Then we may expect a reaction against militarism and a clearer vision of America's mission as the exponent of peace based upon love, friendship and co-operation. I cannot conclude without expressing my appreciation of the courtesy with which Mr. Taft has conducted his part of this discussion. It has been a real pleasure to join him in bringing before the public the issues raised by the League.

Document No. 45 President Wilson's "Peace Without Victory" Speech.
January 22, 1917
Source: U.S. Department of State, *Foreign Relations of the United States, 1917, Supplement I, The World War* (Washington, D.C.: Government Printing Office, 1931), pp. 24-29.

The President's Address to the Senate, January 22, on the Bases of a Durable Peace—Confidential Communication by the German Government of Its Terms of Peace

File No. 763.72119/405a

Address of the President of the United States to the Senate, January 22, 1917 [1]

GENTLEMEN OF THE SENATE: On the 18th of December last I addressed an identic note to the governments of the nations now at war requesting them to state, more definitely than they had yet been stated by either group of belligerents, the terms upon which they would deem it possible to make peace. I spoke on behalf of humanity and of the rights of all neutral nations like our own, many of whose most vital interests the war puts in constant jeopardy. The Central powers united in a reply which stated merely that they were ready to meet their antagonists in conference to discuss terms of peace. The Entente powers have replied much more definitely and have stated, in general terms, indeed, but with sufficient definiteness to imply details, the arrangements, guarantees, and acts of reparation which they deem to be the indispensable conditions of a satisfactory settlement. We are that much nearer a definite discussion of the peace which shall end the present war. We are that much nearer the discussion of the international concert which must thereafter hold the world at peace. In every discussion of the peace that must end this war it is taken for granted that that peace must be followed by some definite concert of power which will make it virtually impossible that any such catastrophe should ever overwhelm us again. Every lover of mankind, every sane and thoughtful man, must take that for granted.

I have sought this opportunity to address you because I thought that I owed it to you, as the council associated with me in the final determination of our international obligations, to disclose to you without reserve the thought and purpose that have been taking form

---

[1] The text of this address was telegraphed to the Ambassadors in belligerent countries Jan. 15 for communication, when notified, to the Foreign Offices and the press.

in my mind in regard to the duty of our Government in the days to come when it will be necessary to lay afresh and upon a new plan the foundations of peace among the nations.

It is inconceivable that the people of the United States should play no part in that great enterprise. To take part in such a service will be the opportunity for which they have sought to prepare themselves by the very principles and purposes of their polity and the approved practices of their Government ever since the days when they set up a new nation in the high and honourable hope that it might in all that it was and did show mankind the way to liberty. They can not in honour withhold the service to which they are now about to be challenged. They do not wish to withhold it. But they owe it to themselves and to the other nations of the world to state the conditions under which they will feel free to render it.

That service is nothing less than this, to add their authority and their power to the authority and force of other nations to guarantee peace and justice throughout the world. Such a settlement cannot now be long postponed. It is right that before it comes this Government should frankly formulate the conditions upon which it would feel justified in asking our people to approve its formal and solemn adherence to a league for peace. I am here to attempt to state those conditions.

The present war must first be ended; but we owe it to candour and to a just regard for the opinion of mankind to say that, so far as our participation in guarantees of future peace is concerned, it makes a great deal of difference in what way and upon what terms it is ended. The treaties and agreements which bring it to an end must embody terms which will create a peace that is worth guaranteeing and preserving, a peace that will win the approval of mankind, not merely a peace that will serve the several interests and immediate aims of the nations engaged. We shall have no voice in determining what those terms shall be, but we shall, I feel sure, have a voice in determining whether they shall be made lasting or not by the guarantees of a universal covenant; and our judgment upon what is fundamental and essential as a condition precedent to permanency should be spoken now, not afterwards when it may be too late.

No covenant of cooperative peace that does not include the peoples of the New World can suffice to keep the future safe against war; and yet there is only one sort of peace that the peoples of America could join in guaranteeing. The elements of that peace must be elements that engage the confidence and satisfy the principles of the American governments, elements consistent with their political faith and with the practical convictions which the peoples of America have once for all embraced and undertaken to defend.

I do not mean to say that any American government would throw any obstacle in the way of any terms of peace the governments now at war might agree upon, or seek to upset them when made, whatever they might be. I only take it for granted that mere terms of peace between the belligerents will not satisfy even the belligerents themselves. Mere agreements may not make peace secure. It will be absolutely necessary that a force be created as a guarantor of the permanency of the settlement so much greater than the force of any nation now engaged or any alliance hitherto formed or projected that no nation, no probable combination of nations, could face or withstand it. If the peace presently to be made is to endure, it must be a peace made secure by the organized major force of mankind.

The terms of the immediate peace agreed upon will determine whether it is a peace for which such a guarantee can be secured. The question upon which the whole future peace and policy of the world depends is this: Is the present war a struggle for a just and secure peace, or only for a new balance of power? If it be only a struggle for a new balance of power, who will guarantee, who can guarantee, the stable equilibrium of the new arrangement? Only a tranquil Europe can be a stable Europe. There must be, not a balance of power, but a community of power; not organized rivalries, but an organized common peace.

Fortunately we have received very explicit assurances on this point. The statesmen of both of the groups of nations now arrayed against one another have said, in terms that could not be misinterpreted, that it was no part of the purpose they had in mind to crush their antagonists. But the implications of these assurances may not be equally clear to all—may not be the same on both sides of the water. I think it will be serviceable if I attempt to set forth what we understand them to be.

They imply, first of all, that it must be a peace without victory. It is not pleasant to say this. I beg that I may be permitted to put my own interpretation upon it and that it may be understood that no other interpretation was in my thought. I am seeking only to face realities and to face them without soft concealments. Victory would mean peace forced upon the loser, a victor's terms imposed upon the vanquished. It would be accepted in humiliation, under duress, at an intolerable sacrifice, and would leave a sting, a resentment, a bitter memory upon which terms of peace would rest, not permanently, but only as upon quicksand. Only a peace between equals can last, only a peace the very principle of which is equality and a common participation in a common benefit. The right state of mind, the right feeling between nations, is as necessary for a lasting peace as is the just settlement of vexed questions of territory or of racial and national allegiance.

The equality of nations upon which peace must be founded if it is to last must be an equality of rights; the guarantees exchanged must neither recognize nor imply a difference between big nations and small, between those that are powerful and those that are weak. Right must be based upon the common strength, not upon the individual strength, of the nations upon whose concert peace will depend. Equality of territory or of resources there of course cannot be; nor any other sort of equality not gained in the ordinary peaceful and legitimate development of the peoples themselves. But no one asks or expects anything more than an equality of rights. Mankind is looking now for freedom of life, not for equipoises of power.

And there is a deeper thing involved than even equality of right among organized nations. No peace can last, or ought to last, which does not recognize and accept the principle that governments derive all their just powers from the consent of the governed, and that no right anywhere exists to hand peoples about from sovereignty to sovereignty as if they were property. I take it for granted, for instance, if I may venture upon a single example, that statesmen everywhere are agreed that there should be a united, independent, and autonomous Poland, and that henceforth inviolable security of life, of worship, and of industrial and social development should be guaranteed to all peoples who have lived hitherto under the power of governments devoted to a faith and purpose hostile to their own.

I speak of this, not because of any desire to exalt an abstract political principle which has always been held very dear by those who have sought to build up liberty in America, but for the same reason that I have spoken of the other conditions of peace which seem to me clearly indispensable—because I wish frankly to uncover realities. Any peace which does not recognize and accept this principle will inevitably be upset. It will not rest upon the affections or the convictions of mankind. The ferment of spirit of whole populations will fight subtly and constantly against it, and all the world will sympathize. The world can be at peace only if its life is stable, and there can be no stability where the will is in rebellion, where there is not tranquility of spirit and a sense of justice, of freedom, and of right.

So far as practicable, moreover, every great people now struggling towards a full development of its resources and of its powers should be assured a direct outlet to the great highways of the sea. Where this can not be done by the cession of territory, it can no doubt be done by the neutralization of direct rights of way under the general guarantee which will assure the peace itself. With a right comity of arrangement no nation need be shut away from free access to the open paths of the world's commerce.

And the paths of the sea must alike in law and in fact be free. The freedom of the seas is the *sine qua non* of peace, equality, and cooperation. No doubt a somewhat radical reconsideration of many of the rules of international practice hitherto thought to be established may be necessary in order to make the seas indeed free and common in practically all circumstances for the use of mankind, but the motive for such changes is convincing and compelling. There can be no trust or intimacy between the peoples of the world without them. The free, constant, unthreatened intercourse of nations is an essential part of the process of peace and of development. It need not be difficult either to define or to secure the freedom of the seas if the governments of the world sincerely desire to come to an agreement concerning it.

It is a problem closely connected with the limitation of naval armaments and the cooperation of the navies of the world in keeping the seas at once free and safe, and the question of limiting naval armaments opens the wider and perhaps more difficult question of the limitation of armies and of all programmes of military preparation. Difficult and delicate as these questions are, they must be faced with the utmost candour and decided in a spirit of real accommodation if peace is to come with healing in its wings, and come to stay. Peace cannot be had without concession and sacrifice. There can be no sense of safety and equality among the nations if great preponderating armaments are henceforth to continue here and there to be built up and maintained. The statesmen of the world must plan for peace and nations must adjust and accommodate their policy to it as they have planned for war and made ready for pitiless contest and rivalry. The question of armaments, whether on land or sea, is the most immediately and intensely practical question connected with the future fortunes of nations and of mankind.

I have spoken upon these great matters without reserve and with the utmost explicitness because it has seemed to me to be necessary if the world's yearning desire for peace was anywhere to find free voice and utterance. Perhaps I am the only person in high authority amongst all the peoples of the world who is at liberty to speak and hold nothing back. I am speaking as an individual, and yet I am speaking also, of course, as the responsible head of a great government, and I feel confident that I have said what the people of the United States would wish me to say. May I not add that I hope and believe that I am in effect speaking for liberals and friends of humanity in every nation and of every programme of liberty? I would fain believe that I am speaking for the silent mass of mankind everywhere who have as yet had no place or opportunity to speak their real hearts out concerning the death and ruin they see to have come already upon the persons and the homes they hold most dear

And in holding out the expectation that the people and Government of the United States will join the other civilized nations of the world in guaranteeing the permanence of peace upon such terms as I have named I speak with the greater boldness and confidence because it is clear to every man who can think that there is in this promise no breach in either our traditions or our policy as a nation, but a fulfilment, rather, of all that we have professed or striven for.

I am proposing, as it were, that the nations should with one accord adopt the doctrine of President Monroe as the doctrine of the world: that no nation should seek to extend its polity over any other nation or people, but that every people should be left free to determine its own polity, its own way of development, unhindered, unthreatened, unafraid, the little along with the great and powerful.

I am proposing that all nations henceforth avoid entangling alliances which would draw them into competitions of power, catch them in a net of intrigue and selfish rivalry, and disturb their own affairs with influences intruded from without. There is no entangling alliance in a concert of power. When all unite to act in the same sense and with the same purpose, all act in the common interest and are free to live their own lives under a common protection.

I am proposing government by the consent of the governed; that freedom of the seas which in international conference after conference representatives of the United States have urged with the eloquence of those who are the convinced disciples of liberty; and that moderation of armaments which makes of armies and navies a power for order merely, not an instrument of aggression or of selfish violence.

These are American principles, American policies. We could stand for no others. And they are also the principles and policies of forward-looking men and women everywhere, of every modern nation, of every enlightened community. They are the principles of mankind and must prevail.

File No. 763.72119/415

Document No. 46 Carlton J.H. Hayes, Proposal for Armed Neutrality instead of Full Belligerency (February 1917)
Source: *The Survey,* XXXVII (Feb. 10, 1917), pp. 535-538.

THE SURVEY

Which?
War without a Purpose?
Or Armed Neutrality with a Purpose?

By Carlton J. H. Hayes

ASSOCIATE PROFESSOR OF HISTORY, COLUMBIA UNIVERSITY

WITH the immediate causes of the present European war and with many, if not all, of its immediate results as between European powers, the United States, I take it, is not concerned. Individually Americans may dislike and denounce the subjection of Belgium to Germany or of Serbia to Austria-Hungary; individually they may likewise dislike and condemn the annexation of Constantinople by Russia or the failure of Great Britain to grant autonomy to Ireland. They may even feel that there is little to choose between entrusting Poland to the "tender mercies" of a Hohenzollern or a Hapsburg and putting it under the sceptre of a "benevolent" Tsar. The European war was not of American making; it is not now being waged directly and purposely either for or against American interests; and the best interests of the United States will not be served by a complete crushing of either group of belligerents.

How, then, is the United States involved in the present war? Only in the general way in which we have been involved in every great struggle that has depended for its issue upon maritime supremacy. Ever since our country declared its independence, Great Britain has asserted and maintained a naval preponderance among all the powers, and on every occasion on which her naval preponderance has been assailed we have willingly or unwillingly been involved. During our own War of Independence, France and Spain went to war with England, and so vexatious became the belligerents' (especially the English) restrictions on neutral trade and commerce by means of the seizure of merchant vessels and the proclamation of paper blockades—so intolerable became the lot of neutrals— that Russia, Denmark, Sweden, Prussia, Austria and Portugal formed an Armed Neutrality, demanding

(1) free passages of neutral ships from port to port and along the coasts of combatant nations,

(2) inviolability of an enemy's goods in neutral ships with the exception of such goods as were contraband of war, and

(3) exact definition of a blockaded port, a merely nominal (paper) blockade, that is, one not enforced by a sufficient number of ships of war in the vicinity of the specified harbor, being declared inadmissible.

The Armed Neutrality League did what it could to enforce its demands by convoying merchantmen and by protesting vehemently and unitedly against violations of its principles. Although it did not have sufficient naval strength to give full force to its decrees in each and every case, it succeeded, nevertheless, in winning recognition of its principles from one group of belligerents (France, Spain, Holland and the United States) and in securing considerable abatement of English pretensions.

Again, during the wars of the French Revolution and of the Napoleonic era, neutrals were confronted with much the same situation. In the earlier stages of this prolonged conflict, the United States, in defense of its neutral commerce, almost came to blows with France. In the later stages of the same general struggle, the United States actually did come to blows with Great Britain. And in the midst of the Franco-British conflict (1800), the Baltic powers revived their Armed Neutrality. This second Armed Neutrality was not large enough or strong enough to resist British attacks upon it, and within a few months it was broken up. Its achievements, like those of America in the War of 1812, were not at the time considered great or decisive.

Yet the Armed Neutrality Leagues of 1780 and 1800 were not without important subsequent results. They served to crystallize neutral sentiment and to force upon the attention of the greatest maritime power demands for a revision of the rules of naval warfare which would have been permanently ignored had they come from any single member of either armed neutrality group. As the event proved, even Great Britain gave adherence in the Paris declaration of 1856 and in the London declaration of 1909 to the principles of the Armed Neutralities.

Now there is another tremendous European war, and neutral interests are again jeopardized, this time mainly by the nature of the naval warfare between Great Britain and Germany. With this phase of the contemporaneous war the United States, as the largest and most influential neutral power, is directly concerned. What exactly have we at stake? And how may we most effectively safeguard our legitimate interests?

What we most clearly have at stake is the freedom of the seas—the recognized and respected right to use the high seas, the arteries of international intercourse, for passenger and non-contraband-goods traffic, and to trade freely and fully without let or hindrance with fellow neutrals and, in so far as non-contraband goods are concerned, with belligerents. In the way of the freedom of the seas stand at the present time both Germany and Great Britain. Both of these powers, together with their respective allies, deny us our "rights."

Rights Denied

FROM the very beginning of the present war Great Britain has sought to check neutral trade with Germany. As early as December 26, 1914, the American government addressed a note to Great Britain, protesting against the detentions and seizures of cargoes and pointing out that British policy was directly responsible for the depression in many American industries. On March 1, 1915, Mr. Asquith stated in the House of Commons that Great Britain and France, in retaliation upon Germany for her declaration of the war zone around the British Isles, would confiscate all goods of "presumed enemy destination, ownership, or origin."

In an extended communication addressed to the British government by Secretary Bryan on March 30, 1915, attention was called to the unusual character of the proposed British blockade and the interference with legitimate neutral commerce which might readily result. The United States government was willing to concede that the changed conditions of naval warfare, especially the operations of submarines, might justify some modification of the old form of "close" blockade, but it was unwilling to concede the right of belligerents to blockade neutral ports. It was further pointed out that alleged illegal acts of Germany could not be offered as an excuse for unlawful acts on the part of Great Britain.

To this protest the British foreign secretary replied politely but evasively. Meanwhile, the closure of Germany to legitimate American trade and even to ordinary American postal correspondence became more and more effective. On October 21, 1915, another note from the United States, couched in much more vigorous language, was addressed to London. It stated that the so-called blockade instituted by the Allies was "ineffective, illegal, and indefensible"; that the "American government cannot submit to the curtailment of its neutral rights"; and that the United States "must insist that the relations between it and His Majesty's government be governed, not by a policy of expediency, but by those established rules of international conduct to which Great Britain in the past has held the United States to account." No real redress of American grievances was forthcoming. On the contrary, the British minister of blockade announced to the Commons on June 28, 1916, that Great Britain had decided to discontinue even "partial enforcement" of the Declaration of London.

But however irksome to neutrals have been the British violations of international law, German violations have been more outrageous because they have been attended by destruction of neutral lives as well as by injury to neutral commerce. Early in the war, Germany's planting of floating mines was a menace to neutral as well as to belligerent traffic. On February 4, 1915, Germany declared the waters around the British Isles a war zone after February 18 and proclaimed her intention of sinking every enemy merchant vessel found in the zone, even if it were impossible to save the crew and passengers. She also stated that neutral ships entering the war zone were in danger. Then, in reply to the American protest, the German government on February 18, 1915, explained that, in view of the illegal methods used by Great Britain in preventing commerce between Germany and neutral countries, even in articles which are not contraband of war, the Imperial government felt justified in using all means within its power to retaliate upon England. The chief means at the disposal of the Germans was the submarine, and it was used with the frightful results we all know. After the sinking of the Lusitania, there could be no question of the hideous character of unrestricted German submarine warfare.

In all these infractions of the rights of neutrals, it cannot be allowed for a moment that either Germany or Great Britain has been actuated by hatred of any neutral. It is absurd to suppose that Great Britain is deliberately violating the commercial rights of neutrals for the mere sake of doing so.

It is equally absurd to imagine that Germany is wilfully destroying the lives of non-combatants for the sheer pleasure of it. The fact of the matter is that Germany and Great Britain are in a death-grapple *with each other* and that each is using the most available weapon for starving out the other.

Common Cause of the Neutrals

IN THE great crisis now confronting the United States, another fact must not be lost sight of. The United States is not the only neutral power. Spain, Holland and the Scandinavian countries have suffered relatively more than we from the infraction of neutral rights; and the Latin-American republics are by no means negligible. Whatever is done by the United States in defense of neutral rights should be done in cooperation with other neutrals.

Neutral rights—those of other countries as well as of the United States—have been flagrantly violated (1) by Great Britain, in that neutral trade with Scandinavian ports and with Holland has been interfered with by the British policy of intercepting all goods of German origin or ultimately destined for Germany, even when the goods have been carried by neutral ships between neutral ports; and (2) by Germany, in that numerous neutral merchantmen have been sunk by German submarines either without warning or without opportunity for safeguarding the lives of passengers, some of whom have been citizens of neutral powers.

It is obvious to any friend of humanity that violations of neutral right which involve loss of life are far more serious at the moment than violations which involve only loss of trade. It is natural, therefore, that Americans should now be moved more against Germany than against Great Britain. It is but natural that the receipt of news of the intention of the German government to resume unrestricted submarine warfare on and after February 1, 1917, should be followed immediately by the exertion of tremendous pressure upon the President of the United States to plunge us into war with Germany. Having in mind the position taken by President Wilson in his earlier notes to Berlin, it can occasion no surprise that he broke off diplomatic relations with Germany.

Breaking off diplomatic relations means little of itself. Unless it is accompanied by positive constructive action, it is merely negative and futile. To me it seems that there are now two main highways, along either of which we may proceed.

On the one hand, we may strive to avenge ourselves upon Germany by allying ourselves with the Entente Powers, a step

340

which will almost inevitably mean accepting their views of
the freedom of the seas; joining our naval units to those of
Great Britain, France, and Italy; sending an expeditionary
force—and later a conscripted army—to the trenches of
Flanders and the Somme; and agreeing to make peace only in
concert with our allies.

But what purpose will be served thereby? We shall be
supplying additional targets for German torpedoes; we shall
be sacrificing thousands of American lives to "avenge" hundreds; we shall be committed to the support of the extreme
peace terms of Russia and Japan as well as those of France
and Great Britain; we shall be assisting in the upbuilding of
states whose future claims to world domination may well be
as dangerous to world peace as the present claims of the most
extreme German spokesman. And, above all, we shall be
losing our opportunity to champion real *neutral* rights against
belligerent pretensions.

Positive Constructive Action

ON THE other hand, we may follow up the rupture of German diplomatic relations with an immediate and earnest attempt to organize an Armed Neutrality. This, if successful,
would mean an agreement among the United States, the Latin-
American republics, Spain, Holland, and the Scandinavian
kingdoms, on a common platform of principles governing commercial intercourse in time of war, and common action in
convoying merchantmen and in defending, by force if necessary, neutral rights.

At the outset, such an Armed Neutrality would devote most
of its energies to safeguarding human life against unlawful
submarine attacks; subsequently it might ameliorate, if not
completely remove, the abuses of blockade, of visit and search,
and of arbitrary extension of lists of contraband. If the
Armed Neutralities of 1780 and 1800 are any guide to an
Armed Neutrality of 1917, the latter might prove successful
in bringing Germany to terms and in convincing the Entente
Powers of the advantages of a modification of their maritime
policy. Best of all, a consensus of neutral opinion and a community of neutral interest would be established in the face of
all belligerents.

The purpose which the United States has in view right now
is to make Germany abandon her unrestricted submarine warfare. If we make war on Germany and throw in our lot with
the Entente Powers, we shall not achieve our purpose; we
shall merely help Great Britain, France, Russia, Italy and
Japan to achieve their purposes. If, however, we succeed in

organizing an Armed Neutrality, we *may* achieve our immediate purpose, and we shall certainly be 'in an infinitely better position both during and after the war to champion neutral rights on land and on sea against any power or any combination of powers which unjustly undertakes to abridge those rights.

Suppose, now, that we elect to organize an Armed Neutrality rather than to declare war against Germany. Some difficulty may be experienced in prevailing upon all neutral powers to participate. Holland, for example, on account of her geographical position, might be very chary about antagonizing her belligerent neighbors. But granting that a majority of neutrals join the United States in forming an Armed Neutrality, what will be the procedure of such a league?

First of all, a declaration of principles must be agreed upon. For a manifesto of this sort there is already abundant precedent in international law and usage. Without attempting to forecast the details of neutral agreement, it may be observed that the declaration should cover at least four points: (1) contraband; (2) blockade; (3) convoy; and (4) submarine warfare. The first three, it might be found, have already been defined quite acceptably to neutrals in the London declaration of 1909. The provisions of the London Declaration were the result of long study on the part of experts in international law; they represent the result of a careful weighing of the interest of belligerents on the one side and of neutrals on the other side during an earlier prevalence of maritime war; and, though never formally ratified by the powers, they were signed at the time by the representatives of the United States, Great Britain, France, Russia, Japan, Austria-Hungary, Italy, Spain and Holland.

The fourth point to be covered by the declaration of the proposed Armed Neutrality—that concerning submarine warfare—would probably involve new applications of old principles, such as the immunity of unarmed merchantmen from attack unless they resisted search or attempted to run away; the inviolability of non-contraband goods on neutral merchantmen; and the safeguarding of the lives of non-combatants. It is obvious that the rigorous enforcement of these doctrines would operate to restrict submarine warfare to attacks on enemy warships and military transports, and to visit and search of merchantmen with a view only to casting overboard recognized contraband of war.

Joint Enforcement

HAVING agreed upon a declaration of principles, the next

thing for the Armed Neutrality to do would be to enforce it as far as possible. Here the chief means would be the naval convoy. For example, an American merchant vessel, or a fleet of American merchant vessels, would depart from the port of New York accompanied by an American warship. The United States government, if it were to take advantage of the principle of convoy as laid down by the Declaration of London, would have to be able to vouch that the ships so convoyed carried nothing contraband—contraband, however, in the sense held by the league of neutrals, not according to the decrees of Germany or Great Britain. If on the way to Liverpool or Southampton, whether within or without the so-called war zone, a German submarine should appear and order the crews and passengers of the merchantmen to take to the life-boats, then the commander of the naval convoy should protest against the patent infringement of international law; and if the submarine attempted to torpedo any ship of the fleet, the American vessels should forthwith retaliate by attempting to destroy the submarine.

If a German submarine should attack any neutral merchantman without warning or without complying with other regulations adopted by the league, thenceforth the very presence of a German submarine in the vicinity of neutral shipping, whether it had attempted to attack or not, could be considered as *prima facie* evidence of an *intent* to attack and all German submarines might be sunk as soon as they were detected. The United States, on account of its relatively large navy, would be expected to perform a larger service than its fellow-neutrals in "potting" submarines; and the Armed Neutrality as a whole might eventually accomplish much towards removing or minimizing the menace of submarine warfare.

Less effective, no doubt, would be the campaign of the Armed Neutrality for the enforcement of its principles in respect of contraband and blockade against the pretensions of the Entente Powers. But some headway might be made. If Great Britain were relieved of the worst menace of submarine warfare and if the neutral powers presented a united front, she, despite her overwhelming naval preponderance, might permit cargoes of non-contraband character to proceed freely under convoy from New York to Rotterdam or Copenhagen or even to such German ports as were not undergoing an effective close-range blockade. The very fact that the cargoes were under convoy would be an official guarantee that they contained no contraband; and the British government would hesitate to order its warships to open fire on an American man-of-war.

But what if the Armed Neutrality, in taking necessary steps to enforce its principles, is met by a German declaration of war? Will not this mean *war* just as much as though the United States should now declare war on Germany? It is my belief that there is a fundamental difference between the two kinds of war. If we declare war against Germany now, we are far more likely to be drawn into an alliance with the Entente Powers than we would be were we later to receive a declaration of war from Germany as an incident to our policy of enforcing our rights and the rights of all neutrals. In the latter case we would certainly be no worse off and we would have performed a noble service to humanity—quite as noble as dying in continental trenches.

It is conceivable that we might be in an actual state of war with Germany without any declaration of war on our part. There is plenty of precedent for such a situation. The Armed Neutralities of 1780 and 1800 are cases in point. Not even British declarations of war swerved the league of 1780 from its purpose. And even more pertinent to America is the instance in 1798 when the United States, to protect its rights at sea, broke off diplomatic relations with France and Congress authorized American frigates to capture French vessels guilty of depredations on American commerce. Actual naval engagements were fought, but no formal declaration of war was made; and within a year France backed down.

It is idle in this hour of national crisis to say merely that the United States should keep out of war. The hour demands well-considered constructive action. By declaring war immediately we shall be taking action, but action that is at once ill-considered and destructive of future world organization and world peace. The United States, in this case, will be last and least on the long list of belligerents. On the other hand, by giving hearty and vigorous support to an Armed Neutrality we shall be taking action which has ample precedent and which promises much that is hopeful for the future. In this case, the United States will be first and foremost among all neutral powers. And a league of neutrals is a better harbinger of future world solidarity than a league of belligerents.

"THE ROAD TO YESTERDAY"
Reproduced from The New York Times of Aug. 16, 1914.

▨ THE ▨
SURVEY

The Sport of Kings

VICTORY

"AND ALL I DID WAS JUST TO GROWL A LITTLE!"

ARMY MEDICAL OFFICER: "AT LAST, A PERFECT SOLDIER!"

"Confronted with the reality, Dante tears up his description of hell."—
From *Berko's Illustrated News (Hungarian), New York city.*

Part III

The Challenge of American Belligerency:
The Anti-War Movement, 1917-1918

Document No. 48   President Wilson's War Message (April 1917)
Source: U.S. Department of State, *Foreign Relations of the United States,*
1917, Supplement I, The World War (Washington, D.C.: U.S. Govt. Printing
Office, 1931), pp. 194-203.

---

*The Secretary of State to the Diplomatic Representatives in all
Countries*

[Circular telegram]

WASHINGTON, *April 2, 1917.*

The President addressed the special session of Congress this evening in regard to the international situation. After briefly reviewing the submarine controversy with Germany, he pointed out
that the present submarine warfare is a warfare against mankind;
that in view of developments, armed neutrality is worse than ineffectual and is only likely to produce what it was meant to prevent;
that we can not choose the path of submission and are arraying ourselves against wrongs which cut to the very roots of human life.
With a profound sense of the solemn and even tragical character
of the step, he advised the Congress to declare the recent course
of the German Government to be in effect nothing less than war
against the Government and people of the United States and proposed that it take immediate steps to put the country in a thorough
state of defense and employ all its power and resources to bring
the German Empire to terms and end the war. This will involve
utmost practicable cooperation in counsel and action with the governments now at war with Germany; the extension of financial
credits, material aid, and addition to armed forces of at least
500,000 men upon principle of universal military service. Legislative proposals along these lines will be promptly introduced. We
have no quarrel with the German people, but only with the autocratic government which has brought on the present situation. The
world must be made safe for democracy which seems to be in the
balance. We have no selfish ends to serve. We desire no conquest,
no dominion; we seek no indemnities for ourselves, no material compensation for the sacrifices we shall freely make. We are but one
of the champions of the rights of mankind.
The following Joint Resolution was immediately introduced and
referred to the Foreign Relations and Foreign Affairs Committees
which meet to-morrow morning for its consideration:

353

Joint Resolution declaring that a state of war exists between the Imperial German Government and the Government and people of the United States and making provision to prosecute the same:

WHEREAS, the recent acts of the Imperial Government are acts of war against the Government and people of the United States;

RESOLVED, by the Senate and House of Representatives of the United States of America in Congress assembled that the state of war between the United States and the Imperial Government which has thus been thrust upon the United States is hereby formally declared; and,

That the President be, and he is hereby, authorized and directed to take immediate steps not only to put the country in a thorough state of defense but also to exert all of its power and employ all of its resources to carry on war against the Imperial German Government and to bring the conflict to a successful termination.

LANSING

Address of the President of the United States Delivered at a Joint Session of the Two Houses of Congress, April 2, 1917 [1]

GENTLEMEN OF THE CONGRESS: I have called the Congress into extraordinary session because there are serious, very serious, choices of policy to be made, and made immediately, which it was neither right nor constitutionally permissible that I should assume the responsibility of making.

On the 3d of February last [2] I officially laid before you the extraordinary announcement of the Imperial German Government that on and after the 1st day of February it was its purpose to put aside all restraints of law or of humanity and use its submarines to sink every vessel that sought to approach either the ports of Great Britain and Ireland or the western coasts of Europe or any of the ports controlled by the enemies of Germany within the Mediterranean. That had seemed to be the object of the German submarine warfare earlier in the war, but since April of last year the Imperial Government had somewhat restrained the commanders of its undersea craft in conformity with its promise then given to us that passenger boats should not be sunk and that due warning would be given to all other vessels which its submarines might seek to destroy, when no resistance was offered or escape attempted, and care taken that their crews were given at least a fair chance to save their lives in their open boats. The precautions taken were meagre and haphazard enough, as was proved in distressing instance after instance in the progress of the cruel and unmanly business, but a certain

---

[1] Reprinted from the *Congressional Record*, Sixty-fifth Cong., 1st sess. (vol. LV); p. 102.

[2] For address of Feb. 3, see *ante*, p. 109.

degree of restraint was observed. The new policy has swept every restriction aside. Vessels of every kind, whatever their flag, their character, their cargo, their destination, their errand, have been ruthlessly sent to the bottom without warning and without thought of help or mercy for those on board, the vessels of friendly neutrals along with those of belligerents. Even hospital ships and ships carrying relief to the sorely bereaved and stricken people of Belgium, though the latter were provided with safe-conduct through the proscribed areas by the German Government itself and, were distinguished by unmistakable marks of identity, have been sunk with the same reckless lack of compassion or of principle.

I was for a little while unable to believe that such things would in fact be done by any government that had hitherto subscribed to the humane practices of civilized nations. International law had its origin in the attempt to set up some law which would be respected and observed upon the seas, where no nation had right of dominion and where lay the free highways of the world. By painful stage after stage has that law been built up, with meagre enough results, indeed, after all was accomplished that could be accomplished, but always with a clear view, at least, of what the heart and conscience of mankind demanded. This minimum of right the German Government has swept aside under the plea of retaliation and necessity and because it had no weapons which it could use at sea except these which it is impossible to employ as it is employing them without throwing to the winds all scruples of humanity or of respect for the understandings that were supposed to underlie the intercourse of the world. I am not now thinking of the loss of property involved, immense and serious as that is, but only of the wanton and wholesale destruction of the lives of noncombatants, men, women, and children, engaged in pursuits which have always, even in the darkest periods of modern history, been deemed innocent and legitimate. Property can be paid for; the lives of peaceful and innocent people can not be. The present German submarine warfare against commerce is a warfare against mankind.

It is a war against all nations. American ships have been sunk, American lives taken, in ways which it has stirred us very deeply to learn of, but the ships and people of other neutral and friendly nations have been sunk and overwhelmed in the waters in the same way. There has been no discrimination. The challenge is to all mankind. Each nation must decide for itself how it will meet it. The choice we make for ourselves must be made with a moderation of counsel and a temperateness of judgment befitting our character and our motives as a nation. We must put excited feeling away. Our motive will not be revenge or the victorious assertion of the physical might of the nation, but only the vindication of right, of human right, of which we are only a single champion.

When I addressed the Congress on the 26th of February last,[1] I thought that it would suffice to assert our neutral rights with arms, our right to use the seas against unlawful interference, our right to keep our people safe against unlawful violence. But armed neutrality, it now appears, is impracticable. Because submarines are in effect outlaws when used as the German submarines have been used against merchant shipping, it is impossible to defend ships against their attacks as the law of nations has assumed that merchantmen would defend themselves against privateers or cruisers, visible craft giving chase upon the open sea. It is common prudence in such circumstances, grim necessity indeed, to endeavour to destroy them before they have shown their own intention. They must be dealt with upon sight, if dealt with at all. The German Government denies the right of neutrals to use arms at all within the areas of the sea which it has proscribed, even in the defense of rights which no modern publicist has ever before questioned their right to defend. The intimation is conveyed that the armed guards which we have placed on our merchant ships will be treated as beyond the pale of law and subject to be dealt with as pirates would be. Armed neutrality is ineffectual enough at best; in such circumstances and in the face of such pretensions it is worse than ineffectual; it is likely only to produce what it was meant to prevent; it is practically certain to draw us into the war without either the rights or the effectiveness of belligerents. There is one choice we can not make, we are incapable of making: we will not choose the path of submission and suffer the most sacred rights of our nation and our people to be ignored or violated. The wrongs against which we now array ourselves are no common wrongs; they cut to the very roots of human life.

With a profound sense of the solemn and even tragical character of the step I am taking and of the grave responsibilities which it involves, but in unhesitating obedience to what I deem my constitutional duty, I advise that the Congress declare the recent course of the Imperial German Government to be in fact nothing less than war against the Government and people of the United States; that it formally accept the status of belligerent which has thus been thrust upon it; and that it take immediate steps not only to put the country in a

---

[1] Extract from address of Feb. 26, *ante*, p. 150.

more thorough state of defense but also to exert all its power and employ all its resources to bring the Government of the German Empire to terms and end the war.

What this will involve is clear. It will involve the utmost practicable cooperation in counsel and action with the governments now at war with Germany, and, as incident to that, the extension to those governments of the most liberal financial credits, in order that our resources may so far as possible be added to theirs. It will involve the organization and mobilization of all the material resources of the country to supply the materials of war and serve the incidental needs of the nation in the most abundant and yet the most economical and efficient way possible. It will involve the immediate full equipment of the Navy in all respects but particularly in supplying it with the best means of dealing with the enemy's submarines. It will involve the immediate addition to the armed forces of the United States already provided for by law in case of war at least 500,000 men, who should, in my opinion, be chosen upon the principle of universal liability to service, and also the authorization of subsequent additional increments of equal force so soon as they may be needed and can be handled in training. It will involve also, of course, the granting of adequate credits to the Government, sustained, I hope, so far as they can equitably be sustained by the present generation, by well conceived taxation.

I say sustained so far as may be equitable by taxation because it seems to me that it would be most unwise to base the credits which will now be necessary entirely on money borrowed. It is our duty, I most respectfully urge, to protect our people so far as we may against the very serious hardships and evils which would be likely to arise out of the inflation which would be produced by vast loans.

In carrying out the measures by which these things are to be accomplished we should keep constantly in mind the wisdom of interfering as little as possible in our own preparation and in the equipment of our own military forces with the duty—for it will be a very practical duty—of supplying the nations already at war with Germany with the materials which they can obtain only from us or by our assistance. They are in the field and we should help them in every way to be effective there.

I shall take the liberty of suggesting, through the several executive departments of the Government, for the consideration of your committees, measures for the accomplishment of the several objects I have mentioned. I hope that it will be your pleasure to deal with them as having been framed after very careful thought by the branch of the Government upon which the responsibility of conducting the war and safeguarding the nation will most directly fall.

While we do these things, these deeply momentous things, let us be very clear, and make very clear to all the world what our motives and our objects are. My own thought has not been driven from its habitual and normal course by the unhappy events of the last two months, and I do not believe that the thought of the nation has been altered or clouded by them. I have exactly the same things in mind now that I had in mind when I addressed the Senate on the 22d of January last [1]; the same that I had in mind when I addressed the Congress on the 3d of February and on the 26th of February. Our object now, as then, is to vindicate the principles of peace and justice in the life of the world as against selfish and autocratic power and to set up amongst the really free and self-governed peoples of the world such a concert of purpose and of action as will henceforth ensure the observance of those principles. Neutrality is no longer feasible or desirable where the peace of the world is involved and the freedom of its peoples, and the menace to that peace and freedom lies in the existence of autocratic governments backed by organized force which is controlled wholly by their will, not by the will of their people. We have seen the last of neutrality in such circumstances. We are at the beginning of an age in which it will be insisted that the same standards of conduct and of responsibility for wrong done shall be observed among nations and their governments that are observed among the individual citizens of civilized states.

We have no quarrel with the German people. We have no feeling towards them but one of sympathy and friendship. It was not upon their impulse that their Government acted in entering this war. It was not with their previous knowledge or approval. It was a war determined upon as wars used to be determined upon in the old, unhappy days when peoples were nowhere consulted by their rulers and wars were provoked and waged in the interest of dynasties or of little groups of ambitious men who were accustomed to use their fellow men as pawns and tools. Self-governed nations do not fill their neighbour states with spies or set the course of intrigue to bring about some critical posture of affairs which will give them an opportunity to strike and make conquest. Such designs can be successfully worked out only under cover and where no one has the right to ask questions. Cunningly contrived plans of deception or aggression, carried, it may be, from generation to generation, can be

[1] Address, ante, p. 24.

worked out and kept from the light only within the privacy of courts or behind the carefully guarded confidences of a narrow and privileged class. They are happily impossible where public opinion commands and insists upon full information concerning all the nation's affairs.

A steadfast concert for peace can never be maintained except by a partnership of democratic nations. No autocratic government could be trusted to keep faith within it or observe its covenants. It must be a league of honour, a partnership of opinion. Intrigue would eat its vitals away; the plottings of inner circles who could plan what they would and render account to no one would be a corruption seated at its very heart. Only free peoples can hold their purpose and their honour steady to a common end and prefer the interests of mankind to any narrow interest of their own.

Does not every American feel that assurance has been added to our hope for the future peace of the world by the wonderful and heartening things that have been happening within the last few weeks in Russia? Russia was known by those who knew it best to have been always in fact democratic at heart, in all the vital habits of her thought, in all the intimate relationships of her people that spoke their natural instinct, their habitual attitude towards life. The autocracy that crowned the summit of her political structure, long as it had stood and terrible as was the reality of its power, was not in fact Russian in origin, character, or purpose; and now it has been shaken off and the great, generous Russian people have been added in all their naïve majesty and might to the forces that are fighting for freedom in the world, for justice, and for peace. Here is a fit partner for a league of honour.

One of the things that has served to convince us that the Prussian autocracy was not and could never be our friend is that from the very outset of the present war it has filled our unsuspecting communities and even our offices of government with spies and set criminal intrigues everywhere afoot against our national unity of counsel, our peace within and without, our industries and our commerce. Indeed it is now evident that its spies were here even before the war began; and it is unhappily not a matter of conjecture but a fact proved in our courts of justice that the intrigues which have more than once come perilously near to disturbing the peace and dislocating the industries of the country have been carried on at the instigation, with the support, and even under the personal direction of official agents of the Imperial Government accredited to the Government of the United States. Even in checking these things and trying to extirpate them we have sought to put the most generous interpretation possible upon them because we knew that their source lay, not in any hostile feeling or purpose of the German people towards us (who were, no doubt, as ignorant of them as we ourselves were), but only in the selfish designs of a Government that did what it pleased and told its people nothing. But they have played their part in serving to convince us at last that that Government entertains no real friendship for us and means to act against our peace and security at its convenience. That it means to stir up enemies against us at our very doors the intercepted note to the German Minister at Mexico City is eloquent evidence.

We are accepting this challenge of hostile purpose because we know that in such a government, following such methods, we can never have a friend; and that in the presence of its organized power, always lying in wait to accomplish we know not what purpose, there can be no assured security for the democratic governments of the world. We are now about to accept gage of battle with this natural foe to liberty and shall, if necessary, spend the whole force of the nation to check and nullify its pretensions and its power. We are glad, now that we see the facts with no veil of false pretence about them, to fight thus for the ultimate peace of the world and for the liberation of its peoples, the German peoples included: for the rights of nations great and small and the privilege of men everywhere to choose their way of life and of obedience. The world must be made safe for democracy. Its peace must be planted upon the tested foundations of political liberty. We have no selfish ends to serve. We desire no conquest, no dominion. We seek no indemnities for ourselves, no material compensation for the sacrifices we shall freely make. We are but one of the champions of the rights of mankind. We shall be satisfied when those rights have been made as secure as the faith and the freedom of nations can make them.

Just because we fight without rancour and without selfish object, seeking nothing for ourselves but what we shall wish to share with all free peoples, we shall, I feel confident, conduct our operations as belligerents without passion and ourselves observe with proud punctilio the principles of right and of fair play we profess to be fighting for.

I have said nothing of the governments allied with the Imperial Government of Germany because they have not made war upon us or challenged us to defend our right and our honour. The Austro-Hungarian Government has, indeed, avowed its unqualified endorsement and acceptance of the reckless and lawless submarine warfare adopted now without disguise by the Imperial German Government, and it has therefore not been possible for this Government to receive Count Tarnowski, the Ambassador recently accredited to this Government by the Imperial and Royal Government of Austria-Hungary; but that Government has not actually engaged in warfare against citizens of the United States on the seas, and I take the liberty, for the present at least, of postponing a discussion of our relations with the authorities at Vienna. We enter this war only where we are clearly forced into it because there are no other means of defending our rights.

It will be all the easier for us to conduct ourselves as belligerents in a high spirit of right and fairness because we act without animus, not in enmity towards a people or with the desire to bring any injury or disadvantage upon them, but only in armed opposition to an irresponsible government which has thrown aside all considerations of humanity and of right and is running amuck. We are, let me say again, the sincere friends of the German people, and shall desire nothing so much as the early reestablishment of intimate relations of mutual advantage between us—however hard it may be for them, for the time being, to believe that this is spoken from our hearts. We have borne with their present government through all these bitter months because of that friendship—exercising a patience and forbearance which would otherwise have been impossible. We shall, happily, still have an opportunity to prove that friendship in our daily attitude and actions towards the millions of men and women of German birth and native sympathy who live amongst us and share our life, and we shall be proud to prove it towards all who are in fact loyal to their neighbours and to the Government in the hour of test. They are, most of them, as true and loyal Americans as if they had never known any other fealty or allegiance. They will be prompt to stand with us in rebuking and restraining the few who may be of a different mind and purpose. If there should be disloyalty, it will be dealt with with a firm hand of stern repression; but, if it lifts its head at all, it will lift it only here and there and without countenance except from a lawless and malignant few.

It is a distressing and oppressive duty, gentlemen of the Congress, which I have performed in thus addressing you. There are, it may be, many months of fiery trial and sacrifice ahead of us. It is a fearful thing to lead this great peaceful people into war, into the most terrible and disastrous of all wars, civilization itself seeming to be in the balance. But the right is more precious than peace, and we shall fight for the things which we have always carried nearest our hearts—for democracy, for the right of those who submit to authority to have a voice in their own governments, for the rights and liberties of small nations, for a universal dominion of right by such a concert of free peoples as shall bring peace and safety to all nations and make the world itself at last free. To such a task we can dedicate our lives and our fortunes, everything that we are and everything that we have, with the pride of those who know that the day has come when America is privileged to spend her blood and her might for the principles that gave her birth and happiness and the peace which she has treasured. God helping her, she can do no other.

Document No. 49 Socialist Party Position on American Belligerency
(April, 1917)
Source: Alexander Trachtenberg, ed., *The American Socialists and the
War* (N.Y.: Rand School of Social Science, 1917), pp. 38-45.

THE "MAJORITY" AND "MINORITY" REPORTS OF THE ST. LOUIS CONVENTION

Since the regular convention of the Socialist Party, whick
was to be held in the summer of 1916, was set aside by the
membership, the party did not have the opportunity from
the beginning of the European war to formulate a nationa
program which would represent the view of the largest majority of the membership.

Upon the formal declaration of war by Congress, the Na
tional Executive Committee issued a call for an emergency
convention to consider the war policy of the Party and to
take such measures as would be deemed advisable to inaugurate a movement for a speedy termination of the war
The call for the emergency convention was accepted with
universal approval and nearly 200 delegates from every par
of the country assembled at St. Louis, Mo., during the sec
ond week of April (7th-14th) and proceeded to shape the
policy of the party on the questions of war and militarism.

Two reports emanated from that convention which are
now before the membership of the party, the so-called "ma
jority" and "minority" reports. The designations are some
what misleading. The Committee on War and Militarisn
of the convention presented a majority and two minority re
ports. The first was signed by eleven members of the Com
mittee and, having received 140 votes, is the majority repor
of the convention. One minority report, signed by three
members of the Committee, and substantially supporting the
position of the majority report, but expressed in different
terms, received 31 votes, while the second minority report
which attempted to justify the present war and was signed
by the remaining member of the Committee, received only
five votes.

Neither of the minority reports having received the required number of votes (50), they could not be submitted
to the membership. Thereupon a statement was drawn up
by those not in accord with the declarations in the majority
report and, having obtained the required number of signatures of delegates (50), was sent forth with the referendum as a substitute for the majority report. It is now before the party as the minority report.

As the voting on these reports is still in progress, we re-
produce both reports as representative of the opinion of the
two groups within the Socialist Party.

MAJORITY REPORT

The Socialist Party of the United States in the present grave crisis, solemnly reaffirms its allegiance to the principle of inter-nationalism and working class solidarity the world over, and proclaims its unalterable opposition to the war just declared by the government of the United States.

Modern wars as a rule have been caused by the commercial and financial rivalry and intrigues of the capitalist interests in the different countries. Whether they have been frankly waged as wars of aggression or have been hypocritically represented as wars of "defense", they have always been made by the classes and fought by the masses. Wars bring wealth and power to the ruling classes, and suffering, death and demoralization to the workers.

They breed a sinister spirit of passion, unreason, race hatred and false patriotism. They obscure the struggles of the workers for life, liberty and social justice. They tend to sever the vital bonds of solidarity between them and their brothers in other countries, to destroy their organizations and to curtail their civic and political rights and liberties.

The Socialist Party of the United States is unalterably opposed to the system of exploitation and class rule which is upheld and strengthened by military power and sham national patriotism. We, therefore, call upon the workers of all countries to refuse support to their governments in their wars. The wars of the contending national groups of capitalists are not the concern of the workers. The only struggle which would justify the workers in taking up arms is the great struggle of the working class of the world to free itself from economic exploitation and political oppression, and we particularly warn the workers against the snare and delusion of so-called defensive warfare. As against the false doctrine of national patriotism we uphold the ideal of inter-national working-class solidarity. In support of capitalism, we will not willingly give a single life or a single dollar; in support of the struggle of the workers for freedom we pledge our all.

The mad orgy of death and destruction which is now con-vulsing unfortunate Europe was caused by the conflict of capi-talist interests in the European countries.

In each of these countries, the workers were oppressed and exploited. They produced enormous wealth but the bulk of it was withheld from them by the owners of the industries. The workers were thus deprived of the means to repurchase the wealth which they themselves had created.

The capitalist class of each country was forced to look for foreign markets to dispose of the accumulated "surplus" wealth. The huge profits made by the capitalists could no longer be profitably reinvested in their own countries, hence, they were driven to look for foreign fields of investment. The geo-graphical boundaries of each modern capitalist country thus became too narrow for the industrial and commercial operations of its capitalist class.

The efforts of the capitalists of all leading nations were there-fore centered upon the domination of the world markets. Im-perialism became the dominant note in the politics of Europe. The acquisition of colonial possessions and the extension of spheres of commercial and political influence became the object of diplomatic intrigues and the cause of constant clashes be-tween nations.

The acute competition between the capitalist powers of the earth, their jealousies and distrusts of one another and the fear of the rising power of the working class forced each of them to

arm to the teeth. This led to the mad rivalry of armament.
which, years before the outbreak of the present war, had turned
the leading countries of Europe into armed camps with standing
armies of many millions, drilled and equipped for war in times
of "peace."

Capitalism, imperialism and militarism had thus laid the
foundation of an inevitable general conflict in Europe. The
ghastly war in Europe was not caused by an accidental event,
nor by the policy or institutions of any single nation. It was
the logical outcome of the competitive capitalist system.

The six million men of all countries and races who have been
ruthlessly slain in the first thirty months of this war, the millions of others who have been crippled and maimed, the vast
treasures of wealth that have been destroyed, the untold misery
and sufferings of Europe, have not been sacrifices exacted in a
struggle for principles or ideals, but wanton offerings upon the
altar of private profit.

The forces of capitalism which have led to the war in Europe
are even more hideously transparent in the war recently provoked by the ruling class of this country.

When Belgium was invaded, the government enjoined upon
the people of this country the duty of remaining neutral, thus
clearly demonstrating that the "dictates of humanity," and the
fate of small nations and of democratic institutions were matters that did not concern it. But when our enormous war
traffic was seriously threatened, our government calls upon us
to rally to the "defense of democracy and civilization."

Our entrance into the European war was instigated by the
predatory capitalists in the United States who boast of the
enormous profit of seven billion dollars from the manufacture
and sale of munitions and war supplies and from the exportation
of American food stuffs and other necessaries. They are also
deeply interested in the continuance of war and the success of
the allied arms through their huge loans to the governments of
the allied powers and through other commercial ties. It is the
same interests which strive for imperialistic domination of the
Western Hemisphere.

The war of the United States against Germany cannot be
justified even on the plea that it is a war in defense of American
rights or American "honor." Ruthless as the unrestricted submarine war policy of the German government was and is, it is
not an invasion of the rights of the American people, as such,
but only an interference with the opportunity of certain groups
of American capitalists to coin cold profits out of the blood and
sufferings of our fellow men in the warring countries of Europe.

It is not a war against the militarist regime of the Central
Powers. Militarism can never be abolished by militarism.

It is not a war to advance the cause of democracy in Europe.
Democracy can never be imposed upon any country by a foreign
power by force of arms.

It is cant and hypocrisy to say that the war is not directed
against the German people, but against the Imperial Government of Germany. If we send an armed force to the battlefields of Europe, its cannon will mow down the masses of the
German people and not the Imperial German Government.

Our entrance into the European conflict at this time will serve
only to multiply the horrors of the war, to increase the toll of
death and destruction and to prolong the fiendish slaughter.
It will bring death, suffering and destitution to the people of
the United States and particularly to the work class. It will
give the powers of reaction in this country, the pretext for an

attempt to throttle our rights and to crush our democratic insti
tutions, and to fasten upon this country a permanent militarism

The working class of the United States has no quarrel with
the working class of Germany or of any other country. The
people of the United States have no quarrel with the people of
Germany or any other country. The American people did not
want and do not want this war. They have not been consulted
about the war and have had no part in declaring war. They
have been plunged into this war by the trickery and treachery
of the ruling class of the country through its representatives in
the National Administration and National Congress, its dema-
gogic agitators, its subsidized press, and other servile instruments of public expression.

We brand the declaration of war by our government as a
crime against the people of the United States and against the
nations of the world.

In all modern history there has been no war more unjustifiable than the war in which we are about to engage.

No greater dishonor has ever been forced upon a people than
that which the capitalist class is forcing upon this nation against
its will.

In harmony with these principles, the Socialist Party em-
phatically rejects the proposal that in time of war the workers
should suspend their struggle for better conditions. On the
contrary, the acute situation created by war calls for an ever
more vigorous prosecution of the class struggle, and we
recommend to the workers and pledge ourselves to the following course of action:

1. Continuous, active, and public opposition to the war
through demonstrations, mass petitions, and all other means
within our power.

2. Unyielding opposition to all proposed legislation for military or industrial conscription. Should such conscription be
forced upon the people, we pledge ourselves to continuous
efforts for the repeal of such laws and to the support of all mass
movements in opposition to conscription. We pledge ourselves
to oppose with all our strength any attempt to raise money for
payment of war expense by taxing the necessaries of life or
issuing bonds which will put the burden upon future generations. We demand that the capitalist class, which is responsible
for the war, pay its cost. Let those who kindled the fire
furnish the fuel.

3. Vigorous resistance to all reactionary measures, such as
censorship of press and mails, restriction of the rights of free
speech, assemblage, and organization, or compulsory arbitration
and limitation of the right to strike.

4. Consistent propaganda against military training and
militaristic teaching in the public schools.

5. Extension of the campaign of education among the
workers to organize them into strong, class-conscious, and
closely unified political and industrial organizations, to enable
them by concerted and harmonious mass action to shorten this
war and to establish lasting peace.

6. Widespread educational propaganda to enlighten the
masses as to the true relation between capitalism and war, and
to rouse and organize them for action, not only against present
war evils, but for the prevention of future wars and for the
destruction of the causes of war.

7. To protect the masses of the American people from the
pressing danger of starvation which the war in Europe has
brought upon them, and which the entry of the United States

has already accentuated, we demand—

(a) The restriction of food exports so long as the present shortage continues, the fixing of maximum prices and whatever measures may be necessary to prevent the food speculators from holding back the supplies now in their hands;

(b) The socialization and democratic management of the great industries concerned with the production, transportation, storage, and the marketing of food and other necessaries of life:

(c) The socialization and democratic management of all land and other natural resources now held out of use for monopolistic or speculative profit.

These measures are presented as means of protecting the workers against the evil results of the present war. The danger of recurrence of war will exist as long as the capitalist system of industry remains in existence. The end of wars will come with the establishment of socialized industry and industrial democracy the world over. The Socialist Party calls upon all the workers to join it in its struggle to reach this goal, and thus bring into the world a new society in which peace, fraternity, and human brotherhood will be the dominant ideals.

MINORITY REPORT

Congress has declared that a state of war exists between this nation and Germany. War between the two nations is a fact.

We opposed the entrance of this republic into the war, but we failed. The political and economic organizations of the working class were not strong enough to do more than protest.

Having failed to prevent the war by our agitation, we can only recognize it as a fact and try to force upon the government, through pressure of public opinion, a constructive program.

Our aim now must be to minimize the suffering and misery which the war will bring to our own people, to p   our rights and liberties against reactionary encroachments, and to promote an early peace upon a democratic basis, advantageous to the international working class.

Furthermore we must seize the opportunity presented by war conditions to advance our program of democratic collectivism. Every one of the other belligerent nations has discovered through the war that capitalism is inherently inefficient. To secure a maximum of efficiency, whether for military or civil needs, it has been found necessary to abandon the essential principle of capitalist industry. The warring nations have had to give up the organization and operation of industry and primary economic functions for profit, and to adopt the Socialist principle of production for use. Thus the war has demonstrated the superior efficiency of collective organization and operation of industry.

Guided by this experience, we would so reorganize our economic system as to secure for our permanent domestic needs the greatest possible results from the proper utilization of our national resources.

In furtherance of these aims we propose the following:

1. We propose that the Socialist Party shall establish communication with the Socialists within the enemy nations, to the end that peace may be secured upon democratic terms at the earliest possible moment.

2. We demand that there be no interference with freedom of speech, freedom of the press, and freedom of assemblage.

3. We demand that dealings between the government and the workers in all of the industries and services taken over and

operated by the government shall be conducted through their organizations with due regard to the right of organization of those not yet organized.

4. We demand that conscription, if it come at all, shall begin with wealth. All annual incomes in excess of $5,000 should be taken by the government and used to pay the current expenses of the war. If it is just to conscript a human being, it is just to conscript wealth. Money is not as sacred as human life.

5. We demand that there shall be no conscription of men until the American people shall have been given the right to vote upon it. Under the British empire the people of Australia were permitted to decide by ballot whether they should be con-- scripted. We demand for the American people the same right.

6. We demand that the government seize and operate for the benefit of the whole people, the great industries concerned with production, transportation, storage and marketing of the food and other. necessities of the people.

7. We demand that the government seize all suitable vacant and, and have the same cultivated for the purpose of furnishing ood supplies for the national use.

8. We demand that the government take over and operate .ll land and water transport facilities; all water powers and rrigation plants; mines, forests and oil fields; and all industrial nonopolies; and that this be done at once, before the nation .hall suffer çalamity from the failure of their capitalist direction .nd management under war pressure.

Document No. 50   The Quakers and the War (1917)
Source: *The Friends' Intelligencer,* LXXIV (April 14, 1917), p. 231.

STATEMENT OF NEW YORK FRIENDS.

To FRIENDS AND OTHERS:

The undersigned are members of the Society of Friends, commonly called Quakers.

In the solemn crisis in which our country now finds itself, upon the threshold of a great war, we desire to present to our fellow-members and to our fellow-citizens certain principles which we believe are fundamental as to our conduct.

The Society of Friends has from its beginning advocated freedom of speech and liberty of conscience. It has upheld the personal accountability of each person to his Maker. It has supported democracy as that form of government which best maintains the liberty of the individual, earnestly seeking the right to follow the dictates of his own conscience. It has consistently opposed oppression and wrong, and the endeavor to impose beliefs and laws adverse to men's conscience. We believe these principles are likewise fundamental in our American democracy.

War and military power being ready instruments in the hands of oppressors, and the militant and combative spirit being, as we hold, contrary to the spirit of God and the teachings of Jesus, Friends have endeavored to bring to the hearts of men the benign influences of peace and that spirit which shall do away with the causes of all wars, and which develops the highest manhood.

Friends point to the bloody course of the present war, with its examples of faithlessness and ruthlessness, as an exposition of what comes to the world when the ambitious, autocratic spirit of domination controls the minds of men.

In order to restrain the ruthless warfare waged, not only upon foes but upon nations which have with unexampled patience shown their desire to remain friends, the President of the United States has deemed it wise to ask Congress to grant to him the right and the means to use the power of this nation to endeavor to restore the principles of peace, stating the objects to be " to vindicate the principles of peace and justice in the world as against selfish and autocratic power, and to set up among the really free and self-governed peoples of the world such a concert of purpose and of action as will henceforth ensure the observance of those principles."

With those objects we believe the members of the Society of Friends unqualifiedly agree, and in the war will give this government their hearty unwavering support.

There will be work for Friends and other lovers of peace. We can serve in various capacities without hatred or animus, and we hope that the time is near when all peoples shall be free of autocratic ambitions and militarism, and will co-operate in maintaining peace in the world.

We believe that in the work before us we could follow the words of Lincoln: " With malice toward none, with charity for all, with firmness in the right, as God gives us to see the right, let us strive on to finish the work we are in, to bind up the nation's wounds, to care for him who shall have borne the battle, and for his widow and his orphan, to do all that may achieve and cherish a just and lasting peace among ourselves and with all nations."

WILSON M. POWELL,	WILL WALTER JACKSON,
HENRY M. HAVILAND,	DANIEL T. MERRITT,
THOMAS T. SMITH,	JOHN C. PERCY,
EDWARD CORNELL,	STEPHEN VALENTINE,
CHARLES MC DOWELL,	J. JAY WATSON,
JOHN P. BROOMELL,	WALTER MENDELSON,
JOHN L. CARVER,	CLARENCE A. CLOUGH,
ALBERT R. LAWTON,	CHARLES F. UNDERHILL,
WILLIAM T. SMITH,	BENJAMIN I. CARHART,
WILLIAM P. SMITH,	J. HIBBERD TAYLOR,
HENRY C. TURNER,	ANDREW MAYER, JR.
A. WRIGHT CHAPMAN,	

Dated New York, April 6, 1917.

Document No. 51 The American Peace Society and the War (1917)
Source: *The Advocate of Peace,* LXXIX (May, 1917), p. 137.

ARE WE "A GOOD LOSER"?

" **A** GOOD loser is the old American Peace Society," says an editorial in the old Springfield *Republican;* and yet in one sense the American Peace Society is by this war no loser at all. The plan for international organization and a governed world, outlined first by William Ladd, and maintained these many years by the Society he founded, stands today as intact as ever and more intelligently understood and appreciated withal. Only in so far as the popular mind is for the time diverted from thoughts of the ultimate peace to thoughts of the present war are we in any sense losers; and that that diversion is only temporary and possibly helpful is shown by the increasing diligence with which plans for a lasting peace, based upon our ancient principles, are being formulated by all the nations at war.

If we have not lost, it is, we believe, because our Society has granted unqualified and spontaneous support to our government in this crisis. It might easily become folly for us to oppose with mere tactics of obstruction our fellow-citizens, earnest for peace as we, even though their path toward it be other than that which we would take. Who will not go our way, we shall go his, so long as the goal is the same; and our hope is to convince him of our sincerity and sympathy. We may say, further, that we do not seek merely to follow the government. We aim to go side by side with it in its effort to win peace as best it can.

We believe that our fellow-citizens will neither fail to recognize our purpose nor to continue their support. In any event, it is gratifying to note that the American Peace Society's action has already aroused comment of a most favorable and encouraging sort. Among others, we choose to present the friendly criticism of such a paper of widely recognized sterling qualities as the Springfield *Republican.* This is what this paper says editorially in its issue of March 31:

A Sane Position

The position now taken by the American Peace Society might sanely be taken by every citizen after he has had his say, in the present crisis, on the issue of peace or war. At the recent meeting of the Society's Executive Committee it was voted that the decision as to whether the United States should enter the war should be left entirely to the United States Government. "The American Peace Society cannot decide this question," it was deliberately affirmed.

That was not an easy conclusion to reach, for the American Peace Society is the oldest one in the world, and it has been stoutly fighting war nearly one hundred years.

After leaving the momentous decision to the government, moreover, the Society's Executive Committee concluded that there was still something to think of, and that was "loyalty to the land which makes our work for international justice possible." There is something in loyalty; a peace society need not secede.

A good loser is the old American Peace Society. There is no despair in its attitude. It has seen too many wars come and go. There will be work for it in that future sure to come, when the whole civilized world will spend a generation investigating, analyzing, and judging its own blood-guilt and its own shame.

If there be anything to add to this frank statement, it is that the Society's work does not wait for the future. We have our work now, for "support" such as we pledge means more than getting out of the way merely. In the measure that our members stand by us and lend us the strength of their sympathy and cooperation, we shall render a support that will count and of which none may be ashamed; and this is a matter for each individual member of this Society and for each of our readers to take closely to heart.

Document No. 52   Resolutions of the People's Council (1917)
Source: Pamphlet in the Swarthmore College Peace Collection, Swarthmore, Pa.

RESOLUTIONS

of the

First American Conference for Democracy and Terms of Peace

NEW YORK CITY
May 30 and 31, 1917

Published by
THE ORGANIZING COMMITTEE
People's Council of America
for Democracy and Peace
2 WEST 13th ST.   NEW YORK CITY

INTRODUCTORY.

The First American Conference for Democracy and Terms of Peace was held in New York City, May 30 and 31, 1917. It was called together to consider the urgent and vital questions arising not only from the war, but also from the hopeful manifestations of a desire for a just and enduring peace which now emanate from Europe and which are seen most vividly in the new-born Russian Republic.

The spontaneous and enthusiastic response to the Call for the Conference amply justified the hopes of its sponsors. Six sessions were held covering two days and concluding with one of the largest mass meetings ever held in Madison Square Garden. The meetings were attended by delegates from 43 states of the Union. They comprised earnest men and women of every class, profession and trade—Jewish rabbi and Christian clergy, university professors, suffragists and day laborers, Socialists, Democrats, and Republicans, single taxers and social workers, the extreme individualist representing himself alone and the president of an organization representing 500,000 workers. Over 15,000 took part in the mass meeting. In addition there were letters of encouragement from hosts who were unable to attend in person.

The resolutions adopted by the Conference after careful deliberation follow. They are the guide of the Organizing Committee of the People's Council of America for Democracy and Peace.

PREAMBLE

United in our love for America, we are convinced that we can best serve our country by urging upon our countrymen the adoption of the following policies:

I. PEACE

The Conference favors an early, general and democratic peace, to be secured through negotiation in harmony with the principles outlined by the President of the United State and by revolutionary Russia, and accepted substantially by the progressive and democratic forces of France, England,

Italy, Germany, Austria and other countries, namely:

(a) No forcible annexation of territory.
(b) No punitive indemnities.
(c) Free development of all nationalities.

We favor international reorganization for the maintenance of peace. As steps leading thereto, we suggest: The adjudication of disputes among nations; simultaneous disarmament; freedom of the seas and international waterways; protection of small nations; and other similar measures.

2. STATEMENT OF TERMS

We urge the Government of the United States immediately to anounce its war aims in definite and concrete terms upon the above principles and to make efforts to induce the Allied countries to make similar declarations, thus informing our public for what concrete objects they are called upon to fight, and thereby forcing a definite expression of war aims on the part of the Central Powers.

We demand that this country shall make peace the moment its announced aims shall have been achieved, and that it shall not carry on war for the territorial and imperialistic ambitions of other countries. Further, we demand that it shall make no agreement with other governments limiting its freedom of action nor any agreement or understanding looking toward an economic war after the war.

3. AMERICAN LIBERTIES

The first victims of war are the people's liberties. It was to preserve these liberties that our forefathers framed the first amendment to the constitution, forbidding Congress to abridge "the freedom of speech or of the press, or the right of the people peaceably to assemble and to petition the government for a redress of grievances."

We hereby protest to the President and Congress against the abridgement of these rights, and call upon the American people to defend them. We shall oppose with all legal means at our disposal the censorship of newspapers and of other printed matter or interference with their distribution by the postal department.

We demand that private mail shall not be tampered with. The invasion of homes or offices without search warrant and the seizure of private letters and documents is clearly a violation of the constitution of the United States. We protest against the suppression of any public meetings of American citizens. To imprison citizens without warrant or charge is a practical suspension of the writ of habeas corpus.

We also declare that all Americans are entitled to passports to neutral countries. Legislation now pending in Congress, if passed, will make this country more autocratic than Russia under the rule of the czar.

Secret diplomacy must be abolished. We demand democratic control of our foreign policy. We call for a referendum on questions of war and conscription. We insist on discussion in Congress, in the press and in public meetings of the terms of all alliances, agreements and treaties. It seems to be the intention of the government now to forbid even the discussion of the terms of peace in the press and in public meetings.

4. CONSCRIPTION

We pledge ourselves to work for the repeal of all laws for compulsory military training and compulsory service and to oppose the enactment of all such laws in the future.

Inasmuch as we believe conscription laws to be unconstitutional (violating the Thirteenth Amendment to the Constitution of the United States) we appeal to the Congress of the United States to amend the Conscription Act so as to grant exemption to all conscientious objectors, whether or not they be members of recognized religious organizations.

Inasmuch as young men of conscriptable age are inquiring whether or not military registration on June 5th will subject them immediately to military law and will compel them to work without the protection of labor laws under any conditions which the military executive may force upon them; and inasmuch as the legal branch of the War Department has thus far refused to answer questions concerning the status of these men after registration.

This conference hereby appeals to the Government for a full and unmistakable pronouncement on this point.

5. INDUSTRIAL STANDARDS.

The standard of living of American workers prior to the war was low enough, as revealed by the report of the industrial relations commission and other impartial investigators.

The long struggle that has been waged to reduce hours, to raise wages, to abolish child labor, to protect the life, limbs and health of the wage-earners, has created definite minimum labor standards. A nation-wide assault on these standards is now in progress. Labor laws are being suspended or repealed; cheap alien labor is to be imported; women are replacing the men who leave for the front. We call upon the working people to resist this assault by insisting that the labor laws be preserved and enforced; by maintaining the rights gained through the labor movements; by opposing the importation of cheap alien labor and prisoners of war, and by insisting that where women take the place of men they receive' men's wages.

To furnish the vast profits that American organized business is exacting from the American people, the cost of living has been increased until it is undermining American standards. We, therefore, demand that Congress provide forthwith the machinery for the fixing of maximum prices on the necessities of life and minimum wages which will insure health, efficiency, comfort and education.

Taxation of the necessities of life invariably reduces standards of living. We, therefore, demand that none of the revenue required for the prosecution of the war shall come from the taxation of necessaries.

Industrial plutocracy makes for war—industrial democracy for peace. This brings with it autocratic control of industry in the interest of the ruling classes. The American people, joining hands with the new democracy of Russia, must lay the basis for permanent world peace by establishing industrial democracy.

6. PERMANENT ORGANIZATION.

Resolved, That the Conference elect an organizing committee of eight members, with' power to add to their number, and with the understanding that this organizing committee organize a permanent delegated People's Council from all sympathetic groups, to give immediate and permanent effect to the resolutions of the First American Conference for Democracy and Terms of Peace.

Resolved, that this committee recommend the appointment by the chairman of this conference of a committee which shall go at once to Washington to present the resolutions of the conference and ask the president for the terms on which the administration would be willing to make peace.

Resolved, That the organizing committee arrange for a similar conference on democracy and terms of peace in Illinois immediately, and for a similar conference in California as soon as practicable thereafter, as originally intended in connection with this conference.

Resolved, That the organizing committee be instructed to create at once a committee on international co-operation, representing all the democratic forces in the United States, to work in co-operation with the democratic forces of other countries, both during and after the war.

Resolved, That the organizing committee be instructed to see to it that legal defense of all American liberties in war time is effectively organized throughout the United States.

———

Document No. 53 Jane Addams, "Patriotism and Pacifists in War Time"
Source: *City Club Bulletin*, Chicago, Vol. X, No. 9, June 16, 1917.

"PATRIOTISM AND PACIFISTS IN WAR TIME"
JANE ADDAMS

Miss Jane Addams, on May 15, presented to the City Club her views on the present world situation and the part which "pacifists" should play in it. She said:

"THE position of the pacifist in time of war is most difficult, and necessarily he must abandon the perfectly legitimate propaganda he maintained before war was declared. When he, with his fellow countrymen, is caught up by a wave of tremendous enthusiasm and is carried out into a high sea of patriotic feeling, he realizes that the virtues which he extols are brought into unhappy contrast to those which war, with its keen sense of a separate national existence, places in the foreground.

"Nevertheless, the modern peace movement, since it was inaugurated three hundred years ago, has been kept alive throughout many great wars and during the present war some sort of peace organization has been maintained in all of the belligerent nations. Our Woman's International Committee for Permanent Peace, for instance, of which I have the honor to be chairman, is in constant communication with our branches organized since this war began in such fighting nations and colonies as Australia, Austria, Belgium, Canada, Finland, Germany, Great Britain, Ireland, Hungary, British India, Italy, France, Poland and Russia, in addition to the neutral countries of Europe and one or two of South America.

"Surely the United States will be as tolerant to pacifists in time of war as those countries have been, some of which are fighting for their very existence, and fellow-citizens, however divided in opinion, will be able to discuss those aspects of patriotism which endure through all vicissitudes.

"Before taking up the subject of this paper, it may be well to state that there are many types of pacifists, from the extreme left, composed of non-resistants, through the middle-of-the-road groups, to the extreme right, who can barely be distinguished from mild militarists; and that in our movement, as well as in many others, we must occasionally remind ourselves of Emerson's saying, that the test of a real reformer is his ability to put up with the other reformers.

"In one position, however, we are all agreed, and to this as to an abstract proposition, we must hold at all times, even after war has been declared: that war, although exhibiting some of the noblest qualities of the human spirit, yet affords no solution for vexed international problems; and that moreover after war has been resorted to, its very existence, in spite of its superb heroisms and sacrifices which we also greatly admire, tends to obscure and confuse those faculties which might otherwise find a solution.

"In the stir of the heroic moment when a nation enters war, men's minds are driven back to the earliest obligations of patriotism, and almost without volition the emotions move along the worn grooves of blind admiration for the soldier and of unspeakable contempt for him who, in the hour of danger, declares that fighting is unnecessary. We pacifists are not surprised, therefore, when apparently striking across and reversing this popular conception of patriotism, that we should not only be considered incapable of facing reality, but that we should be called traitors and cowards. It makes it all the more incumbent upon us, however, to demonstrate, if we can, that in our former advocacy we urged a reasonable and vital alternative to war, and that our position now does not necessarily imply lack of patriotism or cowardice.

"To take up the three charges in order:

PACIFISTS AND "PASSIVISM"

"First: The similarity of sound between the words 'passive' and 'pacifism' is often misleading, for most pacifists agree with such statements as that made by Mr. Brailsford in *The New Republic* of March 17th—that wonderful journal, *The New Republic*, from which so many preachers are now taking their texts in preference to the New Testament. Mr. Brailsford, an Englishman, said: 'This war was an act of insurgence against the death in life which acquiesces in hampered conditions and unsolved problems. There was in this concerted rush to ruin and death the force of a rebellious and unconquerable life. It was bent on a change, for it knew that the real denial and surrender of life is not a physical death but the refusal to move and progress.' Agreeing substantially with this analysis of the causes of the present war, we pacifists, so far from passively wishing nothing to be done, contend on the contrary that this world crisis should be utilized for the creation of an international government able to make the necessary political and economic changes when they are due; we feel that it is unspeakably stupid that the nations should have failed to create an international organization through which each one, without danger to itself, might recognize and even encourage the impulse toward growth in other nations.

"Pacifists believe that in the Europe of 1914, certain tendencies were steadily pushing towards large changes which in the end made war, because the system of peace had no way of effecting those changes without war, no adequate international organization which could cope with the situation. The conception of peace founded upon the balance of power or the undisturbed *status quo,* was so negative that frustrated national impulses and suppressed vital forces led to war, because no method of orderly expression had been devised.

"We are not advocating the mid-Victorian idea that good men from every country meet together at The Hague or elsewhere, where they shall pass a resolution, that 'wars hereby cease' and that 'the world hereby be federated.' What we insist upon is that the world can be organized politically by its statesmen as it has been already organized into an international fiscal system by its bankers or into an international scientific association by its scientists. We ask why the problem of building a railroad to Bagdad, of securing corridors to the sea for a land-locked nation, or warm water harbors for Russia, should result in war. Surely the minds of this generation are capable of solving such problems as the minds of other generations have solved their difficult problems. Is it not obviously because such situations transcend national boundaries and must be approached in a spirit of world adjustment, while men's minds, still held apart by national suspicions and rivalries, are unable to approach them in a spirit of peaceful adjustment?

"The very breakdown exhibited by the present war reinforces the pacifists' contention that there is need of an international charter—a Magna Charta indeed —of international rights, to be issued by the nations great and small, with large provisions for economic freedom.

THE PATRIOTISM OF PACIFISTS

"In reply to the old charge of lack of patriotism, we claim that we are patriotic from the historic viewpoint as well as by other standards. American pacifists believe—if I may go back to those days before the war, which already seem so far away—that the United States was especially qualified by her own particular experience to take the leadership in a peaceful organization of the world. We then ventured to remind our fellow citizens that when the founders of this republic adopted the federal constitution and established the Supreme Court, they were entering upon a great political experiment of whose outcome they were by no means certain. The thirteen colonies somewhat slowly came into the federation, and some of them consented very reluctantly to the use of the supreme court. Nevertheless, the great political experiment of the United States was so well established by the middle of the 19th century, that America had come to stand to the world for the principle of federal government and for a supreme tribunal whose decisions were binding upon sovereign states.

"We pacifists hoped that the United States might perform a similar service in the international field, by demonstrating that the same principles of federation and of an interstate tribunal might be extended among widely separated nations as they had already been established between contiguous states. Stirred by enthusiasm over the great historical experiment of the United States, it seemed to us that American patriotism might rise to a supreme effort. We hoped that the United States might refuse to follow the beaten paths of upholding the rights of a separate nationalism by war, because her own experience for more than a century had so thoroughly committed her to federation and to peaceful adjudication as to every-day methods of government. The President's speech before the Senate embodied such a masterly restatement of these early American principles that thousands of his fellow citizens dedicated themselves anew to finding a method for applying them in the wider and more difficult field of international relationships.

THE TASK OF ORGANIZATION

"We also counted upon the fact that this great war had challenged the validity of the existing status between nations as it had never been questioned before, and that radical changes were being proposed by the most conservative of men and of nations. As conceived by the pacifist, the constructive task laid upon the United States in the recent crisis called for something more than diplomacy and the old type of statesmanship.

"It demanded a penetration which might discover a more adequate moral basis for the relationship between nations and the sustained energy to translate the discovery into political action. The exercise of the highest political intelligence, we hoped, might not only establish a new scale of moral values, but might hasten to a speedy completion for immediate use, that international organization which has been so long discussed and so ardently anticipated. For there is another similarity between

the end of the 18th century and the present time; quite as the Declaration of Independence and the adoption of the Constitution had been preceded by much philosophic writing on the essential equality of all men and on the possibility of establishing self government among them, so the new internationalism has long had its thinkers who have laid a foundation of abstract principle. Then, as now, however, the great need was not for more writing, nor even for able propaganda, but for a sober attempt to put them into practice, to translate them into concrete acts.

AMERICAN PRECEDENTS

"We were more hopeful of this from the fact that the test of experience had already been applied by the United States to such a course of action, at least so far as to substitute adjudication for war. Four times before now has our country become involved in the fringe of European wars, and in three instances the difficulties were peacefully adjudicated.

"In 1798, when the French Revolution had pulled most of Europe into war, George Washington, who was then President—perhaps because he was so enthusiastic over our Supreme Court—refused to yield to the clamor of his countrymen to go to war on the side of France, our recent friend, against Great Britain, our recent enemy, and sent Chief Justice John Jay over to London to adjust the difficulties which had arisen in connection with our shipping. Because John Jay was successful in his mission, George Washington became for the time so unpopular that he publicly expressed the wish that he had never been born—although he does not seem to have permanently lost his place in the hearts of his countrymen.

"Four years later, when France violated our neutral rights on the seas, John Adams, as President, sent commissioners to Paris who adjudicated the matter. Although keeping the peace made Adams so unpopular that he failed of his second term, many years later, as an old man, he said that his tombstone might well be inscribed with the words: 'He kept the peace with France.'

"Adams' successor, Thomas Jefferson, encountered the same difficulty, and in spite of grave mistakes, succeeded in keeping the country out of war. He was finally rewarded by the peaceful acquisition of the vast Louisiana territory.

"The War of 1812 was the result of a disregard of neutral rights incident to the Napoleonic upheaval, and made the first break in the chain of international adjudications instituted by Chief Justice Jay, which had become known as the American plan.

"Although both England and France had violated our rights at sea, the United States was drawn into war with England at the moment when she was in a death grapple with Napoleon, and so irrational is war, that in the final terms of peace, the treaty did not mention the very matter upon which war had been declared. Perhaps, however, three adjudications out of five instances in which the shipping of the United States has become involved in European war, is as much as can be hoped for.

PACIFISTS AGAINST ISOLATION

"With such a national history back of us, as pacifists we are thrown into despair over our inability to make our position clear when we are accused of wishing to isolate the United States and to keep our country out of world politics. We are, of course, urging a policy exactly the reverse, that this country should lead the nations of the world into a wider life of co-ordinated political activity; that the United States should boldly recognize the fact that the vital political problems of our time have become as intrinsically international in character as have the commercial and social problems so closely connected with them; that modern wars are not so much the result of quarrels between nations as of the rebellion against international situations inevitably developed through the changing years, which admit of adequate treatment only through an international agency not yet created. The fact that such an agency has been long desired, the necessity for it clearly set forth by statesmen in all the civilized nations, and that a splendid beginning had already been made at The Hague, makes the situation only more acute.

AMERICA'S RESOURCES FOR LEADERSHIP

"We had also hoped much from the varied population of the United States, for whether we will or not, our very composition would make it easier for us than for any other nation to establish an international organization founded upon understanding and good will, did we but possess the requisite courage and intelligence to utilize it.

"There are in this country thousands of emigrants from the Central Powers, to whom a war between the United States and the fatherland means exquisite torture. They and their inheritances are a part of the situation which faces us. They are a source of great strength in an international venture, as they are undoubtedly a source of weakness in a purely nationalistic position of the old-fashioned sort. These ties of blood, binding us to all the nations of the earth, afford a unique equipment for a great international task if the United States could but push forward into the shifting area of internationalism.

"Modern warfare is an intimately social and domestic affair. The civilian suffering and, in certain regions, the civilian mortality, is as great as that endured by the soldiers. There are thousands of our fellow citizens who cannot tear their minds away from Poland, Galicia, Syria, Armenia, Serbia, Roumania, Greece, where their own relatives are dying from diseases superinduced by hardship and hunger. To such sore and troubled minds war had come to be a hideousness which belongs to Europe alone and was part of that privation and depression which they had left behind them when they came to America. Newly immigrated Austrian subjects of a dozen nationalities came to their American friends during the weeks of suspense, utterly bewildered by the prospect of war. They had heard not three months before that the President of the United States did not believe in war—for so the Senate speech has been interpreted by many simple minds —and they had concluded that whatever happened, some more American way would be found.

"The multitude of German subjects who have settled and developed certain parts of the United States had, it seems to me, every right to be considered as an important factor in the situation, before war was declared. President Wilson himself said, in February, after the U-boat campaign had been announced, that he was giving due weight to the legitimate rights of the American citizens of German descent. The men of '48 are as truly responsible for our national ideals as the Puritans of New England, the Quakers of Pennsylvania, or the Russian revolutionists of the '90s. How valuable that gallant spirit of '48, spreading as it did from one European country to another, could be made in an international venture it is difficult to estimate.

"It has been said that this great war 'will prove the bloody angle at which mankind turns from centuries of warfare to the age of peace.' But certainly this will not happen automatically nor without leadership founded upon clear thinking and international sympathies.

"It is very easy to go to war for a well defined aim which changes imperceptibly as the war progresses, and to continue the war or even end it on quite other grounds. Shifting aims is one of the inherent characteristics of war as an institution.

"Pacifists hoped that this 'revolution in international relationships, which has been steadily approaching for three hundred years and is long over-due might have been obtained without our participation in the war; but we also believe that it may be obtained after the war, if the United States succeeds in protecting and preserving the higher standards of internationalism.

NATIONAL UNSELFISHNESS

"Pacifists recognize and rejoice in the large element of national unselfishness and in the recognition of international obligation set forth by President Wilson as reasons for our participation in the great war. We feel that the exalted sense of patriotism in which each loses himself in the consciousnes of a national existence, has been enlarged by an alliance with nations across the Atlantic and across the Pacific with whom we are united in a common purpose. Let the United States, by all means, send a governmental commission to Russia; plans for a better fiscal system to bewildered China; food to all nations wherever little children are starving; but let us never forget that the inspiring and overwhelming sense of a common purpose, which an alliance with fifteen or sixteen nations gives us, is but a forecast of what might be experienced if the genuine international alliance were achieved, including all the nations of the earth.

"In so far as we and our allies are held together by the consciousness of a common enemy and the fear of a common danger, there is a chance for the growth of the animosity and hatred which may yet overwhelm the attempt at international organization to be undertaken after the war, as it has defeated so many high-hearted attempts in the past.

"May we not say in all sincerity that for thirty-three months Europe has been earnestly striving to obtain through patriotic wars, that which can finally be secured only through international organization? Millions of men, loyal to one international alliance, are gallantly fighting millions of men loyal to another international alliance, because of Europe's inability to make an alliance including them all. Can the United States discharge her duty in this situation save as she finally makes possible the establishment of a genuine international government?

AMERICA'S SENSE OF FAILURE

"Ever since the European war began the United States has been conscious of a failure to respond to a moral demand she has vaguely felt that she was shirking her share in a world effort toward the higher good; she has had black moments of compunction and shame for her own immunity and safety. Can she hope through war to assuage the feverish thirst for action she has felt during all those three years? There is no doubt that she has made the correct diagnosis of her case, of her weariness with a selfish, materialistic life, and of her need for concerted, self-forgetting action. But is blood-letting a sufficiently modern remedy in such a diagnosis? Will she lose her sense of futility and her consciousness of moral failure, when thousands of her young men are facing the dangers of war? Will she not at the end of this war still feel her inadequacy and sense of failure unless she is able to embody in a permanent organization the cosmopolitanism which is the essence of her spirit? Will she be content, even in war time, to organize food supplies of one group of nations and to leave the women and children of any nation still starving?

"Is not the government of the United States somewhat in the position of those of us who have lived for many years among immigrants? It is quite impossible for us to ask just now whether the parents of a child who needs food are Italians, and therefore now our allies, or Dalmatians, and therefore now our 'alien enemies.' Such a question is as remote as if during the Balkan war we had anxiously inquired whether the parents were Macedonians or Montenegrins, although that was then a distinction of paramount importance to thousands of our neighbors.

"It has been officially declared that we are entering this war 'to make the world safe for democracy.' While we are still free to make terms with our allies, are we not under obligation to assert that the United States owes too much to all the nations of the earth whose sons have developed our raw prairies into fertile fields, to allow the women and children of any of them to starve?

"It is told of the recent Irish uprising that after Sheehy Skeffington had been arrested, an English soldier was placed on guard in the house lest Mrs. Skeffington and her little boy might destroy possibly incriminating papers; that the soldier, after standing for a long time in the presence of the woman and child, finally shifted his position and, looking uneasily at Mrs. Skeffington, said; 'You see, I didn't enlist exactly for this.'

"Would it not be possible for the United States to tell her allies that she had not enlisted in this great war for the purpose of starving women and children? When the United States entered the war the final outcome was apparently to be decided by food supply rather than by force of arms. Could Germany hold out during the spring and early summer until the new crop was garnered? Could England feed herself were the U-boat campaign in any degree successful, were the terrible questions in men's minds.

"For decades civilized nations had confidently depended upon other nations for their supply of cattle and of grain until long continued war brought the primitive fear of starvation back into the world with so many other obsolete terrors.

NATIONAL BOUNDARIES AND FOOD SUPPLY

"Such an international organization as the United States is now creating in connection with her allies for the control of their common food supply, is clearly transcending old national bounds. It may be a new phase of political unification in advance of all former achievements, or it may be one of those shifting alliances for war purposes, of which European history affords so many examples. Simply because food is so strategic, as it were, we lay ourselves open to the latter temptations. Could we not free ourselves from this and at the same time perform a great service if we urge that an international commission sit at Athens during the rest of this war, as an international commission sat in London during the Balkan wars? Such a commission might at once insist upon a more humane prosecution of the war, at least so far as civilian populations are concerned, a more merciful administration of the lands occupied, and distribution of foodstuffs to all conquered peoples.

MILITARY COERCION OR SOCIAL CONTROL?

"The United States has to her credit a long account of the spread of democratic institutions during the years when she was at peace with the rest of the world. Her own experiment as a republic was quickly followed by France, and later by Switzerland, and to the south of her a vast continent contains no nation which fails—through many vicissitudes though it be—to maintain a republican form of government.

"It has long been the aim of this government of ours and of similar types of government the world over to replace coercion by the full consent of the governed, to educate and strengthen the free will of the people through the use of democratic institutions, and to safeguard even the rights of minorities. This age-long process of obtaining the inner consent of the citizen to the outward acts of his government is of necessity violently interrupted and thrown back in war time; but we all realize that some day it must be resumed and carried forward again, perhaps on an international basis. Let us strive to keep our minds clear regarding it.

"Some of us once dreamed that the cosmopolitan inhabitants of this great nation might at last become united in a vast common endeavor for social ends. We hoped that this fusing might be accomplished without the sense of opposition to a common enemy which is an old method of welding people together, better fitted for military than for social use. If this for the moment is impossible, let us at least place the spirit of cooperation above that of bitterness and remember the wide distinction between social control and military coercion.

"It is easy for all of us to grow confused in a moment like this for the pacifist, like the rest of the world, has developed a high degree of suggestibility; we too share that sensitiveness to the feelings, the opinion, and the customs of our own social group which is said to be an inheritance from an almost prehuman past. An instinct which once enabled the man-pack to survive when it was a question of keeping a herd together, or of perishing off the face of the earth is perhaps not under-developed in any of us.

ARE PACIFISTS COWARDS?

"When as pacifists we urge a courageous venture into international ethics, which will require a fine valor as well as a high intelligence, we experience a sense of anti-climax when we are told that because we do not want war, we are so cowardly as to care for 'safety first,' that we place human life, physical life, above the great ideals of national righteousness.

"But surely that man is not without courage who, seeing that which is invisible to the majority of his fellow countrymen, still asserts his conviction and is ready to vindicate its spiritual value over against the world. Each advance in the zigzag line of human progress has traditionally been embodied in small groups of individuals, who have ceased to be in harmony with the *status quo* and have demanded modifications. Such modifications did not always prove to be in the line of progress, but whether they were or not, they always excited opposition, which from the nature of the case was never so determined as when the proposed changes touched moral achievements which were greatly prized and had been secured with much difficulty.

"Bearing in mind the long struggle to secure and maintain national unity, the pacifist easily understands why his theories seem particularly obnoxious just now, although in point of fact our national unity is not threatened, and would be finely consummated in an international organization.

PEACE AND JUSTICE

"With visions of international justice filling our minds, pacifists are always a little startled when those who insist that justice can only be established by war, accuse us of caring for peace irrespective of justice. Many of the pacifists in their individual and corporate capacity have long striven for social and political justice with a fervor perhaps equal to that employed by the advocates of force, and we realize that a sense of justice has become the keynote to the best political and social activity in this generation. Although this ruling passion for juster relations between man and man, group and group, or between nation and nation, is not without its sterner aspects, among those who dream of a wider social justice throughout the world there has developed a conviction that justice between men or between nations can be achieved only through understanding and fellowship, and that a finely tempered sense of justice, which alone is of any service in modern civilization, cannot be secured in the storm and stress of war. This is not only because war inevitably arouses the more primitive antagonisms, but because the spirit of fighting burns away all of those impulses, certainly towards the enemy, which foster the will to justice.

"We believe that the ardor and self sacrifice so characteristic of youth could be enlisted for the vitally energetic role which we hope our beloved country will inaugurate in the international life of the world. We realize that it is only the ardent spirits, the lovers of mankind, who will be able to break down the suspicion and lack of understanding which has so long stood in the way of the necessary changes upon which international good order depends; who will at last create a political organization enabling nations to secure without war, those high ends which they now gallantly seek to obtain upon the battlefield.

"With such a creed, can the pacifists of today be accused of selfishness when they urge upon the United States not isolation, not indifference to moral issues and to the fate of liberty and democracy, but a strenuous endeavor to lead all nations of the earth into an organized international life worthy of civilized men?"

Document No. 54   Government Censorship and *The Masses* magazine (1917)
Source: *The Masses* (September, 1917).

What Happened to the August Masses

1. August issue presented for mailing at New York post office, July 3d.

2. Copies of August issue forwarded to Washington for "examination." The Solicitor of the Post Office Department, the Attorney General, and Judge Advocate General Crowder, of the United States Army, conferred about excluding it from the mails and decided that this should be done.*

3. Letter received July 5th from T. G. Patten, postmaster of New York City, informing us that:

   "according to advices received from the Solicitor of the Postoffice Department, the August issue of The Masses is unmailable under the Act of June 15th, 1917."

4. The business manager of THE MASSES interviewed in Washington Solicitor Lamar, who refused to state what provisions of the Espionage Act the August MASSES violated, or what particular parts 'of the magazine violated the law. (July 6th.)

5. THE MASSES retained as counsel Gilbert E. Roe.' Bill in equity to federal court, to enjoin postmaster from excluding the magazine from the mails, filed July 12th. Motion made returnable before Judge Learned Hand on July 16.

6. Hearing postponed till July 21st, the Post Office Department being unprepared.

---

* Date of conference unknown; rumor that the Generals, in spite of pressure of war-business, celebrated Independence Day by deciding to suppress THE MASSES, cannot be verified.

7. Argument lasting all day, July 21st, on motion for injunction.

The Postoffice Department was represented by Asst. U. S.
District Attorney Barnes. He explained that the Department
construed the Espionage Act as giving it power to exclude
from the mails anything which might interfere with the successful conduct of the war.

Four cartoons and four pieces of text in the August issue
were specified as violations of the law. The cartoons were
Boardman Robinson's "Making the World Safe for Democracy,"
H. J. Glintenkamp's Liberty Bell and Conscription cartoons,
and one by Art Young on Congress and Big Business. The
Conscription cartoon was considered by the Department "the
worst thing in the magazine." The text objected to was: "A
Question," an editorial by Max Eastman; "A Tribute," a poem
by Josephine Bell; a paragraph in an article on "Conscientious
Objectors"; and an editorial, "Friends of American Freedom."

Gilbert E. Roe, on behalf of THE MASSES, urged that the
Espionage Act was not intended to prohibit political criticism or discussion, and that to permit the Postoffice Department to use it as cover for arbitrary acts of suppression, would
be to recognize a censorship set up without warrant of law.

8. Preliminary injunction against postmaster granted by Judge
Hand.

Judge Hand, in an extended decision, sustained THE MASSES'
contention at all points. The construction placed by the postal
authorities on the Espionage Act was shown to be invalid.
The specific provisions of the law, he points out, are not violated by the magazine. Its cartoons and editorials "fall within
the scope of that right to criticise, either by temperate reasoning or by immoderate and indecent invective, which is normally
the privilege of the individual in countries dependent upon the
free expression of opinion as the ultimate source of authority."
The expression of such opinion may militate against the success of the war, but Congress has not seen fit to exclude it
from the mails, and only Congress has the power to do so.
The pictures and text may tend to prompte disaffection with
the war, but they cannot be thought to counsel insubordination in the military or naval forces "without a violation of
their meaning quite beyond any tolerance of understanding."
The Conscription cartoon may "breed such animosity toward
the Draft as will promote resistance and strengthen the determination of those disposed to be recalcitrant," but it does not
tell people that it is their duty or to their interest to resist
the law. The text expresses "high admiration for those who
have held and are holding out for their convictions even to
the extent of resisting the law." But the expression of such
admiration is not a violation of the Espionage Act.

9. Formal order, requiring postmaster to transmit the Aug-
ust MASSES through the mails; served on District
Attorney, July 25th, with notice that it would be presented to
Judge Hand for signature, under the rule, the following day.

10 *United States Circuit Judge C. M. Hough signed at Windsor, Vt., an order staying execution of Judge Hand's order, and requiring parties to appear before him at Windsor, Vt., Aug. 2, to show cause why stay should not be made permanent pending an appeal which had been taken the same day by Postmaster Patten and which cannot be heard for several months.* Some one must have been waiting before Judge Hough to get his order for a stay at the very time Judge Hand had his order before him for signature. For the orders were signed the same day, and the judges were hundreds of miles apart.

* * * *

That is the history of the case—so far. Our attorney will oppose the staying of Judge Hand's order. If he succeeds, you will get your August issue through the mails—unless the Department thinks of some other way to stop it. If our attorney doesn't succeed, we will have to adopt other ways and means.

We will do our best to reach you. We publish THE MASSES because you want it. THE MASSES is your property. This is your fight as much as it is ours. We are not going to quit. We do not believe you are, either. We need money to help pay expenses. We need subscriptions. We need bundle orders for the magazine for sale or distribution. You know the facts. The way in which you will help us is up to you, .

Conscription

H. J. Glintenkamp.

Document No. 55   Max Eastman, Criticism of Wilson's War Policy (1917)
Source: Pamphlet in the Haverford College Library, Haverford, Pa.

Washington to Petrograd —via Rome

Some observations on President Wilson's reply to Pope Benedict XV by Max Eastman, Editor of "The Masses"

Reprinted from "The Masses" (October, 1917) by

The People's Council of America

2 West 13th Street, New York City

W HEN war was declared we called for some proof that it was a war for democracy. "Will you state your terms of peace with Germany," we said to the President, "making a settlement with the Reichstag, and not with the Imperial Government, the essential and only indispensable item in those terms? If it is a war for democracy, you will."

When Russia appealed to the Allies to declare for a peace upon the vise and democratic basis of "no punitive indemnities, no forcible annexaions, free development for all nationalities," and the President echoed the British government in a flat refusal to consider these terms, declaring that 'past wrongs must be righted," and otherwise vaguely intimating that he vas adopting the whole animus of he British war on Germany, we assumed that our question was answered in the negative. We gave our whole energy to denouncing a var with such an animus. We upported the People's Council, vhich was organized in response o the Russian Council's appeal to .ccede to those terms of peace. And we denounced, as adding insult to injury, the conscription of American citizens to such a war, r to any war whose purposes were ot concretely specified.

When the President made his 'lag Day address, emphasizing the ecessity of breaking up Germany's sphere of influence in the ast—which is simply the necesity of defending England's ex-usive empiry in the world—when he emphasized that and that only, we ere reinforced in our belief that in accepting the war animus, he had oandoned every elevated and just ideal and purpose that had been ex-ressed by him in his Peace without Victory message. We know the nister egotism of the imperial classes in Great Britain, and we fear them hen we contemplate the future of the world, only a little less than we fear erman autocracy. We were amazed at the foolhardy support that our iends were giving to a government apparently unconscious of this danger -unconscious, too, of the rights of its citizens to know what they were ghting for, willing to blindfold its eyes and swallow all the partisan sen-

Russia's Peace Terms:

From the Russian Government's manifesto, March 15, 1917.

"A peace without forcible annexations or punitive indemnities and based on the right of nations to decide their own affairs."

[Since May 30th, Russia's peace terms have been endorsed by the People's Council of America at conferences and mass meetings throughout America.]

timental blather of wartime patriotism. We were amazed and we were
outraged that this thing could be done in the name of democracy.

These things are considerably altered by the President's letter to the
Pope. In that letter he does declare, as we demanded, that he will enter
into peace negotiations as soon as he can treat with a government responsible to the people. And he makes this plainer in a supplementary statement (through Lansing) that he means what is commonly meant by a
"responsible ministry."

He does accede to the Russian peace terms in almost their own
language: "No punitive damages," "no dismemberment of empires," "vindication of the sovereignty both of
those that are weak and those that
are strong."

He does separate our purpose
absolutely from the imperialisti
ambitions of the ruling classes i
the Allied countries, both by th
manifest implications of thes
peace terms, and by dissentin
from the "economic war" again
Germany agreed upon by them i
their Paris conference.

He does state in concrete lan-
uage what it is our citizens a
being drafted for, and this r
moves a little of the insult, at leas
from the injury of conscription.

He still fulminates in a way th
seems a little forgetful of our ov
failings against lies and crim
committed by the enemy, but
good deal of that may be discounted as the necessary self-righteousness
the mood of combat. For he renounces vindictive intentions so complete
as to make us feel that he has recovered, or will recover, at least, when t
day of action comes, the justice and elvation of the Peace without Victo
address. There is high hope, in this letter to the Pope, of permanent ju
peace and international federation for the world.

It is interesting to speculate as to the reasons why President Wils
should ignore the appeal of his ally, the Russian republic, to declare pea
terms for which her free citizens could be persuaded to fight, should ignc
the indignant demand to the same effect of some three millions of his ov

President Wilson's Peace Terms:

From the President's reply to the Pope August 28, 1917.

"*Punitive damages, the dismemberment of empires, the
establishment of selfish and
exclusive economic leagues,
we deem inexpedient, and in
the end worse than futile, no
proper basis for a peace of any
kind, least of all for an enduring peace. That must be based
upon justice and fairness,
and the common rights of
mankind.*"

citizens who elected him, should ignore them placidly for five months, and then grant all that they have been asking, not to them, but to the Pope at Rome. It may be that he has done this inadvertently, as he rather pretends in accusing us of being "deaf" to the repeated statements of his war purposes. But we doubt it. We credit Woodrow Wilson with knowing what is going on. We believe that he understood perfectly well the motive of the People's Council, and that he was not in any wise misled by the criminal and ignorant slanders launched against that movement by the uneducated American press. He knows that he did not state his war purposes until he wrote to the Pope, and he knows that he did state them then, and he knows why.

Perhaps the President's reason for waiting was that he wanted to lend enough money and guarantee enough support to the Allies, so that he would be in a position to tell them what their peace terms were to be. If that was the reason, we make our bow to him as the most astute and really powerful statesman of the world, and we give thanks that he really likes peace better than war.

But perhaps the reason that he finally made this declaration, was that we "pro-Germans" and "traitors" (names which now merely signify people who insist upon using their brains) compelled him to. The agitation conducted by the People's Council was more widespread, more rapid-moving, and more determined, than anything of its kind we have ever seen. It was a startling notice to the Government that the American people could not be led to this war without a plain-spoken guarantee of the purposes for which the war was being fought. The President's letter to the Pope was published two days before the People's Council was to convene. In that letter he yielded the Council's original and chief demand. It may be that the People's Council was in large measure the cause of the wording of his letter—in which case we make our bow to the People's Council.

But these things are only to be guessed at. Woodrow Wilson has established himself in a position of power which enables him to keep his own counsel. He is in very truth—albeit we hope temporarily and only through personal force—the strongest autocrat in the world. And while denouncing his autocracy, and its employment to silence criticism and quell the struggle for liberty within our borders, we are thankful for this evidence that he still intends to use it beyond our borders, if he can, to the great end of eliminating international war from the world.

MAX EASTMAN.

Document No. 56   President Wilson's Fourteen Points Speech (January 8, 1918)
Source: U.S. Department of State, *Foreign Relations of the United States, 1918, Supplement I* (Washington, D.C.: Government Printing Office, 1933), pp. 12-17.

Address of the President of the United States Delivered at a Joint Session of the Two Houses of Congress, January 8, 1918

GENTLEMEN OF THE CONGRESS: Once more, as repeatedly before, the spokesmen of the Central Empires have indicated their desire to discuss the objects of the war and the possible bases of a general peace. Parleys have been in progress at Brest-Litovsk between Russian representatives and representatives of the Central Powers to which the attention of all the belligerents has been invited for the purpose of ascertaining whether it may be possible to extend these parleys into a general conference with regard to terms of peace and settlement.[1] The Russian representatives presented not only a perfectly definite statement of the principles upon which they would be willing to conclude peace but also an equally definite programme of the concrete application of those principles. The representatives of the Central Powers, on their part, presented an outline of settlement which, if much less definite, seemed susceptible of liberal interpretation until their specific programme of practical terms was added. That programme proposed no concessions at all either to the sovereignty of Russia or to the preferences of the populations with whose fortunes it dealt, but meant, in a word, that the Central Empires were to keep every foot of territory their armed forces had occupied,—every province, every city, every point of vantage,—as a permanent addition to their territories and their power. It is a reasonable conjecture that the general principles of settlement which they at first suggested originated with the more liberal statesmen of Germany and Austria, the men who have begun to feel the force of their own peoples' thought and purpose, while the concrete terms of actual settlement came from the military leaders who have no thought but to keep what they have got. The negotiations have been broken off. The Russian representatives were sincere and in earnest. They can not entertain such proposals of conquest and domination.

The whole incident is full of significance. It is also full of perplexity. With whom are the Russian representatives dealing? For whom are the representatives of the Central Empires speaking? Are they speaking for the majorities of their respective

---

[1] See *Foreign Relations*, 1918, Russia, vol. I, pp. 244, 253, 258, 405-408.

parliaments or for the minority parties, that military and imperialistic minority which has so far dominated their whole policy and controlled the affairs of Turkey and of the Balkan states which have felt obliged to become their associates in this war? The Russian representatives have insisted, very justly, very wisely, and in the true spirit of modern democracy, that the conferences they have been holding with the Teutonic and Turkish statesmen should be held within open, not closed, doors, and all the world has been audience, as was desired. To whom have we been listening, then? To those who speak the spirit and intention of the resolutions of the German Reichstag of the 9th [*19th*] of July last,[1] the spirit and intention of the liberal leaders and parties of Germany, or to those who resist and defy that spirit and intention and insist upon conquest and subjugation? Or are we listening, in fact, to both, unreconciled and in open and hopeless contradiction? These are very serious and pregnant questions. Upon the answer to them depends the peace of the world.

But, whatever the results of the parleys at Brest-Litovsk, whatever the confusions of counsel and of purpose in the utterances of the spokesmen of the Central Empires, they have again attempted to acquaint the world with their objects in the war and have again challenged their adversaries to say what their objects are and what sort of settlement they would deem just and satisfactory. There is no good reason why that challenge should not be responded to, and responded to with the utmost candor. We did not wait for it. Not once, but again and again, we have laid our whole thought and purpose before the world, not in general terms only, but each time with sufficient definition to make it clear what sort of definitive terms of settlement must necessarily spring out of them. Within the last week Mr. Lloyd George has spoken with admirable candor and in admirable spirit for the people and Government of Great Britain. There is no confusion of counsel among the adversaries of the Central Powers, no uncertainty of principle, no vagueness of detail. The only secrecy of counsel, the only lack of fearless frankness, the only failure to make definite statement of the objects of the war, lies with Germany and her allies. The issues of life and death hang upon these definitions. No statesman who has the least conception of his responsibility ought for a moment to permit himself to continue this tragical and appalling outpouring of blood and treasure unless he is sure beyond a peradventure that the objects of the vital sacrifice

---

[1] See *ibid.*, 1917, Supplement 2, vol. I, pp. 139–140.

are part and parcel of the very life of society and that the people for whom he speaks think them right and imperative as he does.

There is, moreover, a voice calling for these definitions of principle and of purpose which is, it seems to me, more thrilling and more compelling than any of the many moving voices with which the troubled air of the world is filled. It is the voice of the Russian people. They are prostrate and all but helpless, it would seem, before the grim power of Germany, which has hitherto known no relenting and no pity. Their power, apparently, is shattered. And yet their soul is not subservient. They will not yield either in principle or in action. Their conception of what is right, of what it is humane and honorable for them to accept, has been stated with a frankness, a largeness of view, a generosity of spirit, and a universal human sympathy which must challenge the admiration of every friend of mankind; and they have refused to compound their ideals or desert others that they themselves may be safe. They call to us to say what it is that we desire, in what, if in anything, our purpose and our spirit differ from theirs; and I believe that the people of the United States would wish me to respond, with utter simplicity and frankness. Whether their present leaders believe it or not, it is our heartfelt desire and hope that some way may be opened whereby we may be privileged to assist the people of Russia to attain their utmost hope of liberty and ordered peace.

It will be our wish and purpose that the processes of peace, when they are begun, shall be absolutely open and that they shall involve and permit henceforth no secret understandings of any kind. The day of conquest and aggrandizement is gone by; so is also the day of secret covenants entered into in the interest of particular governments and likely at some unlooked-for moment to upset the peace of the world. It is this happy fact, now clear to the view of every public man whose thoughts do not still linger in an age that is dead and gone, which makes it possible for every nation whose purposes are consistent with justice and the peace of the world to avow now or at any other time the objects it has in view.

We entered this war because violations of right had occurred which touched us to the quick and made the life of our own people impossible unless they were corrected and the world secured once for all against their recurrence. What we demand in this war, therefore, is nothing peculiar to ourselves. It is that the world be made fit and safe to live in; and particularly that it be made safe for every peace-loving nation which, like our own, wishes to live its own life, determine its own institutions, be assured of justice and fair dealing by the other peoples of the world as against force and selfish aggression. All the peoples of the world are in effect partners in this interest, and for our own part we see very clearly that unless justice be done to others it will not be done to us. The programme of the world's peace, therefore, is our programme; and that programme, the only possible programme, as we see it, is this:

I. Open covenants of peace, openly arrived at, after which there shall be no private international understandings of any kind but diplomacy shall proceed always frankly and in the public view.

II. Absolute freedom of navigation upon the seas, outside territorial waters, alike in peace and in war, except as the seas may be closed in whole or in part by international action for the enforcement of international covenants.

III. The removal, so far as possible, of all economic barriers and the establishment of an equality of trade conditions among all the nations consenting to the peace and associating themselves for its maintenance.

IV. Adequate guarantees given and taken that national armaments will be reduced to the lowest point consistent with domestic safety.

V. A free, open-minded, and absolutely impartial adjustment of all colonial claims, based upon a strict observance of the principle that in determining all such questions of sovereignty the interests of the populations concerned must have equal weight with the equitable claims of the government whose title is to be determined.

VI. The evacuation of all Russian territory and such a settlement of all questions affecting Russia as will secure the best and freest cooperation of the other nations of the world in obtaining for her an unhampered and unembarrassed opportunity for the independent determination of her own political development and national policy and assure her of a sincere welcome into the society of free nations under institutions of her own choosing; and, more than a welcome, assistance also of every kind that she may need and may herself desire. The treatment accorded Russia by her sister nations in the months to come will be the acid test of their good will, of their comprehension of her needs as distinguished from their own interests, and of their intelligent and unselfish sympathy.

VII. Belgium, the whole world will agree, must be evacuated and restored, without any attempt to limit the sovereignty which she enjoys in common with all other free nations. No other single act will serve as this will serve to restore confidence among the nations in the laws which they have themselves set and determined for the government of their relations with one another. Without this healing act the whole structure and validity of international law is forever impaired.

VIII. All French territory should be freed and the invaded portions restored, and the wrong done to France by Prussia in 1871 in the matter of Alsace-Lorraine, which has unsettled the peace of the world for nearly fifty years, should be righted, in order that peace may once more be made secure in the interest of all.

IX. A readjustment of the frontiers of Italy should be effected along clearly recognizable lines of nationality.

X. The peoples of Austria-Hungary, whose place among the nations we wish to see safeguarded and assured, should be accorded the freest opportunity of autonomous development.

XI. Rumania, Serbia, and Montenegro should be evacuated; occupied territories restored; Serbia accorded free and secure access to the sea; and the relations of the several Balkan states to one another determined by friendly counsel along historically established lines of allegiance and nationality; and international guarantees of the political and economic independence and territorial integrity of the several Balkan states should be entered into.

XII. The Turkish portions of the present Ottoman Empire should be assured a secure sovereignty, but the other nationalities which are now under Turkish rule should be assured an undoubted security of life and an absolutely unmolested opportunity of autonomous development, and the Dardanelles should be permanently opened as a free passage to the ships and commerce of all nations under international guarantees.

XIII. An independent Polish state should be erected which should include the territories inhabited by indisputably Polish populations, which should be assured a free and secure access to the sea, and whose political and economic independence and territorial integrity should be guaranteed by international covenant.

XIV. A general association of nations must be formed under specific covenants for the purpose of affording mutual guarantees of political independence and territorial integrity to great and small states alike.

In regard to these essential rectifications of wrong and assertions of right we feel ourselves to be intimate partners of all the governments and peoples associated together against the Imperialists. We cannot be separated in interest or divided in purpose. We stand together until the end.

For such arrangements and covenants we are willing to fight and to continue to fight until they are achieved; but only because we wish the right to prevail and desire a just and stable peace such as can be secured only by removing the chief provocations to war, which this programme does remove. We have no jealousy of German greatness, and there is nothing in this programme that impairs it. We grudge her no achievement or distinction of learning or of pacific enterprise such as have made her record very bright and very enviable. We do not wish to injure her or to block in any way her legitimate influence or power. We do not wish to fight her either with arms or with hostile arrangements of trade if she is willing to associate herself with us and the other peace-loving nations of the world in covenants of justice and law and fair dealing. We wish

400

her only to accept a place of equality among the peoples of the world,—the new world in which we now live,—instead of a place of mastery.

Neither do we presume to suggest to her any alteration or modification of her institutions. But it is necessary, we must frankly say, and necessary as a preliminary to any intelligent dealings with her on our part, that we should know whom her spokesmen speak for when they speak to us, whether for the Reichstag Majority or for the military party and the men whose creed is imperial domination.

We have spoken now, surely, in terms too concrete to admit of any further doubt or question. An evident principle runs through the whole programme I have outlined. It is the principle of justice to all peoples and nationalities, and their right to live on equal terms of liberty and safety with one another, whether they be strong or weak. Unless this principle be made its foundation no part of the structure of international justice can stand. The people of the United States could act upon no other principle; and to the vindication of this principle they are ready to devote their lives, their honor, and everything that they possess. The moral climax of this the culminating and final war for human liberty has come, and they are ready to put their own strength, their own highest purpose, their own integrity and devotion to the test.

Document No. 57   Eugene V. Debs, a Socialist Leader's Condemnation of
the War (1918)
Source: Ronald Radosh, ed., *Debs* in Gerald Emanuel Stearn, general
editor, *Great Lives Observed Series* (Englewood Cliffs, N.J.: Prentice-Hall,
Inc., Copyright, 1971), pp. 66-78. Reprinted by permission.

THE CANTON, OHIO SPEECH [1]

Comrades, friends, and fellow workers, for this very cordial greet-
ing, this very hearty reception, I thank you all with the fullest appreciation of your interest in and your devotion to the cause for which I am
to speak to you this afternoon.

To speak for labor, to plead the cause of the men and women and
children who toil, to serve the working class has always been to me a
high privilege, a duty of love.

I have just returned from a visit over yonder (pointing to the work-
house), where three of our most loyal comrades* are paying the penalty
for their devotion to the cause of the working class. They have come
to realize, as many of us have, that it is extremely dangerous to exercise
the constitutional right of free speech in a country fighting to make
democracy safe in the world.

I realize that, in speaking to you this afternoon, there are certain
limitations placed upon the right of free speech. I must be exceedingly
careful, prudent, as to what I say, and even more careful and prudent
as to how I say it. I may not be able to say all I think, but I am not
going to say anything that I do not think. I would rather a thousand
times be a free soul in jail than to be a sycophant and coward in the
streets. They may put those boys in jail—and some of the rest of us in
jail—but they cannot put the Socialist movement in jail. Those prison
bars separate their bodies from ours, but their souls are here this afternoon. They are simply paying the penalty that all men have paid in all
the ages of history for standing erect, and for seeking to pave the way
to better conditions for mankind.

If it had not been for the men and women, who, in the past, have had
the moral courage to go to jail, we would still be in the jungles. . . .

There is but one thing you have to be concerned about, and that is
that you keep four-square with the principles of the international
Socialist movement. It is only when you begin to compromise that
trouble begins. So far as I am concerned, it does not matter what others
may say, or think, or do, as long as I am sure that I am right with myself and the cause. There are so many who seek refuge in the popular

[1] Delivered at Nimisilla Park, Canton, Ohio, Sunday afternoon, June 16th,
1918. This speech as printed is an abridgement of the original. Omissions consist
solely of local and out-of-date references and repetitions.

* Debs refers to three Cleveland Socialists, Charles E. Ruthenberg, Alfred
Wagenknecht, and Charles Baker, imprisoned because of their opposition to the
war.

side of a great question. As a Socialist, I have long since learned how to stand alone. . . .

I never had much faith in leaders. I am willing to be charged with almost anything, rather than to be charged with being a leader. I am suspicious of leaders, and especially of the intellectual variety. Give me the rank and file every day in the week. If you go to the city of Washington, and you examine the pages of the Congressional Directory, you will find that almost all of those corporation lawyers and cowardly politicians, members of Congress, and misrepresentatives of the masses—you will find that almost all of them claim, in glowing terms, that they have risen from the ranks to places of eminence and distinction. I am very glad I cannot make that claim for myself. I would be ashamed to admit that I had risen from the ranks. When I rise it will be with the ranks, and not from the ranks. . . .

They who have been reading the capitalist newspapers realize what a capacity they have for lying. We have been reading them lately. They know all about the Socialist party . . . except what is true. Only the other day they took an article that I had written—and most of you have read it—most of you members of the party, at least—and they made it appear that I had undergone a marvelous transformation. I had suddenly become changed—had in fact come to my senses; I had ceased to be a wicked Socialist, and had become a respectable Socialist, a patriotic Socialist—as if I had ever been anything else.

What was the purpose of this deliberate misrepresentation? It is so self-evident that it suggests itself. The purpose was to sow the seeds of dissension in our ranks; to have it appear that we were divided among ourselves; that we were pitted against each other, to our mutual undoing. But Socialists were not born yesterday. They know how to read capitalist newspapers, and to believe exactly the opposite of what they read.

Why should a Socialist be discouraged on the eve of the greatest triumph in all the history of the Socialist movement? It is true that these are anxious, trying days for us all—testing days for the women and men who are upholding the banner of labor in the struggle of the working class of all the world against the exploiters of all the world; a time in which the weak and cowardly will falter and fail and desert. They lack the fiber to endure the revolutionary test; they fall away; they disappear as if they had never been. On the other hand, they who are animated by the unconquerable spirit of the social revolution; they who have the moral courage to stand erect and assert their convictions; stand by them; fight for them; go to jail or to hell for them, if need be— they are writing their names, in this crucial hour—they are writing their names in fadeless letters in the history of mankind. . . .

Are we opposed to Prussian militarism? Why, we have been fighting it since the day the Socialist movement was born; and we are going to continue to fight it, day and night, until it is wiped from the face of the earth. Between us there is no truce—no compromise.

But, before I proceed along this line, let me recall a little history, in which I think we are all interested.

In 1869 that grand old warrior of the social revolution, the elder Liebknecht, was arrested and sentenced to prison for three months, because of his war, as a Socialist, on the Kaiser and on the Junkers that rule Germany. In the meantime the Franco-Prussian war broke out. Liebknecht and Bebel were the Socialist members in the Reichstag. They were the only two who had the courage to protest against taking Alsace-Lorraine from France and annexing it to Germany. And for this they were sentenced two years to a prison fortress charged with high treason; because, even in that early day, almost fifty years ago, these leaders, these forerunners of the international Socialist movement were fighting the Kaiser and fighting the Junkers of Germany. They have continued to fight them from that day to this. Multiplied thousands of Socialists have languished in the jails of Germany because of their heroic warface upon the despotic ruling class of that country. . . .

I hate, I loathe, I despise Junkers and junkerdom. I have no earthly use for the Junkers of Germany, and not one particle more use for the Junkers in the United States.

They tell us that we live in a great free republic; that our institutions are democratic; that we are a free and self-governing people. This is too much, even for a joke. But it is not a subject for levity; it is an exceedingly serious matter.

To whom do the Wall Street Junkers in our country marry their daughters? After they have wrung their countless millions from your sweat, your agony and your life's blood, in a time of war as in a time of peace, they invest these untold millions in the purchase of titles of broken-down aristocrats, such as princes, dukes, counts, and other parasites and no-accounts. Would they be satisfied to wed their daughters to honest workingmen? To real democrats? Oh, no! They scour the markets of Europe for vampires who are titled and nothing else. And they swap their millions for the titles, so that matrimony with them becomes literally a matter of money.

These are the gentry who are today wrapped up in the American flag, who shout their claim from the housetops that they are the only patriots, and who have their magnifying glasses in hand, scanning the country for evidence of disloyalty, eager to apply the brand of treason to the men who dare to even whisper their opposition to junker rule in the United States. No wonder Sam Johnson declared that "patriotism is the last refuge of the scoundrel." He must have had this Wall Street gentry in mind, or at least their prototypes, for in every age it has been the tyrant, the oppressor, and the exploiter who has wrapped himself in the cloak of patriotism, or religion, or both to deceive and overawe the people. . . .

I know Tom Mooney intimately—as if he were my own brother. He is an absolutely honest man. He had no more to do with the crime with which he was charged and for which he was convicted than I had. And if he ought to go to the gallows, so ought I. If he is guilty every man who belongs to a labor organization or to the Socialist party is likewise guilty.

What is Tom Mooney guilty of? I will tell you. I am familiar with his record. For years he has been fighting bravely and without compromise the battles of the working class out on the Pacific coast. He refused to be bribed and he could not be browbeaten. In spite of all attempts to intimidate him he continued loyally in the service of the organized workers, and for this he became a marked man. The henchmen of the powerful and corrupt corporations concluding finally that he could not be bought or bribed or bullied, decided he must therefore be murdered. That is why Tom Mooney is today a life prisoner, and why he would have been hanged as a felon long years ago but for the world-wide protest of the working class. . . .

Who appoints our federal judges? The people? In all the history of the country, the working class have never named a federal judge. There are 121 of these judges and every solitary one holds his position, his tenure, through the influence and power of corporate capital. The corporations and trusts dictate their appointment. And when they go to the bench, they go, not to serve the people, but to serve the interests that place them and keep them where they are.

Why, the other day, by a vote of five to four—a kind of craps game—come seven, come 'leven—they declared the child labor law unconstitutional—a law secured after twenty years of education and agitation on the part of all kinds of people. And yet, by a majority of one, the Supreme Court, a body of corporation lawyers, with just one exception, wiped that law from the statute books, and this in our so-called Democracy, so that we may continue to grind the flesh and blood and bones of puny little children into profits for the junkers of Wall Street. And this in a country that boasts of fighting to make the world safe for democracy! The history of this country is being written in the blood of the childhood the industrial lords have murdered. . . .

How stupid and short-sighted the ruling class really is! Cupidity is stone blind. It has no vision. The greedy, profit-seeking exploiter cannot see beyond the end of his nose. He can see a chance for an "opening"; he is cunning enough to know what graft is and where it is, and how it can be secured, but vision he has none—not the slightest. He knows nothing of the great throbbing world that spreads out in all directions. He has no capacity for literature; no appreciation of art; no soul for beauty. That is the penalty the parasites pay for the violation of the laws of life. . . . Every move they make in their game of greed but hastens their own doom. Every blow they strike at the Socialist movement reacts upon themselves. Every time they strike at us, they hit themselves. It never fails. Every time they strangle a Socialist paper they add a thousand voices proclaiming the truth of the principles of Socialism and the ideals of the Socialist movement. They help us in spite of themselves.

Socialism is a growing idea, an expanding philosophy. It is spreading over the entire face of the earth. It is as vain to resist it as it would be to arrest the sunrise on the morrow. It is coming, coming, coming all along the line. Can you not see it? If not, I advise you to consult an oculist. There is certainly something the matter with your vision. It is the mightiest movement in the history of mankind. What a privilege to serve it! I have regretted a thousand times that I can do so little for the movement that has done so much for me. The little that I am, the little that I am hoping to be, I owe to the Socialist movement. It has given me my ideas and ideals, my principles and convictions, and I would not exchange one of them for all of Rockefeller's blood-stained dollars. It has taught me how to serve—a lesson to me of priceless value. It has taught me the ecstasy in the handclasp of a comrade. It has enabled me to hold high communion with you, and made it possible for me to take my place side by side with you in the great struggle for the better day; to multiply myself over and over again; to thrill with a fresh-born manhood; to feel life truly worth while; to open new avenues of vision; to spread out glorious vistas; to know that I am kin to all that throbs; to be class-conscious, and to realize that, regardless of nationality, race, creed, color, or sex, every man, every woman who toils, who renders useful service, every member of the working class without an exception, is my comrade, my brother and sister—and that to serve them and their cause is the highest duty of my life. . . .

Yes, my comrades, my heart is attuned to yours. Aye, all our hearts now throb as one great heart responsive to the battle cry of the social revolution. Here, in this alert and inspiring assemblage our hearts are with the Bolsheviki of Russia. Those heroic men and women, those unconquerable comrades have by their incomparable valor and sacrifice added fresh lustre to the fame of the international movement. . . . The very first act of the triumphant Russian revolution was to proclaim a state of peace with all mankind, coupled with a fervent moral appeal, not to kings, not to emperors, rulers or diplomats, but to *the people* of all nations. . . . When the Bolsheviki came into power and went through the archives they found and exposed the secret treaties— the treaties that were made between the Czar and the French Government, the British Government and the Italian Government, proposing, after the victory was achieved, to dismember the German Empire and destroy the Central Powers. These treaties have never been denied nor repudiated. Very little has been said about them in the American press. I have a copy of these treaties, showing that the purpose of the Allies is exactly the purpose of the Central Powers, and that is the conquest and spoliation of the weaker nations that has always been the purpose of war.

Wars throughout history have been waged for conquest and plunder. In the Middle Ages when the feudal lords who inhabited the castles whose towers may still be seen along the Rhine concluded to enlarge their domains, to increase their power, their prestige, and their wealth

406

they declared war upon one another. But they themselves did not go to war any more than the modern feudal lords, the barons of Wall Street go to war. The feudal barons of the Middle Ages, the economic predecessors of the capitalists of our day, declared all wars. And their miserable serfs fought all the battles. The poor, ignorant serfs had been taught to revere their masters; to believe that when their masters declared war upon one another, it was their patriotic duty to fall upon one another and to cut one another's throats for the profit and glory of the lords and barons who held them in contempt. And that is war in a nutshell. The master class has always declared the wars; the subject class has always fought the battles. The master class has had all to gain and nothing to lose, while the subject class has had nothing to gain and all to lose—especially their lives. . . .

And here let me emphasize the fact—and it cannot be repeated, too often—that the working class who fight all the battles, the working class who make the supreme sacrifices, the working class who freely shed their blood and furnish the corpses, have never yet had a voice in either declaring war or making peace. It is the ruling class that invariably does both. They alone declare war and they alone make peace.

> Yours not to reason why;
> Yours but to do and die.

That is their motto and we object on the part of the awakening workers of this nation. . . .

What a compliment it is to the Socialist movement to be persecuted for the sake of the truth! The truth alone will make the people free. And for this reason the truth must not be permitted to reach the people. The truth has always been dangerous to the rule of the rogue, the exploiter, the robber. So the truth must be ruthlessly suppressed. That is why they are trying to detroy the Socialist movement; and every time they strike a blow they add a thousand new voices to the hosts proclaiming that Socialism is the hope of humanity and has come to emancipate the people from their final form of servitude. . . .

We do not attack individuals. We do not seek to avenge ourselves upon those opposed to our faith. We have no fight with individuals as such. We are capable of pitying those who hate us. We do not hate them; we know better; we would freely give them a cup of water if they needed it. There is no room in our hearts for hate, except for the system, the social system in which it is possible for one man to amass a stupendous fortune doing nothing, while millions of others suffer and struggle and agonize and die for the bare necessities of existence. . . .

It is the minorities who have made the history of this world. It is the few who have had the courage to take their places at the front, who have been true enough to themselves to speak the truth that was in them, who have dared oppose the established order of things, who have espoused the cause of the suffering, struggling poor, who have upheld without regard to personal consequences the cause of freedom and righteousness. It is they, the heroic, self-sacrificing few who have made the history of the race and who have paved the way from barbarism to civilization. The many prefer to remain upon the popular side. They lack the courage and vision to join a despised minority that stands for a principle; they have not the moral fiber that withstands, endures, and finally conquers. They are to be pitied and not treated with contempt for they cannot help their cowardice. But, thank God, in every age and in every nation there have been the brave and self-reliant few, and they have been sufficient to their historic task; and we, who are here today, are under infinite obligations to them because they suffered, they sacrificed, they went to jail, they had their bones broken upon the wheel, they were burned at the stake and their ashes scattered to the winds by the hands of hate and revenge in their struggle to leave the world better for us than they found it for themselves. We are under eternal obligations to them because of what they did and what they suffered for us and the only way we can discharge that obligation is by doing the best we can for those who are to come after us. . . .

The heart of the International Socialist never beats a retreat.

They are pressing forward, here, there and everywhere, in all the zones that girdle the globe. Everywhere these awakening workers, these class-conscious proletarians, these hardy sons and daughters of honest toil are proclaiming the glad tidings of the coming emancipation; everywhere their hearts are attuned to the most sacred cause that ever challenged men and women to action in all the history of the world. Everywhere they are moving toward democracy and the dawn; marching toward the sunrise, their faces all aglow with the light of the coming day. These are the Socialists, the most zealous and enthusiastic crusaders the world has ever known. They are making history that will light up the horizon of coming generations, for their mission is the emancipation of the human race. They have been reviled; they have been ridiculed, persecuted, imprisoned, and have suffered death, but they have been sufficient to themselves and their cause, and their final triumph is but a question of time. . . .

If you would be respected you have got to begin by respecting yourself. Stand up squarely and look yourself in the face and see a man! Do not allow yourself to fall into the predicament of the poor fellow who, after he had heard a Socialist speech concluded that he too ought to be a Socialist. The argument he had heard was unanswerable. "Yes," he said to himself, "all the speaker said was true and I certainly ought to join the party." But after a while he allowed his ardor to cool and he soberly concluded that by joining the party he might anger his boss and lose his job. He then concluded: "I can't take the chance." That night he slept alone. There was something on his conscience and it resulted in a dreadful dream. Men always have such dreams when they betray themselves. A Socialist is free to go to bed with a clear conscience. He goes to sleep with his manhood and he awakens and walks forth in the morning with his self-respect. He is unafraid and he can look the whole world in the face without a tremor and without a blush. But this poor weakling who lacked the courage to do the bidding of his reason and conscience was haunted by a startling dream and at midnight he awoke in terror, bounded from his bed and exclaimed: "My God, there is nobody in this room." He was absolutely right. There was nobody in that room.

How would you like to sleep in a room that had nobody in it? It is an awful thing to be nobody. That is certainly a state of mind to get out of, the sooner the better. . . .

To turn your back on the corrupt Republican party and the corrupt Democratic party—the gold-dust lackeys of the ruling class counts for something. It counts for still more after you have stepped out of those popular and corrupt capitalist parties to join a minority party that has an ideal, that stands for a principle, and fights for a cause. This will be the most important change you have ever made and the time will come when you will thank me for having made the suggestion. It was the day of days for me. I remember it well. It was like passing from midnight darkness to the noontide light of day. It came almost like a flash and found me ready. It must have been in such a flash that great, seething, throbbing Russia, prepared by centuries of slavery and tears and martyrdom, was transformed from a dark continent to a land of living light.

There is something splendid, something sustaining and inspiring in the prompting of the heart to be true to yourself and to the best you know, especially in a crucial hour of your life. You are in the crucible today, my Socialist comrades! You are going to be tried by fire, to what extent no one knows. If you are weak-fibered and faint-hearted you will be lost to the Socialist movement. We will have to bid you good-bye. You are not the stuff of which revolutions are made. We are sorry for you unless you chance to be an "intellectual." The "intellectuals," many of them, are already gone. No loss on our side nor gain on the other.

I am always amused in the discussion of the "intellectual" phase of this question. It is the same old standard under which the rank and file are judged. What would become of the sheep if they had no shepherd to lead them out of the wilderness into the land of milk and honey?

Oh, yes, "I am your shepherd and ye are my mutton."

They would have us believe that if we had no "intellectuals" we would have no movement. They would have our party, the rank and file, controlled by the "intellectual" bosses as the Republican and Democratic parties are controlled. These capitalist parties are managed by "intellectual" leaders and the rank and file are sheep that follow the bellwether to the shambles. . . .

The capitalist system affects to have great regard and reward for i.tellect, and the capitalists give themselves full credit for having superior brains. When we have ventured to say that the time would come when the working class would rule they have bluntly answered "Never! it requires brains to rule." The workers of course have none. And they certainly try hard to prove it by proudly supporting the political parties of their masters under whose administration they are kept in poverty and servitude. . . .

It is true that they have the brains that indicates the cunning of the fox, the wolf, but as for brains denoting real intelligence and the measure of intellectual capacity they are the most woefully ignorant people on earth. Give me a hundred capitalists and let me ask them a dozen simple questions about the history of their own country and I will prove to you that they are as ignorant and unlettered as any you may find in the so-called lower class. They know little of history; they are strangers to science; they are ignorant of sociology and blind to art but they know how to exploit, how to gouge, how to rob, and do it with legal sanction. They always proceed legally for the reason that the class which has the power to rob upon a large scale has also the power to control the government and legalize their robbery. I regret that lack of time prevents me from discussing this phase of the question more at length.

They are continually talking about your patriotic duty. It is not *their* but *your* patriotic duty that they are concerned about. There is a decided difference. Their patriotic duty never takes them to the firing line or chucks them into the trenches.

And now among other things they are urging you to "cultivate" war gardens, while at the same time a government war report just issued shows that practically 52 percent of the arable, tillable soil is held out of use by the landlords, speculators, and profiteers. They themselves do not cultivate the soil. They could not if they would. Nor do they allow others to cultivate it. They keep it idle to enrich themselves, to pocket the millions of dollars of unearned increment. Who is it that makes this land valuable while it is fenced in and kept out of use? It is the people. Who pockets this tremendous accumulation of value? The landlords. And these landlords who toil not and spin not are supreme among American "patriots."

In passing I suggest that we stop a moment to think about the term "landlords." "LANDLORD!" Lord of the Land! The Lord of the land is indeed a super-patriot. This lord who practically owns the earth tells you that we are fighting this war to make the world safe for democracy —he, who shuts out all humanity from his private domain; he, who profiteers at the expense of the people who have been slain and mutilated by multiplied thousands, under pretense of being the great Americans patriot. It is he, this identical patriot who is in fact the arch-enemy of the people; it is he that you need to wipe from power. It is he who is a far greater menace to your liberty and your well-being than the Prussian junkers on the other side of the Atlantic Ocean.

Fifty-two percent of the land kept out of use, according to their own figures! They tell you that there is an alarming shortage of flour and that you need to produce more. They tell you further that you have got to save wheat so that more can be exported for the soldiers who are fighting on the other side, while half of your tillable soil is held out of use by the landlords and profiteers. What do you think of that? . . .

Let us illustrate a vital point. Here is the coal in great deposits all about us; here are the miners and the machinery of production. Why should there be a coal famine upon the one hand and an army of idle and hungry miners on the other hand? Is it not an incredibly stupid situation, an almost idiotic if not criminal state of affairs?

In the present system the miner, a wage-slave, gets down into a pit three or four hundred feet deep. He works hard and produces a ton of coal. But he does not own an ounce of it. That coal belongs to some mine-owning plutocrat who may be in New York or sailing the high seas in his private yacht; or he may be hobnobbing with royalty in the capitals of Europe, and that is where most of them were before the war was declared. The industrial captain, so-called, who lives in Paris, London, Vienna, or some other center of gayety, does not have to work to revel in luxury. He owns the mines and he might as well own the miners.

That is where you workers are and where you will remain as long as you give your support to the political parties of your masters and exploiters. You vote these miners out of a job and reduce them to corporation vassals and paupers.

We Socialists say: "Take possession of the mines in the name of the people." Set the miners at work and give every miner the equivalent of all the coal he produces. Reduce the work day in proportion to the development of productive machinery. That would at once settle the matter of a coal famine and of idle miners. But that is too simple a proposition and the people will have none of it. The time will come, however, when the people will be driven to take such action for there is no other efficient and permanent solution of the problem. . . .

Of course that would be Socialism as far as it goes. But you are not in favor of that program. It is too visionary because it is so simple and practical. So you will have to continue to wait until winter is upon you before you get your coal and then pay three prices for it because you insist upon voting a capitalist ticket and giving your support to the present wage-slave system. The trouble with you is that you are still in a capitalist state of mind.

Lincoln said: "If you want that thing, that is the thing you want"; and you will get it to your heart's content. But some good day you will wake up and realize that a change is needed and wonder why you did not know it long before. Yes, a change is certainly needed, not merely a change of party but a change of system; a change from slavery to freedom and from despotism to democracy, wide as the world. When this change comes at last, we shall rise from brutehood to brotherhood, and to accomplish it we have to educate and organize the workers industrially and politically. . . .

There are few men who have the courage to say a word in favor of the IWW. I have. Let me say here that I have great respect for the IWW. Far greater than I have for their infamous detractors.

It is only necessary to label a man "IWW" to have him lynched. War makes possible all such crimes and outrages. And war comes in spite of the people. When Wall Street says war the press says war and the pulpit promptly follows with its *Amen*. In every age the pulpit has been on the side of the rulers and not on the side of the people. That is one reason why the preachers so fiercely denounce the IWW. . . .

Political action and industrial action must supplement and sustain each other. You will never vote the Socialist republic into existence. You will have to lay its foundations in industrial organization. The industrial union is the forerunner of industrial democracy. In the shop where the workers are associated is where industrial democracy has its beginning. Organize according to your industries! Get together in every department of industrial service! United and acting together for the common good your power is invincible.

When you have organized industrially you will soon learn that you can manage as well as operate industry. You will soon realize that you do not need the idle masters and exploiters. They are simply parasites. They do not employ you as you imagine but you employ them to take from you what you produce, and that is how they function in industry. You can certainly dispense with them in that capacity. You do not need them to depend upon for your jobs. You can never be free while you work and live by their sufferance. You must own your own tools and then you will control your own jobs, enjoy the products of your own labor and be free men instead of industrial slaves.

Organize industrially and make your organization complete. Then unite in the Socialist party. Vote as you strike and strike as you vote.

Your union and your party embrace the working class. The Socialist party expresses the interest, hopes, and aspirations of the toilers of all the world.

Get your fellow workers into the industrial union and the political party to which they rightfully belong, especially this year, this historic year in which the forces of labor will assert themselves as they never have before. This is the year that calls for men and women who have the courage, the manhood, and womanhood to do their duty.

Get into the Socialist party and take your place in its ranks; help to inspire the weak and strengthen the faltering, and do your share to speed the coming of the brighter and better day for us all.

When we unite and act together on the industrial field and when we vote together on election day we shall develop the supreme power of the one class that can and will bring permanent peace to the world. We shall then have the intelligence, the courage, and the power for our great task. In due time industry will be organized on a cooperative basis. We shall conquer the public power. We shall then transfer the title deeds of the railroads, the telegraph lines, the mines, mills, and great industries to the people in their collective capacity; we shall take possession of all these social utilities in the name of the people. We shall then have industrial democracy. We shall be a free nation whose government is of and by and for the people.

And now for all of us to do our duty! The clarion call is ringing in our ears and we cannot falter without being convicted of treason to ourselves and to our great cause.

Do not worry over the charge of treason to your masters, but be concerned about the treason that involves yourselves. Be true to yourself and you cannot be a traitor to any good cause on earth.

Yes, in good time we are going to sweep into power in this nation and throughout the world. We are going to destroy all enslaving and degrading capitalist institutions and recreate them as free and humanizing institutions. The world is daily changing before our eyes. The sun of capitalism is setting; the sun of Socialism is rising. It is our duty to build the new nation and the free republic. We need industrial and social builders. We Socialists are the builders of the beautiful world that is to be. We are all pledged to do our part. We are inviting—aye challenging you in the name of your own manhood and womanhood to join us and do your part.

In due time the hour will strike and this great cause triumphant —the greatest in history—will proclaim the emancipation of the working class and the brotherhood of all mankind.

Part IV

*Plans for Postwar
Reconstruction and Disarmament—
The Peace Movement Reborn,
1919-1922*

Document No. 58 President Wilson's First Draft of the League Covenant (1918)
Source: Ray S. Baker, *Woodrow Wilson and the World Settlement* (3 vols.; Garden City, N.Y.: Doubleday, 1922), III, pp. 88-93.

COVENANT.

PREAMBLE.

In order to secure peace, security, and orderly government by the prescription of open and honorable relations between nations, by the firm establishment of the understandings of international law as the actual rule of conduct among governments, and by the maintenance of justice and a scrupulous respect of all treaty obligations in the dealings of all organized peoples with one another, the Powers signatory to this covenant and agreement jointly and severally adopt this constitution of the League of Nations.

ARTICLE I.—The action of the Signatory Powers under the terms of this agreement shall be effected through the instrumentality of a Body of Delegates which shall consist of the ambassadors and ministers of the contracting Powers accredited to H. and the Minister for Foreign Affairs of H. The meetings of the Body of Delegates shall be held at the seat of government of H. and the Minister for Foreign Affairs of H. shall be the presiding officer of the Body.

Whenever the Delegates deem it necessary or advisable, they may meet temporarily at the seat of government of B. or of S., in which case the Ambassador or Minister to H. of the country in which the meeting is held shall be the presiding officer *pro tempore.*

ARTICLE II.—The Body of Delegates shall regulate their own procedure and shall have power to appoint such committees as they may deem necessary to inquire into and report upon any matters which lie within the field of their action.

They shall organize a Secretariat to act as their ministerial agency, and the expense of the maintenance of the Secretariat shall be borne as they may prescribe.

In all matters covered by this Article the Body of Delegates may decide by a majority vote of the whole Body.

ARTICLE III.—The Contracting Powers unite in guaranteeing to each other political independence and territorial integrity; but it is understood between them that such territorial readjustments, if any, as may in the future become necessary by reason of changes in present racial conditions and aspirations or present social and political relationships, pursuant to the principle of self-determination, and also such territorial readjustments as may in the judgment of three-fourths of the Delegates be demanded by the welfare and manifest interest of the peoples concerned, may be effected, if agreeable to those peoples; and that territorial changes may in equity involve material compensation. The Contracting Powers accept without reservation the principle that the peace of the world is superior in- importance to every question of political jurisdiction or boundary.

Article IV.—(H. 21.) The Contracting Powers recognize the principle that the establishment and maintenance of peace will require the reduction of national armaments to the lowest point consistent with domestic safety and the enforcement by common action of international obligations; and the Delegates are directed to formulate at once plans by which such a reduction may be brought about. The plan so formulated shall be binding when, and only when, unanimously approved by the Governments signatory to this Covenant.

The Contracting Powers further agree that munitions and implements of war shall not be manufactured by private enterprise or for private profit, and that there shall be full and frank publicity as to all national armaments and military or naval programmes.

ARTICLE V.—The Contracting Powers agree that all disputes arising between or among them of whatever nature, which shall not be satisfactorily settled by diplomacy, shall be referred for arbitration to three arbitrators, one of the three to be selected by each of the parties to the dispute, when there are but two such parties, and the third by the two thus selected. When there are more than two parties to the dispute, one arbitrator shall be named by each of the several parties and the arbitrators thus named shall add to their number others of their own choice, the number thus added to be limited to the number which will suffice to give a deciding voice to the arbitrators thus added in case of a tie vote among the arbitrators chosen by the contending parties. In case the arbitrators chosen by the contending parties cannot agree upon an additional arbitrator or arbitrators, the additional arbitrator or arbitrators shall be chosen by the Body of Delegates.

On the appeal of a party to the dispute the decision of the arbitrators may be set aside by a vote of three-fourths of the Delegates, in case the decision of the arbitrators was unanimous, or by a vote of two-thirds of the Delegates in case the decision of the arbitrators was not unanimous, but unless thus set aside shall be finally binding and conclusive.

When any decision of arbitrators shall have been thus set aside the dispute shall again be submitted to arbitrators chosen as heretofore provided, none of whom shall, however, have previously acted as arbitrators in the dispute in question, and the decision of the arbitrators rendered in this second arbitration shall be finally binding and conclusive without right of appeal.

ARTICLE VI.—(H. 14.) Any power which the Body of Delegates shall declare to have failed to submit any dispute to arbitration under the terms of Article V of this Covenant or to have refused or failed to carry out any decision of such arbitration shall thereupon lose and be deprived of all rights of commerce and intercourse with any of the Contracting Powers.

ARTICLE VII.—If any Power shall declare war or begin hostilities, or take any hostile step short of war, against another Power before submitting the dispute involved to arbitrators as herein provided, or shall declare war or begin hostilities, or take any hostile step short of war, in regard to any dispute which has been decided adversely to it by arbitrators chosen and empowered as herein provided, the Contracting Powers hereby bind themselves not only to cease all commerce and intercourse with that Power but also to unite in blockading and closing the frontiers of that power to commerce or intercourse with any part of the world and to use any force that may be necessary to accomplish that object.

ARTICLE VIII.—(H. 5, 7, 8.) Any war or threat of war, whether immediately affecting any of the Contracting Powers or not, is hereby declared a matter of concern to the League of Nations and to all the Powers signatory hereto, and those Powers hereby reserve the right to take any action that may be deemed wise and effectual to safeguard the peace of nations.

The Delegates shall meet in the interest of peace whenever war is rumoured or threatened, and also whenever the Delegate of any Power shall inform the Delegates that a meeting and conference in the interest of peace is advisable.

The Delegates may also meet at such other times and upon such other occasions as they shall from time to time deem best and determine.

ARTICLE IX.—(H. 16, 17.)   In the event of a dispute arising between one of the Contracting Powers and a Power not a party to this Covenant, the Contracting Power involved hereby binds itself to endeavour to obtain the submission of the dispute to judicial decision or to arbitration.   If the other Power will not agree to submit the dispute to judicial decision or to arbitration, the Contracting Power shall bring the matter to the attention of the Body of Delegates.   The Delegates shall in such case, in the name of the League of Nations, invite the Power not a party to this Covenant to become *ad hoc* a party and to submit its case to judicial decision or to arbitration, and if that Power consents it is hereby agreed that the provisions hereinbefore contained and applicable to the submission of disputes to arbitration shall be in all respects applicable to the dispute both in favour of and against such Power as if it were a party to this Covenant.

In case the Power not a party to this Covenant shall accept the invitation of the Delegates to become *ad hoc* a party, it shall be the duty of the Delegates immediately to institute an inquiry into the circumstances and merits of the dispute involved and to recommend such joint action by the Contracting Powers as may seem best and most effectual in the circumstances disclosed.

ARTICLE X.—(H. 18.)   If hostilities should be begun or any hostile action taken against the Contracting Power by the Power not a party to this Covenant before a decision of the dispute by arbitrators or before investigation, report, and recommendation by the Delegates in regard to the dispute, or contrary to such recommendation, the Contracting Powers shall thereupon cease all commerce and communication with that Power and shall also unite in blockading and closing the frontiers of that Power to all commerce or intercourse with any part of the world, employing jointly any force that may be necessary to accomplish that object. The Contracting Powers shall also unite in coming to the assistance of the Contracting Power against which hostile action has been taken, combining their armed forces in its behalf.

ARTICLE XI.—(H. 19.) In case of a dispute between states not parties to this Covenant, any Contracting Power may bring the matter to the attention of the Delegates, who shall thereupon tender the good offices of the League of Nations with a view to the peaceable settlement of the dispute.

If one of the states, a party to the dispute, shall offer and agree to submit its interests and cause of action wholly to the control and decision of the League of Nations, that state shall *ad hoc* be deemed a Contracting Power. If no one of the states, parties to the dispute, shall so offer and agree, the Delegates shall of their own motion take such action and make such recommendation to their governments as will prevent hostilities and result in the settlement of the dispute.

ARTICLE XII.—(H. 22.) Any Power not a party to this Covenant may apply to the Body of Delegates for leave to become a party. If the Delegates shall regard the granting thereof as likely to promote the peace, order, and security of the World, they may act favourably on the application, and their favourable action shall operate to constitute the Power so applying in all respects a full signatory party to this Covenant.

ARTICLE XIII.—(H. 23.) The Contracting Powers severally agree that the present Covenant and Convention is accepted as abrogating all treaty obligations *inter se* which are inconsistent with the terms hereof, and solemnly engage that they will not enter into any engagements inconsistent with the terms hereof.

In case any of the Powers signatory hereto or subsequently admitted to the League of Nations shall, before becoming a party to this covenant, have undertaken any treaty obligations which are inconsistent with the terms of this Covenant, it shall be the duty of such Power to take immediate steps to procure its release from such obligations.

Document No. 59   The Treaty of Versailles, the Covenant of the League of Nations (1919)
Source: U.S. Congress, 67th Cong.; 4th Sess., *Treaties, Sen. Doc. 348* (Washington, D.C.: Government Printing Office, 1923), pp. 3336-3345.

THE COVENANT OF THE LEAGUE OF NATIONS.

The High Contracting Parties,

In order to promote international co-operation and to achieve international peace and security

by the acceptance of obligations not to resort to war,

by the prescription of open, just and honourable relations between nations,

by the firm establishment of the understandings of international law as the actual rule of conduct among Governments, and

by the maintenance of justice and a scrupulous respect for all treaty obligations in the dealings of organised peoples with one another,

Agree to this Covenant of the League of Nations.

ARTICLE 1.

The original Members of the League of Nations shall be those of the Signatories which are named in the Annex to this Covenant and also such of those other States named in the Annex as shall accede without reservation to this Covenant.   Such accession shall be effected by a Declaration deposited with the Secretariat within two months of the coming into force of the Covenant.   Notice thereof shall be sent to all other Members of the League.

Any fully self-governing State, Dominion or Colony not named in the Annex may become a Member of the League if its admission is agreed to by two-thirds of the Assembly, provided that it shall give effective guarantees of its sincere intention to observe its international obligations, and shall accept such regulations as may be prescribed by the League in regard to its military, naval and air forces and armaments.

Any Member of the League may, after two years' notice of its intention so to do, withdraw from the League, provided that all its international obligations and all its obligations under this Covenant shall have been fulfilled at the time of its withdrawal.

ARTICLE 2.

The action of the League under this Covenant shall be effected through the instrumentality of an Assembly and of a Council, with a permanent Secretariat,

ARTICLE 3.

The Assembly shall consist of Representatives of the Members of the League.

The Assembly shall meet at stated intervals and from time to time as occasion may require at the Seat of the League or at such other place as may be decided upon.

The Assembly may deal at its meetings with any matter within the sphere of action of the League or affecting the peace of the world.

At meetings of the Assembly each Member of the League shall have one vote, and may have not more than three Representatives.

ARTICLE 4.

The Council shall consist of Representatives of the Principal Allied and Associated Powers, together with Representatives of four other Members of the League. These four Members of the League shall be selected by the Assembly from time to time in its discretion. Until the appointment of the Representatives of the four Members of the League first selected by the Assembly, Representatives of Belgium, Brazil, Spain and Greece shall be members of the Council.

With the approval of the majority of the Assembly, the Council may name additional Members of the League whose Representatives shall always be members of the Council; the Council with like approval may increase the number of Members of the League to be selected by the Assembly for representation on the Council.

The Council shall meet from time to time as occasion may require, and at least once a year, at the Seat of the League, or at such other place as may be decided upon.

The Council may deal at its meetings with any matter within the sphere of action of the League or affecting the peace of the world.

Any Member of the League not represented on the Council shall be invited to send a Representative to sit as a member at any meeting of the Council during the consideration of matters specially affecting the interests of that Member of the League.

At meetings of the Council, each Member of the League represented on the Council shall have one vote, and may have not more than one Representative.

ARTICLE 5.

Except where otherwise expressly provided in this Covenant or by the terms of the present Treaty, decisions at any meeting of the Assembly or of the Council shall require the agreement of all the Members of the League represented at the meeting.

All matters of procedure at meetings of the Assembly or of the Council, including the appointment of Committees to investigate particular matters, shall be regulated by the Assembly or by the Council and may be decided by a majority of the Members of the League represented at the meeting.

The first meeting of the Assembly and the first meeting of the

Council shall be summoned by the President of the United States of America.

ARTICLE 6.

The permanent Secretariat shall be established at the Seat of the League. The Secretariat shall comprise a Secretary General and such secretaries and staff as may be required.

The first Secretary General shall be the person named in the Annex: thereafter the Secretary General shall be appointed by the Council with the approval of the majority of the Assembly.

The secretaries and staff of the Secretariat shall be appointed by the Secretary General with the approval of the Council.

The Secretary General shall act in that capacity at all meetings of the Assembly and of the Council.

The expenses of the Secretariat shall be borne by the Members of the League in accordance with the apportionment of the expenses of the International Bureau of the Universal Postal Union.

ARTICLE 7.

The Seat of the League is established at Geneva.

The Council may at any time decide that the Seat of the League shall be established elsewhere.

All positions under or in connection with the League, including the Secretariat, shall be open equally to men and women.

Representatives of the Members of the League and officials of the League when engaged on the business of the League shall enjoy diplomatic privileges and immunities.

The buildings and other property occupied by the League or its officials or by Representatives attending its meetings shall be inviolable.

ARTICLE 8.

The Members of the League recognise that the maintenance of peace requires the reduction of national armaments to the lowest point consistent with national safety and the enforcement by common action of international obligations.

The Council, taking account of the geographical situation and circumstances of each State, shall formulate plans for such reduction for the consideration and action of the several Governments.

Such plans shall be subject to reconsideration and revision at least every ten years.

After these plans shall have been adopted by the several Governments, the limits of armaments therein fixed shall not be exceeded without the concurrence of the Council.

The Members of the League agree that the manufacture by private enterprise of munitions and implements of war is open to grave objections. The Council shall advise how the evil effects attendant upon such manufacture can be prevented, due regard being had to the necessities of those Members of the League which are not able to manufacture the munitions and implements of war necessary for their safety.

The Members of the League undertake to interchange full and frank information as to the scale of their armaments, their military, naval and air programmes and the condition of such of their industries as are adaptable to war-like purposes.

ARTICLE 9.

A permanent Commission shall be constituted to advise the Council on the execution of the provisions of Articles 1 and 8 and on military, naval and air questions generally.

ARTICLE 10.

The Members of the League undertake to respect and preserve as against external aggression the territorial integrity and existing political independence of all Members of the League. In case of any such aggression or in case of any threat or danger of such aggression the Council shall advise upon the means by which this obligation shall be fulfilled.

ARTICLE 11.

Any war or threat of war, whether immediately affecting any of the Members of the League or not, is hereby declared a matter of concern to the whole League, and the League shall take any action that may be deemed wise and effectual to safeguard the peace of nations. In case any such emergency should arise the Secretary General shall on the request of any Member of the League forthwith summon a meeting of the Council.

It is also declared to be the friendly right of each Member of the League to bring to the attention of the Assembly or of the Council any circumstance whatever affecting international relations which threatens to disturb international peace or the good understanding between nations upon which peace depends.

ARTICLE 12.

The Members of the League agree that if there should arise between them any dispute likely to lead to a rupture, they will submit the matter either to arbitration or to inquiry by the Council, and they agree in no case to resort to war until three months after the award by the arbitrators or the report by the Council.

In any case under this Article the award of the arbitrators shall be made within a reasonable time, and the report of the Council shall be made within six months after the submission of the dispute.

ARTICLE 13.

The Members of the League agree that whenever any dispute shall arise between them which they recognise to be suitable for submission to arbitration and which cannot be satisfactorily settled by diplomacy, they will submit the whole subject-matter to arbitration.

Disputes as to the interpretation of a treaty, as to any question of international law, as to the existence of any fact which if established would constitute a breach of any international obligation, or as to the extent and nature of the reparation to be made for any such breach, are declared to be among those which are generally suitable for submission to arbitration.

For the consideration of any such dispute the court of arbitration to which the case is referred shall be the Court agreed on by the parties to the dispute or stipulated in any convention existing between them.

The Members of the League agree that they will carry out in full good faith any award that may be rendered, and that they will not resort to war against a Member of the League which complies therewith. In the event of any failure to carry out such an award, the Council shall propose what steps should be taken to give effect thereto.

ARTICLE 14.

The Council shall formulate and submit to the Members of the League for adoption plans for the establishment of a Permanent Court of International Justice. The Court shall be competent to hear and determine any dispute of an international character which the parties thereto submit to it. The Court may also give an advisory opinion upon any dispute or question referred to it by the Council or by the Assembly.

ARTICLE 15.

If there should arise between Members of the League any dispute likely to lead to a rupture, which is not submitted to arbitration in accordance with Article 13, the Members of the League agree that they will submit the matter to the Council. Any party to the dispute may effect such submission by giving notice of the existence of the dispute to the Secretary General, who will make all necessary arrangements for a full investigation and consideration thereof.

For this purpose the parties to the dispute will communicate to the Secretary General, as promptly as possible, statements of their case with all the relevant facts and papers, and the Council may forthwith direct the publication thereof.

The Council shall endeavour to effect a settlement of the dispute, and if such efforts are successful, a statement shall be made public giving such facts and explanations regarding the dispute and the terms of settlement thereof as the Council may deem appropriate.

If the dispute is not thus settled, the Council either unanimously or by a majority vote shall make and publish a report containing a statement of the facts of the dispute and the recommendations which are deemed just and proper in regard thereto.

Any Member of the League represented on the Council may make public a statement of the facts of the dispute and of its conclusions regarding the same.

If a report by the Council is unanimously agreed to by the mem-

427

bers thereof other than the Representatives of one or more of the parties to the dispute, the Members of the League agree that they will not go to war with any party to the dispute which complies with the recommendations of the report.

If the Council fails to reach a report which is unanimously agreed to by the members thereof, other than the Representatives of one or more of the parties to the dispute, the Members of the League reserve to themselves the right to take such action as they shall consider necessary for the maintenance of right and justice.

If the dispute between the parties is claimed by one of them, and is found by the Council, to arise out of a matter which by international law is solely within the domestic jurisdiction of that party, the Council shall so report, and shall make no recommendation as to its settlement.

The Council may in any case under this Article refer the dispute to the Assembly. The dispute shall be so referred at the request of either party to the dispute, provided that such request be made within fourteen days after the submission of the dispute to the Council.

In any case referred to the Assembly, all the provisions of this Article and of Article 12 relating to the action and powers of the Council shall apply to the action and powers of the Assembly, provided that a report made by the Assembly, if concurred in by the Representatives of those Members of the League represented on the Council and of a majority of the other Members of the League, exclusive in each case of the Representatives of the parties to the dispute, shall have the same force as a report by the Council concurred in by all the members thereof other than the Representatives of one or more of the parties to the dispute.

ARTICLE 16.

Should any Member of the League resort to war in disregard of its covenants under Articles 12, 13 or 15, it shall *ipso facto* be deemed to have committed an act of war against all other Members of the League, which hereby undertake immediately to subject it to the severance of all trade or financial relations, the prohibition of all intercourse between their nationals and the nationals of the covenant-breaking State, and the prevention of all financial, commercial or personal intercourse between the nationals of the covenant-breaking State and the nationals of any other State, whether a Member of the League or not.

It shall be the duty of the Council in such case to recommend to the several Governments concerned what effective military, naval or air force the Members of the League shall severally contribute to the armed forces to be used to protect the covenants of the League.

The Members of the League agree, further, that they will mutually support one another in the financial and economic measures which are taken under this Article, in order to minimise the loss and inconvenience resulting from the above measures, and that they will mutually support one another in resisting any special measures aimed at one of their number by the covenant-breaking State, and that they will take the necessary steps to afford passage through their territory to the forces of any of the Members of the League which are co-operating to protect the covenants of the League.

Any Member of the League which has violated any covenant of the League may be declared to be no longer a Member of the League by a vote of the Council concurred in by the Representatives of all the other Members of the League represented thereon.

ARTICLE 17.

In the event of a dispute between a Member of the League and a State which is not a Member of the League, or between States not Members of the League, the State or States not Members of the League shall be invited to accept the obligations of membership in the League for the purposes of such dispute, upon such conditions as the Council may deem just. If such invitation is accepted, the provisions of Articles 12 to 16 inclusive shall be applied with such modifications as may be deemed necessary by the Council.

Upon such invitation being given the Council shall immediately institute an inquiry into the circumstances of the dispute and recommend such action as may seem best and most effectual in the circumstances.

If a State so invited shall refuse to accept the obligations of membership in the League for the purposes of such dispute, and shall resort to war against a Member of the League, the provisions of Article 16 shall be applicable as against the State taking such action.

If both parties to the dispute when so invited refuse to accept the obligations of membership in the League for the purposes of such dispute, the Council may take such measures and make such recommendations as will prevent hostilities and will result in the settlement of the dispute.

ARTICLE 18.

Every treaty or international engagement entered into hereafter by any Member of the League shall be forthwith registered with the Secretariat and shall as soon as possible be published by it. No such treaty or international engagement shall be binding until so registered.

ARTICLE 19.

The Assembly may from time to time advise the reconsideration by Members of the League of treaties which have become inapplicable and the consideration of international conditions whose continuance might endanger the peace of the world.

ARTICLE 20.

The Members of the League severally agree that this Covenant is accepted as abrogating all obligations or understandings *inter se* which are inconsistent with the terms thereof, and solemnly undertake that they will not hereafter enter into any engagements inconsistent with the terms thereof.

In case any Member of the League shall, before becoming a Member of the League, have undertaken any obligations inconsistent with the terms of this Covenant, it shall be the duty of such Member to take immediate steps to procure its release from such obligations.

ARTICLE 21.

Nothing in this Covenant shall be deemed to affect the validity of international engagements, such as treaties of arbitration or regional understandings like the Monroe doctrine, for securing the maintenance of peace.

ARTICLE 22.

To those colonies and territories which as a consequence of the late war have ceased to be under the sovereignty of the States which formerly governed them and which are inhabited by peoples not yet able to stand by themselves under the strenuous conditions of the modern world, there should be applied the principle that the well-being and development of such peoples form a sacred trust of civilisation and that securities for the performance of this trust should be embodied in this Covenant.

The best method of giving practical effect to this principle is that the tutelage of such peoples should be entrusted to advanced nations who by reason of their resources, their experience or their geographical position can best undertake this responsibility, and who are willing to accept it, and that this tutelage should be exercised by them as Mandatories on behalf of the League.

The character of the mandate must differ according to the stage of the development of the people, the geographical situation of the territory, its economic conditions and other similar circumstances.

Certain communities formerly belonging to the Turkish Empire have reached a stage of development where their existence as independent nations can be provisionally recognised subject to the rendering of administrative advice and assistance by a Mandatory until such time as they are able to stand alone. The wishes of these communities must be a principal consideration in the selection of the Mandatory.

Other peoples, especially those of Central Africa, are at such a stage that the Mandatory must be responsible for the administration of the territory under conditions which will guarantee freedom of conscience and religion, subject only to the maintenance of public order and morals, the prohibition of abuses such as the slave trade, the arms traffic and the liquor traffic, and the prevention of the establishment of fortifications or military and naval bases and of military training of the natives for other than police purposes and the defence of territory, and will also secure equal opportunities for the trade and commerce of other Members of the League.

There are territories, such as South-West Africa and certain of the South Pacific Islands, which, owing to the sparseness of their population, or their small size, or their remoteness from the centres of civilisation, or their geographical contiguity to the territory of the Mandatory, and other circumstances, can be best administered under the laws of the Mandatory as integral portions of its territory, subject to the safeguards above mentioned in the interests of the indigenous population.

In every case of mandate, the Mandatory shall render to the Council an annual report in reference to the territory committed to its charge.

The degree of authority, control, or administration to be exercised by the Mandatory shall, if not previously agreed upon by the Members of the League, be explicitly defined in each case by the Council.

A permanent Commission shall be constituted to receive and examine the annual reports of the Mandatories and to advise the Council on all matters relating to the observance of the mandates.

ARTICLE 23.

Subject to and in accordance with the provisions of international conventions existing or hereafter to be agreed upon, the Members of the League:

(a) will endeavour to secure and maintain fair and humane conditions of labour for men, women. and children, both in their own countries and in all countries to which their commercial and industrial relations extend, and for that purpose will establish and maintain the necessary international organisations;

(b) undertake to secure just treatment of the native inhabitants of territories under their control;

(c) will entrust the League with the general supervision over the execution of agreements with regard to the traffic in women and children, and the traffic in opium and other dangerous drugs;

(d) will entrust the League with the general supervision of the trade in arms and ammunition with the countries in which the control of this traffic is necessary in the common interest;

(e) will make provision to secure and maintain freedom of communications and of transit and equitable treatment for the commerce of all Members of the League. In this connection, the special necessities of the regions devastated during the war of 1914–1918 shall be borne in mind;

(f) will endeavour to take steps in matters of international concern for the prevention and control of disease.

ARTICLE 24.

There shall be placed under the direction of the League all international bureaux already established by general treaties if the parties to such treaties consent. All such international bureaux and all commissions for the regulation of matters of international interest hereafter constituted shall be placed under the direction of the League.

In all matters of international interest which are regulated by general conventions but which are not placed under the control of international bureaux or commissions, the Secretariat of the League shall, subject to the consent of the Council and if desired by the parties, collect and distribute all relevant information and shall render any other assistance which may be necessary or desirable.

The Council may include as part of the expenses of the Secretariat the expenses of any bureau or commission which is placed under the direction of the League.

ARTICLE 25.

The Members of the League agree to encourge and promote the establishment and co-operation of duly authorised voluntary national Red Cross organizations having as purposes the improvement of health, the prevention of disease and the mitigation of suffering throughout the world.

ARTICLE 26.

Amendments to this Covenant will take effect when ratified by the Members of the League whose Representatives compose the Council and by a majority of the Members of the League whose Representatives compose the Assembly.

No such amendment shall bind any Member of the League which signifies its dissent therefrom, but in that case it shall cease to be a Member of the League.

ANNEX.

I. ORIGINAL MEMBERS OF THE LEAGUE OF NATIONS SIGNATORIES OF THE TREATY OF PEACE.

UNITED STATES OF AMERICA.
BELGIUM.
BOLIVIA.
BRAZIL.
BRITISH EMPIRE.
    CANADA.
    AUSTRALIA.
    SOUTH AFRICA.
    NEW ZEALAND.
    INDIA.
CHINA.
CUBA.
ECUADOR.
FRANCE.
GREECE.
GUATEMALA.

HAITI.
HEDJAZ.
HONDURAS.
ITALY.
JAPAN.
LIBERIA.
NICARAGUA.
PANAMA.
PERU.
POLAND.
PORTUGAL.
ROUMANIA.
SERB-CROAT-SLOVENE STATE.
SIAM.
CZECHO-SLOVAKIA.
URUGUAY.

ARGENTINE REPUBLIC.
CHILI.
COLOMBIA.
DENMARK.
NETHERLANDS.
NORWAY.
PARAGUAY.

PERSIA.
SALVADOR.
SPAIN.
SWEDEN.
SWITZERLAND.
VENEZUELA.

II. FIRST SECRETARY GENERAL OF THE LEAGUE OF NATIONS.

The Honourable Sir James Eric DRUMMOND, K. C. M. G., C. B.

Document No. 60   Hamilton Holt, "The League or Bolshevism?" (1919)
Source: *The Independent,* XCVIII (April 5, 1919), pp. 3-4.

THE LEAGUE OR BOLSHEVISM?

BY HAMILTON HOLT

ARE American people aware that Europe is on the verge of a volcano? No one, I think, can have visited England, France and Germany, as I have during the past three months, without realizing that this is the case. The Allies have won the war, but while the delegates at Paris are engaged in winning the peace, the Bolshevik cloud grows blacker and blacker on the horizon, till today it overshadows all Europe. As the hope of Europe turned to America in those dark days of April, May and June last year when the fate of civilization trembled in the balance, so again today the world looks to America to save her from perhaps a greater menace.

Owing to the inventions of steam and electricity which have annihilated time and space the world has become a small neighborhood in which what concerns one concerns all. It is only by concerted action, by a League of Nations that will substitute coöperation for competition in international affairs, that there can be the slightest hope of the future peace of the world. This is the belief of the soldiers who have fought, as well as of those who have stayed at home. Even the governments at last realize that no single nation, no matter how powerful and prepared, can guarantee its own peace, to say nothing of the peace of the world. Without a League Europe knows she must return to the old system of alliances, with its colossal armaments, secret diplomacy and mutual hates and suspicions. Once such a reversion to pre-war conditions is seen inevitable or even likely the people will revolt. The issue before the world therefore is a League of Nations or Bolshevism.

Everywhere I went men asked me if it were possible that America would refuse to join the League of Nations. They had heard that President Wilson did not have the American people unanimously behind him. Was it true? Would America fail the world now after autocracy had been dethroned and it only required patience and an unselfish will to inaugurate a new era of coöperation and peace on earth?

I did not meet a single man in Europe who thought a League could succeed for a moment if the United States was not a member. I met many who assured me that if America refused to join revolutions would follow everywhere. Europe's foremost democrat, Premier Venizelos of Greece, told me that should our Senate refuse to ratify the Covenant, all liberal and humane men everywhere would despair. Ex-Premier Bourgeois, France's spokesman on the Commission that drafted the Covenant, begged me the night before I left to make plain to the American people that Europe was lost if the United States would not continue to play its full part in saving civilization. The work so heroically begun by our boys at Seicheprey, Cantigny, Chateau Thierry, St. Mihiel and the Argonne must not now be left uncompleted.

It was my great privilege to have been present at Paris when the Covenant was born. Colonel House was good enough to appoint me liaison officer between the American Peace Commission and the League to Enforce Peace. Consequently I saw the progress of the Covenant from day to day on its course thru the Commission. Had I been permitted to divulge what I learned when I learned it, I should have got many a "beat" on the thousand or more journalists assembled at the Conference.

It has been intimated by Senator Lodge and others that the Covenant is a British document. Nonsense. I read in advance the original English "secret" draft brought by Lord Robert Cecil to Paris, and while I must say that it was the most admirably worked out proposal presented by any delegation, the Covenant as it stands today is more American than English. I have taken the trouble to underline in red ink those portions of the Covenant whose words are taken bodily from the American original draft which I have in my possession, and my copy is streaked with red from beginning to end. And if I had underlined the American ideas as well as the precise words that were adopted the Covenant would be more red than black.

Of course political exigencies made it necessary that Mr. Wilson should carry a draft of the Covenant home with him in his pocket. Consequently the Covenant bears internal testimony of haste in its construction. Mr. Taft was quite

435

right when he said, "Undoubtedly the Covenant needs revision. It is not symmetrically arranged, its meaning has to be dug out, and the language is ponderous and in diplomatic patois." I myself while on the sea voyage home was able to formulate what I believe to be forty-seven distinct improvements in the Covenant, most of them, of course, in the interest of clarity and precision, but some of them fundamental.

It is inconceivable that the Peace Conference will not amend the draft in many particulars. I am, consequently, quite sure that the Commission will be most grateful for any constructive criticisms from any responsible groups or individuals anywhere on earth. This is evidenced by the fact that the neutral nations have been officially invited to make suggestions. The neutrals have gladly availed themselves of this opportunity and already some thirty concrete proposals have been presented, many of which will no doubt be adopted. With the full approval of the various official peace Commissions a Conference was held in London on March 11 and 12 when representatives of the various League of Nations societies from the Allied countries assembled to discuss the Covenant article by article to see what improvements those groups who have been giving most attention to the subject for the past four years might have to offer. I attended this conference as a representative of the League to Enforce Peace and many important suggestions were made there that I am sure will be useful to the Commissioners at Paris. Even Bourgeois of France and Venizelos of Greece, both framers of the Covenant, thought it important enough to leave their pressing work at Paris to participate in our unofficial conference.

On my return home I find a far greater amount of discussion going on in respect to the minutiæ of the Covenant than was the case in Europe. There the disposition was to insist passionately on the establishment of a League of Nations, provided that it was a real League with "teeth in it," but to leave the technical details to be settled by the experts. The discussion here seems also more active and thorogoing. This is all to the good. The more criticism we can offer that will make the document simple, precise and powerful, the better. The activity of the Senators is to be praised, if not always their arguments. Not only is it the right of the Senators under the constitution to give advice, but it is their duty. On that we must all agree. But it is also the right and duty of the people to be heard. This is probably the first time in history, as President Lowell has well pointed out, when the people have been invited in to take part in such a discussion. The day of open diplomacy has at last arrived.

But what we object to is not the criticism that will help the delegates to perfect and strengthen the Covenant, but the criticism that would weaken and destroy it. Most of the senatorial criticism seems to be of the latter kind. It is apparently not the intention of many of our Senators to see what the United States can put into the League but what she can get out of it.

Our young men with all the ardor and idealism of youth crost the ocean to offer their lives to save the world from autocratic tyranny. Our old men at home now urge their country to play safe. Luckily Woodrow Wilson has the spirit of youth. He would have the United States give its all, that in giving it may gain. I had an interview with him at the Murat Palace while the Covenant was still in committee. He told me he would sign no document to which the Senate could "reasonably" object on constitutional grounds. Apparently if the Senate objected on other grounds he was ready for a fight.

The fact is that all the trouble at the Peace Conference, like trouble everywhere else in the world, is owing to human selfishness. The Peace Conference has been accused of "unconscionable" delays. The truth is that all the delays have been made by those blind reactionaries of Europe who are trying to avoid the obligations they assumed when they agreed to accept our President's fourteen points. Wilson and Lloyd George would have been measurably nearer the goal of peace today had it not been for the machinations of those selfish individuals, groups, classes and nations who have been trying to play at the peace table the old diplomatic game of getting something at the expense of the other fellow. And these reactionaries, I am ashamed to say, have of late dared to show their heads the more openly owing to the attitude of some of our Senators and public men who have left no stone unturned to divide our country on this greatest of all issues and to discredit the President.

As for the charge, that the drafting of the Covenant has delayed the signing of the peace treaty, that is without any foundation whatsoever. The Commission that drafted the Covenant is of course the one commission that has done its job extra expeditiously.

I hope to discuss the Covenant later in some detail, but here I wish to say that even without a single amendment it is unquestionably the greatest document since the Declaration of American Independence. It should be amended without doubt, but better not a syllable changed than that it should be emasculated at the behest of timidity, selfishness or partizan advantage. Our forefathers took no counsel of cowardice from the tories of their day when they signed the immortal document that brought forth the United States of America. If now we take no counsel of cowardice from our senatorial reactionaries, but pledge "our lives, our fortunes and our sacred honor" to the Declaration of Interdependence so nobly championed by Presidents Wilson and Taft, and the host of great men in Europe and Asia, then the United Nations of the World will result.

Document No. 61 President Wilson's Statement to the Senate Foreign Relations Committee (August, 1919)
Source: U.S. Senate, Senate Document No. 76, 66th Cong., 1st Sess. (Washington, D.C.: Government Printing Office, 1919), pp. 3-7.

TREATY OF PEACE WITH GERMANY.

TUESDAY, AUGUST 19, 1919.

UNITED STATES SENATE,
COMMITTEE ON FOREIGN RELATIONS,
Washington, D. C.

CONFERENCE AT THE WHITE HOUSE.

The committee met at the White House at 10 o'clock a. m., pursuant to the invitation of the President, and proceeded to the East Room, where the conference was held.

Present: Hon. Woodrow Wilson, President of the United States, and the following members of the committee: Senators Lodge (chairman), McCumber, Borah, Brandegee, Fall, Knox, Harding, Johnson, of California, New, Moses, Hitchcock, Williams, Swanson, Pomerene, Smith, and Pittman.

STATEMENT OF THE PRESIDENT.

The PRESIDENT. Mr. Chairman, I have taken the liberty of writing out a little statement in the hope that it might facilitate discussion by speaking directly on some points that I know have been points of controversy and upon which I thought an expression of opinion would not be unwelcome. I am absolutely glad that the committee should have responded in this way to my intimation that I would like to be of service to it. I welcome the opportunity for a frank and full interchange of views.

I hope, too, that this conference will serve to expedite your consideration of the treaty of peace. I beg that you will pardon and indulge me if I again urge that practically the whole task of bringing the country back to normal conditions of life and industry waits upon the decision of the Senate with regard to the terms of the peace.

I venture thus again to urge my advice that the action of the Senate with regard to the treaty be taken at the earliest practicable moment because the problems with which we are face to face in the readjustment of our national life are of the most pressing and critical character, will require for their proper solution the most intimate and disinterested cooperation of all parties and all interests, and can not be postponed without manifest peril to our people and to all the national advantages we hold most dear. May I mention a few of the matters which can not be handled with intelligence until the country knows the character of the peace it is to have? I do so only by a very few samples.

439

The copper mines of Montana, Arizona, and Alaska, for example, are being kept open and in operation only at a great cost and loss, in part upon borrowed money; the zinc mines of Missouri, Tennessee, and Wisconsin are being operated at about one-half their capacity; the lead of Idaho, Illinois, and Missouri reaches only a portion of its former market; there is an immediate need for cotton belting, and also for lubricating oil, which can not be met—all because the channels of trade are barred by war when there is no war. The same is true of raw cotton, of which the Central Empires alone formerly purchased nearly 4,000,000 bales. And these are only examples. There is hardly a single raw material, a single important foodstuff, a single class of manufactured goods which is not in the same case. Our full, normal profitable production waits on peace.

Our military plans of course wait upon it. We can not intelligently or wisely decide how large a naval or military force we shall maintain or what our policy with regard to military training is to be until we have peace not only, but also until we know how peace is to be sustained, whether by the arms of single nations or by the concert of all the great peoples. And there is more than that difficulty involved. The vast surplus properties of the Army include not food and clothing merely, whose sale will affect normal production, but great manufacturing establishments also which should be restored to their former uses, great stores of machine tools, and all sorts of merchandise which must lie idle until peace and military policy are definitively determined. By the same token there can be no properly studied national budget until then.

The nations that ratify the treaty, such as Great Britain, Belgium, and France, will be in a position to lay their plans for controlling the markets of central Europe without competition from us if we do not presently act. We have no consular agents, no trade representatives there to look after our interests.

There are large areas of Europe whose future will lie uncertain and questionable until their people know the final settlements of peace and the forces which are to administer and sustain it. Without determinate markets our production can not proceed with intelligence or confidence. There can be no stabilization of wages because there can be no settled conditions of employment. There can be no easy or normal industrial credits because there can be no confident or permanent revival of business.

But I will not weary you with obvious examples. I will only venture to repeat that every element of normal life amongst us depends upon and awaits the ratification of the treaty of peace; and also that we can not afford to lose a single summer's day by not doing all that we can to mitigate the winter's suffering, which, unless we find means to prevent it, may prove disastrous to a large portion of the world, and may, at its worst, bring upon Europe conditions even more terrible than those wrought by the war itself.

Nothing, I am led to believe, stands in the way of the ratification of the treaty except certain doubts with regard to the meaning and implication of certain articles of the covenant of the league of nations; and I must frankly say that I am unable to understand why such doubts

440

should be entertained. You will recall that when I had the pleasure of a conference with your committee and with the Committee of the House of Representatives on Foreign Affairs at the White House in March last the questions now most frequently asked about the league of nations were all canvassed with a view to their immediate clarification. The covenant of the league was then in its first draft and subject to revision. It was pointed out that no express recognition was given to the Monroe doctrine; that it was not expressly provided that the league should have no authority to act or to express a judgment on matters of domestic policy; that the right to withdraw from the league was not expressly recognized; and that the constitutional right of the Congress to determine all questions of peace and war was not sufficiently safeguarded. On my return to Paris all these matters were taken up again by the commission on the league of nations and every suggestion of the United States was accepted.

The views of the United States with regard to the questions I have mentioned had, in fact, already been accepted by the commission and there was supposed to be nothing inconsistent with them in the draft of the covenant first adopted—the draft which was the subject of our discussion in March—but no objection was made to saying explicitly in the text what all had supposed to be implicit in it. There was absolutely no doubt as to the meaning of any one of the resulting provisions of the covenant in the minds of those who participated in drafting them, and I respectfully submit that there is nothing vague or doubtful in their wording.

The Monroe doctrine is expressly mentioned as an understanding which is in no way to be impaired or interfered with by anything contained in the covenant and the expression "regional understandings like the Monroe doctrine" was used, not because anyone of the conferees thought there was any comparable agreement anywhere else in existence or in contemplation, but only because it was thought best to avoid the appearance of dealing in such a document with the policy of a single nation. Absolutely nothing is concealed in the phrase.

With regard to domestic questions article 16 of the covenant expressly provides that, if in case of any dispute arising between members of the league the matter involved is claimed by one of the parties "and is found by the council to arise out of a matter which by international law is solely within the domestic jurisdiction of that party, the council shall so report, and shall make no recommendation as to its settlement." The United States was by no means the only Government interested in the explicit adoption of this provision, and there is no doubt in the mind of any authoritative student of international law that such matters as immigration, tariffs, and naturalization are incontestably domestic questions with which no international body could deal without express authority to do so. No enumeration of domestic questions was undertaken because to undertake it, even by sample, would have involved the danger of seeming to exclude those not mentioned.

The right of any sovereign State to withdraw had been taken for granted, but no objection was made to making it explicit. Indeed, so soon as the views expressed at the White House conference were laid before the commission it was at once conceded that it was best not to leave the answer to so important a question to inference. No proposal was made to set up any tribunal to pass judgment upon the question whether a withdrawing nation had in fact fulfilled "all its international obligations and all its obligations under the covenant." It was recognized that that question must be left to be resolved by the conscience of the nation proposing to withdraw; and I must say that it did not seem to me worth while to propose that the article be made more explicit, because I knew that the United States would never itself propose to withdraw from the league if its conscience was not entirely clear as to the fulfillment of all its international obligations. It has never failed to fulfill them and never will.

Article 10 is in no respect of doubtful meaning when read in the light of the covenant as a whole. The council of the league can only "advise upon" the means by which the obligations of that great article are to be given effect to. Unless the United States is a party to the policy or action in question, her own affirmative vote in the council is necessary before any advice can be given, for a unanimous vote of the council is required. If she is a party, the trouble is hers anyhow. And the unanimous vote of the council is only advice in any case. Each Government is free to reject it if it pleases. Nothing could have been made more clear to the conference than the right of our Congress under our Constitution to exercise its independent judgment in all matters of peace and war. No attempt was made to question or limit that right. The United States will, indeed, undertake under article 10 to "respect and preserve as against external aggression the territorial integrity and existing political independence of all members of the league," and that engagement constitutes a very grave and solemn moral obligation. But it is a moral, not a legal, obligation, and leaves our Congress absolutely free to put its own interpretation upon it in all cases that call for action. It is binding in conscience only, not in law.

Article 10 seems to me to constitute the very backbone of the whole covenant. Without it the league would be hardly more than an influential debating society.

It has several times been suggested, in public debate and in private conference, that interpretations of the sense in which the United States accepts the engagements of the covenant should be embodied in the instrument of ratification. There can be no reasonable objection to such interpretations accompanying the act of ratification provided they do not form a part of the formal ratification itself. Most of the interpretations which have been suggested to me embody what seems to me the plain meaning of the instrument itself. But if such interpretations should constitute a part of the formal resolution of ratification, long delays would be the inevitable consequence, inasmuch as all the many governments concerned would have to accept, in effect, the language of the Senate as the language of the treaty before ratification would be complete. The assent of the German Assembly at Weimar would have to be obtained, among the rest, and

I must frankly say that I could only with the greatest reluctance approach that assembly for permission to read the treaty as we understand it and as those who framed it quite certainly understood it. If the United States were to qualify the document in any way, moreover, I am confident from what I know of the many conferences and debates which accompanied the formulation of the treaty that our example would immediately be followed in many quarters, in some instances with very serious reservations, and that the meaning and operative force of the treaty would presently be clouded from one end of its clauses to the other.

Pardon me, Mr. Chairman, if I have been entirely unreserved and plain-spoken in speaking of the great matters we all have so much at heart. If excuse is needed, I trust that the critical situation of affairs may serve as my justification. The issues that manifestly hang upon the conclusions of the Senate with regard to peace and upon the time of its action are so grave and so clearly insusceptible of being thrust on one side or postponed that I have felt it necessary in the public interest to make this urgent plea, and to make it as simply and as unreservedly as possible.

Document No. 62   William I. Hull, professor at Swarthmore, The Need for an Amended Covenant (1919)
Source: *The Advocate of Peace*, LXXXI (November, 1919), pp. 321-323.

THE PROPOSED LEAGUE OF NATIONS
Seven Fundamental Amendments
By WILLIAM I. HULL

I. Adoption and Amendment

The Government of the League of Nations proposed at Paris was offered to the world by the victors in the World War. Like the treaties of peace, it was a dictated and not a negotiated document. It was virtually decided upon, moreover, by three men—the spokesmen of Great Britain, France, and the United States. Two other "great powers" and twenty-two small powers, which were allied or associated against Germany in the war, accepted it after it was decided upon. The four central powers and the twenty-five neutral nations were not consulted in its formation; thirteen of the neutral powers were simply given the option of accepting or rejecting it, while the four central powers, Russia, and eleven of the neutral powers were not even invited to "accede" to it.

These uninvited States may be admitted at some indefinite time in the future, provided a two-thirds vote of the assembly admits them, and provided that they are "fully self-governing," that they have given "effective guarantees of their sincere intention to observe their international obligations," and that they shall accept such regulations in regard to their armaments as the League may prescribe.

When the Constitution of the United States was adopted, it was not drafted by the three leading delegates from the three largest States, and the other ten States bidden to "take it or leave it"; nor was it handed down by the victors to the defeated and the neutrals in a recent war. A constitutional convention was held: twelve of the thirteen States were represented in it, and all of them participated in a free and equal discussion and vote upon the various features of the proposed Constitution. This inclusive and mutual procedure was followed in the two Hague conferences.

Reason and experience show that constitutions which are "war-babies," the children of violence and victory, have a stormy and precarious infancy and seldom reach maturity or old age. The constitution of a world league of nations should not be created by a "treaty" among a handful of allies. The third Hague Conference should be summoned and the world's fifty-six States, fully represented and freely participating in its deliberations, should continue to work out together the world constitution.

The Covenant as it stands at present can be amended only by unanimous vote of the nine powers represented in the council, and by a majority of the members of the league whose representatives compose the assembly. Moreover, any State that rejects an amendment must cease to be a member of the league; thus the covenant provides for its own nullification, and an easy means of secession and disunion is planted in the bosom of the league at its birth. The Constitution of the United States can be amended by a three-fourths vote of the States, regardless of their size and "power," and the States which vote against the amendment are not excluded from the Union.

Some means can be found, but only as the result of mutual consideration and concession, in a world assembly to provide for the adoption of future amendments to the world constitution as they are dictated by world needs, and at the same time to prevent a resort to nullification, expulsion, secession, or disunion.

II. National Armaments

The founders of the American Union recognized the plain fact that the Constitution could not be made to work, nor the Union to survive, unless the rival method of settling disputes among the States, namely, a resort to arms, were eliminated. Article I, section 10, of the Constitution accordingly forbids the States, without the consent of the Congress, to keep troops or ships of war in time of peace, or to engage in war, unless actually invaded, or in such imminent danger as will not admit of delay.

William Penn foresaw this necessity of restricting national armaments to national purposes, if international government is ever to become a success; and President Wilson, in his address to the United States Senate, January 22, 1917, declared: "There can be no sense of safety and equality among the nations if great preponderating armaments are henceforth to continue here and there to be built up and maintained. The statesmen of the world must plan for peace, and nations must adjust and accommodate their policy to it as they have planned for war and made ready for pitiless contest and rivalry. *The question of armaments, whether on land or sea, is the most immediately and intensely practical question connected with the future fortunes of nations and of mankind.*" In accordance with this declaration, he stated one of his Fourteen Points as follows:

"IV. Adequate guarantees given and taken that national armaments will be reduced to the lowest point consistent with domestic safety."

Instead of giving and taking adequate guarantees for the reduction and limitation of armaments, the Covenant merely refers this vitally important question to consideration and recommendation by the council, which can act only by unanimous consent. How long it would take this council to solve the problem is a matter of anxious conjecture. In view of the many militaristic tasks imposed by the treaties of peace upon the council, the delay is likely to be long enough to prove fatal to the infant league and its judicial and conciliatory, as distinguished from its military, organs and functions. Meanwhile the nations have taken up again and with renewed vigor their mad competition in the building up of armaments on land and sea and air and in the multitude of measures looking toward military "preparedness."

The treaty with Germany lays down a precise and radical program for the reduction and limitation of armaments *in Germany;* the foremost, essential amendment of the revised Covenant is the application of this program to the rest of the world.

III. Mandatories

Together with the competitive increase in armaments, the prime cause of the recent war, as of numerous other wars,

445

was the rivalry among the "great powers" in the appropriation and exploitation of the "backward" lands and peoples of the earth. President Wilson's demand (in his fourteen points), that these lands and peoples should become the wards of the entire family of nations and should be given a fair degree of self-determination, was practically nullified by the demand of Great Britain, France, Italy, and Japan for the spoils which war has usually assigned to the victors.

The Covenant, it is true, endeavors to provide for international supervision of the mandatory power by laying down certain principles of conduct in its dealings with the backward people assigned to it and by demanding an annual report of those dealings. But, so far from appointing genuinely international commissions to administer these backward lands in the interest of their own people and of the whole world, the League is not even to appoint the mandatory powers. It is simply to recognize the *status quo*. As a consequence, three or four of the great powers of Europe and Asia have been (ever since the armistice) conniving, bargaining, threatening, and even fighting to get their clutches upon as many of these backward lands as possible before the League gets under way. They have attempted to cajole the United States into accepting a mandatory over Armenia, or Constantinople, or some portion of central Africa, hoping thereby to entangle our government in the general scramble and thus secure its sanction for their great game of grab. The United States Government, so far as is known, has thus far eluded the snare; but how difficult it will prove to induce the mandatory powers "to haul down the flag," to release their dead-man's grip upon the lands and peoples thus brought within their "sphere of influence," let Korea, Manchuria, Egypt, Morocco, Fiume, the Philippines, and scores of other protectorates, vassal states and hinterlands answer.

The American Union, to which the claimant States ceded their western lands, affords a fine example, in this respect as in others, to the League of Nations.

IV. The International Assembly

The Constitution of the United States placed a national legislature in the foreground of the Union, and made this legislature representative of both the people and the States. The Covenant of the League of Nations provides that the international legislature shall have not more than three representatives from each State, that each State shall have one vote, and that action shall be taken only by unanimity. Not only is the international assembly thus cribbed, cabined, and confined, but the real power of the League is vested in its executive council; hence President Wilson has correctly characterized the assembly as "a debating society."

To make the world safe for democracy, the world constitution must be amended by the creation of an assembly which shall be genuinely representative of the *peoples* of the world, even if an international "Connecticut Compromise" be found necessary to preserve the equality of States. The world assembly must be given genuine legislative power—within its own sphere, of course—and must be given control over the international executive. Through a *responsible* government only can the peoples really rule.

The Covenant has taken one real step in the direction of basing the machinery of the League upon vital human needs, namely, its provision that all existing international bureaus shall be placed under the direction of the League, and its establishment of an international conference and commission on labor; but it has neglected to provide for the fundamental need of a world production and a world distribution of food, clothing, and shelter, and for the next most important need, namely, that of an education which shall result in the eradication of mutual ignorance, misunderstanding, and hatred among the nations, and thus remove the roots of war. The international assembly must be given the power to legislate for these and other prime necessities of a world which has become a neighborhood and which should become a brotherhood.

V. The International Council

Since the real power of the League is vested in the council, it is doubly unfortunate that this body is constituted as it is. The five "great powers," victors in the recent war—namely, Great Britain, the United States, France, Italy, and Japan—are to be permanently represented in the council, while four other members are to be chosen by the assembly. Thus five States are to have a perpetual majority in the council, while the other fifty-one States in the family of nations are to be in a permanent minority. *If* and *when* both council and assembly shall consent, the 575 millions of Chinese, Russians, and Germans (*i. e.*, one-third of the earth's population) may have permanent representatives in the council; and, under the same condition, the fifty-one "outside" States may increase their four representatives to some indefinite number.

Would the American Union ever have been formed or endured if five of the States had thus monopolized eleven-twelfths of the power of the Union?

One of President Wilson's fundamental principles (September 27, 1918) declared that "there can be no leagues or alliances or special covenants and understandings within the general and common family of the League of Nations."

The so-called League of Nations proposed at Paris is a partial alliance, and, like the Holy Alliance, the Concert of Europe, the Triple Alliance, and the Entente Cordiale, is inimical to a genuine League of Nations. As Prussia dominated the twenty-five other States of the German Empire, so the "Big Five," or, in practice, the "Big Three," or the "Big Two," would endeavor, under the Covenant as it now stands, to dominate the forty-five or fifty other States of the world.

Fortunately, two of the "Big Five" are republics and two others are limited monarchies, only one being still a military autocracy. Hence the nefarious designs of the Holy Alliance and other partial alliances, which reddened Europe's soil with blood and crushed in iron bands the spirit of liberty, appear to be, and may be in reality, remote; but eternal vigilance will continue to be the price of liberty, especially in view of the iniquities incorporated within the treaties of peace, which the League of Nations, or the alliance of the great powers, will be called upon to enforce.

The Covenant, therefore, should be wholly divorced from the peace treaties: its council should be made genuinely international; and the League established by it should at once begin to remove from the treaties the numerous and inevitable causes of future wars which are embedded in their ruthless violation of national self-determination, freedom of trade, and international justice.

VI. The International Court and Non-military Sanctions

The two prime objects of a league of nations are, first, to provide adequate means of international co-operation, and, second, to substitute for war a judicial means of settling international disputes. The substitution of judicial settlement for war is the world's pressing, immediate need. The world has long cherished a vision of an international court; the amended Covenant of the League of Nations must realize that vision.

Isaiah prophesied that court; William Penn planned it; the Hague conferences created it; the dozen years before 1914 saw it settle fifteen disputes among the nations; the appeal to arms in the World War crushed it to earth; like Truth, it must and shall rise again.

The Covenant of Paris, instead of fulfilling one of its most imperative duties by lifting the court again to its feet and giving it larger development and renewed vigor, simply referred it to the council! And with this shelving reference is coupled the shackling proviso that resort to it shall be purely voluntary on the part of the nations, while at the same time the Covenant lays no real curb on the court's fatal rival, preparedness for war.

A genuine, permanent, international court, competent to try all justiciable disputes and supplied with proper means and methods (like those of the arbitration treaties of 1911) of bringing disputant States before it—such was the great achievement which all the world confidently expected of the Paris Covenant and which it callously put aside. To attempt to preserve the peace by peaceful means, without providing adequately for those means, is like playing "Hamlet" with Hamlet left out.

This great error of omission must be speedily corrected, and it must be corrected as the founders of the American Union corrected one of the prime defects of the old Confederation, namely, by providing for the court in the Constitution itself. What would the American Union have been, how long would it have lasted amidst the conflicting interests and contending passions of the States, without the keystone of its arch, the Supreme Court of the United States? Eighty-seven times it has settled disputes between and among the States. Not one of its decisions has been rejected by the States; and at the same time it has not possessed one shred of military force, either to compel defendant States to appear before its tribunal or to enforce its decisions!

Our twentieth century has at its disposal at least seven great sanctions for its judicial process, aside from the military sanction. These have proved entirely adequate for the acceptance of our Supreme Court's decisions, and, when national armaments are duly curbed, they will prove entirely adequate for the enforcement of the international court's decisions.

When our Constitution was adopted there were then, as now, many people who had a blind confidence in the efficiency of military force, and in that alone, to insure obedience to law and to judicial decisions. It was accordingly proposed in the first draft of the Constitution that the national legislature should be given the power and right "to call forth the force of the Union against any member of the Union failing to fulfill its duty under the articles thereof." Two days after this proposal was made, it was expressly rejected for the reasons, offered by Mason and Madison, that punishment

448

could not, in the nature of things, be executed on States collectively: that governments must operate directly on individuals and punish only the guilty: that the use of force is impracticable, unjust, and inefficient when applied to people collectively and not individually: that the use of force against a State would look more like a declaration of war than an infliction of punishment, and would probably be considered by the party attacked as a dissolution of all previous compacts by which it might be bound; and that a Union of the States containing such an ingredient would provide for its own destruction.

The unresisting acceptance by the nations of more than 240 awards of international arbitral tribunals in the entire absence of any military power by which to enforce them; the rich experience of the United States with a government resting upon individuals instead of upon States, and the present attempt to secure the conviction and punishment of those individuals responsible for the recent war are all significant of the logic and justice of restraining or punishing delinquent individuals and of avoiding attempt to constrain or punish whole States comprising the innocent and the guilty alike.

VII. The Monroe Doctrine

The great and constantly growing problem of the Monroe Doctrine should have been settled by the Covenant of the League of Nations. Under the cloak of its name and prestige, imperialism has grown apace in the United States during the past score of years. While we have warned off the Old World powers against acquiring by any means the territory of our Latin American neighbors, we have ourselves taken over the Panama Canal Zone, Porto Rico, the Virgin Isles, Hawaii, Samoa, Guam, and the Philippines, and there is an insistent demand that we should take over the other half of Mexico which we did not take at the close of the Mexican War of 1848. While we have warned off the Old World powers against any intervention in the political affairs of our sister republics, we have ourselves made protectorates of Cuba, Haiti, the Dominican Republic, Panama, Honduras, and Nicaragua.

So great had the evil consequences of our imperialism in the New World become under the shadow of the Monroe Doctrine that President Wilson yielded to the demand that we should give security against our power and pass a self-denying ordinance against ourselves. In his address to the United States Senate, January 22, 1917, he said: "I am proposing, as it were, that the nations should with one accord adopt the doctrine of President Monroe as the doctrine of the world: that no nation should seek to extend its polity over any other nation or people, but that every people should be left free to determine its own polity, its own way of development, unhindered, unthreatened, unafraid, the little along with the great and powerful."

In accord with this proposition, the Covenant as first adopted at Paris included, in Article 10, the following pledge: "The members of the League undertake to respect and preserve as against external aggression the territorial integrity and existing political independence of all members of the League." But when the super-patriotic and ultra-nationalistic Senators at Washington heard of this self-denying ordinance they insisted upon an exemption of the United States from the mutual pledge, and the President yielded to their clamor or to the advice of his own party advisers and inserted in the final draft of the Covenant Article 21. which reads as follows: "Nothing in this Covenant shall be deemed to affect the validity of international engagements, such as treaties of arbitration or regional understandings like the Monroe Doctrine, for securing the maintenance of peace."

Thus, the Covenant leaves the door wide open for the creation within the League itself of "regional understandings," or partial alliances. concerts, ententes, and the like. all of which have been formed, of course, "for securing the maintenance of peace": and it lays no restraining hand upon the economic exploitation and political imperialism which may be anticipated in Mexico and in Central and Northern and South America, under the name of the Monroe Doctrine of the United States, or in Shantung, Manchuria, Siberia, and the Mongolian provinces of China, under the name of the Monroe Doctrine of Japan.

This defect in the Covenant must also be remedied, this prolific cause of tyranny and war within the League be removed. The Constitution of the United States did not evade the great issue of territorial integrity and political self-determination. but embodied in Article IV. section 4, this warning to predatory States within the Union as well as outside: "The United States shall guarantee to every State in this Union a republican form of government, and shall protect each of them against invasion." There is no danger now that Massachusetts may conquer Rhode Island, or that Texas may dictate the government of Oklahoma. There should be as little danger that the United States may conquer Mexico, or that Great Britain may strangle the self-government of Persia.

Document No. 63   The Rev. Anna Garlin Spencer, "Woman and the Peace
Treaty" (1919)
Source: *The Advocate of Peace,* LXXXI (December, 1919), pp. 359-360.

WOMAN AND THE PEACE TREATY

By REV. ANNA GARLIN SPENCER

An Address Given at the National Council of Women of the United States, St. Louis

We call the attention of our readers to the importance of
the *National Council of Women of the United States,* one of
twenty-five such Councils across the world. It represents at
least 10,000,000 women among its thirty national organizations within this country. Its President is Mrs. Philip North
Moore, of St. Louis.—THE EDITORS.

IN VIEW of what the National and International Councils of Women have already declared in respect to
internationalism, we are not here holding a meeting to
discuss a new question of the form of a proposed League
of Nations; we, are here with a history.

The National and International Councils of Women
were born in 1888. The International Council held its
first quinquennial session, in 1893, in Chicago; the second in London in 1899; the third in Paris in 1904; the
fourth in Canada in 1909, and the fifth in Rome in 1914.
We should have had a meeting in 1919, but circumstances
which you all know have postponed it until September,
1920, when it will be held in Christiania, Norway.

At every session of the International Council resolutions in favor of international arrangements for the prevention of war have been passed and great meetings held
in which the principles and methods by which to carry
out these principles of internationalism were presented.
The first committee which the International Council of
Women formed was a Committee on Peace and Arbitration. It was at first thought that the International and
National Councils would meet only for purposes of conference, and that anything that savored of propaganda
should be shut out; but so eagerly insistent were the
women of the world who came together at that great
meeting in Chicago, held in connection with the World's
Columbian Exposition, to express one great desire which
they held in common, that a Committee on Peace and

Arbitration was formed; and before the 1899 meeting was reached every one of the National Councils in membership in the International had already established a Committee on Peace and Arbitration, as such committees were then universally called.

When it was first proposed to have a Committee on Peace and Arbitration, a woman rose in the International Council meeting and said: "Why have a Peace Committee, when the Constitution of the International Council of Women is in itself a peace document?" and quoted the Covenant of that body as follows:

"We; women of all nations, sincerely believing the best good of humanity will be advanced by greater unity of thought, sympathy, and purpose, and that an organized movement of women will best conserve the highest good of the family and of the State, do hereby unite ourselves in a Federation of workers, to further the application of the Golden Rule to society, custom, and law."

I once stood on the platform in a great meeting in New York City beside a man who said: "There is no need for peace societies, for the Christian Church is a Universal Peace Society." Yet, neither the preamble of the Constitution of the International Council of Women nor the profession of faith in a universal fatherhood and a universal brotherhood has kept us from war, and therefore the International Council of Women was right in definitely pledging help to prevent war.

In 1895, when the International Committee was appointed, the fourteen nations then represented in the Councils had each an important member on that International Committee. Such has been the custom ever since, and our own May Wright Sewall served with distinguished ability and full consecration as the representative for many years of our own country on the International Committee, and then as International Committee Chairman of Peace and Arbitration.

In the agenda of the second quinquennial a very important resolution was proposed and it was passed at the meeting, viz:

"*Resolved*, That the International Council of Women do take steps in every country to further advance by every means in its power the movement toward international arbitration."

The National Council of Women of the United States undertook a special work in connection with its own Committee on Peace and Arbitration the first year after the first Hague Conference was called. They set apart a day in May to come together to celebrate the coming of the nations together in a peace conference. This was the simple resolution passed in 1903:

"Whereas the Hague Conference of Peace and Arbitration convened on the 18th of May: Therefore

"*Resolved*, That that day be universally conserved as Peace and Arbitration Day."

The first year over 390 meetings were held; the second year over 700 were held. I myself ceased to keep tab upon these meetings, but there were on one day at least over 3,500 reports that reached us of meetings held on this day to celebrate the establishment of the Peace Conference. You say it was all in vain. It was not all in vain. It sowed the seeds, the harvest of which will be reaped later on.

The resolutions that were passed at these different meetings each year were identical resolutions, and they were sent out from May Wright Sewall's study, and we all had the same resolutions presented at the same time all over the country. Some of us spoke at two or three meetings each day, but they were arranged so that there should be a great unanimity in the celebration. This is the resolution:

"*Resolved*, That American women assembled on May 18, 1903, for the purpose of considering the fruits of war and the fruits of peace, do solemnly pledge themselves to meet annually to hold a demonstration on behalf of peace and arbitration. They commit themselves to adopting as their own that ideal of loving brotherhood which can be realized only by the cessation of international hostilities. They repudiate war as a means of settling things; they send greetings to the women of all other countries who this day may be assembled to attest similar convictions. They rejoice that women throughout the world are beginning to feel their responsibility for human conditions outside of the home as well as in its sacred walls."

During this war, especially since the signing of the armistice, a great movement, said to represent in petitions hundreds of thousands of women, has been established in this country to protest against the horrible violations and outrages of women in the recent war, and asking that measures be taken to personally punish personal offenders. These women thought they were doing a new thing, but the International Council of Women was more than a decade in advance of them. This Council sent to all the governments of the countries represented in its constituent membership a demand that the special cruelties and outrages which women have always suffered in all wars should in some way be provided against, and that personal responsibility for such wrongs should be insisted upon. The present war has proved that the spirit that inflames men's passions in one direction renders it extremely difficult for any law to prevent these special outrages upon women.

In one of the International Councils the question of the Boer War came up, and that was as difficult to reconcile with the Golden Rule as our recent war has been. It is very difficult to make our principles of religion work when we have a condition demanding wholesale slaughter. They somehow do not fit together, and so, at the last quinquennial in Rome, before this war began, there were rumors of war, and there was fear of war, and there was mutual suspicion between the nations, representatives of which were assembled in the Council. Instead of the public meeting which had been planned, only small meetings were held, because those nearer the centers of government in Europe felt it inadvisable to have a great public demonstration for world peace.

That meeting of the women at Rome was in May, 1914, and you know how soon thereafter the storm broke.

In 1907 the first great International Peace Congress was held in this country, in New York. It was the first International Peace Congress in which women were asked to take a special part, and I had the great honor of being chairman of the Woman's Committee, which had given to it one of the great mornings on that great occasion. At that time I asked Mrs. May Wright Sewall to report in print, because I wanted to put into the hands of every one present the record of what women had tried to do in this particular, and the addresses on that occasion were worthy of women and worthy of the theme.

It was a fresh voice that was heard on that occasion, the voice of the reserve forces of humanity becoming articulate.

The Committee on Peace and Arbitration of this National Council has been renamed the Committee on Permanent Peace. It was suggested that it ought to be the Committee on Promotion of Peace, and some of us would like very much if it could be a Committee on League of Nations and Women's Share in its work; but we are here with a tale of attempts and beginnings only.

This meeting has not been asked to put itself on record by any resolution concerning the proposed League of Nations which could be a divisive element in our membership; but I venture the hope that every woman will go from here and study the Covenant and the Treaty. It was my privilege to conduct a number of classes of study last winter in New York, where men and women came together to wrestle with that great document, and it seemed to us that we could see how different interests had played against one another and how difficult it had been to get an agreement. There are things in the Treaty that, to my mind, are deplorable, and have clouded what might and should have come to us for decision as to the League itself. We have all wondered how any newborn League could carry some of the heavy burdens which would be placed upon it by the provisions of the Treaty.

I wish to say here I hope that every woman in this Council will disassociate herself from the type of opposition which the League is meeting in many quarters in our country. It is all right, if you believe so, to say that the Covenant is not good enough; but I beg you not to believe that it is too good, and not to take the ground of those who say that because it binds us in fellowship with all the nations of the world therefore we will not have it.

My complaint of it is that the Treaty that accompanies the Covenant is not good enough; but I see no other way by which to begin to clarify and rectify the mistakes that have been made in the first flush of victory, and the first recoil from the dangers and difficulties of war, except to begin to try to live together. I once knew a man who was very slow. He had a very quick wife, and, of course, it is very difficult for a lightning express to accommodate itself to a freight train, so often there would be a great deal of, I will not say friction, but there would be some excited talk when the wife would try to get him to move faster. Once he said: "Why, don't be impatient; I am beginning to get ready to commence to go." It looks to me as if, at worst, the League of Nations was beginning to get ready to commence to go, and I think that through the proverbial quickness, I would not say impatience, of women we may make it go a little faster. At any rate, we must work with all our might, must we not, for some effective organization—the world to substitute law for war and to build good-will into the fabric of the common life.

Document No. 64 Scott Nearing, Socialist Economist, Criticizes the League of Nations (1919)
Source: Leaflet in the Swarthmore College Peace Collection, Swarthmore, Pa.

The League of Nations
AS SEEN BY AN ECONOMIST
By Scott Nearing

PEACE on earth will not be established through the World League plan, read by President Wilson to the Peace Conference. The document is a weak compromise that ignores the vital factors underlying international relations.

The draft of the League Constitution is a purely political document. It ignores economic factors entirely. The great capitalist nations of the world that are asked to endorse the plan are interested primarily in markets, shipping and investments. The document contains no reference to any of these subjects, and is, therefore, fundamentally incomplete. **Commercial and financial rivalries will breed wars in the future as they have bred them in the past.** This fact has been acknowledged by President Wilson; it has been insisted upon by the Navy League, and preached for years by leading economists all over the world yet the League Constitution does not cover economic questions. A political document of this character might have had some reason for existence in 1815. Today, it is archaism.

The plan is faulty in other important respects. First, it is undemocratic. Treaties are not to be published till after they are made— the processes of diplomacy are still secret. There is no provision for the democratic selection of the members of the delegate body. Under the Constitution as drawn, all of them may be appointed by the Governments. The people may have no voice in choosing them. Again, out of the nine votes of the Executive Council, five are to belong permanently to the United States, France, Italy, Great Britain and Japan. In short, the decisions of the League may all be reached by hand-picked diplomats of the old school from the "big five" allied nations.

The plan is arbitrary. It contains no provision for and no suggestion of self-determination. Ireland, India, the Philippines and China will be no freer after the plan is adopted than before.

The plan is imperialistic. The "big five" are to take the German Colonies in addition to their present possessions. The allied empires will still be empires.

The plan is weak. It takes no stand on the question of armaments, other than to state that they must be "fair" and "reasonable." Evidently, the members of the "big five" are not yet ready to "bury the hatchet."

The plan is ineffective. No adequate means are provided for the enforcement of the League's decisions. The organization contemplated is weaker than that of the Thirteen Colonies under the Articles of Confederation.

The League plan is political treaty of the old variety, providing for a continuation of the alliance among the victorious Allies. This alliance will inevitably force a defensive alliance of Russia, Germany and the other socialist countries of Europe, so that the world will be arrayed in two camps—capitalist nations against socialist nations. It is this class conflict alone that will hold the League together. Lacking such a compelling motive, the plan will hold until commercial and financial rivalries among the members of the League grow bitter and sharp. Then, like thousands of similar treaties, this one will go into the discard while the world busies itself with the next great war.

—*From "The World Tomorrow" March, 1919.*

Document No. 65   The Rev. Norman Thomas, editor of the magazine of the
Fellowship of Reconciliation, urges Amnesty for political prisoners (1919)
Source: Leaflet in the Swarthmore College Peace Collection, Swarthmore,
Pa.

AMNESTY!

By NORMAN THOMAS
Editor "The World To-morrow"

There are in the United States some hundreds of Political Prisoners under the Federal laws alone; no one knows how many more there are under
the various State laws. By Political Prisoners we mean men and women whose
offense primarily involves not a crime against the common law but their
loyalty to or expression of conscientious convictions. In the United States
this term includes somewhere between 100 and 200 conscientious objectors
still in jail, as well as the men and women convicted under the Espionage
Law, under which law not one German spy, so far as can be learned, was
ever sentenced.

In practice, the Espionage Law was a weapon of attack not only against
the Socialist Party and the I. W. W., which were opposed to the war, but
also against the Non-Partisan League which supported it. It was a weapon
in the struggle against radicals rather than against Germans. That its victims
still remain in jail and that the law itself is still on the statute books proves
this fact. America, unlike France, Italy and England, was never in immediate
or imminent danger from the external foe or internal heretic. Yet to-day
neither England, nor France, nor Italy has in her jails any considerable number of these prisoners of conscience. That shame is reserved for the United
States. Not only are these men and women denied their liberties, but they
are confined with criminals in jails utterly unfit for the imprisonment of the
worst offenders against society. Eugene V. Debs was deliberately transferred
from the comparatively easy routine of life in a West Virginia penitentiary
to the iron discipline of Atlanta. This, with the full knowledge of the fact
that he is a man well on in years, not robust in health, who finds the heat of
the Atlanta climate peculiarly hard to bear. His offense was simply this, that
during the war he declared that it was an economic struggle, which the President of the United States now says ought to be a matter of common knowledge to every child. Supposing Mr. Debs was unwise in saying what he did
when he did, is that any reason, simply from the standpoint of expediency,
why he should be confined now that the war is won? What is true of one
conspicuous man is true in a greater or less degree of many inconspicuous
folk who have shared the same fate. That fate in case after case has included
positive torture. This is particularly true, for instance, of those conscientious
objectors who have been confined in solitary cells under conditions deliberately
intended to break men. One such prisoner has spent 107 days in solitary out
of little more than a year. Others have been for as much as eleven con-
secutive weeks in solitary, half the time on a diet of bread and water.

The continuance of these conditions is a prime cause of violent unrest.
It makes mock of our professions not only of democracy, but of humanity.
It proves that as a people we are afraid of thought; that we who were willing
to fight a great war in behalf of the word "democracy" will not tolerate that
dissent of opinion and open discussion of problems upon which all true democracy rests. These political Prisoners are for the most part heroes and martyrs
in the struggle for industrial freedom. It is, therefore, peculiarly the duty of
Organized Labor to secure a General Amnesty. Labor's attitude in this matter is an acid test of its own wisdom and idealism. But not only Organized
Labor but all loyal Americans are challenged by the very existence of a class
of Political Prisoners.

Heretics, whether religious, scientific, political or economic are often obnoxious to a complacent majority. Over and over again the heretic has been wrong. Yet all progress begins with a heretical minority. In confining her political heretics in jail, America is denying her own hope of peaceful progress. Immediate Amnesty is not a matter of mercy but of right, a partial atonement for a great wrong. We demand it not merely or chiefly in justice to some of the bravest of our fellow citizens, but for the sake of the life and honor of the American Democracy. While these Political Prisoners are confined in jails, penitentiaries, or internment camps, we are not free.

Write to your Congressman and Senator demanding that he use his influence to obtain AMNESTY for POLITICAL PRISONERS. Attend AMNESTY demonstrations and spread the cry "AMNESTY" among your friends and fellow-workers. Have them do likewise.

Document No. 66 Report on the Zurich Congress of the Women's International League for Peace and Freedom (1919)
Source: The Women's International League for Peace and Freedom, *Towards Peace and Freedom* (August, 1919), pp. 6-19, a pamphlet in the Swarthmore College Peace Collection, Swarthmore, Pa.

The Congress in Session

THE Congress which met at Zürich on May 12th, 1919, was the first international meeting of organized women which has ever come together to discuss a treaty or to make representations to a Conference of the Powers on the subject of peace. They met to carry out a resolution passed by the Women's International Congress at The Hague in April, 1915, by which it was decided that an international meeting of women for the purpose of presenting practical proposals should be held at the same place and at the same time as the Conference which framed the terms of the Peace settlement after the war.

The first Women's Conference had met to consider what could be done internationally even during the war for the establishment of permanent peace in the future, the repressing of hatred and revenge, and the promotion of mutual understanding between the nations. It was called by a group of Dutch women, and delegations from twelve countries succeeded, under conditions of the greatest difficulty, in arriving at The Hague. From Great Britain only two were present, the rest having been prevented from sailing at the last moment by the closing of the North Sea. The resolutions passed at that Conference formed the basis of the policy of the Women's International League for Permanent Peace. Briefly stated, the policy stood for the principles of a just peace, for the settling of international disputes by other means than war, and the claim that women should have a voice in the affairs of the nations.

Four years separated the first Congress from the Conference at Zürich. During the interval women in the neutral countries were prominent in pressing for a Conference of neutral powers in the hope of hastening peace by mediation, but the attempt was unsuccessful. When it was decided that the Conference of the Powers to frame the peace was to meet at Paris, it was obviously impossible under existing conditions to hold an international Congress there at the same time. The German women, however, urged the holding of an allied Conference of women, even should they themselves be excluded. After months of delay and uncertainty it was found possible to hold an International Conference and at the shortest possible notice it was decided that it should meet in Zürich.

To the last moment it was uncertain as to how many of the National Sections would be represented. Telegrams to the officers poured in during the days preceding the Congress saying that delegates would be prevented from attending. Germany was in revolution, Hungary was in revolution. The French delegation was prevented from travelling by the action of the Government, though permission was given at the last moment. The Australian delegation sailed, but the ship did not stop at Naples, and they were obliged to come *via* London. From Russia there was no news at all. Though there were delays in Great Britain in obtaining passports, the obstructions attending the first Congress were absent. The whole atmosphere surrounding the idea of a Women's Congress had changed. This was due partly to the growth of pacifist ideals, partly to the changed outlook with regard to women which the war had brought, and partly, no doubt, to the fact of their political emancipation. The Jingo press was silent, after hysterical outbursts for over four years, and ridicule gave way to genuine interest as to the tone and policy which women were likely to adopt.

By a remarkable coincidence the delegates met at Zürich on the very day on which the terms of the Peace Treaty were published in Paris.

In most countries the difficulties had been overcome by dint of sheer determination. Those who were not expected appeared, the delegates finally numbering 147 in all, and including women well known in all branches of life—political, literary, educational, and social.

"THE BEST FORMULATIONS"

The resolutions passed at The Hague, though regarded in many quarters as unrealizable at the time, had been received with interest and appreciation by the statesmen of the belligerent and neutral countries and were strikingly similar to the Fourteen Points subsequently enumerated by President Wilson.

"The best formulations I have so far seen," was President Wilson's comment, as reported by Miss Addams at one of the opening meetings of the Congress. It was the elaboration of these "formulations," their application to feminist and educational programmes, and, above all, to the immediate question of the Peace Settlement, the Blockade, and the League of Nations, that occupied the more important sessions of the Congress.

On the resolution on the Peace Terms there was little

461

difference of opinion and criticism was unrelenting. This was a foregone conclusion for the gloom of the settlement in the act of being announced from Paris hung like a shadow over the whole Congress.

The breach of faith by the Allies in tearing up. President Wilson's Fourteen Points; the proposals for one-sided disarmament; for bartering about millions of Germans "like chattels and pawns in a game"; the tacit sanction of the secret treaties, the crushing financial and economic proposals; with such terms linked to the Covenant Mrs. Snowden declared that the League of Nations would be "like a boat with a hole in it." There could be no security without a real basis of International agreement. The resolution was passed with little discussion, an additional proposal being made that meetings of protest should be organized in the various countries on the return of the delegates.

Next to the Peace Terms the question of the blockade dominated the whole Congress. In moving the resolution on this subject Mrs. Pethick Lawrence described the state of Europe—maddened by hunger and misery—worse than anything which had ever occurred in the world's history since the Plague, and maintained that the raising of the blockade was insufficient, that the Nations must pool their resources and jointly carry out the provisioning of the peoples, developing international organization for the saving of life, instead of destroying it. Both these resolutions were forwarded to the representatives of the Powers at Paris.

In reply to the resolution on the blockade, President Wilson wired to Miss Addams, "Your message appeals both to my head and to my heart, and I hope most sincerely that means may be found, though the present outlook is extremely unpromising because of infinite difficulties." During the discussion on both these subjects great restraint was shown by the delegates from the Central Empires. They refrained from voting on the Peace Terms, they spoke very little of their sufferings from hunger; but at the non-official gatherings, speech after speech, through mere statement of fact, emphasized the state of starvation and misery into which the blockade had plunged large tracts of Europe.

THE LEAGUE OF NATIONS

The discussions on the League of Nations continued throughout the week's Session, the proposals on this subject falling mainly under two headings : amendments for incorporation in the treaty of peace, and recommendations which might form a programme for future propaganda. Three committees worked on the subject and each presented a draft resolution to the Congress. The warmest supporters of the Covenant were found amongst the American delegation : though conscious of its imperfections, they maintained that the Covenant " was a vehicle of Life " and that it represented a real effort of statesmanship; they supported it as embodying principles similar to those passed at The Hague in 1915, urged that there was no satisfactory alternative to oppose to it, and that without this form of co-operation progress would be stultified.

The opponents of the Paris Covenant, including delegates from the U.S.A. and some from Great Britain, while welcoming the fact that the idea of a League of Nations was so generally accepted, declared that in its present form it was a league of conquerors against the conquered, that it maintained the old discredited system of the Balance of Power, excluded some nations from membership, and would not save the world from future wars. They therefore regarded it as useless as an instrument of peace.

Between these two sections was another which took the medium line expressed in French by one of the delegates, " L'Enfant est né, la grande chose c'est de ne pas le tuer." The British delegation appointed a group which prepared a medium draft embodying many of the amendments proposed in an able pamphlet on the League of Nations by Mrs. Swanwick. The proposals from the various committees were discussed in detail, and ultimately referred to a new Committee which made the final draft. This laid down certain conditions, which the Congress declared it was essential to incorporate in the Covenant if the League were to be of any value as an instrument of peace. The following were included : membership to be open to any State desiring to join and willing to perform the duties of membership : immediate reduction of armaments ; adherence to the principle of self-determination in matters of nationality and territorial adjustment; free access to raw materials for all nations on equal terms and provision for easier amendment of the constitution of the League of Nations. Another resolution welcomed the provision in the Covenant for the admission of women to all positions in connexion with the League. The differences of opinion on the League of Nations were more acute than on any other subject, and in the debates certain marked characteristics became apparent.

In other Conferences it has been usual to regard the Anglo-Saxons as the advance guard on political questions. In the Zürich Conference there was a strong element which repudiated the idea of progressing step by step and coupled average opinion in Great Britain and America with the traditions of the old régime which they believed to be passing away.

PACIFISTS AND REVOLUTION

The discussion on the attitude of pacifists to revolutionary movements brought this out still more clearly. While accepting special responsibility to counsel against violence the Congress declared its belief that there was a fundamentally just demand underlying most of the revolutionary movements and its sympathy with the workers who were everywhere seeking to make an end of exploitation and to claim their world. The attitude of the women from the revolutionary countries, in face of the huge changes impending in the world, was remarkable. Many of them had been through terrible experiences unknown to the rest of Europe. Loathing militarism, they welcomed the promise of the coming democracy, and appeared in some cases to have unbounded faith in the dawn of the new era. In the Central Empires progress had been sudden and complete; at one bound they had gained equal opportunity for men and women alike, and some of the highest posts in the Government had been thrown open and actually occupied by women.

Other delegates took a less optimistic view, and their sufferings were expressed in the words of an Austrian woman—"it is not only our countries which are desolated, but our souls." The morals of their cities under political pressure and the miseries of famine were "the morals of of a sinking ship." One and all agreed that progress and freedom must be achieved without violence and the reports from the German delegates of their efforts to avoid bloodshed were amongst the most interesting records of the Congress.

Further resolutions dealt with the right of Ireland to self-determination, with protection for Jews and national minorities, with political amnesty, with the right of asylum, and with Conscientious Objectors. The Feminist Charter and the educational programme appear on pp. 18 and 19. A Labour Charter was also presented, and referred to the National Sections for study.

Not a moment was wasted in discussion on the responsibility for the war. Throughout the proceedings the voting showed little concern with national feeling and opinion cut right across the National Sections.

It was the German women who denounced the invasion of Belgium, the deportations, and the Brest Litovsk Treaty. It was the women from the Allied countries who denounced the blockade and the injustices of the Peace Treaty. The time for discussion on subjects covering so wide an area was entirely inadequate yet all agreed that the Congress was fully successful; the basis of agreement and harmony on essential matters of feeling and outlook was so complete that everyone felt that a load of oppression had been lifted and that the foundation of friendship and loyalty had emerged from the furnace clearer and stronger than ever before.

The most moving incident during the whole Congress occurred when Mlle Mélin, one of the French delegates, arrived at the last moment from Carignan. Standing on the platform while business was suspended, she told with marvellous power of her own experience in the Ardennes, how her home had been devastated, how she had seen youths driven under the machine-guns and slaughtered. With passionate emotion she denounced war as the common enemy of women and, calling on all to use every effort to annihilate it and to renounce all desire for vengeance and a peace of conquest, she appealed to "Les forces de demain." "I greet you, forces of the future, not men nor women anywhere, not nationalities. War alone is our enemy." In a moment Gustava Heymann rose, and with clasped hands the two women stood together pledging themselves, with every delegate in the Congress, to live and work for international fellowship.

"The whole Congress," said an Italian pressman, "gave me an impression of youth and freshness." There was an atmosphere of relief and buoyancy in this experience of re-union and of the first attempt to reconstruct on truer and better lines. The very phraseology of war seemed ridiculous and to belong to another world. The younger generation, full of hope and energy, was already out on the open road speaking a new language and the older women, loved, trusted, and experienced in the life-long struggle for freedom, were ready to lead once more, and, where necessary, to follow : to forge, as Miss Ashton said, "the first links in the golden chain that would some day bind the world."

Evening Meetings

AT the public meetings held in the evenings at the University and the St. Peter's Kirche the full sympathy and warm interest of the townspeople were evident. Both buildings were crowded out. The younger element from the University and the town was conspicuous and the hope and determination of the young men and women students to work out their own international ideals was admirably put by Fräulein Bäer, from Germany.

Miss JANE ADDAMS, in her opening speech, sketched the evolution of ideas of law and order in social life through the conditions imposed on men's predatory instincts by the mere necessity of providing food for their children. Through women and the care of children had come the curbing of the instinct which in primitive races caused men to rove and destroy. Just as the family had tended to concentrate his energies on one spot and on the more human responsibilities of fatherhood, so perhaps now out of the horrors of war and destruction would emerge again, through women and the primitive cry for food, a restraining influence which might again seek to create a home and rebuild the suffering nations on the lines of a higher social and moral evolution. The world had been brought to its knees by hunger and in this women must see their opportunity for developing their powers of co-operation in international life.

The child was the symbol of that need and the world would be led through the child to realize at last that one human life was as sacred as another. Apparently, they had not yet learned to come together on that higher plane. They had not yet learned that the human and spiritual needs of the race were so blended that they could not be separated.

Some had feared that the spiritual bonds themselves might break under the strain, but if this was not to be they must turn the material needs of the world to the highest purpose; they must remember that the distribution of food itself was a holy thing and that when women, as sisters, pleaded for the raising of the blockade they were pleading for the restoration of the normal balance of the world. Women had still to be taught that the conditions of the world were not altogether creditable to men and especially must they remember this at a time when the humanitarian needs appealed to them so overwhelmingly, lest they might be tempted to leave the field of politics in order to attend to material needs only.

In reviewing their efforts over the last four years, the members of the Women's International League must never forget what they have striven for; the failure to meet and act must not discourage them: and, though their efforts for a neutral conference had been in vain, the recommendations made at The Hague had been widely taken up. They might fail and fail again, but they must still go on learning to use the moral energy which they knew was a vital thing. For that purpose they had come together and met in genuine friendship. If they failed once more they must come together again to tell of their failures; but they knew that though institutions might perish their principles were bound to triumph, and in that cause they were ready in this crisis to go forth once more to the great task.

The need for instant action was emphasized in the speeches which followed.

Frau BEER ANGERER (Vienna), in a speech of great restraint, expressed the hope that a mere statement of the facts of misery, disease, and death, as they presented themselves in Vienna, might produce some effect where the cry of millions had failed. Giving terrible details of suffering, she described Vienna as a " city of death," with a constantly falling supply of milk, the life of the mothers themselves failing. Children between five and six years old were often unable to walk. What was the use, she asked in conclusion, of prolonging negotiations and discussions on the things of the past, when fresh things were being inflicted daily on the young and the coming generation ?

Frau KULKE, of Vienna, described the morals of the cities, where starvation was causing mortality and disease, as " the morals of a sinking ship." Not only were the countries desolated, but the souls of the nations. Perhaps those present could not realize the impression which a well ordered city such as Zürich made on the inhabitants of cities of their own country—devastated, desolated, starving and racked with misery and disease. They might well have lost faith when they thought of the policy of moral and political degradation which had been carried out ; but there, at the Conference of Women, it was possible to revive it, and believe even in a League of Mankind ultimately founded on love. But the men who were now directing the affairs of the world were not turning their hand to this task and women from all countries and all nations must undertake it themselves.

Mrs. SNOWDEN said she was glad to know that the last speaker realized that it was not by the will of one single woman in England or Scotland or Wales that this evil thing, the blockade, had been inflicted upon the children of Austria. Mothers must go down on their spiritual knees to the mothers of Austria when they considered what these children were called upon to suffer. If men and women could only settle their affairs over the dead bodies of children, then it was time for all women to get together and confer. To-night they were discussing the League of Nations. She had never been an enthusiastic supporter of a paper league. It could never reflect the thoughts of the mass of people in the world. The present League of Nations was not a perfect scheme ; it was at best only half a league ; it was like a boat with a hole in it. It included only a few nations, whereas it should include all who wished to be included. Possibly the nations might come in later, but would they ? Not if the treaty were bad, and in that case the League of Nations would be condemned as heartily as the Treaty of Peace itself, and the idea for which they went to war would be made contemptible.

They had not fought to establish protectorates in Egypt and to steal German colonies, or to steal the German fleet. She was willing to admit all that critics might say of Germany. She would baffle militarism and oppose it wherever it existed and with all the power she had. But because other countries had done wrong it was no reason why we should not do right. What were we doing with the principle of self-determination in East Prussia, Silesia, Poland, and the Saar Basin ? Every man and woman who thought quite agreed with her when she condemned this policy of the Peace Treaty. The economic conditions were an insult to the world. The League of Nations would continue to be a League of conquerers against conquered, and create Alsace-Lorraines all over Europe. It would put civilization back if the Entente persisted in this. Peace could not be established on injustice.

Dr. ANITA AUGSBURG urged that women should undertake constructive work. The vote would help towards attaining permanent peace, but it would be useless if they did not obtain influence in other directions in the life of the State. She recommended that they should concentrate their energies on restoring the devastated areas. Women must seek to make their spirit penetrate everywhere and obtain representation in all Government bodies replacing personal ambitions by a consciousness of wider solidarity.

Mrs. TERRELL (America) spoke for the coloured races, for the black women whose husbands, she said, were fighting in the war for liberty—a liberty they themselves did not possess, for in the State to which she belonged 400,000 black men had been conscripted. She appealed especially to mothers to interest their children in the fate of the black children abroad.

Miss ASHTON described the difficulties which women had laboured under in Great Britain. Since the last Congress at The Hague the tactics of the Government had been to keep the people separate. The women had struggled to unite and have intercourse, but for them this had been particularly difficult, as they were not organized. Now at last they had met, and it was the business of the Women's International League to make co-operation and friendship between the women of all nations increasingly possible. Each nation must wish only to produce the finest race possible and for the raising of the whole human race the international spirit was one of the greatest forces. If women could make a chain round the world it would be impossible to separate them. For that union they must work and for the recognition of the equality of every unit of humanity, both industrial and national. The nearer they came to that idea the nearer would they be to solving the great difficulties which lay in the problems before them.

At the last of the evening meetings on May 16, in the St. Peter's Kirche, Mrs. Swanwick (President of the British Section of the Women's International League) reviewed the work since its inauguration at The Hague in 1915. In Great Britain the same groups of women had been attracted as in many other countries—suffragists, peace workers and social workers. They had come to perceive that the foundation of their needs and desires were so as to ensure the attendance of women as voting delegates from every country. It was further decided that, should these proposals not be adopted, the Women's International League for Peace and Freedom should continue to bring them before the League of Nations till they are formally included in its policy. The League of Nations was also to be urged to set up a Commission of an equal number of men and women to investigate the question of marriages between persons of different nationality.

The Feminist programme also emphasized the importance of giving due weight to the value of women's work in the home in connexion with questions of land laws, taxes, and tariffs. The Congress further recommended to the consideration of its national sections the whole question of population, considering it was not yet ripe for decision, but laying it down that full information, scientific and other, should be made available on the subject.

Question of Education

ONE of the most interesting proposals for the future scope of the W.I.L.P.F. was embodied in the following Resolution:—

INTERNATIONAL COUNCIL FOR EDUCATION.

Believing that the basis for peace between nations is a fuller and wider education of the peoples this Council resolves that a permanent International Council for Education be instituted for the purpose of promoting the idea of world organization and international ethics and citizenship. The Congress asks its Officers to appoint an International Committee which shall create the preparatory machinery of the Council, secure the financial support, and draw up a programme indicating the general principle upon which the work of the Council shall be based.

No detailed educational programme was adopted, but the following draft was recommended to the National Sections for study:—

The events of the last four years have proved that our civilization has completely failed. Our lives have been dominated by a purely materialistic philosophy, by a policy of sheer force and violence.

The International Congress for Permanent Peace seeks to establish a basis for a new human civilization. Properly to accomplish this, we must begin with the education of the peoples. Respect for human life, the sacred character of the individual personality, must become fundamental in our thinking. Only men and women of high moral and intellectual standing can be trusted with so sacred a task. The Congress recommends the following means toward this end :—

(a) The development of an international spirit. Under this head comes the exclusion from school books, &c., of anything which tends to hinder international understanding, to injure national pride, or to arouse hate and scorn for foreign peoples. The history of civilization should be fundamental to all instruction ; the young should be made familiar with the evolution of peoples and with lives of the great men of all times. Instruction in civics should develop a world consciousness and give an introduction to the duties of world-citizenship.

The introduction of national literature at the same time with a first acquaintance with the masterpieces of other countries.

The preparation and distribution of books exciting to hate should be discouraged. International commissions to examine such books are proposed.

Instruction in foreign languages should be supplemented by the introduction of an auxiliary world-language. Especially attention should be paid to comparative studies of the psychology of peoples. The establishment of a free International University and of an International Normal School is desirable.

The existing exchange of professorships and exchange of students should be extended. A period of residence in foreign countries should so far as practicable be required as part of the preparation for teaching. Higher schools for women should train the woman as a world-citizen for her responsible task as mother of humanity.

There should be established in all countries :

Numerous clubs, unions, and summer courses for foreigners, without distinction of nationality ; circulating libraries for foreign books ; internationally organized associations of professors and students ; exchange lectures on the experience of various countries in special fields might become the basis of a permanent institute for international information.

(b) Development of physical culture, not in the form of military drill, but as a method of developing the strength and efficiency of the human race.

Resolutions presented to the Peace Conference in Paris

I. ON FAMINE AND BLOCKADE

THIS International Congress of Women regards the famine, pestilence, and unemployment, extending throughout great tracts of Central and Eastern Europe and into Asia, as a disgrace to civilization.

It therefore urges the Governments of all the Powers assembled at the Peace Conference immediately to develop the inter-allied organizations formed for purposes of war into an international organization for purposes of peace, so that the resources of the world—food, raw materials, finance, transport—shall be made available for the relief of the people of all countries from famine and pestilence.

To this end it urges that immediate action be taken—

(1) To raise the blockade, and

(2) If there is insufficiency of food or transport :

(a) To prohibit the use of transport from one country to another for the conveyance of luxuries until the necessaries of life are supplied to all peoples.

(b) To ration the people of every country so that the starving may be fed.

The Congress believes that only immediate international action on these lines can save humanity, and bring about the permanent reconciliation and union of the peoples.

II. ON THE TREATY OF PEACE

1. Peace Terms

This International Congress of Women expresses its deep regret that the terms of peace proposed at Versailles should so seriously violate the principles upon which alone a just and lasting peace can be secured, and which the democracies of the world had come to accept.

By guaranteeing the fruits of the secret treaties to the conquerors, the terms of peace tacitly sanction secret diplomacy, deny the principles of self-determination, recognize the right of the victors to the spoils of war, and create all over Europe discords and animosities, which can only lead to future wars.

By the demand for the disarmament of one set of belligerents only, the principle of justice is violated, and the rule of force is continued.

By the financial and economic proposals a hundred million people of this generation in the heart of Europe are condemned to poverty, disease, and despair, which must result in the spread of hatred and anarchy within each nation.

With a deep sense of responsibility, this Congress strongly urges the Allied and Associated Governments to accept such amendments of the Terms as shall bring the Peace into harmony with those principles first enumerated by President Wilson upon the faithful carrying out of which the honour of the Allied peoples depend.

2. League of Nations

This Congress holds, that the peaceful progress of the world can only be assured when the common interests of humanity are recognized in the establishment of a League of Nations, which shall represent the will of the people and promote international co-operation. It therefore records its satisfaction that the idea of a League of Nations, regarded as impracticable by the majority of people at the time of the Congress of Women at the Hague in 1915, has become so widely accepted; that, incorporated in the armistice terms of November 11, 1918, it was agreed to, both by the Allied and Associated Powers, and by Germany. But the Congress regrets that the Covenant of the League, now submitted by the Allied and Associated Powers, in many respects does not accord with the Fourteen Points laid down as the basis for the present negotiations, contains certain provisions that will stultify its growth, and omits others which are essential to world peace.

Essential Conditions omitted from the Covenant.

The Congress declares, that to be a real instrument of peace capable of development, rather than one which sets up conditions tending to produce war, the League of Nations should embody certain fundamental principles, now omitted from the Covenant.

In order to avoid future wars, it urges the immediate adoption of these following essential conditions :—

(a) Membership freely open, from the time of the establishment of the League to any State desiring to join and willing to perform the duties of membership.

(b) The number of Nations to be included in the executive body to be not less than eleven.

(c) Immediate reduction of armaments on the same terms for all member States.

(d) Abolition of conscription in all States joining the League.

(e) Adherence to the principle of self-determination in

471

territorial adjustments and matters of nationality, whether sanctioned by the secret treaties, by the treaty embodying the Covenant of the League of Nations, or by later treaties.

(f) The right of direct presentation to the League by Nationalities and Dependencies within any government of their desires as to self-government.

(g) Free access to raw materials for all nations on equal terms.

(h) Abrogation of regional understandings, like the " Monroe Doctrine " and " other international engagements," in so far as inconsistent with the Covenant of the League.

(i) Provision for easier amendment of the Constitution.

ENDORSEMENT OF CERTAIN PRINCIPLES NOW IN THE COVENANT.

The Congress welcomes the recognition in the Covenant of certain principles which it has held since its foundation, but believes that they cannot be put into practice unless the above essential conditions are also included.

These principles are :—

(a) Establishment of machinery for arbitration and conciliation.

(b) Abolition of secret treaties.

(c) Provision for the revision of treaties which have become inapplicable, and for changing certain international conditions, which, if continued, may endanger the peace of the world.

(d) Recognition of the necessity for the reduction of armaments, and for publicity concerning their manufacture.

(e) Abrogation of certain obligations inconsistent with the Covenant.

(f) Promotion of " Freedom of Transit," and of equal trading opportunities for all members of the League.

(g) Organization by the League of international resources to combat disease, and to improve health.

ADDITIONAL PRINCIPLES TO STRENGTHEN THE LEAGUE.

This Congress considers that the League will be greatly strengthened as an instrument of peace when the nations composing it agree to the adoption, in addition to the essential principles enumerated above, of the following principles not now found in the Covenant :—

(a) Total disarmament (land, sea, air).

(b) Enforcement of the decisions of the League by other means than military pressure or food blockade.

(c) Registration and review of all existing treaties and international engagements within a specified time, and the abrogation of such as are not thus registered.

(d) National ratification of treaties only by an elected legislative body.

(e) Executive power of the League to be democratically elected.

(f) Universal free trade.

(g) Adoption of a plan of world economy for the production and distribution of the necessities of life at the smallest cost.

(h) Abolition of the protection of the investments of the capitalists of one country in the resources of another.

(i) Guaranteeing the representation and protection of the civil and political rights of minorities within each nation, including those of language, religion, and education.

(j) The requirement that all backward races under the tutelage of more advanced nations should be put under the guardianship of the League, and that the Mandatory Powers be required to promote the development and power of self-government of their wards.

(k) Complete freedom of communication and travel.

(l) Abolition of child labour.

(m) Agreement between the nations in the League to the abolition of governmental censorship.

(n) Establishment of full equal suffrage and the full equality of women with men politically, socially, and economically.

WOMEN'S POSITION IN A LEAGUE OF NATIONS.

The Congress welcomes the international recognition of women in the proposals put forward by the Allied and Associated Powers, providing in their draft for a Covenant of a League of Nations for the admission of women to all positions " in connexion with the League," this making them eligible for the Assembly, the Executive Council, and the Commissions therein proposed, and urges that this be explicitly stated in the Covenant.

(3) Women's Charter

That the Peace Conference be urged to insert in the Peace Treaty the following Women's Charter :—

The Contracting Parties recognize that the status of women—social, political, and economic—is of supreme international importance.

They hold that the natural relation between men and women is that of interdependence and co-operation, and that it is injurious to the community to restrict women to a position of dependence, to discourage their education or development, or to limit their opportunities.

They hold that the recognition of women's service to the world not only as wage-earners but as mothers and home-makers, is an essential factor in the building up of the world's peace.

They recognize that differences in social development and tradition make strict uniformity with respect to the status of the women difficult of immediate attainment. But, holding as they do, that social progress is dependent upon the status of women in the community, they think that there are certain principles which all communities should endeavour to apply.

Among these principles the following seem to the Contracting Parties to be of special and urgent importance :—

(a) That suffrage should be granted to women, and their equal status with men upon legislative and administrative bodies, both national and international, recognized ;

(b) That women, equally with men, should have the protection of the law against slavery, such as still exists in some parts of Eastern Europe, Asia, and Africa ;

(c) That on marriage a woman should have full personal and civil rights, including the right to the use and disposal of her own earnings and property, and should not be under the tutelage of her husband ;

(d) That the mother should have the same right of guardianship of her children as the father ;

(e) That a married woman should have the same right to retain or change her nationality as a man ;

(*f*) That all opportunities for education should be open to both sexes ;

(*g*) That women should have the same opportunity for training and for entering industries and professions as men ;

(*h*) That women should receive the same pay as men for the same work ;

(*i*) That the traffic in women should be suppressed, the regulation of vice abolished, and an equal moral standard recognized ;

(*j*) That the responsibility not only of the mother, but also of the father, of a child born out of wedlock should be recognized ;

(*k*) That there should be adequate economic provision for the service of motherhood ;

(*l*) That no political or industrial quarrel should deprive the mother of food for her children.

Without claiming that these principles are complete, the Contracting Parties are of opinion that they are well fitted to guide the policy of the League of Nations, and that, if adopted by the communities which are members of the League, they will confer lasting benefits upon the whole world.

(4) On Women and General Labour Conference

Since the General Labour Conference to be set up under the Treaty of Peace deals with questions which directly affect large numbers of wage-earning women in all countries, this International Congress of Women calls attention to Article 3 of the Report of the Commission on International Labour Legislation, which proposes that this General Labour Conference should consist of representatives from each country, namely, two Government delegates, one representative of employers, and one of employees, and urges that, in the interest of these women workers, this Article should be amended so as to provide that at least one representative from each country shall be a woman.

(5) On Women's Vote in Plebiscites

This International Congress of Women urges that the following clause be inserted in the Peace Treaty :—

" That in any plebiscite taken under the Treaty of Peace or a League of Nations women should have the same right to vote as men."

III. ON PRESENT MILITARY ACTION IN RUSSIA AND HUNGARY

This International Congress of Women, recognizing the right of each nation to determine its own form of government on the lines laid down in President Wilson's Fourteen Points, urges the immediate cessation of attack upon Russia and Hungary, whether by armed force, by supply of munitions or money, or by blockade.

It protests against the warfare now being waged, without open declaration of war, upon peoples who are experimenting in a new social and economic order, which may prove to have a great contribution to make to the world, and which has not yet had a fair trial.

IV. ON AMNESTY FOR WAR PRISONERS

This International Congress of Women urges all the belligerent nations immediately to proclaim an amnesty for political prisoners, including conscientious objectors to military service, and requests that, where necessary, public funds be given to ensure the return of prisoners of war from Siberia and other remote places.

NOTE.—Space prevents the printing of all the resolutions passed. These will be given in the Official Report.

The Delegations

Of the 21 National Sections of the Women's International League, 15 were represented at the Congress, the delegations being as follows: America sent 27, Australia 3, Austria 4, Denmark 6, England 26, France 4, Germany 25. Holland 5, Hungary 2, Ireland 3, Italy 1, Norway 6, Roumania 1, Sweden 11, Switzerland 23.

Document No. 67 The American Peace Society Urges a Third Hague Conference (1919)
Source: *Advocate of Peace,* LXXXI (November, 1919), pp. 307-309.

OUR WAY OUT—A CONFERENCE OF THE NATIONS

W HAT is now seen to have been inevitable from the outset has happened. The Paris plans for a League to Enforce Peace, like all similar plans heretofore in history, have gone awry. Readers familiar with the ADVOCATE OF PEACE will understand something of the reasons. A League to Enforce Peace never has succeeded; we believe it never can. As we have frequently argued, it is a contradiction in terms, and it has in it from the outset the canker of failure. Laws can provide for the coercion of individuals; but there is but one way to coerce a State, and that is by war. Nations cannot be expected to set over themselves voluntarily the machinery of organized warfare, controlled by foreigners, and operative at any time against themselves. The League of Nations as proposed out of the Paris Conference, a scheme which for all practical purposes has been defeated in the United States Senate, represents, we may believe, the last attempt on the part of the nations to set up such an organ, because it is now seen to be wrong in' principle, contrary to the teachings of history, and dangerous to the peace of the world.

And yet the Covenant of the League of Nations brought to America by President Wilson has already rendered the greatest possible benefit to the cause of international peace. Prior to 1914, there was in America little appreciation of other nations, because, outside of a very limited group, there was small knowledge of facts relating to conditions abroad. To be sure, the Hague Conferences of 1899 and 1907 had received no little attention from our State Department, in a measure from the press; and especially from the Mohonk Conferences, the American Society of International Law, the Carnegie Endowment for International Peace, from the five American Peace Congresses initiated by the

American Peace Society, from the Advocate of Peace. In consequence there was a measure of informed opinion in America; but that information was, unfortunately, confined to the few. The discussion about the League of Nations has changed all that. We believe the hope now of a practical international co-operative effort lies in the direction of a Third Hague Conference. That there is now hope for such a conference lies in the fact that, thanks to the Covenant of the League of Nations and to the United States Senate, there is at last a widely educated body of public opinion in America concerning the aims, methods, and possibilities of a rational international organization. There are ninety-six men in the United States Senate quite fully informed in all such matters. The members of Congress cannot possibly have escaped learning many things about international affairs heretofore unfamiliar to them. Our newspapers and magazines have given to us all in America a new vision and a new body of opinion about nations outside our own. This educated intelligence, not confined to our own country, is the hope of the peace of the world.

If, in 1899, the nations of the earth could meet, pass laws for themselves, set up an international tribunal which has already settled some eighteen international difficulties; if, in 1907, practically all of the nations of the earth could meet, adopt laws for themselves and agree with practical unanimity upon the principle that nations rest upon law, and that the peace of the world depends upon the judicial settlement of international disputes: if they could agree then, as they did, that there should be periodic Hague conferences, and plan, as many of them did, for a third such conference, it would for these reasons seem the part of ordinary sense to take up the international problem of solving international disputes where it was left off in 1907.

The peace of the world depends upon the society of all the nations governing themselves by mutual consent under law. There is no other way.

A Third Hague Conference, certainly a conference of the society of all the nations, is therefore not only the natural next step in the evolution of international co-operation, it is the inevitable step. There is already

477

much ground broken for such a conference. With all the history at hand, and with all the benefits of the limitless discussions over the Paris treaty fresh in our minds, such a conference might well be called within a year.

The final act of the Peace Conference of 1907 recommended to the powers the assembling of a Third Peace Conference, and called the attention of the powers to the necessity of preparing a program for such a conference a sufficient time in advance to insure its deliberations being conducted with the necessary authority and expedition. To this end the Conference recommended the selection of a preparatory committee by the governments, which committee should be charged with the task of collecting the various proposals to be submitted to the committee, and ascertaining what subjects were ripe for embodiment in an international regulation, and of preparing a program which the governments should decide upon in sufficient time to enable it to be carefully examined by the countries interested. This committee, the suggestion continued, should further be entrusted with the task of proposing a system of organization and procedure for the Conference itself.

Acting upon this recommendation, President Taft appointed an Advisory Committee to the United States, which committee submitted, in June, 1912, an elaborate and suggestive program as a basis of recommendation by the United States to such a preparatory committee. This report is still in the State Department. December 10, 1913, Elihu Root, speaking for a number of others, some of whom had taken part in the Hague conferences, wrote the Secretary of State urging "greater activity of preparation on the part of other powers." In his letter Mr. Root pointed out that the proposal for periodic conferences was American in its origin, and that the United States, accordingly, is especially interested that future conferences should take place automatically. Mr. Root urged the selection by the United States of its member of the international committee provided for by the final act of 1907, and pointed out that if that were done, "The United States would be free from any imputation of lack of interest in this step which so great a proportion of the people of our country regard as of the highest importance." As a result of this suggestion from Mr. Root, President Wilson, in a letter by the Secretary of State, January 31, 1914, instructed the diplomatic officers of the United States accredited to the governments which took part in the second international peace conference at the Hague, to "propose to the governments to which you are respectfully accredited, that the duties of the international preparatory committee shall be committed to the Administrative Council of the Permanent Court of Arbitration at The Hague, this Council being composed of the Netherlands Minister of Foreign Affairs and the diplomatic representatives of the contracting powers accredited to The Hague. To this Council the task of preparation for the conference may readily and appropriately be committed. The place at which the Council sits leaves nothing to be desired from the point of view of convenience, while the entrusting of the work to a competent body already in existence would result in an appreciable saving both in time and in expense. If the membership of the Council were found to be too large for the efficient carrying on of the work in detail, this difficulty could at once be solved by the appointment of subcommittees to deal with particular subjects."

February 5, 1914, the United States Government announced that it had taken steps toward the calling of a Third Hague Conference to meet in the summer of 1915. Communications were opened with the Dutch Government to that end. A Citizens' National Committee was formed to support the action of the government. On the 19th of March, 1914, a resolution was favorably reported to the House of Representatives by the Foreign Affairs Committee, calling upon the Secretary of State to advise the House of Representatives what steps had been taken toward the calling of a Third Hague Conference. On the 28th of May, 1914, Hon. Andrew D. White, speaking at the Twentieth Mohonk Conference, made an impassioned and reasoned speech, urging the importance of calling a Third Hague Conference. July 2. the Dutch Government invited the nations which took part in the Second Hague Conference to choose delegates to serve on a committee to arrange the program of the Third Conference. A meeting of this committee was called for June, 1915.

The principle of the Root Arbitration treaties is still active. The treaties embodying the principle of delay in case of disputes between this country and twenty-one other nations are still in force. Peace can rest securely only upon the judicial settlement of international disputes. These great principles salvaged from the war indicate the direction for advance. They are highly important matters for the early consideration of the Society of Nations.

These familiar facts are enumerated here because they indicate in a measure America's most intelligent interest in the cause of an international effort to establish a peace of justice between the nations.

With the rich history of those conferences to inspire us; with the reasons for the failure of the Paris Conference to warn us; with the great body of informed public opinion, not only in this country, but everywhere, to point the way; with the problem of peace of the world most vitally to the front among the aspirations of men, our personal view is that the United States Congress should request the President of the United States to enter again into communication with foreign governments looking toward the earliest possible meeting of a Third Hague Peace Conference.

Document No. 68   William L. Chenery, ."Conscription in Peace Times," (1920)
Source: *The Survey,* XLIII (Feb. 14, 1920), pp. 575-576.

Conscription in Peace Times

By *William L. Chenery*

THE Army Reorganization bill as reported by the Senate Committee on Military Affairs is as significant from an industrial as from a military point of view. In truth it is an understatement to say that certain unobtrusive provisions of the measure concern the economic development of the country much more intimately than they do the national defense against some external enemy. For that reason, if for no other, the proposal which is now being advocated by Senator Wadsworth and opposed by Representative Mondell, Republican leader in the House, should be clearly understood by all ·those citizens who would preserve the United States as a land of individual freedom.

Two arguments have risen to the surface of the discussion of the Army Reorganization bill. The first is that presented by its advocates. In a word it is " Now or Never." If this opportunity is lost, say those who support Senator Wadsworth, it may never again be possible to write such a measure upon the statute books of the nation. This line of reasoning is not the most persuasive conceivable. If the merits of the Senate proposal are real, the American people can be relied upon to act wisely even though haste is foresworn. If, on the other hand, the good points of the bill are overbalanced by its evils, surely nothing is to be gained by thoughtless action.

The chief argument so far advanced by those who agree with Representative Mondell in opposing the bill is that of economy. These say, not without reason, that taxes are high. They assert that governmental economy is of first importance at this particular moment in our history. Without retrenchment, it is argued, it is futile to hope for any lowering of the burdensome cost of living. The passage of the Wadsworth bill, they say, will call for enormous expenditures. The precise cost is debatable, but the opponents of the measure are convinced that it will be not less than a half a billion dollars from the very outset and probably more.

Neither the importunate plea of those who say "Now or Never" nor the argument of the opposition who urge the universal desire for public economy goes to the heart of the matter. If the Army Reorganization measure were as necessary as those for whom Senator Wadsworth speaks think it is, it might be cheap at any price. If it is as dangerous as others believe it to be, it ought to be rejected on its proved demerits. For it is undeniably freighted with consequences of the highest import to the welfare of our nation. No single measure except a declaration of war has perhaps contained within itself such momentous implications of change.

Not without guile, in this suggested reorganization of the army, two far reaching policies are offered. These are:

1. The establishment of a system of universal military training.
2. The enactment of a permanent draft system.

Were the measure to be accepted by Congress, further discussion either of universal military training or of conscription would be vain. The choice would have been made and the consequences would have to be endured even though these rendered the industrial workers of the nation infinitely more servile than any plan for compulsory arbitration or the abolition of trade unionism could possibly effect.

It should be recognized at the outset moreover that the enactment of a draft system in peace times for peace purposes is a very different thing from the approval of such a system for the emergency of war. During the World War no other method of distributing the burden of national service seemed practical. The American people accepted for the purpose of overthrowing the German autocracy the draft act. Defeating Hohenzollernism, however, is one thing; choking off industrial evolution is quite another. Americans who were willing to make any sacrifice to thwart the will of German militarism, by the same token, refuse to set up a system, which whatever its immediate purpose, could only have the effect of preventing the economic development of the country along the lines of American political theories.

The sections of the Army Reorganization bill, dealing with compulsory military training and service, as digested by the Legislative Reference Service of the Library of Congress, are as follows:

SECTION 51. *Military Training.* All male citizens of territorial United States, and all aliens who have declared intention to become citizens, to be subject, on becoming 18, or within three years thereafter, to military or naval training for four months, exclusive of time for mobilization, etc. (committee amendment; such time limited to ten days); or, with their consent, for two months additional; training to begin at eighteen, or be deferred, at election of individual; expressed preference for Army or Navy to be followed as far as practicable. [Where climatic conditions, etc., permit], two training periods to be held each year; recruits allowed to elect training periods, subject to regulations prescribed by President. (Committee amendment; omit phrase in brackets.) System of training to become effective in calendar year 1921. All who do not begin training by 21 because of exemption, etc., to begin as soon thereafter as possible, but not after reaching 26.

Male aliens resident in United States not less than one year and qualified for citizenship except as to length of residence and prior declaration of intention, and who if citizens would be liable for training, to have choice of

(1) voluntarily undergoing the prescribed training; certificate of completion of such training, if presented within six months to a naturalization court, to entitle such alien to naturalization without payment of fees, etc.; or

(2) claiming exemption on ground of alienage, except as provided by treaty; such alien to be thereafter barred from citizenship.

SECTION 52. *Classes of Training.* Military training, and any preparatory education herein required, to include general educational and appropriate vocational training, hygiene, American history, etc., and such instruction " as may be adapted to qualify those receiving it for the performance of their duties as citizen-soldiers "; to be adapted to climatic and industrial conditions, etc., of the particular training area. Recruits to be subject to physical and psychological tests, to determine whether training should be with combat or special troop units. Regulations to be prepared by committee of General Staff and an equal number of other persons, not less than three, including veteran officers eligible as reserve officers, physicians, etc. Training in Navy to be subject to regulations prescribed by President.

SECTION 53. *Preparatory Educational Training.* Induction into service for a maximum of two months additional authorized for preparatory education of any persons not " sufficiently instructed in the English language to be able to profit by the military training herein provided."

SECTION 54. *Pay During Training,* including preparatory educational period, to be $5 a month, besides transportation, food, etc.

SECTION 55. *Exceptions from Liability to Training:*

(a) persons exempted by treaty;

(b) citizens or subjects of enemy country or of an ally of such country;

(c) persons with dependents [provided no suitable provision is made for them by law.]

Committee amendment; omit clause in brackets and add the following: in case person called for training has dependents in sense of act of May 18, 1917 (40 Stat. 76-83), such dependents to be paid " the amount provided by said law," without requiring allotment from the recruit.

(d) persons in military or naval service, or who have served therein for four months, including only such service as may be prescribed by regulation;

(e) persons incapable, from physical, mental or moral defect, of profiting by the training; but corrective measures may be taken in such cases.

SECTION 56. *Registration for Military Training* required (under regulations prescribed by President) of all male citizens, and all male residents of the United States, except in Alaska and insular possessions, upon reaching age of 17. Preparatory education provided for in Sec. 53 may be required at any time after registration; any person physically fit may, with consent of parents, take initial training after registration and before becoming 18.

SECTION 57. *Application of Existing Law.* Provisions of acts of May 18, 1917 (40 Stat. 79, 80, Secs. 4, 6) relating to registration, exemptions, etc., to be extended and made applicable where necessary and applicable in carrying out provisions of the bill. Regulations to be made by President; but compensation of members of local boards limited to $4 a day; assistants to $2.50, and to rate current in locality.

SECTION 58. *Assignment of Reservists.* Upon completion of prescribed training, all reservists to be assigned to local organization of National Guard or organized reserves, and transferred upon change of residence; assignments to be made to branches elected by reservists, so far as needs of service permit.

Persons assigned to National Guard to enlist for three years, taking oath prescribed in Sec. 63, below; to be transferred to unorganized reserves upon expiration of enlistment unless re-enlisting in National Guard. Reservists not to be assigned to National Guard without their consent; total number assigned in any one year limited to one-third authorized strength of National Guard.

Reservists assigned to organized reserves to serve for five years and be thereafter transferred to unorganized reserves; organized reserves subject to two annual periods of mobilization and training of not over two weeks each; but reservists desiring to qualify as officers or non-commissioned officers may receive additional training, and be continued in reserves (committee amendment, from year to year) for ten years.

Thus at the age of seventeen boys will be registered. Thereafter they will be in the control of the military leaders of the nation. Citizens will have become " citizen-soldiers." What the soldier gains in discipline the citizen loses in freedom. A graceful concession is made to the farmer opposition, however, by providing that the four months' training may be given in winter as well as in summer. Boys from the industrial districts would thus go to summer camps while sons of farmers would get their training during the infertile days of winter.

The full import of the Wadsworth bill is, albeit, revealed in the section which reenacts conscription as a permanent policy. Here is the digest provided by the Library of Congress:

SECTION 73. *Liability for Active Military Service,* in national emergency declared by Congress and proclaimed by the President, to be as follows:
(a) National Guard and organized reserves to be subject to call for immediate service for period of emergency;
(b) all other male citizens, or resident aliens who have within seven years declared intention to become citizens, between 18 and 45, except permanent personnel of Army, Navy and Marine Corps and persons excepted in Section 55 (a) and (b), to be subject to call for immediate service, in order determined by classification under Section 74.

SECTION 74. *Classification for Service.* Persons subject to service under Section 73 to be classified so as to
(a) constitute special classes;
(a) give deferred classification for those in essential industries;

(c) give deferred classificatiqn on account of dependent relatives in case of special hardship;

(d) provide adequate supply of specially qualified men for military and naval establishments;

(e) except the following classes (on claim therefor) ;

(1) regularly ordained ministers of religion;

(2) members of a "well recognized religious sect or organization " of at least five years' standing, whose declared creed during that time forbids any participation in war; such exception not to release them from noncombatant service;

(3) Federal, State, District of Columbia, county and municipal officers whose functions render exception advisable, including reasonable police forces.

Exception or deferred classification to cease when cause no longer exists.

SECTION 75. *Registration.* President authorized to require registration, in national emergency, of male citizens and residents, except permanent personnel of Army, Navy, and Marine Corps, organized reservists and recruits in training, diplomatic representatives, consuls, attachés, etc., and such other officers of foreign governments as may be excepted by regulation. Place of registration and information to be given (which may be required to be under oath) to be prescribed by the President.

In that sentence which authorizes the President " in national emergency " to require the registration of male citizens and residents between eighteen and forty-five the secret of the Military Reorganization bill is revealed. A national emergency is a flexible phrase. When in 1910 the French railway men struck Premier Briand called the railway workers to military service. The strike was effectually broken. That is one way of handling industrial questions. Another way is to forbid trade unionism. Still another is to enact laws for compulsory arbitration. A fourth is the system to which America has been more or less committed. That consists in ascertaining what are the causes of dissention and in dealing with the causes. In his message to Congress last December, President Wilson aligned himself with those who believe in ascertaining and in removing the causes of industrial unrest rather than in repressing their manifestations. It is indisputable that these sections of the Wadsworth measure could be utilized to suppress any expression of the grievances of workers.

In truth the industrial rather than the military aspect of world affairs offers the principal excuse for the consideration of such a measure as the Wadsworth bill at this time. Whatever the arguments for universal military training and for conscription were prior to the World War it is certainly obvious that no foreign enemy has either the resources or the will to invade America at the present time or in the immediate future. The strength of the American navy is greater than that of any conceivable invader. Germany was the enemy which compelled France to adopt conscription. Universal military service saved France and Europe against Germany. France, however, was preparing against a known enemy. Against whom must we mobilize our entire manpower?

Germany had no enemy threatening invasion. The men who claimed the God given right to rule Germany, however, foisted conscription upon the empire. None can now argue that conscription saved Germany. It did not even preserve the economic or the social status quo within the nation. The part which conscription played in the final overthrow of the Hohenzollerns and vanquishment of the German nation was indeed preeminent. The possession of unneeded military power bred that lust for aggrandizement which obtained its full expression when the Kaised forced war upon the entire world. German conscription created aggressive imperialism and destroyed the feudal autocracy which expected to benefit by it. If the United States were in the position of France after 1870 universal military training and conscription would be perhaps inescapable. The only rational explanation of military policies such as those offered by Senator Wadsworth lies therefore in the domestic rather than in the foreign field.

It is a curious time for the United States to consider embarkation upon such a sea of trouble. The overweening military power of Europe lies in the dust. Out of the destruction, the League of Nations, weak perhaps, but comparably no weaker than was the confederation of the Thirteen Colonies, is emerging. Methods of maintaining the peace of the world are being developed. European nations which because of utter fear of invasion were compelled to accept conscription are preparing to give it up. The war against war has been won, the method of mutual reduction in armament having been provided in the structure of the League of Nations. The determination of nations associated with the United States to reduce their military forces has been plainly expressed. Should we cooperate with them in reducing the size of armies or force them to meet a new competition?

Document No. 69   Defeat of the Treaty of Versailles; Failure to Muster Two-thirds Necessary for Approval. March 19, 1920
Source: U.S. *Congressional Record,* 66th Cong., 2nd Sess., Volume LIX, Part 5 (March 19, 1920), p. 4599.

The roll call having been concluded, it resulted—yeas 49, nays 35. as follows:

YEAS—49.

Ashurst	Gore	Myers	Spencer
Ball	Hale	New	Sterling
Beckham	Henderson	Nugent	Sutherland
Calder	Jones, Wash.	Owen	Trammell
Capper	Kellogg	Page	Wadsworth
Chamberlain	Kendrick	Phelan	Walsh, Mass.
Colt	Kenyon	Phipps	Walsh, Mont.
Curtis	Keyes	Pittman	Warren
Dillingham	King	Pomerene	Watson
Edge	Lenroot	Ransdell	Wolcott
Elkins	Lodge	Smith, Ga.	
Fletcher	McLean	Smith, Md.	
Frelinghuysen	McNary	Smoot	

NAYS—35.

Borah	Gronna	McCormick	Shields
Brandegee	Harris	McKellar	Simmons
Comer	Harrison	Moses	Smith, S. C.
Culberson	Hitchcock	Norris	Stanley
Dial	Johnson, Calif.	Overman	Swanson
Fernald	Johnson, S. Dak.	Reed	Thomas
France	Kirby	Robinson	Underwood
Gay	Knox	Sheppard	Williams
Glass	La Follette	Sherman	

NOT VOTING—12.

Cummins	Harding	Nelson	Poindexter
Fall	Jones, N. Mex.	Newberry	Smith, Ariz.
Gerry	McCumber	Penrose	Townsend

The PRESIDENT pro tempore. Upon agreeing to the resolution of ratification the yeas are 49 and the nays are 35. Not having received the affirmative votes of two-thirds of the Senators present and voting, the resolution is not agreed to, and the Senate does not advise and consent to the ratification of the treaty of peace with Germany.

The resolution of ratification voted upon and rejected is as follows:

Resolution of ratification.

Resolved (two-thirds of the Senators present concurring therein), That the Senate advise and consent to the ratification of the treaty of peace with Germany concluded at Versailles on the 28th day of June, 1919, subject to the following reservations and understandings, which are hereby made a part and condition of this resolution of ratification, which ratification is not to take effect or bind the United States until the said reservations and understandings adopted by the Senate have been accepted as a part and a condition of this resolution of ratification by the allied and associated powers and a failure on the part of the allied and associated powers to make objection to said reservations and understandings prior to the deposit of ratification by the United States shall be taken as a full and final acceptance of such reservations and understandings by said powers:

1. The United States so understands and construes article 1 that in case of notice of withdrawal from the League of Nations, as provided in said article, the United States shall be the sole judge as to whether all its international obligations and all its obligations under the said covenant have been fulfilled, and notice of withdrawal by the United States may be given by a concurrent resolution of the Congress of the United States.

2. The United States assumes no obligation to preserve the territorial integrity or political independence of any other country by the employment of its military or naval forces, its resources, or any form of economic discrimination, or to interfere in any way in controversies between nations, including all controversies relating to territorial integrity or political independence, whether members of the league or not, under the provisions of article 10, or to employ the military or naval forces of the United States, under any article of the treaty for any purpose, unless in any particular case the Congress, which, under the Constitution, has the sole power to declare war or authorize the

employment of the military or naval forces of the United States, shall, in the exercise of full liberty of action, by act or joint resolution so provide.

3. No mandate shall be accepted by the United States under article 22, part 1, or any other provision of the treaty of peace with Germany, except by action of the Congress of the United States.

4. The United States reserves to itself exclusively the right to decide what questions are within its domestic jurisdiction and declares that all domestic and political questions relating wholly or in part to its internal affairs, including immigration, labor, coastwise traffic, the tariff, commerce, the suppression of traffic in women and children and in opium and other dangerous drugs, and all other domestic questions, are solely within the jurisdiction of the United States and are not under this treaty to be submitted in any way either to arbitration or to the consideration of the council or of the assembly of the League of Nations, or any agency thereof, or to the decision or recommendation of any other power.

5. The United States will not submit to arbitration or to inquiry by the assembly or by the council of the League of Nations, provided for in said treaty of peace, any questions which in the judgment of the United States depend upon or relate to its long-established policy, commonly known as the Monroe doctrine; said doctrine is to be interpreted by the United States alone and is hereby declared to be wholly outside the jurisdiction of said League of Nations and entirely unaffected by any provision contained in the said treaty of peace with Germany.

6. The United States withholds its assent to articles 156, 157, and 158, and reserves full liberty of action with respect to any controversy which may arise under said articles.

7. No person is or shall be authorized to represent the United States, nor shall any citizen of the United States be eligible, as a member of any body or agency established or authorized by said treaty of peace with Germany, except pursuant to an act of the Congress of the United States providing for his appointment and defining his powers and duties.

8. The United States understands that the reparation commission will regulate or interfere with exports from the United States to Germany, or from Germany to the United States, only when the United States by act or joint resolution of Congress approves such regulation or interference.

9. The United States shall not be obligated to contribute to any expenses of the League of Nations, or of the secretariat, or of any commission, or committee, or conference, or other agency, organized under the League of Nations or under the treaty or for the purpose of carrying out the treaty provisions, unless and until an appropriation of funds available for such expenses shall have been made by the Congress of the United States: *Provided*, That the foregoing limitation shall not apply to the United States' proportionate share of the expense of the office force and salary of the secretary general.

10. No plan for the limitation of armaments proposed by the council of the League of Nations under the provisions of article 8 shall be held as binding the United States until the same shall have been accepted by Congress, and the United States reserves the right to increase its armament without the consent of the council whenever the United States is threatened with invasion or engaged in war.

11. The United States reserves the right to permit, in its discretion, the nationals of a covenant-breaking State, as defined in article 16 of the covenant of the League of Nations, residing within the United States or in countries other than such covenant-breaking State, to continue their commercial, financial, and personal relations with the nationals of the United States.

12. Nothing in articles 296, 297, or in any of the annexes thereto or in any other article, section, or annex of the treaty of peace with Germany shall, as against citizens of the United States, be taken to mean any confirmation, ratification, or approval of any act otherwise illegal or in contravention of the rights of citizens of the United States.

13. The United States withholds its assent to Part XIII (articles 387 to 427, inclusive) unless Congress by act or joint resolution shall hereafter make provision for representation in the organization established by said Part XIII, and in such event the participation of the United States will be governed and conditioned by the provisions of such act or joint resolution.

14. Until Part I, being the covenant of the League of Nations, shall be so amended as to provide that the United States shall be entitled to cast a number of votes equal to that which any member of the league and its self-governing dominions, colonies, or parts of empire, in the aggregate shall be entitled to cast, the United States assumes no obligation to be bound, except in cases where Congress has previously given its consent, by any election, decision, report, or finding of the council or assembly in which any member of the league and its self-governing dominions, colonies, or parts of empire, in the aggregate have cast more than one vote.

The United States assumes no obligation to be bound by any decision, report, or finding of the council or assembly arising out of any dispute between the United States and any member of the league if such member, or any self-governing dominion, colony, empire, or part of empire united with it politically has voted.

15. In consenting to the ratification of the treaty with Germany the United States adheres to the principle of self-determination and to the resolution of sympathy with the aspirations of the Irish people for a government of their own choice adopted by the Senate June 6, 1919, and declares that when such government is attained by Ireland, a consummation it is hoped is at hand, it should promptly be admitted as a member of the League of Nations.

Document No. 70 Senator Gilbert Hitchcock, "The League or Bolshevism?" (1920)
Source: *The Independent,* CIII (Aug. 28, 1920), pp. 235-236.

© *John T. McCutcheon in Chicago Tribune*

The red peril

Kirby in New York World

The guardian angel

The League or Bolshevism?
We Must Choose

A Message from the United States Government to the American People

By Senator Gilbert M. Hitchcock

Former Chairman of the Committee on Foreign Relations

THE question of whether the United States shall enter the League of Nations has been appealed from the Senate, the representatives of the people, who after more than a year of controversy found themselves unable to make the decision, to the people themselves. The real issue is daily bcoming clearer. It does not relate to the terms upon which we shall enter the League. The issue is whether there shall be a League, with the United States in its member- ship, competent to fulfil the desire of the world for permanent peace.

Let us strip aside the quibbles, behind which the ene- mies of the League of Nations have attempted to hide their real purpose. Let us get back to the essentials of the matter. Thru all the ages down to the present the world has been afflicted with the curse of war. The greater part of the money spent by governments, here and elsewhere, has been for the burdens of war. This has continued thru all the centuries. Do the people of the United States realize that 92 per cent of our appropriations for the fiscal year of 1920—the enormous total of $5,279,621,262—were for obligations arising from war and for current military and naval needs?

Every generation has sent its men out to slaughter. Fifty wars have raged in the old world during the last hundred years. In the United States we have not been free from war's curse. In addition to the Revolution, the Civil war and the Indian wars, we have had the war with Mexico, the war with Spain and the war with Germany. We have been a peace-loving people. We have bent our efforts to keep out of war, yet we have not escaped its awful effects.

We came out of the world war with the conviction that we are a part of the world; that whenever the world is again convulsed with conflict we are going to suffer and probably be drawn into the whirlpool. We cannot stand aloof. We must, therefore, consider and give our solemn answer to the question: Shall it be war and preparations for war or a League of Nations to preserve international peace?

A League of Nations already exists. Twenty-nine powers are in its membership, but it needs no resort to speculation to assert that without the adherence of the United States the League will lack sufficient strength to carry out the purposes for which it was conceived. And so by their votes the American people are to decide not merely whether the United States shall take membership in it, but the fate of the whole enterprize.

Before the war the United States and the four great nations associated with us in the formation of this League for peace, were spending some twelve hundred million dollars a year upon preparations for war. If the league fails, the world will sag back into the despair and desperation of a constant prospect of renewed war. Every nation will become an armed camp. Military and naval preparations will go forward upon an unheard of scale. The burdens of the people will be enormously increased. These are merely the preparations for war. What of war itself?

First there is the money cost. The nations that bore the principal burdens of the European war expended for the purposes of destruction more than one hundred and forty thousand million dollars. Their peoples will stagger under this burden for generations to come, if no relief is afforded in the cost of war preparations.

The war cost 6,000,000 lives and millions more of cripples. Hundreds of towns were destroyed and millions of wives were widowed. Pestilence and famine have come after. Law and order have been overthrown in various parts of the world. Bolshevism and anarchy have been propagated. The confidence of men in their governments has been shaken. It will never be restored until the governments of earth join together in a solemn compact that will guard against the recurrence of such a disaster. These, and not the quibbles of politicians, are the things we should have in mind as we cast our votes in November.

Narrow-visioned men attack the League of Nations as a form of internationalism. They object to internationalism. They are too late. Internationalism is here. We have not to choose between nationalism and internationalism, but the form of internationalism we will take. Our choice lies between the internationalism of justice, honor and peace, and mutual support between the civilized nations of the world, and the internationalism of Bolshevism.

Men will not forever tolerate recurring wars over controversies capable of quick adjustment by peaceful means. They will not for long submit to demands that they lay down their lives in unnecessary and useless slaughter. Taxpayers will not indefinitely comply with laws that take their savings for the purposes of destruction.

Have the opponents of the League been blind to the rising tide of protest against war among the peoples of all the civilized world? If we refuse to give support to the internationalism of governments, uniting to end wars, we soon will be face to face with the internationalism of men who have taken things into their own hands.

In the United States we have, as yet, seen no marked tendency in this direction, but there is a lesson for us in the things that have come to pass in Europe. We can no longer ignore the fact that Russia's millions are thoroly committed to the communistic theory. France and Italy are coming increasingly under the control of socialistic ideas and socialistic leaders. No other leaders can long hold control in the existing state of public opinion in those countries. Germany has been reorganized into a socialistic nation of 75,-000,000 souls. We are impressed with the growth of socialism in Great Britain and the adoption of socialistic ideas by British statesmen.

For this development in the nations of Europe, war and preparations for war, the burdens and the horrors of war are largely responsible. It spreads across frontiers as readily as trade and commerce and much more irresistibly. If war and war preparations are to continue to be the principal business and the chief expense of national government, we will not be immune from the development of socialism and Bolshevism on an impressive scale in the United States. It will not be confined as in the past to soap box oratory. It will seize the political power.

I repeat, therefore, that we are called upon to choose between the internationalism of a League of Nations, a society of states whose standards are mutual protection, with honor, justice, liberty and self-government, and the internationalism of the Bolshevist.

Washington, D. C.

Document No. 71   Elihu Root's Plan for a World Court (1920)
Source: *The Literary Digest,* LXVII (Oct. 2, 1920), pp. 15-17.

THE "ROOT PLAN" FOR A WORLD COURT

"**N**O LEAGUE-BORN COURT!" exclaims the militant Republican New York *Sun,* in outright repudiation of the so-called "Root plan" for an International Court of Justice, which many important Republican papers assumed would furnish the Republican substitute for the League. The trouble arises from publication of the complete draft of the plan by the Council of the League. *The Sun* head-lined its cable dispatch of the text from London, "Root's Plan for World Court is Like, Harding's—Excels Hague Scheme—Diplomacy not Factor." But on further examination *The Sun* finds that it is neither a direct extension of the Hague Tribunal nor a substitute for the League: "It is an integral part of the League's machinery, and a scion of the Wilson Covenant itself." The Republican platform calls for no such tribunal to be accepted by the people of the United States "in lieu of their own judgment and their own power," declares *The Sun,* nor does that paper believe that "any such purpose as lurks behind Mr. Root's conception of a League-born Court can for a moment be entertained by Senator Harding when its significance has become apparent." *The Sun* does not hesitate to call down Mr. Root, Republican ex-Secretary of State, saying:

"No scheme of international jurisprudence that is superimposed upon a Wilson League of Nations or that grows out of the Covenant upon which President Wilson and Governor Cox insist, can be made by any

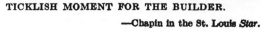

TICKLISH MOMENT FOR THE BUILDER.

—Chapin in the St. Louis *Star*.

jugglery of phrase or any sophistry of logic acceptable to the American sentiment that is now so imperiously manifesting itself whenever and wherever it gets a chance at the ballot-box.

"This is the plain fact of the case. It is not within the intellectual powers of Elihu Root, great tho they are, to make the fact any different. If Mr. Root thinks the contrary, his thought does not represent the youth and vigor of the party. He is not in touch with the people and is not in their world. He does not represent them and is not in sympathy with them."

If Mr. Root has not pleased the "bitter-enders," it is also apparent that other Republican papers consider this stage of the campaign a time for speaking rather cautiously, maintaining a waiting attitude, or refraining from immediate comment altogether, like the New York *Tribune*. Naturally, the Democrats make the most of their opportunity to play Root against Harding, "*The Sun* having duly convicted Elihu Root of heresy," according to the New York *World*. This strong Democratic paper describes the Republican dilemma thus: "From the recesses of the front porch, Senator Harding set up an international court that exists only in his bucolic imagination. Elihu Root has set up a real court as part of the machinery of the League of Nations, and Republicans have been telling us that Root was creating the Republican foreign policy. Are they now prepared to follow him and abandon Harding, or, like *The Sun and New York Herald*, will they throw the Root court overboard in order to continue their partizan filibuster against the League of Nations?" *The World* points out that the Root court "can no more be separated from the League than the judiciary department of the United States can be separated from the rest of the government." This Court, modeled on the United States Supreme Court, "has no existence except as a part of the League of Nations":

"Of course, the Root plan is an integral part of the League's machinery. It could not be otherwise. This Court is created by the Covenant of the League. Its decisions, if they are to be enforced, must be enforced by the members of the League acting in concert. No other court can be established which is worth the serious attention of the civilized world.

"*The Sun and New York Herald* is of the opinion that 'the Permanent Court of International Justice is not open to acceptance by the United States so long as acceptance of the Court involves acceptance of the Wilson League.' We may have very little to say about it. If the Root Court is set up by the League of Nations we shall have to accept its decisions whether we are a member or not. What the Court says is international law will be international law, and what we say to the contrary will avail little.

"The main question in relation to this Court is whether the United States as a member of the League will have a hand in naming the judges, or whether, because of its refusal to join the League, it will have no voice whatever, but will be subject to the Court's findings."

In submitting the Court plan to the thirty-seven member nations of the League for action at the first meeting of the Assembly in November, the Council calls attention to the significance of the achievement of the Commission of International Jurists who formulated the draft:

"The scheme has been arrived at after prolonged discussion by a most competent tribunal. Its members represented widely different national points of view; they all signed the report. Its fate has therefore been very different from that of the plans for a Court of Arbitral Justice, which were discust without result in 1907. Doubtless the agreement was not arrived at without difficulty. Variety of opinions, even among the most competent experts, is inevitable on a subject so perplexing and complicated. Some mutual concessions are therefore necessary if the failure of thirteen years ago is not to be repeated. The Council would regard an irreconcilable difference of opinion on the merits of the scheme as an international misfortune of the gravest kind. It would mean that the League was publicly compelled to admit its incapacity to carry out one of the most important of the tasks

"ANYWAY, THERE ARE NO DEMOCRATS HERE."
—Fitzpatrick in the St. Louis *Post-Dispatch*.

which it was invited to perform. The failure would be great and probably irreparable, for, if agreement proves impossible under circumstances apparently so favorable, it is hard to see how and when the task of securing it will be successfully resumed."

The plan establishes a permanent Court of International Justice at The Hague, to which parties shall have direct access, in accordance with Article 14 of the Covenant. This Court shall be in addition to the Court of Arbitration organized by the Hague Convention of 1899 and 1907, and to the special Tribunals of Arbitration to which states are always at liberty to submit their disputes for settlement. As reported in THE LITERARY DIGEST for August 14, the hitherto insuperable difficulty of selecting judges regardless of nationality is met by election by both Council and Assembly of the League. Provision is made for judges of each contesting nationality to sit in cases. The Council proposes salaries of judges and apportionment of expenses, both to be determined by the Assembly. The Court shall have jurisdiction to hear and determine suits between states, be open of right to original signatories of the Covenant and subsequent members of the League, and other states may have access under conditions of the Covenant. The three articles which are said to mark the greatest advance over any previous project are the following:

ARTICLE 33—When a dispute has arisen between states, and it has been found impossible to settle it by diplomatic means, and no agreement has been made to choose another jurisdiction, the party complaining may bring the case before the Court. The Court shall, first of all, decide whether the preceding conditions have been complied with; if so, it shall hear and determine the dispute according to the terms and within the limits of the next article.

ARTICLE 34—Between states which are members of the League of Nations the Court shall have jurisdiction (and this without any special convention giving it jurisdiction) to hear and determine cases of a legal nature concerning:

a. The interpretation of a treaty;

b. Any question of international law;

c. The existence of any fact which, if established, would constitute a breach of an international obligation;

d. The nature or extent of reparation to be made for the breach of an international obligation;

e. The interpretation of a sentence passed by the Court.

The Court shall also take cognizance of all disputes of any kind which may be submitted to it by a general or particular convention between the parties.

In the event of a dispute as to whether a certain case comes within any of the categories above mentioned, the matter shall be settled by the decision of the Court.

ARTICLE 35—The Court shall, within the limits of its jurisdiction as defined in Article 34, apply in the order following:

1. International conventions, whether general or particular, establishing rules expressly recognized by the contesting states.

2. International custom, as evidence of a general practise, which is accepted as law.

3. The general principles of law recognized by civilized nations.

4. Judicial decisions and the teachings of the most highly qualified publicists of the various nations, as subsidiary means for the determination of rules of law.

Provisions for giving advisory opinions on questions or disputes of an international nature are made, and a detailed code of procedure provides for majority decisions; judgment by default; final judgment without appeal, but the Court may be called upon to construe a judgment, and applications for revision are admissible. Judgments are to be made public together with the names of judges who take part in the decision, altho reasons for dissenting opinions or reservations shall not appear in a judgment.

We find scarcely a trace of enthusiasm and few discussions of the merits of the Root plan in Republican papers. The Philadelphia *Evening Public Ledger* states that the new World Court avoids Hague Tribunal pitfalls, takes up the machinery of international peace where it was left incomplete in 1907, and will have the power through the Covenant—lacking heretofore— "to enforce decrees and reach decisions through the application of general principles of justice and international law to specific cases." No accomplishment of the League "is a more hopeful index than that the original commendable purpose back of its formation has not been forgotten." Assuming that Mr. Harding's policy has contact with Mr. Root's work in an endeavor "to formulate something that will be practical and acceptable to every one," the Detroit *Free Press* says:

"The scheme as put into print shows statesmanship of a sane, far-seeing sort; it gives evidence of construction by expert hands who understand the limitations as well as the great possibilities of international judicial procedure. Accepting it as an expression of Republican policy, it is a direct refutation of the Democratic charge that the Republicans are opposed to peace and desire to kill off the whole League idea. On the contrary, it distinctly recognizes the League idea as one to be properly developed and used."

Since the Hague Tribunal does not guarantee any nation against war, but "recognizes that there are conflicts which a court can not prevent or adjust," the Chicago *Tribune* asserts that it will never count for much with "the true pro-Leaguer." By contrast, Americans "who have kept their feet on the ground" and "insist that the United States shall be strong in her own right" will welcome the proposed High Court as a step forward. The Boston *Transcript* discovers that "for a nation to avail itself of the agencies of the Court and become one of the pillars supporting the Court and its decrees, it is not necessary for the United States to stick its head into the noose of internationalism that the Wilson League of Nations provides." The Pittsburgh *Gazette-Times* declares that "the proposed Court would be of very limited benefit, if it were useful at all, as long as the League of Nations exists. That paramount agency for imposing the will of the strong on the weak without any consideration for justice makes impossible realization of the ideals that lie at the base of the Court concept." The Buffalo *Express* insists that "if the League as it exists is so unamendable that the Court can not be taken out of it and given an independent standing, that is all the more reason for Americans to rejoice that the Senate did not permit the United States to enter the League." The Chicago *News* thinks "the American people will await with interest the comments and suggestions of Mr. Root in respect of the proposed Court." "When the situation has become quite clear," the Springfield (Mass.) *Union* says,

"It will probably be found that the proposed Court is a logical step in a prospective revision of the League Covenant in such a manner as to emphasize the juridical obligations within the League, and to subordinate, if not largely remove, the economic and military obligations of its members—a revision, in short, that would change its essential character, remove the reasonable objections that have been raised against its present form, and permit of its acceptance by this country."

On the Democratic side Mr. Cox promptly finds occasion to say that—

"This Court of International Justice, which Mr. Harding hoped would be a substitute for the League of Nations, now appears as an essential part of the League and one which without the League would have no standing whatever.

"This limb having been cut off, Mr. Harding sitting on the end, we may confidently look forward to another frantic effort from Marion in an attempt to confuse the public and to keep both Senator Johnson—who is against any kind of a League—and Elihu Root—who is not only for the League, but has performed valiant services for the existing League—for the party candidate."

Secretary of State Colby remarks that this Court, which derives its authority from the League, "can not be expanded into an alternative for the League, and there is nothing mysterious about it that could operate as a sort of plank on which Senator Harding might walk ashore." The Louisville *Courier-Journal* says, "The League and the Court are interdependent. They are instruments of each other. The League enforces certain of the judgments of the Court. The Court defines the basis of justice on which the League is to act." The Newark *News* emphasizes the Council's suggestion that if this Hague Court can not be established with the all-important aid of the League, it can not be established at all. In the Council's opinion,

"The establishment of the Court is not such an easy matter as it appears to Mr. Harding, who would reconstruct it without the aid of the League, 'put teeth in it,' and palm it off as a more satisfactory substitute for the League. The sober views of the Council are in refreshing contrast with the hasty, ill-considered suggestions Mr. Harding has dispensed so freely."

Mr. Harding's substitute proposals favoring some association of free nations and a World Court development of the Hague Tribunal appeared in THE LITERARY DIGEST for September 11.

Aside from the favorite contrast of Root and Harding in Democratic papers we read in the Charleston *News and Observer* the assurance that despite the fact that the United States is holding aloof this Court project shows that "the League is gradually

THE NEXT PROBLEM WILL BE TO GET THE ANIMALS TO MAKE THE TRANSFER.

—Darling in *Collier's Weekly*.

being perfected, and the process is of epochal importance."
The Atlanta *Constitution* sums up the situation thus:

"We find the Republicans fighting the League of Nations with
one arm and embracing it under a different name with the other.

"Should the party succeed in defeating the Democrats by this
anomaly, thus fooling the people as to the actual facts, it will
then put the identical League of Nations sought by Mr. Wilson
into effect and claim credit for having done the whole thing."

The Washington *Herald* (Ind.) says:

"Both Candidate Harding and Candidate Cox need to be
more accurate in their references to the facts of recent and present
history. The Hague Conference's bequest to the makers of a
new international judicial tribunal is not truly described by Mr.
Cox when he refers to it as something with 'bats in the belfry
and spiders everywhere,' and the League is not 'dead,' as Mr.
Harding reports it to be."

Document No. 72 Forgiving War-Offenders (1920)
Source: *The Literary Digest,* LXVII (October 2, 1920), pp. 18-19.

FORGIVING WAR - OFFENDERS

THE "CROWD OF MARPLOTS and conspirators" who are confined in State and Federal prisons for opposing the Government during the war should not, in the opinion of a Washington paper, "be dumped upon an already outraged nation." But, argue the friends of these prisoners, the war is really over, the offenders were merely lovers of peace whose souls shrank from the bloodthirstiness of armed conflict, and it is cowardly and tyrannical to keep them in jail now.

Some of our more conservative editors say we should let bygones be bygones and release them, but others hold that they would at once join the "Red" agitators who are trying to stir up Bolshevism here. Of course, the Socialist papers have been calling for their release almost ever since the armistice was signed, but recently such well-known metropolitan dailies as the New York *World,* the New York *Evening Post,* and the Brooklyn *Citizen* alined themselves in this respect with the New York *Call* (Socialist) and the Milwaukee *Leader,* Victor Berger's Socialist daily.

In the first place, we are told by a labor paper, "there is a grave doubt as to the constitutionality of the Espionage Law (under which most of the prisoners, including Eugene V. Debs, were convicted), as the First Amendment of the Constitution expressly prohibits Congress from making any law abridging the rights of free speech and free press." "In no previous war," points out this paper, "has it been found necessary to pass such a law." Attorney-General Palmer, however, recently refused to consider the proposal of Samuel Gompers, president of the American Federation of Labor, and representatives of the Socialist party that a blanket proclamation freeing the prisoners be issued; each case must be reviewed separately, ruled Mr. Palmer. Including per-

ONE WHO HAS BEEN FREED.

"On the day I stept outside the prison walls I took a solemn oath never to rest, never be silent, never cease my labors until every political prisoner is free," says Mrs. Kate Richards O'Hare, whose five-year sentence for violating the Espionage Act was commuted by President Wilson after she had served fourteen months of it.

sons imprisoned by the various States, there are said to be four thousand political prisoners serving sentences at the present time. Their case is thus argued by the Socialist party:

"The men and women convicted of offenses under war-time statutes are not criminals except in a very technical and unnatural sense. They were opposed to the war and the government war-policies, and in the light of the tragic consequences of the war for the whole world the people of this country begin to feel increasingly that the opposition was legitimate and well grounded as it was honest and courageous. Under these circumstances their further incarceration is not justifiable on grounds of sound policy or good morals, but assumes the character of political and class vindictiveness."

"It should not be difficult now to write at a fairer judgment concerning the culpability of these culprits than was possible in the time of war," thinks the New York *World*, which adds that "in nearly all cases where guilt was solely a matter of opinion the penalties inflicted were extremely severe and might properly be modified." The Brooklyn *Citizen* thinks "the common welfare" demands "an early release of all the less important offenders," and the New York *Evening Post*, which reminds us that the prisoners under discussion "did not violate statutes already in existence, but war-statutes," and that "the danger is now past," makes out the following case for them:

"Both the Democratic and Republican candidates have been urged to express their opinions in regard to amnesty for such offenders. We have no hesitation in saying that such amnesty ought to be granted. No good can come from the further confinement of these people. Their punishment serves only to make them martyrs for their followers. Imprisonment itself is of no benefit to them, if we may believe the strong statements of a special committee of the American Prison Association.

"Amnesty is desirable because there is no advantage in further imprisonment, because the existence of a large group of political prisoners is excellent propaganda for the discontented, and because it is one of the first characteristics of a free people, loving liberty, to display tolerance toward those who disagree with it. The amnesty ought not to wait on a Presidential election. It ought to be granted now by the Administration."

Representative of the Socialist attitude is the plea of Mrs. Kate Richards O'Hare, herself a political prisoner until last summer. In *The Appeal to Reason* (Girard, Kan.), Mrs. O'Hare writes:

"On the day I stept outside the prison walls I took a solemn oath never to rest, never be silent, never cease my labors until every political prisoner is free and our benighted, brutal, degenerating prison system is destroyed. I have enjoyed two months of freedom, I have talked with many political prisoners, who like myself have been freed, and I feel more intensely than ever the weight of my vow.

"The question of a general amnesty has nothing to do with whether or not Socialism is politically right or wrong, the I. W. W. sound or unsound in its economic beliefs, or anarchy a practical or impractical social creed. The only question at issue is whether or not wartime usurpation of power by the Administration shall be tolerated in peace and whether we shall be governed by the hysterical dementia of timid officials or clearly exprest and long-tried Constitutional rights.

"Our demand for a general amnesty does not mean that we are asking for the release of criminals or clemency for persons convicted of committing overt acts. We simply demand that persons convicted and serving sentences for the expression of opinion shall be released and restored to all of their legal rights."

"A general amnesty has been granted by practically all the warring nations of Europe, but it 'can not be done' by this so-called free country," caustically remarks the Schenectady *Citizen*, a Socialist daily. And the New York *Call*, which maintains that Congress is to blame for the present plight of the political prisoners, and that the Constitution explicitly prohibits Congress from enacting laws "to gag opinions," goes on to explain:

"Every ruling clique is cowardly in the face of criticism. It will tolerate it if it does not probe fundamentals of the régime in which the clique's material interests are rooted. When fundamental criticism endangers the whole régime of camouflage the ruling clique becomes apprehensive and its one answer is to gag offenders and, if that does not suffice, to jail them.

"This is the explanation of the imprisonment of Eugene V. Debs and other political offenders. They spoke too plainly. They said things that have been verified by events. They have been proved right and their enemies wrong. Just because they told the truth they are dangerous; that is, dangerous to those who dominate by intellectual coercion. They are not dangerous to those in whose name they spoke, the masses, whose better impulses and welfare are imposed upon by the dominant charlatans. The real interests of the masses were exprest by those who have been caged behind prison bars."

One of Mr. Gompers's arguments in behalf of political prisoners was that their cases "should be treated with love and reason and a sense of democracy." The Philadelphia *Public Ledger*, however, points out that "there was neither love nor reason nor a sense of democracy in many of the people who systematically tried to hinder the Government and belittle it in the eyes of enemies at a time when we were exerting all our energies to preserve such freedom as remained in a world ridden by militarists on one hand and by anarchists on the other." Continues *The Ledger:*

"A great many persons now in confinement will probably be released, since, with the end of the war and the repeal of the Espionage Act, their offenses may properly be forgotten. They are 'political prisoners' in the true sense. They held and voiced opinions which made them dangerous in a time of stress and crisis. Others, however, were frank and determined enemies of the Government, and therefore dangerous to the country not because of their opinions alone, but because of an active opposition to rules established in the interest of national safety and moral law. They deserve punishment."

"If there were any evidence that these offenders had learned the lesson in citizenship which they needed, there might be some sympathy for them on the ground that the war is over," remarks the Philadelphia *Bulletin*—

"But there are no proofs of repentance offered, nor any pretense made that any one of the principal beneficiaries of the petition would do differently were the circumstances to recur. Mercy is not asked. The pardon which is asked for is regarded as a sign that the President and the Attorney-General, representing the Government of the United States, have actually condoned the offense of defying its military law in a time of national crisis. And public sentiment, even if it confesses a measure of sympathy for the unfortunates, can hardly agree to that."

"It would be a political misfortune to Mr. Debs and his party if he were pardoned and released before the election," says the Springfield *Republican*, which does not think the appeals of the Socialist party for their leader's release are "entirely sincere." And we read in the Washington *Post:*

"Mercy is warranted frequently where the offender admits his wrong-doing and expresses sincere regret, but in the cases of Debs and Berger and their 'comrades' there are no such expressions. They remain contumacious. They voice the same contempt for the law that they did when they fought for Germany by weakening the American defenses; they would turn to sowing the seeds of discord and strife and preaching revolution and disrespect for established authority that they have shown in the past. Mercy is a noble sentiment, but it will be frightfully abused if extended to all violators of the Espionage Act."

Document No. 73   Jane Addams, "Feed the World and Save the League,"
(1920)
Source: *The New Republic* (Nov. 24, 1920).

Feed the World
and Save the League

IN Bertrand Russell's recent report of his experiences in Russia, he said: "Contact with
those who had no doubts, has intensified a
thousandfold my own doubts not only of commun-
ism, but of any creed so firmly held that for its sake
men are willing to inflict wide-spread misery."

The statement recalls a similar one put into the
mouth of Danton by Romain Rolland in his play
of that name; "There is no danger in any state as
great as that of men with principles. They don't
try to do good but to be in the right; no suffering troubles them. Their only morality, their
only political ideal, is to impress their ideas upon
others."

Have the advocates of the League of Nations
fallen into the state of mind thus described? Does
the common man distrust the League because it is
slow to relieve the wide-spread misery in Europe;
because it so cautiously refuses to become the tentative instrument of a longed for new era; because
it threatens to become one more of those abortive
efforts "to end war" which fail because they have
nothing tangible and human upon which to focus
scattered moral energies and no popular drive with
which to make effective moral ideas upon a more
extended scale than that to which the time has become accustomed?

As the revolutionists have learned from the war
the ready use of arms in pressing their claims, is it

not possible that the united governments from their war experience in the increased production and distribution of foods, may have learned what the great underlying demand of the oppressed actually is, and also to use the training of war to meet it reasonably and quickly?

If this demand could be recognized and acknowledged as in a great measure valid, what a much needed change in the world's affairs might take place, not as it now threatens to occur under the leadership of men driven desperate by hunger, but with the help of men who are trained in the daily processes of world wide commerce; men working wholeheartedly to meet adequately and scientifically a world obligation but newly formulated on an international scale, although long recognized in piecemeal fashion. The great danger ahead of the League of Nations is implicit in the fact that its first work involves the guaranteeing of a purely political peace and a dependence upon the old political motives. Whereas if from the very first it could perform an act of faith, if it evinced the daring to meet new demands which could be met in no other way, then and then only would it become the necessary instrumentality to carry on the enlarged life of the world and gradually be recognized as indispensable.

Since the cessation of war, there is all over the world a sense of loss in motive power, the consciousness that there is no driving force equal to that furnished by the heroism and self-sacrifice demanded in war time. Yet the great purposes of the League of Nations could be made sufficiently appealing to absorb these to the full. What could afford a more primitive, genuine and abiding motive than feeding the people of the earth on an international scale? It would utilize all the courage and self-sacrifice evolved by warfare and turn into immediate efficiency all that international co-operation which performed such miracles of production in the prosecution of the war. Both are ready to its hand. The British Labor party has pointed out the beginning of international order as follows: "During the period of the war we had great international bodies for the control and distribution of shipping, credit, and raw material in accordance not with capacity to pay, but with vital need. Only so could the common enemy be met. There was in these arrangements the beginnings of an organized economic government of the world, a real international society, subjecting to a common control those things essential to the common life. Here was a world-government actually in being."

If the League of Nations had maintained the system, remedied its defects, enlarged its functions, and democratized its administration, the de facto beginnings of an organized economic government of the world would have been constituted. The eighteenth century phrases in which diplomatic intercourse has been so long conducted would have dropped away as not fitted to discuss the need of an internationally guaranteed loan, the functions of an Economic Council for the control of food stuffs and raw material, the fuel shortage, credits granted to enemy and liberated countries alike for reconstruction purposes, the effect of malnutrition on powers of production, the irreparable results of "hunger oedema." Some brave spirit might even point out that it is useless to hold an International Labor Congress in order to raise the standard of life and wages throughout the world, if famine continues steadily to depress that standard throughout the great manufacturing regions of Europe. Out of his wide experience in feeding devastated Europe, Mr. Hoover once, perhaps hastily, said: "There are certain foundations of industry in

Europe that, no matter what the national or personal ownership or control may be, yet partake of the nature of public utilities in which other nations have a moral right." Certainly such a situation presents material for a statesmanship which is genuine and straightforward, and contains a tremendous appeal to the common man.

If this policy of feeding the hungry were once adopted, the League might at last feel the zeal, the tingle and excitement of reality and through the sheer processes of life become genuinely significant.

We are told by those familiar with the work carried on at the temporary headquarters of the League of Nations in London that "the economic section has for many months been engaged in a world wide study of such questions as coal, production, markets, food and the movement of raw material. At the first meeting of the Assembly a full report will be ready." But how many people may starve to death before those reports are acted upon. It suggests a committee studying the best method of extinguishing fires while precious granaries are burning down.

It is quite obvious that the League must proceed carefully but there are times when even well considered delay is fatal. While these reports are being prepared, the starving people themselves have ceased to look to the League for help, it has lost all that popular confidence and hope which was its greatest asset. How many times do the friends of the League say in its defense: "that is due to the Treaty, the League has not yet begun to function" only to receive the bitter reply, "the same men who wrote the Treaty, made the League."

Much has been said during the war about primitive emotion and instinctive action, but certainly their use need not be reserved to purposes of destruction. After all, the first friendly communication between tribe and tribe came through the need of food when one or the other was starving and too weak to fight, primitive human pity made the folk way which afterward developed into political relationships.

Why not open the gates and let these primitive emotions flood our devastated world? By all means let the beneficent tide be directed and canalized by the League of Nations which is, after all, the outgrowth of century-old dreams. The great stumbling block always in the way of its earlier realization and the crux of its actual survival now, is the difficulty in interpreting it to the understanding of the common man, grounding it in his affections, appealing to his love for human kind. To such men, who, after all, compose the bulk of the citizens in every nation participating in the League, the abstract policies of it make little appeal although they would gladly contribute their utmost to feed the starving, as the two and a half million French trade unionists regularly tax themselves for the children of Austria; as the British Labor party insists that the British foreign policy shall rest "upon a humane basis, really caring for all mankind, including colored men, women and children"; as the German workmen recommend that "all commodities of first necessity be pooled so that each people gets its share"; or as the American Federation of Labor declares its readiness to "give a mighty service in common effort for all human kind."

So far as the working man in any country has expressed himself, it is all in this direction. In addition to the organized workers, millions of earth's humblest toilers whose lives are consumed in securing the daily needs of existence for themselves and their families, go stumbling towards the light of better international relations largely because "Man is constantly seeking a new and finer adjustment between his inner emotional demands and the practical arrangements of the world in which he lives." It is absurd for us, as advocates of the League, to complain that it is difficult to endear it to "the people" when it is precisely the people who are most ready for an act of faith, to whom it seems most natural to feed the hungry. It may take years to popularize the principles of the League, but citizens of civilized nations have already received much religious instruction. "To do the will" on an international scale might result in that world wide religious revival which the war in spite of many predictions, has as yet failed to evoke. It would certainly establish the sort of League of which thousands of people dreamed when they hailed the President of the United States as the Savior of Europe. Why are we, its advocates, so slow to tap this reservoir of moral power which alone could adequately motive the great undertaking? We fail to remember that to confound principles with people, indicates that we understand neither religion nor our fellow-men.

JANE ADDAMS

Document No. 74 Woodrow Wilson's Acceptance of the Nobel Peace Prize
(1920)
Source: Frederick W. Haberman, ed., *Peace, 1901-1925; Nobel Lectures*
(Amsterdam: Elsevier Publishing Co. for the Nobel Foundation, 1972), pp.
294-296. Reprinted by permission of the Elsevier Publishing Company.

Acceptance

by Albert G. Schmedeman, American Minister

The Peace Prize for 1919, reserved in that year, was awarded in 1920 to
Woodrow Wilson in recognition of his Fourteen Points peace program and
his work in achieving inclusion of the Covenant of the League of Nations
in the 1919 Treaty of Versailles. Since President Wilson was not present at
the award ceremony on December 10, 1920, Albert G. Schmedeman, United
States minister in Oslo, accepted the prize in his behalf. Mr. Schmedeman's
speech[1], which included the reading of a message from President Wilson,
follows:

Mr. President, I have the honor to inform you that I am the bearer of a
telegram from Woodrow Wilson, President of the United States, in which
he requests me to express his thanks and appreciation for the honor which
has been conferred upon him by the Nobel Peace Committee of the Storting
in awarding him the prize for the year 1919. Therefore, I have the honor,
Mr. President, to request that permission will be granted me to read the
message and make a few remarks to the honorable body.

I have been instructed by President Wilson to convey the following message[2] of appreciation to President [Chairman] Løvland and the members
of the Nobel Peace Committee of the Storting:

«In accepting the honor of your award I am moved not only by a profound gratitude for the recognition of my [sincere and] earnest efforts in
the cause of peace, but also by a very poignant humility before the vastness
of the work still called for by this cause.

May I not take this occasion to express my respect for the far-sighted
wisdom of the founder in arranging for a continuing system of awards? If

1. Taken from the text in *Les Prix Nobel en 1919-1920*, with two minor emendations
based on the text in *Forhandlinger i Stortinget* (nr. 502) for December 10, 1920 [Pro-
ceedings of the Norwegian Parliament].
2. The text and punctuation of the telegram are taken from *Les Prix Nobel en 1919-
1920* and verified in *Forhandlinger i Stortinget* (nr. 502); the words in brackets are from
the *New York Times* (December 11, 1920) version of the text.

there were but one such prize, or if this were to be the last, I could not of course accept it. For mankind has not yet been rid of the unspeakable horror of war. I am convinced that our generation has, despite its wounds, made notable progress. But it is the better part of wisdom to consider our work as one[1] begun. It will be a continuing labor. In the indefinite course of [the] years before us there will be abundant opportunity for others to distinguish themselves in the crusade against hate and fear and war.

There is indeed a peculiar fitness in the grouping of these Nobel rewards. The cause of peace and the cause of truth are of one family. Even as those who love science and devote their lives to physics or chemistry, even as those who would create new and higher ideals for mankind in literature, even so with those who love peace, there is no limit set. Whatever has been accomplished in the past is petty compared to the glory and promise of the future.

Woodrow Wilson»

I regret that I am unable to address this honorable body in the Norwegian language; even if I were, there are no words which can fully express my appreciation for the high honor conferred upon my country by the award of the Nobel Peace Prize for the year 1919 by the Nobel Committee of the Storting to one of America's greatest statesmen, Woodrow Wilson, President of the United States of America. This honor which has been bestowed on President Wilson is one of significance and of utmost satisfaction to me – an occasion which will always remain in my memory. To have the privilege of accepting, on behalf of the President of the United States, this evidence of appreciation of his efforts to replace discord with harmony by appealing to the highest moral forces of each nation, is an event to be cherished.

It is unnecessary for me to dwell upon any of those achievements of President Wilson which justify the bestowal of this honor upon him; his comprehensive understanding of international affairs and his discerning and convincing methods of procedure in matters affecting the welfare and success of entire peoples, which, due to his earnest and forceful endeavors, resulted in the formation of the League of Nations, are well known to us all. He, perhaps as much as any public man, is conscious of the fact that the time is

---

1. *Les Prix Nobel* and *Forhandlinger i Stortinget* read «one»; *N.Y. Times* reads «only»; the context suggests «only» as the proper reading.

past when each nation can live only unto itself, and his labors have been inspired with the idea and hope of making peace universal a living reality. It is impossible to make a proper estimate of Woodrow Wilson and his great work for international peace until time has revealed much that must, for the present, be a sealed book.

Let me assure you, members of the Norwegian Storting, that words fail to convey the deep emotion which stirs within me at this time, when it falls within my province to receive this testimonial on behalf of the President of the United States of America. No more fitting word of appreciation could be voiced than that contained in the President's message, in which he acknowledges the great honor that has been conferred upon him by the Nobel Peace Committee of the Storting.

President Wilson, who notified the Nobel Committee that ill health prevented his visiting Oslo, did not deliver a Nobel lecture.

Document No. 75   War-Time Offenders Out of Jail (1920)
Source: *The Literary Digest* (Dec. 11, 1920), p. 20.

WAR-TIME OFFENDERS OUT OF JAIL

"**S**HIRKERS, SKULKERS, AND INGRATES," are some of the harsh appellations applied by the Grand Rapids *Press* to the thirty-three "conscientious objectors" released by Secretary of War Baker in time to enjoy Thanksgiving dinner at home. "Presumably, following Mr. Baker's usual custom, they were given full back pay and new suits of clothes," adds this paper. These "C. O's," as they are designated by some editors, "were the worst of the lot, for they not only declined to fight for their country, but refused to do any work whatever, altho displaying hearty appetites at meal-time." "These men stood in the way of the nation's safety," charges *The American Legion Weekly* (New York); "they had the choice between self and sacrifice, and they chose to be selfish at a time when selfishness needed to be submerged in the name of public necessity." "The action of Secretary Baker constitutes an insult to every loyal member of the American Expeditionary Forces, and it aroused a feeling of resentment which marred an otherwise placid Thanksgiving day," declares the Washington *Post*. And *The Post* further unburdens itself in a scathing arraignment of Secretary Baker and the "cringing, skulking cowards" whom he released:

"Doubtless Secretary of War Baker feels entirely justified in extending clemency to the thirty-three conscientious objectors who have just been given the freedom enjoyed by some six hundred others of their ilk. But if 'the quality of mercy is not strained,' why does Secretary Baker not extend his clemency further and open the doors of military prisons to all offenders except murderers? For there is no type of criminal so repulsive to the patriotic citizen as the cringing, skulking coward who refuses to fight for his flag and country.

"Under the operation of the law, these men were sentenced to long terms of imprisonment, but after the armistice the Administration's policy of leniency began to develop and one by one they were released until but thirty-three remained. Now these have been given their freedom.

"This action is the culminating act of a Secretary of War who has been apparently unable to understand the spirit of America. These recalcitrants now turned loose are Americans, not enemy aliens. It was as much their duty to defend America in war as it would be to assist in putting out a fire or defending their families against invaders. For every one of them who skulked and shirked his duty, another American boy suffered extra risk and assumed extra duty.

"It is not the fault of these skulkers that the United States did not lose the war. They have no right to enjoy the liberty that they refused to fight for and which others earned for them."

But, declares Secretary Baker:

"Each case has been considered on its merits, and the principle on which they have been considered is to remit so much of the sentence as exceeds the normal peace-time penalty for the offenses charged.

"The major part of these men have been in confinement for more than two years. Those last discharged were men who had refused to do any sort of work while in confinement."

However, points out *The American Legion Weekly*, "the severity of this penance can hardly be expected to impress those soldiers who have been in hospitals for two years and more with tuberculosis contracted in the service," and the Grand Rapids *Press* reminds us that there are numbers of soldiers "who faced Hun bullets in France, and who, for some infraction of military discipline, were sentenced to long terms in prison, and still are imprisoned." "Why not extend amnesty to them, too?" asks the Michigan paper.

The Commander of the American Legion, however, says he is glad these prisoners have been released by Secretary Baker, and gives his reasons:

"I am glad that Secretary Baker has released these men; glad that he completed the job he started long ago of releasing the men who refused the first duty of citizenship, who proved untrue to American ideals, and who outlawed themselves forever in the estimation of all American patriots.

"I am glad he got them off his mind, for they seemed to be his first consideration. I hope that Mr. Baker will now find time to consider the cases of the men who served their country; who went to France to fight and who did not object to serving their country; men who went A. W. O. L. in France and are serving long prison terms as the result of courts martial.

"Let Mr. Baker consider that in the one case men refused even to bear arms and think what that would have meant for the nation had every one adopted that attitude.

"Let him then consider that men who were willing to fight are serving long terms as the result of indiscretions that are minor compared with the crime of refusing to fight."

The New York *Evening World*, on the contrary, thinks "Secretary Baker's administration has been excellent; certainly it has been courageous. He steered his course between the perils of Prussianism on one hand and sentimentalism on the other." This paper's morning namesake believes that "the release of these prisoners . . . was an act of clemency dictated by common sense," and it reminds us that there is a difference between the "slacker" and the conscientious objector. Says *The World*:

"For the conscientious objector who went to prison there may be excuses that can not hold good for the slacker who evaded service by running away in the hope of beating the law. The true conscientious objector was capable of a kind of moral courage or obstinacy that rendered him the fitting object of a certain respect. The slacker's first instincts were those of cowardice or disloyalty.

"It is a distinction that should be kept in mind by all who have joined in condemning in advance Secretary Baker's course in freeing the conscientious objectors. In their case certainly the law has been vindicated, and by their long imprisonment they have paid the required penalty for denying an obligation of citizenship that the average young man was proud to meet."

"Their continued imprisonment would do no particular good," agrees the Washington *Star*, and it reminds the released men that "they are now fully identified before the country and must take their chances for rehabilitation in public esteem." Furthermore, thinks *The Star*, "their path will not be one of primroses in the best of circumstances."

President Wilson, it is recalled by *The Nation* (New York), declined to pardon Eugene V. Debs, Socialist candidate for President in the last election, on the ground that "it would set a bad precedent and would encourage others to oppose the Government in the event of another war." Therefore, points out *The American Legion Weekly*, Secretary Baker's action, should another emergency arise, "will show the prospective conscientious objectors how easily a fellow can get away with it."

At about the same time the conscientious objectors were being freed, what the Boston *Transcript* calls "A Scandalous Pardon" was granted by the President to Franz Rintelen (sometimes known as von Rintelen), the German spy who was captured by the British as he was trying to escape from this country, and turned over to the United States Government upon the assurance that he would be punished for his activities as a spy. "This pardon stains the national honor," asserts this Boston paper, and the Troy *Record* agrees that "a man like Rintelen deserved more to be shot than to have his sentence commuted." His release "will put a premium on plotting," thinks the Richmond (Va.) *News-Leader*, which reminds us that "Rintelen was a spy, a conspirator; not a prisoner of war." Of his many activities in this country before we entered the war, we read in the New York *Tribune:*

"Von Rintelen was tried three times and three times convicted. First, for having conspired to suppress legal American trade; secondly, for fraudulently obtaining a passport; thirdly, for conspiring to destroy ships going from our ports to those of the Allies by putting fire bombs in their cargoes. There were other even more heinous acts connected with the activities of von Rintelen, but the foregoing were the formal accusations. Of his guilt there was no pretense of doubt. He was in the category of a pirate. He was a guerrilla who sought to butcher the citizens of another land with which his country was at peace."

Document No. 76 Senator Borah's Resolution for a Disarmament
Conference (1920)
Source: U.S. *Congressional Record,* 66th Cong., 3rd Sess., Vol. LX, Part I
(Dec. 14, 1920), p. 310.

REDUCTION OF NAVAL ARMAMENT—DISARMAMENT.

Mr. BORAH. I introduce a joint resolution which I ask
may be read and referred to the Committee on Foreign Relations.

The joint resolution (S. J. Res. 225) authorizing the President
of the United States to advise the Governments of Great Britain
and Japan that the Government of the United States is ready to
take up with them the question of disarmament, etc., was read
the first time by its title and the second time at length and
referred to the Committee on Foreign Relations, as follows:

Whereas a representative and official of the Japanese Government has
advised the world that the Japanese Government could not consent
even to consider a program of disarmament on account of the naval
building program of the United States; and

Whereas by this statement the world is informed and expected to believe that Japan sincerely desires to support a program of disarmament, but can not in safety to herself do so on account of the attitude and building program of this Government; and

Whereas the only navies whose size and efficiency requires consideration on the part of this Government in determining the question of
the size of our Navy are those of Great Britain and of Japan, two
Governments long associated by an alliance; and

Whereas the United States is now and has ever been in favor of a
practical program of disarmament: Now, therefore, be it

*Resolved by the Senate and House of Representatives of the United
States of America in Congress assembled,* That the President of the
United States is requested, if not incompatible with the public interests, to advise the Governments of Great Britain and Japan, respectively, that this Government will at once take up directly with their
Governments and without waiting upon the action of any other nation
the question of disarmament, with a view of quickly coming to an understanding by which the building naval programs of each of said Governments, to wit, that of Great Britain, Japan, and the United States,
shall be reduced annually during the next five years 50 per cent of the
present estimates or figures.

Second, that it is the sense of the Congress, in case such an understanding can be had, that it will conform its appropriation and building
plans to such agreement.

Resolved further, That this proposition is suggested by the Congress
of the United States to accomplish immediately a substantial reduction
of the naval armaments of the world.

Document No. 77 Arthur Deerin Call of the American Peace Society Gives an Optimistic Forecast (1921)
Source: *The Advocate of Peace,* LXXXIII (April, 1921), pp. 140-145.

THREE FACTS IN AMERICAN FOREIGN POLICY

By ARTHUR DEERIN CALL

TRUE SANITY in international matters may mean to be in tune with the Infinite; it certainly means to be in tune with the finite. As perhaps never before, international morality is simply intelligence applied to the common good. The World War has had at least one beneficent effect; it has concentrated the thoughts of men upon the mysteries of foreign policy. It is evident now to us all that the well-being of every man is very closely related to the aspirations and behavior of nations, that the foreign policy of States is the concern of every one of us. In untangling the skein of international relationships we may well begin at home, for there are three facts in American foreign policy, as John Hay expressed, principles of "limpid simplicity," which are of no little concern to the weal of the world.

I

AMERICA AND THE WAR SYSTEM

America a Protest

America is itself a protest against the war system. American citizenship is made up in no small measure of persons who have come to this country, or whose ancestors came to this country, for the purpose of getting rid of the recurring devastations peculiar to European wars. Life, liberty, pursuit of happiness, health, justice, education—these are more distinctly American than even wealth and sky-scrapers. America knows that these things thrive only where peace thrives. Men of other nations have known this, but with America the belief has often been a passion. America's participation in the World War was a rebuke to the war system. We insist that the Old World methods of war shall not interfere with these prime American aims. The first objection to war is that wars may be won and justice defeated; brute force may have its way and at the same time do violence to right. That is the great iniquity of war. It is the basis of our America's objection to that precarious method of settling disputes.

True, the opposition to war did not begin in America. The will to end war is of a long historical growth. Something of that long development should be familiar, more familiar than it now is.

When, as set forth in the 14th chapter of Genesis, four kings waged war with five others in the Vale of Siddim, there were evidently in operation two leagues to enforce peace. In the very first book of his Aeneid, Virgil reveals Jupiter unrolling the fates, when wars shall cease and the gates of Janus be closed "with fast iron bars." The words in the second chapter of Isaiah, referring to the time when "They shall beat their swords into plowshares and their spears into pruning hooks;" when "nation shall not lift its sword against nation, neither shall they learn war any more," are repeated not only in the fourth chapter of Micah; they voice the age-long hope of men.

Throughout history leaders among men have struggled to show the way to overthrow war. Not always actuated by the highest motives in particular instances, enthusiasts, favoring primarily the countries to which they happened to belong, often concerned to preserve situations developed out of the blood of arms, they have, nevertheless, revealed the one common purpose to establish a more permanent peace.

For example, Pierre Dubois in his *De Recuperatione Terre Sancte,* written in 1305-7, elaborates the course for occupying and retaining the Holy Land through the means of a league to enforce peace. Again, in 1311, the poet Dante Alighieri wrote his *De Monarchia,* a work in which he defends the principle of monarchy, but upon the basis that "the human race is ordered for the best when it is most free," and that "universal peace is the best of those things which are ordained for our beatitude." And there was George von Podébrad, who in his *Traité d'Alliance et Confederation,* etc., written 1460-63, insisted that "peace cannot exist apart from justice," and "justice cannot exist apart from peace." Von Podébrad submitted a plan for a league to enforce peace, especially for the purpose of bringing about "a true, pure, and lasting peace, union, and love among Christians, and to defend the religion of Christ against the unspeakably monstrous Turk." Then, about the year 1515, Erasmus wrote his treatise on war, which has been placed "among the most famous writings of the most illustrious writers of his age." It is a treatise "against war." It begins with these words: "It is both an elegant proverb, and among all others, by the writings of many excellent authors, full often and solemnly used, *Dulce bellum inexpertis,* that is to say, War is sweet to them that know it not." Colet, founder of St. Paul's School, Thomas More and others of a similar mind, were friends of Erasmus at that time and joined with him for the most part in his opposition to war. But Erasmus surpassed them all in his persistent and unequivocal condemnation of "war, pestilence, and the theologians," the three great enemies with which he says he had to contend throughout his life.

But America's opposition to war is backed not only by treatises of the long ago; there have been the various plans and projects for the practical realization of the peace goal of the philosophers.

Seventeenth Century

In the seventeenth century there were four outstanding projects for a league to enforce peace.

1

Addressing himself to the monarchs and sovereign princes of that time, Emeric Crucé, wrote in 1623 what he called the "New Cyneas," which was a "discourse of the occasions and means to establish a general peace and the liberty of commerce throughout the whole world." Crucé grants that to assure perpetuity to universal peace "is very difficult." He says: "It seems that calm weather cannot last long in the ocean of our affairs, where the impetuous winds of ambition excite so many storms. Suppose, for instance, that peace is signed to-day; that it is published to the whole world; how do we know that posterity will ratify the articles? Opinions are changeable, and the actions of the men of the present time do not bind their successors." And yet he urges the necessity of choosing a city "where all sovereigns should have perpetually their ambassadors, in order that the differences that might arise should be settled by the judgment of the whole assembly." With his congress of ambassadors backed by a collective force, he proposes the establishment of a universal peace. He says: "We have raised enough storms. It is time to give calm and serenity to this great ocean by throwing upon it the oil of perfect reconciliation."

2

Hugo Grotius wrote his treatise "On the Law of War and Peace" in 1625. In this work Grotius urges conference and arbitration for the settlement of disputes between nations, and, drawing upon the experience of the Druids, points out the necessity that measures "be taken to compel the disputants to accept peaceful settlement on equitable terms."

In 1638 appeared "The Great Design" of Henry IV.
This influential project, taken from the Memoirs of the
Duke of Sully, who is probably its author, is a plan to
maintain by force a status created by force, a political
scheme for the government of all Europe.

The influence of this ambitious "Design" was marked.
Because of it William Penn was inspired in 1693 to
write his "Present and Future Peace of Europe." Even
the gentle Penn's "Dyet," founded upon the principle
that justice "is a better procurer of peace than war"—
indeed, that "peace is maintained by justice, which is a
fruit of government, as government is from society, and
society from consent"—provided for the compulsion of
recalcitrant States.

Eighteenth Century

In the eighteenth century there were some five other
plans for ending war, with, however, a gradually diminishing emphasis upon force as an agency for peace.

1

Either in 1712 or 1713 appeared Charles Irenee Castel
de Saint-Pierre's "Project for the Establishment of a
Permanent Peace in Europe." This, too, was an outgrowth of the great "Design." Here, too, is a plan for
the maintenance by force of a status created for the most
part by force. But the first article of the project shows
the author's purpose to be the establishment of a "security against the great misfortunes of foreign wars."

2

In 1736 Cardinal Jules Alberoni of Italy set forth a
plan for establishing a perpetual diet at Ratisbon for the
purpose of subjugating the Turk and overcoming the
"tyranny and bondage of the infidels."

3

In 1756 Jean Jacques Rousseau wrote his "Epitome
of Abbé de Saint Pierre's Project for Perpetual Peace,"
published in 1761, in which he expresses his sympathy
with an irrevocable European alliance backed by force.
With no little eloquence he pictures a state of peace resulting from the proposed confederacy, and also of the
"state of war which results from the present impolitic
state of Europe." The same year that Rousseau wrote
his "Epitome" he wrote also his "Judgment of Perpetual

Peace," published in 1782, in which, granting that "perpetual peace is at present a very absurd project," he nevertheless concludes that "if a Henry IV and a Sully are given to us, perpetual peace will become again a reasonable project."

4

Between 1786 and 1789 Jeremy Bentham wrote "A Plan for an Universal and Perpetual Peace." In it he proposes "a common court of judicature for the decision of differences between the several nations." As he says, saving the credit and honor of contending parties, being in every way conformable to their interests, and being inconsonant with no practice, such an arrangement could not "be justly styled visionary." Bentham believed that force would be of little account in the success of his project.

5

In his philosophical essay entitled "Eternal Peace," written in 1795, Immanuel Kant proposed a representative league for the realization of public law backed only by the sanction of public opinion. Founding his plan upon the proposition that the "civil constitution in every State shall be republican," and expressing the opinion that the law of nations should "be founded on the federation of free States . . . 'the guaranty of eternal peace is furnished by no lesser power than the great artist Nature herself, *Natura dœdala rerum.*"

A Constructive Peace Movement

The work of these men of many centuries was not wasted. America's opposition to war is seen to have a great background; it has developed directly from such a history.

And this opposition has not been confined to "brittle-minded" persons. Benjamin Franklin frequently expressed his opposition to war. George Washington wrote in 1785: "My first wish is to see this plague to mankind banished from the earth." The Federal Convention of 1787 was called primarily for the purpose of maintaining peace between thirteen not altogether friendly States. The Monroe Doctrine, enunciated in 1823, was promulgated in the interests of "peace and safety."

The Peace Movement, technically so called, began with the establishment of peace societies in 1815, and that in America. These societies multiplied, and in 1828, upon the initiative of William Ladd, they were amalgamated in the American Peace Society. In 1840 this same William Ladd wrote "An Essay on a Congress of Nations for the Adjustment of International Disputes without Resort to Arms." In this "Essay" Mr. Ladd proposed two things: a congress of nations and a court of nations. This essay by Mr. Ladd contained the foundations of practically all that had been accomplished in the direction of international organization prior to the World War, including the achievements in arbitration and the record of the Hague Conferences of 1899 and 1907. Whether or not the British Empire and continental Europe can be organized for peace after the American pattern, no man can say. Whether or not the continental States of Europe can be brought together, even in a loose federation for peace, is also a problem. But of this the world may be assured: William Ladd's plan needs to be known of men; for, to quote a leading authority in this field, William Ladd "certainly gives the only rational plan that has ever been presented, of advancing the cause of peace by means of international conferences in which a court of justice should be established, and the law, little by little, recommended to the States which the court is to apply." No man has demonstrated more fully than William Ladd the protest against war that is America.

If these plans and projects to which we have referred were for the most part theoretical, there have been practical achievements as well, and often on a large scale. Pan-Americanism, with all its setbacks, is a real achievement in the direction of practical international peace. The Universal Postal Union is an international achievement of great consequence to the common weal. Prior to the war, there were in the neighborhood of 1,000 international organizations concerned with concrete interests. The practical confederations, such as arose under the articles of the Swiss Confederation, in 1291, and under the Union of Utrecht, in 1579, were a part of the movement which led to the Articles of Confederation of the United States of America, in 1777; and thence to the Constitution of the United States, in 1787. The years 1776 and 1787 reveal America as the flower of this age-long aspiration of the race, the will to end war.

II

AMERICA'S INTERNATIONAL BACKGROUND

Based Upon Experience

America is an international fact, representing within herself centuries of concrete international experiences. From 1492 to 1787 was a period of 275 years. From

1787 to 1921 represents a period of only 134 years—approximately eight generations before our Federal Convention as against approximately four generations since that time. During those first eight generations men of this hemisphere were schooled increasingly in matters relating to international affairs. Boundaries, public debts, dishonesties, inefficiencies, countless irritations and ambitions produced their interstate disputes, contests, and settlements. The varying tariffs brought troubles of an international character in their wake. Connecticut taxing imports from Massachusetts higher than imports from Great Britain produced an international problem of no little seriousness. Some States drew separate treaties with the Indians, and that contrary to agreement; and there were various other violations of contract, some ending in war. Shortly prior to 1787 the people of this country received from abroad little but disdain. Economic difficulties became so acute that during upwards of a hundred years various plans of union were proposed and some tried, revealing the international mindedness of those earlier Americans. The step-by-step development was significantly international. Looking back across it all, one is impressed with the remark of C. Ellis Stevens in his "Sources of the Constitution of the United States," in which he says: "Yet it is a characteristic of the race both in England and in America that it has never really broken with the past. Whatever of novelty may appear from time to time, there is ever under all the great and steady force of historic continuity."

1787

The year 1787 may properly be said to be an epoch in the evolution of international achievement. That convention, called to meet on the second Monday of May, found itself faced with the problem of setting up a more perfect union of thirteen free, sovereign, and independent States, preserving the separate powers of the union and of the States, and maintaining at the same time the independence of each. That was a very suggestive international situation. That all-American conference was an international conference; for the States were free, sovereign, and independent—sometimes arrogantly so. Some of them were small, some large. Some of the questions arising between them were in nature justiciable, some were non-justiciable. Whether or not they should set up a government with power to coerce the States by force of arms was at the outset discussed and decided in the negative. Faced with such international questions, that international conference of 1787 met them and solved them. Such was the method of the solution, such the wisdom of the action, we can truthfully say that the United States of America is today the oldest international organization, as it is the oldest government in the world, for since 1787 the English constitution has been radically changed; France has had at least six constitutions, Spain three, and so on down the list. America is not only an international fact representing an outgrowth of international concrete experiences, it is the product of the one successful international conference which has proved adequate to its purpose. As James Brown Scott has phrased it, referring to the services of James Madison: "The Constitution of the more perfect union has succeeded, and if different States and kingdoms should be inclined to substitute the regulated interdependence of States for their unregulated independence, they need only turn for light and leading to the little man of Montpelier, who has preserved for all time an exact account of what took place in the conference of the States in Philadelphia in the summer of 1787."

If in 1787 delegates from twelve free, sovereign, and independent States could meet and successfully solve the questions of representation as between large and small States, establishing a system under which every State is equal in law if not in influence, it ought to be possible for other and similarly free, sovereign, and independent States to do as much. If instructed delegates from those twelve free, sovereign, independent States, voting as States, could adjust all questions of procedure within the conference, fix upon a mutually satisfactory method of ratification, by the provisions of which the States were bound only by their own consent, it would seem reasonable that a similar thing may be done again. If, now, as a result of that international conference, forty-eight free, sovereign, independent States can live peacefully with each other under a more perfect union, providing for a division of legislative, judicial, and executive powers, and subordinating the military arm to civil control, that fact should be of interest for all States belonging to the society of nations. If under this system of union it be a fact that there is no first among equals, no State with privileges or functions not common to all, it must be granted that such a beneficent arrangement is possible.

Coercion of States

But of still greater significance for the nations of the world is the fact that America has demonstrated the desirability and the feasibility of eliminating any plan for the coercion of States by force of arms. Coercion there is; but it is confined to the coercion of individuals only. All attempts to organize States, giving to some central power the authority to coerce member States, have usually led to war; they have invariably failed. As already said, a plan for the coercion of States was presented, debated, and discarded in the Federal Convention of 1787. Madison, Hamilton, and Ellsworth condemned unequivocally any proposal looking toward a union of States with power to coerce the States by arms. There is a coercion of the States in America, but it is coercion by the only conceivable force calculated to avoid war—a force greater than the force of arms, because it is the force which makes and directs arms—that is, the force of public opinion, what Washington called "a decent respect to the opinions of mankind."

Organization for Peace

America is the one outstanding union of States organized for peace. That peace was the motive of the "founding Fathers" is apparent from many provisions of the Constitution. The States delegated and relinquished their rights to lay taxes or duties on "articles exported from any State"; they agreed that "No preference shall be given by any regulation of commerce or revenue to the ports of one State over those of another"; in Article I, section 10, they eschewed "alliances"; they set up an organization under which no State, without the consent of Congress, shall "keep troops or ships of war in time of peace, enter into any agreement or compact with another State or with a foreign power, or engage in war, unless actually invaded or in such imminent danger as will admit of no delay." America has realized disarmament, therefore, because the States of the Union have conferred upon the agent of their creation, the Government of the Union, their former right to raise troops; and they have given to their agent the task of preserving a republican form of government, and of protecting each State against invasion. Thus we have here an "Article X" rationally drawn for the preservation of peace.

The importance of this is that, while the United States of America has organized the States for peace, Europe seems to have missed the lesson. Europe is organized for war, and that to the continuous danger of the rest of the world. Europe must organize for peace if she is to escape war. Leading men in Europe are beginning to see this, and more clearly as they study the experience in America. A Belgian publicist has recently agreed that it would have been possible in Paris to form a loose confederation of the continental States of Europe upon the basis of our Union. A distinguished Austrian, now in this country, has granted the same thing. Switzerland, with a citizenship of French, Germans, and Italians, preserved her neutrality during the World War and showed what can be done under a régime of justice. A Europe organized for war may become a Europe organized for peace. Our own Benjamin Franklin saw this truth as a result of his experiences in the Federal Convention, for in October, 1787, he wrote to a friend in Europe:

"I send you enclos'd the propos'd new Federal Constitution for these States. I was engag'd 4 Months of the last Summer in the Convention that form'd it. It is now sent by Congress to the several States for their Confirmation. If it succeeds, I do not see why you might not in Europe carry the Project of good Henry the 4th into Execution, by forming a Federal Union and One Grand Republick of all its different States & Kingdoms; by means of a like Convention; for we had many interests to reconcile."

Thus America is an international fact, representing an outgrowth of international concrete experiences—a fact of consequence to all men concerned with the peace of the world. We, like Patrick Henry, can know no way of judging the future but by the past. Alliances, "holy" and otherwise, have proved ephemeral. The American Union is an example of permanence. Thus America is of the essence of the forward look. Evidently this was the thought in the mind of President Harding, who in his inaugural address said: "When the governments of earth shall have established a freedom like our own and shall have sanctioned the pursuit of peace as we have practiced it, I believe the last sorrow and the final sacrifice of international warfare will have been written."

III

AMERICA AND THE THREE EQUILIBRIUMS

We have seen that one of the facts of America's foreign policy is the fact that America is itself a protest against the war system. We have just said that another fact of American foreign policy is the fact of its own successful international experiences. There is a third fact at the basis of American foreign policy, and that fact is that America is a series of at least three vital equilibriums.

Anarchy and Tyranny

In the first place, America is an equilibrium between anarchy and tyranny. These two contending forces have come down to us out of a long past, Sophists and Cynics against Aristotle and the other defenders of constitutionalism. As has been frequently pointed out, Greece believed strongly in the freedom of the nation's parts. But through the centuries there arose too much freedom of the parts, and the result was that Greece fell because of anarchy. On the other hand, there was Rome, made up of people strongly inclined toward a highly centralized form of government. Then through the centuries the Roman State became too strong and finally fell, because of tyranny. These two tendencies met in the Renaissance, the Reformation, the French Revolution—indeed, in the Federal Convention of 1787. The Federalists were the Romans, the Anti-Federalists the Greeks, in that convention. One came forth the progenitor of the Republican, and the other of the Democratic party. Because the United States has mapped her course thus far successfully between these two opposing forces, veering now toward tyranny and then toward anarchy, yet avoiding each, the United States has, because of its equilibrium, survived.

Large and Small States

America is also an equilibrium between large and small States. Because both large and small States are equally represented in the Senate, most vitally concerned with foreign relations, the small States have been satisfied. Because the representation has been based on population in the House of Representatives, where bills of appropriation arise, the large States have been satisfied. And because all States, large and small, are equal before the law, large and small States have no irreconcilable divergencies of interest. This equilibrium was found to be necessary before the more perfect union could come into being. It has made it possible for that more perfect union to survive.

Rights and Duties

Finally, America represents an equilibrium between rights and duties. In faith and practice America adopts the principle that every State has the right to exist; and that, therefore, it is the duty of every State to commit no unlawful act calculated to jeopardize the existence of another. America accepts the principle that every State has a right to its independence; and that, therefore, it is the duty of every State never to interfere with that right in another. America believes that every State has a right to equality with other States before the law; and that, therefore, it is the duty of every State to respect this right in other States. America believes that every State has a right not only to its territory, but to jurisdiction over it; and that, therefore, it is the duty of every State to violate neither of these rights in another State. America believes that every State has the right to expect protection in its rights from other States; and that, therefore, it is the duty of every State to respect and protect other States. America believes that every State has the right to a hearing under the law; and that, therefore, it is the duty of every State to uphold the law. These are not matters of theory only; they have been adopted by the American Institute of International Law, by the American Peace Society; they have been upheld by the decisions of the highest courts; they are accepted facts in American political and legal practice. Thus America is an equilibrium between the rights and duties of States.

American Faiths

All this is but another way of saying that America believes in government only as it is a government of laws and not of men. Therefore America cannot arouse any interest in an international organization that does not include all civilized States. America cannot believe in a League of Nations organized for the purpose of doing violence to the existence, independence, or equality of other States. America can conceive of no international organization as an agency for peace if it be set up to infringe upon the rights of other States, and especially if it be organized on the principle of maintaining international order by the coercion of arms. The American Revolution was fought for the purpose of overthrowing an imposed control. America sees the peace of the world to lie in the direction not of executive action, but of law and conciliation. Force, brute force, is not a guarantor of world peace. Any league with adequate force at its disposal is a superstate, impossible of realization within any reasonable time.

America has refused, America will always refuse, to promise in advance to pool her armed forces in contingencies now impossible of definition, contingencies which when they arise may prove to be different from anything now experienced or foreseen. At least America ought so to refuse. America stands for inclusive international organization, not for a limited league of the powerful. America does not believe in the subordination of the judiciary to the will of the executive.

531

America believes in conference, law, friendly composition, arbitration, judicial settlement, the only methods known to be capable of maintaining the equilibriums essential to the permanence of States. And all this is but another way of saying that, for Americans, government, national or international, can rest successfully only on the free consent of the governed. That, after all, is the significant fact of 1787, of America's participation in The Hague conferences of 1899 and 1907. It is the reason for the outcome of the elections of November 2, 1920.

CONCLUSION

Thus American foreign policy rests upon three outstanding facts: She is herself a protest against the war system; she is herself an international entity developed out of concrete international experiences; she survives because she is balanced—thus far safely—between those opposing forces which have destroyed all international organizations hitherto. Therefore, if human beings are to demand, legislate, achieve and live a greater health, a finer happiness, a more creative service for all in an advancing world democracy; if they are to attain unto those wider significances of what it means to live; if they are to build up a world-life that shall be more humane, more just, more free; then, indeed, they must apply their minds and wills unto this answer to the cry of the ages, this contribution peculiarly successful, assuredly enduring, supremely hopeful; this permanent illustration of a workable foreign policy capable of application everywhere, the United States of America. The world's most vivid expression of opposition to the war system is America. The most successful machinery for the maintenance of peace between States is America. This needs to be more generally known and appreciated. America's libation on the altar of world fate is America.

Document No. 78   James Brown Scott Analyzes the Harding Foreign Policies (1921)
Source: *American Journal of International Law*, XV (1921), pp. 232-234.

EDITORIAL COMMENT

THE FOREIGN POLICY OF THE UNITED STATES

During the past few years, especially since the entrance of the United States into the World War on April 6, 1917, the question has been much mooted whether the policy of interested isolation, which had characterized American relations from the earliest days of the Republic, was to be continued, or whether the United States would cease its isolation and take an active part in the world's affairs, not merely in its own interest, but in the interest of the states of the world.

Many there were who thought that conditions had changed to such a degree that the policy of other days should be consciously renounced for a policy more in harmony with what were thought to be the needs of the more modern world. The recent treaty between Germany and its enemies, concluded at Paris during the course of 1919, and signed at Versailles on June 28, 1919, by American representatives, pledged the United States to an active participation not merely in the affairs of Europe, but in the affairs of the world at large. This treaty was twice considered by the Senate of the United States with a view to its advice and consent, and twice that advice and consent were refused. The question was one, however, upon which it was thought advisable to consult the people of the United States directly.

The advantages and disadvantages of the Treaty of Versailles—of the old policy and of the new departure—were debated from one end of the country to the other, and United States Senator Warren G. Harding, of Ohio, was elected President, by 404 electoral votes out of a total vote of 531; and by a popular vote of 16,138,914, in a total vote of 26,661,606.

What is to be the policy of the new administration? For Mr. Harding is a Republican, the Senate is Republican, and the House of Representatives is Republican.

Of this administration Mr. Harding is the mouthpiece of the United States in foreign affairs, although a treaty or convention to bind the United States must be "by and with the advice and consent of the Senate," and then only "provided two-thirds of the Senators present concur." The President may propose: the Senate disposes.

On March 4, 1921, Mr. Harding, having taken the oath of office as President of the United States, stated that policy in so far as he was then able to declare it, and as it depended upon him to frame it, in the inaugural address which he delivered to his fellow-countrymen from the steps of the Capitol.

In the first place, he seems to have stated in his own language, the policy to be found in Washington's farewell address to his countrymen, and in Jefferson's first inaugural address. Thus, in the first three paragraphs devoted to this phase of the subject, he said:

The recorded progress of our republic, materially and spiritually, in itself proves the wisdom of the inherited policy of noninvolvement in Old World affairs. Confident of our ability to work out our own destiny, and jealously guarding our right to do so, we seek no part in directing the destinies of the Old World. We do not mean to be entangled. We will accept no responsibility except as our own conscience and judgment, in each instance, may determine.

Our eyes never will be blind to a developing menace, our ears never deaf to the call of civilization. We recognize the new order in the world, with the closer contacts which progress has wrought. We sense the call of the human heart for fellowship, fraternity, and coöperation. We crave friendship and harbor no hate. But America, our America, the America builded on the foundation laid by the inspired fathers, can be a party to no permanent military alliance. It can enter into no political commitments, nor assume any economic obligations which will subject our decisions to any other than our own authority.

I am sure our own people will not misunderstand, nor will the world misconstrue. We have no thought to impede the paths to closer relationship. We wish to promote understanding. We want to do our part in making offensive warfare so hateful that governments and peoples who resort to it must prove the righteousness of their cause or stand outlaws before the bar of civilization.[1]

Mr. Harding did not mean, however, to convey the impression that the United States would stand aloof and refuse to enter into an association of nations. He sought to make clear in the next three paragraphs of his address, the kind of an association which he had in mind, and the purposes for which it was to be formed. Thus:

We are ready to associate ourselves with the nations of the world, great and small, for conference, for counsel; to seek the expressed views of world opinion; to recommend a way to approximate disarmament and relieve the crushing burdens of military and naval establishments. We elect to participate in suggesting plans for mediation, conciliation, and arbitration, and would gladly join in that expressed conscience of progress which seeks to clarify and write the laws of international relationship, and establish a world court for the disposition of such justiciable questions as nations are agreed to submit thereto. In expressing aspirations, in seeking practical plans, in translating humanity's new concept of righteousness and justice and its hatred of war into recommended action we are ready most heartily to unite, but every commitment must be made in the exercise of our national sovereignty.

Since freedom impelled, and independence inspired, and nationality exalted, a world supergovernment is contrary to everything we cherish and can have no sanction by our

<hr>

[1] Congressional Record, March 4, 1921, p. 2.

republic. This is not selfishness; it is sanctity. It is not aloofness; it is security. It is not suspicion of others; it is patriotic adherence to the things which made us what we are.

To-day, better than ever before, we know the aspirations of humankind, and share them. We have come to a new realization of our place in the world, and a new appraisal of our nation by the world. The unselfishness of these United States is a thing proven, our devotion to peace for ourselves and for the world is well established, our concern for preserved civilization has had its impassioned and heroic expression. There was no American failure to resist the attempted reversion of civilization; there will be no failure to-day or to-morrow.

Finally, he completed this portion of his address in three further paragraphs:

The success of our popular government rests wholly upon the correct interpretation of the deliberate, intelligent, dependable popular will of America. In a deliberate questioning of a suggested change of national policy, where internationality was to supersede nationality, we turned to a referendum to the American people. There was ample discussion, and there is a public mandate in manifest understanding.

America is ready to encourage, eager to initiate, anxious to participate in any seemly program likely to lessen the probability of war, and promote that brotherhood of mankind which must be God's highest conception of human relationship. Because we cherish ideals of justice and peace, because we appraise international comity and helpful relationship no less highly than any people of the world, we aspire to a high place in the moral leadership of civilization, and we hold a maintained America, the proven republic, the unshaken temple of representative democracy, to be not only an inspiration and example but the highest agency of strengthening good will and promoting accord on both continents.

Mankind needs a world-wide benediction of understanding. It is needed among individuals, among peoples, among governments, and it will inaugurate an era of good feeling to mark the birth of a new order. In such understanding men will strive confidently for the promotion of their better relationships, and nations will promote the comities so essential to peace.

Mr. Harding's task during the ensuing four years will be, in so far as he deems it advisable, or conditions permit, to translate these words into facts. Whether it can be done, or how far it can be done, perhaps he himself does not know at present. It is a chart, as it were, for the Ship of State, should it put to sea under his guidance.

For the moment, both at home and abroad, all is expectancy.

JAMES BROWN SCOTT.

TREATY OF PEACE WITH GERMANY
August 25, 1921

(U. S. Statutes at Large, Vol. XXXXII, p. 1939)

The United States of America and Germany:

Considering that the United States, acting in conjunction with its co-belligerents, entered into an Armistice with Germany on November 11, 1918, in order that a Treaty of Peace might be concluded;

Considering that the Treaty of Versailles was signed on June 28, 1919, and came into force according to the terms of its Article 440, but has not been ratified by the United States;

Considering that the Congress of the United States passed a Joint Resolution, approved by the President July 2, 1921, which reads in part as follows:

"Resolved by the Senate and House of Representatives of the United States of America in Congress Assembled:

"That the state of war declared to exist between the Imperial German Government and the United States of America by the joint resolution of Congress approved April 6, 1917, is hereby declared at an end.

"Section 2. That in making this declaration, and as a part of it, there are expressly reserved to the United States of America and its nationals any and all rights, privileges, indemnities, reparations or advantages, together with the right to enforce the same, to which it or they have become entitled under the terms of the Armistice signed November 11, 1918, or any extensions or modifications thereof; or which were acquired by or are in the possession of the United States of America by reason of its participation in the war or to which its nationals have thereby become rightfully entitled; or which, under the Treaty of Versailles, have been stipulated for its or their benefit; or to which it is entitled as one of the Principal Allied and Associated

powers; or to which it is entitled by virtue
of any Act or Acts of Congress; or otherwise."

. . . Being desirous of restoring the friendly
relations existing between the two Nations
prior to the outbreak of war:

Have for that purpose appointed their
plenipotentiaries:

The President of the United States of
America

    Ellis Loring Dresel, Commissioner of the
        United States of America to Germany,
        and

    The President of the German Empire

        Dr. Friedrich Rosen, Minister for For-
        eign Affairs,

Who, having communicated their full
powers, found to be in good and due form
have agreed as follows:

Art. 1. Germany undertakes to accord to
the United States, and the United States shall
have and enjoy, all the rights, privileges, indemnities, reparations or advantages specified in the aforesaid Joint Resolution of the
Congress of the United States of July 2,
1921, including all the rights and advantages
stipulated for the benefit of the United
States in the Treaty of Versailles which the
United States shall fully enjoy notwithstanding the fact that such Treaty has not been
ratified by the United States.

Art. 2. With a view to defining more particularly the obligations of Germany under
the foregoing Article with respect to certain
provisions in the Treaty of Versailles, it is
understood and agreed between the High
Contracting Parties:

(1) That the rights and advantages stip-
ulated in that Treaty for the benefit of the
United States, which it is intended the
United States shall have and enjoy, are those
defined in Section 1 of Part IV, and Parts V,
VI, VIII, IX, X, XI, XII, XIV, and XV.

The United States, in availing itself of the
rights and advantages stipulated in the provisions of that Treaty mentioned in this
paragraph, will do so in a manner consistent
with the rights accorded to Germany under
such provisions.

(2) That the United States shall not be
bound by the provisions of Part 1 of that

Treaty, nor by any provisions of that Treaty, including those mentioned in Paragraph (1) of this Article, which relate to the Covenant of the League of Nations, or by the Council or by the Assembly thereof, unless the United States shall expressly give the assent to such action.

(3) That the United States assumes no obligations under or with respect to the provisions of Part II, Part III, Sections 2 to 8 inclusive of Part IV, and Part XIII of that Treaty.

(4) That, while the United States is privileged to participate in the Reparation Commission, according to the terms of Part VIII of that Treaty, and in any other Commission established under the Treaty or under any agreement supplemental thereto, the United States is not bound to participate in any such commission unless it shall elect to do so.

(5) That the periods of time to which reference is made in Article 440 of the Treaty of Versailles shall run, with respect to any act or election on the part of the United States, from the date of the coming into force of the present Treaty.

Art. 3. The present Treaty shall be ratified in accordance with the constitutional forms of the High Contracting Parties and shall take effect immediately on the exchange of ratifications, which shall take place as soon as possible at Berlin.

In witness whereof, the respective plenipotentiaries have signed this Treaty and have hereunto affixed their seals.

Done in duplicate in Berlin this twenty-fifth day of August, 1921.

Ellis Loring Dresel.
Rosen.

Document No. 80 *The Nation* Assesses the Possibilities of the Disarmament Conference (1921)
Source: *The Nation* (July 27, 1921).

The Disarmament Conference and Its Possibilities

WITH the English protests against the sending of Lloyd George and Lord Curzon to represent Great Britain at the Washington disarmament conference we heartily sympathize, not because, like the London *Times* and Lord Northcliffe, we wish to attack Mr. Lloyd George's personal character, but because we believe with our London namesake that the less the coming conference smacks of Versailles and its personalities the better it will be for the conference and the world. For that reason we trust that neither M. Briand nor M. Viviani nor M. Tardieu will come over to speak for France. And on our side we sincerely hope that there will be no Elihu Root and no James Brown Scott and no Nicholas Murray Butler as part of our delegation. If this conference is to be dominated by the Europeans who helped to plunge the world into its misery and have proceeded to make the situation worse ever since there will be little hope that the meeting can achieve anything thoroughgoing. As for the Root type of mind, with all respect for its profound learning and its mastery of international law, what the hour calls for is younger men—men who at least dimly realize that the world stands at the threshold of a new order and are yet young enough to count upon witnessing the results of their handiwork.

Above all we trust that there will be no generals and no admirals assigned or appointed to the conference by any member of it. It was the German admirals and generals, who, as Joseph H. Choate testified, wrecked the Second Hague Conference. The best of these men in all countries are partisans unable to free themselves from professional prejudices and usually wedded to the idea that nothing can be done to cure the human being of his propensity to fight. Indeed, it is from these and from certain other vested interests that we may expect to have the question asked with increasing frequency as to what practical result the conference can accomplish.

Well, there are many practical things that can be done even if the conference balks at the chief task before it— the abolition of all naval forces save a few ships manned not for fighting purposes but for the police and rescue work of the seas, and the abolition of all armies. Take the submarine. Even naval officers have been urging that this weapon be banned for all time; and as for battleships the rapidly enlarging doubt as to whether they have any value in view of the development of aircraft—doubts stimulated by the American experiments now going on—ought to make it easy for the nations invited to agree upon the barring of all further battleship construction. It is this type of craft that has run up the costs of navies so enormously, the latest types costing between 40 and 50 millions of dollars apiece; moreover, those that are building will be years behind the times in their technical construction the day they are launched.

The danger will be, of course, that the various nations will endeavor to manipulate affairs so that they may be left each of them in the strongest naval position. Hence the only way to reduce them all to absolute equality is to abolish all the navies. We admit that the question of aircraft is more difficult because of the fact that commercial airplanes can speedily be made into death-dealing instruments. None the less, control of this branch of the military and naval service is by no means impossible. During the war Lloyd George solemnly promised the British miners that as soon as the struggle was over he would limit the making of all arms and ammunition and the building of all warships to state-owned arsenals and dockyards. The present advantage of this is that it would make very easy the control of one nation by the other nations, that is, it would not be possible for a country to conceal from its rivals what it might be doing in the making of arms and ammunition if it must carry on those activities in government arsenals which could neither be increased in number nor enlarged in size without the fact becoming public property. In Germany today the Allies are relying upon the extreme radicals and the Socialists to keep them informed as to just what the German Government is really doing in the way of carrying out the decrees of the Treaty of Versailles concerning disarmament. Fortunately there are and there will be in the United States, as well as in other countries, similar pacifist and radical forces which will tend to render any underhand work by any government impossible of concealment.

Again there is the matter of poison gas and the new so-called chemical warfare which the Allies denounced as. a crime against humanity when Germany used it, but which we and they since have embraced with joy. This is the easiest kind of warfare for a disarmed nation to prepare for in short order, for there are many factories that can be utilized for this foul purpose with but slight changes. No one who has read Mr. Will Irwin's "The Next War" can fail to realize that if this sort of warfare is not immediately stopped it will endanger not merely whole nations—men, women, and children—but civilization itself if war on a great scale should occur again.

As for the armies, there are a number of measures that suggest themselves, such as the forbidding of conscription and the limitation of standing armies to a fixed percentage per one hundred thousand of population. Doubtless here England will present the most difficult problem since she insists upon holding great nations like Egypt and India in forcible subjection. But any one can conjure up obstacles; the encouraging thing is that necessity is the whip that drives. If the European nations do not disarm they can hardly escape bankruptcy. Curiously enough, and happily, too, it is, according to the Washington correspondent of the New York *Globe*, the fortunate situation of disarmed Germany which is also compelling the Allies to act; they see that Germany, freed from her crushing military taxes, will be able to get ahead in her economic reconstruction far more rapidly than the Allies. Indeed, Senator Borah has brought out the astonishing fact, which ought to be printed in large type on the front page of every American news-paper, that if we go on with our present armament burdens the people of the United States will have to disburse exactly as much for them during the next thirty years as will the Germans if they pay the 33 billions of dollars imposed by the Allies! Exactly the same burden placed upon Germany as penalty for her share in the war is, in other words, to be voluntarily assumed by the American taxpayers as their tribute to Mars. Was there ever greater folly? Every sane American ought to make it clear to the President that thoroughgoing and radical disarmament on sea and land is what this country wishes and proposes to obtain from the conference.

Document No. 81 National Council on the Limitation of Armament, Leaflet for Disarmament Campaign (1921)
Source: Leaflet in the Swarthmore College Peace Collection, Swarthmore, Pa.

An Efficient Disarmament Campaign

1 Organize a representative local disarmament committee.

2. Help your church to turn men's minds from might to right.

3. Give prizes for disarmament essays in the local schools.

4. Buy Will Irwin's "The Next War", ($1.50) at your book store.
Read it!   Lend it!

5. Become a well-informed speaker on disarmament.
Free information at the address below.

6. Write a letter to "the Editor" in favor of disarmament.

7. Distribute literature on disarmament.
Free pamphlets and leaflets at the address below.

8. Present books to your public library for a disarmament shelf.
You can get a list at the address below.

9. Devise an attractive disarmament window for your store.

10. Show a set of these 20 posters everywhere.
Sold for $1.00

11. Talk disarmament instead of hard times.

12. March with the rest in an "End War" parade.

13. Have a disarmament lecture in your lodge or club.

14. Add your letter to the pile on the President's desk.

What will you do?

For further information, write to
THE NATIONAL COUNCIL ON LIMITATION OF ARMAMENT
1811 Eye Street N. W., Washington, D. C.

Document No. 82   Jane Addams on the Washington Conference (1921)
Source: Clipping from *The Chicago Tribune,* Dec. 19, 1921, located in the
Swarthmore College Peace Collection, Swarthmore, Pa., the Jane Addams
Papers.

MISS JANE ADDAMS ON THE WOMAN'S LEAGUE MASSMEETING.

Chicago, Dec. 16.—In response to various inquiries as to the resolutions actually passed at the massmeeting held last Sunday in Washington under the auspices of the national section of the Women's International league, I take advantage of your friendly column to give the following information:

Six resolutions were passed, only one of which related even remotely to the four powers pact; it read as follows:

" We recognize the peace of the world rests upon the coöperation of all races and we urge that in all conferences or agreements in regard to keeping the peace of the Pacific, China be included on a basis of complete equality."

This resolution had been considered in our conference on Saturday before the evening papers had brought out the terms of the four powers pact. The Sunday massmeeting amended it by inserting the words " all nations " after the words " all races," but nothing was " condemned."

One heard naturally much interesting discussion in Washington concerning the new pact. Among our own membership as among other citizens there were two points of view. On the one hand, those people who viewed the pact as a treaty of the new regional type regarded it as a great advance that an open agreement of four powers should supplant the more or less secret agreement between Japan and Great Britain. On the other hand, people who interpreted the pact as in the nature of an alliance were quite sure that it would in time provoke a counter alliance composed of China, Russia, and other powers, and that the Pacific ocean would thus become subjected to the same balance of power theory which had previously dominated Europe. In either case, our group was naturally much pleased that the four power pact contained no military sanctions and stressed the use of conferences.

The parade following the meeting had been arranged by a local committee and was described by one of the Washington papers as " led by a group of girls from the Western high school bearing banners and torches alternately." The fifty

banners had been carried by the New
York Peace society Nov. 11, 1921, in one
of those protests against war which
characterized the entire country at that
moment of high enthusiasm. The local
committee assured us that in a city so
accustomed to demonstrations as Washington, their use in a parade after a
massmeeting would be understood as such
a general protest. The banners bore no
reference to the current work of the
conference on the limitation of armaments which our organization, uniting
with the majority of our fellow citizens,
very much admires; we, too, believe this
historic gathering to be an earnest of the
time when friendly conference and joint
responsibility will supersede the secrecy
and suspicion leading to war.

If, as THE TRIBUNE informs me, a
formal statement was given out from the
league after the parade which expressed
the league's condemnation of the new alliance, such a statement was unauthor-
ized and represent the view of a minority or of the individual who gave it out.

JANE ADDAMS.

Editor's note—The statement to which
Miss Addams refers in her last paragraph
was issued at the headquarters of the league
an hour after the meeting. In our opinion,
it completely vindicates The Tribune's report.
It says, in part:
" Stirred by the ringing resolutions which
condemned the idea of a four power alliance
and demanded that the United States should
not be a party to any alliance that did not
include all the nations of the world, several
hundred men and women who had been attending a disarmament massmeeting at the
new Masonic Temple auditorium grabbed the
banners which had been used as decorations
and marched to the Pan-American building
as a protest against the action of the conference. . . .
" The ringing appeal which stirred the
men and women at the massmeeting to demonstrate their disapproval of the four power
alliance was made by Miss Margaret Crooks.
" Miss Crooks called upon all those who
disbelieved in the four power alliance to
march upon the Pan-American building to
indicate their protest."
Miss Addams was in the procession.

Document No. 83   The Five-Power Treaty at the Washington Disarmament Conference (1922)
Source: U.S. Congress, 67th Cong.; 4th Sess., *Treaties, Conventions, International Acts, Protocols, and Agreements, 1910-1923, Senate Document No. 348,* (Washington, D.C.: Government Printing Office, 1923), III, pp. 3100-3107.

1922.

TREATY BETWEEN THE UNITED STATES OF AMERICA, THE BRITISH EMPIRE, FRANCE, ITALY, AND JAPAN LIMITING NAVAL ARMAMENT.

Signed at Washington February 6, 1922; ratification advised by the Senate March 29, 1922 (legislative day of March 16).

(Not in force on March 4, 1923.)

ARTICLES.

The United States of America, the British Empire, France, Italy and Japan;

Desiring to contribute to the maintenance of the general peace, and to reduce the burdens of competition in armament:

Have resolved, with a view to accomplishing these purposes, to conclude a treaty to limit their respective naval armament, and to that end have appointed as their Plenipotentiaries:

The President of the United States of America:
Charles Evans Hughes,
Henry Cabot Lodge,
Oscar W. Underwood,
Elihu Root,
    Citizens of the United States;
His Majesty the King of the United Kingdom of Great Britain and Ireland and of the British Dominions beyond the Seas, Emperor of India:
    The Right Honourable Arthur James Balfour, O. M., M. P., Lord President of His Privy Council;
    The Right Honourable Baron Lee of Fareham, G. B. E., K. C. B., First Lord of His Admiralty;
    The Right Honourable Sir Auckland Campbell Geddes, K. C. B., His Ambassador Extraordinary and Plenipotentiary to the United States of America;
and
for the Dominion of Canada:
    The Right Honourable Sir Robert Laird Borden, G. C. M. G., K. C. ;
for the Commonwealth of Australia:
    Senator the Right Honourable George Foster Pearce, Minister for Home and Territories for the Dominion of New Zealand:
    The Honourable Sir John William Salmond, K. C., Judge of the Supreme Court of New Zealand;
for the Union of South Africa:
    The Right Honourable Arthur James Balfour, O. M., M. P.;
for India:
    The Right Honourable Valingman Sankaranarayana Srinivasa Sastri, Member of the Indian Council of State;
The President of the French Republic:
    Mr. Albert Sarraut, Deputy, Minister of the Colonies;
    Mr. Jules J. Jusserand, Ambassador Extraordinary and Plenipotentiary to the United States of America, Grand Cross of the National Order of the Legion of Honour;
His Majesty the King of Italy:
    The Honourable Carlo Schanzer, Senator of the Kingdom;
    The Honourable Vittorio Rolandi Ricci, Senator of the Kingdom, His Ambassador Extraordinary and Plenipotentiary at Washington;
    The Honourable Luigi Albertini, Senator of the Kingdom:
His Majesty the Emperor of Japan:
    Baron Tomosaburo Kato, Minister for the Navy, Junii, a member of the First Class of the Imperial Order of the Grand Cordon of the Rising Sun with the Paulowina Flower;
    Baron Kijuro Shidehara, His Ambassador Extraordinary and Plenipotentiary at Washington, Joshii, a member of the First Class of the Imperial Order of the Rising Sun;
    Mr. Masanao Hanihara, Vice Minister for Foreign Affairs, Jushii, a member of the Second Class of the Imperial Order

of the Rising Sun;

Who, having communicated to each other their respective full powers, found to be in good and due form, have agreed as follows:

CHAPTER I. GENERAL PROVISIONS RELATING TO THE LIMITATION OF NAVAL ARMAMENT.

ARTICLE I.

The Contracting Powers agree to limit their respective naval armament as provided in the present Treaty.

29479—S. Doc. 348, 67–4——41

ARTICLE II.

The Contracting Powers may retain respectively the capital ships which are specified in Chapter II, Part 1. On the coming into force of the present Treaty, but subject to the following provisions of this Article, all other capital ships, built or building, of the United States, the British Empire and Japan shall be disposed of as prescribed in Chapter II, Part 2.

In addition to the capital ships specified in Chapter II, Part 1, the United States may complete and retain two ships of the *West Virginia* class now under construction. On the completion of these two ships the *North Dakota* and *Delaware* shall be disposed of as prescribed in Chapter II, Part 2.

The British Empire may, in accordance with the replacement table in Chapter II, Part 3, construct two new capital ships not exceeding 35,000 tons (35,560 metric tons) standard displacement each. On the completion of the said two ships the *Thunderer*, *King George V*, *Ajax* and *Centurion* shall be disposed of as prescribed in Chapter II, Part 2.

ARTICLE III.

Subject to the provisions of Article II, the Contracting Powers shall abandon their respective capital ship building programs, and no new capital ships shall be constructed or acquired by any of the Contracting Powers except replacement tonnage which may be constructed or acquired as specified in Chapter II, Part 3.

Ships which are replaced in accordance with Chapter II, Part 3, shall be disposed of as prescribed in Part 2 of that Chapter.

ARTICLE IV.

The total capital ship replacement tonnage of each of the Contracting Powers shall not exceed in standard displacement, for the United States 525,000 tons (533,400 metric tons); for the British Empire 525,000 tons (533,400 metric tons); for France 175,000 tons (177,800 metric tons); for Italy 175,000 tons (177,800 metric tons); for Japan 315,000 tons (320,040 metric tons).

ARTICLE V.

No capital ship exceeding 35,000 tons (35,560 metric tons) standard displacement shall be acquired by, or constructed by, for, or within the jurisdiction of, any of the Contracting Powers.

ARTICLE VI.

No capital ship of any of the Contracting Powers shall carry a gun with a calibre in excess of 16 inches (406 millimetres).

ARTICLE VII.

The total tonnage for aircraft carriers of each of the Contracting Powers shall not exceed in standard displacement, for the United States 135,000 tons (137,160 metric tons); for the British Empire 135,000 tons (137,160 metric tons); for France 60,000 tons (60,960 metric tons); for Italy 60,000 tons (60,960 metric tons); for Japan 81,000 tons (82,296 metric tons).

ARTICLE VIII.

The replacement of aircraft carriers shall be effected only as prescribed in Chapter II, Part 3, provided, however, that all aircraft carrier tonnage in existence or building on November 12, 1921, shall be considered experimental, and may be replaced, within the total tonnage limit prescribed in Article VII, without regard to its age.

ARTICLE IX.

No aircraft carrier exceeding 27,000 tons (27,432 metric tons) standard displacement shall be acquired by, or constructed by, for or within the jurisdiction of, any of the Contracting Powers.

However, any of the Contracting Powers, may, provided that its total tonnage allowance of aircraft carriers is not thereby exceeded, build not more than two aircraft carriers, each of a tonnage of not more than 33,000 tons (33,528 metric tons) standard displacement, and in order to effect economy any of the Contracting Powers may use for this purpose any two of their ships, whether constructed or in course of construction, which would otherwise be scrapped under the provisions of Article II. The armament of any aircraft carriers exceeding 27,000 tons (27,432 metric tons) standard displacement shall be in accordance with the requirements of Article X, except that the total number of guns to be carried in case any of such guns be of a calibre exceeding 6 inches (152 millimetres), except anti-aircraft guns and guns not exceeding 5 inches (127 millimetres), shall not exceed eight.

ARTICLE X.

No aricraft carrier of any of the Contracting Powers shall carry a gun with a calibre in excess of 8 inches (203 millimetres). Without prejudice to the provisions of Article IX, if the armament carried includes guns exceeding 6 inches (152 millimetres) in calibre the total number of guns carried, except anti-aircraft guns and guns not exceeding 5 inches (127 millimetres), shall not exceed ten. If alternatively the armament contains no guns exceeding 6 inches (152 millimetres) in calibre, the number of guns is not limited. In either case the number of anti-aircraft guns and of guns not exceeding 5 inches (127 millimetres) is not limited.

Article XI.

No vessel of war exceeding 10,000 tons (10,160 metric tons) standard displacement, other than a capital ship or aircraft carrier, shall be acquired by, or constructed by, for, or within the jurisdiction of, any of the Contracting Powers. Vessels not specifically built as fighting ships nor taken in time of peace under government control for fighting purposes, which are employed on fleet duties or as troop transports or in some other way for the purpose of assisting in the prosecution of hostilities otherwise than as fighting ships, shall not be within the limitations of this Article.

Article XII.

No vessel of war of any of the Contracting Powers, hereafter laid down, other than a capital ship, shall carry a gun with a calibre in excess of 8 inches (203 millimetres).

Article XIII.

Except as provided in Article IX, no ship designated in the present Treaty to be scrapped may be reconverted into a vessel of war.

Article XIV.

No preparations shall be made in merchant ships in time of peace for the installation of warlike armaments for the purpose of converting such ships into vessels of war, other than the necessary stiffening of decks for the mounting of guns not exceeding 6 inch (152 millimetres) calibre.

Article XV.

No vessel of war constructed within the jurisdiction of any of the Contracting Powers for a non-Contracting Power shall exceed the limitations as to displacement and armament prescribed by the present Treaty for vessels of a similar type which may be constructed by or for any of the Contracting Powers; provided, however, that the displacement for aircraft carriers constructed for a non-Contracting Power shall in no case exceed 27,000 tons (27,432 metric tons) standard displacement.

Article XVI.

If the construction of any vessel of war for a non-Contracting Power is undertaken within the jurisdiction of any of the Contracting Powers such Power shall promptly inform the other Contracting Powers of the date of the signing of the contract and the date on which the keel of the ship is laid; and shall also communicate to them the particulars relating to the ship prescribed in Chapter II, Part 3, Section I (b), (4) and (5).

Article XVII.

In the event of a Contracting Power being engaged in war, such Power shall not use as a vessel of war any vessel of war which may be under construction within its jurisdiction for any other Power, or which may have been constructed within its jurisdiction for another Power and not delivered.

Article XVIII.[1]

Each of the Contracting Powers undertakes not to dispose by gift, sale or any mode of transfer of any vessel of war in such a manner that such vessel may become a vessel in the Navy of any foreign Power.

Article XIX.

The United States, the British Empire and Japan agree that the status quo at the time of the signing of the present Treaty, with regard to fortifications and naval bases, shall be maintained in their respective territories and possessions specified hereunder:

(1) The insular possessions which the United States now holds or may hereafter acquire in the Pacific Ocean, except (a) those adjacent to the coast of the United States, Alaska and the Panama Canal Zone, not including the Aleutian Islands, and (b) the Hawaiian Islands;

(2) Hongkong and the insular possessions which the British Empire now holds or may hereafter acquire in the Pacific Ocean, east of the meridian of 110° east longitude, except (a) those adjacent to the coast of Canada, (b) the Commonwealth of Australia and its Territories, and (c), New Zealand;

(3) The following insular territories and possessions of Japan in the Pacific Ocean, to wit: the Kurile Islands, the Bonin Islands, Amami-Oshima, the Loochoo Islands, Formosa and the Pescadores, and any insular territories or possessions in the Pacific Ocean which Japan may hereafter acquire.

The maintenance of the status quo under the foregoing provisions implies that no new fortifications or naval bases shall be established in the territories and possessions specified that no measures shall be taken to increase the existing naval facilities for the repair and maintenance of naval forces, and that no increase shall be made in the coast defenses of the territories and possessions above specified. This restriction, however, does not preclude such repair and replacement of worn-out weapons and equipment as is customary in naval and military establishments in time of peace.

ARTICLE XX.

The rules for determining tonnage displacement prescribed in Chapter II, Part 4, shall apply to the ships of each of the Contracting Powers.

---

[1] The following resolution, recorded in the Committee on Limitation of Armament and reported by its direction to the full Conference, was spread upon the record by unanimous assent at the Sixth Plenary Session, February 4, 1922:

"It should therefore be recorded in the minutes of the subcommittee and before the full Conference that the Powers signatory of the Treaty of Naval Limitation regard themselves in honor bound not to sell any ships between the present date and the ratification of the Treaty when such a sale would be a breach of Article XVIII."

CHAPTER II. RULES RELATING TO THE EXECUTION OF THE TREATY— DEFINITION OF TERMS.

PART 1. CAPITAL SHIPS WHICH MAY BE RETAINED BY THE CONTRACTING POWERS.

In accordance with Article II ships may be retained by each of the Contracting Powers as specified in this Part.

Ships which may be retained by the United States.

Name:	Tonnage.
Maryland	32, 600
California	32, 300
Tennessee	32, 300
Idaho	32, 000
New Mexico	32, 000
Mississippi	32, 000
Arizona	31, 400
Pennsylvania	31, 400
Oklahoma	27, 500
Nevada	27, 500
New York	27, 000
Texas	27, 000
Arkansas	26, 000
Wyoming	26, 000
Florida	21, 825
Utah	21, 825
North Dakota	20, 000
Delaware	20, 000
Total tonnage	500, 650

On the completion of the two ships of the *West Virginia* class and the scrapping of the *North Dakota* and *Delaware*, as provided in Article II, the total tonnage to be retained by the United States will be 525,850 tons.

Name:	Tonnage.
Royal Sovereign	25, 750
Royal Oak	25, 750
Revenge	25, 750
Resolution	25, 750
Ramillies	25, 750
Malaya	27, 500
Valiant	27, 500
Barham	27, 500
Queen Elizabeth	27, 500
Warspite	27, 500
Benbow	25, 000
Emperor of India	25, 000
Iron Duke	25, 000
Marlborough	25, 000
Hood	41, 200
Renown	26, 500
Repulse	26, 500
Tiger	28, 500
Thunderer	22, 500
King George V	23, 000
Ajax	23, 000
Centurion	23, 000
Total tonnage	580, 450

On the completion of the two new ships to be constructed and the scrapping of the *Thunderer, King George V, Ajax* and *Centurion,* as provided in Article II, the total tonnage to be retained by the British Empire will be 558,950 tons.

Ships which may be retained by France.

Name:	Tonnage (metric tons).
Bretagne	23, 500
Lorraine	23, 500
Provence	23, 500
Paris	23, 500
France	23, 500
Jean Bart	23, 500
Courbet	23, 500
Condorcet	18, 890
Diderot	18, 890
Voltaire	18, 890
Total tonnage	221, 170

France may lay down new tonnage in the years 1927, 1929, and 1931, as provided in Part 3, Section II.

Ships which may be retained by Italy.

Name:	Tonnage (metric tons).
Andrea Doria	22, 700
Caio Duilio	22, 700
Conte Di Cavour	22, 500
Giullo Cesare	22, 500
Leonardo Da Vinci	22, 500
Dante Alighieri	19, 500
Roma	12, 600
Napoli	12, 600

Vittorio Emanuele	12, 600
Regina Elena	12, 600
Total tonnage	182, 800

Italy may lay down new tonnage in the years 1927, 1929, and 1931, as provided in Part 3, Section II.

Ships which may be retained by Japan.

Name:	Tonnage.
Mutsu	33, 800
Nagato	33, 800
Hiuga	31, 260
Ise	31, 260
Yamashiro	30, 600
Fu-So	30, 600
Kirishima	27, 500
Haruna	27, 500
Hiyel	27, 500
Kongo	27, 500
Total tonnage	301, 320

Document No. 84   Free Speech and Jailed Speakers (1923)
Source: *Literary Digest,* LXXVII (June 16, 1923), pp. 10-13.

FREE SPEECH AND JAILED SPEAKERS

A NEW PHASE IN THE PERSISTENT CAMPAIGN for the release of all persons serving prison sentences for violations of the war-time espionage act was reached the other day, when a petition signed by forty-eight prominent men and women, among them five Governors of States, eleven college presidents, several editors, and many well-known Protestant, Catholic and Jewish clergymen, was presented to President Harding. According to an announcement given out to the press in Washington by the Joint Amnesty Committee, this petition asks for the release of all persons (said to be 52 in number) serving prison sentences for "political" offenses, and would include all the I. W. W. agitators who were convicted of violating war laws, involving the use of free-speech privileges. At the same time it is added that some of the petitioners confine their applications for executive clemency to the "Chicago and Wichita I. W. W. cases" (thus leaving out the more widely condemned Pacific coast cases). According to the dispatches the signers include:

"The governors of Montana, Oklahoma, Arizona, Kansas and Colorado; the .presidents of Vassar, Mount Holyoke, Smith, University of Wyoming, Oberlin, Trinity, Bryn Mawr, Swarthmore, Temple University (Philadelphia), St. Stephen's College (New York), and the Catholic University of America. Other educators include Francis B. Sayre of the Harvard Law school, son-in-law of former President Wilson, and Dr. Richard C. Cabot of Harvard, medical authority who served in France, and who signed the petition so far as the Chicago and Wichita I. W. W. cases were concerned. Editors include William Allen White, Emporia *Gazette*; Herbert Bayard Swope, New York *World;* Lewis Gannett, *The Nation*; Glenn Frank, *Century Magazine*, and Herbert Croly, *The New Republic.*"

The petition's statement that the "continued imprisonment of men in America for political offenses involving only the voicing of unorthodox opinion, in many cases exprest solely by membership in an organization, is a violation of American principles of freedom" is sharply criticized by a wide-spread section of the press. "Forgetting the men at the front," is the point of view taken by the Chicago *Tribune*, which, after emphasizing the war-time emergency during which these men were sentenced, concludes:

"Free speech is a precious privilege. But it should never be extended for the imperilment of the lives of patriots or the cause of the nation at grips with a foe."

Naturally, this point of view, besides being reflected in several other papers, is more or less characteristic of American Legion utterances. *The American Legion Weekly,* describing the prisoners as "men who obstructed America's conduct of the World War and were justly jailed on that account," says:

"The American Legion has always taken the stand that there is no essential difference between a war criminal and any other criminal. Having committed a crime against the security of our national Government in time of war, a man has demonstrated that he is a menace to our security at any time, because conditions which brought about the war can not, unhappily, be forever removed."

The adjutant of the Pennsylvania posts of the Legion, taking the view that the petition was an "outrage against all the men who fought for their country in the Great War" is quoted further in the Philadelphia *North American,* as saying:

"If these prisoners are to be released, then we citizens who love our country, we who have served it and are willing to serve it again should be locked up. It is not fair to mix the two groups."

The two points most generally emphasized by other papers opposing the petition, such as the Birmingham *Age-Herald* and the Buffalo *Express,* are that the men imprisoned were either criminals, just as dangerous as any others, or "slackers" who preferred imprisonment to the Army.

Considering the point of view of the Department of Justice, which has remained apparently unchanged through two administrations, Charles G. Ross, in a special dispatch to the New York *World* and the St. Louis *Post-Dispatch,* quotes them as follows:

"In justification of its policy of dealing separately with the cases of the war prisoners, the Department contends that it can not be expected to recommend the release of men whose previous acts and present beliefs warrant the assumption that they would if given freedom become a menace to society. The Department holds that it has, in fact, been generous in the dealings with the prisoners, approximately fifty in the political prisoners' cases having been released since the present Administration came into power. It points also to what it describes as a liberal form of parole offered in a number of cases—a form requiring

SERVING A TWENTY-YEAR SENTENCE

Ralph Chaplin, one of our "political prisoners."
A poem of his, written in Leavenworth penitentiary,
ends with these stanzas:

Mourn not your captive·comrades who must dwell,
  Too strong to strive,
Within each steel-bound coffin of a cell,
  Buried alive.

But rather mourn the apathetic throng—
  The cowed and meek—
Who see the world's great anguish and its wrong
  And dare not speak!

the prisoner to report at stated intervals and binding him to observe the laws of the United States, on penalty of having his parole revoked on executive order of the President."

On the other hand a tremendous amount of very powerful and intelligent public opinion in this country has come out unequivocally for general amnesty. Scores of organizations such as the Women's Industrial League, the Federal Council of Churches, the Chicago Church Federation, the American Federation of Labor, the Women's Trade Union, the Committee of 48, the World War Veterans, the Central Conference of American Rabbis, the Methodist Federation for Social Service and the Private Soldiers' and Sailors' Legion, have gone on record for general amnesty. Petitions said to contain more than a million names have been presented to the President and various government officials. Among them they seem to have raised some grave issues which include especially: (1) Legality of the convictions; (2) the issue of free speech; (3) danger of war bitterness; and (4) "political" prisoners.

As to the convictions, we quote again from the last-mentioned dispatch as follows:

"Three groups of prisoners were brought to trial by the Government in prosecutions of the I. W. W. during the war, on charges of conspiracy to obstruct the war and draft act. At Chicago in the Haywood trial, one hundred were convicted, of whom twenty-two are still in prison. In the so-called Wichita case, twenty-five were convicted, of whom four are still in prison, and at Sacramento forty-six were convicted, of whom twenty-two are still in prison. All the I. W. W. prisoners are at Leavenworth."

In the Chicago and Wichita cases it appears there were five counts in the indictments—three industrial, charging conspiracy to practise sabotage against the war or to intimidate persons in the executions of contracts, and two war counts charging conspiracy to refuse draft registration, to desert military service, or to obstruct the war by the oral or printed expression of their views. It is on this last count that all the remaining prisoners are in jail, the Court of Appeals in general having reversed convictions on industrial charges.

The Sacramento case is different because all those now in jail refused to make any defense, feeling, according to one of the attorneys, that "both courts and juries were prejudiced against 'war offenses' and to offer defense would be futile." The indictments were the same except that overt acts including the transportation of dynamite and the setting of fires were charged. A general verdict of guilty was returned and a general sentence imposed.

To quote still from the *World* article, Major Alexander Sidney Lanier, of the Military Intelligence Division of the General Staff, U. S. Army, read and summarized, as part of his official duties, 44,000 typewritten pages comprising the record in the Chicago I. W. W. case, and concluded that not one of the men was properly convicted on the evidence. Senator George Wharton Pepper, of Pennsylvania, a constitutional lawyer and generally accounted conservative in his views, is reported to have said of this same trial:

"I am satisfied myself that in not one of the twenty-eight cases I looked into did the evidence justify a continuance of restraint, and I then recommended to the Attorney-General and also direct to the President that unconditional amnesty be granted to these men."

As to the question raised that the trials were influenced by prejudice, Mr. Ross cites the contention of the American Civil Liberties Union that of the twenty-five prisoners released at Christmas, 1921, only six were members of the I. W. W., and all but one of the six were aliens subject to deportation or had recanted, altho all the prisoners had been jailed for conspiracy to obstruct the war, not for belief in the I. W. W.

This leads to the more widely discust question of free speech, concerning which Senator Borah, in an address last March to a large audience of World War Veterans, is quoted as follows:

"There is a much broader principle, my friends, involved in this matter, one of far deeper concern, than the freedom of fifty-three (there were then fifty-three) men. At the bottom of the controversy there lies the question

559

of what constitutes free speech and free press under the American flag."

It is this point of view, together with the general proposition that after all, the war is over, that is emphasized by papers like the Boston *Post*, Columbus *Ohio State Journal*, Springfield *Republican*, and Baltimore *Evening Sun*. According to the Baltimore paper:

"Profiteers have recently been pardoned and German spies, including the leader of them in this country, have had their liberty restored, but the radical talkers are still in durance vile. It would appear that the most heinous crime in this country is to say what one thinks."

"Freedom of speech, press and assemblage," the Milwaukee *Leader* points out, "is guaranteed by the first Amendment of the Constitution," and other papers reecho this point of view.

The career of the Socialist leader, Eugene Debs, since his release from prison not so long ago, is taken as the principal argument against the petition by papers like the New Haven *Journal-Courier* and the Detroit *News*. Every time Debs opens his mouth, they say, he gives ample illustration that he and his comrades are "unrepentant and persistent enemies of America, saturated with the crime of treason."

There remains the important question of "political" prisoners. The Wichita *Eagle*, at the heart of the Wichita section of the controversy, and laying great stress on the signature to the petition, along with William Allen White's, of "every person who may be called a humanitarian of note in the United States," maintains that this country and Russia are the only ones on earth which confine political prisoners, and that we alone retain war prisoners.

Representing a diametrically opposed point of view, the Peoria *Journal* roundly asseverates that there is no such thing under our system as a "political prisoner." Each of the fifty-two prisoners was convicted of violation of the

Espionage Law of June 15, 1917, it continues. They were guilty then of a "wilful attempt to cause insubordination, disloyalty, mutiny, or refusal of duty in the military or naval forces of the United States." This law was upheld by the Supreme Court. To release them now, en bloc, it concludes, would be a "confession to insurgency that laws are passed not for public, but for despotic purposes."

With so sharply contrasted a divergence in the press of the country and, perhaps, popular sentiment as well, it is obvious that President Harding and Attorney-General Daugherty have a difficult decision before them. A widely circulated plan to solve the problem by a workable compromise seems to have been made by Judge Alton B. Parker. We quote the plan as given in the Richmond *Times-Dispatch*. After pointing out that a pardon carries with it official forgiveness of the crime in question with a restoration of citizenship, whereas a commutation of sentence gives freedom only, the paper goes on to say:

"Judge Parker in his well-considered communication to the President recommends that all the twenty-year sentences imposed upon political prisoners be commuted to expire in ten years. This would make them subject immediately to parole, under our penal system. It is further proposed that thereafter the Government offer parole to the men, 'if they will by oath or affirmation promise to support the Constitution of the United States and the Constitutions of their respective States.'

"If the prisoners agree to this proposal and renew their allegiance to their Government, they may return to their homes and engage again in support of their families. If, after their release, they violate their oath, they may forfeit their parole and may be again incarcerated. Any prisoner who refuses to take the oath, thereby pronouncing himself an enemy of his country, would be required to serve out his time."

Document No. 85 Anti-War Cartoons and Posters, 1919-1922
Source: The Swarthmore College Peace Collection, Swarthmore, Pa.

The Seven Ages of Man

Four drawings made in 1918

by ROCKWELL KENT

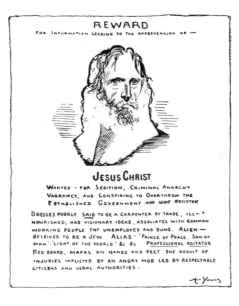

The Appropriation Pie

(From Labor, December 11, 1920)

United States Appropriations, 1920

I. Past Wars	$3,855,482,586	68%
II. Future Wars	1,424,138,677	25%
III. Civil Departments	181,087,225	3%
IV. Public Works	168,203,557	3%
V. Education and Science	57,093,661	1%
Total	$5,686,005,706	100%

(Analysis by Dr. Edward B. Ross, of the United States Bureau of Standards)

Why Add to His Load?

NAVAL APPROPRIATIONS

1900	.	.	.	.	$61,000,000
1905	.	.	.	.	100,000,000
1910	.	.	.	.	131,000,000
1915	.	.	.	.	149,000,000
1921	.	.	.	.	437,000,000
1922	.	.	.	.	?

(Over)

Drawn by Rollin Kirby

The Wise Men

Will they follow the star?

How Nations Gamble

"The United States, Great Britain and Japan are now actually engaged in a naval race. They are building navies with mad speed and piling taxes upon the people at a rate and to an amount never before dreamed of in time of peace."

—*Senator Borah, in the Nation's Business, September, 1921.*

"In its moral aspect, as mass homicide, war is appalling, but in its economic aspect it is preposterous.....

"We came as near as anyone to winning that war, and we are losers. Fifty years from now we will still be paying its debts."

From a review of "The Next War," by Will Irwin, in the September, 1921, issue of
The Nation's Business, the official organ of the Chamber of Commerce of the United States.

The Next Generation—"How About Schools?"

Distributed by the
Women's International League for Peace and Freedom
SECTION FOR THE UNITED STATES

National Office
125 East 37th Street, New York

Courtesy of the New York Evening Post

What's the Use?

Distributed by the

Women's International League for Peace and Freedom
SECTION FOR THE UNITED STATES

National Office
125 East 37th Street, New York

Courtesy of the New York Evening Post

DISARM!

Part V

Suggested Reading

Part V
Suggested Reading

Addams, Jane. *Peace and Bread in Time of War*. N.Y.: The Macmillan Co., 1922.

Bailey, Thomas A. *Woodrow Wilson and the Great Betrayal*. N.Y., 1945.

Bartlett, Ruhl. *The League to Enforce Peace*. Chapel Hill, N.C.: Univ. of North Carolina Press, 1944.

Bates, Scott, ed. *Poems of War Resistance: From 2300 B.C. to the Present*. N.Y.: Grossman, 1969.

Beale, Howard K. *Theodore Roosevelt and the Rise of America to World Power*. Baltimore: The Johns Hopkins Press, 1956.

Beales, A.C.F. *The History of Peace*. N.Y.: The Dial Press, 1931.

Bell, Sidney. *Righteous Conquest: Woodrow Wilson and the Evolution of the New Diplomacy*. Port Washington, N.Y., 1972.

Boothe, Leon E. "Anglo-American Pro-League Groups Lead Wilson, 1915-1918," *Mid-America*, LI (1969), pp. 92-107.

Bourne, Randolph S. *War and the Intellectuals; Collected Essays, 1915-1919*. Edited by Carl Resek. N.Y.: Harper, 1964.

Buckley, Thomas H. *The United States and the Washington Conference, 1921-1922*. Knoxville, Tenn., 1970.

Buehrig, E.H., ed. *Wilson's Foreign Policy in Perspective*. Bloomington, Ind., 1957.

Campbell, John P. "Taft, Roosevelt, and the Arbitration Treaties of 1911," *Journal of American History*, LIII (1966), pp. 279-298.

Cantor, Milton. "The Radical Confrontation with Foreign Policy: War and Revolution, 1914-1920," in Alfred F. Young, ed., *Dissent: Explorations in the History of American Radicalism*. DeKalb: Northern Illinois University Press, 1968.

Chambers, John W. "Conscripting for Colossus: The Adoption of the Draft in the United States in World War I." Doctoral Dissertation, Columbia University, 1973.

SUGGESTED READING

Chatfield, Charles. *For Peace and Justice: Pacifism in America, 1914-1941.* Knoxville: Univ. of Tennessee Press, 1971.

Chatfield, Charles, ed. *Peace Movements in America.* N.Y.: Schocken Books, 1973.

Coletta, Paolo E. *William Jennings Bryan: Progressive Politician and Moral Statesman, 1909-1915.* Lincoln, Neb.: Univ. of Nebraska Press, 1969.

Cook, Blanche Wiesen. "Woodrow Wilson and the Anti-militarists, 1914-1917." Doctoral Dissertation. The Johns Hopkins University, 1970.

Cooper, John Milton, Jr. *The Vanity of Power: American Isolationism and World War I, 1914-1917.* Westport, Conn.: The Greenwood Press, 1969.

Curti, Merle. *Peace or War, The American Struggle, 1636-1936.* N.Y.: Norton, 1936.

Davis, Calvin D. *The United States and the First Hague Peace Conference.* Ithaca, N.Y.: Cornell University Press, 1962.

DeBenedetti, Charles. "Peace was His Profession: James T. Shotwell and American Internationalism," in Frank J. Merli and Theodore A. Wilson, eds., *Makers of American Diplomacy.* 2 vols., N.Y.: Charles Scribner's Sons, 1974, II, pp. 81-101.

DeConde, Alexander, ed., *Isolation and Security: Ideas and Interests in Twentieth-Century American Foreign Policy.* Durham, N.C.: Duke Univ. Press, 1957.

Degen, Marie L. *The History of the Women's Peace Party.* Baltimore: The Johns Hopkins Press, 1939.

Dubin, Martin D. "The Development of the Concept of Collective Security in the American Peace Movement, 1899-1917." Doctoral Dissertation. Indiana University, 1960.

Dubofsky, Melvyn. *We Shall Be All: A History of the Industrial Workers of the World.* Chicago: University of Chicago Press, 1969.

Dudden, A.P., ed., *Woodrow Wilson and the World of Today.* Philadelphia, 1957.

Ekirch, Arthur A., Jr. *The Civilian and the Military.* N.Y.: Oxford University Press, 1956.

Ellis, L. Ethan. *Republican Foreign Policy, 1921-1933.* New Brunswick, N.J.: Rutgers University Press, 1968.

SUGGESTED READING

Ferrell, Robert H. *Peace in Their Time: The Origins of the Kellogg-Briand Pact.* New Haven: Yale University Press, 1952.

Filene, Peter. "The World Peace Foundation and Progressivism, 1910-1918," *New England Quarterly,* XXXVI (December, 1963), pp. 478-501.

Farrell, John C. *Beloved Lady: A History of Jane Addams' Ideas on Reform and Peace.* Baltimore: The Johns Hopkins Press, 1967.

Herman, Sondra R. *Eleven Against war: Studies in American Internationalist Thought, 1898-1921.* Stanford: Stanford University Press, 1969.

Holcombe, Arthur N. "Edwin Ginn's Vision of World Peace," *International Organization,* XIX (1965), pp. 1-19.

Jessup, Philip C. *Elihu Root.* 2 vols. N.Y.: Dodd, Mead, 1938.

Johnson, Donald. *Challenge to American Freedoms, World War I and the Rise of the American Civil Liberties Union.* Lexington, Ky.: University of Kentucky Press, 1963.

Johnson, Joseph E. and Bush, Bernard, eds. *Perspectives on Peace, 1910-1960.* N.Y.: Praeger, 1960.

Kuehl, Warren F. *Seeking World Order: The United States and International Organization to 1920.* Nashville: Vanderbilt University Press, 1969.

Leopold, Richard W. *The Growth of American Foreign Policy: A History.* N.Y.: Knopf, 1962.

Levin, N. Gordon, Jr. *Woodrow Wilson and World Politics: America's Response to War and Revolution.* N.Y.: Oxford University Press, 1968.

Libby, Frederick J. *To End War: The Story of the National Council for the Prevention of War.* Nyack, N.Y.: Fellowship Publications, 1969.

Link, Arthur S. *The Higher Realism of Woodrow Wilson and other Essays.* Nashville: Vanderbilt Univ. Press, 1971.

_____. *Wilson: Campaigns for Progressivism and Peace, 1916-1917.* Princeton: Princeton Univ. Press, 1965.

_____. *Wilson the Diplomatist: A Look at his Major Foreign Policies.* Baltimore: The Johns Hopkins University Press, 1957.

_____. *Woodrow Wilson and the Progressive Era, 1910-1917.* N.Y.: Harper, 1963.

SUGGESTED READING

Lutzker, Michael A. "The Practical Peace Advocates: An Interpretation of the American Peace Movement, 1898-1917." Doctoral Dissertation, Rutgers University, 1969.

Marchand, C. Roland. *The American Peace Movement and Social Reform, 1898-1918.* Princeton: Princeton University Press, 1972.

Margrave, Robert N. "The Policy of the United States Respecting the Development of International Adjudication." Doctoral Dissertation, American University, 1950.

May, Ernest R. *The World War and American Isolation, 1914-1917.* Cambridge, Mass.: Harvard University Press, 1959.

Mayer, Arno J. *Politics and Diplomacy of Peacemaking: Containment and Counterrevolution at Versailles, 1918-1919.* N.Y., 1967.

Mets, David R. "A Case Study in Arms Control: Naval Limitation before Pearl Harbor and Post-war Arms-Control Theory." Doctoral dissertation, University of Denver, 1972.

Meyer, Ernest L. *"Hey! Yellowbacks!" The War Diary of a Conscientious Objector.* N.Y., 1930.

Megargee, Richard. "The Diplomacy of John Bassett Moore: Realism in American Foreign Policy." Doctoral Dissertation, Northwestern University, 1963.

Noggle, Burl. *Into the Twenties: The United States from Armistice to Normalcy.* Urbana: Univ. of Illinois Press, 1974.

O'Connor, Raymond G. *Perilous Equilibrium: The United States and the London Naval Conference of 1930.* Lawrence, Kans.: Univ. of Kansas, 1962.

Olson, William C. "Theodore Roosevelt's Conception of an International League," *World Affairs Quarterly,* XXIX (January, 1959), pp. 329-353.

Patterson, David S. "The Travail of the American Peace Movement, 1887-1914." Doctoral dissertation, University of California, Berkeley, 1968.

_____. "Woodrow Wilson and the Mediation Movement, 1914-17," *The Historian,* XXXIII (August, 1971), pp. 535-556.

Peterson, H.C. and Fite, Gilbert C. *Opponents of War, 1917-1918.* Madison, Wis.: University of Wisconsin Press, 1957.

SUGGESTED READING

Perkins, Dexter. *America's Quest for Peace*. Bloomington: Indiana University Press, 1963.

Radosh, Ronald, ed. *Debs* in Gerald Emanuel Stearn, general editor, *Great Lives Observed*. Englewood Cliffs, N.J.: Prentice-Hall, 1971.

Randall, Mercedes M. *Improper Bostonian: Emily Green Balch*. N.Y.: Twayne Publishers, 1964.

Scholes, Walter V. and Marie V. *The Foreign Policies of the Taft Administration*. Columbia, Mo.: Univ. of Missouri Press, 1970.

Shaver, Barbara McKay. "American Policy and European Collective Security, 1921-1925." Doctoral dissertation, University of Colorado, 1972.

Stone, Ralph. *The Irreconcilables: The Fight against the League of Nations*. N.Y.: Norton, 1970.

Stromberg, Roland N. "Uncertainties and Obscurities about the League of Nations," *Journal of the History of Ideas*, XXXIII (January-March, 1972), pp. 139-154.

Tate, Merze. *The Disarmament Illusion; The Movement for a Limitation of Armaments to 1907*. N.Y.: Macmillan, 1942.

Thomas, Norman. *The Conscientious Objector in America*. N.Y., 1923.

Trow, C.W. "Woodrow Wilson and the Mexican Interventionist Movement of 1919," *Journal of American History*, LVIII (1971), pp. 46-72.

Vinson, John C. *The Parchment Peace: The United States Senate and the Washington Conference, 1921-1922*. Athens, Ga.: University of Georgia Press, 1955.

_____. *Referendum for Isolation: Defeat of Article Ten of the League of Nations Covenant*. Athens: University of Georgia Press, 1961.

Weinstein, James, "Anti-War Sentiment and the Socialist Party, 1917-1918," *Political Science Quarterly*, LXXIV (1959), pp. 215-239.

Whitney, Edson L. *The American Peace Society: A Centennial History*. Washington, D.C.: American Peace Society, 1928.

Wreszin, Michael. *Oswald Garrison Villard: Pacifist at War*. Bloomington, Ind., 1965.